Databases Illuminated

Second Edition

Catherine Ricardo, Iona College

JONES & BARTLETT
LEARNING

World Headquarters

Jones & Bartlett Learning	Jones & Bartlett Learning Canada	Jones & Bartlett Learning International
40 Tall Pine Drive	6339 Ormindale Way	Barb House, Barb Mews
Sudbury, MA 01776	Mississauga, Ontario L5V 1J2	London W6 7PA
978-443-5000	Canada	United Kingdom
info@jblearning.com		
www.jblearning.com		

Jones & Bartlett Learning books and products are available through most bookstores and online booksellers. To contact Jones & Bartlett Learning directly, call 800-832-0034, fax 978-443-8000, or visit our website, www.jblearning.com.

Substantial discounts on bulk quantities of Jones & Bartlett Learning publications are available to corporations, professional associations, and other qualified organizations. For details and specific discount information, contact the special sales department at Jones & Bartlett Learning via the above contact information or send an email to specialsales@jblearning.com.

Production Credits
Publisher: Cathleen Sether
Senior Acquisitions Editor: Timothy Anderson
Senior Editorial Assistant: Stephanie Sguigna
Production Director: Amy Rose
Senior Marketing Manager: Andrea DeFronzo
Associate Marketing Manager: Lindsay White
V.P., Manufacturing and Inventory Control: Therese Connell
Composition: Northeast Compositors, Inc.
Cover and Title Page Design: Kristin E. Parker
Cover Image: © ErickN/ShutterStock, Inc.
Printing and Binding: Malloy, Inc.
Cover Printing: Malloy, Inc.

Library of Congress Cataloging-in-Publication Data
Ricardo, Catherine M.
  Databases illuminated / Catherine M. Ricardo. — 2nd ed.
     p. cm.
  Includes bibliographical references and index.
  ISBN 978-1-4496-0600-8 (casebound)
  1. Database management. I. Title.
  QA76.9.D3R514 2011
  005.74—dc22
                        2010052808

6048
Printed in the United States of America
15 14 13 12 11   10 9 8 7 6 5 4 3 2

Dedication

To my beloved husband, Henry

Contents

3.3.3 Multivalued Attributes 66
3.3.4 Composite Attributes 66
3.3.5 Derived Attributes 67

3.4 Keys 68

3.4.1 Superkeys 68
3.4.2 Candidate Keys 69
3.4.3 Primary Keys 69

3.5 Relationships 70

3.5.1 Degree of Relationships 71
3.5.2 Attributes of Relationship Sets 74
3.5.3 Cardinality of a Relationship 74
3.5.4 Showing Cardinalities on an E-R Diagram 76
3.5.5 Participation Constraints 78

3.6 Roles 79

3.7 Existence Dependency and Weak Entities 80

3.8 A Sample E-R Diagram 82

3.9 Chapter Summary 85

Exercises 87

4. The Relational Model 93

Chapter Objectives 93

4.1 Advantages of the Relational Model 94

4.2 Relational Data Structures 95

4.2.1 Tables 95
4.2.2 Mathematical Relations 97
4.2.3 Database Relations and Tables 99
4.2.4 Properties of Relations 100
4.2.5 Degree and Cardinality 100
4.2.6 Relation Keys 101

6.   Normalization   211

15.   Data Warehouses and Data Mining   593

Preface

Purpose of This Book

Since the publication of the first edition of this book in 2004, databases have become an even more central part of the framework of modern computer systems, and the study of database systems, design, and management is an essential part of the education of computer science and information science students. A database course should provide a strong theoretical background, practice in database design, and experience creating and developing a working database. This book is designed to help students integrate theoretical material with practical knowledge, using an approach that has a firm theoretical basis applied to practical database implementation.

Structure

Theoretical foundations are presented early and the concepts are used repeatedly throughout the book, including the chapters that deal with implementation. Logical database design is given full consideration. The entity-relationship model is introduced early and then mapped to the relational model. Relational normalization is studied in detail, and many examples of the normalization process are discussed. The object-oriented model is presented using UML as a vehicle for logical design. The enhanced entity-relationship model is presented, and mapped to both relational and object-relational models. XML and the semi-structured data model are introduced in Chapter 13. A continuing example of a university database is incorporated throughout the text, to illustrate concepts and techniques and to provide both continuity and contrast. Other examples are presented as needed. Purely relational, object-relational, and object-oriented database systems are described and used for implementation of the examples. Details of database management systems are described so that students can learn the specifics of these real-life systems, down to the physical implementation level. Microsoft® Access® is used initially in the examples, but Oracle® is introduced as the material is developed. However, the examples are suitable for use with any relational or object-relational DBMS. InterSystems Caché® DBMS is used to illustrate object-oriented databases.

Purpose of the Sample Project and Student Projects

The various approaches are integrated in a sample project that is a unique feature of this book. Starting at the end of the first chapter, students can visit the Student Companion Website to see a sample project that is developed as the book progresses. This project is independent of the examples that are presented in the chapter text or in exercises. The design begins with a description of the application: a database needed by an art gallery. At the end of the first chapter, students see how the information needs are specified. After the students study planning techniques in Chapter 2, they see how to create a complete user-oriented data dictionary and how other planning tools could be used. When they learn about logical models, they see the step-by-step development of an E-R diagram at the end of Chapter 3. They see the steps involved in mapping the diagram to the relational model after Chapter 4, and normalizing the model after Chapter 6. Complete details of creating and manipulating a purely relational Oracle database using SQL are presented for the relational model after Chapter 5. The E-R diagram is expanded to a complete EE-R diagram and mapped to an object-relational database after Chapter 8, using the object-relational features of Oracle. The EE-R diagram is transformed into a UML diagram after Chapter 7, which includes the design and creation of an object-oriented database using ODL and also InterSystems Caché DBMS. The sample project is extended after Chapter 12 to show a distributed design that might be used in a client-server environment or a true distributed environment. Details of creating a simple website for the art gallery are provided after Chapter 13 using PL/SQL, JDBC, Caché, and XML. Thus, every important technique of planning, design, and implementation is illustrated using real-life systems. The sample project section is always connected to continuing student projects, which require students to emulate the steps of the sample.

From my experiences assigning similar projects while teaching database courses, I have found that students learn most effectively by creating a working database and developing their own continuing projects to incorporate new concepts, and that they benefit by seeing samples as they progress. Such realistic experiences provide insights that no amount of lecturing can produce. Later chapters deal with topics of database security, concurrency control, recovery techniques, query optimization, distributed databases, social and ethical issues, data warehouses, and data mining. Online appendices cover physical data organization, the network model, the hierarchical model, and other specialized material.

Learning Features

The writing style is conversational. Each chapter begins with a statement of learning objectives. Examples and applications are presented throughout the text. Illustrations are used both to clarify the material and to vary the presentation. Exercises, including lab exercises where appropriate, appear at the end of each chapter and on the Student Companion Website, with solutions provided in the Instructor's Guide. The sample project on the Student Companion Website is an important part of the text, providing an application of the material just presented. The student projects that follow the sample are introduced after the first chapter, and students are expected to choose one, or have one assigned, and to develop that project to parallel the sample as they progress. Student projects may be done individually or in a group. Access, Oracle, and Caché implementations of the example databases used in the text, and of the sample project, are available on the book's website; solutions for the student projects, since they are intended to be used as assignments, are not included there. Resources for student laboratory exercises are also available on the website. Chapter summaries are included in the text to provide a rapid review or preview of the material and to help students understand the relative importance of the concepts presented. The Instructor's Guide contains Microsoft® PowerPoint® presentations for each chapter, solutions for the student projects, copies of figures, full statements of objectives for each chapter, alternative student projects, quizzes, chapter tests, comprehensive examinations for multiple chapters, and solutions to exercises.

Audience

The material is suitable for junior or senior computer science majors or information science majors with a good technical background. Students should have completed at least one year of programming, including data structures. The book could also be used as an introductory database text for graduate students or for self study.

Mapping to Curriculum Guidelines

Although this book was based on the author's experiences, it fits the ACM-IEEE Curriculum Guidelines well. It covers the topics and supports the learning objectives listed in the IS 2010 Curriculum Guidelines for IS 2010.2, Data and Information Management. It also supports the guidelines of ACM Computer Science Curriculum 2008, An Interim Revision of CS2001. This revision retains the basic structure and guidelines of the 2001 recommendations, while including some new trends that have emerged since the first report. These include more attention to security, concurrency, and net-centric computing, all of which are addressed in this text. CC2001 provides a model database course, CS270T, for the topic-based curriculum. The course includes three areas, Human-Computer Interaction (HCI), Information Management (IM), and Social and Professional Issues (SP). The units included in CS270T are listed below, along with the corresponding chapters in the book.

IM1 Information models and systems (3 core hours)—Chapters 1, 2

IM2 Database systems (3 core hours)—Chapter 2

IM3 Data modeling (4 core hours)—Sections 2.7, 13.4; Chapters 3, 4, 7, 8, Appendices B, C

IM4 Relational databases (5 hours)—Chapter 4

IM5 Database query languages (4 hours)—Sections 4.5, 7.5, 8.7; Chapters 6, 11, 13; Appendices B, C

IM6 Relational database design (4 hours)—Chapter 6

IM7 Transaction processing (3 hours)—Chapter 10

IM8 Distributed databases (3 hours)—Chapters 12, 13

IM9 Physical database design (3 hours)—Appendix A

HCI Foundations of human–computer interaction (2 core hours)—Chapter 14

SP6 Intellectual property (3 core hours)—Chapter 14

SP7 Privacy and civil liberties (2 core hours)—Chapters 9, 14

Elective topics (1 hour)—Chapter 15

In addition to the text's coverage, the sample project and student projects also provide practice in data modeling, database design, human–computer interaction, relational databases, database query languages, distributed databases, web-based databases, and physical database design. Some aspects of security, privacy, and civil liberties are discussed in the sample project, and similar issues will arise and should be treated in the student projects.

Acknowledgments

Many people have offered useful comments, advice, and encouragement during the writing of this book. I am grateful to students and colleagues throughout the world who used the first edition and provided comments that have helped shape this book, especially Mary Courtney, Pace University and Stephen D'Alessio and Smiljana Petrovic, Iona College.

For his encouragement and support for this project, I am grateful to Tim Anderson, Senior Acquisitions Editor at Jones & Bartlett Learning. I would also like to thank the editorial and production staff at Jones & Bartlett Learning, especially Amy Rose.

Finally I would like to thank my family, especially my husband, Henry, for his love, patience, and understanding and for his active help in critiquing and proofreading the manuscript.

CHAPTER 1

Introductory Database Concepts

Chapter Objectives

In this chapter you will learn the following:

- How databases are used
- The major functions of a database management system
- Advantages of using an integrated database system
- Roles in the integrated database environment
- The history of information systems

1.1   Uses of Databases

Databases play a major role in today's computing environment, with applications both in everyday life and in highly specialized environments. They can be found in organizations of all sizes, ranging from large corporations and government agencies to small businesses and even homes. Your everyday activities often involve contact with databases.

- When you visit a **consumer website** that allows online browsing and ordering of goods you are accessing a database.

- When you visit an interactive **customer service** website, such as a utility company's or a health insurer's homepage, you are able to access information about your own records of services provided.

- Using **online banking**, you can retrieve database records about deposits, withdrawals, bill payments, and other transactions for your accounts.

- When you use a **credit card**, the transaction approval process involves consulting a database to verify that your card has not been lost or stolen and to approve your purchase.

- When you buy goods in a **supermarket** or **retail store**, scanners are used to read universal product codes or other identifiers of merchandise as input to a database.

- For making travel plans, you may access an **airline reservations system** in which a database is used to keep track of scheduled flights and passenger reservations. Hotels and rental car companies also have centralized reservation systems to accept reservations for any of their locations, using an integrated database system.

- **Healthcare providers** may use their databases to do third-party billing, automatically verifying your coverage and submitting insurance claims for covered expenditures. Your **medical records** and **billing data** are probably kept in a database. When you have a prescription filled, your pharmacist may use a database to record information about the prescription, check for interactions with drugs you are currently using, and print the label and receipt.

- Your **employment records** may be kept in a database and your payroll is probably produced using a database that stores information about each pay period and data about the year's gross pay, tax deductions, and taxes withheld, among other things.

- Your **school records** may be kept in a database that is updated each term to record your registration in, completion of, and grade for each class.

- To do research, you can use a **bibliographic database** in which you enter keywords that describe the subject of interest.

- More specialized databases may store data for **geographic information systems**, **software development** and deployment, **scientific research**, **decision support systems**, **customer relations management**, and other advanced applications. Database technology is also used in **search engines** to make identification and retrieval of data on the Internet more efficient.

As this short overview of activities demonstrates, databases are used to satisfy the information needs of many organizations and individuals in a variety of areas. However, a poorly designed database may fail to provide the required information or may provide outdated, flawed, or contradictory information. In order to maximize their potential benefits, it is important to understand the theoretical foundations, internal structure, design, and management of databases.

1.2 A Sample Database

For the present, we describe a **database** as a collection of related stored data. It can be large or small, single-user or multi-user. As an example, let us consider a simple database that records information about university students, the classes they take during one semester, and the professors who teach the classes. The information kept for each student includes the student's ID, name, major, and total number of credits earned. Using **Microsoft Access** for this example, we have a **table** for this data as shown in Figure 1.1(a). The `Student` table has five columns, named `stuId`, `lastName`, `firstName`, `major`, and `credits`. Each row of the table shows the student ID, last name, first name, major, and number of credits for one student. The values of these

FIGURE 1.1(a)

The Student Table

Student

stuId	lastName	firstName	major	credits
S1001	Smith	Tom	History	90
S1002	Chin	Ann	Math	36
S1005	Lee	Perry	History	3
S1010	Burns	Edward	Art	63
S1013	McCarthy	Owen	Math	0
S1015	Jones	Mary	Math	42
S1020	Rivera	Jane	CSC	15

FIGURE 1.1(b)

The Faculty Table

Faculty

facId	name	department	rank
F101	Adams	Art	Professor
F105	Tanaka	CSC	Instructor
F110	Byrne	Math	Assistant
F115	Smith	History	Associate
F221	Smith	CSC	Professor

FIGURE 1.1(c)

The Class Table

Class

classNumber	facId	schedule	room
ART103A	F101	MWF9	H221
CSC201A	F105	TuThF10	M110
CSC203A	F105	MThF12	M110
HST205A	F115	MWF11	H221
MTH101B	F110	MTuTh9	H225
MTH103C	F110	MWF11	H225

items for each student are placed in the columns with the corresponding names. The Faculty table has columns named facId, name, department, and rank, as shown in Figure 1.1(b). Each row of that table gives the faculty

Enroll		
stuId	classNumber	grade
S1001	ART103A	A
S1001	HST205A	C
S1002	ART103A	D
S1002	CSC201A	F
S1002	MTH103C	B
S1010	ART103A	
S1010	MTH103C	
S1020	CSC201A	B
S1020	MTH101B	A

FIGURE 1.1(d)

The Enroll Table

ID, last name, department, and rank of one faculty member. Class information kept for each class offered includes the class number, the faculty ID of the professor, the schedule, and the room, in appropriate columns as shown in the Class table in Figure 1.1(c). These three tables alone do not allow us to determine which classes a student is taking. To represent the fact that a student is enrolled in a particular class, we need another table, which we call Enroll, pictured in Figure 1.1(d). The columns of Enroll are stuId, classNumber, and grade. Notice that the Enroll table represents the **relationship** between Student and Class, telling us which rows of these tables are related (i.e., which students take which classes). For example, the first row, with values S1001, ART103A, tells us that the student whose ID is S1001 is enrolled in the class whose class number is ART103A. The last column of the row tells us the grade each student earned in each class. Since these represent current enrollments, we will assume that the grade is the mid-term grade. At the end of the semester, it can be changed to the final grade. Note that we did not put student names as well as the IDs in this table, because they are already in the Student table, and we want to avoid the redundancy and possible inconsistency that storing the names twice would cause. The tables shown were created using Access, and we can use Access to update them, to ask questions (called queries) about the data in them, to create reports about the data, and to do many other functions. As an example of a query, suppose we want the names of all students enrolled in ART103A. First, how do we find the answer to the question visually? Looking at the database, we see that the Enroll table tells us which students are enrolled in ART103A. However, it gives us the stuId of each student, not the name. Student names appear on the Student table. One plan for answering the question is to look at the Enroll table and find all the rows where the value of classNumber is ART103 and make note of the stuId values in those rows, namely, S1001, S1002, and S1010. Then we look at the Student table and find the rows containing those values in the stuId column. We find the answer to the question by listing the lastName and firstName values in those rows, giving us Smith Tom, Chin Ann, and Burns Edward. Access provides a **query tool** that allows us to check off which columns are included in a query and to specify conditions for the records in the results. Figure 1.2 shows the results of executing the preceding query using this tool. We can also use the **reporting tool** in Access to generate a variety of reports. Figure 1.3 shows a typical report called Class Lists that shows each class number, the ID and name of the fac-

FIGURE 1.2

Results of the Query: "Find names of all students enrolled in ART103A"

Query1	
lastName	**firstName**
Smith	Tom
Chin	Ann
Burns	Edward

FIGURE 1.3

Class Lists Report

Class Lists					
classNumber	**facId**	**name**	**stuId**	**lastName**	**firstName**
ART103A	F101	Adams	S1001	Smith	Tom
			S1002	Chin	Ann
			S1010	Burns	Edward
CSC201A	F105	Tanaka	S1002	Chin	Ann
			S1020	Rivera	Jane
HST205A	F115	Smith	S1001	Smith	Tom
MTH101B	F110	Byrne	S1020	Rivera	Jane
MTH103C	F110	Byrne	S1002	Chin	Ann
			S1010	Burns	Edward

ulty member teaching the class, and the IDs and names of all the students in
that class.

1.3   The Integrated Database Environment

Before integrated databases were created, **file processing** systems were
used, and data used by an organization's application programs was stored
in separate files. Typically, a department that needed an application program worked with the organization's data processing department to create
specifications for both the program and the data needed for it. Often the
same data was collected and stored independently by several departments
within an organization, but not shared. Each application had its own data
files that were created specifically for the application, and that belonged to
the department for which the application was written. (Note: although the
word *data* is plural in standard English, it is customary to use it as both sin-
gular and plural in database literature, as in "data is" and "data are".) More
recently, the widespread use of microcomputer-based databases can create
a similar scenario, where individuals or departments set up their own databases or spreadsheets containing data, creating isolated "islands of information" within an organization. Having multiple copies of the same data
within isolated files or small databases can lead to flawed, outdated, or contradictory information, creating confusion for users. Most organizations
can benefit by having their data integrated into a single database. In this
book, we assume the typical database is a large one belonging to a business
or organization, which we will call the **enterprise**. However, the techniques
described apply to databases of all sizes. An **integrated database** is a collection of related data that can be used simultaneously by many departments
and users in an enterprise. It is typically a large database that contains all
the data needed by an enterprise for a specific group of applications or
even for all of its applications stored together, with as little repetition as
possible. Several different types of records may appear in the database.
Information about the structure of the records and the logical connections
between the data items and records is also stored in the database, so that
the system "knows," for example, which faculty record is connected to a
particular class record. This "data about data" is called **metadata**. The database is not owned by a single department, but is a shared resource. The
database is managed by a **database administrator** (DBA), who is responsible for creating and maintaining the database to satisfy the needs of users.
All access to the database is controlled by a software package called the
Database Management System (DBMS). The DBMS has programs that set

up the storage structures, load the data, accept data requests (queries) from programs and users, format retrieved data so that it appears in the form the program or user expects, hide data that a particular user should not have access to, accept and perform updates, allow concurrent use of the data without having users interfere with each other, and perform backup and recovery procedures. These are just some of the many functions of the database management system.

Figure 1.4 illustrates an integrated database environment for the sample University database. Here, all the data about students, classes, faculty, and enroll-

FIGURE 1.4

The Integrated Database Environment

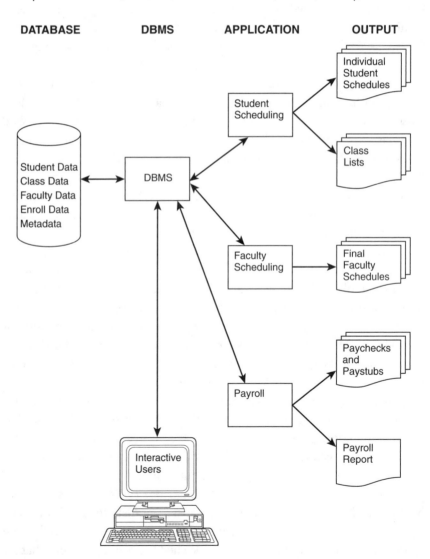

ments is stored in a single database. The data is integrated, so that the data items are stored in compatible formats and information about logical connections between them is also stored. The database contains this metadata, including a description of its own structure so the DBMS "knows" what data items exist and how they are structured. It is shared by many users, usually concurrently. All access to the data is through the DBMS. The applications programs, which might be written in different programming languages, go through the DBMS, which can present data in the form each program expects. In addition to providing support for applications, the DBMS provides a user interface for interactive queries. Authorized users can question the database directly, using the query language of the particular DBMS.

1.4   Roles in the Integrated Database Environment

Many individuals or groups are involved in the operations of a large database system. They play different roles, depending on the way they interact with the database, as depicted in Figure 1.5.

- End Users

    The database is designed, created, and maintained to serve the information needs of **end users**, people who use the data to perform their jobs. Regardless of the elegance of the database design or the sophistication of the hardware and software used, if the database does not provide adequate information to users, it is a failure. Ultimately, it is the users who judge the success of the system. Users can be categorized according to the way they access data. Sophisticated users (also called **casual users**) are trained in the use of the interactive query language, and access data by entering queries at workstations. Such users are authorized by the DBA to see a portion of the database called a **view** and to operate on data included in that view. The flexibility of the query language allows them to perform many different operations on the database, limited only by the view they have been assigned and their authorizations. Casual users may perform retrieval, insertion, deletion, or update operations through the query language, provided they are authorized to do so. **Naive users** do not use the interactive query language, but access data through application programs that

FIGURE 1.5

**Roles in the Database
Environment**

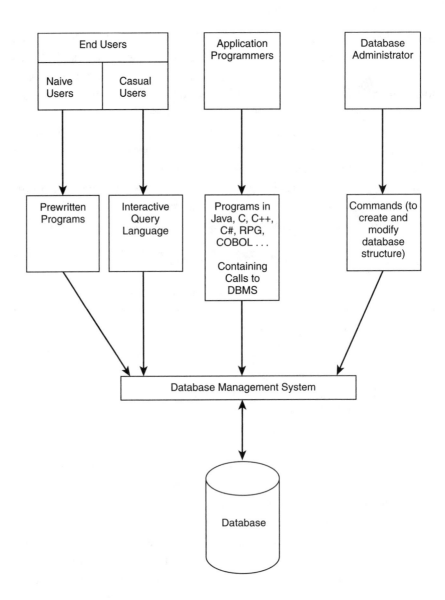

have been written for them. They invoke the programs by entering
simple commands or choosing options from a menu. They do not
need to know any details of the structure or language of the database system. They interact with the system in a less sophisticated
way, restricting their access to operations performed by the programs. The programs themselves may perform update or retrieval
operations. An even larger group of **secondary users** may use the

information in the database, without interacting directly with it, by receiving output that they use in their work.

For example, in a university Registrar's Office, clerks may be naive users, while the registrar may be a casual user. The clerks perform simple, repetitive tasks such as printing out student transcripts, perhaps by choosing an option such as PRINT OUT TRANSCRIPT from a menu. The TRANSCRIPT program would prompt the clerk for the student ID or other identifying information, and complete its task without further instructions from the clerk. The registrar uses the query language to ask one-of-a-kind questions such as, "How many students are registered for six or more classes this semester?" If there is no pre-written program in the DBMS system to answer this question, the registrar writes statements in the query language of that particular database. The students who receive printed transcripts, and the professors who receive class rosters, are secondary users.

- Applications Programmers
  This group includes programmers who write batch, or interactive, applications for other users. Their application programs may be written in a variety of host programming languages such as Java, C, C++, C#, Visual BASIC, or COBOL. Each program that accesses the database contains statements that call the database management system to perform updates or retrievals on the database. Some sophisticated end users who have both the knowledge of the programming language, and who have permission to do so, are able to write applications for their own use.

- Database Administrator
  The database administrator is the individual or group responsible for designing, creating the structure of, and maintaining the database. In many cases the database is designed by a specialist, and the DBA takes over responsibility once the design is complete. The database designer begins the design process by interviewing users to determine their data needs. He or she examines the current system, analyzes the organization and its information needs, and develops a tentative model for the database. The model is refined and improved as the designer, in consultation with users, becomes

more aware of their data needs and learns more about the functioning of the organization. When a satisfactory design is developed, the DBA implements it. Once again, users are consulted to determine whether the operational system is adequate. The design, refinement, and redesign of the system are all team efforts, with the designer, DBA, and users working together to develop the best data resource for the organization. The DBA interacts with the operational database as a "superuser," one who controls and accesses information about the structure and use of the database itself, as opposed to end users, who access the data within the database. Chapter 2 contains a more detailed description of the functions of the database administrator.

1.5   Advantages of the Integrated Database Approach

The integrated database approach has several advantages compared with the "islands of information" typical of file processing or small isolated databases:

1. Sharing of Data
    The database belongs to the entire enterprise, which now has control over the data it needs to conduct its business. Many users can be authorized to access the same piece of information.

2. Control of Redundancy
    Information is integrated so that multiple copies of the same data are not stored unless necessary. Some limited redundancy is permitted, but the database management system "knows about" that repetition. A database ordinarily does not have multiple copies of entire records, unlike a file system, where different departments may have duplicates of entire files.

3. Data Consistency
    One effect of eliminating or controlling redundancy is that the stored data is consistent. If a data item appears only once, any update to its value needs to be performed only once, and all users will have access to the same new value. If the system has some controlled redundancy, when it receives an update to an item that

appears more than once, it will automatically update every occurrence of that item, keeping the database consistent.

4. Improved Data Standards

The DBA can define and enforce organization-wide standards for representation of data in the database. There may be rules governing the format of all data items, conventions on data names, documentation standards, update procedures, backup procedures, and permitted usage of the database.

5. Better Data Security

An organization's database is a valuable corporate resource that should be protected from intentional or accidental misuse. Data security is the protection of the database from unauthorized access by persons or programs that might misuse or damage the data. A database system allows security restrictions to be defined and enforced on several levels. All authorized access to the database is through the DBMS, which can require that users go through security procedures or use passwords to gain access to the database. Each user is provided with a view of a predefined portion of the database. The DBMS knows what data items the user is permitted to access, and the type of access allowed, whether retrieval only, update or deletion of existing records, or insertion of new records. To preclude the possibility of having a user bypass the DBMS and gain access to data in an illegal manner, the DBMS can encrypt the data before storing it.

6. Improved Data Integrity

Database management systems allow the DBA to define integrity constraints—consistency rules that the database must obey. These constraints apply to items within a record (intra-record constraints), or to records that are related to one another (inter-record constraints), or they might be general business constraints. The DBMS is responsible for never allowing a record insertion, deletion, or update that violates an integrity constraint.

7. Balancing of Conflicting Requirements

Each department or individual user has data needs that may be in conflict with those of other users. The DBA is aware of the needs of all users and can make decisions about the design, use, and maintenance of the database that provide the best solutions for the organization as a whole.

8. Faster Development of New Applications

A well-designed database provides an accurate model of the operations of the organization. When a new application is proposed, it is likely that the data required is already stored in the database. If so, the DBMS can provide data in the form required by the program. Development time is reduced because no file creation phase is needed for the new application, as it is when file processing systems are used.

9. Better Data Accessibility

In addition to providing data for programs, most database management systems allow interactive access by users. They provide query languages that permit users to ask ad hoc questions and to obtain the desired information.

10. Economy of Scale

When all of the organization's data requirements are satisfied by one database instead of many separate files, the size of the combined operation provides several advantages. The portion of the budget that would ordinarily be allocated to various departments for their data design, storage, and maintenance costs can be pooled, possibly resulting in a lower total cost. The pooled resources can be used to develop a more sophisticated and powerful system than any department could afford individually. Any improvement to the database benefits many users.

11. More Control over Concurrency

If two users are permitted to access data simultaneously, and at least one of them is updating data, it is possible that they will interfere with each other. Integrated database management systems have subsystems to control concurrency so that transactions are not lost or performed incorrectly.

12. Better Backup and Recovery Procedures

In a database environment, the database records are normally backed up (copied) on a regular basis. As transactions are performed, any updates are recorded to a log of changes called the

recovery log. If the system fails, the backup and log are used to bring the database to the state it was in just prior to the failure. The system is therefore self-recovering.

1.6   Historical Developments in Information Systems

The need to record data goes back to earliest recorded history. We see evidence of attempts to provide permanent records of transactions in Sumarian clay tables, in artifacts left by the Babylonians, in ancient Egyptian hieroglyphics, and even in cave paintings. Paper records or other written forms have been used for centuries to record information about family histories, treaties and other agreements, household or business inventories, school enrollment, employee records, payment for goods or services, census data, and many other facets of life.

The use of **punched cards** for data storage was introduced in 1890, when US census data was collected and stored on punched cards for the first time. As the time for the 1890 census approached, the country's population had increased so much that it was anticipated there would not be sufficient time to complete the census before 1900, when a new one would begin. The Census Bureau sponsored a competition to spur ideas about ways to make the census more efficient. Herman Hollerith, an employee at the bureau, proposed the use of punched cards to record census responses from each household and to facilitate processing of the responses. Such cards were already in use in the silk weaving industry in Lyon, France to control the Jacquard loom, which wove patterns in silk fabric. Hollerith designed a method of using the same technology to store the census data and to examine its patterns. He won the competition and because of his design the census was completed in record time—and a new technique for data processing was invented. After that success, mechanical punched-card equipment was used for many years for storing, sorting, analyzing, and reporting data, and punched cards served as an input medium for computers for both programs and data.

Punched paper tape was used to store both computer programs and data beginning in the early 1940s, when the earliest electro-mechanical and electronic computers were developed. Starting about 1950, **magnetic tape** was developed and used for input for early computers, including the UNIVAC 1, the first commercially available computer. Decks of punched cards, loops of punched paper tape, or reels of magnetic tape were all used in essentially the same way, both for storing programs and providing a method of storing and inputting data. Data on these mediums could be read only in the order in which it was stored. This type of **sequential file processing** was extremely efficient but not very flexible. Payroll was usually the first application that a business chose to automate, because of the complex calculations and reporting requirements that were tedious for human beings to perform.

Figure 1.6 provides an overview of a payroll application using sequential file processing. A **master file** containing relatively permanent payroll data for each employee was kept in order by a key field, perhaps Employee Number. The records in this file might also contain items such as the employee name, address, weekly salary, exemptions, tax deductions, year-to-date totals for gross pay, taxes, and take-home pay. Each week a **transaction file** containing new data such as the number of hours worked that week, any changes in salary, deductions or other data, and any other new information needed for this week's payroll would be prepared. Often magnetic tape was used for the master file, and punched cards for the transaction file. Both files had to be in the same order, by Employee Number. A program would read a master record, then read the transaction record for

FIGURE 1.6

A Sequential File Processing System

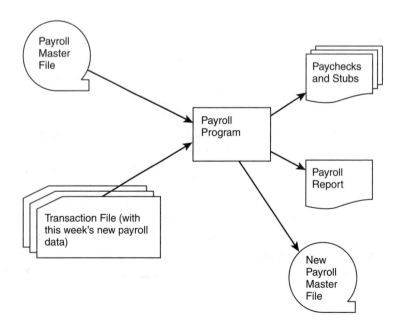

the same employee, and complete the payroll processing for that person. In the process, the information on the old master record would be changed to reflect new data, and a new record would be written to a new master tape. At the end of the program, the new tape would become the current master tape, and it would be used the following week. This is referred to as an **old master/new master** or a **father/son** system. The type of processing described here, where a set of records is submitted as a unit to a program that then operates on them without further human intervention, is referred to as **batch processing**. Sequential storage devices are sufficient for use in batch processing.

Magnetic disk storage was available by the late 1950s, making **direct access** (nonsequential access) of records possible. Since records could now be retrieved directly without passing through previous ones, programs no longer required that the order of access match the physical order of the records. Updates could be made to the disk, without rewriting the entire file. Programming languages, including COBOL and PL/1, were developed during the 1960s for commercial data processing that used data stored on both tape and disk. Originally, simple file organizations were used to organize data on these secondary storage devices, but as applications became more complex, more sophisticated methods of storing and retrieving data were needed. Two competing database models, the network and the hierarchical, were developed at this time. However, file systems continued to be used for many applications.

The **hierarchical model** for databases was developed during the 1960s as an ad hoc solution to immediate needs of real applications. The oldest hierarchical database management system, IBM's IMS, was developed to organize and store information needed by the space program for the Apollo moon landing project. North American Aviation, (which became Rockwell), and IBM worked jointly to produce the first version of IMS, which was released in 1968. Early versions of IMS were designed to be used with magnetic tape devices, but later magnetic disk became the standard. IMS soon became the dominant hierarchical database management system in the marketplace and was for many years the most widely used of all DBMSs, until it was replaced by relational systems. The original SABRE airline reservation system was based on IMS. The hierarchical model used a tree structure familiar to programmers who are accustomed to working with files, and provided efficient, predictable performance.

One of the oldest database management systems, Integrated Data Store (IDS) was developed at General Electric by Charles Bachman during the early 1960s using the **network model**. This database management system influenced the development of the database field for many years. The Conference on Data Systems Languages (**CODASYL**), an organization consisting of representatives of major hardware and software vendors and users, was formed to try to standardize many aspects of data processing. It had successfully written standards for the COBOL language. In the late 1960s it formed a subgroup called the Database Task Group (**DBTG**) to address the question of standardization for database management systems. Influenced by IDS, the group proposed a network-based model and specifications for data definition and data manipulation languages. In 1971 its first official report was submitted to the American National Standards Institute (ANSI), which refused to accept or reject the proposed standard. The 1971 report was succeeded by several newer versions, but it remained the principal document describing a network-based model generally referred to as the CODASYL model or the DBTG model, and several popular database management systems were based on it. In addition, it provided the vocabulary and framework for discussion of database issues, establishing for the first time the notion of a layered database architecture and common terminology. The most widely used network-based system was IDMS from Cullinet. Others included PRIME DBMS from PRIME Computer, IDS II from Honeywell, DMS 170 from Control Data Corporation, DC, DMSII and DMS1100 from UNISYS, and DBMS 20 from Digital Equipment Corporation.

Although the hierarchical and network models were powerful and efficient, they were complex, requiring users to understand data structures and access paths to data. They were designed for use with programs rather than for interactive access by users, so ad hoc queries were not supported. The logic required to locate the desired records was contained in the applications, not in the database. They were also not based on a solid theoretical foundation, but were solutions built on existing file systems.

The **relational model** was first proposed by E. F. Codd in 1970, in a paper called "A Relational Model of Data for Large Shared Data Banks." It was the first model based on abstract notions from mathematics, which provided a strong theoretical base. Early research on the model was done at the IBM Research Laboratory in San Jose, California. System R, a prototype relational database management system, was developed by IBM researchers during the late 1970s, and the research results, including the development of a new language, SQL (Structured Query Language) were widely published. At about the same time, The Peterlee Relational Test Vehicle, was developed at the IBM UK Scientific Laboratory. Another important research project based on the relational model was **INGRES**, developed at the University of California at Berkeley. The research led to a "university" version of INGRES, as well as a commercial product. Recognizing the value of the model, Larry Ellison founded a company to use the results of the System R project and released ORACLE, the first commercial relational DBMS in 1979. IBM did not initially recognize the commercial potential of the relational model, probably due to the tremendous success of IMS, which it continued to promote as its primary database product. IBM finally released its first commercial relational DBMS, called SQL/DS in 1981, followed by the announcement of DB2 in 1983. The widespread use of microcomputers beginning in the 1980s led to the development of PC-based database management systems, which were all relational. Among early microcomputer-based relational database management systems were dBase, R:Base, Foxpro, and Paradox. SQL, the language developed for System R, has become the standard data language for relational-model databases, with ANSI-approved standards published starting in 1986, with major revisions in 1992 and 1999, and further expansions in 2003, 2006, and 2008. Microsoft's Access, which uses the relational model, is now the most widely used microcomputer-based database management system. Oracle, DB2, and Informix (both from IBM), Sybase, Microsoft's SQL Server, MySQL, and PostGreSQL all of which use the relational model, are currently the most popular enterprise database management systems.

The relational model uses simple tables to organize data. However, it does not allow database designers to express some important distinctions when they model an enterprise. In 1976, P. P. Chen developed a new type of model, the **entity-relationship** (ER) model. This is an example of a **semantic model**, one that attempts to capture the meaning of the data it represents. It is most often used in the design phase for relational databases. The Entity-Relationship model itself has been extended several times to make it semantically richer. Other semantic models for databases, including the object-oriented model, were developed to try to capture more of the meaning in data.

The need to store and manipulate complex data that is not easy to model using the simple tables of the relational model, as well as the development of programming languages using the object-oriented paradigm, led to the development of **object-oriented** databases in the 1990s. These databases were developed to handle the data required for advanced applications such as geographical information systems, multimedia, computer-aided design and computer-aided manufacturing (CAD/CAM), and other complex environments. Object-oriented programming languages including both Java and C++ were extended to allow the creation of persistent objects that could be stored in a database. UML (Unified Modeling Language) was created to express the concepts and plan the design of object-oriented databases. Object-oriented DBMSs include ObjectStore, Versant, Objectivity, and Caché. Despite the popularity of object-oriented programming languages, object-oriented database management systems were not widely adopted. Instead, relational database management systems such as Oracle and DB2 added object-oriented capabilities to their products, and the SQL language was extended to include some object capabilities, resulting in hybrid **object-relational** databases, which have become the leading products in the field.

Data warehouses were developed in the 1990s to provide a method of capturing data consolidated from many databases. A data warehouse usually stores historical data about an organization, for the purpose of **data mining**, a process of analyzing the data statistically to enable the organization to unearth the trends that may be present in its own records.

The widespread use of the Internet has had a tremendous impact on database development. The World Wide Web connects users to a rich and constantly expanding network of databases or other data sources such as spreadsheets, data files, or documents, providing access to digital libraries, multimedia resources, educational resources, and much more. E-commerce websites provide interactive access by customers to databases of information about products and services throughout the world. The need to exchange data between these Internet-based resources led to the adoption of Extensible Markup Language (**XML**) as a standard for data exchange. The **semi-structured data model** is used for describing the format of data residing in differently structured or relatively unstructured data stores. It is useful when the data sources either have no fixed structure or have a structure that is defined within the data itself rather than in separate metadata. XML databases provide a system for handling the data within diverse data sources.

1.7   Chapter Summary

Databases are used in hundreds of thousands of organizations ranging from large government agencies to small businesses. The study of the theory, design, and management of databases enables us to maximize their potential benefits.

In a typical database, data is stored in a format that makes it easy to access, either for individual queries or large reports. In an integrated database environment, all data is kept in a single repository called the database, and managed by the database administrator (DBA). All access to the database is through the database management system (DBMS), a software package that sets up storage structures, loads data, provides access for programs and interactive users, formats retrieved data, hides certain data, does updates, controls concurrency, and performs backup and recovery for the database. Data in a database is integrated, self-describing, and shared concurrently by many users. The DBMS provides a program interface and a user interface for interactive queries that are expressed in the query language of the particular DBMS. People in the integrated database environment include end users, application programmers, and the DBA, all of whom interact with the database in different ways.

Some of the advantages of the integrated database approach are sharing of data, control of redundancy, data consistency, improved data standards, better data security, improved data integrity, balancing of conflicting requirements, faster development of new applications, better data accessibility, economy of scale, more control over concurrency, and better backup and recovery procedures.

The development of information systems depended on technological advances in hardware and software. Starting with punched cards, storage technology moved on to paper tape, magnetic tape, magnetic disk, and newer devices. Sequential file processing, required for tape, was replaced by direct file processing once direct-access devices such as disks were developed. The hierarchical database model was developed from file processing technology, and the first hierarchical database management system, IMS, was created by IBM and North American Aviation to handle the vast amount of data needed for the Apollo moon landing project. IDS, based on the network model, was developed by Charles Bachman at General Electric, and was the inspiration for the CODASYL DBTG standardization proposals. The relational model was proposed by E. F. Codd, and a prototype called System R, was developed, along with SQL, as the standard relational data language. The entity-relationship model was developed by P. P. Chen to be a semantic model, capturing more of the meaning of data than the relational model. Object-oriented models were developed to allow representation of more complex data items needed for advanced database applications. Hybrid object-relational systems add some object features to relational databases. Data warehouses allow collection of data from many databases, providing an organization with a rich data resource for data mining. The widespread use of the Internet and the growth of e-commerce have made databases more accessible to the public, and has led to the creation of the semi-structured data model and the use of XML as a standard for data exchange.

Exercises

1.1   Give four examples of database systems other than those listed in Section 1.1.

1.2   Name five tasks performed by the DBMS.

1.3   List three functions that you can perform with a database that you cannot perform with a spreadsheet.

1.4   Distinguish between a database and a database management system.

1.5   List five advantages of a database system and give an example of each.

1.6   List three responsibilities of the DBA.

1.7   Give an example of an end user and describe a typical task that a user can perform on a database.

1.8   Provide an example of an application besides payroll that might use sequential batch processing and draw a diagram similar to Figure 1.6.

1.9   Briefly define each of the following terms used in database systems:

a. integrated database

b. enterprise

c. metadata

d. concurrent use

e. query

f. end user

g. data redundancy

h. data consistancy

i. integrity constraint

j. data encryption

k. economy of scale

l. backup

m. recovery log

n. user view

o. semantic model

p. SQL

q. XML

r. data mining

On the Companion Website:

- Lab Exercises
- Sample Project
- Student Projects

CHAPTER 2

Database Planning and Database Architecture

Chapter Objectives

In this chapter you will learn the following:

- The distinction between data and information

- The four levels of discussion about data

- The steps in staged database design

- The functions of a database administrator

- The distinction between DDL and DML

- The rationale for and contents of the three-level database architecture

- The meaning of logical and physical data independence

- Characteristics of
  various data
  models

2.1   Data as a Resource

If you were asked to identify the resources of a typical business organization, you would probably include capital equipment, financial assets, and personnel, but you might not think of data as a resource. When a corporate database exists, the data it contains is a genuine corporate resource. Since the database contains data about the organization's operations (called **operational data**) that is used by many departments, and since it is professionally managed by a DBA, there is an increased appreciation of the value of the data itself, independent of the applications that use it. A **resource** is any asset that is of value to an organization and that incurs costs. An organization's operational data clearly fits this definition. To appreciate the value of an organization's data more fully, imagine what would happen if the data were lost or fell into the hands of a competitor. Many organizations, such as banks and brokerage houses, are heavily dependent on data, and would fail very quickly if their data were lost. Most businesses would suffer heavy losses if their operational data were unavailable. In fact, an organization depends on the availability of operational data in managing its other resources. For example, decisions about the purchase, lease, or use of equipment; financial investments and financial returns; and staffing needs should be made on the basis of information about the organization's operations. The recognition of data as a corporate resource is an important objective in developing an integrated database environment. The database protects the data resource by providing data security, integrity, and reliability controls through the DBMS.

2.2   Characteristics of Data

In order to appreciate the importance of data as a corporate resource, we need to examine its characteristics more closely.

2.2.1   Data and Information

We often think of data as information, but these two terms have slightly different meanings. The term **data** refers to the bare facts recorded in the database. **Information** is processed data that is in a form that is useful for making decisions. Information is derived from the stored data by re-arranging, selecting, combining, summarizing, or performing other operations on the data. For example, if we simply print out all the stored items in the database shown in Figure 1.1, without the column headings that identify what they represent, we have data. However, if we print a formatted report such as the one in Figure 1.3, showing the data in some order that helps us make a decision, we have information. In practice, most people use the two terms interchangeably.

2.2.2   Levels of Discussing Data

When we discuss data, it is important to distinguish between the real world, the small part of the real world that the database is concerned with, the inherent structure of that portion of the world, the structure of the database, and the data stored in the database. There are actually four levels of discussion or abstraction to be considered when we talk about databases.

We begin with the **real world**, or reality. On this first level, we talk about the **enterprise**, the organization for which the database is designed. The enterprise might be a corporation, government agency, university, bank, brokerage house, school, hospital, or other organization. As the enterprise functions in the real world, there is too much detail involved to keep track of all the facts needed for decision making by direct observation. Instead, we identify those facets of the enterprise that we need to keep track of for decision making. The part of the real world that will be represented in the database is called a **miniworld** or a **universe of discourse**. For the miniworld, we begin to develop a **conceptual model**, which forms the second level of data discussion. We identify **entities** which are persons, places, events, objects, or concepts about which we collect data. For the organizations mentioned previously, we could choose entities such as customers, employees, students, bank accounts, investments, classes, or patients. We group similar entities into **entity sets**. For example, for the set of all customers we form the entity set we might call Customers. Similarly, we might have entity sets called Employees, Students, Accounts, Investments, Classes, and Patients—each consisting of all entity instances of the corresponding type. A conceptual model may have many entity sets. Each entity has certain **attributes**, which are characteristics or properties to describe the entity and that the organization considers important. For the Student entity set, attributes might include student ID, name, address, telephone number, major, credits passed, grade point average, and adviser. Some entities may have **relationships** or associations with other entities. For example, in a university, students are related to classes by being enrolled in those classes, and faculty members are related to classes by teaching them. The conceptual model will represent these relationships by connecting the entity sets in some manner. The concepts of entity, attribute, and relationship will be discussed in more detail in Chapter 3. The conceptual model is often represented by a diagram such as an ER or UML diagram. The model should be designed to be a useful picture of the organization and its operations for the miniworld of interest.

The structure of the database, called the **logical model** of the database, is the third level of discussion. The logical model is also called the **intension** of the database, and it is relatively permanent. The **database schema** is a written description of the logical model. The schema may change occasionally if new data needs arise, a process called **schema evolution**. On this level, we talk about **metadata**, or data about data. For each entity set in the conceptual model, we have a **record type** (or equivalent representation, such as a class) in the logical model of the database. For example, for the Student entity set in the university, we would have a `Student` record type. A record type contains several **data item types**, each of which represents an attribute of an entity. For the `Student` record type, the data item types could be `stuId`, `stuName`, `address`, `phone`, `major`, `credits`, `gpa`, and `adviser`. A **data item** is the smallest named unit of stored data. Other words sometimes used for data item are data element, field, or attribute. Data items are sometimes grouped together to form **data aggregates**, which are named groups of data items within a record. Data aggregates allow us to refer to the group of data items as a whole or to the individual items in the group. A **record** is a named collection of related data items and/or data aggregates. Relationships must also be represented in the logical model.

Information about the logical structure of the database is stored in a DBMS **data dictionary**, also called a **data directory** or **system catalog**. This repository of information contains descriptions of the record types, data item types, and data aggregates in the database, as well as other information. The data dictionary is actually a database about the database. However, a DBMS system catalog usually does much more than simply store the description of the database structure. For some systems, the system catalog is actively involved in all database accesses.

The fourth level of discussion concerns actual data in the database itself. It consists of **data instances** or occurrences. For each entity occurrence in the miniworld, there will be an occurrence of a corresponding record in the database. For each student in the university, there is a student record occurrence. So, while there is only one Student record type, which is described in the data dictionary and corresponds to the Student entity set, there may be thousands of Student record occurrences, corresponding to individual student entities, in the database itself. Similarly, there will be many instances of each of the data item types that correspond to attributes. A **file** (sometimes called a data set) is a named collection of record occurrences. For example, the Student file may contain 5000 Student records. Finally, the **database** may be thought of as a named collection of related files. The data stored in the database at a given moment is called an **extension** of the database, or a **database instance** or **database state**. The extension changes whenever records are added, deleted, or updated. The extension should always be a **valid state**, which means it should satisfy all the constraints specified in the schema. The intension of the database is actually a complex abstract data structure that formally defines all possible extensions. Figure 2.1 summarizes the four levels of discussion of data.

2.2.3   Data Sublanguages

The language that is used to describe a database to a DBMS is part of a **data sublanguage**. A data sublanguage consists of two parts: a **data definition language** (DDL) and a **data manipulation language** (DML). The DDL is used to describe the database, while the DML is used to process the database. These languages are called sublanguages because they have limited functionality, lacking many features of general purpose programming

Realm	Objects	Examples
Real World Containing Miniworld	Enterprise	Corporation, university, bank
	Some aspects of the enterprise	Human resources Student enrollment Customers and accounts
Conceptual Model	Entity Attribute Entity set Relationship	a student, a class name, schedule all students, all classes Student entity relates to Class entity by being enrolled in it
Logical Model Metadata: data definitions, stored in Data Dictionary	Record type Data item type Data aggregate	Student record type, Class record type stuId, classNumber address, consisting of street, city, state, ZIP
Data Ocurrences stored in the database	Student record occurrence Data item occurrence File Database	Record of student Tom Smith 'S1001','Smith','Tom','History',90 Student file with 5000 Student records University database containing Student file, Class file, Faculty file, . . .

FIGURE 2.1

Four Levels of Discussing Data

languages. The data sublanguage commands can be embedded within a **host** program, a general purpose language program in, for example, C, C++, C#, Java, COBOL, Fortran, or Ada. There are standards for most of the widely used general purpose languages as host languages for standard data sublanguages. In addition, most data sublanguages allow non-embedded or interactive commands for access from workstations.

2.3   Stages in Database Design

The process of analyzing the organization and its environment, developing a database model, and implementing that model requires an appropriate methodology. Traditional systems analysis provides a possible approach, but a staged database design approach offers a better solution. The database should be designed in such a way that it can evolve, changing to meet the future information needs of the organization. This evolution is possible when the designer develops a true conceptual model of the organization with the following characteristics:

- The model faithfully mirrors the operations of the organization.

- It is flexible enough to allow changes as new information needs arise.

- It supports many different user views.

- It is independent of physical implementation.

- It does not depend on the data model used by a particular database management system.

A well-designed conceptual database model protects the data resource by allowing it to evolve so that it serves both today's and tomorrow's information needs. Even if the database management system chosen for implementation is replaced, the logical model may change, but the conceptual model of the enterprise can survive. The staged database design approach is a top-down method that begins with general statements of needs, and progresses to more and more detailed consideration of problems. Different problems are considered at different phases of the project. Each stage

FIGURE 2.2

Steps in Staged Database
Design

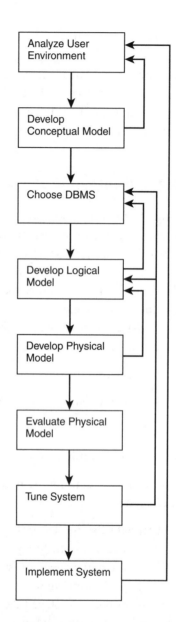

uses design tools that are appropriate to the problem at that level. Figure
2.2 shows the major design stages. They are

1.   Analyze the user environment.
     The first step in designing a database is to determine the current
     user environment. The designer studies all current applications,

determines their input and output, examines all reports generated by the present system, and interviews users to determine how they use the system. After the present system is thoroughly understood, the designer works closely with present users and potential users of the new system to identify their needs using these same methods. The designer considers not only present needs but possible new applications or future uses of the database. The result of this analysis is a model of the user environment and requirements.

2. Develop a conceptual data model.
Using the model of the user environment, the designer develops a detailed conceptual model of the database—identifying the entities, attributes, and relationships that will be represented. In addition to the conceptual model, the designer has to consider how the database is to be used. The types of applications and transactions, the kinds of access, the volume of transactions, the volume of data, the frequency of access, and other quantitative data must be specified. Other constraints such as budgetary restrictions and performance requirements must also be identified. The result of this phase is a set of database specifications.

3. Choose a DBMS.
The designer uses the specifications and knowledge of available hardware and software resources to evaluate alternative database management systems and chooses the system that best satisfies the specifications.

4. Develop the logical model.
The designer maps the conceptual model to the data model used by the chosen DBMS, creating the logical model.

5. Develop the physical model.
The designer plans the layout of data considering the structures supported by the chosen DBMS, and hardware and software resources available.

6. Evaluate the physical model.
The designer estimates the performance of all applications and transactions, considering the quantitative data previously identified, information about the performance characteristics of hardware and software to be used, and priorities given to applications

and transactions. It can be helpful to develop a **prototype**, implementing a selected portion of the database so that user views can be validated and performance measured more accurately.

7. Perform tuning if indicated by the evaluation.
    Adjustments such as modifying physical structures or optimizing software can be done to improve performance.

8. Implement the physical model.
    If the evaluation is positive, the designer then implements the physical design and the database becomes operational.

The loops in Figure 2.2 provide opportunities for feedback and changes at various stages in the design process. For example, after developing the conceptual model, the designer communicates with user groups to make sure their data requirements are represented properly. If not, the conceptual model must be adjusted. If the conceptual model does not map well to a particular data model, another should be considered. For a particular DBMS, there might be several possible logical mappings that can be evaluated. If the physical model is not acceptable, a different mapping or a different DBMS can be considered. If the results of the performance evaluation are not satisfactory, additional tuning and evaluation may be performed. The physical model can be changed if tuning does not produce the required performance. If repeated tuning and optimization are not sufficient, it might be necessary to change the way the logical model is mapped to the DBMS or to consider a different database management system. Even after the system is implemented, changes might be needed to respond to changing user needs or a changing environment.

2.4   Design Tools

Many methodologies exist that can make the database design process easier for both designers and users. They vary from general techniques described in the software engineering literature to commercial products to automate the design process. For example, **CASE** (Computer-Aided Software Engineering) packages include various tools for system analysis, project management, and design that can be very useful in the database design process. They are helpful for collecting and analyzing data, designing the data model, designing applications, and implementing the database, including prototyping, data conversion, generating application code, generating reports, and testing. **Project management software** is another type of tool that can be applied effectively to database development.

2.4.1   Data Dictionary

A DBMS data dictionary, as discussed in Section 2.2.2, is a repository of information that describes the logical structure of the database. It contains **metadata**, or data about the data in the database. It has entries for all the types of objects that exist in the database. If the data dictionary is part of the DBMS, it is referred to as an **integrated** data dictionary or **system catalog**. A system catalog is always consistent with the actual database structure, because it is maintained automatically by the system. It can perform many functions throughout the life of the database. If the data dictionary is available without a particular DBMS, we refer to it as a **freestanding** data dictionary. A freestanding data dictionary can be a commercial product or a simple file developed and maintained by the designer. For example, CASE packages often include a data dictionary tool, and freestanding data dictionaries are available even for non-database environments. Both integrated and freestanding data dictionaries have advantages and disadvantages, but a freestanding dictionary is helpful in the initial design stages, before the designer has chosen a particular DBMS. It allows the designer to enjoy the advantages of having this tool without committing to a particular implementation. A major disadvantage is that once the database is created, adjustments to its structure may not be entered into the freestanding data dictionary and, over time, the dictionary will not be an accurate reflection of the database structure.

A freestanding data dictionary is useful in the early design stages for collecting and organizing information about data. Each data item, its source(s), its name(s), its uses, its meaning, its relationship to other items, its format, and the identity of the person or group responsible for entering it, updating it, and maintaining its correctness must be determined. The data dictionary provides an effective tool for accomplishing these tasks. The database administrator (DBA) can begin development of the data dictionary by identifying data items, securing agreement from users on a definition of each item, and entering the item in the dictionary. Since users should not be aware of other users' data, the DBA should control access to the dictionary.

A freestanding data dictionary is useful for the following:

- Collecting and storing information about data in a central location. This helps management to gain control over data as a resource.

- Securing agreement from users and designers about the meanings of data items. An exact, agreed-upon definition of each item should be developed for storage in the data dictionary.

- Communicating with users. The data dictionary greatly facilitates communication, since exact meanings are stored. The dictionary also identifies the persons, departments, or groups having access to or interest in each item.

- Identifying redundancy and inconsistency in data item names. In the process of identifying and defining data items, the DBA may discover **synonyms**, which are different names for the same item. The database can accept synonyms, but the system must be aware of them. The DBA might also discover **homonyms**, which are identical names for different data items. These are never permitted in a database.

- Keeping track of changes to the database structure. Changes such as creation of new data items and record types or alterations to data item descriptions should be recorded in the data dictionary.

- Determining the impact of changes to the database structure. Since the data dictionary records each item, all its relationships, and all its users, the DBA can see what effects a change would have.

- Identifying the sources of and responsibility for the correctness of each item. A general rule for data entry is that data should be captured as near to its source as possible. The persons or departments that generate or capture values for each data item and those responsible for updating each item should be listed in the data dictionary.

- Recording the external, logical, and internal schemas and the mappings between them. This aspect will be discussed in Section 2.6.

- Recording access control information. A data dictionary can record the identities of all those who are permitted to access each item, along with the type of access-retrieval, insertion, update, or deletion.

- A DBMS system catalog can also perform all these functions, but it is also useful for providing audit information. The system catalog can be used to record each access, allowing usage statistics to be collected for auditing the system and spotting attempted security violations.

Note that not all data dictionaries provide support for all of these functions, and some provide additional functions. Some just store the schema, some control documentation, while some system catalogs are "meta-systems" that control access to the database, generate system code, and keep statistics on database usage as well.

2.4.2 Project Management Software

This type of software provides a set of tools that can be used to plan and manage a project, especially when there are many people working on it. There are usually several types of graphs and charts available, such as **Gantt charts** and **PERT charts**, which are similar. The user specifies the objectives and scope of the project, identifies the major tasks and phases, indicates dependencies among the tasks, identifies the resources available, and sets a timeline for completion of the tasks and phases of the project. The software can be used to generate calendars, to produce graphs with many different views of the progress of the project, and to provide a means of communication among the project staff, using either intranet or Internet access. An example is Microsoft Project.

2.5   Database Administration

The database administrator is responsible for the design, operation, and management of the database. In many cases, the conceptual design is done by a database designer, and the DBA implements the design, develops the system, and manages it. The DBA must be technically competent, a good manager, a skilled communicator, and must have excellent interpersonal and communication skills. The DBA has many functions that vary according to the stage of the database project. Major functions include planning, designing, developing, and managing the database.

2.5.1   Planning and Design

- **Preliminary Database Planning.** If the DBA or database designer is chosen early enough in the project, he or she should participate in the preliminary investigation and feasibility study.

- **Identifying User Requirements.** The DBA or designer examines all transactions and all reports generated by the present system and consults with users to determine whether they satisfy their information needs. He or she works with present and potential users to design new reports and new transactions. The frequency of reports and transactions and the timeframe within which they must be produced are also recorded. The DBA uses his or her knowledge of the long-term and short-term objectives of the organization to prioritize user requirements.

- **Developing and Maintaining the Data Dictionary.** As he or she determines data needs of users, the DBA or designer stores data item names, sources, meanings, usage, and synonyms in the data dictionary. The DBA revises the data dictionary as the project progresses.

- **Designing the Conceptual Model.** The DBA or designer identifies all entities, attributes, and relationships that are to be represented in the database, and develops a conceptual model that is an accurate reflection of the miniworld.

- **Choosing a DBMS.** The DBA considers the conceptual model and other database specifications and the hardware and software available, and chooses the DBMS that best fits the environment and meets the specifications.

- **Developing the Logical Model.** There may be several ways the conceptual model could be mapped to the data model used by the DBMS. The DBA chooses the one that appears to be most appropriate.

- **Developing the Physical Model.** There may be several ways the logical model could be mapped to the data structures provided by the DBMS and to physical devices. The DBA evaluates each mapping by estimating performance of applications and transactions. The best mapping becomes the physical model.

2.5.2 Developing the Database

- **Creating and Loading the Database.** Once the physical model is developed, the DBA creates the structure of the database using the data definition language for the chosen DBMS. He or she establishes physical data sets, creates libraries, and loads the data into the database.

- **Developing User Views.** The DBA attempts to satisfy the data needs of all users. A user's view may be identical to the one requested in the initial design stages. Often, however, users' requests change as they begin to understand the system better. If the view does not coincide with the user's request, the DBA should present cogent reasons why the request has not been met and secure agreement on the actual view.

- **Writing and Maintaining Documentation.** When the database is created, the DBA makes sure all documentation accurately reflects the structure of the database. Some database documentation is written automatically by the system catalog as the database is created.

- **Developing and Enforcing Data Standards.** Since the database is shared by many users, it is important that standards be defined and enforced for the benefit of all. Users who are responsible for inserting and updating data must follow a standard format for entering data. The user interface should be designed to make it easy for users to follow the standards by displaying default values, showing acceptable ranges for items, and so on. Typical data standards include specifications for null values, abbreviations, codes, punctuation, and capitalization. The system can automatically check for errors and range restrictions, uniqueness of key values, and relationships between data values in a single record, between records in the same file, and between records in different files.

- **Developing and Enforcing Application Program Standards.** The DBA must develop security and privacy standards for applications and make sure they are subject to the audit mechanism, make proper use of the high-level data manipulation language, and fit the application development facilities provided by the DBMS. These standards apply both to old applications that are converted for use with the database and to new applications.

- **Developing Operating Procedures.** The DBA is responsible for establishing procedures for daily startup of the DBMS (if necessary), smooth running of database operations, logging of transactions, periodic backups, security and authorization procedures, recording hardware and software failures, taking performance measurements, shutting down the database in an orderly fashion in case of failure, restarting and recovering after failure, and shutting down at the end of each day (if necessary). Since these procedures are performed by operators, the DBA must consult with the operations manager to ensure that operators are trained in all aspects of database operations.

- **Doing User Training.** End users, application programmers, and systems programmers who access the database should participate in training programs so that they can learn to use it most effectively. Sessions may be conducted by the DBA, the vendor of the DBMS, or other technical trainers, either onsite or in a training center.

2.5.3   Database Management

- **Monitoring Performance.** The DBA is responsible for collecting and analyzing statistics on database performance and responding to user complaints and suggestions regarding performance. The running time for applications and the response time for interactive queries should be measured, so that the DBA can spot problems in database use. Usually, the DBMS provides facilities for recording this information. The DBA continually compares performance to requirements and makes adjustments when necessary.

- **Tuning and Reorganizing.** If performance begins to degrade as changes are made to the stored data, the DBA can respond by adding or changing indexes, reorganizing files, using faster storage devices, or optimizing software. For serious performance problems, he or she may have to reorganize the entire database.

- **Keeping Current on Database Improvements.** The DBA should be aware of new features and new versions of the DBMS that become available. He or she should evaluate these new products and other hardware and software developments to determine whether they would provide substantial benefits to the organization.

2.6   The Three-Level Database Architecture

In Section 2.3, we presented a staged database design process that began with the development of a conceptual model and ended with a physical model. Now we are ready to examine these and related concepts more closely. When we discuss a database, we need some means of describing different aspects of its structure. An early proposal for a standardized vocabulary and architecture for database systems was developed and published in 1971 by the Database Task Group appointed by the Conference on Data Systems and Languages, or CODASYL DBTG. As a result of this and later reports, databases can be viewed at three levels of abstraction. The levels form a layered **three-level architecture** and are described by three **schemas**, which are written descriptions of their structures. The purpose of the three-level architecture is to separate the user's model from the physical structure of the database. There are several reasons why this separation is desirable:

- Different users need different views of the same data.

- The way a particular user needs to see the data may change over time.

- Users should not have to deal with the complexities of the database storage structures.

- The DBA should be able to make changes to the conceptual model of the database without affecting all users.

- The DBA should be able to change the logical model, including data structures and file structures, without affecting the conceptual model or users' views.

- Database structure should be unaffected by changes to the physical aspects of storage, such as changes to storage devices.

Figure 2.3 shows a simplified version of the three-level architecture of database systems. The way users think about data is called the **external level**. The **internal level** is the way the data is actually stored using standard data structures and file organizations. However, there are many different users' views and many physical structures, so there must be some method of mapping the external views to the physical structures. A direct mapping is undesirable, since changes made to physical structures or storage devices would require a

FIGURE 2.3

Simplified Three-Level Architecture for Database Systems

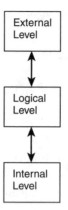

corresponding change in the external to physical mapping. Therefore there is a middle level that provides both the mapping and the desired independence between the external and physical levels. This is the **logical** level.

2.6.1   External Views

The **external level** consists of many different **external views** or **external models** of the database. Each user has a model of the real world represented in a form that is suitable for that user. Figure 2.4 presents a more detailed picture of the three-level database architecture. The top level of Figure 2.4 shows several external views. A particular user interacts with only certain aspects of the miniworld, and is interested in only some entities, and only some of their attributes and relationships. Therefore, that user's view will contain only information about those aspects. Other entities or other attributes or relationships may actually be represented in the database, but the user will be unaware of them. Besides including different entities, attributes, and relationships, different views may have different representations of the same data. For example, one user may believe dates are stored in the form month, day, year, while another may believe they are represented as year, month, day. Some views might include **virtual** or calculated data, data not actually stored as such, but created when needed. For example, age may not be actually stored, but dateOfBirth may be, and age may be calculated by the system when the user refers to it. Views may even include data combined or calculated from several records. An **external record** is a record as seen by a particular user, a part of his or her external view. An external view is actually a collection of external records. The external views are described in **external schemas** (also called **subschemas**) that are written in the data definition language (DDL). Each

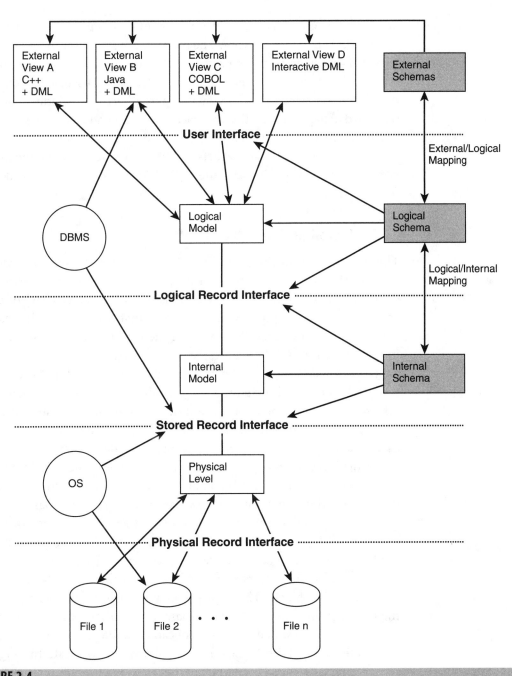

FIGURE 2.4

Three-Level Database Architecture

user's schema gives a complete description of each type of external record that appears in that user's view. The schemas are stored for use by the system data catalog in retrieving records. They should also be kept in source form as documentation. The DBMS uses the external schema to create a **user interface**, which is both a facility and a barrier. An individual user sees the database through this interface. It defines and creates the working environment for that user, accepting and displaying information in the format the user expects. It also acts as a boundary below which the user is not permitted to see. It hides the logical, internal, and physical details from the user.

2.6.2   Logical and Conceptual Models

The middle level in the three-level architecture is the **logical level**, as shown in Figure 2.4. This model includes the entire information structure of the database, as seen by the DBA. It is the "community view" of data, and includes a description of all of the data that is available to be shared. It is a comprehensive model or view of the workings of the organization in the miniworld. All the entities, with their attributes and relationships, are represented in the logical model using the data model that the DBMS supports. The model includes any constraints on the data and semantic information about the data meanings. The logical model supports the external views, in that any data available to any user must be present in or derivable from the logical model. The logical model is relatively constant. When the DBA originally designs it, he or she tries to determine present and future information needs and attempts to develop a lasting model of the organization. Therefore, as new data needs arise, the logical model might already contain the objects required. If that is not the case, the DBA expands the logical model to include the new objects. A good logical model will be able to accommodate this change and still support the old external views. Only users who need access to the new data should be affected by the change. The **logical schema** is a complete description of the information content of the database. It is written in DDL, compiled by the DBMS, and stored in the system catalog and in source form as documentation. The DBMS uses the logical schema to create the **logical record interface**, which is a boundary below which everything is invisible to the logical level and which defines and creates the working environment for the logical level. No internal or physical details such as how records are stored or sequenced cross this boundary. The logical model is actually a collection of logical records.

The logical data model is the heart of the database. It supports all the external views and is, in turn, supported by the internal model. However, the internal model is merely the physical implementation of the logical model. The logical model is itself derived from the conceptual model. Developing the conceptual model is the most challenging, interesting, and rewarding part of database design. The database designer must be able to identify, classify, and structure elements in the design. The process of **abstraction**, which means identifying common properties of a set of objects rather than focusing on details, is used to categorize data. In computer science, abstraction is used to simplify concepts and hide complexity. For example, abstract data types are considered apart from their implementation; the behavior of queues and stacks can be described without considering how they are represented. The designer can look at different levels of abstraction, so that an abstract object on one level becomes a component of a higher level abstraction. During the conceptual design process, there might be many errors and several false starts. Like many other problem-solving processes, conceptual database design is an art, guided by knowledge. There may be many possible solutions, but some are better than others. The process itself is a learning situation. The designer gradually comes to understand the workings of the organization and the meanings of its data, and expresses that understanding in the chosen model. If the designer produces a good conceptual model, it is a relatively easy task to convert it to a logical model and complete the internal and physical design. If the conceptual model is a good one, the external views are easy to define as well. If any data that a user might be interested in is included in the conceptual model, it is an easy task to put it into the user's external view. On the other hand, a poor conceptual model can be hard to implement, particularly if data and relationships are not well defined. It will also be inadequate to provide all the needed external models. It will continue to cause problems during the lifetime of the database, because it will have to be "patched up" whenever different information needs arise. The ability to adjust to change is one of the hallmarks of good conceptual design. Therefore, it is worthwhile to spend all the time and energy necessary to produce the best possible conceptual design. The payoff will be felt not only at the logical and internal design stages but in the future.

2.6.3   Internal Model

The **internal level** covers the physical implementation of the database. It includes the data structures and file organizations used to store data on physical storage devices. The DBMS chosen determines, to a large extent, what structures are available. It works with the operating system access methods to lay out the data on the storage devices, build the indexes, and/or set the pointers that will be used for data retrieval. Therefore, there is actually a physical level below the one the DBMS is responsible for—one that is managed by the operating system under the direction of the DBMS. The line between the DBMS responsibilities and the operating system responsibilities is not clear cut and can vary from system to system. Some DBMSs take advantage of many of the operating system access method facilities, while others ignore all but the most basic I/O managers and create their own alternative file organizations. The DBA must be aware of the possibilities for mapping the logical model to the internal model, and choose a mapping that supports the logical view and provides suitable performance. The **internal schema**, written in DDL, is a complete description of the internal model. It includes such items as how data is represented, how records are sequenced, what indexes exist, what pointers exist, and what hashing scheme, if any, is used. An **internal record** is a single stored record. It is the unit that is passed up to the internal level. The **stored record interface** is the boundary between the physical level, for which the operating system may be responsible, and the internal level, for which the DBMS is responsible. This interface is provided to the DBMS by the operating system. In some cases where the DBMS performs some operating system functions, the DBMS itself may create this interface. The physical level below this interface consists of items only the operating system knows, such as exactly how the sequencing is implemented and whether the fields of internal records are actually stored as contiguous bytes on the disk. The operating system creates the **physical record interface**, which is a lower boundary where storage details, such as exactly what portion of what track contains what data, are hidden.

The data dictionary/directory not only stores the complete external, logical, and internal schemas, but it also stores the mappings between them. The **external/logical mapping** tells the DBMS which objects on the logical level correspond to which objects in a particular user's external view. There may be differences in record names, data item names, data item order, data types, and so forth. If changes are made to either an external view or the logical model, the mappings must be changed. Similarly, the **logical/internal mapping** gives the correspondence between logical objects and internal ones, in that it tells how the logical objects are physically represented. If the stored structure is changed, the mapping must be changed accordingly.

To understand the distinctions among the three levels, we will examine what each level receives and passes on when we request the record of a particular employee. Refer to Figure 2.5 along with Figure 2.6. When User A requests a record such as the (external) record of Employee 101, the DBMS intercepts the request. Once the DBMS receives the request, it checks the user's external view and the external/logical mapping. Both the views and the mapping are stored in object form in the system catalog, so the checking can be accomplished easily. The DBMS also checks the user's authorization to access the items and to perform the operations requested. If there is no such authorization, the request is denied. If the user is authorized, the DBMS notes what logical level objects are needed, and the request is passed down to the logical level. Next, the logical/internal mapping is checked to see what internal structures correspond to the logical items. Once again, the system catalog has stored both of the models and the mapping. The DBMS identifies the internal objects that are required, and it passes the request to the operating system.

On the physical level, an employee record is contained in a physical record, a page or block that can hold several employee records. This is the unit that is brought to the buffer from the disk. The operating system is responsible for performing the basic job of locating the correct block for the requested record and managing its retrieval. When the retrieval is complete, the proper block is in the buffer, and the operating system passes to the DBMS the exact location within the buffer at which the stored record appears. The DBMS reads only the requested employee record, not all the records in the block. However, it sees the complete stored record, exactly as it is coded or encrypted, together with any embedded blanks and pointers that may appear in it, but without its header. This is a description of an internal record, which is the unit that passes up through the stored record interface. The DBMS uses the logical/internal mapping to decide what items to pass up through the logical record interface to the logical level.

FIGURE 2.5

Retrieving Record of E101 for User A

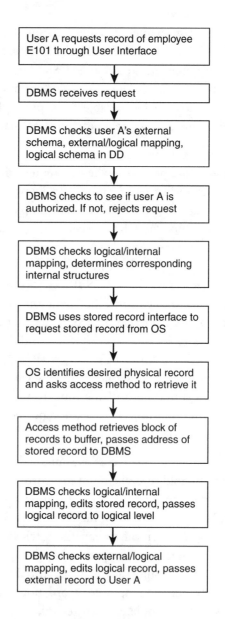

At the logical level, the record appears as a logical record, with encryption and special coding removed. Pointers that are used for establishing relationships do not appear on the logical level, since that level is only concerned with the existence of relationships, not how they are implemented. Similarly, pointers used for sequencing are not of interest on the logical level, nor are indexes. The logical level record therefore contains only the

External Employee Record:		
employeeName	empNumber	dept
JACK JONES	E101	Marketing

Logical Employee Record:				
empId	lastName	firstName	dept	salary
E101	Jones	Jack	12	55000

Stored Employee Record:						
empId	lastName	firstName	dept	salary	forward pointer	backward pointer
E101bbbbbb**Jones**bbbbbb**Jack**bbbbbbbbbb**12**bbbbbbbbb**55000**bbbb**10101**bbbbbb**10001**						

Physical Record:				
Block header	rec of E90	rec of E95	**rec of E101**	rec of E125

FIGURE 2.6

Differences in External, Logical, Stored, and Physical Record

information for that particular employee, but it contains all the fields stored for the employee, in the order in which they are stored. The DBMS checks the external/logical mapping to decide what the user's external record should look like.

When the record is passed up through the user interface to the external level, certain fields can be hidden, some can have their names changed, some can be rearranged, some can appear in a form different from their stored form, and some can be virtual, created from the stored record. Some external records might be combinations of stored records, or the result of operations such as calculations on stored records. The user then performs operations on the external record. That is, he or she can manipulate only those items that appear in the external record. These changes, if legal, are eventually made to the stored record. Figure 2.5 summarizes the steps in this process, and Figure 2.6 illustrates the differences in the appearance of the employee record as it is passed up to the external level.

2.6.4 Data Independence

A major reason for the three-level architecture is to provide **data independence**, which means that upper levels are unaffected by changes to lower

FIGURE 2.7

Logical and Physical Data
Independence

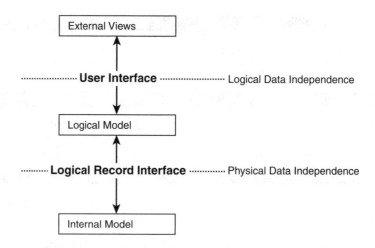

levels. There are two kinds of data independence: **logical** and **physical**. Logical data independence refers to the immunity of external models to changes in the logical model. Logical model changes such as addition of new record types, new data items, and new relationships should be possible without affecting existing external views. Of course, the users for whom the changes are made need to be aware of them, but other users should not be. In particular, existing application programs should not have to be rewritten when logical level changes are made.

Physical data independence refers to the immunity of the logical model to changes in the internal model. Internal or physical changes such as a different physical sequencing of records, switching from one access method to another, changing the hashing algorithm, using different data structures, and using new storage devices should have no effect on the logical model. On the external level, the only effect that may be felt is a change in performance. In fact, deterioration in performance is the most common reason for internal model changes. Figure 2.7 shows where each type of data independence occurs.

2.7   Overview of Data Models

A **data model** is a collection of tools often including a type of diagram and specialized vocabulary for describing the structure of the database. There is much disagreement over what constitutes a data model, and that is reflected in the dozens of proposed models and methodologies found in the literature. A data model provides a description of the database structure including the data, the relationships, constraints, and sometimes data semantics or meanings.

2.7.1 The Entity-Relationship Model

The Entity-Relationship model is an example of a **semantic model**. Semantic models are used to describe the conceptual and external levels of data, and are independent of the internal and physical aspects. In addition to specifying what is to be represented in the database, they attempt to incorporate some meanings or semantic aspects of data such as explicit representation of objects, attributes, and relationships, categorization of objects, abstractions, and explicit data constraints. Some of the concepts of the E-R model were introduced in Section 2.2.2, when we described the four levels of abstraction in the discussion of data. The model was introduced by Chen in the mid 1970s and is widely used for conceptual design. It is based on identifying **entities** that are representations of real objects in the miniworld. Entities are described by their attributes and are connected by relationships. We described entities as persons, places, events, objects, or concepts about which we collect data. A more abstract description is that an entity is any object that exists and is distinguishable from other objects. The **attributes** are qualities or characteristics that describe the entities and distinguish them from one another. We defined an **entity set** as a collection of entities of the same type. Now we also define a **relationship set** as a set of relationships of the same type, and we add the fact that relationships themselves might have **descriptive attributes**. The E-R model also allows us to express constraints, or restrictions, on the entities or relationships. Chapter 3 contains a more complete description of the E-R model, including details about constraints.

One of the most useful and attractive features of the E-R model is that it provides a graphical method for depicting the conceptual structure of the database. E-R diagrams contain symbols for entities, attributes, and relationships. Figure 2.8 shows some of the symbols, along with their names, meanings, and usages. Figure 2.9 illustrates a simple E-R diagram for a students and classes database similar to the one we discussed in Section 1.2. It shows an entity set called Student, with the attributes stuId (the primary key, which is a unique identifier for each student entity instance), lastName, firstName, major, and credits. Class information, to be kept for each class offered during the current term, includes the classNumber (primary key), the schedule, and the room. The Student and Class entity sets are connected by a relationship set, Enroll, which tells us which students

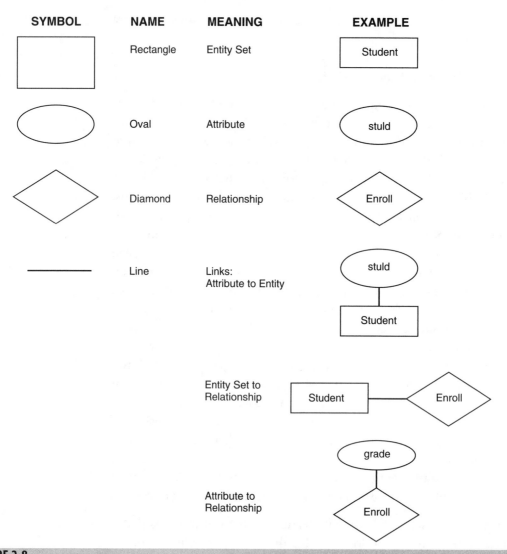

FIGURE 2.8

Basic Symbols for E-R Diagrams

are enrolled in which classes. It has its own descriptive attribute, grade. Note that grade is not an attribute of Student, since knowing the grade for a student is meaningless unless we know the course as well. Similarly, grade is not an attribute of Class, since knowing that a particular grade was given for a class is meaningless unless we know to which student the grade was given. Therefore, since grade has meaning only for a particular combination of student and class, it belongs to the relationship set. Since

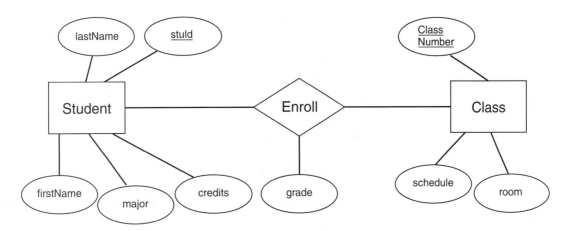

FIGURE 2.9
Simplified E-R Diagram

the E-R model describes only a conceptual structure for the database, we do not attempt to describe how the model could or should be represented internally. Therefore, the material in Section 2.2.2 in which we described data items, records, and files is not part of the E-R model itself.

2.7.2 Relational Model

The relational model is an example of a **record-based model**, one that essentially pictures what the logical records will look like. Record-based models are used to describe the external, logical, and to some extent the internal levels of the database. They allow the designer to develop and specify the logical structure and provide some options for implementation of the design. However, they do not provide much semantic information such as categorization of objects, relationships, abstraction, or data constraints. The relational model was proposed by Codd in 1970 and is widely used, because of its simplicity and its power. The relational model began by using the theory of relations in mathematics and adapting it for use in database theory. The same type of theoretical development of the subject, complete with formal notation, definitions, theorems, and proofs that we usually find in mathematics can be applied to databases using this model. The results of this theoretical development are then applied to practical considerations of implementation. In the relational model, entities are represented as relations, which are physically represented as tables, and attributes as columns of those tables. Some relationships may also be represented as relations or tables. Figure 1.1 (a)–(d) showed a sample relational database for data about students, faculty, and their classes. We will study the relational model, including SQL, the standard language for the model, in later chapters. Two older record-based models are the **network** and the **hierarchical** models mentioned in Section 1.6. They are primarily of historic interest, since they are no longer widely used for developing new databases. However, many legacy databases based on these models still exist, with code that is still being used and that must be maintained.

2.7.3   Object-Oriented Model

The object-oriented model is a semantic model. It is based on the notion of an **object**, which, like an entity, is a representation of some person, place, event, or concept in the real world that we wish to represent in the database. While entities have only attributes, objects have both a **state** and a **behavior**. The state of an object is determined by the values of its attributes (instance variables). The behavior is the set of functions (methods) defined for the object. A **class** is similar to an entity set and consists of the set of objects having the same structure and behavior. The object-oriented model uses **encapsulation**, incorporating both data and functions in a unit where they are protected from modification from outside. Classes can be grouped into hierarchies, For example, we could define a Person class with attributes such as FirstName, LastName, and ID and methods such as ChangeName. We could then create a Student class and a Faculty class as subclasses of Person. The subclasses inherit the attributes and methods of the parent, so in this example, every Student object and every Faculty object has the attributes and methods of Person. They can also have their own attributes and methods. For example, the Student class can have its own additional attribute, Major, and a method changeMajor. Classes can also participate in relationships of various types. For example, the Student class can be related to the Course class. Unified Modeling Language (UML) class diagrams are usually used for representing object-oriented data models. Figure 2.10 shows an example of a simple OO data model. Every object in a database must have a unique **object identifier** that functions as a permanent primary key, but that does not take its value from any of the object's attributes. An important difference between program objects and database objects is **persistence**. Unlike a program object that exists only while the program is executing, a database object remains in existence after execution of an application program completes.

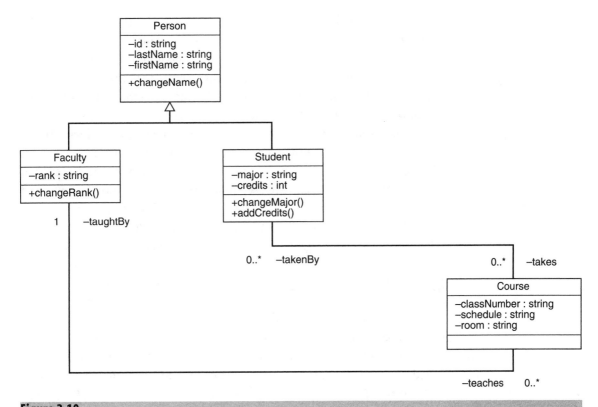

Figure 2.10

A Class Diagram

2.7.4   Object-Relational Model

The object-relational model extends the relational model by adding complex data types and methods as well as other advanced features. Instead of atomic, single-valued attributes as required in the relational model, this model allows attributes to be structured and have sets or arrays of values. It also permits methods and type inheritance. The SQL language was extended to create and manipulate the more complex data types and facilities that this model supports. Therefore the language used to manage an object-relational database is closer to the type of language used for relational databases than that used for strictly object-oriented databases.

2.7.5   Semistructured Data Model

Most data models require that entity sets (or classes or records, depending on the model) have the same structure. The structure is defined in the schema, and remains unchanged unless the DBA changes the schema. By contrast, the semi-structured model allows a collection of nodes, each containing data, possibly with different schemas. The node itself contains information about the structure of its contents. Semi-structured databases are especially useful when existing databases having different schemas must be integrated. The individual databases can be viewed as documents, and XML (Extensible Markup Language) tags can be attached to each document to describe its contents. XML is a language similar to HTML (Hypertext Markup Language), but is used as a standard for data exchange rather than data presentation. XML tags are used to identify elements, sub-elements, and attributes that store data. The schema can be specified using a Document Type Definition (DTD) or by an XML schema that identifies the elements, their attributes, and their relationships to one another.

2.8   Chapter Summary

A corporation's operational data is a corporate resource, an asset that is of value to the organization and incurs cost. A database, which is shared by many users, protects operational data by providing data security, integrity constraints, reliability controls, and professional management by a DBA.

Data means facts, while information is processed data. There are four levels of discussion about data: **reality** (the real world) containing the **miniworld** (Universe of Discourse) that we are modeling, the abstract **conceptual model** of the miniworld, the **logical model** or **intention** of the database with its **metadata** (data about data), and the **database extension**, with **data instances**.

A staged approach to database design is a top-down approach that allows the designer to develop a conceptual model that mirrors the operations of the organization, allows changes, supports many user views, is independent of physical implementation, and does not depend on the model of a particular DBMS. This approach allows the database to evolve as needs change. In staged database design the designer must analyze the user environment, develop a conceptual data model, choose the DBMS, create the logical model by mapping the conceptual model to the data model of the DBMS, develop the internal and physical models, evaluate the physical model, perform tuning if needed, and implement the physical model. Steps may be repeated until the design is satisfactory.

Design methodologies can be general techniques or commercial products such as **CASE** packages. A **data dictionary** can be **integrated** (the DBMS system catalog) or **freestanding** (independent of a DBMS). A data dictionary is a valuable tool for collecting and organizing information about data.

The **DBA** must be technically competent, a good manager, and have excellent interpersonal and communication skills. He or she has primary responsibility for planning, designing, developing, and managing the operating database.

Standard database architecture uses three levels of abstraction: **external, logical**, and **internal**. An **external view** is the model seen by a particular user. An **external schema** is an external model description written in the **data definition language**, which is part of the **data sublanguage** for the DBMS being used. The **user interface** creates the user's working environment and hides lower levels from the user. The **logical schema** is a complete DDL description of the logical model. It specifies the information content of the database, including all record types and fields. It is derived from the conceptual model. A good conceptual model results in a logical model that is easy to implement and supports the desired external views. The **logical record interface** is a boundary below which the logical level cannot see. The **internal schema** is a DDL description of the internal model. It specifies how data is represented, how records are sequenced, what indexes and pointers exist, and what hashing scheme is used. The **stored record interface** is the boundary below which the DBMS does not see. The operating system should be responsible for all physical details below this interface, including creating a **physical record interface** for itself to handle low-level physical details such as track placement. The **external/logical mapping** tells how the external views correspond to the logical items. The **logical/internal** mapping tells how logical items correspond to internal ones. **Data independence** makes each level immune to changes on lower levels. **Logical data independence** means that the logical level can be changed without changing external views. **Physical data independence** means internal and physical changes will not affect the logical model.

Some data models are the **entity-relationship, object-oriented, object-relational**, and **semistructured** models. There are also **record-based** models, including the **relational** as well as the older **network** and **hierarchical** models. The entity-relationship model uses **E-R diagrams** to show entity sets, attributes of entities, relationship sets, and descriptive attributes of relationships. The relational model uses **tables** to represent data and relationships. The object-oriented model uses the concept of a **class**, having attributes and methods. An **object** is created as an instance of a class. Object-oriented databases contain **persistent** objects. Object-relational databases are extensions of relational model databases to allow complex objects and methods. Semistructured databases consist of nodes that are self-describing using XML.

Exercises

2.1   Name four resources of a typical business organization.

2.2   Distinguish between data and information.

2.3   Identify the four levels of abstraction in discussing data. For each, give an example of an item that appears on that level.

2.4   Distinguish between an entity set and an entity instance.

2.5   Distinguish between a record type and a record occurrence.

2.6   What level of data abstraction is represented in the data dictionary? Give examples of the types of entries that would be stored there.

2.7   Explain why a staged design approach is appropriate for database design.

2.8   Name five desirable characteristics of a conceptual model of an enterprise.

2.9   Name the eight major design stages in staged database design, along with the activities and possible outcomes of each.

2.10   Explain what is meant by saying staged database design is a "top-down" method.

2.11   Explain how a CASE package can be used in database design.

2.12   Name two advantages and two disadvantages of the following:

      a. integrated data dictionaries

      b. freestanding data dictionaries

2.13 Explain why users should not have access to the data dictionary.

2.14 Name eight uses for a data dictionary.

2.15 What types of skills must a database administrator possess? For what tasks are they needed?

2.16 List the major functions of the DBA.

2.17 Define each of the following terms:

a. operational data

b. corporate resource

c. metadata

d. entity

e. attribute

f. data item

g. data aggregate

h. data record

i. data file

j. data sublanguage

k. prototype

l. system tuning

m. CASE

n. integrated data dictionary

o. data dictionary synonym

p. data dictionary homonym

q. data standards

r. DBA

2.18 Describe the three-level architecture for databases.

2.19 Describe the two parts of data sublanguages.

2.20 Give five reasons why it is desirable to separate the physical representation from the external structure of a database.

2.21   Distinguish between the following: user interface, logical record interface, stored record interface, physical record interface.

2.22   Describe each of the following: external schema, logical schema, internal schema.

2.23   Explain the purpose of the external/logical mapping and of the logical/internal mapping.

2.24   Distinguish between logical and physical data independence, and give examples of possible changes they allow.

2.25   Explain why the logical model is called the heart of the database.

2.26   Describe abstraction and explain how it is used in database design.

2.27   Distinguish between the intension and extension of a database.

2.28   Explain how record-based data models differ from semantic models.

On the Companion Website:

- Lab Exercises
- Sample Project
- Student Projects

CHAPTER 3

The Entity-Relationship Model

Chapter Objectives

In this chapter you will learn the following:

- The meaning of enterprise schema, entity type, entity set, and entity instance

- The meaning of attribute and domain

- The meaning of null, multivalued, composite, and derived attributes

- The meaning of superkey, candidate key, primary key, alternate key, and secondary key

- The meaning of relationship type, relationship set, and relationship instance

- How to represent entities, attributes, and relationships on an E-R diagram

3.1   Purpose of the E-R Model

The entity-relationship model was developed by P. P. Chen in 1976 to facilitate database design by allowing the designer to express the conceptual properties of the database in an **enterprise schema**. Therefore, it is not limited to the data definition language of any particular DBMS. It uses its own E-R diagrams to express the structure of the model. Some of the diagram symbols and their uses were described in Figure 2.8 and Figure 2.9. Because of its independence from a DBMS, the enterprise schema will be valid regardless of the management system chosen, and it can remain correct even if the DBMS is changed. We will view the diagrams as design tools that can be useful in implementing a variety of systems. We note that the discussion of the E-R model here differs slightly from that of Chen's. We have added concepts and used terminology that will be useful in later discussions.

The E-R model was classified in Section 2.7 as a semantic model, one that attempts to capture meaning as well as structure. The items in the model represent "things" in the miniworld, the part of the real world that the database is to model, including relationships between real-world "things." The model describes the environment of the miniworld in terms of **entities**, **attributes**, and **relationships**. Figure 2.8 shows the basic symbols for E-R diagrams. A **rectangle** is used to represent an entity, an **oval** to represent an attribute, and a **diamond** to represent a relationship. These elements are connected by lines, as shown in Figure 2.8 and Figure 2.9. Figure 3.1 is an enhanced version of Figure 2.9, showing a simplified E-R diagram for a university database that represents

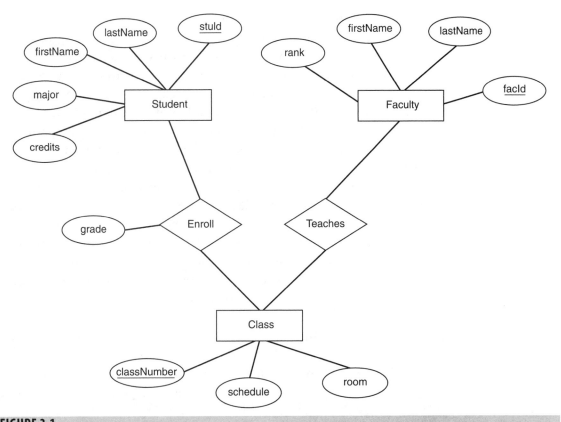

FIGURE 3.1

A Simplified E-R diagram for the University Database

information about students, faculty, and classes. The Student entity set, shown as a rectangle, has attributes stuId, lastName, firstName, major, and credits, each shown as an oval connected to the rectangle for the Student entity. The Faculty entity set has attributes facId, lastName, firstName, and rank. The class entity set has attributes classNumber, schedule, and room. The diamond marked Enroll shows there is a relationship between students and the classes they are taking. The Teaches relationship connects faculty to the classes they are teaching.

3.2   Entities

We will not give a formal definition of the term **entity** but, informally, we describe it as any object that exists and can be distinguished from other objects. It can represent a person, place, event, object, or concept in the real world that we plan to model in the database. It may be a physical object or an abstraction. Different designers may disagree about what entities exist in the miniworld. Entity **instances** represent a particular student, a specific class, an individual customer, a particular employee, an account, a patient, a conference, an invention, or a club, depending on what the enterprise is and what parts of it we wish to represent. Applying abstraction, we can identify the common properties of entity instances that are of interest in the database, and define an **entity type**, which is a representation in the data model of a category of entities. For example, if the enterprise is a university, we can consider all students in the university and identify the common properties of interest for the Student entity type. The entity type forms the **intension** of the entity, the permanent definition part. A collection of entities of the same type is called an **entity set**. The set must be **well-defined**, meaning that it must be possible to determine whether a particular entity instance belongs to it or not. All the entity instances that fulfill the definition at the moment form the **extension** of the entity. The members of the Student entity set change as students come and go, but the student entity type remains constant. Entity sets can intersect, that is, have common members. For example, in the model of the university we might have a faculty entity type and an administrator entity type. A particular person may satisfy the definition of both types, being simultaneously both a faculty member and an administrator in the university, and would therefore be an instance in both of these entity sets. As shown in Figure 3.1, an entity set is represented in E-R diagrams by a rectangle having the name of the entity inside.

3.3 Attributes

The **attributes** of an entity represent the defining properties or qualities of the entity type. For the student entity type, the defining properties might be the student's ID, name, major, and number of credits accumulated. The attributes are the representation in the model of those properties, namely stuId, lastName, firstName, major, and credits. Normally, an entity instance will have a value for each of its attributes. An attribute is represented in an E-R diagram by an oval with the name of the attribute inside. A line connects the attribute oval to the rectangle for the entity set it describes. Figure 3.1 shows several examples of attributes connected to their entity sets. Just as with entities, different designers may disagree about the attributes for an entity set. For example, another designer may choose to include stuAddress, stuPhone, and stuStatus, but not credits. In addition, what appears to be an attribute to one designer may be an entity to another. For example, major might be seen as an entity in a different design. In choosing whether an object should be an entity or an attribute, the designer should consider whether the object describes another object and whether it has values for its instances. In that case, it is best to represent the object as an attribute. If it is difficult to identify possible values, the object is more likely to be an entity.

3.3.1 Domains

The set of values permitted for each attribute is called the **domain** of that attribute. For the Student example, the domain of the credits attribute might be the set of integer values between 0 and 150 inclusive, depending on how the university computes credit hours. The domain of the lastName attribute is somewhat more difficult to define, since it consists of all legal last names of students. It is certainly a string, but it might consist not only of letters but also apostrophes, blanks, hyphens, or other special characters. Different attributes may have the same domains. For example, a subset of the set of positive integers is often used as a domain for attributes with quite different meanings, such as credits and age. An attribute actually maps an entity set to the domain of the attribute. For example, the attribute credits is a function that takes the set of students, and maps each student to a specific value in the domain {0,. . .,150}. Figure 3.2 illustrates credits as a function majoring the Student entity set to the credits domain. (Note: This figure is not part of an E-R diagram, but a means of illustrating this concept visually.) You may notice that the word domain as used here does not fit the mathematical notion of domain as the set on which a function is defined. In fact, the domain of the attribute is actually the range of a mathematical function. A particular entity instance could be described as a set of ordered pairs, with each pair being the name of an attribute and the value of the attribute. For a specific student, such a set might be {(stuId, S1001), (lastName, Smith), (firstName, Jack), (major, History), (credits, 90)}. The named attribute itself and its domain are part of the intension of the model, while the attribute values are part of the extension.

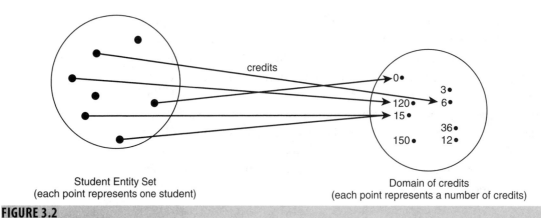

FIGURE 3.2

Credits as Mapping of Student Entity to Credits Domain

3.3.2   Null Values

Sometimes the value of an attribute is unknown at the present time or is undefined for a particular instance. In a database, some attributes may be permitted to have **null values** for some entity instances. In that case, the entity instance will not map to the domain of the attribute, although other instances of the same entity set will map to the attribute domain. In Figure 3.2 some members of the student entity set were not connected by arrows to the domain of credits. Note that values of zero or a blank string for a character-string field are considered to be non-null entries. Null means no value.

3.3.3   Multivalued Attributes

Some attributes may have **multiple values** for an entity instance. For example, students may have more than one email address. If it is possible for any entity instance to have multiple values for a particular attribute, we use a **double oval** around the attribute's name. The double oval should not be interpreted to mean that all instances must have multiple values, only that some instances may. Figure 3.3 illustrates how the multiple email addresses for a student would appear on an E-R diagram.

3.3.4   Composite Attributes

Some attributes can be decomposed into smaller elements. For example address can be broken down into street, city, state, and zip. If we examine

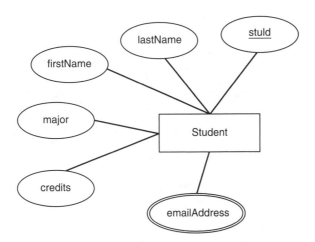

FIGURE 3.3
Student Entity Set with Multivalued Attribute emailAddress

classNumber, we see that it consists of a department code, a course number within that department, and a letter for a section. If we used stuName as an attribute, we could decompose that into firstName and lastName. Similarly, telephoneNumber might be decomposed into areaCode, phoneNumber, or into countryCode, areaCode, exchange, and extension. An attribute is a **composite** attribute if it is possible to decompose it further. We indicate that an attribute is a composite by writing its name in an oval in the usual manner, and then drawing ovals for the individual components, which we connect by lines to the composite attribute's oval. Figure 3.4 illustrates address as a composite attribute.

3.3.5 Derived Attributes

We might sometimes want to include in a design an attribute whose value can be calculated when needed. For example, we might want to treat age as if it were an attribute, but if we already stored dateOfBirth there is no need to store age as well, since it is easily calculated. Attributes that are not to be stored, but whose values are to be calculated or obtained from other sources, are called **derived**. These are indicted by a **dashed oval** on an E-R diagram. Figure 3.4 also shows age as a derived attribute. Attributes can also be derived from other entities or from relationships. For example, we could have an attribute currentEnrollment for Class, showing the number of students enrolled. The value could be derived from the number of enrollment relationships for the class entity. If we had stored Department as an entity, we could have a derived attribute, numberOfFaculty, which

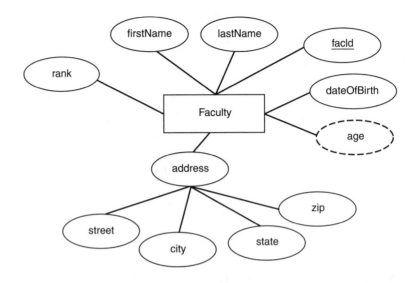

would hold a count of the faculty members for each department. This could be derived from the faculty entity.

3.4 Keys

Intuitively, we think of a **key** as a data item that allows us to tell records apart. We need a more exact definition of the concept of key. We begin with the notion of a superkey.

3.4.1 Superkeys

A **superkey** is an attribute or a set of attributes that uniquely identifies an entity. This means it always allows us to tell one entity instance from another. For example, for the Student entity set, {stuId} is a superkey because it can be used to uniquely identify each student. If you have a list of all students—with their IDs, last names, first names, majors, and credits—and you are told the stuId value, there is only one student on the list with that value. If you are told the student's last name, you might not be sure which student to choose, since two or more students might have the same last name. Therefore {lastName} is not a superkey. If you have a superkey, then any set of attributes containing that superkey is also a superkey. Therefore, the combination of stuId and credits, written {stuId,credits}, is also a superkey. Note that a superkey provides unique identification for all extensions of the database, not just for one or two examples. We can use examples to help us fix our ideas about superkeys, but an example might be misleading. For instance, it might happen that at the moment no two students in the university have the same last name and we might incorrectly infer from the particular extension that {lastName} is a superkey. To identify a superkey requires that we consider the meaning of the attributes, a semantic notion, before deciding whether we have uniqueness over all extensions. Superkeys represent a constraint that prevents two entities from ever having the same value for those attributes. It represents an assumption we make about the miniworld we are using in the model.

3.4.2 Candidate Keys

Since a superkey such as {stuId,credits} might contain extra attributes that are not necessary for unique identification of entity instances, we are interested in finding superkeys that do not contain these extra attributes. In this example, the extra attribute is clearly credits. A **candidate key** is one that does not contain extra attributes. We define a candidate key as a superkey such that no proper subset of its attributes is itself a superkey. In our example, {stuId,credits} is not a candidate key because it contains a subset, {stuId}, that is a superkey. However, {stuId} by itself is a candidate key, since it has no proper subset that uniquely identifies entities. There may be several candidate keys for an entity set. If we stored social security numbers of students, then {socSecNo} would also be a candidate key, provided each student had a social security number. Note that a candidate key can consist of a single attribute, as {stuId} and {socSecNo} both do, or it can be a combination of attributes. For example, the combination {lastName,firstName,address}, if it is always unique, can be a candidate key for some entity set. When a key consists of more than one attribute, we call it a **composite key**. For convenience, we will now drop the set braces in identifying keys, and simply list the attribute(s) in the key.

3.4.3 Primary Keys

An entity set might have several candidate keys. The database designer chooses among them and identifies one of them as the normal way of identifying entities and accessing records. This becomes the **primary key**. In other words, the primary key is the "successful" candidate key—the one actually chosen. The primary key may be a single attribute key or a composite key. Often, the other candidate keys become **alternate keys**, whose unique values provide another method of accessing records. The term **secondary key** usually means an attribute or set of attributes whose values, not necessarily unique, are used as a means of accessing records. In our example, stuId might be the primary key for the Student entity set. If socSecNo is also stored, it might be an alternate key. The attribute lastName can be used as a secondary key. While duplicate last names are allowed, we can use the last name to help us find a student record if we do not know the student ID or social security number. Usually an index is created on a secondary key field, permitting quick retrieval of records with a particular value of the indexed attribute. The records can then be examined individually to find the one desired. For the Class entity set, course# might be the primary key, and facId might be the primary key for the Faculty entity set. An important characteristic of a primary key is that none of its attributes have null values. If we permitted null values in keys, we would be unable to tell entities apart, since two entities with null values for the same key attribute might be indistinguishable. This follows from the definition of candidate key, which specified that no subset of a candidate key is itself a candidate key, so all attributes in a candidate key are necessary for unique identification of entity instances. To ensure data correctness, we also have to insist that no attribute of a candidate key be permitted to have null values. In creating a database, typically we identify the primary key so that the system will enforce the no null and uniqueness properties, and we enforce the key status of candidate keys by specifying that they be unique. We underline the primary key of an entity in the E-R diagram, as shown in Figure 3.1.

For the sake of completeness, we note here that there is a concept called **foreign key**. However, it belongs to the relational model, and it is not part of the Entity-Relationship model. We will discuss it in Chapter 4.

3.5   Relationships

Entities are often linked by associations or **relationships**, which are connections or interactions among the entity instances. A student may be related to a class by being enrolled in that class. By abstraction, we can identify the common properties of certain relationships and define a **relationship type** and a corresponding well-defined **relationship set** as the collection of relationships of that type. The relationships that satisfy the requirements for membership in the relationship set at any moment are the **instances**, or members, of the relationship set. As with entities and attributes, the relationship type is part of the **intension** and the instances are part of the **extension** of the model. For example, we have a relationship type that links each student with each of the classes in which he or she is enrolled. We then have an Enroll relationship set, which contains all instances of the relationship. The name given to a relationship set is chosen by the designer. It is a good practice to choose a verb that captures the meaning of the relationship. If no name is given, we will refer to the relationship by using the names of the related entities, with a hyphen between them, e.g., Student-Class or Department-Faculty. Figure 3.1 shows two relationships, Enroll and Teaches, represented by diamonds on the E-R diagram.

3.5.1 Degree of Relationships

Enroll is an example of a **binary** relationship set, one that links two entity instances and therefore has a degree of two. It is possible to describe this relationship set more formally as a set of ordered pairs, in which the first element represents a student and the second a class that the student is taking. At a given moment, the instances of this relationship set might be thought of as

```
Enroll = { (The student with Id S1001, The class with classNumber ART103A),
           (The student with Id S1020, The class with classNumber CS201A),
           (The student with Id S1002, The class with classNumber CS201A),
           (The student with Id S1010, The class with classNumber ART103A),
           (The student with Id S1002, The class with classNumber ART103A),
           (The student with Id S1020, The class with classNumber MTH101B),
           (The student with Id S1001, The class with classNumber HST205A),
           (The student with Id S1010, The class with classNumber MTH103C),
           (The student with Id S1002, The class with classNumber MTH103C) }
```

Each ordered pair shows that a particular student is enrolled in a particular class. For example, the first pair shows that the student whose ID is S1001 is enrolled in the class with class number ART103A. The set of the ordered pairs of the related entities is the relationship set, and each ordered pair is an instance of the relationship.

The entity sets involved in a relationship set need not be distinct. For example, we could define a roommate relationship within the Student entity set.

Such a relationship is called **recursive**. Assuming only two students share a room, this would be a binary relationship called Roommate of the form

```
Roommate = {(Student1, Student2) | Student1 ∈ Student, Student2 ∈
Student, Student1 is the roommate of Student2}.
```

Instances of this relationship would be ordered pairs of students, as in

```
Roommate = { (The student with Id S1001, The student with Id S1020),
             (The student with Id S1020, The student with Id S1001),
             (The student with Id S1002, The student with Id S1005),
             . . . }
```

If we had an entity set of employees, we might have a recursive Manages relationship that links each employee to his or her manager, who is also an employee. That set would be defined as

```
Manages = {(Employee1, Employee2) | Employee1 ∈ Employee, Employee2 ∈
Employee, Employee1 is the manager of Employee2}.
```

Instances would be ordered pairs of employees, as in

```
Manages = { (The Employee with Id E101, The Employee with Id E301),
            (The Employee with Id E101, The Employee with Id E421),
            The Employee with Id E102, The Employee with Id E555),
            . . . }
```

Figure 3.5 shows the recursive Manages relationship between members of the Employee entity set.

A relationship might involve more than two entity sets. For example, we could have a **ternary** relationship (with degree three), one involving three entity sets, linking courses, faculty, and textbooks that the faculty members use in the course. For this example, we assume that the same course could be taught by different professors who can choose to use different books. Then the relationship set could be defined as a set of ordered triples, in which the first element represents a course, the second a faculty member, and the third a textbook. Using course numbers to represent

Figure 3.5

The Recursive Manages Relationship

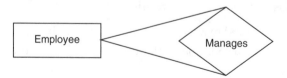

course entities, faculty IDs to represent faculty entities, and isbn numbers to represent textbooks, this relationship, which we call Course-Faculty-Text, might be thought of as

```
Course-Faculty-Text= { (ART103, F101, '0-89134-573-6'),
                       (CSC201, F105, '0-13-101634-1'),
                       (CSC203, F105, '0-13-090955-5'),
                       (HST205, F115, '0-78-531220-4'),
                       (MTH101, F110, '0-618-04239-3'),
                       (MTH103, F110, '0-618-733214-6')}
```

Here, each ordered triple is an instance that shows that a particular text is used in a particular course that is taught by a particular professor. For example, the ordered triple (ART103, F101, '0-89134-573-6'), means that the course ART103, when taught by the professor whose ID is F101, uses the text with isbn '0-89134-573-6' as the textbook. Figure 3.6 illustrates how a ternary relationship appears on an E-R diagram.

Although most relationships in a data model are binary or at most ternary, we could define a relationship set linking any number of entity sets. Therefore, the general relationship set of degree n can be thought of as a subset of an n-ary relation of the form

$$\{(e_1, e_2, \ldots e_n) \mid e_1 \in E_1, e_2 \in E_2, \ldots, e_n \in E_n\}$$

where the E_i are entity sets, the e_i are entity instances, and each ordered n-tuple represents an instance of the relationship. You may recognize the

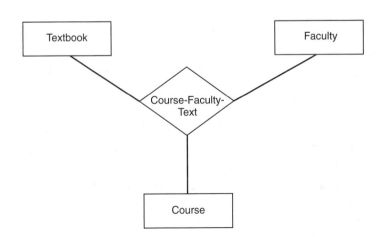

FIGURE 3.6
A Ternary Relationship

notation used for the cross-product or Cartesian product of sets in mathematics. In fact, a relationship set is a subset of the Cartesian product of the entity sets involved; that is, if R is a relationship set and $E_1, E_2, \ldots, E_2$ are entity sets, then

$$R \subset E_1 \times E_2 \times \ldots \times E_n$$

3.5.2   Attributes of Relationship Sets

Sometimes a relationship set has **descriptive attributes** that belong to the relationship rather than to any of the entities involved. For example, in Figure 3.1, the attribute grade is a descriptive attribute for the Enroll relationship set. On an E-R diagram, we place a descriptive attribute of a relationship in an oval and connect it to the relationship diamond. Since students are still enrolled in the classes, we will assume this attribute represents the mid-term grade. The attribute grade does not describe the Student entity, since each student can have grades for several classes, nor does it describe the Class entity, since there are different grades given in a particular class for different students. For a grade to have meaning, it must be associated with a particular student for a particular class.

3.5.3   Cardinality of a Relationship

It is important to identify restrictions or constraints on relationships so that the possible extensions of the relation correspond to real-world connections or associations. Two types of constraints on relationships are participation constraints and cardinality. The **cardinality** of a relationship is the number of entities to which another entity can map under that relationship. Let X and Y be entity sets and R a binary relationship from X to Y. If there were no cardinality constraints on R, then any number of entities in X could relate to any number of entities in Y. Usually, however, there are restrictions on the number of corresponding entities. We distinguish four types of binary relationships.

1.   **one-to-one.** A relationship R from X to Y is **one-to-one** if each entity in X is associated with at most one entity in Y and, conversely, each entity in Y is associated with at most one entity in X. An example of a one-to-one relationship is the Chairperson to Department relationship. Each chairperson chairs at most one department, and each department has at most one chairperson. In family life, an example of a one-to-one relationship is the monog-

amous marriage relationship. At any given time, each husband is married to only one wife, and each wife to one husband.

2. **one-to-many.** A relationship R from X to Y is **one-to-many** if each entity in X can be associated with many entities in Y but each entity in Y is associated with at most one entity in X. The word "many" applies to the possible number of entities another is associated with. For a given instance, there might be zero, one, two, or more associated entities, but if it is *ever* possible to have more than one, we use the word "many" to describe the association. The relationship between Faculty and Class is one-to-many, assuming there is no team teaching. Each faculty member can teach several classes, but each class is taught by only one faculty member. In a family, the traditional mother-to-child relationship is one-to-many. A mother can have many children, but each child has only one (birth) mother.

3. **many-to-one.** A relationship R from X to Y is **many-to-one** if each entity in X is associated with at most one entity in Y, but each entity in Y can be associated with many entities in X. The relationship between Student and his or her major is many-to-one, assuming there are no double or triple majors. Each student can have at most one major, but a major can have many student majors in it. In family life, the child-to-birth mother relationship is many-to-one. Each child has at most one birth mother, but each birth mother can have many children. A many-to-one relationship is actually the same as a one-to-many, but viewed from the opposite side.

4. **many-to-many.** A relationship R from X to Y is **many-to-many** if each entity in X can be associated with many entities in Y and each entity in Y can be associated with many entities in X. The relationship between Student and Class is many-to-many. Each student can be enrolled in many classes (i.e., more than one), and each class can have many students enrolled in it. In a family, the grandparent-to-grandchild relationship illustrates a many-to-many relationship. A grandparent can have many grandchildren, and a grandchild can have many grandparents.

If entity sets A, B, and C are related in a ternary relationship, R, we can determine cardinality constraints for each entity set in the relationship. For each particular combination of B and C entities, if there is only one A value, then A participates as a "one." If there can be more than one A value for a particular B-C combination, then A participates as a "many." Similarly, B participates as a "one" or a "many" depending on how many B values can exist for each A-C combination, and C participates as a "one" or a "many" depending on the number of C values for each A-B combination. The notion can be extended to any degree relation.

3.5.4   Showing Cardinalities on an E-R Diagram

In an E-R diagram, lines connect the rectangles representing entity sets to the diamonds representing the relationship sets that show their association. There are several alternate methods of showing the cardinality of the relationship. The traditional one, shown as Method 1 at the top in Figure 3.7 is to put a "1" to show a "one" relationship cardinality and an "M" or "N" to show a "many" cardinality on the line connecting an entity to a relationship set. Thus if one faculty member is associated with each class, the line between the Faculty entity set rectangle and the Faculty-Class relationship set diamond has a "1" on it. Since many classes can be associated with the faculty member, the line between the Faculty-Class relationship set diamond and the Class rectangle has an "M" on it. If we choose to represent the one-to-one Chairperson-Department relationship, we would put a "1" on the line connecting the Chairperson rectangle to the Chairperson-Department relationship set diamond, and another "1" on the line connecting the relationship set diamond to the Department rectangle. For the Enroll relationship, we would have an "M" from the Student entity set rectangle to the Enroll diamond and an "N" from the Enroll diamond to the Class entity set rectangle.

An alternate notation to the "1" is to put a single-headed arrow on the line from a relationship diamond pointing to an entity set rectangle that participates as a "one" and a double-headed arrow on the line pointing to an entity set that participates as a "many." Some authors or diagram-drawing software tools use a single arrow for a "one" and no arrowhead for a "many," while others use a "big dot" at the end of a "many" line and nothing at the end of a "one" line. Still another notation is to use lines to connect related entities, without a diamond, with a branched "crow's foot" at the end for a "many," and an unbranched end for a "one." Figure 3.7 summarizes these methods applied to these three examples. We will use the traditional notation in our E-R diagrams.

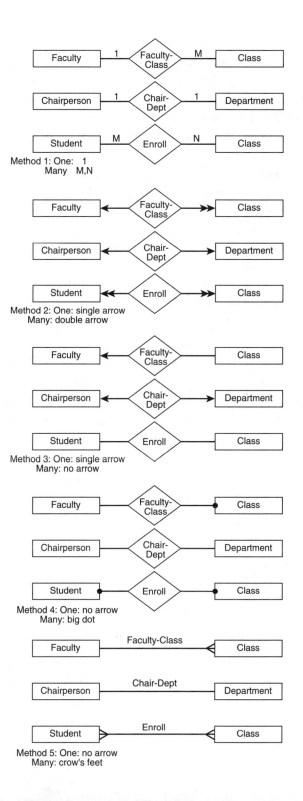

FIGURE 3.7

Showing Cardinalities on an E-R Diagram

For ternary relations, we place a "1" or an "M" or "N" on the arc from an entity to the relationship set, depending on whether the entity participates as a "one" or as a "many." We determine the participation by asking, "For each combination of the other two entities, how many of these participate?" Figure 3.8 shows the cardinalities for the Course-Faculty-Textbook ternary relationship. It indicates that for each Faculty-Course combination, there is at most one text, for each combination of faculty and text there may be many courses, and for each combination of course and text there may be many faculty. So the diagram tells us that many professors teach the same course, and each one can use exactly one text for that course, but two professors can choose the same text or different texts for the same course if they wish. Also, a professor may choose to use the same text for different courses.

3.5.5   Participation Constraints

It is possible that not all members of an entity set participate in a relationship. For example, some faculty members may not be teaching this semester, or some students may not be enrolled in any class this semester, although they are maintaining their student status. If every member of an entity set must participate in a relationship, refer to this as **total participation** of the entity set in the relationship. We denote this by drawing a double line from the entity rectangle to the relationship diamond. A single line indicates that some members of the entity set may not participate in the relationship, a situation called **partial participation**. For example, if there are students who do not take classes, the participation of Student in

FIGURE 3.8

Cardinalities for Ternary Relationship

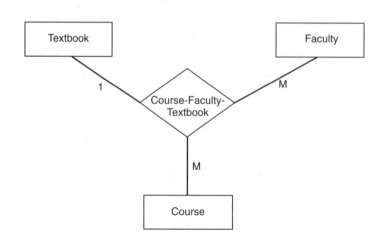

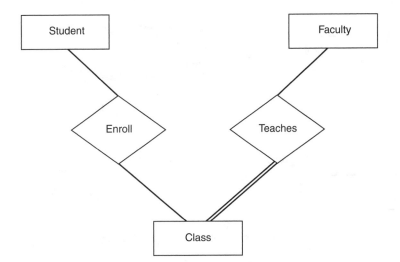

FIGURE 3.9

Total vs. Partial Participation in a Relationship

the Enroll relationship is partial, and the line linking the Student entity set rectangle to the Enroll relationship diamond is a single line. A double line would imply that a person is not a student unless he or she is enrolled in some class. The single lines in Figure 3.9 show that some students may not be enrolled in any class, some classes may have no students enrolled, and some faculty members may not be teaching any class. However, the double line shows that every class must have a faculty member teaching it. There are also alternate methods of representing participation constraints.

3.6 Roles

In a relationship, each entity has a function called its **role** in the relationship. Usually it is clear from the context what role an entity plays in a relationship. Thus in the relationship connecting Faculty and Class, it is understood that the Faculty entity plays the "is the teacher of" role in the relationship, while the Class entity plays the "is taught by" role. When an entity set is related to itself, we have a **recursive** relationship, and it is necessary to indicate the roles that members play in the relationship. The Manages relationship between a manager–employee and the other employees he or she manages, discussed in Section 3.5.1, is a recursive one-to-many relationship. The manager plays the "manages" role and the other employees play the "is managed by" role. Figure 3.10(a) shows this

FIGURE 3.10(a)

Recursive Relationship

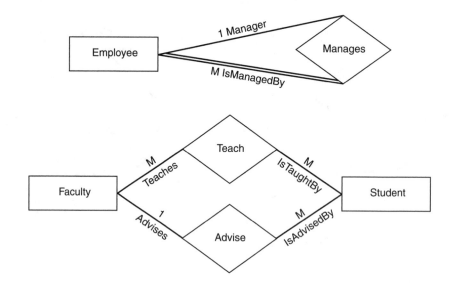

FIGURE 3.10(b)

Entity Sets with Two Relationships

relationship with the roles identified. Note that it is a one-to-many relationship in which every employee has to have a manager (total participation) but not every manager has to have employees, perhaps because some managers might manage other resources. Another instance where role names are helpful occurs when the same two entity sets are related in two different ways. For example, suppose we wanted to represent two different relationship types between faculty members and students. One type would be the usual Teacher–Student relationship, in which the Faculty entity has the "teaches" role and the Student entity has the "is taught by" role. Another is the Advisor relationship, in which the Faculty entity has the "advises" role and the Student entity has the "is advised by" role. When entity sets are connected by multiple relationships, the roles can be written on the appropriate links. Figure 3.10(b) shows two entity sets, Faculty and Student, connected by two relationships, with roles appearing on the links. Although not necessary in all cases, we can use role names to help clarify any relationship, whether required or not.

3.7   Existence Dependency and Weak Entities

At times we need to store data about an entity that we would not be interested in unless we had a related entity already in the database. For example, we would not need to store data about sales orders unless we had customers. An existence constraint, or **existence dependency**, can occur between two entities. If X and Y are entities and each instance of Y must have a corresponding instance of X, then we say that Y is **existence dependent** on X. This means a Y entity cannot exist without some X entity. If Y is existence dependent on X, then Y must have **total participation** in its relationship set with X. A special type of existence dependency occurs when the dependent entity set does not have a candidate key, and its instances are indistinguishable without a relationship with another entity. For example, assume that teaching evaluations of faculty members are conducted by senior faculty or by the dean, and the ratings are stored in the database. For simplicity, we assume a single rating is given for each evaluation, so that an evaluation entity has attributes Date, RaterName, and Rating. Since there might be several instances with identical values for all three attributes, an Evaluation entity must be associated with the correct Faculty instance to have meaning. In this case, X (Faculty, in this example) is referred to as the **strong entity** (also called the parent, owner, or dominant entity) and Y (Rating, in this example) is referred to as the **weak entity** (also called the child, dependent, or subordinate entity). A weak entity is depicted in the E-R diagram by drawing a double rectangle around the entity, and making the relationship diamond a double diamond. Figure 3.11 shows the E-R diagram with the weak Evaluation entity and its identifying relationship. When an entity is weak, it has no primary key of its own,

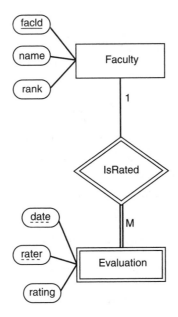

FIGURE 3.11
Weak Entity Set

but is unique only in reference to its relationship to its owner. However, it often has a partial key, also called a **discriminator**, that allows us to uniquely identify the weak entities that belong to the same owner. The partial key may be a single attribute or a composite. For Evaluation, Date alone cannot be sufficient, if it is possible for a faculty member to be evaluated by two different people on the same date. Therefore, we will use the combination of Date and RaterName as the discriminator. The discriminator is indicated by a dashed underline on the E-R diagram.

3.8   A Sample E-R Diagram

Figure 3.12 shows an E-R diagram incorporating many of the entities and relationships discussed in this chapter. The entities and attributes are:

- Student: stuId, lastName, firstName, major, credits

We are assuming each student has a unique ID and has at most one major.

- Department: deptCode, deptName, office

We are assuming that each department has a unique code and a unique name, and that each department has one office designated as the departmental office.

- Faculty: facId, lastName, firstName, rank

We are assuming that facId is unique and that every faculty member must belong to a department. One faculty member in each department is the chairperson.

- Class: classNumber, sched, room

We are assuming the classNumber consists of a department code, a number that identifies the course within the department, and a section code. We are keeping data for current classes only. If we want to store historical data about past class offerings or data about planned classes, we would need to add a date attribute.

- Textbook: isbn, author, title, publisher

We assume a book can have multiple authors.

- Evaluation: date, rater, rating

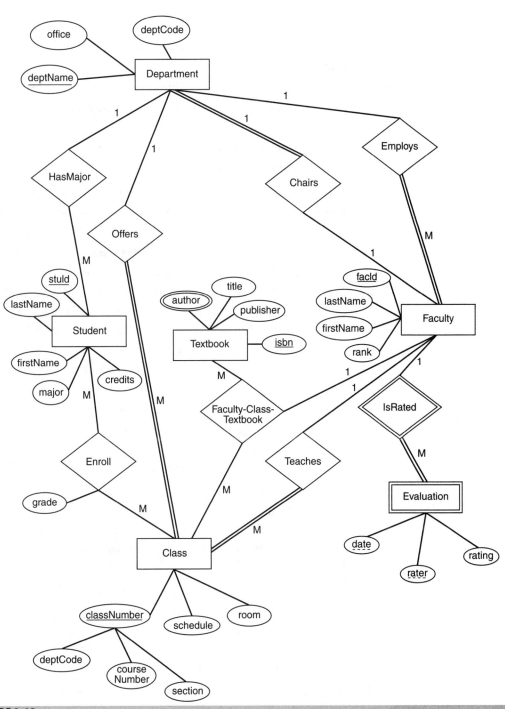

FIGURE 3.12

An E-R Diagram

Evaluation is a weak entity, dependent on Faculty.

Note that we do not make the enterprise one of the entities. We have no entity set called university, since this is the entire enterprise. Everything in the diagram represents some facet of the university. The relationship sets are:

1. HasMajor, which is a one-to-many relationship that connects students to their major departments. We are assuming students have at most one major. Not every department has majors, and not every student has declared a major.

2. Offers, which is a one-to-many relationship that connects departments to the classes they offer. Only offerings for the current semester are kept in this database. A department may have no class offerings this semester, but every class has a department that offers it.

3. Enroll, which is a many-to-many relationship that connects students to the classes in which they are enrolled. We are assuming only current enrollments are kept. Grade is a descriptive attribute for this relationship set. Since the students are still enrolled in the classes, this attribute represents a mid-term grade. Some students are not enrolled in any class, and some class offerings may have no students enrolled.

4. Employs, which is a one-to-many relationship that connects departments to faculty members assigned to them. Faculty members must belong to exactly one department. A department might or might not have faculty assigned to it, but it can also have many faculty.

5. Chairs, which is a one-to-one relationship that connects departments to faculty. One faculty member in each department is the chairperson of the department. Every department must have a chairperson, but not every faculty member must be a chairperson. We are assuming a chairperson is a regular faculty member who has the additional responsibility of chairing the department.

6. Teaches, which is a one-to-many relationship that connects faculty members to the classes they teach. We assume a faculty member may teach zero or many classes, and each class has exactly one faculty member assigned to it.

7. IsRated, a one-to-many relationship between Faculty and the weak entity, Evaluation. Not every faculty member has a rating, but every rating must belong to a faculty member.

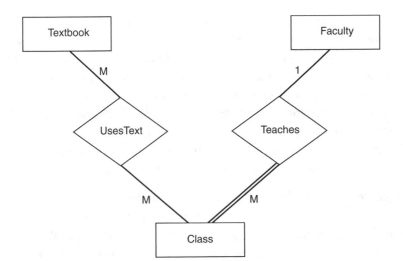

FIGURE 3.13

Example of Two Binary Relationships Replacing the Ternary Relationship

8. Faculty-Class-Textbook, which is a ternary relationship among
    the three entities. Note that we have changed our assumptions
    from our earlier example called Course-Faculty-Text. Here we are
    showing Class, not Course. Class includes the section, so there is
    only one faculty member for the section. Also, we assume a faculty
    member may be using several textbooks for the class. We could
    have used two binary relationships, the Teaches one that already
    exists connecting Faculty and Class, and a new one UsesText, con-
    necting Class and Textbook, as indicated in Figure 3.13. However,
    the meaning would be slightly different. The UsesText binary rela-
    tionship would indicate that the class would use that text regard-
    less of who the instructor is, while the ternary relationship
    indicates that the text depends on the instructor. The cardinalities
    are more difficult to identify in a ternary relationship than in a
    binary one, but the ones pictured in Figure 3.12 preserve the
    meanings. To identify the cardinality for each entity, it is necessary
    to determine how many instances of that entity are related to each
    combination of instances of the other two entities.

3.9   Chapter Summary

The **entity-relationship** model uses **E-R diagrams** to represent an enterprise
schema, a conceptual level description that is independent of any DBMS. An
entity is any distinguishable object in the miniworld that the database mod-

els. Entities are categorized into **entity types**, and a collection of entities of the same type forms an **entity set**. The individual entities that belong to the set at a given moment are **entity instances**. On an E-R diagram, a **rectangle** represents an entity set. **Attributes** are representations of properties of the real-world entities. They are represented as **ovals** on an E-R diagram. The set of values permitted for an attribute are its domain. The attribute is actually a mapping of the entity set into the domain of the attribute. **Null** values occur when an entity instance is missing a value for a particular attribute. Attributes can also be **multivalued**, **composite**, and/or **derived**.

A **superkey** is an attribute set that uniquely identifies entity instances. A minimal superkey, one with no proper subset that is also a superkey, is called a **candidate key**. The **primary key** of an entity is the candidate key that the designer chooses for unique identification. The other candidate keys can become **alternate keys**. A **secondary key**, which provides another way to access records, might or might not have unique values. A **composite key** is one that has more than one attribute. No attribute of a primary key can have null values.

A **relationship** is an association or interaction between entities. A **relationship set** consists of all relations of a given relationship type. Relationships have a **degree**, which is the number of entity instances in each occurrence of the relationship. Relationships may be **binary**, linking two entities, **ternary**, linking three entities, or *n*-ary, linking *n* entities. Binary relationship instances can be represented as ordered pairs, ternary instances as ordered triples, and *n*-ary instances as ordered *n*-tuples of entity instances. A relationship set is a subset of the Cartesian product of the related entity sets. A **diamond** is used to represent a relationship set on an E-R diagram. A relationship set may have descriptive attributes. On an E-R diagram, a descriptive attribute appears in an oval connected to the relationship diamond. Relationships have **cardinality constraints**, which specify how many entity instances may be related in the entire relationship set. For binary relationships, these may be one-to-one, one-to-many, many-to-one, or many-to-many. For ternary or higher-degree relationships, cardinality is determined for each entity by examining how many instances of that entity can occur for each combination of the other entities in the relationship. Cardinalities can be shown on E-R diagrams in several ways, the usual one being to write "1" or "M" on the arc from each entity set to the relationship diamond to indicate the cardinality of the participation of that entity set. Relationships also have **participation constraints**, which can be **total**, indicating that all members of the entity set must participate in the relationship, or **partial**, if not all members have to participate. A single line is used for partial participation and a double line for total participation.

If a relationship is **recursive**, i.e., defined on a single entity set, or if two entity sets are related in more than one way, the **role** or function an entity plays in a relationship can be identified. This is done by placing the role name on the line from the entity set to the relationship diamond on the E-R diagram.

An entity is **existence dependent** on another if it cannot exist in the database without a corresponding instance of the other entity. If such an entity has no key of its own, but must use the primary key attribute of the entity it depends on, it is called **weak**. The entity it depends on is called **strong**. A weak entity is shown on an E-R diagram within a double rectangle with its identifying relationship shown as a double diamond.

Exercises

3.1   Define each of the following terms.

    a. entity type

    b. entity set

    c. well-defined set

    d. intension of an entity

    e. extension of an entity

    f. attribute

    g. domain of an attribute

    h. null value

    i. superkey

    j. candidate key

    k. composite key

    l. primary key

    m. alternate key

    n. secondary key

    o. relationship type

p. relationship set

q. binary relationship

r. ternary relationship

s. *n*-ary relationship

t. cardinality of a relationship

u. recursive relationship

v. existence dependency

w. weak entity

3.2   Consider the entity set Employee with attributes empId, soc-SecNo, empName, jobtitle, and salary

a. Show how the entity set and its attributes would be represented on an E-R diagram.

b. Describe the domain of the salary attribute, making assumptions as needed.

c. Identify a superkey for the Employee entity set.

d. Identify all candidate keys for the entity set.

e. Identify a primary key for the entity set and underline it on the E-R diagram.

3.3   a. Assume in the same enterprise as in Exercise 3.2, that there is an entity set called Project with attributes projName, startDate, end-Date, and budget. Show how this entity set and its relationship to Employee would be represented on the E-R diagram. Assume you want to represent the number of hours an employee is assigned to work on a project, and show that in the diagram.

b. Stating any necessary assumptions, make a decision about the cardinality and participation constraints of the relationship, and add appropriate symbols to the E-R diagram.

c. Assume there is another entity called Department to be added. Each employee works for only one department. Projects are not directly sponsored by a department. Making up attributes as needed, add this entity and appropriate relationship(s) to the diagram.

3.4   Design a database to keep data about college students, their academic advisors, the clubs they belong to, the moderators of the
clubs, and the activities that the clubs sponsor. Assume each student is assigned to one academic advisor, but an advisor counsels
many students. Advisors do not have to be faculty members. Each
student can belong to any number of clubs, and the clubs can
sponsor any number of activities. The club must have some student members in order to exist. Each activity is sponsored by
exactly one club, but there might be several activities scheduled
for one day. Each club has one moderator, who might or might
not be a faculty member. Draw a complete E-R diagram for this
example. Include all constraints.

3.5   A dentist's office needs to keep information about patients, the
number of visits they make to the office, work that must be performed, procedures performed during visits, charges and payments for treatment, and laboratory supplies and services. Assume
there is only one dentist, so there is no need to store information
about the dentist in the database. There are several hundred
patients. Patients make many visits, and the database should store
information about the services performed during each visit, and
the charges for each of the services. There is a standard list of
charges, kept outside the database. The office uses three dental
laboratories that provide supplies and services, such as fabricating
dentures. Draw a complete E-R diagram for this example.

3.6   An interior design firm would like to have a database to represent
its operations. A client (customer) requests that the firm perform
a job such as decorating a new home, redecorating rooms, locating and purchasing furniture, and so forth. One of the firm's dec-
orators is placed in charge of each job. For each job, the firm
provides an estimate of the amount of time and money required
for the entire job. Some of the work for a job, such as planning
furniture placement, is done by the decorator in charge of the job.
In addition, the firm might hire contractors to work on a daily or
hourly basis on a particular job. A job might also include several
activities, such as painting, installing floor covering, fabricating
draperies, wallpapering, constructing, installing cabinets, and so
on. These activities are done by contractors hired by the firm. The

contractor provides an estimate for each activity. An activity or job might also require materials such as paint or lumber, and the firm has to keep track of the cost of materials for each activity or job, in order to bill the client. The database should store the estimated costs and actual costs of all activities and all jobs. Draw a complete E-R diagram for this example

3.7   An automobile body repair shop needs to keep information about its operations. Customers initially bring their cars to the shop for an estimate of repairs. A mechanic looks at the car and estimates the cost and time required for the entire job. If the customer accepts the estimate, a job number is assigned and the customer's name and contact information; the car's license plate number, make, model, and year; and a list of the repairs needed are recorded. The customer then makes an appointment to bring in the car on a specified date. When the car is brought in for repairs, the work begins. The shop keeps track of the charges for parts and labor as they accumulate. Only one mechanic works on the car for the entire job. A job might include several repairs (e.g., replacing the left fender, painting the passenger door). The time actually spent for each repair is recorded and used to calculate the cost of labor, using a fixed hourly rate. Draw a complete E-R diagram for this example.

3.8   A database is needed to keep track of the operations of a physical therapy center. Every patient must be referred by a physician and have a prescription for physical therapy in order to receive treatments. A patient may have different physicians at different times. The database keeps all information about prescriptions and treatments, both past and current. When appointments are made, the information about scheduled date and time is recorded. No patient is ever scheduled for two visits on one day. The center has several physical therapists, and a patient may be treated by different physical therapists at different visits. When a patient makes a visit at an appointed time, the name of the therapist, the treatment, the date, time, and the equipment used are all recorded for that visit. Each of these has only one value for the visit. This information will be used later for insurance billing, which is not part of this database. Draw a complete E-R diagram for this example.

On the Companion Website:

- Additional Design Exercises
- Lab Exercises
- Sample Project
- Student Projects

CHAPTER 4

The Relational Model

Chapter Objectives

In this chapter you will learn the following:

- Some advantages of the relational model

- How tables are used to represent data

- Characteristics of database relations

- The meaning of entity integrity and referential integrity

- The categories of relational languages

- How to write queries in relational algebra

- How views are defined in the relational model

- How to transform an E-R diagram into a relational model

4.1　Advantages of the Relational Model

Section 1.6 describes the history of the relational model, which replaced earlier hierarchical and network database systems. Those earlier models were based on file systems, and the databases created using them required that the application programs contain details about the layout of data in the database. Therefore whenever the database was reorganized, the applications had to be rewritten. There was no data independence. The relational model removed such details from the applications, providing a logical view and creating true data independence for the first time.

The relational model is based on the mathematical notion of a **relation**. Codd and others extended the notion to apply to database design. Thus they were able to take advantage of the power of mathematical abstraction and of the expressiveness of mathematical notation to develop a simple but powerful structure for databases. The relational model is the subject of a large body of research literature.

Much of the literature treats the model theoretically, developing aspects of the model by using the mathematical approach of theorem and proof. This abstract approach has the advantage that the results are general, meaning they do not depend on a particular example, and can be applied to many different applications. Fortunately, we can use the results of the theory to design relational models without necessarily following the intricate process of theorem proving. The theory assists in database design by identifying potential flaws in proposed designs, and providing tools to allow us to correct those flaws. Chapter 6 contains a detailed discussion of some of these techniques.

The basic structure of the relational model is simple, making it easy to understand on an intuitive level. It allows separation of the conceptual and physical levels, so that conceptual design can be performed without considering storage structures. Users and designers find that the model allows them to express conceptual data notions in a manner that is easily understood. Data operations are also easy to express, and do not require users to be familiar with the storage structures used. The model uses a few very powerful commands to accomplish data manipulations that range from the simple to the complex. For these reasons, the relational model has quickly become the most popular model for databases large and small.

4.2   Relational Data Structures

The data structures used in the relational model are tables with relationships among them.

4.2.1   Tables

The relational model is based on the concept of a **relation**, which is physically represented as a **table** or two-dimensional array. In this model, tables are used to hold information about the objects to be represented in the database. Using the terms of the Entity Relationship model, both entity sets and relationship sets can be shown using tables. A relation is represented as a two-dimensional table in which the rows of the table correspond to individual records and the columns correspond to attributes. For example, the Student relation is represented by the `Student` table, having columns for attributes `stuId`, `lastName`, `firstName`, `major`, and `credits`. Figure 4.1(a), which

Student				
stuId	**lastName**	**firstName**	**major**	**credits**
S1001	Smith	Tom	History	90
S1002	Chin	Ann	Math	36
S1005	Lee	Perry	History	3
S1010	Burns	Edward	Art	63
S1013	McCarthy	Owen	Math	0
S1015	Jones	Mary	Math	42
S1020	Rivera	Jane	CSC	15

FIGURE 4.1
The University Tables

FIGURE 4.1(a)
The Student Table

Faculty			
facId	**name**	**department**	**rank**
F101	Adams	Art	Professor
F105	Tanaka	CSC	Instructor
F110	Byrne	Math	Assistant
F115	Smith	History	Associate
F221	Smith	CSC	Professor

FIGURE 4.1(b)
The Faculty Table

FIGURE 4.1(c)

The Class Table

Class			
classNo	facId	schedule	room
ART103A	F101	MWF9	H221
CSC201A	F105	TuThF10	M110
CSC203A	F105	MThF12	M110
HST205A	F115	MWF11	H221
MTH101B	F110	MTuTh9	H225
MTH103C	F110	MWF11	H225

FIGURE 4.1(d)

The Enroll Table

Enroll		
stuId	classNo	grade
S1001	ART103A	A
S1001	HST205A	C
S1002	ART103A	D
S1002	CSC201A	F
S1002	MTH103C	B
S1010	ART103A	
S1010	MTH103C	
S1020	CSC201A	B
S1020	MTH101B	A

is a copy of Figure 1.1(a), shows an instance of the Student table. Note that the column names, stuId, lastName, firstName, major, and credits, are the same as the attribute names. As you can see from this example, a column contains values of a single attribute; for example, the stuId column contains only IDs of students. The **domain** of an attribute is the set of allowable values for that attribute. Domains may be distinct, or two or more attributes may have the same domain. Each row of the table corresponds to an individual record or entity instance. In the relational model, each row is called a **tuple**.

A table that represents a relation has the following characteristics:

- Each cell of the table contains only one value.

- Each column has a distinct name, which is the name of the attribute it represents.

- The values in a column all come from the same domain, since they are all values of the corresponding attribute.

- Each tuple or row is distinct; there are no duplicate tuples.

- The order of tuples or rows is immaterial.

To show what these restrictions mean, we use the Student table as an example. Since each cell should contain only one value, it is illegal to store multiple values for an attribute of a single entity. For example, we cannot store two majors for a student in a single cell. The column names written at the tops of the columns correspond to the attributes of the relation. The values in the stuId column are all from the domain of stuId; we would not allow a student's name to appear in this column. There can be no duplicate rows, because each individual student is represented just once. The rows can be interchanged at will, so the records of S1001 and S1002 can be switched, with no change in the relation.

4.2.2 Mathematical Relations

To understand the strict meaning of the term relation, we need to review some notions from mathematics. Suppose we have two sets, $D_1 = \{1, 3\}$ and $D_2 = \{a, b, c\}$. We could form the **Cartesian product** of these two sets, written $D_1 \times D_2$, which is the set of all ordered pairs such that the first element is a member of D_1 and the second element is a member of D_2. Another way of thinking of this is to find all combinations of elements with the first from D_1 and the second from D_2. Thus we find the following:

D₁ × D₂ = {(1,a), (1,b), (1,c), (3,a), (3,b), (3,c)}

A relation is simply some subset of this Cartesian product. For example,

R = {(1,a), (3,a)}

is a relation. Often, we specify which ordered pairs will be in the relation by giving some rule for their selection. For example, **R** includes all those ordered pairs in which the second element is *a*, so we could write **R** as,

R = {(x,y) | x ∈ D₁, y ∈ D₂, and y = a}

Using these same sets, we could form another relation, **S**, in which the first element is always 3. Thus,

S = {(x,y) | x ∈ D₁, y ∈ D₂, and x = 3}

Alternatively, **S** = {(3, *a*), (3, *b*), (3, *c*)}, since there are only three ordered pairs in the Cartesian product that satisfy the condition.

We could extend the notion of a relation to three sets in a natural way. Let **D₁**, **D₂**, and **D₃** be three sets. Then the Cartesian product **D₁ × D₂ × D₃** of these three sets is the set of all ordered triples such that the first element is from **D₁**, the second element is from **D₂**, and the third element is from **D₃**. A relation is then any subset of this Cartesian product. For example, suppose we define the sets as,

D₁ = {1,3}   D₂ = {2,4,6}   D₃ = {3,6,9}
Then D₁ × D₂ × D₃ = {(1,2,3), (1,2,6), (1,2,9), (1,4,3), (1,4,6), (1,4,9),
(1,6,3), (1,6,6), (1,6,9), (3,2,3), (3,2,6), (3,2,9), (3,4,3), (3,4,6),
(3,4,9), (3,6,3), (3,6,6), (3,6,9)}

A relation is any subset of these ordered triples. For example, we could define a relation **T** as those ordered triples in which the third element is the sum of the first two. Then we have,

T = {(x,y,z) | x ∈ **D₁**, y ∈ **D₂**, z ∈ **D₃** and z = x + y}
or T = {(1,2,3), (3,6,9}.

We can go beyond three sets and define a general relation on *n* domains. Let **D₁**, **D₂**, . . ., **Dₙ** be *n* sets. Their Cartesian product is defined as,

D₁ × **D₂** × . . . × **Dₙ** = {(d₁,d₂, . . ., dₙ) | d₁∈ **D₁**, d₂∈ **D₂**, . . ., dₙ ∈ **Dₙ**}

The Cartesian product is usually written,

$$\prod_{i=1}^{n} D_i$$

A relation on the *n* sets is any set of *n*-tuples chosen from this Cartesian product. Notice that in defining relations we had to specify the domains, or the sets from which we chose values.

4.2.3   Database Relations and Tables

Applying these concepts to databases, let $A_1, A_2, \ldots, A_n$ be attributes with domains $D_1, D_2, \ldots, D_n$. A relation schema R is such a set of attributes with their corresponding domains. Thus the set $\{A_1, A_2, \ldots, A_n\}$ with corresponding domains $\{D_1, D_2, \ldots, D_n\}$ is a relation schema. A **relation r** on a relation schema R is a set of mappings from the attribute names to their corresponding domains. Thus relation r is a set of n-tuples $(A_1:d_1, A_2:d_2, \ldots, A_n:d_n)$ such that $d_1 \in D_1, d_2 \in D_2, \ldots, d_n \in D_n$. Each element in one of these n-tuples consists of an attribute and a value of that attribute. Normally, when we write out a relation as a table, we list the attribute names as column headings and simply write out the tuples using values chosen from the appropriate domains, so we think of the n-tuples as having the form $(d_1, d_2, \ldots, d_n)$. In this way we can think of a relation in the relational model as any subset of the Cartesian product of the domains of the attributes. A table is simply a representation of such a relation.

For our university example, the relation `Student` would have attributes `stuId`, `lastName`, `firstName`, `major`, and `credits`, each with their corresponding domains. The `Student` relation is any subset of the Cartesian product of the domains, or any set of 5-tuples in which the first element is a student ID, the second is a student's last name, the third is a student's first name, the fourth is a major, and the fifth is a number of credits. Some of the 5-tuples are:

```
{
(S1001, Smith, Tom, History, 90),
(S1002, Chin,  Ann, Math,    36),
. . .}
```

More properly, these 5-tuples are:

```
{
(stuId:S1001, lastName:Smith, firstName:Tom, major:History, credits:90),
(stuId:S1002, lastName:Chin, firstName:Ann, major:Math, credits:36),
. . .}
```

The `Student` table, shown in Figure 4.1(a) is a convenient way of writing out all the 5–tuples that satisfy the relation at the moment. The 5-tuples are, of course, the rows of the table, which explains why table rows in the relational model are called **tuples**. The table, with all its rows written out, is an instance or **extension** of the relation. The structure of the table, together with a specification of the domains and any other restrictions on possible values, shows the **intension** of the relation, also called the **database schema**. Strictly speaking, the schema also includes domains, views, character sets, constraints, stored procedures, authorizations, and other related information. We can represent relation schemas by giving the name of each relation, followed by the attribute names in parentheses, as in,

```
Student (stuId, lastName, firstName, major, credits)
```

The attribute stuId is underlined because it is customary to underline the primary key in the relation schema.

4.2.4   Properties of Relations

Most of the characteristics specified for tables result from the properties of mathematical relations. Since a relation is a set, the order of elements does not count. Therefore, in a table, the order of rows is immaterial. In a set, no elements are repeated. Similarly, in a table, there are no duplicate rows. When we found the Cartesian products of sets with simple, single-valued elements such as integers, each element in each tuple was single valued. Similarly, each cell of a table contains only one value. In a relation, the possible values for a given position are determined by the domain on which the position is defined. In a table, the values in each column must come from the same attribute domain. In a mathematical relation, the order of elements in a tuple is important. For example, the ordered pair (1,2) is quite different from the ordered pair (2,1), as you realize when you locate the two points in a plane using Cartesian coordinates. However, in tables, the order of columns is immaterial. We consider the Student table to be the same even if we put the columns in different order, as long as we use the same data. The reason is that the column headings tell us which attribute the value belongs to. However, once the structure of the table is chosen, the order of elements within the rows of the extension must match the order of column names.

4.2.5   Degree and Cardinality

The number of columns in a table is called the **degree** of the relation. The degree of the Student relation is five, since the Student table has five columns. This means each row of the table is a 5–tuple, containing 5 values.

A relation with only one column would have degree one and be called a **unary** relation. A relation with two columns is called **binary**, one with three columns is called **ternary** and, after that, the term *n*-**ary** is usually used. The degree of a relation is part of the intension of the relation and never changes.

By contrast, the number of rows in a table, called the **cardinality** of the relation, changes as new tuples are added or old ones are deleted. The cardinality is a property of the extension of the relation, the particular instance of the relation at any given moment.

We note that the meaning of these terms differs from their meanings for the E-R model discussed in Chapter 3.

4.2.6   Relation Keys

Since a relation is a set and a set has no duplicate elements, it is always possible to tell elements of a set apart. In a database relation, the tuples are the set elements, so it must always be possible to tell tuples apart. This means that there must always be some attribute, or some combination of attributes, that makes the tuples distinct. Therefore there will always be a superkey for every relation, and this implies that there will always be a minimal superkey, which means there is always a candidate key. Therefore we can always find a primary key for every relation. In the worst case, the entire set of attributes would need to be examined to tell tuples apart. Usually, however, some smaller set of attributes is sufficient to distinguish among tuples. Applying our definitions from Chapter 3, a **superkey** for a relation is an attribute or a set of attributes that uniquely identifies a tuple, a **candidate key** is a superkey such that no proper subset is a superkey, and a **primary key** is the candidate key that is actually chosen to uniquely identify tuples. Note that an instance of the table cannot be used to prove that an attribute or combination of attributes is a candidate key. The fact that there are no duplicates for the values that appear at a particular moment does not guarantee that duplicates are not possible. However, the presence of duplicates in an instance can be used to show that some attribute combination is not a candidate key. Identifying a candidate key requires that we consider the meaning of the attribute(s) involved so that we can make a decision about whether duplicates are possible in the miniworld. Only by using this semantic information and identifying the assumptions for the model can we be sure that an attribute or combination of attributes is a candidate key.

A **foreign key** is an attribute or attribute combination of a relation that is not the primary key of that relation but that is the primary key of some relation, usually a different one. Foreign keys are very important in the relational model, because they are used to represent logical connections between relations. Consider an employee relation with schema,

Employee(<u>empId</u>, lastName, firstName, departmentName)

and also a Department relation with schema,

Department(<u>departmentName</u>, office)

The attribute departmentName, which is a primary key in the Department relation, is a foreign key in Employee. Notice that although it has unique values in the Department table, it is not unique in the Employee table, since several employees may belong to the same department. Having that attribute in the Employee table allows us to tell what department an employee belongs to. When we have a foreign key, we call the relation in which the attribute or combination is the primary key its **home relation**. Department is the home relation for departmentName.

In the tables shown in Figure 4.1(a)–(d), facId is a foreign key in Class. It is not the primary key of that table, but it is the primary key of a different table, Faculty. Having that attribute in the Class table allows us to connect a class with the faculty member who teaches it, showing the relationship between these tables. In the Enroll table, stuId is a foreign key. It is not, by itself, the primary key of Enroll, but it is the primary key of Student. Similarly, classNo is a foreign key in Enroll, but it is the primary key of Class. These two attributes in Enroll allow us to tell what classes a student is enrolled in, and what students are enrolled in each class.

The home relation does not have to be a separate table. For example, suppose an employee schema appears as,

Employee(<u>empId</u>, firstName, lastName, managerEmpId)

Although empId is the primary key of this table, managerEmpId is a foreign key that actually refers to the empId of another tuple in the same table. Each employee's record contains the empId of that person's manager, which of course occurs in the manager's employee record as his or her `empId`.

4.3 Integrity Constraints: domain, key, foreign key, general constraints

It is important to preserve the **integrity**, which means the correctness and internal consistency, of the data in the database by not allowing users to enter data that would make the database incorrect. The relational model allows us to define **integrity constraints (ICs)**, which are rules or restrictions that apply to all instances of the database. A **legal state** of the database is one that obeys all the integrity constraints. Part of the job of a database management system is to enforce the integrity constraints—to ensure that any data entered creates a legal instance of the database.

Since every attribute has an associated domain, there are restrictions on the set of values allowed for attributes of relations. These are called **domain constraints**, and they can be enforced in SQL by defining the domain for an attribute when we create a table. An alternative is to use one of the built-in data types, and to add a constraint called the CHECK option, which allows us to specify that the value of an attribute must be within a specified set of values, or that it must obey a condition that we specify using logical predicates.

A primary key constraint, called **entity integrity**, states that in a relation no attribute of a primary key can have a null value. By definition, a primary key is a minimal identifier that is used to uniquely identify tuples. This means that no subset of the primary key is sufficient to provide unique identification of tuples. If we were to allow a null value for any part of the primary key, we would be demonstrating that not all of the attributes are needed to distinguish between tuples, which would contradict the definition. All relation keys, both primary and candidate, must have unique values. In SQL, we can identify the primary key using a primary key constraint when we create the table. The system will then enforce both the non-null and uniqueness constraints automatically. For candidate keys, most systems allow us to specify both a uniqueness constraint and a not null constraint.

An integrity rule called **referential integrity** applies to foreign keys. Referential integrity states that, if a foreign key exists in a relation, then either the foreign key value must match the primary key value of some tuple in its home relation, or the foreign key value must be completely null. SQL allows us to specify foreign key constraints when we create a table.

There are several other types of constraints, referred to as **general constraints**, which we will discuss in later chapters. Constraints are enforced by the database management system whenever changes are made to the data. The system verifies that the changes do not violate the constraints before permitting them to be accepted in the table.

4.4   Representing Relational Database Schemas

A relational database schema can have any number of relations. We can represent relation schemas by giving the name of each relation, followed by the attribute names in parentheses, with the primary key underlined. There is no simple standard way of indicating foreign keys unambiguously, but we will use italics to indicate that an attribute is a foreign key, or part of a foreign key. Unfortunately, this method will not always tell us clearly what the home relation is. Also, if we have composite foreign keys we would have difficulty identifying exactly what the foreign key is. The clearest way of showing foreign keys is by drawing arrows from the foreign keys to the primary keys they refer to. Recall that the schema actually also includes domains, views, character sets, constraints, stored procedures, authorizations and other related information, so our representation is actually only a part of the schema. For the university example, a simple database might contain relations for `Student`, `Class`, `Faculty`, and `Enroll`. The relation schemas would be written as:

```
Student (stuId, lastName, firstName, major, credits)
Class (classNo, facId, schedule, room)
Faculty (facId, name, department, rank)
Enroll(stuId,classNo, grade)
```

The relation schema gives us the table name for each relation and column headings for each of its attributes. The logical model schema is the set of all these schemas for the database. Figure 4.1 shows an instance of this database.

Notice that some attributes, such as foreign keys, appear in more than one relation. For example, `stuId` appears in both `Student` and `Enroll`. When we want to distinguish between the two appearances of `stuId`, we use the relation name, followed by a period, followed by the attribute name. The two qualified names for `stuId` are `Student.stuId` and `Enroll.stuId`. An even more explicit name would start with the database name, then the table name, then the attribute name, as in `University.Student.stuId`. When an attribute appears in more than one relation, its appearance usually represents a relationship or interaction between tuples of the two relations. These common attributes play an important role in performing data manipulation, as we shall see in later sections.

4.5   Relational Data Manipulation Languages

There are a variety of languages used by relational database management systems.

4.5.1   Categories of DMLs

Some of the languages are **procedural** or proscriptive, meaning the user tells the system exactly how to manipulate the data. **Relational algebra** is an example of a procedural language that we will discuss. Others are **nonprocedural** or declarative, which means the user states what data is needed but not exactly how it is to be located. **Relational calculus** and **SQL** are nonprocedural languages. Some languages are **graphical**, allowing the user to give an example or illustration of what data should be found. **QBE** (QueryByExample) is a graphical language that allows users to provide examples of data they would like retrieved. Another category is **fourth-generation language** (4GL), which allows a complete customized application to be created using a few commands in a user-friendly, often menu-driven, environment. Some systems accept a variety of **natural language**, sometimes called a **fifth-generation language**, a restricted version of natural English to allow the user to enter requirements for an application, and have the system use artificial intelligence to produce a solution.

Both relational algebra and relational calculus are formal, non-user-friendly languages. They are not implemented in their native form in database management systems, but both have been used as the basis for other, higher level data manipulation languages for relational databases such as SQL. We introduce relational algebra here because it illustrates the basic operations required of any data manipulation language, and it serves as the standard of comparison for other relational languages.

4.5.2   Relational Algebra

Relational algebra is a theoretical language with operators that are applied on one or two relations to produce another relation. Thus, both the operands and the result are tables. Three very basic operations, SELECT, PROJECT, and JOIN, allow us to perform most of the data retrieval operations that interest us. We will use the university database example from Figure 4.1 to illustrate these operations. There are several variations of syntax of relational algebra commands, and we will use a fairly simple English-like one here and present it informally. We also include the more formal symbolic notation for the commands. There are many variations of the operations that are included in relational algebra. We assume we have the option of assigning the results to a table that we name in the command. (Note: In a more formal discussion, we would use a special "rename" operation to do this.)

The SELECT Operator, σ

The SELECT command is applied to a single table and takes rows that meet a specified condition, copying them into a new table. Informally, the general form is:

SELECT *tableName* WHERE *condition* [GIVING *newTableName*]

Note: The square brackets indicate that the part of the statement enclosed in them is optional.

Symbolically, the form is:

[*newTableName* =] σ predicate (*table-name*)

or simply

σ_θ(*table-name*)

For example, if we wanted to find all information in the Student table about student S1013, we would write informally,

SELECT Student WHERE stuId = 'S1013' GIVING Result

or symbolically,

Result = σ STUID='S1013' (Student)

The command produces a new table that we call `Result`, which looks like this:

Result:

stuId	lastName	firstName	major	credits
S1013	McCarthy	Owen	Math	0

The SELECT operation can be used to find more than one row. For example, to find all classes that meet in room H225, we would write,

```
SELECT Class WHERE room = 'H225' GIVING Answer
```

or symbolically,

```
Answer = σ room='H225' (Class)
```

This command produces the following table:

Answer:

classNo	facId	schedule	room
MTH101B	F110	MTuTh9	H225
MTH103C	F110	MWF11	H225

Note that the operation is performed on an existing table, *tableName,* and produces a new table that is a horizontal subset of the old one and which we can name and indicate by *newTableName.* The old table still continues to exist under its old name and both it and the new table are available for additional operations. If we simply wish to find and display the rows that satisfy the condition, but do not plan further operations on the new table, we omit its name. The selection predicate is referred to as the **theta-condition.** The Greek letter theta, written θ, is often used in mathematics to represent any kind of operator. It was used by the developers of relational theory to represent predicates involving any of the comparison operators, namely,

```
<, <=, >, >=, =, ≠, ∧ (AND), ∨ (OR), ¬ (NOT)
```

We can form complex selection predicates by using more than one comparison operator in the θ-condition. For example, to find all math majors who have more than 30 credits, we write:

```
SELECT Student WHERE major = 'Math' AND credits> 30
```

or symbolically,

$$\sigma_{\text{major='Math'} \wedge \text{credits} > 30}(\text{Student})$$

This command produces the following unnamed table:

stuId	lastName	firstName	major	credits
S1002	Chin	Ann	Math	36
S1015	Jones	Mary	Math	42

The PROJECT Operator, Π

The PROJECT command also operates on a single table, but it produces a vertical subset of the table, extracting the values of specified columns, eliminating duplicates, and placing the values in a new table. Informally, its form is,

PROJECT tableName OVER (colName, . . ., colName) [GIVING newTableName]

or, symbolically,

[newTableName =] Π colName, . . ., colName (tableName)

To illustrate projection over a single column, we find all the different majors that students have by the command,

```
PROJECT Student OVER major GIVING Temp
```

or Temp = Π_{major}(Student)

The resulting table, Temp, looks like this:

```
Temp   major
       History
       Math
       Art
       CSC
```

Notice that we get all the values that appear in the major column of the Student table, but duplicates have been eliminated.

When we project over two or more columns, duplicates of combinations of values are eliminated. For example, suppose we want to find the rooms where each faculty member teaches. We could do so by using the command,

```
PROJECT Class OVER (facd,room)
```

or,

$\Pi_{\text{facId,room}}$ (Class)

This gives the result in an unnamed table,

facId	room
F101	H221
F105	M110
F115	H221
F110	H225

While we have repetition in the room values, with H221 appearing twice, we notice that the repeated room values appear with different `facId` values. As long as the combination has not appeared before, it is added to the projection. Notice that the third and the last rows of `Class` did not contribute to the projection result, since their combination of values for `facId` and `room` appeared previously.

We can combine the SELECT and PROJECT operations to give us only specific columns of certain rows, but doing so requires two steps. For example, suppose we want to see the names and IDs of all history majors. Since we want only history majors, we need a SELECT, but since we want only certain columns of those records, we need a PROJECT. We can express the query as,

```
SELECT Student WHERE major = 'History' GIVING Temp
PROJECT Temp OVER (lastName, firstName, stuId) GIVING Result
```

After the first command is executed, we have the table,

Temp:

stuId	lastName	firstName	major	credits
S1001	Smith	Tom	History	90
S1005	Lee	Perry	History	3

The second command is performed on this temporary table, and the result is,

Result:

lastname	firstname	stuid
Smith	Tom	S1001
Lee	Perry	S1005

Notice that the PROJECT operation allowed us to change the order of the columns in the final result. We could have written the commands symbolically as,

$$\Pi_{lastName, firstName, stuId}(\sigma_{major='History'}(Student))$$

Note that we can compose the operations using the result of the first as the argument for the second. The intermediate table resulting from the selection operation, which we called `Temp` when we used the English-like syntax, does not need a name when we use symbolic notation, since we use the expression as an operand. Observe that we could not reverse the order of the SELECT and PROJECT. If we had done the PROJECT first, we would have an intermediate table with only `lastName`, `firstName`, and `stuId` columns, so we could not then try to do a SELECT on `major` on the intermediate table, since it does not contain that attribute.

The Natural Join If a relational database schema has two related tables, they have a common column or columns. For example, the `Student` table and the `Enroll` table both have `stuId`, which shows that there is a relationship between the tables. We often wish to find the rows of the two tables that have the same values in the common column. For example, suppose we want to find information about all the classes each student is enrolled in. We begin with the `Student` table and for each row, find each `Enroll` record with the same `stuId`, and combine the two matching rows. This operation is called the natural join. It is a binary operator, symbolized by |x|, which we place between the two tables that participate in the join, as in

    Student |x| Enroll

Using our informal syntax, we can write this as

    Student JOIN Enroll

The result of this natural join is shown in Figure 4.2. Note that the `Student` rows appear more than once if students are enrolled in multiple classes. As another example, we note that `Class` and `Faculty` also have a common attribute, `facId`. We form the natural join `Faculty |x| Class` by examining each `Faculty` record and combining it with any `Class` record having the same `facId`.

The resulting table shown in Figure 4.3 gives us all the details about faculty members and the classes they teach. The natural join allows us to recombine pieces of information about an entity, even though they appear on different tables. We do not keep the data about faculty and classes in a single table, because we would have a lot of repetition in the table. If the tables in a natural join have more than one column in common, the values must match in all the corresponding columns to enter the natural join. Other types of joins

			Student Natural Join Enroll				
stuId	lastName	firstName	major	credits	classNo	grade
S1001	Smith	Tom	History	90	HST205A	C
S1001	Smith	Tom	History	90	ART103A	A
S1002	Chin	Ann	Math	36	MTH103C	B
S1002	Chin	Ann	Math	36	CSC201A	F
S1002	Chin	Ann	Math	36	ART103A	D
S1010	Burns	Edward	Art	63	MTH103C	
S1010	Burns	Edward	Art	63	ART103A	
S1020	Rivera	Jane	CSC	15	MTH101B	A
S1020	Rivera	Jane	CSC	15	CSC201A	B

FIGURE 4.2

Student |X| Enroll

			Faculty Natural Join Class			
facId	name	department	rank	classNo	schedule	room
F101	Adams	Art	Professor	ART103A	MWF9	H221
F105	Tanaka	CSC	Instructor	CSC203A	MThF12	M110
F105	Tanaka	CSC	Instructor	CSC201A	TuThF10	M110
F110	Byrne	Math	Assistant	MTH103C	MWF11	H225
F110	Byrne	Math	Assistant	MTH101B	MTuTh9	H225
F115	Smith	History	Associate	HST205A	MWF11	H221

FIGURE 4.3

Faculty |X| Class

are described in the student website for this book. However, since the natural join is the most commonly used, we will simply refer to it as the join.

Complex Queries

More complicated queries can require use of the SELECT, PROJECT, and JOIN commands. For example, suppose we want to find the classes and grades of student Ann Chin. We notice that the `Student` table contains the student's name, but not classes or grades, while the `Enroll` table contains the classes and grades, but not the name. Whenever we need to use more than one table to answer a query, we will use a join. If the result needs to contain only some, but not all, columns of the original tables, we also need a PROJECT. If not all rows will be used, we need a SELECT as well. To decide what operations to do and in what order, examine the tables to see how you would answer the question "by hand" and then try to formulate the operations required in terms of relational algebra commands. To find the classes and grades for Ann Chin, we start with the `Student` table, and locate the record for Ann Chin (a SELECT operation). We then consult the `Enroll` table, look for records with `stuId` that matches Ann Chin's `stuId` (a JOIN operation), and read off only the `classNo` and `grade` values (a PROJECT operation). One way to find the data required is the following, expressed using our English-like language:

```
SELECT Student WHERE lastName='Chin' AND firstName ='Ann' GIVING Temp1
Temp1 JOIN Enroll GIVING Temp2
PROJECT Temp2 OVER (classNo, grade) GIVING Answer
```

or symbolically as,

$$\Pi_{classNo,grade}((\sigma_{lastName='Chin'\wedge firstName='Ann'}(\text{Student}))|x|\text{Enroll})$$

After the SELECT in the first line we have this result:

Temp1:

stuId	lastName	firstName	major	credits
S1002	Chin	Ann	Math	36

After the JOIN in the second line we have this result:

Temp2:

stuId	lastName	firstName	major	credits	classNo	grade
S1002	Chin	Ann	Math	36	ART103A	D
S1002	Chin	Ann	Math	36	CSC201A	F
S1002	Chin	Ann	Math	36	MTH103C	B

After the PROJECT in the third line, we have this result:

Answer:

classNo	grade
CSC201A	F
ART103A	D
MTH103C	B

You may have observed that all we really needed from `Temp1` was the `stuId` column, since this was used for the comparison for the join, and none of the other columns was used later. Therefore, if we preferred, we could have used a PROJECT on `Temp1` to give us only the `stuId` column before doing the JOIN, as in,

$$\Pi_{classNo,grade}(\Pi_{stuId}(\sigma_{lastName='Chin' \wedge firstName='Ann'}(Student)) \mid x \mid Enroll)$$

A third way to do the query is,

```
Student JOIN Enroll GIVING Tempa
SELECT Tempa WHERE lastName='Chin' AND firstName = 'Ann' GIVING Tempb
PROJECT Tempb OVER (classNo, grade)
```

or,

$$\Pi_{classNo,grade}(\sigma_{lastName='Chin' \wedge firstName='Ann'}(Student \mid x \mid Enroll))$$

This method is less efficient, since the first line requires 54 comparisons to form a joined table, a relatively slow operation. Doing the selection first reduces the number of comparisons to nine, thus optimizing the query.

We can do joins of joined tables. Suppose we want to find the IDs of all students in Professor Adams' classes. We need data from the `Faculty`, `Class`, and `Enroll` tables to answer this query. One method is,

```
SELECT Faculty WHERE name = 'Adams' GIVING Temp1
Temp1 JOIN Class GIVING Temp2
Temp2 JOIN Enroll GIVING Temp3
PROJECT Temp3 OVER stuId GIVING Result
```

or symbolically,

$$\Pi_{stuId}(((\sigma_{name='Adams'}(Faculty)) \mid x \mid Class) \mid x \mid Enroll)$$

In this example, `Temp2` has seven columns and `Temp3` has nine columns. Since only one of the `Faculty` columns, `facId`, is used for the join and none of its other columns is needed later, we could do a PROJECT before the first join. Alternatively, since only one of `Temp2`'s columns, `classNo`, is needed for the join and none of its other columns is used again, we could do a PROJECT between the two joins.

Products

For two tables, A and B, the product, A TIMES B, written A X B, is formed much like the Cartesian product, by concatenating each row of A with every row of B, regardless of whether there are common columns or common values. The columns of the product consist of all the columns of A followed by all the columns of B, and the number of rows in the product is the number of rows of A times the number of rows of B. For example, we can form

```
Student X Enroll
```

which will consist of all possible combinations of `Student` rows with `Enroll` rows, regardless of the values of `stuId`.

Theta Join

The theta join of two tables is defined as the result of performing a select operation on their product. For example, we might want to select only the tuples of `Student  X  Enroll` where the number of credits is greater than 50. We write this theta join as

```
Student Xcredits>50 Enroll
```

This is equivalent to $\sigma_{credits>50}$(`Student  X  Enroll`)

The predicate in the select, `credits>50`, is referred to as the theta condition, written θ. If A and B are relations, the abstract representation of their theta join is A X_θ B.

Set Operations

Since relations are sets of n-tuples, relational algebra includes a version of the basic set operations of union, intersection, and set difference. For these binary operations to be possible, the two relations on which they are performed must be **union compatible**, which means that they must have the same degree, and the attributes in the corresponding position in both relations must have the same domains. The result of each of the set operations is a new table with the same structure as the two original tables. For example, suppose we have two tables for faculty. `MainFac` contains records of faculty members who teach at the main campus and `Branch-Fac` contains records of faculty members who teach at the branch campus. Some faculty may teach at both locations, so their records would appear in both tables. The set union

```
MainFac ∪ BranchFac
```

consists of all the tuples in either relation or both relations.

The set intersection

`MainFac ∩ BranchFac`

is the set of tuples in both relations simultaneously, and the set difference

`MainFac - BranchFac`

is the set of tuples in `MainFac` but not in `BranchFac`.

Several additional operators have been defined for relational algebra.

On the Companion Website:

- Additional Operators

4.6 Views

The actual tables in the schema for a relational database, the logical-level tables, are called **base tables**.

In the standard three-level architecture, the top level consists of external views. An external view is the structure of the database as it appears to a particular user. In the relational model, the word "view" has a slightly different meaning. Rather than being the entire external model of a user, a view is either a subset of a base table or a virtual table—one that does not actually exist but can be constructed by performing operations such as relational algebra selection, projection, or join or other calculations on the values of base tables. Thus, an external model can consist of both actual base tables and views derived from tables.

The view mechanism is desirable because it allows us to hide portions of the database from certain users. The user is not aware of the existence of any attributes that are missing from his or her view. It also permits users to access data in a "customized" manner. The view should be designed to create an external model that the user finds familiar and comfortable. For example, a user might need enrollment records that contain student names as well as the three attributes already in `Enroll`. This view would be created by joining the `Enroll` and `Student` tables, and then projecting on the four attributes of interest. Another user might need to see `Student` records without the `credits` attribute. For this user, a projection is done so that his or her view does not have the `credits` column. Attributes may be renamed, so that the user accustomed to calling the ID of students by the name `stuNumber` can see that column heading, and the order of columns can be changed, so that `lastName, firstName` can appear as the first and second columns in a view. Selection operations can also be used to create a view. For example, a department chairperson can see faculty records for only that department. Here, a select operation is performed so that only a horizontal subset of the `Faculty` table is seen. View tables are not permanently stored as such. Instead, their definitions are stored in the data dictionary and the system creates the view dynamically as the user requests it. When the user finishes with a view, the view table may be erased, but the base tables from which it was created remain.

Although all of the previous examples demonstrate that a view provides logical independence, views allow more significant logical independence when the logical level is reorganized. If a new column is added to a base table, existing users can be unaware of its existence if their views are defined to exclude it. When a new table is added, there is no change to the external models of existing users. However, if an existing table is rearranged or split up, a view can be defined so that users can continue to see their old models. In the case of splitting up a base table, the old table can be recreated by defining a view from the join of the new base tables, provided the split is done in such a way that the original can be reconstructed. We can ensure that this is possible by placing the primary key in both of the new tables. Thus, if we originally had a `Student` table of the form,

```
Student(stuId, lastName, firstName, ssn, major, credits)
```

we could reorganize this into two new tables,

```
PersonalStu(stuId, lastName, firstName, ssn)
AcademicStu(stuId, major, credits)
```

Users and applications could still access the data using the old table structure, which would be recreated by defining a view called `Student` as the natural join of `personalStu` and `academicStu`, with `stuId` as the common column.

Many views act as "windows" into tables, allowing the user to see portions of base tables. Others that contain joined, calculated, or summary information from base tables are not windows, but more like "snapshots," pictures of the data as it existed when the view was invoked during the session. In the "window" case, the view is dynamic, meaning changes made to the base table that affect view attributes are immediately reflected in the view. When users make permitted changes to the "window" view, those changes are made to the base tables. There are restrictions on the types of modifications that can be made through views. For example, a view that does not contain the primary key should not be updateable at all. Also, views constructed from summary information are not updateable. When a view user writes a DML command, he or she uses the view name, and the system automatically converts the command into an equivalent one on the base tables. The necessary external/logical mapping information is stored in the data dictionary. The (permitted) operations are performed on the base tables, and the system returns results in the form that a user expects, based on the view used.

4.7 Mapping an E-R Model to a Relational Schema

An E-R diagram can be converted to a relational model fairly easily. Both entities and relationships must be represented in the relational schema. For example, to convert the University E-R diagram to a relational model, refer to Figure 3.12 and map as follows. We begin with the entity sets.

- The **strong entity sets** shown as rectangles become relations represented by base tables. The table name is the same as the entity name written inside the rectangle. For strong entity sets, **non-composite, single-valued attributes**, represented by simple ovals, become attributes of the relation, or column headings of the table. The strong entity sets, Department, Student, and Faculty can be represented by the following tables:

```
Department (deptName, deptCode, office)
Student (stuId, lastName, firstName, major, credits)
Faculty (facId, lastName, firstName, rank)
```

- For E-R attributes that are **composites**, the pure relational model does not directly allow us to represent the fact that the attribute is a composite. Instead, we can simply make a column for each of the simple attributes that form the composite, or we can choose to leave the composite as a single attribute. For example, if we had a composite, address, we would not have a column with that name, but instead have individual columns for its components: street, `city`, `state`, and `zip`. For example, if we included an address in the `Student` table, we could use the schema,

```
Student1 (stuId, lastName, firstName, street, city, state, zip, major,
credits)
```

or, keeping address as a single attribute,

```
Student2 (stuId, lastName, firstName, address, major, credits)
```

The second choice would make it more difficult to select records on the basis of the value of parts of the address, such as zip code or state. In Figure 3.12, we saw that `className` is actually a composite consisting of `deptCode`, `courseNumber`, and `section`. Here, we are choosing to leave that composite as a single attribute. Therefore for the present we form the `Class` table as,

```
Class (className, schedule, room)
```

- **Multivalued** attributes pose a special problem when converting to a pure relational model, which does not allow multiple values in a cell. The usual solution is to remove them from the table and to create a separate relation in which we put the primary key of the entity, along with the multivalued attribute. The key of this new table is the combination of the key of the original table and the multivalued attribute. The key of the original table becomes a foreign key in the new table. If there are multiple multivalued attributes in the original table, we have to create a new table for each one. These new tables are treated as if they are weak entities, with the original table (without the multivalued attributes) acting as the owner entity. It is convenient to name the new tables using the plural form of the multivalued attribute name. As an illustration of how to handle multivalued attributes, let us consider what we would do if students could have more than one major. To represent this, we would change the `Student` table by removing `major` from it, and create instead two tables,

```
Student3(stuId, lastName, firstName, credits)
StuMajors(stuId, major)
```

Another solution is to put in additional columns for the multiple values in the original table. Using this solution, if students could have at most two majors, the `Student` table would become,

```
Student4(stuId, lastName, firstName, major1, major2, credits)
```

However, we are assuming that students have at most one major, so we will retain the original `Student` table instead.

If telephone numbers were included for faculty, and faculty members could have more than one telephone number stored in the database, the multiple column solution would produce the schema,

```
Faculty2 (facId, lastName, firstName, rank, phone, alternatePhone)
```

In Figure 3.12, we saw that the attribute `author` for `Textbook` can have multiple values. We will choose the first method, representing the authors in a separate table, giving us,

```
Textbook(isbn, title, publisher)
TextAuthors(isbn, author)
```

- **Weak entity sets** are also represented by tables, but they require additional attributes. Recall that a weak entity is dependent on another (owner) entity and has no candidate key consisting of just its own attributes. Therefore, the primary key of the corresponding owner entity is used to show which instance of the owner entity a weak entity instance depends on. To represent the weak entity, we use a table whose attributes include all the attributes of the weak entity, plus the primary key of the owner entity. The weak entity itself should have a discriminant—some attribute or attribute set that, when coupled with the owner's primary key, enables us to tell instances apart. We use the combination of the owner's primary key and the discriminant as the key. In Figure 3.12, the weak entity set, `Evaluation`, is given the primary key of its owner entity set, `Faculty`, resulting in the table,

```
Evaluation(facId, date, rater, rating)
```

- **Relationship sets** must be represented in the tables as well, either by foreign keys or by a separate relationship table, depending on the cardinality and degree of the relationship in the E-R model.

    - If A and B are **strong entity sets** and **binary relationship** A:B is **one-to-many**, we place the key of A (the one side) in the table for B (the many side), where it becomes a foreign key. `Teaches` is a one-to-many relationship set connecting the strong entity sets, `Class` and `Faculty`.

We use a foreign key to represent this relationship, by placing `facId`, the key of the "one" side, `Faculty`, in the table for the "many" side, `Class`. We therefore change the `Class` table to,

`Class (classNo, facId, schedule, room)`

- Notice that in the resulting base table each `Class` row will have one `facId` cell that tells us who the teacher is. If we had tried to represent the relationship the opposite way, by placing the `courseNumber` in the `Faculty` table, it would not work. Since a faculty member may teach many courses, a row in the Faculty table would need several values in the `courseNumber` cell, which is not allowed.

- All strong entity sets that have a **one-to-one** relationship should be examined carefully to determine whether they are actually the same entity. If they are, they should be combined into a single entity. If A and B are truly separate entities having a one-to-one relationship, then we can put the key of either relation in the other table to show the connection (i.e., either put the key of A in the B table, or vice-versa, but not both). For example, if students can get a parking permit to park one car on campus, we might add a Car entity, which would have a one-to-one relationship with Student. Each car belongs to exactly one student and each student can have at most one car. The initial schema for `Car` might be,

`Car(licNo, make, model, year, color)`

We assume `licNo` includes the state where the car is licensed. To store the one-to-one relationship with `Student`, we could put `stuId` in the `Car` table, getting,

`Car(licNo, make, model, year, color, stuId)`.

Alternatively, we could add `licNo` to the `Student` table but not both.

- For a binary relationship, the only time that we cannot use a foreign key to represent the relationship set is the **many-to-many** case. Here, the connection must be shown by a separate relationship table. The `Enroll` relationship is a many-to-many relationship. The table that represents it must contain the primary keys of the associated `Student` and `Class` entities, `stuId` and `classNo` respectively. Since the relationship also has a descriptive attribute, `grade`, we include that as well. The relationship table is,

`Enroll(`<u>`stuId, classNo`</u>`, grade)`

Note that we would need a relationship table even if there were no such descriptive attribute for the M:M relationship. For such a relationship, the table consists entirely of the two keys of the related entities.

- When we have a **ternary**, or *n***-ary relationship** involving three or more entity sets, we construct a table for the relationship, in which we place the primary keys of the related entities. If the ternary or *n*-ary relationship has a descriptive attribute, it goes in the relationship table. Figure 3.12 showed a ternary relationship, `Faculty-Class-Textbook`. We represent it by the table,

`Faculty-Class-Textbook(facId, `<u>`classNo, isbn`</u>`)`

We choose the combination of `classNo` and `isbn` as the key because, as the diagram shows, for each combination of `classNo` and `isbn` values, there is only one `facId`. So for a ternary or higher-order relationship table, we examine the cardinalities involved and choose as the key the attribute or combination that guarantees unique values for rows of the table.

- When we have a **recursive** relationship, its representation depends on the cardinality. If the cardinality is many-to-many, we must create a relationship table. If it is one-to-one or one-to-many, the foreign key mechanism can be used. For example, `Chair-Member` could have been included as a one-to-many recursive relationship on `Faculty`.

We could represent this relationship by placing the attribute `chairFacId` as a foreign key in the `Faculty` table. The `Faculty` table would then have the structure,

`Faculty(`<u>`facID`</u>`, lastName, firstName, department, rank,`
`chairFacId``)`.

If we assume each student can have exactly one roommate, we could represent the one-to-one recursive roommate relationship by adding an attribute to the Student table, as in

```
Student(stuId, lastName, firstName, major, credits,
    roommateStuId)
```

There are eight relationship sets represented in Figure 3.12 by diamonds. To represent the 1:M HasMajor relationship set connecting Department to Student we would place the primary key of the "one" side, Department, in the table for the "many" side, Student. We note that Student already contains major. If the names of all major programs are actually just the department names then this is a foreign key already, so we do not need to add deptName as well. If that is not the case, i.e., program majors can differ from department names, then we would need to add the department name as a foreign key in Student.

Offers is a one-to-many relationship that connects Department to Class.

We can represent this relationship by putting the key of Department, deptName, in the Class table. Note that if we had chosen to split the composite attribute classNumber into its components initially, deptName would have been an attribute in Class already. This example shows how an early design decision can resurface as a problem at a later stage of development.

Employs is a one-to-many relationship that represents the association between Department and Faculty.

We use the foreign key mechanism, adding deptName as an attribute in the Faculty table, making that table,

```
Faculty(facId, lastName, firstName, deptName, rank)
```

Chairs is a one-to-one relationship that connects Department to Faculty. We will push the primary key of Faculty into Department as a foreign key, making the Department schema,

```
Department(deptName, deptCode, office, chairFacId)
```

As indicated previously, the ternary relationship connecting Textbook, Faculty, and Class should be represented by a table. The isRated relationship connects the weak entity Evaluation to its owner, `Faculty`. It will be represented by having the primary key of the owner entity in the weak entity's table as part of its primary key.

Our entire schema, then, is:

```
Department (deptName, deptCode, office, chairFacId)
Student (stuId, lastName, firstName, major, credits)
Class (classNumber, facId, sched, room, deptName)
Textbook (isbn, title, publisher)
TextbookAuthors (isbn, author)
Faculty (facId, lastName, firstName, deptName, rank)
Evaluation (facId, date, rater, rating)
Enroll (stuId, classNumber, grade)
Textbook-Class-Faculty (isbn, classNumber, facId)
```

4.8   Chapter Summary

A mathematical **relation** is defined as a subset of the Cartesian product of sets. In database terms, a relation is any subset of the Cartesian product of the domains of the attributes. A relation is normally written as a set of **n-tuples**, in which each element is chosen from the appropriate domain. Relations are physically represented as **tables**, with the rows corresponding to individual records and the columns to the attributes of the relation. The structure of the table, with domain specifications and other constraints is the **intension** of the database, while the table with all its rows written out is an instance or **extension** of the database. Properties of database relations are: Each cell is single-valued, column names are distinct, a column's values all come from the same domain, row order is immaterial, and there are no duplicate rows.

The **degree** of a relation is the number of attributes or columns. A **unary** relation has one column, a **binary** relation has two, a **ternary** relation has three and an **n-ary** relation has n columns. The **cardinality** of a relation is the number of rows or tuples. Degree is a property of the intension, while cardinality is a property of the extension of a relation. A **superkey** is a set of attributes that uniquely identifies tuples of the relation, while a **candidate key** is a minimal superkey. A **primary key** is the candidate key chosen for use in identification of tuples. A relation must always have a primary key. A **foreign key** is an attribute of a relation that is not the primary key of that relation, but that is the primary key of some (usually other) relation, called its **home relation**. **Entity integrity** is a constraint that states that no attribute of a primary key may be null. **Referential integrity** states that foreign key values must match the primary key values of some tuple in the home relation or be completely null. Other integrity rules include **domain constraints, table constraints,** and **general constraints**.

Relational data manipulation languages may be **procedural** or **nonprocedural, graphical, fourth-generation,** or **fifth-generation. Relational algebra** is a formal procedural language. Its most commonly used operators include select, project, and natural join. Many other relational algebra operators exist.

A **base table** is one that is part of the logical schema and actually exists. A **view** in the relational model is not a complete external model, but a **virtual table** or a subtable of a base table. The view protects security and allows the designer to customize a user's model. Views can be created dynamically when the user makes a data request.

In converting an E-R to a relational model, strong entities become tables having a column for each of the entity's simple, single-valued attributes. Composite attributes can either be stored as a single attribute, or the simple attributes that comprise the composite can be represented by a column, with no representation of the composite. Each multivalued attribute is removed and placed in a separate table, along with the primary key of the original table. Tables for weak entities have columns for the key attributes of the associated owner entity as well as for the attributes of the weak entity. One-to-many binary relationships can be represented by placing a foreign key in the table of the many side and one-to-one on either side. Many-to-many binary relations require a separate relationship table, consisting of the primary keys of the related entity sets, plus a column for each descriptive attribute of the relation (if any). Ternary and *n*-ary relationships are best represented as separate tables. Recursive relationships can be represented by foreign keys, provided they are one-to-one or one-to-many, or by a separate relationship table, if they are many-to-many relationships.

Exercises

4.1   Let S = {red, yellow, green} and T = {plaid, stripe, dot}. Find the Cartesian product of S and T.

4.2 Let Q = {Tom, Mary, Jim} and R = {walking, running}. Create a relation with Q and R as domains.

4.3 Consider the relation schema containing book data for a bookstore: Book (title, author, isbn, publisher, pubDate, pubCity, qtyOnHand)

a. Write out the table for an instance of this relation.

b. Identify a superkey, a candidate key, and the primary key, writing out any assumptions you need to make to justify your choice.

4.4 Consider the following database instance that contains information about employees and the projects to which they are assigned:

Emp

empId	lastName
E101	Smith
E105	Jones
E110	Adams
E115	Smith

Assign

empId	projNo	hours
E101	P10	200
E101	P15	300
E105	P10	400
E110	P15	700
E110	P20	350
E115	P10	300
E115	P20	400

Proj

projNo	projName	budget
P10	Hudson	500000
P15	Columbia	350000
P20	Wabash	350000
P23	Arkansas	600000

Show ALL the tables (including the intermediate ones) that would be produced by each of the following relational algebra commands:

a. SELECT Emp WHERE lastName = 'Adams' GIVING T1

T1 JOIN Assign GIVING T2

Symbolically this is,

$(\sigma_{lastName='Adams'}(Emp)) |\times| Assign$

b. SELECT Proj WHERE budget > 400000 GIVING T1

T1 JOIN Assign GIVING T2

PROJECT T2 OVER empId GIVING T3

Symbolically this is,

$\Pi_{empId}((\sigma_{budget>400000}(Proj)) |\times| Assign)$

c. PROJECT Assign OVER projNo GIVING T1

T1 JOIN Proj GIVING T2

PROJECT T2 OVER budget GIVING T3

Symbolically this is,

$\Pi_{budget}(\Pi_{projNo}(Assign) |\times| Proj)$

4.5 Consider the following schema for a database that keeps information about business trips and their associated expenses by employees:

EMPLOYEE (<u>SSN</u>, Name, DeptNo, JobTitle, Salary)

TRIP(<u>TripId</u>, DepartureCity, DestinationCity, DepartureDate, ReturnDate, *SSN*)

EXPENSE(*TripId*, <u>Item</u>, Date, Amount)

Write relational algebra queries for each of the following:

a. Get a list of all the different destination cities where the employees have taken trips.

b. Find all the employee information for employees who work in Department 10.

c. Get complete trip records (but not their associated expenses) for all trips with departure dates after January 1 of the current year.

d. Find the names of all employees who have departed on trips from London.

e. Find the SSN of all employees who have any single expense item of more than $1000 for any trip.

f. Find the names of all employees who have any expense item with value "Entertainment."

g. Find the destination cities of all trips taken by employees who have the job title of "Consultant."

h. Find the names and departments of all employees who have a single expense item of over $1000 since January 1 of this year.

i. Find the items and amounts of all expenses for a trip to Cairo beginning on January 3 of this year taken by employee Jones.

j. Find the names, departments, and job titles of all employees who have any expense item with value "Service Charge" for trips taken to Melbourne last year, along with the date and amount of the expense.

4.6   Design a relational database schema corresponding to the diagram shown in Figure 4.4.

4.7   Design a relational database schema for the data described in Exercises 3.2 and 3.3.

4.8   Design a relational database schema for the data described in Exercise 3.4.

4.9   Design a relational database schema for the data described in Exercise 3.5.

4.10   Design a relational database schema for the data described in Exercise 3.6.

4.11   Design a relational database schema for the data described in Exercise 3.7.

4.12   Design a relational database schema for the data described in Exercise 3.8.

On the Companion Website:

- Additional Design Exercises
- Sample Project
- Student Projects

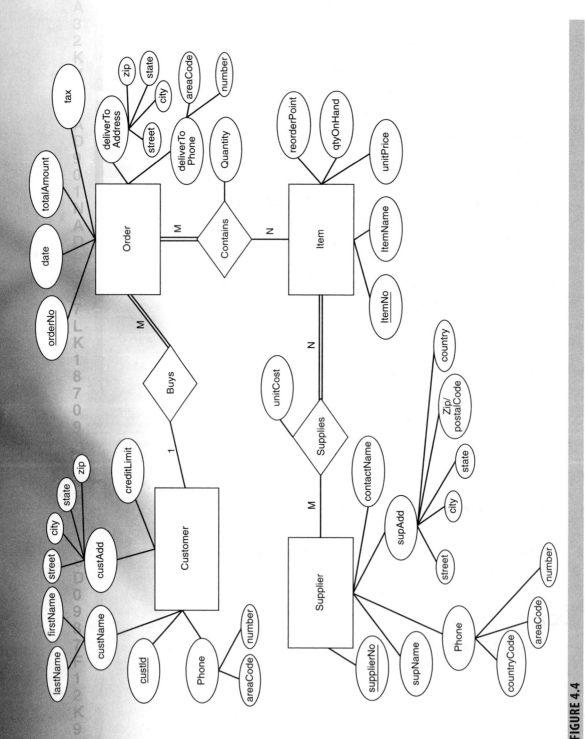

FIGURE 4.4

E-R Diagram for CustomerOrder Example

CHAPTER 5

Relational Database Management Systems and SQL

Chapter Objectives

In this chapter you will learn the following:

- The history of relational database systems and SQL

- How the three-level architecture is implemented in relational systems

- How to create and modify a relational database using SQL DDL

- How to retrieve and update data using SQL DML

- How to enforce constraints in relational databases

- How to create and manipulate relational views

- How SQL is used in programming

- The structure and
  functions of a
  system catalog

5.1   Brief History of SQL in Relational Database Systems

As described in Section 1.6, the relational model was first proposed by
E. F. Codd in 1970. D. D. Chamberlin and others at the IBM San Jose
Research Laboratory developed a language now called SQL, or Structured
Query Language, as a data sublanguage for the relational model. Originally spelled SEQUEL, the language was presented in a series of papers
starting in 1974, and it was used in a prototype relational system called
System R, which was developed by IBM in the late 1970s. Under the direction of Larry Ellison, an early commercial relational database management system, ORACLE, was developed in the late 1970s using SQL as its
language. INGRES, another early prototype relational database management system, was developed at the University of California at Berkeley.
System R was evaluated and refined over a period of several years, and it
became the basis for IBM's first commercially available relational database
management system, SQL/DS, which was announced in 1981. IBM's DB2,
also using SQL as its language, was released in 1983. Microsoft SQL Server,
MySQL, Informix, Sybase, PostGreSQL, Microsoft Access, and many other
relational database management systems have also incorporated SQL.

Both the American National Standards Institute (ANSI) and the International Standards Organization (ISO) adopted SQL as a standard language
for relational databases and published specifications for the SQL language
starting in 1986. This standard is usually called SQL1. A minor revision,
called SQL-89, was published three years later. A major revision, SQL2,
was adopted by both ANSI and ISO in 1992. The current SQL3 standard
was developed over time, with major parts published in 1999, 2003, 2006,
and 2008. New features included object-oriented data management capabilities, triggers, new data types, support for XML, and other capabilities.

Most vendors of relational database management systems have added features to the standard and use their own extensions of the language, creating a variety of dialects around the standard. Since some parts of the SQL3 standard are optional, not all vendors provide the full set of features described in the standard. This chapter will focus on the most widely used strictly relational features that are available in most relational DBMSs.

SQL has a complete data definition language (DDL) and data manipulation language (DML) described in this chapter, and an authorization language, described in Chapter 9. Readers should note that different implementations of SQL vary slightly from the syntax presented here, but the basic notions are the same. Commands given in this chapter generally use the Oracle syntax, and may need slight modifications to run on other DBMSs.

5.2 Architecture of a Relational Database Management System

Relational database management systems support the standard three-level architecture for databases described in Section 2.6. As shown in Figure 5.1, relational databases provide both logical and physical data independence because they separate the external, logical, and internal levels. The logical level for relational databases consists of base tables that are physically stored. These tables are created by the database administrator using a CREATE TABLE command, as described in Section 5.3. A base table can have any number of indexes, either created by the system itself or created by the DBA using the CREATE INDEX command. An index is used to speed up retrieval of records based on the value in one or more columns. An index lists the values that exist for the indexed column(s), and gives the location of the records that have those values, thus speeding up retrieval of records based on the value of the column. Most relational database management systems use B trees or B+ trees for indexes. On the physical level, the base tables and their indexes are represented in files. The physical representation of the tables may not correspond exactly to our notion of a base table as a two-dimensional object consisting of rows and columns like a spreadsheet. However, the rows of the table do correspond to physically stored records, although their order and other details of storage may be different from our concept of them. The database management system, not the operating system, controls the internal structure of both the data files and the indexes. The user is generally unaware of what indexes exist, and

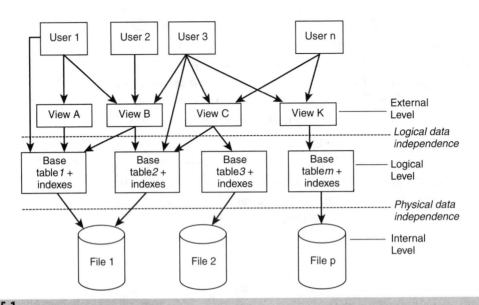

FIGURE 5.1

Three Level Architecture for Relational Databases

has no control over which index will be used in locating a record. Once the base tables have been created, the DBA can create "views" for users, using the CREATE VIEW command, described in Section 5.8. As described in Section 4.6, relational views can be either "windows" into base tables or "virtual tables," not permanently stored, but created when the user needs to access them. Users are unaware of the fact that their views are not physically stored in table form. In a relational system, the word "view" means a single virtual table. This is not exactly the same as our term "external view," which means the database as it appears to a particular user. In our terminology, an external view may consist of several base tables and/or views. Users should be unaware of the fact that their views are not physically stored in table form.

One of the most useful features of a relational database is that it permits dynamic database definition. The DBA, and users he or she authorizes to do so, can create new tables, add columns to old ones, create new indexes, define views, and drop any of these objects at any time. The flexibility of relational databases encourages users to experiment with various structures and allows the system to be modified to meet their changing needs. This enables the DBA to ensure that the database is a useful model of the enterprise throughout its life cycle.

5.3   Defining the Database: SQL DDL

The most important SQL Data Definition Language (DDL) commands are the following:

    CREATE TABLE

    CREATE INDEX

    ALTER TABLE

    RENAME TABLE

    DROP TABLE

    DROP INDEX

On the Companion Website:

- All SQL DDL commands are shown here.

These statements are used to create, change, and destroy the structures that make up the logical model. These commands can be used at any time to make changes to the database structure. Additional commands are available to specify physical details of storage, but we will not discuss them here, since they are specific to the system. There are also commands to create and destroy views, which we will discuss in Section 5.8.

5.3.1   CREATE TABLE

This command is used to create the base tables that form the heart of a relational database. Since it can be used at any time during the lifecycle of the system, the database developer can start with a small number of tables and add to them as additional applications are planned and developed. A base table is fairly close to the abstract notion of a relational table. It consists of one or more **column headings**, which give the **column name** and **data type**, and zero or more **data rows**, which contain one data value of the specified data type for each of the columns. As in the abstract relational model, the rows are considered unordered. However, the columns are ordered left-to-right, to match the order of column definitions in the CREATE TABLE command. A simple form of the command is:

CREATE TABLE [schema-name.] *base-table-name* (*colname datatype* [*column constraints*]

[,*colname datetype* [*column constraints*]]

. . .

[*table constraints*]

[*storage specifications*]);

Here, *base-table-name* is a user-supplied name (an identifier) for the table. No SQL keywords may be used, and the table name must be unique within the database. For each column, the user must specify a name that is unique within the table, and a data type. In Oracle, identifiers must be at most 30 characters long, begin with an alphabetic character, and contain only alphanumeric characters (but _, $, and # are permitted, although the last two are discouraged). Either uppercase or lowercase letters may be used, but Oracle will always display them as uppercase. While various character sets can be used for the database, it is wise to use the ASCII set for identifiers for platform portability. The maximum number of columns for an Oracle table is 1000. Note that each line ends with a comma, except the last, which ends with a semicolon. The optional storage specifications section allows the DBA to name the tablespace where the table will be stored. If the tablespace is not specified, the database management system will create a default space for the table.

Figure 5.2 shows the commands to create the base tables for a database for the University example. To execute these commands in Oracle, the user should be using the SQL Plus facility. The commands can be keyed in at the prompt, or can be written using a text editor, and copied into SQL Plus for execution. The schema is

```
Student(stuId, lastName, firstName, major, credits)
Faculty(facId, name, department, rank)
Class(classNumber, facId, schedule, room)
Enroll(classNumber, stuId, grade)
```

Data Types

The available data types vary from DBMS to DBMS. Built-in data types for strictly relational tables in Oracle include various numeric types, fixed-length and varying-length character strings, datetime types, large object types, and others. One of the most common data types in a strictly relational Oracle database is VARCHAR2(n), which stores varying length

```
CREATE TABLE Student     (
     stuId        VARCHAR2(6),
     lastName     VARCHAR2(20)  NOT NULL,
     firstName    VARCHAR2(20)  NOT NULL,
     major        VARCHAR2(10),
     credits      NUMBER(3) DEFAULT 0,
     CONSTRAINT Student_stuId_pk PRIMARY KEY (stuId),
CONSTRAINT Student_credits_cc CHECK ((credits>=0) AND (credits < 150)));

CREATE TABLE Faculty     (
     facId        VARCHAR2(6),
     name         VARCHAR2(20)  NOT NULL,
     department   VARCHAR2(20),
     rank         VARCHAR2(10),
     CONSTRAINT Faculty_facId_pk PRIMARY KEY (facId));

CREATE TABLE Class       (
     classNumber VARCHAR2(8),
     facId        VARCHAR2(6)   NOT NULL,
     schedule     VARCHAR2(8),
     room         VARCHAR2(6),
     CONSTRAINT Class_classNumber_pk PRIMARY KEY (classNumber),
     CONSTRAINT Class_facId_fk FOREIGN KEY (facId) REFERENCES Faculty
     (facId) ON DELETE SET NULL,
     CONSTRAINT Class_schedule_room_uk UNIQUE (schedule, room));

CREATE TABLE Enroll      (
     stuId        VARCHAR2(6),
     classNumber VARCHAR2(8),
     grade        VARCHAR2(2),
     CONSTRAINT Enroll_classNumber_stuId_pk PRIMARY KEY
     (classNumber, stuId),
     CONSTRAINT Enroll_classNumber_fk FOREIGN KEY (classNumber)
     REFERENCES Class (classNumber) ON DELETE CASCADE,
     CONSTRAINT Enroll_stuId_fk FOREIGN KEY (stuId) REFERENCES Student
     (stuId)ON DELETE CASCADE);
```

Figure 5.2

SQL DDL Statements to Create Oracle Tables for the University Example

 See the Companion Website for all SQL Code

strings of maximum size n bytes. The user must specify a size n up to 4000 bytes. For fixed-length strings, the type CHAR(n) can be used, with the maximum allowable size of 2000 bytes. For fixed-point numbers the data type NUMBER(p,s) is used, where p is the precision (the maximum number of significant digits) and s is the scale. In most cases, p is the total number of digits and s is the number of digits to the right of the decimal point, if any. For integers, the s is omitted. Floating-point numbers can also be specified as NUMBER, with no precision or scale specified, or as FLOAT(p), where p is the precision measured in binary digits. The DATE type is used to store dates and times. In Oracle, values of dates are entered using the default format 'dd-mon-yy' as in '02-DEC-11', where the month is represented using a three-letter abbreviation. Microsoft Access supports several types of NUMBER, as well as TEXT, MEMO, DATE/TIME, HYPERLINK, YES/NO, and others.

Column and Table Constraints

The database management system has facilities to enforce data correctness, which the DBA should make use of when creating tables. Recall from Section 4.3 that the relational model uses integrity constraints to protect the correctness of the database, allowing only legal instances to be created. These constraints protect the system from data entry errors that would create inconsistent data. Although the table name, column names, and data types are the only parts required in a CREATE TABLE command, optional constraints can and should be added, both at the column level and at the table level.

The **column constraints** also called **in-line constraints** because they are defined on the same line as the column include options to specify NULL/NOT NULL, UNIQUE, PRIMARY KEY, FOREIGN KEY, REF, CHECK, and DEFAULT for any column, immediately after the specification of the column name and data type. If we do not specify NOT NULL, the system will allow the column to have null values, meaning the user can insert records that have no values for those fields. When a null value appears in a field of a record, the system is able to distinguish it from a blank string or zero value, and treats it differently in computations and logical comparisons. It is desirable to be able to insert null values in certain situations; for example, when a college student has not yet declared a major we might want to set the `major` field to null. However, the use of null values can create complications, especially in operations such as joins, so we should use NOT NULL when it is appropriate. We can optionally specify that a given field is to have unique values by writing the UNIQUE constraint. In that case, the system will reject the insertion of a new record that has the same value in that field as a record that is already in the database. If the primary key is not composite, it is also possible to specify PRIMARY KEY as a column constraint, simply by adding the words PRIMARY KEY after the data type for the column. For example, for the `stuId` column specification in the `Student` table, we could write

```
stuId VARCHAR2(6) PRIMARY KEY,
```

Clearly no duplicate values are permitted for the primary key. Neither are null values, since we could not distinguish between two different records if they both had null key values, so the specification of PRIMARY KEY in SQL carries an implicit NOT NULL constraint as well as a UNIQUE constraint. However, we may wish to ensure uniqueness for candidate keys as well, and we should specify UNIQUE for them when we create the table. The system automatically checks each record we try to insert to ensure that data items for columns that have been described as unique do not have values that duplicate any other data items in the database for those columns. If a duplication might occur, it will reject the insertion. It is also desirable to specify a NOT NULL constraint for candidate keys, when it is possible to ensure that values for these columns will always be available. The CHECK constraint can be used to specify a condition that the rows of the table are not permitted to violate, in order to verify that values provided for attributes are appropriate. A REF constraint is used when a column references an object, and is not a strictly relational feature, so we will defer discussion of it. We can also specify a default value for a column, if we wish to do so. Every record that is inserted without a value for that field is then given the default value automatically. We can optionally provide a name for any constraint. If we do not, the system will automatically assign a name. However, a user-defined name is preferable, since it gives us an opportunity to choose a meaningful name, which is useful if we wish to modify it later. In that case we precede the constraint name by the keyword CONSTRAINT. For example, in defining the `credits` column in the `Student` table, we could create a default value of 0 and create a CHECK constraint called `Student_credits_cc` by writing directly in the column definition line

```
credits NUMBER(3)DEFAULT 0 CONSTRAINT Student_credits_cc CHECK ((credits>=0)
AND (credits < 150))
```

We gave the constraint a name `Student_credits_cc`, which follows the recommended form of identifying the table, the column(s), and the type of constraint (cc), keeping within the 30-character limit for identifiers. The abbreviations pk, fk, nn, uk, and cc are often used in constraint names to refer to the type of constraint defined.

Table constraints also called **out-of-line constraints**, appear after all the columns have been declared, and can include the specification of a primary key, foreign keys, uniqueness, references, checks, and general constraints that can be expressed as conditions to be checked, but not NOT NULL, which is always a column constraint. Note that in Figure 5.2 we used out-of-line constraints for all but the NOT NULL specifications. If the primary key is a composite, it must be identified using a table constraint rather than a column constraint, although even a primary key consisting of a single column can be identified as a table constraint. The PRIMARY KEY constraint enforces the unique and NOT NULL constraints for the column(s) identified as the primary key. The FOREIGN KEY constraint requires that we identify the referenced table where the column or column combination appears. For the `Class` table in Figure 5.2 we specified that `facId` is a foreign key for which the `Faculty` table is the home table by writing

```
CONSTRAINT Class_facId_fk FOREIGN KEY (facId) REFERENCES Faculty(facId)
```

In an out-of-line constraint we must use the keyword CONSTRAINT, which can be optionally followed by an identifier. Then we specified the type of constraint, FOREIGN KEY and, in parentheses, the column of the current table, `facId` in `Class`. The required keyword REFERENCES is followed by the name of the home relation and, in parentheses, the name of the corresponding column in that home relation, `facId` in `Faculty`. This is necessary because it is possible the column has a different name in the home relation.

The SQL standard allows us to specify what is to be done with records containing the foreign key values when the records they relate to are deleted in their home table. For the University example, what should happen to a `Class` record when the record of the faculty member assigned to teach the class is deleted? The DBMS could automatically:

- Delete all `Class` records for that faculty member, an action performed when we specify ON DELETE CASCADE in the foreign key specification in SQL.

- Set the `facId` in the `Class` record to a null value, an action performed when we write ON DELETE SET NULL in SQL.

- Not allow the deletion of a `Faculty` record if there is a `Class` record that refers to it, an action performed when we do not specify an action.

As shown in Figure 5.2, for the `Class` table we have chosen ON DELETE SET NULL. Also note the choices we made for the `Enroll` table, for changes made to both `classNumber` and `stuId`.

The table uniqueness constraint mechanism can be used to specify that the values in a combination of columns must be unique. For example, to ensure that no two classes have exactly the same schedule and room, we wrote:

```
CONSTRAINT Class_schedule_room_uk UNIQUE (schedule, room)
```

There are SQL commands to disable, enable, alter, or drop contraints, provided we know their names.

5.3.2 CREATE INDEX

We can optionally create indexes for tables to facilitate fast retrieval of records with specific values in a column. An index keeps track of what values exist for the indexed column, and which records have those values. For example, if we have an index on the `lastName` column of the `Student` table, and we write a query asking for all students with the last name of Smith, the system will not have to scan all Student records to pick out the desired ones. Instead, it will read the index, which will point it to the records with the desired name. A table can have any number of indexes, which are stored as B trees or B+ trees in separate index files, usually close to the tables they index. Indexes can be created on single fields or combinations of fields. However, since indexes must be updated by the system every time the underlying tables are updated, additional overhead is required. Aside from choosing which indexes will exist, users have no control over the use or maintenance of indexes. The system chooses which, if any, index to use in searching for records. A simple form of the command for creating an index is:

```
CREATE [UNIQUE] INDEX indexname ON basetablename (colname [order]
[,colname [order]] . . .) [CLUSTER] ;
```

If the UNIQUE specification is used, uniqueness of the indexed field or combination of fields will be enforced by the system. Although indexes can be created at any time, we may have a problem if we try to create a unique index after the table has records stored in it, because the values stored for the indexed field or fields may already contain duplicates. In this case, the system will not allow the unique index to be created. To create the index on `lastName` for the `Student` table we would write:

```
CREATE INDEX Stu_lastName_ix ON STUDENT (lastName);
```

The name of the index should be chosen to indicate the table and the field or fields used in the index. Up to 32 columns, regardless of where they appear on the table, may be used in an index. The first column named determines major order, the second gives minor order, and so on. For each column, we may specify that the order is ascending, ASC, or descending, DESC. If we choose not to specify order, ASC is the default. If we write,

```
CREATE INDEX Fac_dept_name_ix ON Faculty (department ASC, name ASC);
```

then an index file called `Fac_dept_name_ix` will be created for the `Faculty` table. Entries will be in alphabetical order by department. Within each department, entries will be in alphabetical order by faculty name.

Some DBMSs allow an optional CLUSTER specification for only one index for each table. If we use this option, the system will store records in physical order by the values of the indexed field. Records with the same values for the indexed field(s) will be close together physically, on the same page or adjacent pages. If we create a clustered index for the field(s) used most often for retrieval, we can substantially improve performance for those applications needing that particular order of retrieval, since we will be minimizing seek time and read time. However, it is the system, not the user, that chooses to use a particular index, even a clustered one, for data retrieval.

By default, Oracle creates a clustered index on the primary key of each table that is created. The user should create additional indexes on any field(s) that are often used in queries, to speed up execution of those queries. Foreign key fields, which are often used in joins, are good candidates for indexing. Besides the usual type of indexes described here, Oracle allows more advanced indexes to be created.

5.3.3 ALTER TABLE, RENAME TABLE

Once a table has been created, users might find it more useful if it contained an additional data item, did not have a particular column, had different data types, or had other constraints. The dynamic nature of a relational database structure makes it possible to change existing base tables. For example, to add a new column on the right of the table, we use a command of the form:

ALTER TABLE *basetablename* ADD *columnname datatype constraints*;

An ALTER TABLE ..ADD command causes the new field to be added to all records already stored in the table, and null values to be assigned to that field in all existing records. Notice we cannot use the NOT NULL specification for the column unless we also specify a DEFAULT value.

Suppose we want to add a new column, cTitle, to our Class table. We can do so by writing

ALTER TABLE Class ADD cTitle VARCHAR2(30);

The schema of the Class table would then be:

Class(classNumber,facId,schedule,room,cTitle)

All old Class records would now have null values for cTitle, but we could provide a title for any new Class records we insert, and update old Class records by adding titles to them. We can also drop columns from existing tables by the command:

ALTER TABLE *basetablename* DROP COLUMN *columnname*;

To drop the cTitle column and return to our original structure for the Class table, we would write:

ALTER TABLE Class DROP COLUMN cTitle;

We can also modify the properties of columns in a table, changing the data type, size, default value, or constraints, using the command

ALTER TABLE *basetablename* MODIFY COLUMN *colname* [*new specifications*];

The new specifications for the column use the same wording as they would in a CREATE TABLE command. The data type can be changed only if all rows of the table contain null values for the column being modified. The size or precision can always be increased even if there are non-null values stored, but they can be decreased only if no existing rows violate the new specifications.

If we want to add, drop, or change a constraint, we can use the same ALTER TABLE command, using the same wording for the constraint clause as in the CREATE TABLE command. For example, if we created the Class table and neglected to make facId a foreign key in Class, we could add the constraint at any time by writing:

```
ALTER TABLE Class ADD CONSTRAINT Class_facId_fk FOREIGN KEY (facId) REFERENCES
Faculty (facId) ON DELETE SET NULL;
```

We could drop an existing named constraint using the ALTER TABLE command. For example, to drop the check condition on the credits attribute of Student that we created earlier, we could write:

```
ALTER TABLE Student DROP CONSTRAINT Student_credits_cc;
```

We can change the name of an existing table easily by the command:

```
RENAME TABLE old-table-name TO new-table-name;
```

To rename a column, use the ALTER TABLE command as in

```
ALTER TABLE Student RENAME COLUMN stuId TO studentNo;
```

5.3.4   DROP Statements

Tables can be dropped at any time by the SQL command:

```
DROP TABLE basetablename;
```

When this statement is executed, the table itself and all records contained in it are removed. In addition, all indexes and, as we will see later, all views that depend on it are dropped. Naturally, the DBA confers with potential users of the table before taking such a drastic step. Any existing index can be destroyed by the command:

```
DROP INDEX indexname;
```

The effect of this change may or may not be seen in performance. Recall that users cannot specify when the system is to use an index for data retrieval. Therefore, it is possible that an index exists that is never actually used, and its destruction would have no affect on performance. However, the loss of an efficient index that is used by the system for many retrievals would certainly affect performance. When an index is dropped, any access plans for applications that depend on it are marked as invalid. When an application calls them, a new access plan is devised to replace the old one.

5.4   Manipulating the Database: SQL DML

SQL's query language is **declarative**, or **non-procedural**, which means that it allows us to specify what data is to be retrieved without giving the procedures for retrieving it. It can be used as an interactive language for queries, embedded in a host programming language, or as a complete language in itself for computations using SQL/PSM (Persistent Stored Modules).

The SQL DML statements are:

> SELECT
>
> UPDATE
>
> INSERT
>
> DELETE

On the Companion Website:

- All SQL DML commands shown here.

5.4.1   Introduction to the SELECT Statement

The SELECT statement is used for retrieval of data. It is a powerful command, performing the equivalent of relational algebra's SELECT, PROJECT, and JOIN, as well as other functions, in a single, simple statement. The general form of SELECT is,

```
SELECT   [DISTINCT] col-name [AS newname], [,col-name..] . . .
FROM     table-name [alias] [,table-name] . . .
[WHERE   predicate]
[GROUP BY col-name [,col-name] . . . [HAVING predicate]]
```

or,

```
[ORDER BY col-name [,col-name] . . .];
```

The result may have duplicate rows. Since duplicates are allowed, it is not a relation in the strict sense, but is referred to as a **multi-set**. As indicated by the absence of square brackets, the SELECT and the FROM clauses are required, but not the WHERE or the other clauses. The many variations of this statement will be illustrated by the examples that follow, using the Student, Faculty, Class, and/or Enroll tables as they appear in Figure 5.3

- Example 1. Simple Retrieval with Condition

  Question: Get names, IDs, and number of credits of all Math majors.

  Solution: The information requested appears on the Student table. From that table we select only the rows that have a value of 'Math' for major. For those rows, we display only the lastName, firstName, stuId, and credits columns. Notice we are doing the equivalent of relational algebra's SELECT (in finding the rows) and PROJECT (in displaying only certain columns). We are also rearranging the columns.

  SQL Query:

  ```
  SELECT    lastName, firstName, stuId, credits
  FROM      Student
  WHERE     major = 'Math';
  ```

  Result:

lastName	firstName	stuId	credits
Chin	Ann	S1002	36
McCarthy	Owen	S1013	0
Jones	Mary	S1015	42

Notice that the result of the query is a table or a multi-set.

- Example 2. Use of Asterisk Notation for "all columns"

  Question: Get all information about CSC Faculty.

  Solution: We want the entire Faculty record of any faculty member whose department is 'CSC'. Since many SQL retrievals require all columns of a single table, there is a short way of expressing "all columns," namely by using an asterisk in place of the column names in the SELECT line.

  SQL Query:

  ```
  SELECT    *
  FROM      Faculty
  WHERE     department = 'CSC';
  ```

Student				
stuld	lastName	firstName	major	credits
S1001	Smith	Tom	History	90
S1002	Chin	Ann	Math	36
S1005	Lee	Perry	History	3
S1010	Burns	Edward	Art	63
S1013	McCarthy	Owen	Math	0
S1015	Jones	Mary	Math	42
S1020	Rivera	Jane	CSC	15

Faculty			
facId	name	department	rank
F101	Adams	Art	Professor
F105	Tanaka	CSC	Instructor
F110	Byrne	Math	Assistant
F115	Smith	History	Associate
F221	Smith	CSC	Professor

Class			
classNumber	facId	schedule	room
ART103A	F101	MWF9	H221
CSC201A	F105	TuThF10	M110
CSC203A	F105	MThF12	M110
HST205A	F115	MWF11	H221
MTH101B	F110	MTuTh9	H225
MTH103C	F110	MWF11	H225

Enroll		
stuld	classNumber	grade
S1001	ART103A	A
S1001	HST205A	C
S1002	ART103A	D
S1002	CSC201A	F
S1002	MTH103C	B
S1010	ART103A	
S1010	MTH103C	
S1020	CSC201A	B
S1020	MTH101B	A

FIGURE 5.3

The University Database (Same as Figure 1.1)

On the Companion Website:

- SQL Script for All Four Tables and Queries

Result:

facId	name	department	rank
F105	Tanaka	CSC	Instructor
F221	Smith	CSC	Professor

Users who access a relational database through a host language are usually advised to avoid using the asterisk notation. The danger is that an additional column might be added to a table after a program was written. The program will then retrieve the value of that new column with each record and will not have a matching program variable for the value, causing a loss of correspondence between database variables and program variables. It is safer to write the query as:

```
SELECT     facId, name, department, rank
FROM       Faculty
WHERE      department = 'CSC';
```

- Example 3. Retrieval without Condition, Use of "Distinct," Use of Qualified Names

  Question: Get the course number of all courses in which students are enrolled.

  Solution: We go to the Enroll table rather than the Class table, because it is possible there is a Class record for a planned class in which no one is enrolled. From the Enroll table, we could ask for a list of all the classNumber values, as follows.

  SQL Query:

  ```
  SELECT     classNumber
  FROM       Enroll;
  ```

  Result:

  classNumber
  ART103A
  CSC201A
  CSC201A
  ART103A
  ART103A
  MTH101B
  HST205A
  MTH103C
  MTH103C

Since we did not need a predicate, we did not use the WHERE line. Notice that there are several duplicates in our result; it is a multi-set, not a true relation. Unlike the relational algebra PROJECT, the SQL SELECT does not eliminate duplicates when it "projects" over columns. To eliminate the duplicates, we need to use the DISTINCT option in the SELECT line. If we write,

```
SELECT DISTINCT classNumber
FROM Enroll;
```

The result would be:

classNumber
ART103A
CSC201A
HST205A
MTH101B
MTH103C

In any retrieval, especially if there is a possibility of confusion because the same column name appears on two different tables, we specify *tablename.colname*. In this example, we could have written:

```
SELECT    DISTINCT Enroll.classNumber
FROM      Enroll;
```

Here, it is not necessary to use the qualified name, since the FROM line tells the system to use the `Enroll` table, and column names are always unique within a table. However, it is never wrong to use a qualified name, and it is sometimes necessary to do so when two or more tables appear in the FROM line.

- Example 4: Retrieving an Entire Table

    Question: Get all information about all students.

    Solution: Because we want all columns of the `Student` table, we use the asterisk notation. Because we want all the records in the table, we omit the WHERE line.

    SQL Query:

```
SELECT    *
FROM      Student;
```

Result: The result is the entire `Student` table.

- Example 5. Use of "ORDER BY" and AS

  Question: Get names and IDs of all `Faculty` members, arranged in alphabetical order by name. Call the resulting columns Faculty-Name and FacultyNumber.

  Solution: The ORDER BY option in the SQL SELECT allows us to order the retrieved records in ascending (ASC—the default) or descending (DESC) order on any field or combination of fields, regardless of whether that field appears in the results. If we order by more than one field, the one named first determines major order, the next minor order, and so on.

  SQL Query:

```
SELECT      name AS FacultyName, facId AS FacultyNumber
FROM        Faculty
ORDER BY    name;
```

  Result:

FacultyName	FacultyNumber
Adams	F101
Byrne	F110
Smith	F115
Smith	F221
Tanaka	F105

The column headings are changed to the ones specified in the AS clause. We can rename any column or columns for display in this way. Note the duplicate name of 'Smith'. Since we did not specify minor order, the system will arrange these two rows in any order it chooses. We could break the "tie" by giving a minor order, as follows:

```
SELECT      name AS FacultyName, facId AS FacultyNumber
FROM        Faculty
ORDER BY    name, department;
```

Now the Smith records will be reversed, since F221 is assigned to CSC, which is alphabetically before History. Note also that the field that determines ordering need not be one of the ones displayed.

- Example 6. Use of Multiple Conditions

Question: Get names of all math majors who have more than 30 credits.

Solution: From the `Student` table, we choose those rows where the major is 'Math' and the number of credits is greater than 30. We express these two conditions by connecting them with 'AND.' We display only the `lastName` and `firstName`.

SQL Query:

```
SELECT      lastName, firstName
FROM        Student
WHERE       major = 'Math' AND credits > 30;
```
Result:

lastName	firstName
Chin	Ann
Jones	Mary

The predicate can be as complex as necessary by using the standard comparison operators =, <>, <, <=, >, >= and the standard logical operators AND, OR, and NOT, with parentheses, if needed or desired, to show order of evaluation.

5.4.2 SELECT Using Multiple Tables

- Example 7. Natural Join

Question: Find IDs and names of all students taking ART103A.

Solution: This question requires the use of two tables. We first look in the `Enroll` table for records where the `classNumber` is 'ART103A.' We then look up the `Student` table for records with matching `stuId` values, and join those records into a new table. From this table, we find the `lastName` and `firstName`. This is similar to the JOIN operation in relational algebra. SQL allows us to do a natural join, as described in Section 4.6.2, by naming the tables involved and expressing in the predicate the condition that the records should match on the common field.

SQL Query:

```
SELECT    Enroll.stuId, lastName, firstName
FROM      Student, Enroll
WHERE     classNumber = 'ART103A'
          AND Enroll.stuId = Student.stuId;
```

Result:

stuId	lastName	firstName
S1001	Smith	Tom
S1002	Chin	Ann
S1010	Burns	Edward

Notice that we used the qualified name for `stuId` in the SELECT line. We could have written `Student.stuId` instead of `Enroll.stuId`, but we needed to use one of the table names, because `stuId` appears on both of the tables in the FROM line. We did not need to use the qualified name for `classNumber` because it does not appear on the `Student` table. The fact that it appears on the `Class` table is irrelevant, as that table is not mentioned in the FROM line. Of course, we had to write both qualified names for `stuId` in the WHERE line.

Why is the condition "`Enroll.stuId=Student.stuId`" necessary? The answer is that it is essential. Without that condition, the result will be a Cartesian product formed by combining all Enroll records with all Student records, regardless of the values of `stuId`. Note that some relational DBMSs allow the phrase

```
FROM Enroll NATURAL JOIN Student,
```

(or equivalent), which essentially adds the condition that the common columns are equal. However, since not all systems support this option, it is safest to specify the condition directly in the WHERE clause.

- Example 8. Natural Join with Ordering

  Question: Find `stuId` and `grade` of all students taking any course taught by the `Faculty` member whose `facId` is F110. Arrange in order by `stuId`.

  Solution: We need to look at the `Class` table to find the `classNumber` of all courses taught by F110. We then look at the `Enroll` table for records with matching `classNumber` values, and get the join of the tables. From this we find the corresponding stuId and grade. Because we are using two tables, we will write this as a join.

SQL Query:

```
SELECT    stuId, grade
FROM      Class, Enroll
WHERE     facId = 'F110' AND Class.classNumber = Enroll.classNumber
ORDER BY  stuId ASC;
```

Result:

stuId	grade
S1002	B
S1010	
S1020	A

- Example 9. Natural Join of Three Tables

  Question: Find course numbers and the names and majors of all students enrolled in the courses taught by Faculty member F110.

  Solution: As in the previous example, we need to start at the Class table to find the classNumber of all courses taught by F110. We then compare these with classNumber values in the Enroll table to find the stuId values of all students in those courses. Then we look at the Student table to find the names and majors of all the students enrolled in them.

  SQL Query:

```
SELECT    Enroll.classNumber, lastName, firstName, major
FROM      Class, Enroll, Student
WHERE     facId = 'F110'
          AND Class.classNumber = Enroll.classNumber
          AND Enroll.stuId = Student.stuId;
```

  Result:

classNumber	lastName	firstName	major
MTH101B	Rivera	Jane	CSC
MTH103C	Chin	Ann	Math
MTH103C	Burns	Edward	Art

This was a natural join of three tables, and it required two sets of common columns. We used the condition of equality for both of the sets in the WHERE line. You may have noticed that the order of the table names in the FROM line corresponded to the order in which they appeared in our plan of solution, but that is not necessary. SQL ignores the order in which the tables are named in the FROM line. The same is true of the order in which we write the various conditions that make up the predicate in the WHERE line. Most sophisticated relational database management systems choose which table to use first and which condition to check first, using an optimizer to identify the most efficient method of accomplishing any retrieval before choosing a plan.

- Example 10. Use of Aliases

  Question: Get a list of all courses that meet in the same room, with their schedules and room numbers.

  Solution: This requires comparing the `Class` table with itself, and it would be useful if there were two copies of the table so we could do a natural join. We can pretend that there are two copies of a table by giving it two "aliases," for example, A and B, and then treating these names as if they were the names of two distinct tables. We introduce the "aliases" in the FROM line by writing them immediately after the real table names. Then we have the aliases available for use in the other lines of the query.

SQL Query:

```
SELECT   A.classNumber, A.schedule, A.room, B.classNumber, B.schedule
FROM     Class A, Class B
WHERE    A.room = B.room AND A.classNumber < B.classNumber ;
```

Result:

A.classNumber	A.schedule	A.room	B.classNumber	B.schedule
CSC201A	TuThF10	M110	CSC203A	MThF12
ART103A	MWF9	H221	HST205A	MWF11
MTH101B	MTuTh9	H225	MTH103C	MWF11

Notice we had to use the qualified names in the SELECT line even before we introduced the "aliases." This is necessary because every column in the `Class` table now appears twice, once in each copy. We added the second condition "`A.classNumber < B.classNumber`" to keep every class from being included, since every class obviously satisfies the requirement that it meets in the same room as itself. It also keeps records with the two classes reversed from appearing. For example, because we have,

ART103A   MWF9   H221   HST205A   MWF11

we do not need the record

HST205A   MWF11   H221   ART103A   MWF9

Incidentally, we can introduce aliases in any SELECT, even when they are not required.

- Example 11. Other Joins

  Question: Find all combinations of students and faculty where the student's major is different from the faculty member's department.

  Solution: This unusual request is to illustrate a type of join in which the condition is not an equality on a common field. In this case, the fields we are examining, `major` and `department`, do not even have the same name. However, we can compare them since they have the same domain. Since we are not told which columns to show in the result, we use our judgment.

  SQL Query:

```
SELECT   stuId, S.lastName, S.firstName, major, facId, F.name, department
FROM     Student S, Faculty F
WHERE    S.major <> F.department;
```

  Result:

stuId	S.lastName	S.firstName	major	facId	F.name	department
S1001	Smith	Tom	History	F101	Adams	Art
S1001	Smith	Tom	History	F105	Tanaka	CS
S1001	Smith	Tom	History	F110	Byrne	Math
S1001	Smith	Tom	History	F221	Smith	CS
S1010	Burns	Edward	Art	F202	Smith	History
....						
....						
....						
S1013	McCarthy	Owen	Math	F221	Smith	CS

As in relational algebra, a join can be done on any two tables by simply forming the Cartesian product. Although we usually want the natural join as in our previous examples, we might use any type of predicate as the condition for the join. If we want to compare two columns, however, they must have the same domains. Notice that we used qualified names in the WHERE line. This was not really necessary, because each column name was unique, but we did so to make the condition easier to follow.

- Example 12. Using a Subquery with Equality

Question: Find the numbers of all the courses taught by Byrne of the Math department.

Solution: We already know how to do this by using a natural join, but there is another way of finding the solution. Instead of imagining a join from which we choose records with the same `facId`, we could visualize this as two separate queries. For the first one, we would go to the `Faculty` table and find the record with `name` of Byrne and `department` of Math. We could make a note of the corresponding `facId`. Then we could take the result of that query, namely F110, and search the `Class` table for records with that value in `facId`. Once we found them, we would display the `classNumber`. SQL allows us to sequence these queries so that the result of the first can be used in the second, shown as follows:

SQL Query:

```
SELECT     classNumber
FROM       Class
WHERE      facId =
           (SELECT     facId
            FROM       Faculty
            WHERE      name = 'Byrne' AND department = 'Math');
```

Result:

```
classNumber
MTH101B
MTH103C
```

Note that this result could have been produced by the following SQL query, using a join:

```
SELECT     classNumber
FROM       Class, Faculty
WHERE      name = 'Byrne' AND department = 'Math' AND Class.facId
           = Faculty.facId;
```

A subquery can be used in place of a join, provided the result to be displayed is contained in a single table and the data retrieved from the subquery consists of only one column. When you write a subquery involving two tables, you name only one table in each SELECT. The query to be done first, the subquery, is the one in parentheses, following the first WHERE line. The main query is performed using the result of the subquery. Normally you want the value of some field in the table mentioned in the main query to match the value of some field from the table in the subquery. In this example, we knew we would get only one value from the subquery, since facId is the key of Faculty, so a unique value would be produced. Therefore, we were able to use equality as the operator. However, conditions other than equality can be used. Any single comparison operator can be used in a subquery from which you know a single value will be produced. Since the subquery is performed first, the SELECT . . . FROM . . . WHERE of the subquery is actually replaced by the value retrieved, so the main query is changed to the following:

```
SELECT    classNumber
FROM      Class
WHERE     facId = ('F110');
```

- Example 13. Subquery Using 'IN'

  Question: Find the names and IDs of all Faculty members who teach a class in Room H221.

  Solution: We need two tables, Class and Faculty, to answer this question. We also see that the names and IDs both appear on the Faculty table, so we have a choice of a join or a subquery. If we use a subquery, we begin with the Class table to find facId values for any courses that meet in Room H221. We find two such entries, so we make a note of those values. Then we go to the Faculty table and compare the facId value of each record on that table with the two ID values from Class, and display the corresponding facId and name.

  SQL Query:

```
SELECT    name, facId
FROM      Faculty
WHERE     facId IN
          (SELECT    facId
           FROM      Class
           WHERE     room = 'H221');
```

Result:

name	facId
Adams	F101
Smith	F115

In the WHERE line of the main query we used IN, rather than =, because the result of the subquery is a set of values rather than a single value. We are saying we want the `facId` in `Faculty` to match any member of the set of values we obtain from the subquery. When the subquery is replaced by the values retrieved, the main query becomes:

```
SELECT      name, facId
FROM        Faculty
WHERE       FACID IN ('F101','F115');
```

The IN is a more general form of subquery than the comparison operator, which is restricted to the case where a single value is produced. We can also use the negative form 'NOT IN', which will evaluate to true if the record has a field value that is not in the set of values retrieved by the subquery.

- Example 14. Nested Subqueries

Question: Get an alphabetical list of names and IDs of all students in any class taught by F110.

Solution: We need three tables, `Student`, `Enroll`, and `Class`, to answer this question. However, the values to be displayed appear on one table, `Student`, so we can use a subquery. First we check the `Class` table to find the `classNumber` of all courses taught by F110. We find two values, MTH101B and MTH103C. Next we go to the `Enroll` table to find the `stuId` of all students in either of these courses. We find three values, S1020, S1010, and S1002. We now look at the `Student` table to find the records with matching `stuId` values, and display the `stuId`, `lastName`, and `firstName`, in alphabetical order by name.

SQL Query:

```
SELECT      lastName, firstName, stuId
FROM        Student
WHERE       stuId IN
            (SELECT     stuId
             FROM       Enroll
```

```
WHERE      classNumber IN
           (SELECT classNumber
           FROM    Class
           WHERE   facId = 'F110'))
ORDER BY lastName, firstName ASC;
```

Result:

lastName	firstName	stuId
Burns	Edward	S1010
Chin	Ann	S1002
Rivera	Jane	S1020

In execution, the most deeply nested SELECT is done first, and it is replaced by the values retrieved, so we have:

```
SELECT     lastName, firstName, stuId
FROM       Student
WHERE      stuId IN
           (SELECT  stuId
           FROM     Enroll
           WHERE    classNumber IN
                    ('MTH101B', 'MTH103C'))
ORDER BY   lastName, firstName ASC;
```

Next the subquery on `Enroll` is done, and we get:

```
SELECT     lastName, firstName, stuId
FROM       Student
WHERE      stuId IN
           ('S1020', 'S1010', 'S1002')
ORDER BY   lastName, firstName ASC;
```

Finally, the main query is done, and we get the result shown earlier. Note that the ordering refers to the final result, not to any intermediate steps. Also note that we could have performed either part of the operation as a natural join and the other part as a subquery, mixing both methods.

- Example 15. Query Using EXISTS

  Question: Find the names of all students enrolled in CSC201A.

  Solution: We already know how to write this using a join or a subquery with IN. However, another way of expressing this query is to use the existential quantifier, EXISTS, with a subquery.

SQL Query:

```
SELECT    lastName, firstName
FROM      Student
WHERE     EXISTS
          (SELECT  *
          FROM     Enroll
          WHERE    Enroll.stuId = Student.stuId
          AND      classNumber = 'CSC201A');
```

Result:

lastName	firstName
Chin	Ann
Rivera	Jane

This query could be phrased as "Find the `lastName` and `firstName` of all students such that there exists an `Enroll` record containing their `stuId` with a `classNumber` of CSC201A." The test for inclusion is the existence of such a record. If it exists, the "EXISTS (SELECT FROM . . .;" evaluates to true. Notice we needed to use the name of the main query table (`Student`) in the subquery to express the condition `Student.stuId = Enroll.stuId`. In general, we avoid mentioning a table not listed in the FROM for that particular query, but it is necessary and permissible to do so in this case. This form is called a **correlated** subquery, since the table in the subquery is being compared to the table in the main query.

- Example 16. Query Using NOT EXISTS

  Question: Find the names of all students who are not enrolled in CSC201A.

  Solution: Unlike the previous example, we cannot readily express this using a join or an IN subquery. Instead, we will use NOT EXISTS.

  SQL Query:

```
SELECT    lastName, firstName
FROM      Student
WHERE     NOT EXISTS
          (SELECT  *
          FROM     Enroll
          WHERE    Student.stuId = Enroll.stuId
          AND      classNumber = 'CSC201A');
```

Result:

lastName	firstName
Smith	Tom
Lee	Perry
Burns	Edward
McCarthy	Owen
Jones	Mary

We could phrase this query as "Select student names from the `Student` table such that there is no `Enroll` record containing their stuId values with `classNumber` of CSC201A."

5.4.3 SELECT with Other Operators

- Example 17. Query Using UNION

Question: Get IDs of all `Faculty` who are assigned to the History department or who teach in Room H221.

Solution: It is easy to write a query for either of the conditions, and we can combine the results from the two queries by using a UNION operator. The UNION in SQL is the standard relational algebra operator for set union, and works in the expected way, eliminating duplicates.

SQL Query:

```
SELECT    facId
FROM      Faculty
WHERE     department = 'History'
UNION
SELECT    facId
FROM      Class
WHERE     room ='H221';
```

Result:

facId
F101
F115

In addition to UNION, SQL supports the operations INTERSECT and MINUS, which perform the standard set operations of set intersection and set difference, and UNION ALL, which operates like UNION, except that it does not eliminate duplicate rows.

- Example 18. Using Aggregate Functions

  Question: Find the total number of students enrolled in ART103A.

  Solution: Although this is a simple question, we are unable to express it as an SQL query at the moment, because we have not yet seen any way to operate on collections of rows or columns. We need some functions to do so. SQL has five commonly used built-in aggregate functions: COUNT, SUM, AVG, MAX, and MIN. Several more advanced functions exist, but are not as commonly used. For this query, we will use COUNT, which returns the number of values in a column.

  SQL Query:

  ```
  SELECT     COUNT (DISTINCT stuId)
  FROM       Enroll
  WHERE      classNumber = 'ART103A';
  ```

  Result:

  3

The built-in functions operate on a single column of a table. Each of them eliminates null values first, and operates only on the remaining non-null values. The functions return a single value, defined as follows:

COUNT	returns the number of values in the column
SUM	returns the sum of the values in the column
AVG	returns the mean of the values in the column
MAX	returns the largest value in the column
MIN	returns the smallest value in the column.

COUNT, MAX, and MIN apply to both numeric and nonnumeric fields, but SUM and AVG can be used on numeric fields only. The collating sequence is used to determine order of nonnumeric data. If we want to eliminate duplicate values before starting, we use the word DISTINCT before the column name in the SELECT line. COUNT(*) is a special use of the COUNT. Its purpose is to count all the rows of a table, regardless of whether null values or duplicate values occur. If we use DISTINCT with

MAX or MIN it will have no effect, because the largest or smallest value remains the same even if two tuples share it. However, DISTINCT usually has an effect on the result of SUM or AVG, so the user should understand whether or not duplicates should be included in computing these. Function references appear in the SELECT line of a query or a subquery.

Additional Function Examples:

Example (a) Find the number of departments that have faculty in them. Because we do not wish to count a department more than once, we use DISTINCT here.

```
SELECT    COUNT(DISTINCT department)
FROM      Faculty;
```

Example (b) Find the average number of credits students have. We do not want to use DISTINCT here, because if two students have the same number of credits, both should be counted in the average.

```
SELECT    AVG(credits)
FROM      Student;
```

Example (c) Find the student with the largest number of credits. Because we want the student's credits to equal the maximum, we need to find that maximum first, so we use a subquery to find it.

```
SELECT    stuId, lastName, firstName
FROM      Student
WHERE     credits =
          (SELECT   MAX(credits)
           FROM     Student);
```

Example (d) Find the ID of the student(s) with the highest grade in any course. Because we want the highest grade, it might appear that we should use the MAX function here. A closer look at the table reveals that the grades are letters A, B, C, etc. For this scale, the best grade is the one that is earliest in the alphabet, so we actually want MIN. If the grades were numeric, we would have wanted MAX.

```
SELECT    stuId
FROM      Enroll
WHERE     grade =
          (SELECT   MIN(grade)
           FROM     Enroll);
```

Example (e) Find names and IDs of students who have less than the average number of credits.

```
SELECT    lastName, firstName, stuId
FROM      Student
WHERE     credits <
          (SELECT   AVG(credits)
           FROM     Student);
```

- Example 19. Using an Expression and a String Constant

  Question: Assuming each course is three credits list, for each student, the number of courses he or she has completed.

  Solution: We can calculate the number of courses by dividing the number of credits by three. We can use the expression credits/3 in the SELECT to display the number of courses. Since we have no such column name, we will use a string constant as a label. String constants that appear in the SELECT line are simply printed in the result.

  SQL Query:

```
SELECT    stuId, 'Number of courses =', credits/3
FROM      Student;
```

  Result:

<u>stuId</u>

```
S1001 Number of courses =  30
S1010 Number of courses =  21
S1015 Number of courses =  14
S1005 Number of courses =   1
S1002 Number of courses =  12
S1020 Number of courses =   5
S1013 Number of courses =   0
```

By combining constants, column names, arithmetic operators, built-in functions, and parentheses, the user can customize retrievals.

- Example 20. Use of GROUP BY

  Question: For each course, show the number of students enrolled.

  Solution: We want to use the COUNT function, but need to apply it to each course individually. The GROUP BY allows us to put together all the records with a single value in the specified field.

Then we can apply any function to any field in each group, provided the result is a single value for the group.

SQL Query:

```
SELECT      classNumber, COUNT(*)
FROM        Enroll
GROUP BY    classNumber;
```

Result:

classNumber	
ART103A	3
CSC201A	2
MTH101B	1
HST205A	1
MTH103C	2

Note that we could have used COUNT(DISTINCT stuId) in place of COUNT(*) in this query.

- Example 21. Use of HAVING

Question: Find all courses in which fewer than three students are enrolled.

Solution: This is a question about a characteristic of the groups formed in the previous example. HAVING is used to determine which groups have some quality, just as WHERE is used with tuples to determine which records have some quality. You are not permitted to use HAVING without a GROUP BY, and the predicate in the HAVING line must have a single value for each group.

SQL Query:

```
SELECT      classNumber
FROM        Enroll
GROUP BY    classNumber
HAVING      COUNT(*) < 3 ;
```

Result:

classNumber
CSC201A
HST205A
MTH101B
MTH103C

- Example 22. Use of LIKE and NOT LIKE

Question: Get details of all MTH courses.

Solution: We do not wish to specify the exact course numbers, but we want the first three letters of `className` to be MTH. SQL allows us to use LIKE in the predicate to show a pattern string for character fields. Records whose specified columns match the pattern will be retrieved.

SQL Query:

```
SELECT      *
FROM        Class
WHERE       classNumber LIKE 'MTH%';
```

Result:

classNumber	facId	schedule	room
MTH101B	F110	MTUTH9	H225
MTH103C	F110	MWF11	H225

In the pattern string, we can use the following symbols:

% The percent character stands for any sequence of characters of any length >= 0.

_ The underscore character stands for any single character.

All other characters in the pattern stand for themselves.

Examples:

- `classNumber LIKE 'MTH%'` means the first three letters must be MTH, but the rest of the string can be any characters.

- `stuId LIKE 'S_ _ _ _'` means there must be five characters, the first of which must be an S.

- `schedule LIKE '%9'` means any sequence of characters, of length at least one, with the last character a nine.

- `classNumber LIKE '%101%'` means a sequence of characters of any length containing 101. Note the 101 could be the first, last, or only characters, as well as being somewhere in the middle of the string.

- `name NOT LIKE 'A%'` means the name cannot begin with an A.

- Example 23. Use of NULL

Question: Find the `stuId` and `className` of all students whose grades in that course are missing.

Solution: We can see from the `Enroll` table that there are two such records. You might think they could be accessed by specifying that the grades are not A, B, C, D, or F, but that is not the case. A null grade is considered to have "unknown" as a value, so it is impossible to judge whether it is equal to or not equal to another grade. If we put the condition "WHERE grade <>'A' AND grade <>'B' AND grade <>'C' AND grade <>'D' AND grade <>'F'" we would get an empty table back, instead of the two records we want. SQL uses the logical expression,

columnname IS [NOT] NULL

to test for null values in a column.

SQL Query:

```
SELECT     classNumber,stuId
FROM       Enroll
WHERE      grade IS NULL;
```

Result:

classNumber	stuId
ART103A	S1010
MTH103C	S1010

Notice that it is illegal to write "WHERE grade = NULL," because a predicate involving comparison operators with NULL will evaluate to "unknown" rather than "true" or "false." Also, the WHERE line is the only one on which NULL can appear in a SELECT statement.

5.4.4 Operators for Updating: UPDATE, INSERT, DELETE

The UPDATE operator is used to change values in records already stored in a table. It is used on one table at a time, and can change zero, one, or many records, depending on the predicate. Its form is:

```
UPDATE     tablename
SET        columnname = expression
           [,columnname = expression] . . .
[WHERE     predicate];
```

Note that it is not necessary to specify the current value of the field, although the present value may be used in the expression to determine the new value.

- Example 1. Updating a Single Field of One Record

  Operation: Change the major of S1020 to Music.

  SQL Command:

  ```
  UPDATE    Student
  SET       major = 'Music'
  WHERE     stuId = 'S1020';
  ```

- Example 2. Updating Several Fields of One Record

  Operation: Change Tanaka's department to MIS and rank to Assistant.

  SQL Command:

  ```
  UPDATE    Faculty
  SET       department = 'MIS',
            rank = 'Assistant'
  WHERE     name = 'Tanaka';
  ```

- Example 3. Updating Using NULL

  Operation: Change the major of S1013 from Math to NULL.

  To insert a null value into a field that already has an actual value, we must use the form:

  SET *columnname* = NULL

  SQL Command:

  ```
  UPDATE    Student
  SET       major = NULL
  WHERE     stuId = 'S1013';
  ```

- Example 4. Updating Several Records

  Operation: Change grades of all students in CSC201A to A.

  SQL Command:

  ```
  UPDATE    Enroll
  SET       grade = 'A'
  WHERE     classNumber = 'CSC201A';
  ```

- Example 5. Updating All Records

Operation: Give all students three extra credits.

SQL Command:

```
UPDATE   Student
SET      credits = credits + 3;
```

Notice we did not need the WHERE line, because all records were to be updated.

- Example 6. Updating with a Subquery

Operation: Change the room to B220 for all courses taught by Tanaka.

SQL Command:

```
UPDATE   Class
SET      room = 'B220'
WHERE    facId =
         (SELECT  facId FROM Faculty WHERE name = 'Tanaka');
```

The INSERT operator is used to put new records into a table. Normally, it is not used to load an entire table, because the database management system usually has a load utility to handle that task. However, the INSERT is useful for adding one or a few records to a table. Its form is:

```
INSERT
INTO      tablename [(colname [,colname]. . .)]
VALUES    (value [,value] . . .);
```

Note that the column names are optional if we are inserting values for all columns in their proper order. We can also write DEFAULT in place of an actual value provided the column has a default specified.

- Example 1. Inserting a Single Record, with All Fields Specified

Operation: Insert a new `Faculty` record with ID of F330, name of Jones, department of CSC, and rank of Instructor.

SQL Command:

```
INSERT
INTO      Faculty (facId, name, department, rank)
VALUES    ('F330', 'Jones', 'CSC', 'Instructor');
```

- Example 2. Inserting a Single Record, without Specifying Fields

  Operation: Insert a new student record with ID of S1030, name of Alice Hunt, major of art, and 12 credits.

  SQL Query:

```
INSERT
INTO    Student
VALUES  ('S1030', 'Hunt', 'Alice', 'Art', 12);
```

Notice it was not necessary to specify field names, because the system assumes we mean all the fields in the table. We could have done the same for the previous example.

- Example 3. Inserting a Record with Null Value in a Field

  Operation: Insert a new student record with ID of S1031, name of Maria Bono, zero credits, and no major.

  SQL Command:

```
INSERT
INTO    Student (lastName, firstName, stuId, credits)
VALUES  ('Bono', 'Maria', 'S1031', 0);
```

Notice we rearranged the field names, but there is no confusion because it is understood that the order of values matches the order of fields named in the INTO, regardless of their order in the table. Also notice the zero is an actual value for `credits`, not a null value. `major` will be set to null, since we excluded it from the field list in the INTO line.

- Example 4. Inserting Multiple Records

  Operation: Create and fill a new table that shows each course and the number of students enrolled in it.

  SQL Command:

```
CREATE TABLE Enrollment
   (classNumber VARCHAR2(7) NOT NULL,
    Students NUMBER(3));
INSERT
INTO Enrollment     (classNumber, Students)
   SELECT           classNumber, COUNT(*)
   FROM             Enroll
   GROUP BY         classNumber;
```

Here, we created a new table, `Enrollment`, and filled it by taking data from an existing table, `Enroll`. If `Enroll` is as it appears in Figure 5.3, `Enrollment` now looks like this:

Enrollment	classNumber	Students
	ART103A	3
	CSC201A	2
	MTH101B	1
	HST205A	1
	MTH103C	2

The `Enrollment` table is now available for the user to manipulate, just as any other table would be. It can be updated as needed, but it will not be updated automatically when the `Enroll` table is updated.

- Example 5. Inserting DATE values and SYSDATE

    The simplest way to insert dates in Oracle is to use the default format 'dd-mon-yy' as in '01-JAN-12'. For example, for the schema

    ```
    Employee(empId, lastName, firstName, birthDate, hireDate)
    ```

    if we have specified the DATE datatype for both `birthDate` and `hireDate`, we could insert an employee record by writing

    ```
    INSERT
    INTO EMPLOYEE
    VALUES(1001, 'Hynes','Susan','15-OCT-1985','01-JUN-2010');
    ```

    If we wish to set the `hireDate` value to the date the record is inserted, we can use the SYSDATE function, which returns the current system date and time, accurate to the second, as in

    ```
    INSERT
    INTO EMPLOYEE
    VALUES(1001, 'Hynes','Susan','15-OCT-1981',SYSDATE);
    ```

    If we use TRUNC(SYSDATE) the time part is set to 00:00. Oracle has several date/time functions, including some that allow users to convert between the DATE and STRING datatypes. For example, to convert a date value to a character string, we use the TO_CHAR function, which requires two arguments. The first is the date value and the second is a format string that shows what part of the date should be returned and in what format it should appear. For example, if we wished to find an employee name and the year part of the birthDate field, we could write

```
SELECT firstName, lastName, TO_CHAR(birthDate, 'YYYY') AS YEAR
FROM Employee
WHERE empId = 1001;
```

This will return

FIRSTNAME	LASTNAME	YEAR
Susan	Hynes	1985

In place of 'YYYY' we could use just 'YY' to express the year as two digits, 'MM', 'MON', or 'MONTH' to find the month expressed as either two digits, a 3-letter abbreviation, or spelled out, and 'DD' for the number of the day of the month.

The function TO_DATE converts a string into a DATE format, which allows Oracle to do date arithmetic such as comparing dates or finding the interval between dates. For example, to store the string '01/01/2012' as a `hireDate`, we could write

```
INSERT
INTO Employee (empId, firstName, lastName, hireDate)
VALUES(1002, 'Scott','Kane',TO_DATE('01/01/2012','MM/DD/YYYY'));
```

The format string here has the same variations as those of the TO_CHAR function.

- Example 6. Creating and Using Sequences

In Access if you create a table without a primary key, you are given the option to have Access create a primary key column. If you accept the option, the column will be called ID and its data type will be AutoNumber. Whenever you add a new record to the table, the ID value will be automatically set, starting with 1 for the first record and increasing by 1 each time a new record is inserted. Oracle has a similar but much more flexible mechanism called a sequence. To use a sequence, we first have to create one, using the command

```
CREATE SEQUENCE seqname [START WITH n] [INCREMENT BY n];
```

For example, for the `Employee` table, we could have chosen to create a sequence to generate empId values

```
CREATE SEQUENCE empId_seq START WITH 1001 INCREMENT BY 1;
```

Note that a sequence is not tied to a particular table, so we do not need to identify a table or attribute for it, nor does it disappear if we drop the table we created the sequence to use in. The default value for both the starting number and increment (*n*) is 1. To generate numbers for the sequence we use *seqname*.NEXTVAL. To find the current value of a sequence, we use *seqname*.CURRVAL. These values are called pseudocolumns, and they perform as if they were regular columns of a table. To see the value of CURRVAL, use the command

```
SELECT empId_seq.CURRVAL from DUAL;
```

We could have inserted the two records shown earlier using the commands

```
INSERT
INTO Employee
VALUES (empId_seq.NEXTVAL, 'Hynes','Susan','15-OCT-1981',SYSDATE);

INSERT
INTO Employee(empId, firstName, lastName, hireDate)
VALUES (empId_seq.NEXTVAL,
'Scott','Kane',TO_DATE('01/01/2012','MM/DD/YYYY'));
```

Once the values generated by the sequence have been entered into the table, we can treat them as ordinary integers, querying and editing them as needed, even updating the `empId` field, an operation that is not permitted using Access AutoNumber fields. We could even insert records in the usual way, bypassing the sequence, although this is not advisable, since the sequence values will be unaffected by our inserts. We can use CURRVAL to obtain the sequence value. For example, if we have just entered an employee record and we want to enter the employee's empId into an existing Assignment table such as

```
Assignment(empId, projNo, hoursAssigned)
```

we could do so by writing

```
INSERT
INTO Assignment
VALUES (empId_seq.CURRVAL, 'J10', 30);
```

That will not change the value of `empId_seq.NEXTVAL`, which will increase the next time it is used. Any sequence can be dropped by writing a drop command such as

```
DROP SEQUENCE empId_seq;
```

This statement will not affect any values already entered into tables using the sequence. They reside there as if they had been entered in the usual way.

The DELETE is used to erase records. The number of records deleted may be zero, one, or many, depending on how many satisfy the predicate. The form of this command is:

```
DELETE
FROM      tablename
WHERE     predicate;
```

- Example 1. Deleting a Single Record

  Operation: Erase the record of student S1020.

  SQL Command:

  ```
  DELETE
  FROM      Student
  WHERE     stuId = 'S1020';
  ```

- Example 2. Deleting Several Records

  Operation: Erase all enrollment records for student S1020.

  SQL Command:

  ```
  DELETE
  FROM      Enroll
  WHERE     stuId = 'S1020';
  ```

- Example 3. Deleting All Records from a Table

  Operation: Erase all the class records.

If we delete `Class` records and allow their corresponding `Enroll` records to remain, we would lose referential integrity, because the `Enroll` records would then refer to classes that no longer exist. However, if we have created the tables using Oracle and the commands shown in Figure 5.2, the delete command will not work on the `Class` table unless we first delete the `Enroll` records for any students registered in the class, because we wrote,

```
CONSTRAINT Enroll_classNumber_fk FOREIGN KEY (classNumber) REFERENCES Class
  (classNumber);
```

for the Enroll table. However, assuming that we have deleted the `Enroll` records, then we can delete `Class` records.

SQL Command:

```
DELETE
FROM    Class;
```

This would remove all records from the `Class` table, but its structure would remain, so we could add new records to it at any time.

- Example 4. DELETE with a Subquery

Operation: Erase all enrollment records for Owen McCarthy.

SQL Command:

```
DELETE
FROM    Enroll
WHERE   stuId =
        (SELECT  stuId
         FROM    Student
         WHERE   lastName = 'McCarthy'
                 AND firstName = 'Owen');
```

Since there were no such records, this statement will have no effect on `Enroll`.

5.4.5 Creating and Using Views

Views are an important tool for providing users with a simple, customized environment and for hiding data. As explained in Section 5.2, a relational view does not correspond exactly to the general external view, but can be either a "window" into a base table or a virtual table derived from one or more underlying base tables. It does not exist in storage in the sense that the base tables do, but is created by selecting specified rows and columns from the base tables, and possibly performing operations on them. The view is dynamically produced as the user works with it. To make up a view, the DBA decides which data the user needs to access, determines what base tables contain it, and creates one or more views to display the attributes and rows the user should see. Views allow a dynamic external model to be created for the user easily. The reasons for providing views rather than allowing all users to work with base tables are as follows:

- Views allow different users to see the data in different forms, permitting an external model that differs from the logical model.

- The view mechanism provides a simple authorization control device, easily created and automatically enforced by the system. View users are unaware of, and cannot access, certain data items.

- Views can free users from complicated DML operations, especially in the case where the views involve joins. The user writes a simple SELECT statement using the view in place of a base table in the FROM clause, and the system takes care of the details of the corresponding more complicated operations on the base tables to support the view.

- If the database is restructured on the logical level, the view can be used to keep the user's model constant. For example, if the table is split by projection and the primary key appears in each resulting new table, the original table can always be reconstructed when needed by defining a view that is the join of the new tables.

The following is the most common form of the command used to create a view:

```
CREATE VIEW viewname
    [(viewcolname [,viewcolname] . . .)]
    AS  SELECT    colname [,colname] . . .
        FROM      basetablename [,basetablename] . . .
        WHERE     condition;
```

The view name is chosen using the same rules as the table name, and should be unique within the database. Column names in the view can be different from the corresponding column names in the base tables, but they must obey the same rules of construction. If we choose to make them the same, we need not specify them twice, so we leave out the *viewcolname* specifications. In the AS SELECT line, also called the subquery, we list the names of the columns from the underlying base tables that we wish to include in the view. The order of these names should correspond exactly to the *viewcolnames,* if those are specified. However, columns chosen from the base tables may be rearranged in any desired manner in the view. As in the usual SELECT . . . FROM . . . WHERE, the condition is a logical predicate that expresses some restriction on the records to be included. A more general form of the CREATE VIEW uses any valid subquery in place of the SELECT we have described.

- Example 1. Choosing a Vertical and Horizontal Subset of a Table

  Assume a user needs to see IDs and names of all History majors. We can create a view for this user as follows:

```
CREATE VIEW HISTMAJ (last, first, StudentId)
    AS SELECT lastName, firstName, stuId
       FROM    Student
       WHERE   major = 'History';
```

Here we renamed the columns from our base table. The user of this view need not know the actual column names.

On the Companion Website:

- SQL code for all view examples

- Example 2. Choosing a Vertical Subset of a Table

If we would like a table of all courses with their schedules and room, we could create this as follows:

```
CREATE VIEW     ClassLoc
AS SELECT       classNumber, schedule, room
FROM            Class;
```

Notice we did not need a condition here, since we wanted these parts of all Class records. This time we kept the names of the columns as they appear in the base table.

- Example 3. A View Using Two Tables

Assume a user needs a table containing the IDs and names of all students in course CSC101. The virtual table can be created by choosing records in Enroll that have a classNumber of CSC101, matching the stuId of those records with the stuId of the Student records, and taking the corresponding last-Name, and firstName from Student. We could express this as a join or as a subquery.

```
CREATE VIEW ClassList
    AS SELECT  Student.stuId,lastName, firstName
       FROM    Enroll, Student
       WHERE   classNumber = 'CSC101'
               AND Enroll.stuId = Student.stuId;
```

- Example 4. A View of a View

We can define a view derived from a view. For example, we can ask for a subset of the ClassLoc (virtual) table by writing:

```
CREATE VIEW ClassLoc2
    AS SELECT    classNumber, room
        FROM     ClassLoc;
```

- Example 5. A View Using a Function

In the SELECT statement in the AS line we can include built-in functions and GROUP BY options. For example, if we want a view of Enroll that gives classNumber and the number of students enrolled in each class, we write:

```
CREATE VIEW ClassCount (classNumber, TotCount)
    AS SELECT    classNumber, COUNT(*)
        FROM     Enroll
                 GROUP BY classNumber;
```

Notice we had to supply a name for the second column of the view, since there was none available from the base table.

This could also have been done by using an alias for the second column as in

```
CREATE VIEW ClassCount2
    AS SELECT    classNumber, COUNT(*) AS Totcount
        FROM     Enroll
                 GROUP BY classNumber;
```

- Example 6. Operations on Views

Once a view is created, the user can write SELECT statements to retrieve data through the view. The system takes care of mapping the user names to the underlying base table names and column names, and performing whatever functions are required to produce the result in the form the user expects. Users can write SQL queries that refer to joins, ordering, grouping, built-in functions, and so on, of views just as if they were operating on base tables. Since the SELECT operation does not change the underlying base tables, there is no restriction on allowing authorized users to perform SELECT with views. The following is an example of a SELECT operation on the ClassLoc view:

```
SELECT  *
FROM    ClassLoc
WHERE   room LIKE 'H%';
```

INSERT, DELETE, and UPDATE can present problems with views. For example, suppose we had a view of student records such as:

```
StudentVw1(lastName, firstName, major, credits)
```

If we were permitted to insert records, any records created through this view would actually be `Student` records, but would not contain `stuId`, which is the key of the `Student` table. Since `stuId` would have the NOT NULL constraint, we would have to reject any records without this field. However, if we had the following view,

```
StudentVw2(stuId, lastName, firstName, credits)
```

we should have no problem inserting records, since we would be inserting `Student` records with a null major field, which is allowable. We write:

```
INSERT
INTO      StudentVw2
VALUES    ('S1040', 'Levine', 'Adam', 30);
```

However, the system should actually insert the record into the `Student` table.

Now let us consider inserting records into the view `ClassCount`, as described earlier in Example 5. This view used the COUNT function on groups of records in the `Enroll` table. Obviously, this table was meant to be a dynamic summary of the `Enroll` table, rather than being a row and column subset of that table. It would not make sense for us to permit new `ClassCount` records to be inserted, since these do not correspond to individual rows or columns of a base table.

The problems we have identified for INSERT apply with minor changes to UPDATE and DELETE as well. As a general rule, these three operations can be performed on views that consist of actual rows and columns of underlying base tables, provided the primary key is included in the view, and no other constraints are violated. INSTEAD OF triggers, which are described in Section 5.2.2, can be used to ensure that the database updates the underlying tables.

To modify an existing view definition, the following command, which is nearly identical to the original CREATE VIEW, is used

```
CREATE OR REPLACE VIEW viewname AS subquery
```

5.5   Active Databases

The DBMS has more powerful means of ensuring integrity in a database than the column and table constraints discussed in Section 5.3. An **active database** is one in which the DBMS monitors the contents in order to prevent illegal states from occurring, using constraints and triggers.

5.5.1   Enabling and Disabling Constraints

The column and table constraints described in Section 5.3 are specified when the table is created, and are checked whenever a change is made to the database, to ensure that the new state is a valid one. Changes that could result in invalid states include insertion, deletion, and updating of records. Therefore, the constraints are checked by the DBMS whenever one of these operations is performed, usually after each SQL INSERT, DELETE, or UPDATE statement. This is called the IMMEDIATE mode of constraint checking, and it is the default mode. However, there are times when a transaction or application involves several changes and the database will be temporarily invalid while the changes are in progress—while some but not all of the changes already have been made. For example, assume we have a Department table in our University example with a `chairPerson` column in which we listed the `facId` of the chairperson, and we make it a foreign key, by writing:

```
CREATE TABLE Department (
    deptName        VARCHAR2(20),
    chairPerson     VARCHAR2(6),
    CONSTRAINT Department_deptName_pk PRIMARY KEY(deptName),
    CONSTRAINT Department_facId_fk FOREIGN KEY (chairPerson) REFERENCES Faculty (facId));
```

For the Faculty table definition in Figure 5.2, we already have a NOT NULL for the department, but now we could make `department` a foreign key with the new `Department` table as the home table, by writing:

```
ALTER TABLE Faculty ADD CONSTRAINT Faculty_department_fk FOREIGN KEY
    department REFERENCES Department(deptName);
```

What will happen when we try to create a new department and add the faculty for that department to the `Faculty` table? We cannot insert the department record unless we already have the chairperson's record in the

`Faculty` table, but we cannot insert that record unless the department record is already there, so each SQL INSERT statement would fail.

In Oracle, we can enable or disable constraints to allow such operations to succeed, using a statement such as:

```
ALTER TABLE DEPARTMENT DISABLE CONSTRAINT Department_facId_fk;
```

This will allow us to insert the Department record without a chairperson's facId, so we can then insert the faculty records with the appropriate department name. We can then update the Department record and insert the facId of the chairperson.

At the end, we should write,

```
ALTER TABLE DEPARTMENT ENABLE CONSTRAINT Department_facId_fk;
```

to allow enforcement again.

If we are using an application to enter data we can also choose to defer constraint checking until the end of the transactions, using statements such as

```
SET CONSTRAINT Department_facId_fk DEFERRED;
```

or

```
SET CONSTRAINT Faculty_department_fk DEFERRED;
```

which will defer the checking until the end of the current transaction.

5.5.2 SQL Triggers

Like constraints, **triggers** allow the DBMS to monitor the database. However, they are more flexible than constraints, apply to a broader range of situations, and allow a greater variety of actions. A trigger consists of three parts:

- An **event**, which is normally some change made to the database
- A **condition**, which is a logical predicate that evaluates to true or false
- An **action**, which is some procedure that is done when the event occurs and the condition evaluates to true, also called **firing the trigger**

A trigger has access to the inserted, deleted, or updated data that caused it to fire (i.e., to be activated or raised), and the data values can be used in the code both for the condition and for the action. The prefix :OLD is used to refer to the tuple just deleted or to the values replaced in an update. The prefix :NEW is used to refer to the tuple just inserted or to the new values in an update. Triggers can be fired either before or after the execution of the insert, delete, or update operation. We can also specify whether the trigger is fired just once for each triggering statement, or for each row that is changed by the statement. (Recall that, for example, an update statement may change many rows.) In Oracle, you specify the SQL command (INSERT, DELETE, or UPDATE) that is the event; the table involved; the trigger level (ROW or STATEMENT); the timing (BEFORE or AFTER); and the action to be performed, which can be written as one or more SQL commands in PL/SQL. Section 5.7 discusses PL/SQL in more detail. The Oracle trigger syntax has the form:

```
CREATE OR REPLACE TRIGGER trigger_name
    [BEFORE/AFTER] [INSERT/UPDATE/DELETE] ON table_name
    [FOR EACH ROW] [WHEN condition]
    [DECLARE local_variable_name datatype [:= initial_value]]
    BEGIN
        trigger body
    END;
```

To create the trigger in Oracle, the user can key in the code for the trigger directly in SQL Plus, or use a text editor and copy it into SQL Plus, placing a forward slash at the end to compile and execute the code.

For this example, let us add to the Class table two additional attributes, currentEnroll, which shows the number of students actually enrolled in each class, and maxEnroll, which is the maximum number of students allowed to enroll. The new table, RevClass, is shown in Figure 5.4(a), along with a new version of the Enroll table, RevEnroll. Since currentEnroll is a derived attribute, dependent on the RevEnroll table, its value should be updated when there are relevant changes made to RevEnroll. Changes that affect currentEnroll are:

1. A student enrolls in a class

2. A student drops a class

RevClass					
classNumber	facId	schedule	room	currentEnroll	maxEnroll
ART103A	F101	MWF9	H221	3	25
CSC201A	F105	TuThF10	M110	2	20
CSC203A	F105	MThF12	M110	0	20
HST205A	F115	MWF11	H221	1	35
MTH101B	F110	MTuTh9	H225	1	25
MTH103C	F110	MWF11	H225	2	25

On the Companion Website:
- All SQL Code

RevEnroll		
stuId	classNumber	grade
S1001	ART103A	A
S1001	HST205A	C
S1002	ART103A	D
S1002	CSC201A	F
S1002	MTH103C	B
S1010	ART103A	
S1010	MTH103C	
S1020	CSC201A	B
S1020	MTH101B	A

FIGURE 5.4(a)

Tables for Triggers

3. A student switches from one class to another

In an active database, there should be triggers for each of these changes. For change (1), we should increment the value of currentEnroll by one. We can refer to the classNumber of the new RevEnroll record by using the prefix :NEW. The corresponding trigger is shown in Figure 5.4(b) Note that we did not use the WHEN because we always want to make this

Figure 5.4(b)

**Trigger for Student
Enrolling in a Class**

```
create or replace trigger ADDENROLL
after insert on revenroll
for each row
begin
        update revclass
        set currentenroll=currentenroll+1
        where revclass.classnumber=:new.classnumber;
exception
        when no_data_found then
                DBMS_OUTPUT.PUT_LINE('No data found');
        when others then
                DBMS_OUTPUT.PUT_LINE('Error-'|| SQLERRM);
end;
/
```

change after a new enrollment record is inserted, so no condition was needed. For change (2), we need to decrement the value of currentEnroll by one, and we use the prefix :OLD to refer to the RevEnroll record being deleted. The trigger is shown in Figure 5.4(c). Change (3) could be

Figure 5.4(c)

**Trigger for Student
Dropping Classes**

```
create or replace trigger DROPENROLL
after delete on revenroll
for each row
begin
        update revclass
        set currentenroll=currentenroll-1
        where revclass.classnumber=:old.classnumber;
exception
        when no_data_found then
                DBMS_OUTPUT.PUT_LINE('No data found');
        when others then
                DBMS_OUTPUT.PUT_LINE('Error-'|| SQLERRM);
end;
/
```

```
create or replace trigger MYSWITCHENROLL
after update of classnumber on revenroll
for each row
begin
        update revclass
        set currentenroll=currentenroll+1
        where revclass.classnumber=:new.classnumber;
        update revclass
        set currentenroll=currentenroll-1;
exception
        when NO_DATA_FOUND then
                DBMS_OUTPUT.PUT_LINE('No data found');
        when others then
                DBMS_OUTPUT.PUT_LINE('Error-' || SQLERRM);
END;
/
```

Figure 5.4(d)

Trigger for Student Changing Classes

treated as a drop followed by an enrollment, but instead we will write a trigger for an update to demonstrate an action with two parts, as shown in Figure 5.4(d).

While these triggers are sufficient if there is room in a class, we also need to consider what should happen if the class is already fully enrolled. The value of `maxEnroll` should have been examined before we allowed a student to enroll in the class, so we need to check that value before we do change (1) or change (3). Assume that if a change would cause a class to be overenrolled, we wish to print out a message with the student's ID, the class number, the current enrollment, and maximum enrollment. The action should be taken before we make the change. The trigger is shown in Figure 5.5.

Oracle provides an INSTEAD OF form that is especially useful when a user tries to update the database through a view. This form specifies an action to be performed instead of the insert, delete, or update that the

Figure 5.5

Trigger to Check for Overenrollment

```
SET SERVEROUTPUT ON;
create or replace trigger ENROLL_REQUEST
before insert or update of classNumber on revenroll
for each row
declare
        numStu   number;
        maxStu   number;
begin
        select    maxEnroll into maxStu
        from      RevClass
        where     RevClass.classNumber =:NEW.classNumber;

        select    currentEnroll +1 into numStu
        from      RevClass
        where     RevClass.classNumber=:NEW.classNumber;

        if numStu > maxStu THEN
DBMS_OUTPUT.PUT_LINE('Student ' || :NEW.stuld ||' has requested ' ||:NEW.classNumber ||'
which currently has' ||TO_CHAR(numstu)||' students and has a maximum enrollment of'
||TO_CHAR(maxStu));

        end if;

exception
        when no_data_found then
                DBMS_OUTPUT.PUT_LINE('No data found');
        when others then
                DBMS_OUTPUT.PUT_LINE('Error-'|| SQLERRM);
end;
/
```

user requested. If a user tries to update a view, we can use an INSTEAD OF trigger to make sure the underlying base table(s) are updated. For example, in Section 5.4 we defined `StudentVw2` that consisted of `stuId`, `lastName`, `firstName`, and `credits`. The following trigger will ensure that any update to the view is performed on the Student table instead.

```
CREATE TRIGGER InsertStuVw2
      INSTEAD OF INSERT ON StudentVw2
      FOR EACH ROW
BEGIN
      INSERT
      INTO  Student(stuId, lastname, firstname, credits)
      VALUES (:NEW.stuId,:NEW.lastName, :NEW.firstName, :NEW.Credits);
END;
```

Triggers can also be used to provide an audit trail for a table, recording all changes, the time they were made, and the identity of the user who made them, an application that will be discussed in Section 9.6.

Triggers are automatically enabled when they are created. They can be disabled by the statement

```
ALTER TRIGGER <trigger-name> DISABLE;
```

After disabling, they can enabled again by the statement

```
ALTER TRIGGER <trigger-name> ENABLE;
```

They can be dropped by the statement

```
DROP TRIGGER <trigger-name>;
```

5.6   Using COMMIT and ROLLBACK Statements

Any changes made to a database using SQL commands are not permanent until the user writes a COMMIT statement. As discussed in Chapter 10, an SQL transaction ends when either a COMMIT statement or a ROLLBACK statement is encountered. The COMMIT makes permanent the changes made since the beginning of the current transaction, which is either the beginning of the session or the time since the last COMMIT or

ROLLBACK. The ROLLBACK undoes changes made by the current transaction. It is wise to write COMMIT often to save changes as you work.

5.7   SQL Programming

For the interactive SQL statements shown so far, we assumed that there was a user interface that provided an environment to accept, interpret, and execute the SQL commands directly. However, most database access is actually performed through programs.

5.7.1   SQL PSMs

Most database management systems include an extension of SQL itself, called **Persistent Stored Modules** (PSM), to allow users to write stored procedures, also called **internal routines**, that are stored on the database server. These facilities are used to write SQL routines that can be saved with the database schema and invoked when needed. In contrast, programs written in a host language are referred to as external routines, and are stored on the client side. Oracle's PL/SQL, which can be accessed from within the SQLPlus environment, is such a facility. In addition, Oracle allows Java stored procedures to reside directly in the database space, providing server-side programming facilities in that language as well. The SQL/PSM standard is designed to provide complete programming language facilities, including constants and control structures, declared variables, assignment statements, and error handling. We have already seen some of these features in our discussion of triggers. However, SQL PSMs can perform much more processing.

SQL/PSM modules include functions, procedures, and temporary relations. To create a named procedure, we write:

```
CREATE [OR REPLACE] PROCEDURE procedure_name (parameter_list){AS | IS}
    declarations of local variables and constants
BEGIN
    executable statements
EXCEPTION
    exception handling
END;
```

We input the code as we did for triggers, either in the SQLPlus window or using a text editor. We add a forward slash (/) after the word END to com-

pile the procedure code. Each parameter in the formal parameter list can
have a name, mode, datatype, and an optional initial value. The name and
data type of the parameter must be specified. The data type of a parameter
should be generic and unconstrained—no length should be specified for
strings, and no precision for numbers. For example, the types NUMBER,
CHAR, and VARCHAR(2) are not followed by a size. The length is determined by the length of the actual parameter passed to it. The mode, which
is optional, may be IN, OUT, or IN OUT, depending on whether it is an
input parameter, an output parameter, or both. If not specified, it defaults
to IN. For example, we write

```
CREATE OR REPLACE PROCEDURE myTest(
    testName    IN          VARCHAR(2),
    testValue   IN    OUT   NUMBER,
    testDate    OUT         DATE)
    AS…
```

A function has a similar declaration, as follows:

```
CREATE [OR REPLACE] FUNCTION function_name (parameter list)
    RETURNS SQLdatatype {AS | IS}
declarations of local variables and constants
BEGIN
    function code (must include a RETURN statement)
EXCEPTION
    exception handling
END;
```

Functions accept only parameters with mode IN, to prevent side effects. The
only value returned should be the one specified in the RETURN statement.

Next are declarations of local variables and constants, if any Declarations
have the form,

```
identifier datatype [:= initial value];
```

as in,

```
mystatus            VARCHAR2(10);        -- uses an SQL datatype
number_of_courses   NUMBER(3) := 0; -- can provide initial value
MAX_CREDITS         CONSTANT   NUMBER(3) := 150;  -- can declare constants
DONE                BOOLEAN :=  false; -- PL/SQL has BOOLEAN datatype
stuNumber           Student.stuId%type;   /* using %, inherits datatype
        of stuId column */
stuLastname         VARCHAR2(20); -- can also specify datatype
```

```
stuFirstName        Student.firstName%type; /* inherits datatype
      of firstName column */
stuCredits          NUMBER(3) NOT NULL := 0;  -- can specify NOT NULL
```

The variables or constants can be the SQL datatypes as well as BOOLEAN, PLS_INTEGER, BINARY_INTEGER, REF_CURSOR, user-defined types, and collection types. Note that we can declare a variable or constant to have the same type as a database attribute, as we did for stuNumber and stuFirstName. When using variables that will get their values from database attributes, this is the safest way to declare their types. We can use the single-line comment delimiter -- or the multi-line /* .....*/ anywhere in the module.

After the BEGIN, the code for the procedure consists of SQL DML (but not DDL) statements, assignment statements, control statements, and error handling. The SQL SELECT statement is modified to include an INTO where we list the declared variables into which the attribute values will be stored as in

```
SELECT stuId, lastName, firstName, credits
INTO stuNumber, stuLastName, stuFirstName, stuCredits
FROM Student
WHERE stuId = 'S1001';
```

The assignment statement permits the value of a constant or an expression to be assigned to a variable. Note that PL/SQL uses := for assigning a value to a declared procedure or function variable, unlike the UPDATE..SET...= , which is used for updating a database attribute. For example, we could write

```
status := 'Freshman';
number_of_courses := stuCredits/3;
```

because these are declared variables, but to enter a new value for credits in the Student table we would use an SQL update command such as UPDATE STUDENT SET CREDITS = 50;

Branches have the form:

```
IF (condition) THEN statements;
    ELSEIF (condition) THEN statements;

    . . .

    ELSEIF (condition) THEN statements;
    ELSE statements;
END IF;
```

for example,

```
IF (Student.credits <30) THEN
    status := 'Freshman';
    ELSEIF (Student.credits <60) THEN
        status := 'Sophomore';
    ELSEIF (Student.credits <90) THEN
        status := 'Junior';
    ELSE status := 'Senior';
END IF;
```

The CASE statement can be used for selection based on the value of a variable or expression.

```
CASE selector
    WHEN value1        THEN statements;
    WHEN value2        THEN statements;
    . . .
END CASE;
```

Repetition is controlled by LOOP ... ENDLOOP, WHILE ... DO ... END WHILE, REPEAT ... UNTIL ... END REPEAT, and FOR ... DO ... END FOR structures. A simple control structure for an iterated loop is

```
FOR loop-variable IN start_value ... end_value LOOP
    loop body
END LOOP;
```

Here the loop variable is local to the loop and does not have to be declared. The start and end values must be constants.

When you compile the PL/SQL module, you will get a message saying either that the compilation was successful or that the procedure was created with compilation errors, but no message showing you the errors. To see your errors for a module just compiled, enter

```
SHOW ERRORS
```

or

```
SHOW ERRORS PROCEDURE procedure-name
```

Once a procedure has been created, it can be executed by the command

```
EXEC procedure_name(actual_ parameter_ list);
```

The actual parameter list consists of the values or variables being passed to the procedure. A function is invoked by using its name, typically in an assignment statement. For example,

```
newVal:= MyFunction(val1, val2);
```

To enable the module to produce output on the client console, it is necessary to first enter the command

```
SET SERVEROUTPUT ON
```

This will allow output produced by the server to be received by the client console. To actually send a message to the client from inside the module, we use the DBMS_OUTPUT.PUT_LINE(*output string*) function, which allows us to display output strings on the console. The || symbol is used to concatenate strings, so you can use TO_CHAR if needed to convert output to a string. For example, we could write

```
DBMS_OUTPUT.PUT_LINE('Student ' || studentNo || ' has' ||
    TO_CHAR(stuCredits)|| ' credits and is a '|| status );
```

or we could write a message indicating success or failure for a requested operation as part of the code.

```
DBMS_OUTPUT.PUT_LINE('New record entered successfully');
```

Figure 5.6 shows a simple procedure to accept a stuId as a parameter and display the student name as output. Note that the RTRIM function removes extra blanks from the first and last name.

A special problem occurs when a SELECT statement returns more than one tuple (a multi-set). Often we wish to be able to process one row at a time from a multi-set, and we create a loop to do so. We need a device called a **cursor**, a symbolic pointer that points to a private area that stores the results of an SQL SELECT or other DML statement. With proper control, it can retrieve one row of a table or multi-set from the private area at a time, provide access to that row to the application, then move on to the next row the next time we enter the loop. Even in single-row SELECT statements, SQL automatically creates a cursor, called an implicit cursor, for us, although we do not control it directly. The simplest form for declaring an explicit cursor is

```
Cursor IS query;
```

Figure 5.7 shows a procedure using a cursor. In this example, to create a cursor to go through student records that we plan to retrieve only, we wrote in the declaration section,

```
Cursor stuCursor IS
    SELECT stuId, lastName, firstName
    FROM student;
```

```
create or replace procedure findname(pstuid char) AS
-- declare program variables
    plastname   char(20);
    pfirstname  char(20);
BEGIN
    -- query to find the first and last name of the student
    SELECT  firstname, lastname
    INTO    pfirstname, plastname
    FROM    Student
    WHERE   stuId = pstuId;

    -- display the name
    DBMS_OUTPUT.PUT_LINE('Student name: ' || RTRIM(pfirstname)
    || ' ' || RTRIM(plastname));

    exception
    when no_data_found then
            DBMS_OUTPUT.PUT_LINE('No data found');
    when others then
            DBMS_OUTPUT.PUT_LINE('Error-' || SQLERRM);

end;
/
```

Figure 5.6

PL/SQL Procedure to Find a Student Name

Code online

If we were planning to update any of the records, we would add a FOR UPDATE just before the final semicolon. Note that this is a declaration, not an executable statement. The SQL query is not executed yet. After declaring the cursor, we write a statement to open it in the executable part of the module. This executes the query so that the multiset of results is created and stored in the private area. Opening the cursor also positions it just before the first tuple of the results set. For this example, we write

```
OPEN stuCursor;
```

We then have a loop of the form

```
LOOP...ENDLOOP
```

in which we have included a check, a line that exits when no data is found. Any other loop control method could have been used instead. Within the

Figure 5.7

Using a Cursor in PL/SQL

Code online

```
SET SERVEROUTPUT ON;
create or replace procedure CURSORSAMPLE
AS
id         char(20);
fname      char(20);
lname      char(20);

cursor stuCursor is
        select stuid, firstname, lastname
        from student;

begin
        open stuCursor;
        LOOP
            fetch stuCursor into id, fname, lname;
            DBMS_OUTPUT.PUT_LINE(id ||  '   ||fname|| '||lname);
        exit when stuCursor%notfound;
        END LOOP;
        close stuCursor;

exception
        when no_data_found then
                DBMS_OUTPUT.PUT_LINE('No data found');
        when others then
                DBMS_OUTPUT.PUT_LINE('Error-' || SQLERRM);

END;
/
```

loop, to retrieve each row of the results, we used the FETCH command, which has the form

        FETCH *cursorname* INTO *hostvariables*;

as in

        FETCH stuCursor INTO id, fname, lname;

The FETCH statement advances the cursor and assigns the values of the attributes named in the SELECT statement to the corresponding declared variables named in the INTO line. After all data has been retrieved (i.e., when `stuCursor%notfound` becomes true), we exit the loop, and close the cursor in a CLOSE statement

```
CLOSE stuCursor;
```

A simpler way to iterate through the results set using a cursor is to use a cursor FOR LOOP. In the following example after we declare the cursor `c1`, the cursor FOR LOOP will open the cursor, perform a fetch for each iteration of the loop as long as the cursor has more rows, and close the cursor when all the rows of the results set have been processed.

```
CURSOR c1 IS
    SELECT lastname, major FROM Student
    WHERE credits > 30;
BEGIN
  FOR person IN c1
  LOOP
    DBMS_OUTPUT.PUT_LINE ('Name = ' || person.lastname || ' has major
= ' || person.major);
  END LOOP;
END;
/
```

The EXCEPTION section is designed to handle errors that occur while the module is executing. Whenever an error occurs, an exception is raised. There are many system-defined exceptions for Oracle, and programmers can also write their own exceptions for possible errors, such as when a user enters data that is not in the expected range. Among the most common system exceptions are NO_DATA_FOUND, which is raised whenever a SELECT statement returns no data, and DUP_VAL_ON_INDEX, which is raised whenever a duplicate key value is entered. The form of the EXCEPTION section is

```
EXCEPTION
  WHEN exception1 THEN sequence_of_statements for exception1
  WHEN exception2 THEN sequence_of_statements for exception2
  ...
  WHEN OTHERS THEN -- optional handler for all other errors
    sequence_of_statements for general errors
END;
```

Figure 5.8 shows a procedure for entering a new student record. If the `stuId` is already in the table, it displays "Duplicate stuId". If any other predefined error occurs, it displays "Error" followed by

Figure 5.8

Exception Handling when Adding a New Student Record

```
SET SERVEROUTPUT ON;

-- Procedure to insert a new student

create or replace procedure addStudent(pstuId char, plastname char,
pfirstname char, pmajor char, pcredits number) AS

BEGIN
insert into student(stuId, lastname, firstname, major, credits)
   values(pstuId, plastname, pfirstname, pmajor, pcredits);

DBMS_OUTPUT.PUT_LINE('New record entered successfully');

exception
   when dup_val_on_index then
      DBMS_OUTPUT.PUT_LINE('Duplicate stuId');
   when others then
      DBMS_OUTPUT.PUT_LINE('Error-' || SQLERRM);

END;
/
```

SQLERRM, a string that holds the error message for that particular error. It is also possible to write exceptions specifically for the module. First the exception must be declared in the declaration section by a statement such as

```
too_expensive              EXCEPTION;
```

In the executable section, a statement should be included saying when the exception should be raised, such as

```
IF price > 99.99 THEN RAISE too_expensive
   ELSE statements for usual processing
ENDIF;
```

In the EXCEPTION section, include the actions to be performed if this exception and others are raised, such as

```
WHEN too_expensive THEN DBMS_OUTPUT.PUT_LINE('Price is too high');
WHEN no_data_found THEN DBMS_OUTPUT.PUT_LINE('Out of data');
when others THEN DBMS_OUTPUT.PUT_LINE('Error-' || SQLERRM);
END;
```

5.7.2 Embedded SQL

Another way that SQL can be used is to embed it in programs written in a general-purpose programming language such as C, C++, Java, COBOL, Ada, Fortran, Visual Basic, and other programming languages, referred to as **host languages**. Unlike PSMs, these programs do not reside in the database space, and are referred to as client-side programs. Any interactive SQL command can be used in an application program, with minor modifications. The programmer writes the source code using both host language statements, which provide the control structures, and SQL statements, which manage the database access. Executable SQL statements are preceded by a prefix such as the keyword EXEC SQL, and end with a terminator such as a semicolon. An executable SQL statement can appear wherever an executable host language statement can appear. The DBMS provides a precompiler, which scans the entire program and strips out the SQL statements, identified by the prefix. The SQL is compiled separately into an access module, and the SQL statements are replaced, usually by simple function calls in the host language. The resulting host language program can then be compiled as usual. Figure 5.9 illustrates this process.

The data exchange between the application program and the database is accomplished through the host-language program variables, for which

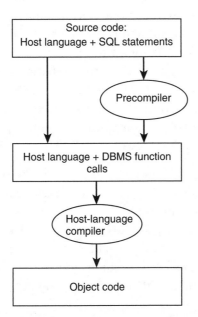

FIGURE 5.9

Processing Embedded SQL Programs

attributes of database records provide values or from which they receive their values. The available datatypes are determined by the host language. These **shared variables** are declared within the program in an SQL declaration section such as the following:

```
EXEC SQL BEGIN DECLARE SECTION;
varchar stuNumber[6];
varchar stuLastName[20];
varchar stuFirstName[20];
varchar stuMajor[10];
int stuCredits;
char SQLSTATE[6];
EXEC SQL END DECLARE SECTION;
```

The first five program variables declared here are designed to match the attributes of the `Student` table. They can be used to receive values from `Student` tuples, or to supply values to tuples. Other common datatypes are `short` and `long` (for integers), `float` and `double` (for floating-point numbers), `char` for a single character and `char[n]` for a string of length n. SQL provides language bindings that specify the correspondence between SQL data types and the data types of each host language.

The last variable declared, SQLSTATE, is a status variable, a character array that is used for communicating warnings and error conditions to the program. When an SQL library function is called, a value is placed in SQLSTATE indicating which error condition may have occurred when the database was accessed. For example, a value of '00000' indicates no error, while a value '02000' indicates that the SQL statement executed correctly but no tuple was found for a query. The value of SQLSTATE can be tested in host language control statements. For example, some processing may be performed if the value is '00000', or a loop may be written to read a record until the value of '02000' is returned. Error handling routines may be written to provide appropriate messages and actions depending on the value of SQLSTATE.

Embedded SQL SELECT statements that operate on a single row of a table are very similar to the interactive statements we saw earlier. For example, a SELECT statement that retrieves a single tuple is modified for the embedded case by identifying the shared variables in an INTO line. Note that when shared variables are referred to within an SQL statement, they are preceded by colons to distinguish them from attributes, which might or might not have the same names. The following example begins with a host-language statement assigning a value to the host variable `stuNumber`. It then uses an SQL SELECT statement to retrieve a tuple from the `Student` table whose `stuId` matches the shared variable `stuNumber` (referred to as `:stuNumber` in the SQL statement). It puts the tuple's attribute values into four shared variables that were declared previously:

```
stuNumber = 'S1001';
EXEC SQL  SELECT  Student.lastName, Student.firstName, Student.major,
Student.credits
    INTO :stuLastName, :stuFirstName, :stuMajor, :stuCredits
    FROM Student
    WHERE Student.stuId = :stuNumber;
```

This segment should be followed by a host-language check of the value of SQLSTATE, to make sure it is 00000 before processing the values, or to do other tasks for other SQLSTATE values.

To insert a database tuple, we can assign values to shared variables in the host language and then use an SQL INSERT statement. The attribute values are taken from the host variables. For example, we could write:

```
stuNumber = 'S1050';
stuLastName = 'Lee';
stuFirstName = 'Daphne';
stuMajor = 'English';
stuCredits = 0;
EXEC SQL    INSERT
            INTO Student (stuId, lastName, firstName, major, credits)
            VALUES(:stuNumber,:stuLastName, :stuFirstName,:stuMajor,
:stuCredits);
```

We can delete any number of tuples that we can identify using the value of a host variable:

```
stuNumber = 'S1015';
EXEC SQL    DELETE
            FROM Student
            WHERE stuId = :stuNumber;
```

We can also update any number of tuples in a similar manner:

```
stuMajor = 'History';
EXEC SQL UPDATE Student
            SET CREDITS = CREDITS + 3
            WHERE major = :stuMajor;
```

An alternative method of handling errors is to include a special SQL communications area, SQLCA, in the host program. Depending on the language, this is done by a statement such as

```
EXEC SQL INCLUDE SQLCA;
```

or

```
#include <sqlca.h>
```

After every executable SQL statement, an error code is returned to the communication area. The programmer can either check the value of the code, or write a WHENEVER directive in the program to handle various errors. It is advisable to place it early in the program. Its form is

```
EXEC SQL WHENEVER <condition><action>;
```

The condition can be NOT FOUND (meaning no rows were returned), SQLERROR, or SQLWARNING. The action can be CONTINUE (appropriate only for a warning, since the program continues to run, turning off the error checking), DO (which can be used to transfer control to an error-handling routine), DO BREAK (which can be used to exit a loop in which the SQL statement appeared), GOTO *labelname*, (which sends control to a labeled statement), or STOP, which terminates the program and disconnects from Oracle.

An **impedance mismatch** can occur when a SELECT statement returns more than one row, since most host languages are not capable of handling sets. A cursor is created and positioned so that it can point to one row in the multi-set at a time. The cursor is declared and opened the same way in embedded SQL as in a PSM. The form for declaring a cursor is:

```
EXEC SQL DECLARE cursorname CURSOR FOR query
[FOR {READ ONLY | UPDATE OF attributeNames}];
```

For example, to create a cursor for a query to find CSC majors, we would write:

```
EXEC SQL DECLARE CSCstuCursor CURSOR FOR
    SELECT stuId, lastName, firstName, credits
    FROM student
    WHERE major='CSC';
```

To open the cursor we write:

```
EXEC SQL OPEN CSCstuCursor;
```

To retrieve a row of the results, we then use the FETCH command, which has the form,

```
EXEC SQL FETCH CSCstuCursor INTO :stuNumber,:stuLastName,
:stuFirstName,:stuCredits
```

A loop controlled by the value of SQLSTATE (e.g., WHILE (SQLSTATE = 00000)) can be created in the host language so that additional rows are accessed. The loop also contains host language statements to do whatever processing is needed. After all data has been retrieved, we exit the loop, and close the cursor in a statement such as:

```
EXEC SQL CLOSE CSCstuCursor;
```

If we plan to update rows using the cursor, we must initially declare it to be updatable by using a more complete declaration such as:

```
EXEC  SQL DECLARE stuCreditsCursor CURSOR FOR
      SELECT stuId, credits
      FROM Student
FOR UPDATE OF credits;
```

We must name in both the SELECT statement and the update attribute list any attribute that we plan to update using the cursor. Once the cursor is open and active, we can update the tuple at which the cursor is positioned, called the **current** of the cursor, by writing a command such as:

```
EXEC SQL UPDATE Student
SET credits = credits + 3
WHERE CURRENT OF stuCreditsCursor;
```

Similarly, the current tuple can be deleted by a statement such as:

```
EXEC SQL DELETE FROM Student
WHERE CURRENT OF stuCreditCursor;
```

5.7.3   Dynamic SQL

Users may wish to be able to specify the type of access they need at run time rather than in a static fashion using compiled code of the type just described. For example, we might want a graphical front end where the user could enter a query that can be used to generate SQL statements that are executed dynamically, like the interactive SQL described earlier. Besides the version of SQL just discussed, which is classified as static, there is a **dynamic SQL**, which allows the type of database access to be specified at run time rather than at compile time. For example, the user may be prompted to enter an SQL command that is then stored as a host-language string. The SQL PREPARE command tells the database management system to parse and compile the string as an SQL command, and to assign the resulting executable code to a named SQL variable. An EXECUTE command is then used to run the code. For example, in the following segment the host-language variable userString is assigned an SQL update command, the corresponding code is prepared and bound to the SQL identifier userCommand, and then the code is executed.

```
char userString[]='UPDATE Student SET credits = 36 WHERE stuId= S1050';
EXEC SQL PREPARE userCommand FROM :userString;
EXEC SQL EXECUTE userCommand;
```

5.7.4   APIs

For embedded SQL, a precompiler supplied by the DBMS compiles the SQL code, replacing it with function calls in the host language. A more flexible approach is for the DBMS to provide an **Application Programming Interface**, API, that includes a set of standard library functions for database processing. The library functions can then be called by the application, which is written in a general purpose language. Programmers use these library functions in essentially the same way they use the library of the language itself. The functions allow the application to perform standard operations such as connecting to the database, executing SQL commands, presenting tuples one at a time, and so on. However, the application would still have to use the precompiler for a particular DBMS and be linked to the API library for that DBMS, so the same program could not be used with another DBMS.

Open Database Connectivity (ODBC) and **JDBC** were created to provide standard ways of integrating SQL code and general-purpose languages by providing a common interface. This standardization allows applications to access multiple databases using different DBMSs. The standard provides a high degree of flexibility, allowing development of client-server applications that work with a variety of DBMSs, instead of being limited to a particular vendor API. Most vendors provide ODBC or JDBC drivers that conform to the standard. An application using one of these standard interfaces can use the same code to access different databases without recompilation. ODBC/JDBC architecture requires four components—the application, driver manager, driver, and data source (normally a database),

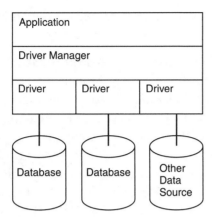

FIGURE 5.10
ODBC/JDBC Architecture

as illustrated in Figure 5.10. The application initiates the connection with the database, submits data requests as SQL statements to the DBMS, retrieves the results, performs processing, and terminates the connection, all using the standard API. A driver manager loads and unloads drivers at the application's request, and passes the ODBC or JDBC calls to the selected driver. The database driver links the application to the data source, translates the ODBC or JDBC calls to DBMS-specific calls, and handles data translation needed because of any differences between the DBMS's data language and the ODBC/JDBC standard, and error-handling differences that arise between the data source and the standard. The data source is the database (or other source, such as a spreadsheet) being accessed, along with its environment, consisting of its DBMS and platform. There are different levels of conformance defined for ODBC and JDBC drivers, depending on the type of relationship between the application and the database. This topic will be discussed in more detail in Chapter 13.

5.8 The System Catalog

The **system catalog** or **system data dictionary** can be thought of as a database of information about databases. It contains, in table form, a summary of the structure of each database as it appears at a given time. Whenever a base table, view, index, constraint, stored module, or other item of a database schema is created, altered, or dropped, the DBMS automatically updates its entries in the catalog. The system also uses the catalog to check authorizations and to store information for access plans for applications. Users can query the data dictionary using ordinary SQL SELECT commands. However, since the data dictionary is maintained by the DBMS itself, the SQL UPDATE, INSERT, and DELETE commands cannot be used on it.

The **Oracle data dictionary** contains information about all schema objects, but access to it is provided through three different views, called USER, ALL, and DBA. In Oracle, each user is automatically given access to all the objects he or she creates. The **USER view** provides a user with information about all the objects created by that user. Users can be given access to objects that are created by others. The **ALL view** provides information about those objects in addition to the one the user has created. The **DBA view**, which provides information about all database objects, is available to the database administrator. Each of the views is invoked by using the appropriate term as a prefix for the object(s) named in the FROM clause in a query. For example, if a user wants a list of the names of all the tables he or she has created, the query is:

On the Companion Website:
- SQL code for all Oracle Catalog queries.

```
SELECT TABLE_NAME
    FROM USER_TABLES;
```

Queries can be written by using the appropriate prefix (USER_, ALL_, DBA_) in the FROM clause, followed by one of the categories CATALOG, CONSTRAINTS, CONS_COLUMNS (columns that have constraints), DICTIONARY, IND_COLUMNS (columns that have indexes), INDEXES, OBJECTS, TAB_COLUMNS (table columns), TRIGGERS, ROLES, PROFILES, SEQUENCES, SOURCE (source code for a module), SYS_PRIVS, USERS, TABLES, TABLESPACES, VIEWS, and other objects in the schema. For each of these categories, each of the three views (USER, ALL, DBA) has several columns. Generally, you can assume that each category has a column for the name of the object, which you can use to write a query such as:

```
SELECT VIEW_NAME
    FROM USER_VIEWS;
```

To determine what all the available columns are, you can use the wild card (*) in the SELECT clause. For example,

```
SELECT *
    FROM USER_TAB_COLUMNS;
```

will display all the recorded information about the columns in the tables you have created. Then you can use the view's column names (e.g., COLUMN_NAME, DATA_TYPE) in a more targeted query, such as:

```
SELECT COLUMN_NAME, DATA_TYPE
    FROM USER_TAB_COLUMNS
    WHERE TABLE_NAME = 'STUDENT';
```

Another way to learn about the objects is to use the DESCRIBE command. Once you know the name of an object (e.g., a table, constraint, column), which you can obtain by one of the methods just illustrated, you can ask for a description of it. For example, you can write,

```
DESCRIBE STUDENT;
```

to see what is known about the Student table, or,

```
DESCRIBE HISTMAJ;
```

to see what is known about the HISTMAJ view that we created earlier. If we want to learn what information is available about constraints in the USER view, we would write:

```
DESCRIBE USER_CONSTRAINTS;
```

We can then write a query using the names of the columns that are displayed, such as:

```
SELECT CONSTRAINT_NAME, CONSTRAINT_TYPE, TABLE_NAME
FROM USER_CONSTRAINTS;
```

For information about triggers, the command,

```
SELECT TRIGGER_NAME, TRIGGER_TYPE
FROM USER_TRIGGERS;
```

provides useful information about them.

5.9 Chapter Summary

Oracle, IBM's DB2, Informix, Sybase, MySQL, SQL Server, Access, and other relational database management systems use **SQL**, a standard relational DDL and DML. On the logical level, each relation is represented by a **base table**. The external level consists of **views**, which are created from subsets, combinations, or other operations on the base tables. A base table can have many indexes defined on it. Dynamic database definition allows the structure to be changed at any time.

SQL DDL commands **CREATE TABLE** and **CREATE INDEX** are used to create the base tables and their indexes. Several built-in **data types** are available for strictly relational databases. **Constraints** can be specified on the column or table level. The **ALTER TABLE** command allows changes to existing tables, such as adding a new column, dropping a column, changing data types, or changing constraints. The **RENAME TABLE** command allows the user to change a table's name. **DROP TABLE** and **DROP INDEX** remove tables and indexes, along with all the data in them, from the database.

The **DML** commands are **SELECT**, **UPDATE**, **INSERT**, and **DELETE**. The SELECT command has several forms, and it performs the equivalent of the relational algebra SELECT, PROJECT, and JOIN operations. Options include **GROUP BY**, **ORDER BY**, **GROUP BY ... HAVING**, **LIKE**, and built-in aggregate functions **COUNT**, **SUM**, **AVG**, **MAX**, and **MIN**. The SELECT statement can operate on joins of tables, and can handle **subqueries**, including correlated subqueries. Expressions and set operations are also possible. The UPDATE command may be used to update one or more fields in one or more records. The INSERT command can insert one or more records, possibly with null values for some fields. The DELETE operator erases records, while leaving the table structure intact.

The **CREATE VIEW** command is used to define a view by selecting fields from existing base tables or previously defined views. The SELECT operation can be used on views, but other DML commands are restricted to certain types of views. A view definition can be destroyed by a DROP VIEW command.

An active database is one where the DBMS actively monitors changes to ensure that only legal instances of the database are created. A combination of constraints and **triggers** may be used to create an active database.

The **COMMIT** statement makes permanent all changes that have been made by the current transaction. The **ROLLBACK** statement undoes all changes that were made by the current transaction. The current transaction begins immediately after the last COMMIT or ROLLBACK, or if neither of these occurred, then at the beginning of the current user session.

SQL is often used in a programming environment rather than interactively. It can be used as a complete language using its own **SQL PSM**s. Oracle's PL/SQL is an example of a complete programming environment for creating SQL PSMs. It can be **embedded** in a host programming language and separately compiled by a **precompiler**. It can be used with a standard API through **ODBC** or **JDBC**.

The **system catalog** or **system data dictionary** is a database containing information about the user's database. It keeps track of the tables, columns, indexes, and views that exist, as well as authorization information and other data. The system automatically updates the catalog when structural changes and other modifications are made.

Exercises

5.1   Write the commands needed to create indexes for the Student, Faculty, Class, and Enroll tables in this chapter.

5.2   For each of the join examples (Examples 7–11) in Section 5.4.2, replace the join by a subquery, if possible. If not possible, explain why not.

Directions for Exercises 5.3–5.25: For the schema that follows, write the indicated commands in SQL. Figure 5.11 shows the DDL for creating these tables. It shows that departmentName is a foreign key in the

```
CREATE TABLE Dept(
departmentName VARCHAR2(15),
mgrId NUMBER(6),
CONSTRAINT Dept_departName_pk PRIMARY KEY (departmentName));

CREATE TABLE Worker (
empId NUMBER(6),
lastName VARCHAR2(20) NOT NULL,
firstName VARCHAR2(15) NOT NULL,
departmentName VARCHAR2(15),
birthDate DATE,
hireDate DATE,
salary NUMBER(8,2),
CONSTRAINT Worker_empId_pk PRIMARY KEY (empId),
CONSTRAINT Worker_departname_fk FOREIGN KEY (departmentName) REFERENCES
Dept(departmentName));
```

Figure 5.11
DDL and Insert Statements for Worker-Project-Assign Example

Figure 5.11
(continued)

```
CREATE TABLE Project(
projNo NUMBER(6),
projName VARCHAR2(20),
projMgrId NUMBER(6),
budget NUMBER (8,2),
startDate DATE,
expectedDurationWeeks NUMBER(4),
CONSTRAINT Project_projNo_pk PRIMARY KEY (projNo),
CONSTRAINT Project_projMgrId_fk FOREIGN KEY(projMgrId) REFERENCES
WORKER(empId));

CREATE TABLE Assign (
projNo NUMBER(6),
empId NUMBER(6),
hoursAssigned NUMBER(3),
rating NUMBER(1),
CONSTRAINT Assign_projNo_empId_pk PRIMARY KEY (projNo, empId),
CONSTRAINT Assign_projNo_fk FOREIGN KEY (projNo) REFERENCES Project(projNo) ON
DELETE CASCADE,
CONSTRAINT Assign_empId_fk FOREIGN KEY (empId) REFERENCES Worker(empId) ON
DELETE CASCADE);

INSERT INTO Dept(departmentName) VALUES('Accounting');
INSERT INTO Dept(departmentName) VALUES('Research');

INSERT INTO Worker VALUES(101,'Smith','Tom','Accounting','01-Feb-1960','06-Jun-
2009',50000);
INSERT INTO Worker VALUES(103,'Jones','Mary','Accounting','15-Jun-1965','20-Sep-
2010',48000);
INSERT INTO Worker VALUES(105,'Burns','Jane','Accounting','21-Sep-1970','12-Jun-
2008',39000);
INSERT INTO Worker VALUES(110,'Burns','Michael','Research','05-Apr-1967','10-Sep-
2009',70000);
INSERT INTO Worker VALUES(115,'Chin','Amanda','Research','22-Sep-1965','19-Jun-
2010',60000);

UPDATE Dept SET mgrId = 101 WHERE departmentName ='Accounting';
UPDATE Dept SET mgrId = 110 WHERE departmentName ='Research';
```

```
INSERT INTO Project VALUES (1001, 'Jupiter', 101, 300000, '01-JUL-2009', 50);
INSERT INTO Project VALUES (1005, 'Saturn', 101, 400000, '01-JUL-2010', 35);
INSERT INTO Project VALUES (1019, 'Mercury', 110, 350000, '15-FEB-2010', 40);
INSERT INTO Project VALUES (1025, 'Neptune', 110, 600000, '01-FEB-2011', 45);
INSERT INTO Project VALUES (1030, 'Pluto', 110, 380000, '15-MAY-2011', 50);


INSERT INTO Assign(projNo,empId, hoursAssigned) VALUES(1001, 101, 30);
INSERT INTO Assign VALUES(1001, 103, 20,5);
INSERT INTO Assign(projNo,empId, hoursAssigned)  VALUES(1005, 103, 20);
INSERT INTO Assign(projNo,empId, hoursAssigned)  VALUES(1001, 105, 30);
INSERT INTO Assign VALUES(1001, 115, 20,4);
INSERT INTO Assign VALUES(1019, 110, 20,5);
INSERT INTO Assign VALUES(1019, 115, 10,4);
INSERT INTO Assign(projNo,empId, hoursAssigned)  VALUES(1025, 110, 10);
INSERT INTO Assign(projNo,empId, hoursAssigned)  VALUES(1030, 110, 10);
```

Figure 5.11
(continued)

`Worker` table, that `mgrId` is a foreign key in the `Dept` table, that `proj-MgrId` is a foreign key in the `Project` table, and that `projNo` and `empId` are foreign keys in the `Assign` table. We assume each department has a manager, and each project has a manager, but these are not necessarily related. (Note: It is recommended that you do Lab Exercise 5.1 in conjunction with these exercises. If Oracle is not available, you can use another relational DBMS, including the freeware MySQL, which you can download. Depending on the product, you may need to make some changes to the DDL. If you do not plan to do Lab Exercise 5.1, you can simply write out the commands.)

On the Companion Website:
- SQL code for Tables for Exer 5.3–5.25

```
Worker (empId, lastName, firstName, departmentName, birthDate, hireDate,
salary)
Dept (departmentName, mgrId)
Project (projNo, projName, projMgrId, budget, startDate,
expectedDurationWeeks)
Assign (projNo, empId, hoursAssigned, rating)
```

5.3 Get the names of all workers in the accounting department.

5.4 Get an alphabetical list of names of all workers assigned to project 1001.

5.5 Get the name of the employee in the research department who has the lowest salary.

5.6   Get details of the project with the highest budget.

5.7   Get the names and departments of all workers on project 1019.

5.8   Get an alphabetical list of names and corresponding ratings of all workers on any project that is managed by Michael Burns.

5.9   Create a view that has project number and name of each project, along with the IDs and names of all workers assigned to it.

5.10   Using the view created in Exercise 5.9, find the project number and project name of all projects to which employee 110 is assigned.

5.11   Add a new worker named Jack Smith with ID of 1999 to the research department.

5.12   Change the hours that employee 110 is assigned to project 1019, from 20 to 10.

5.13   For all projects starting after May 1, 2010, find the project number and the IDs and names of all workers assigned to them.

5.14   For each project, list the project number and how many workers are assigned to it.

5.15   Find the employee names and department manager names of all workers who are not assigned to any project.

5.16   Find the details of any project with the word "urn" anywhere in its name.

5.17   Get a list of project numbers and names and starting dates of all projects that have the same starting date.

5.18   Add a field called `status` to the `Project` table. Sample values for this field are `active`, `completed`, `planned`, `cancelled`. Then write the command to undo this change.

5.19   Get the employee ID and project number of all employees who have no ratings on that project.

5.20   Assuming that `salary` now contains annual salary, find each worker's ID, name, and monthly salary.

5.21   Add a field called `numEmployeesAssigned` to the `Project` table. Use the UPDATE command to insert values into the field to correspond to the current information in the `Assign` table. Then write a trigger that will update the field correctly whenever an assignment is made, dropped, or updated. Write the command to make these changes permanent.

5.22 Write an Oracle data dictionary query to show the names of all the columns in a table called `Customers`.

5.23 Write an Oracle data dictionary query to find all information about all columns named PROJNO.

5.24 Write an Oracle data dictionary query to get a list of names of people who have created tables, along with the number of tables each has created. Assume you have DBA privileges.

5.25 Write an Oracle data dictionary query to find the names of tables that have more than two indexes.

On the Companion Website:

- Lab Exercises

- Sample Project

- Student Projects

CHAPTER 6

Normalization

Chapter Objectives

In this chapter you will learn the following:

- Why relations should be normalized

- The meaning of update, insertion, and deletion anomalies

- The meaning of functional dependency and its relationship to keys

- The definition of first normal form and how to achieve it

- The meaning of full functional dependency

- The definition of second normal form and how to achieve it

- The meaning of transitive dependency

- The definition of third normal form and how to achieve it

- The definition of Boyce-Codd Normal Form and how to achieve it

6.1   Objectives of Normalization

The basic objective of logical modeling is to develop a "good" description of the data, its relationships, and its constraints. For the relational model, this means we must identify a suitable set of relations. However, the task of choosing the relations is a difficult one, because there are many options for the designer to consider. This chapter explains some methods of improving logical design. The techniques presented here are based on a large body of research into the logical design process generally called normalization. When a schema is normalized, each relation has a "theme," relaying facts about a single subject, which can either be an entity or a relationship. All attributes depend on the entire key, and no other non-key attributes in the relation. Each cell of the table contains a single fact about that subject.

The purpose of normalization is to produce a stable set of relations that is a faithful model of the operations of the enterprise. By following the principles of normalization, we achieve a design that is highly flexible, allowing the model to be extended when needed to account for new attributes, entity sets, and relationships. We design the database in such a way that we can enforce certain types of integrity constraints easily. We can also reduce redundancy, both to save space and to avoid inconsistencies in data. We also ensure that the design is free of certain update, insertion, and deletion anomalies. An anomaly is an inconsistent, incomplete, or contradictory state of the database. If these anomalies were present, we would be unable to represent some information, we might lose information when certain updates were performed, and we would run the risk of having data become inconsistent over time.

6.2   Insertion, Update, and Deletion Anomalies

Consider the following relation.

```
NewClass(classNo, stuId, stuLastName, facId, schedule, room, grade)
```

An instance of this relation appears in Figure 6.1. In this example, we will assume that there is only one faculty member for each class (i.e., no team teaching). We also assume each class is always scheduled for the same room. This relation exhibits update, insertion, and deletion anomalies.

- **Update anomaly.** Suppose we wished to change the schedule of ART103A to MWF12. It is possible we might update the first two records of the `NewClass` table but not the third, resulting in an inconsistent state in the database. It would then be impossible to tell the true schedule for that class. This is an update anomaly.

- **Insertion anomaly.** An insertion anomaly occurs when we try to add information about a class for which no student has yet registered. For example, suppose we create a new class, with values MTH110A, F110, MTuTh10, H225 for `classNumber`, `facId`, `schedule`, and `room`. We are unable to record the class information, even though we have the values for these attributes. Since the key is {`classNo, stuId`}, we are not permitted to insert a record with a null value for `stuId`. Because we are not able to represent this class information, we have an insertion anomaly. The same problem would occur if we tried to insert information about a student who had not yet registered for any class.

- **Deletion anomaly.** When we delete the record of the only student taking a particular class, a deletion anomaly occurs. For example, if student S1001 dropped out of HST205A, we would delete the only record with information about that class. It would be desirable to keep the class information, but we cannot do so without a corresponding `stuId`. Similarly, if a student drops the only class he or she is taking, we lose all information about that student.

Research into these anomalies was first done by E. F. Codd, who identified the causes and defined the first three "normal forms." A relation is in a specific normal form if it satisfies the set of requirements or constraints for

FIGURE 6.1

The NewClass Table

classNo	stuId	stuLastName	facId	schedule	room	grade
ART103A	S1001	Smith	F101	MWF9	H221	A
ART103A	S1010	Burns	F101	MWF9	H221	
ART103A	S1006	Lee	F101	MWF9	H221	B
CSC201A	S1003	Jones	F105	TUTHF10	M110	A
CSC201A	S1006	Lee	F105	TUTHF10	M110	G
HST205A	S1001	Smith	F202	MWF11	H221	

that form. Note that the constraints we are discussing here are schema constraints, permanent properties of the relation, not merely of some instance of the relation. They are properties of the intension, not just of a particular extension. Later research by Boyce and Codd led to a refinement of the third of these forms. Additional research by Fagin, Zaniolo, and Delobel (each independently) resulted in the definition of three new normal forms. All of the normal forms are nested, in that each satisfies the constraints of the previous one, but is a "better" form because each eliminates flaws found in the previous form. Our design objective should be to put the schema in the highest normal form that is practical and appropriate for the database. Normalization means putting a relation into a higher normal form. Normalization requires that we have a clear grasp of the semantics of the model. Merely examining an instance or extension is not sufficient, because an instance does not provide enough information about all the possible values or combinations of values for relation attributes.

In attempting to pinpoint the causes of update, insertion, and deletion anomalies, researchers have identified three kinds of dependencies: **functional dependencies**, **multivalued dependencies**, and **join dependencies**. Additional dependency types appear in the research literature.

6.3   Functional Dependency

A **functional dependency (FD)** is a type of relationship between attributes, as described in the following definition:

> **Definition:** If R is a relation schema and A and B are non-empty sets of attributes in R, we say that B is **functionally**

dependent on A if, and only if, each value of A in R has associated with it exactly one value of B in R.

We write this as,

$$A \rightarrow B$$

which we read as "A functionally determines B." The definition says that if two tuples in an extension of R have the same value for A, they must also have the same values for B. More formally, for every pair of tuples, t_1 and t_2, in every instance of R, we have the following rule:

If $t_1.A = t_2.A$ then $t_1.B = t_2.B$

Here, the notation $t_1.A$ means the projection of tuple t_1 onto the attributes of set A. Functional dependency does not mean that A **causes** B or that the value of B can be calculated from the value of A by a formula, although sometimes that is the case. It simply means that if we know the value of A and we examine the table of relation R, we will find only one value of B in all the rows that have the given value of A. Thus, when two rows have the same A value, they must also have the same B value. However, for a given B value, there may be several different A values. A functional dependency is actually a **many-to-one relationship** from attribute set A to attribute set B. It is an **integrity constraint** that every instance of the database must obey. Note that A or B can be sets that consist of a single attribute each. When a functional dependency exists, the set of attributes on the left side of the arrow (A in this example) is called a **determinant** and the set of attributes on the right side of the arrow is called the **dependent**.

To illustrate functional dependency, consider the following relation:

```
NewStudent(stuId, lastName, major, credits, status, socSecNo)
```

Figure 6.2 shows an instance of the relation. This relation stores information about students in a college. Here, we will assume that every student has a unique ID and social security number and that each student has at most one major. We will assume that last names are not unique, that two different students may have the same last name. The attribute `credits` means the number of credits completed, and `status` refers to the year the student is in—freshman, sophomore, junior, or senior. Although we will use this instance to help us detect functional dependencies, we are trying to determine permanent characteristics of the relation, not simply of the instance. Examining the table, we see that if we are given a specific value of `stuId`, there is only one value of `lastName` associated with that particular `stuId`.

NewStudent					
stuId	**LastName**	**major**	**credits**	**status**	**socSecNo**
S1001	Smith	History	90	Senior	100429500
S1003	Jones	Math	95	Senior	010124567
S1006	Lee	CSC	15	Freshman	088520876
S1010	Burns	Art	63	Junior	099320985
S1060	Jones	CSC	25	Freshman	064624738

FIGURE 6.2

Instance of NewStudent Table (assume each student has only one major)

For example, for stuId S1006, the associated lastName is Lee. Because we understand that each student is given a unique ID, we know that this is a characteristic of the relation, not just of this instance, so {lastName} is functionally dependent on {stuId}, and we can write,

{stuId} → {lastName}

However, for a given value of lastName there may be more than one stuId. We note that for the lastName Jones there are two stuId values, S1003 and S1060. Therefore we cannot turn the functional dependency around and write {lastName} → {stuId}. For each of the other attributes, there is only one value associated with a particular value of stuId, so all the attributes are functionally dependent on stuId. We have,

```
{stuId}→ {stuId}
{stuId}→ {lastName}
{stuId}→ { major}
{stuId}→ {credits}
{stuId}→ {status}
{stuId}→ {socSecNo}
```

which we will write in abbreviated form as,

{stuId }→ {stuId, lastName, major, credits, status, socSecNo}

to indicate that each of the attributes on the right is functionally dependent on stuId. Note that we listed stuId as being functionally dependent on itself, a fact that is true of every attribute. Similarly we have,

{socSecNo} → {socSecNo, stuId, lastName, major, credits, status}

We also note that status is functionally dependent on credits. For example, if the value of credits is 15, the status is automatically freshman. We write,

{credits} → {status}

For sets consisting of a single attribute like these, we will write just the attribute name, and drop the set braces. For this case of functional dependency, the determinant, `credits`, does **not** functionally determine all the other attributes of the relation. Note also that the value of `credits` is not necessarily unique. Several students could have the same number of credits, so uniqueness is not a necessary characteristic of determinants. The instance in Figure 6.2 did not really demonstrate the lack of uniqueness of `credits`, which shows that we must be careful in making judgments from instances only. We need to consider the meanings of the attributes and their constraints in identifying functional dependencies. Note that we do not have the FD `status` → `credits`, since, for example, two freshmen may have a different number of credits, as we see in the records of S1006 and S1060.

Certain functional dependencies are called **trivial** because they are always satisfied in every relation. In trivial functional dependencies, the dependent set is a subset of the determinant. If all the attributes in the set on the right-hand side are included in the set on the left-hand side of the dependency, or if the two sides are the same, the FD is trivial. For example, the following FDs are trivial:

```
{A,B}→ A
{A,B}→ B
{A,B}→ {A,B}
```

6.4   Superkeys, Candidate Keys, and Primary Keys

Recall from Chapter 3 that a **superkey** is an attribute or a set of attributes that uniquely identifies an entity. In a table, a superkey is any column or set of columns whose values can be used to distinguish one row from another. Therefore, a superkey is any unique identifier. Since a superkey uniquely identifies each entity, it functionally determines all the attributes of a relation. For the `Student` table in Figure 6.2, {`stuId`} is a superkey. So is the combination of {`stuId,lastName`}. In fact, {`stuId`, *any other attribute*} is a superkey for this relation. The same is true for {`socSecNo`, *any other attribute*}. In fact, any set of attributes containing a superkey is also a superkey. However, a superkey may contain additional attributes that are not needed for uniqueness, and we are interested in finding superkeys that do not contain such extra attributes.

A **candidate key** is a superkey such that no proper subset of its attributes is itself a superkey. Therefore, a candidate key must be a **minimal** identifier. In our example, the superkey {`stuId`, `lastName`} is not a candidate key because it contains a proper subset, {stuId}, that is a superkey. However, stuId by itself is a candidate key. Similarly, socSecNo is a candidate key. A relation may have several candidate keys. We will use the term **composite** key to refer to a key that consists of more than one attribute.

A **primary key** is a candidate key that is actually used to identify tuples in a relation. In our example, stuId might be the primary key and socSecNo an alternate key. These two attributes functionally determine each other, and all of the attributes are functionally dependent on each of them. When making a decision about which candidate key to use as the primary key, it is important to consider which choice is a better representation of the real world in which the enterprise functions. We choose stuId rather than socSecNo because, since the university assigns stuId values, we can always be sure of having that value for each student. It is possible we might not always have a social security number for every student. For example, international students may not have social security numbers. There are also privacy rules that limit the use of social security numbers as identifiers, so it is better to avoid using them as the primary key for the university database. Although not explicitly stated in the definition, an important characteristic of a primary key is that none of its attributes may have null values. If we permitted null values in keys, we would be unable to tell records apart, since two records with null values in the same key field might be indistinguishable. For candidate keys, we should specify that their values are also unique in the database. This helps to ensure the quality of data, since we know that duplicate values would be incorrect for these items. It is also desirable to enforce the "no nulls" rule for candidate keys, provided we can be sure the value of the candidate key will be available.

6.5   Normalization Using Primary Keys

In practice, database designers usually develop an initial logical model for a relational database by mapping an E-R diagram or other conceptual model to a set of relations. They identify the primary key and possibly functional dependencies during the conceptual design process. By mapping the E-R diagram to a relational model using the method described in Section 4.7, the designer creates a relational model that is already fairly well normalized. To complete the relational design process, the designer checks each relation, identifies a set of functional dependencies for it if any exist other than the ones involving the primary key, and normalizes it further if necessary. A well-developed set of rules of thumb, or heuristics, is used to guide the normalization process based on primary keys. In the next section we describe this process, using informal definitions of the normal forms.

6.5.1   First Normal Form

We will use a counterexample to describe first normal form. If we assume that a student is permitted to have more than one major, and we try to store multiple majors in the same field of the student record, our `NewStu` table might appear as in Figure 6.3(a). This example violates the definition of first normal form, which follows.

> **Definition:** A relation is in **first normal form** (1NF) if, and only if, every attribute is single-valued for each tuple.

This means that each attribute in each row, or each "cell" of the table, contains only one value. An alternate way of describing first normal form is to say that the domains of the attributes of the relation are **atomic**. This means that no sets, lists, repeating fields, or groups are allowed in the domain. The values in the domain must be single values that cannot be broken down further. In the table in Figure 6.3(a), we see this rule violated in the records of students S1006 and S1010, who now have two values listed for `major`. This is the first such example we have seen, because all the relations we considered until now were in first normal form. In fact, most of strictly relational theory is based on relations in at least first normal form. It is important to have first normal form so that the relational operators, as we have defined them, will work correctly. For example, if we perform the relational algebra operation `SELECT NewStu WHERE major = 'Math'` on the table in Figure 6.3(a), should the record of student S1006 be included? If we were to do a natural join with some other table using `major` as the joining column, would this record be paired with only those having both CSC and Math as `major`, or with those having either CSC or Math? What would happen on the join if another record had a double major listed as Math CSC? To avoid these ambiguities, we will insist that every relation be written in first normal form. If a relation is not already in 1NF, we can rewrite it, creating a new relation consisting of the key of the original relation, plus the multivalued attribute. Therefore, we would

FIGURE 6.3

First Normal Form Examples

FIGURE 6.3(a)

NewStu Table (assume students can have double majors)

stuId	lastName	major	credits	status	socSecNo
S1001	Smith	History	90	Senior	100429500
S1003	Jones	Math	95	Senior	010124567
S1006	Lee	CSC Math	15	Freshman	088520876
S1010	Burns	Art English	63	Junior	099320985
S1060	Jones	CSC	25	Freshman	064624738

FIGURE 6.3(b)

NewStu2 Table and Majors Table

NewStu2				
stuId	lastName	credits	status	socSecNo
S1001	Smith	90	Senior	100429500
S1003	Jones	95	Senior	010124567
S1006	Lee	15	Freshman	088520876
S1010	Burns	63	Junior	099320985
S1060	Jones	25	Freshman	064624738

Majors	
stuId	major
S1001	History
S1003	Math
S1006	CSC
S1006	Math
S1010	Art
S1010	English
S1060	CSC

stuId	lastName	major1	major2	credits	status	socSecNo
S1001	Smith	History		90	Senior	100429500
S1003	Jones	Math		95	Senior	010124567
S1006	Lee	CSC	Math	15	Freshman	088520876
S1010	Burns	Art	English	63	Junior	099320985
S1060	Jones	CSC		25	Freshman	064624738

FIGURE 6.3(c)

NewStu3 Table with Two Attributes for Major

stuId	lastName	major	credits	status	socSecNo
S1001	Smith	History	90	Senior	100429500
S1003	Jones	Math	95	Senior	010124567
S1006	Lee	CSC	15	Freshman	088520876
S1006	Lee	Math	15	Freshman	088520876
S1010	Burns	Art	63	Junior	099320985
S1010	Burns	English	63	Junior	099320985
S1060	Jones	CSC	25	Freshman	064624738

FIGURE 6.3(d)

NewStu Table Rewritten in 1NF, with {stuId, major} as Primary Key

rewrite the `NewStu` table as in Figure 6.3(b) and create a new `Majors` table. We also note that the key of the new table is not `stuId`, since any student with more than one major appears at least twice. We need `{stuId, major}` to uniquely identify a record in that table.

Another method of normalizing to first normal form in the case where we know the maximum number of repeats an attribute can have is to add new columns for the attribute. For example, if we know students can have at most two majors, we could rewrite `NewStu` with two columns for major, `major1` and `major2`, as shown in Figure 6.3(c). The disadvantage of this approach is that we must know the maximum number of repeats, and that queries become more complex. To form a relational algebra selection on the major, we would need to test both the `major1` and `major2` columns.

An alternate method of making the original table 1NF is to make the multivalued attribute part of the key. Using this method, the new table would contain multiple rows for students with multiple majors, as shown in Figure 6.3(d). This solution can cause difficulties when the designer attempts to put the relation into higher normal forms.

6.5.2   Full Functional Dependency and Second Normal Form

For the relation shown in both Figure 6.1 and Figure 6.4(a), we have the following functional dependencies in addition to the trivial ones:

$$\{classNo, stuId\} \rightarrow \{lastName\}$$
$$\{classNo, stuId\} \rightarrow \{facId\}$$
$$\{classNo, stuId\} \rightarrow \{schedule\}$$
$$\{classNo, stuId\} \rightarrow \{room\}$$
$$\{classNo, stuId\} \rightarrow \{grade\}$$

FIGURE 6.4

Second Normal Form Example

classNo	stuId	lastName	facId	schedule	room	grade
ART103A	S1001	Smith	F101	MWF9	H221	A
ART103A	S1010	Burns	F101	MWF9	H221	
ART103A	S1006	Lee	F101	MWF9	H221	B
CSC201A	S1003	Jones	F105	TUTHF10	M110	A
CSC201A	S1006	Lee	F105	TUTHF10	M110	C
HST205A	S1001	Smith	F202	MWF11	H221	

FIGURE 6.4(a)

The NewClass Table, Not in 2NF

Register				Stu			Class2			
classNo	stuId	grade		stuId	lastName		classNo	facId	schedule	room
ART103A	S1001	A		S1001	Smith		ART103A	F101	MWF9	H221
ART103A	S1010			S1010	Burns		CSC201A	F105	TUTHF10	M110
ART103A	S1006	B		S1006	Lee		HST205A	F202	MWF11	H221
CSC201A	S1003	A		S1003	Jones					
CSC201A	S1006	C								

FIGURE 6.4(b)

The Register, Stu, and Class2 Tables in 2NF

Since there is no other candidate key, we chose {classNo,stuId} for the primary key. Again, ignoring trivial functional dependencies, we also have the functional dependencies,

```
classNo → facId
classNo → schedule
classNo → room
stuId → lastName
```

So we find attributes that are functionally dependent on the key {classNo,stuId}, but also functionally dependent on a subset of that key. We say that such attributes are not **fully** functionally dependent on the key.

> **Definition:** In a relation *R,* attribute *A* of *R* is **fully function-ally dependent** on an attribute or set of attributes *X* of *R* if *A* is functionally dependent on *X* but not functionally dependent on any proper subset of *X.*

In our example, although lastName is functionally dependent on {classNo,stuId}, it is also functionally dependent on a proper subset of that combination, namely stuId. Similarly, facId, schedule, and room are functionally dependent on the proper subset classNo. We note that grade is fully functionally dependent on the combination {classNo,stuId}.

> **Definition:** A relation is in **second normal form** (2NF) if, and only if, it is in first normal form and all the non-key attributes are fully functionally dependent on the key.

Clearly, if a relation is 1NF and the key consists of a single attribute, the relation is automatically 2NF. We have to be concerned about 2NF only when the key is composite. From the definition, we see that the Class relation is not in second normal form since, for example, lastName is not fully functionally dependent on the key {classNo,stuId}. Although there are other non-full functional dependencies here, one is sufficient to show that the relation is not 2NF.

A 1NF relation that is not 2NF can be transformed into an equivalent set of 2NF relations. The transformation is done by performing **projections** on the original relation in such a way that it is possible to get back the original by taking the join of the projections. Projections of this type are called **lossless projections**, and will be discussed in more detail in Section 6.6.3. Essentially, to convert a 1NF relation to 2NF, you identify each of the non-full functional dependencies and form projections by removing the attributes that depend on each of the determinants identified as such. These determinants are placed in separate relations along with their dependent attributes. The original relation will still contain the composite key and any attributes that are fully functionally dependent on it. Even if there are no attributes fully functionally dependent on the key of the original relation, it is important to keep the relation (even with only the key attributes) in order to be able to reconstruct the original relation by a join. This "connecting relation" shows how the projections are related.

Applying this method to our example we first identify all the functional dependencies that concern us. For brevity, we will combine attributes that appear as dependents having the same determinant and we drop the set braces on both sides. It is important to note that when we use this less formal notation, attributes on the right-hand side of the arrow can be "broken up" and listed as separate FDs but attributes on the left-hand side must remain together, since it is the combination of them that is a determinant. The functional dependencies are,

```
classNo → facId, schedule, room
stuId → lastName
classNo, stuId → grade (and, of course, facId, schedule, room, lastName)
```

Using projection, we break up the NewClass relation into the following set of relations:

```
Register (classNo, stuId, grade)
Class2 (classNo, facId, schedule, room)
Stu (stuId, lastName)
```

The resulting relations are shown in Figure 6.4(b). Note that we could reconstruct the original relation by taking the natural join of these three relations. Even if there were no grade attribute, we would need the relation Register(classNo,stuId) in order to show which students are enrolled in which classes. Without it, we could not join Class2 and Stu, which have no common attributes. Using these new relations, we have eliminated the update, insertion, and deletion anomalies discussed earlier. We can change the class schedule for ART103A by updating the schedule column in a single record in Class2. We can add new class information to Class2 without having any student registered in the course, and we can insert new student information by adding a record to Stu, without having to insert class information for that student. Similarly, we can drop a registration record from `Register` and still retain the information about the class in `Class2` and about the student in `Stu`.

6.5.3 Transitive Dependency and Third Normal Form

Although second normal form relations are better than those in first normal form, they may still have update, insertion, and deletion anomalies. Consider the following relation:

```
NewStudent (stuId, lastName, major, credits, status)
```

Figure 6.5(a) shows an instance of this relation. Here, the only candidate key is `stuId`, so we will use that as the primary key. Every other attribute

FIGURE 6.5

Third Normal Form Example

FIGURE 6.5(a)

NewStudent Table Not in 3NF

NewStudent

stuId	lastName	major	credits	status
S1001	Smith	History	90	Senior
S1003	Jones	Math	95	Senior
S1006	Lee	CSC	15	Freshman
S1010	Burns	Art	63	Junior
S1060	Jones	CSC	25	Freshman

FIGURE 6.5(b)

NewStu2 and Stats Tables in 3NF

NewStu2

stuId	lastName	major	credits
S1001	Smith	History	90
S1003	Jones	Math	95
S1006	Lee	CSC	15
S1010	Burns	Art	63
S1060	Jones	CSC	25

Stats

credits	status
15	Freshman
25	Freshman
63	Junior
90	Senior
95	Senior

of the relation is functionally dependent on the key, so we have the following functional dependencies, among others,

```
stuId → status
stuId → credits
```

However, since the number of credits determines `status`, as discussed in Section 6.3, we also have,

```
credits → status
```

Using transitivity we have the logical implication

```
(stuId → credits) ∧ (credits → status)⇒ (stuId → status)
```

Thus, `stuId` functionally determines `status` in two ways, directly and transitively, through the non-key attribute `status`.

> **Definition:** If *A, B,* and *C* are attributes of relation *R*, such that *A* → *B*, and *B* → *C*, then *C* is **transitively dependent** on *A*.

For third normal form, we want to eliminate certain transitive dependencies. Transitive dependencies cause insertion, deletion, and update anomalies. For example, in the `NewStudent` table in Figure 6.5(a), we cannot insert the information that any student with 30 credits has Sophomore status until we have such a student, because that would require inserting a record without a `stuId`, which is not permitted. If we delete the record of the only student with a certain number of credits, we lose the information about the status associated with those credits. If we have several records with the same `credits` value and we change the status associated with that value (for example, making 24 credits now have the status of Sophomore), we might accidentally fail to update all of the records, leaving the database in an inconsistent state. Because of these problems, it is desirable to remove transitive dependencies and create a set of relations that satisfy the following definition.

> **Definition:** A relation is in **third normal form** (3NF) if, whenever a non-trivial functional dependency *X* → *A* exists, then either *X* is a superkey or *A* is a member of some candidate key.

The essence of third normal form is that each non-key attribute is functionally dependent on the entire key, and on no other attribute.

In checking for third normal form, we look to see if any non-candidate key attribute (or group of attributes) is functionally dependent on another non-key attribute (or group). If such a functional dependency exists, we remove the functionally dependent attribute from the relation, placing it in a new relation with its determinant. The determinant can remain in the original relation. For our `NewStudent` example, since the undesirable dependency is credits → status, and credits is not a superkey and status is not part of any candidate key, we form the set of relations:

```
NewStu2 (stuId, lastName, major, credits)
Stats (credits, status)
```

This decompostion is shown in Figure 6.5(b). In fact, we may decide not to store status in the database at all, and calculate the status for those views that need it. In that case, we simply drop the Stats relation. For example, we could add a trigger that uses the value of credits and returns a value for status.

This example did not involve multiple candidate keys. If we had a second candidate key, socialSecurityNumber, in the original relation, we would have, among other FDs

```
socialSecurityNumber → status
```

but this is permissible since socialSecurityNumber is a superkey for the relation, so we would have left the social security number in the NewStu2 relation, along with the stuId and the other attributes there, without violating third normal form.

The definition of third normal form is the original one developed by Codd. It is sufficient for relations that have a single candidate key, but was found to be deficient when there are multiple composite candidate keys. Therefore, an improved definition of third normal form, named for its developers, Boyce and Codd, was formulated to take care of all cases.

6.5.4   Boyce-Codd Normal Form

Boyce-Codd Normal Form is slightly stricter than 3NF.

> **Definition:** A relation is in Boyce-Codd Normal Form (BCNF) if, whenever a non-trivial functional dependency $X \rightarrow A$ exists, then X is a superkey.

Therefore, to check for BCNF, we simply identify all the determinants and verify that they are superkeys. If they are not, we break up the relation by projection until we have a set of relations all in BCNF. For each determinant, we create a separate relation with all the attributes it determines, while preserving the ability to recreate the original relation by joins.

In our earlier examples, we started by making sure our relations were in first normal form, then second, then third. However, using BCNF instead, we can check for that form directly without having to go through the first, second, and third normal forms. Looking back, we see that for our `New-Student` relation shown in Figure 6.5(a), the determinants are `stuId` and `credits`. Since `credits` is not a superkey, this relation is not BCNF. Performing the projections as we did in the previous section, we made a separate relation for the determinant `credits` and the attribute it determined, `status`. We also kept `credits` in the original relation, so that we could get the original relation back by a join. The resulting relations are BCNF. For the relation `NewClass` shown in Figure 6.4(a), we found the determinants `classNo`, which is not (by itself) a superkey, and `stuId`, also not a superkey. Therefore the `NewClass` relation is not BCNF. We therefore created a separate table for each of these determinants and any attribute each determined, namely `Stu` and `Class2`, while also keeping a relation, `Register`, that connects the tables. The relations resulting from the projections are BCNF. If there is only a single candidate key, 3NF and BCNF are identical. The only time we have to be concerned about a difference is when we have multiple composite candidate keys. Let us consider an example involving candidate keys in which we have 3NF but not BCNF.

```
NewFac (facName, dept, office, rank, dateHired)
```

For this example, shown in Figure 6.6(a), we will assume that, although faculty names are not unique, no two faculty members within a single department have the same name. We also assume each faculty member has only one office, identified in `office`. A department may have several faculty offices, and faculty members from the same department may share offices. From these assumptions, we have the following FDs. Again, we are dropping set braces, ignoring trivial FDs, and listing dependents with the same determinant on the right-hand side of the arrow. Recall that when multiple attributes appear on the left-hand side of the arrow it means the combination is a determinant.

```
office → dept
facName, dept → office, rank, dateHired
facName, office → dept, rank, dateHired
```

We have overlapping candidate keys of `{facName,dept}` and `{facName,office}`. If we choose `{facName,dept}` as the primary key of `NewFac`, we are left with a determinant, `office`, that is not a superkey. This violates BCNF. Note that the relation is 3NF since `office` is part of a

FIGURE 6.6

Boyce-Codd Normal Form Example

FIGURE 6.6(a)

NewFac Table in 3NF, but Not BCNF

		Faculty		
facName	**dept**	**office**	**rank**	**dateHired**
Adams	Art	A101	Professor	1975
Byrne	Math	M201	Assistant	2000
Davis	Art	A101	Associate	1992
Gordon	Math	M201	Professor	1982
Hughes	Math	M203	Associate	1990
Smith	CSC	C101	Professor	1980
Smith	History	H102	Associate	1990
Tanaka	CSC	C101	Instructor	2001
Vaughn	CSC	C105	Associate	1995

FIGURE 6.6(b)

Fac1 and Fac2 in BCNF

Fac1	
office	**dept**
A101	Art
C101	CSC
C105	CSC
H102	History
M201	Math
M203	Math

Fac2			
facName	**office**	**rank**	**dateHired**
Adams	A101	Professor	1975
Byrne	M201	Assistant	2000
Davis	A101	Associate	1992
Gordon	M201	Professor	1982
Hughes	M203	Associate	1990
Smith	C101	Professor	1980
Smith	H102	Associate	1990
Tanaka	C101	Instructor	2001
Vaughn	C105	Associate	1995

candidate key. To reach BCNF, we can decompose the `Faculty` relation by projection, making a new table in which `office` is a key, as follows

```
Fac1 (office, dept)
Fac2 (facName, office, rank, dateHired)
```

The key of the first relation is `office`, since a department may have several offices, but each office belongs to only one department. It is clearly BCNF, since the only determinant is the key. The key of the second is {`facName,office`}. It is also BCNF, since its only determinant is the key. Note, however, that our final scheme does not preserve the functional dependency {`facName, dept`} → {`office, rank, dateHired`}, since these attributes do not remain in the same relation.

(Note: If we had chosen {`facName,office`} as the primary key of the original `NewFac` relation, we would have `office` → `dept`. Since `office` is not a superkey, the relation would not be BCNF. In fact, it would not be 2NF, since `dept` would not be fully functionally dependent on the key, {`facName,office`}, since it is functionally dependent on `office` alone.)

Any relation that is not BCNF can be decomposed into BCNF relations by the method just illustrated. However, it might not always be desirable to transform the relation into BCNF. In particular, if there is functional dependency that is not preserved when we perform the decomposition, then it becomes difficult to enforce the functional dependency in the database since two or more tables would have to be joined to verify that it is enforced, and an important constraint is lost. In that case, it is preferable to settle for 3NF, which always allows us to preserve dependencies. Our `New-Fac` relation provided an example in which we lost a functional dependency by normalizing to BCNF. In the resulting relations, the attributes `facName` and `dept` appeared in different relations, and we had no way to express the fact that their combination determines all other attributes.

6.5.5   Comprehensive Example of Functional Dependencies

To summarize the various normal forms defined by functional dependencies, consider the following relation that stores information about projects in a large business:

```
Work (projName, projMgr, empId, hours, empName, budget, startDate, salary,
empMgr, empDept, rating)
```

Figure 6.7(a) shows an instance of this relation.

We make the following assumptions:

1. Each project has a unique name.

2. Although project names are unique, names of employees and managers are not.

3. Each project has one manager, whose name is stored in `projMgr`.

4. Many employees can be assigned to work on each project, and an employee can be assigned to more than one project. The attribute `hours` tells the number of hours per week a particular employee is assigned to work on a particular project.

5. `budget` stores the amount budgeted for a project, and `startDate` gives the starting date for a project.

6. `salary` gives the annual salary of an employee.

7. `empMgr` gives the name of the employee's manager, who might not be the same as the project manager.

8. `empDept` gives the employee's department. Department names are unique. The employee's manager is the manager of the employee's department.

9. `rating` gives the employee's rating for a particular project. The project manager assigns the rating at the end of the employee's work on that project.

Using these assumptions, we find the following functional dependencies to begin with,

```
projName → projMgr, budget, startDate
empId → empName, salary, empMgr, empDept
projName, empId → hours, rating
```

Since we assumed people's names were not unique, `empMgr` does not functionally determine `empDept`. (Two different managers may have the same name and manage different departments, or possibly a manager may manage several departments—see `empMgr` Jones in Figure 6.7(a).) Similarly, `projMgr` does not determine `projName`. However, since department names are unique and each department has only one manager, we need to add,

```
empDept → empMgr
```

FIGURE 6.7

Normalization Example

projName	projMgr	empId	hours	empName	budget	startDate	salary	empMgr	empDept	rating
Jupiter	Smith	E101	25	Jones	100000	01/15/04	60000	Levine	10	9
Jupiter	Smith	E105	40	Adams	100000	01/15/04	55000	Jones	12	
Jupiter	Smith	E110	10	Rivera	100000	01/15/04	43000	Levine	10	8
Maxima	Lee	E101	15	Jones	200000	03/01/04	60000	Levine	10	
Maxima	Lee	E110	30	Rivera	200000	03/01/04	43000	Levine	10	
Maxima	Lee	E120	15	Tanaka	200000	03/01/04	45000	Jones	15	

FIGURE 6.7(a)

The Work Table

Proj			
projName	projMgr	budget	startDate
Jupiter	Smith	100000	01/15/04
Maxima	Lee	200000	03/01/04

Dept	
empDept	empMgr
10	Levine
12	Jones
15	Jones

Emp1			
EmpId	empName	salary	empDept
E101	Jones	60000	10
E105	Adams	55000	12
E110	Rivera	43000	10
E120	Tanaka	45000	15

Work1			
projName	empId	hours	rating
Jupiter	Jones	25	9
Jupiter	Adams	40	
Jupiter	Rivera	10	8
Maxima	Jones	15	
Maxima	Rivera	30	
Maxima	Tanaka	15	

FIGURE 6.7(b)

The Normalized Tables Replacing Work

You may ask whether `projMgr` → `budget`. Although it may be the case that the manager determines the budget in the English sense of the word, meaning that the manager comes up with the figures for the budget, you should recall that functional dependency does not mean to cause or to figure out. Similarly, although the project manager assigns a rating to the employee, there is no functional dependency between `projMgr` and `rating`. (If there were, it would mean that each manager always gives the same ratings to those he or she evaluates. For example, it would mean that if the manager's name is Levine, the employee always gets a rating of 9.)

Since we see that every attribute is functionally dependent on the combination {`projName`, `empId`}, we will choose that combination as our primary key, and see what normal form we have. We begin by checking to see whether it is already in BCNF.

BCNF: We look to see if there is a determinant that is not a superkey. Any one of `empId`, `empDept`, or `projName` is sufficient to show that the `Work` relation is not BCNF. Since we know it is not BCNF, let us begin the normalization process by checking the lower normal forms, normalizing the relation(s) as we go along. At the end, we can see if we have reached BCNF.

First Normal Form: With our composite key, {`projName`, `empID`} each cell would be single valued, so `Work` is in 1NF.

Second Normal Form: We found partial (non-full) dependencies.

```
projName → projMgr, budget, startDate
empId → empName, salary, empMgr, empDept
```

We can take care of these, transforming the relation into an equivalent set of 2NF relations by projection, resulting in,

```
Proj (projName, projMgr, budget, startDate)
Emp (empId, empName, salary, empMgr, empDept)
Work1 (projName, empId, hours, rating)
```

Third Normal Form: Using the set of projections, {`Proj`, `Emp`, `Work1`}, we test each relation to see if we have 3NF. Examining `Proj`, we see that no non-key attribute functionally determines another non-key attribute, so `Proj` is 3NF. In `Emp`, we have a transitive dependency, since `empDept` → `empMgr`, as previously explained. Since `empDept` is not a superkey, nor is `empMgr` part of a candidate key, this violates 3NF. Therefore we need to rewrite `Emp` as,

```
Emp1 (empId, empName, salary, empDept)
Dept (empDept, empMgr)
```

`Work1` has no transitive dependency involving hours or rating, so that relation is already 3NF. Our new set of 3NF relations is therefore,

```
Proj (projName, projMgr, budget, startDate)
Emp1 (empId, empName, salary, empDept)
Dept (empDept, empMgr)
Work1 (projName, empId, hours, rating)
```

Boyce-Codd Normal Form revisited: Our new 3NF set of relations is also BCNF, since, in each relation, the only determinant is the primary key.

Figure 6.7(b) shows the new tables that replace the original `Work` table. Note that they can be joined to produce the original table exactly.

6.6   Properties of Relational Decompositions

Although normalization can be carried out using the heuristic approach based on primary keys and demonstrated in the previous sections, a more formal approach to relational database design is based strictly on functional dependencies and other types of constraints. This approach uses formal normalization algorithms to create relation schemas. To begin, all the attributes in the database are placed in a single large relation called the **universal relation**. Using functional dependencies and other constraints, the universal relation is decomposed into smaller relational schemas until the process reaches a point where no further decomposition is preferred. We would like the results of the decomposition process to have some important qualities, if possible. It is desirable to have each relation schema be in BCNF or at least 3NF. Other important properties include attribute preservation, dependency preservation, and lossless joins.

6.6.1   Attribute Preservation

When the universal relation is constructed it contains, by definition, every attribute in the database. In the process of decomposing the universal relation into smaller relations and moving attributes into them, we want to ensure that every attribute appears in at least one of the relations, so no data item is lost. As we saw in our examples, the database schema usually contains some repetition of attributes in order to represent relationships among the tables.

6.6.2   Dependency Preservation

A functional dependency represents a constraint that should be enforced in the database. Whenever an update is performed, the DBMS should check that the constraint is not violated. For a functional dependency, this would involve checking to see whether the value of the determinant in the new tuple already occurs in the table, and if so, then ensuring that the values of any dependent attributes match those of the already-occurring tuples. It is much easier to check constraints within one table than to check one involving multiple tables, which would require doing a join first. To avoid having to do such joins, we would like to be sure that in a decomposition the functional dependencies involve attributes that are all in the same table, if possible. Given a decomposition of a relation R into a set of individual relations $\{R_1, R_2, . . . , R_n\}$, for each functional dependency $X \rightarrow Y$ in the original relation it is desirable for all the attributes in $X \cup Y$ to appear in the same relation, R_i. This property is called **dependency preservation**. It is always possible to find a dependency preserving decomposition that is 3NF, but it is not always possible to find one that is BCNF, as illustrated by the example shown in Figure 6.6 and discussed in Section 6.5.4.

6.6.3   Lossless Decomposition

In splitting relations by means of projection in our earlier examples, we were very explicit about the method of decomposition to use. In particular, we were careful to use projections that could be undone by joining the resulting tables, so that the original table would result. By the term *original table* we do not mean merely the structure of the table, that is, the column names, but the actual tuples as well. The attributes have to be placed in relations in a manner that preserves all of the information in any extension of the table, not just all of the attributes. Such a decomposition is called a nonloss or **lossless decomposition**, because it preserves all the information in the original relation. Although we have used the word decomposition, we have not written a formal definition, and we do so now.

> **Definition:** A **decomposition** of a relation R is a set of relations $\{R_1, R_2, \ldots, R_n\}$ such that each R_i is a subset of R and the union of all of the R_i is R.

Now we are ready for the definition of lossless decomposition.

> **Definition:** A decomposition $\{R_1, R_2, \ldots, R_n\}$ of a relation R is called a **lossless decomposition** for R if the natural join of $R_1, R_2, \ldots, R_n$ produces exactly the relation R.

Not all decompositions are lossless, because there are projections whose join does not give us back the original relation. As an example of a lossy projection, consider the relation EmpRoleProj(empName, role, projName) shown in Figure 6.8(a). The table shows which employees play which roles for which projects. Just for this example, we are assuming that no two employees have the same name, so, for example, there is only one employee named Smith and only one named Jones. The same employee can have different roles in the same project (Smith is both a programmer and designer for the Amazon project) and in different projects (Smith is only a designer for the Nile project), and different employees can have the same role in the same project (both Jones and Smith are designers on the Amazon project). We can decompose the table by projection into the two tables, Table 1 and Table 2 shown in Figure 6.8(b). However, when we join those two tables, in Figure 6.8(c), we get an extra tuple that did not appear in the original table. This is a **spurious** (false) tuple, one created by the projection and join processes. Since, without the original table, we would have no way of identifying which tuples were genuine and which were spurious, we would actually lose information (even though we have more tuples) if we substituted the projections for the original relation.

We can guarantee lossless decomposition by making sure that, for each pair of relations that will be joined, the set of common attributes is a superkey of one of the relations. We can do this by placing functionally dependent attributes in a relation with their determinants and keeping the determinants themselves in the original relation.

More formally, for binary decompositions, if R is decomposed into two relations $\{R_1, R_2\}$ then the join is lossless if, and only if, either of the following holds in the set of FDs for R, or is implied by the FDs in R:

R1 ∩ R2 → R1 − R2

FIGURE 6.8

Example of Lossy Projection

FIGURE 6.8(a)

Original Table EmpRoleProj

EmpRoleProj

empName	role	projName
Smith	designer	Nile
Smith	programmer	Amazon
Smith	designer	Amazon
Jones	designer	Amazon

FIGURE 6.8(b)

Projections of EmpRoleProj

Table 1

empName	role
Smith	designer
Smith	programmer
Jones	designer

Table 2

role	projName
designer	Nile
programmer	Amazon
designer	Amazon

FIGURE 6.8(c)

Join of Table 1 and Table 2

empName	role	projName	
Smith	designer	Nile	
Smith	designer	Amazon	
Smith	programmer	Amazon	
Jones	designer	Nile	←spurious tuple
Jones	designer	Amazon	

or,

```
R1 ∩ R2 → R2 – R1
```

In the example shown in Figure 6.8, `role` was not a determinant for either `projName` or `empName`, so the intersection of the two projections, `role`, did not functionally determine either projection. We saw many examples of lossless projection when we normalized relations.

The test for the lossless join property for the general case is much more complex than that for the binary decomposition case. However, if we limit our projections to successive binary projections, each of which is lossless, the final result will also be lossless. If we have a decomposition D consisting of the set $\{R_1, R_2\}$ which has the lossless join property (easily confirmed by the test for the binary case), and R_2 in turn has a lossless projection $\{T_1, T_2\}$ (also easily tested since it is binary), then the decomposition D_2 consisting of $\{R_1, T_1, T_2\}$ is lossless. We can use this process repeatedly until the final decomposition is shown to be lossless.

6.6.4   Decomposition Algorithm for Boyce-Codd Normal Form with Lossless Join

It is always possible to find a decomposition, D, that is Boyce-Codd Normal Form and that has the lossless join property. The process involves finding each violation of BCNF and removing it by decomposing the relation containing it into two relations. The process is repeated until all such violations are removed. The algorithm is

Given a universal relation R and a set of functional dependencies on the attributes of R:

1. $D \leftarrow R;$

2. while there is some relation schema S in D that is not already BCNF
    {
        a. Find a functional dependency X→ Y in S that violates BCNF
        b. Replace S by two relation schemas (S-Y) and (X,Y)
    }

On the Companion Website:

- Higher Normal Forms
- Formal Relational Design

6.7   The Normalization Process

As we stated at the beginning of this chapter, the objective of normalization is to find a stable set of relations that are a faithful model of the enterprise. We found that normalization eliminated some problems of data representation and resulted in a good schema for the database. There are two different processes that could be used to develop the set of normalized relations, called analysis and synthesis. Most designers choose instead to start with an Entity-Relationship diagram and work from there.

6.7.1 Analysis

The analysis or decomposition approach begins with a list of all the attributes to be represented in the database and assumes that all of them are in a single relation called the universal relation for the database. The designer then identifies functional dependencies among the attributes and uses the techniques of decomposition explained in this chapter to split the universal relation into a set of normalized relations. Our normalization examples in Section 6.5 were all decomposition examples. In particular, in Section 6.5.5 we considered an example in which we had a single relation called Work. Work was actually a universal relation, since all the attributes to be stored in the database were in it. We then wrote out our assumptions and identified four functional dependencies. The functional dependencies enabled us to perform lossless projections, so that we developed a set of relations in BCNF that preserved all functional dependencies. All the constraints expressed in our list of assumptions and all the dependencies we identified in our discussion were considered in developing the final set of relations. This example illustrates the process of analysis from a universal relation. The algorithm given in Section 6.6.4 for finding a lossless BCNF decomposition is an analysis algorithm.

6.7.2 Synthesis

Synthesis is, in a sense, the opposite of analysis. In analysis we begin with a single big relation and break it up until we reach a set of smaller normalized relations. In synthesis we begin with attributes and combine them into related groups, using functional dependencies to develop a set of normalized relations. If analysis is a top-down process, then synthesis is bottom-up. Additional information about this approach is available on the companion website for this text.

6.7.3 Normalization from an Entity-Relationship Diagram

In practice, when a complete E-R diagram exists, the process of normalization is significantly more efficient than either pure analysis or pure synthesis. Using the mapping techniques discussed in Section 4.7, the resulting set of tables is usually fairly well normalized. The designer can begin by checking each relation to see if it is BCNF. If not, the determinants that cause the problems can be examined and the relation normalized using the analysis method described here.

6.8 When to Stop Normalizing

Regardless of the process used, the end result should be a set of normalization relations that form lossless joins and, if possible, preserve dependencies over common attributes. An important question is how far to go in the normalization process. Usually, we try to reach DKNF. However, if that process results in a decomposition that does not preserve dependencies, we may settle for 3NF. It is always possible to find a dependency preserving lossless decomposition for 3NF. Even so, there may be valid reasons for choosing not to implement 3NF as well. For example, if we have attributes that are almost always used together in applications and they end up in different relations, then we will always have to do a join operation when we use them. A familiar example of this occurs in storing addresses. Assume we are storing an employee's name and address in the relation,

```
Emp (empId, lastName, firstName, street, city, state, zip)
```

As usual we are assuming names are not unique. We have the functional dependency,

```
zip → city, state
```

which means that the relation is not 3NF. We could normalize it by decomposition into,

```
Emp1 (empId, name, street, zip)
Codes (zip, city, state)
```

However, this would mean that we would have to do a join whenever we wanted a complete address for a person. In this case, we might settle for 2NF and implement the original EMP relation. This is purely a design decision and depends on the needs of the applications and the performance requirements for the database. These should be taken into account in deciding what the final form will be.

6.9   Chapter Summary

This chapter dealt with a method for developing a suitable set of relations for the logical model of a relational database. **Functional dependencies** were found to produce problems involving **update**, **insertion**, and **deletion anomalies**. *A* set of attributes *B* is said to be **functionally dependent** on a set of attributes *A* in a relation *R* if each *A* value has exactly one *B* value associated with it.

Normalization is often done by starting with a set of relations designed from the mapping of an E-R diagram and using heuristic methods to create an equivalent set of relations in a higher normal form. **First normal form** means that a relation has no multiple-valued attributes. We can normalize a relation that is not already in 1NF by creating a new table consisting of the key and the multivalued attribute, by adding additional columns for the expected number of repeats, or by "flattening," making the multivalued attribute part of the key. Relations in 1NF can have update, insertion, and deletion anomalies, due to **partial dependencies** on the key. If a non-key attribute is not **fully functionally dependent** on the entire key, the relation is not in **second normal form**. In that case, we normalize it by projection, placing each determinant that is a proper subset of the key in a new relation with its dependent attributes. The original composite key must also be kept in another relation. Relations in 2NF can still have update, insertion, and deletion anomalies. **Transitive dependencies**, in which one or more non-key attribute functionally determines another non-key attribute, cause such anomalies. **Third normal form** is achieved by eliminating transitive dependencies using projection. The determinant causing the transitive dependency is placed in a separate relation with the attributes it determines. It is also kept in the original relation. In third normal form, each non-key attribute is functionally dependent only on the entire key. **Boyce-Codd Normal Form** requires that every determinant be a superkey. This form is also achieved by projection, but in some cases the projection will separate determinants from their functionally dependent attributes, resulting in the loss of an important constraint. If this happens, 3NF is preferable.

Three desirable properties for relational decompositions are **attribute preservation**, **dependency preservation**, and **lossless decomposition**. Lossy projections can lose information because when they are undone by a join, spurious tuples can result. For binary projections, we can be sure a decomposition is lossless if the intersection of the two projections is a determinant for one of them. For binary decompositions, there is a simple test for lossless decomposition. However, if decomposition is done by repeated binary decomposition, the simple test can be applied to each successive decomposition.

In analysis we begin with a relation, identify dependencies, and use projection to achieve a higher normal form. The opposite approach, called synthesis, begins with attributes, finds functional dependencies, and groups together functional dependencies with the same determinant, forming relations.

In deciding what normal form to choose for implementation, we consider attribute preservation, lossless projection, and dependency preservation. We generally choose the highest normal form that allows for all of these. We must also balance performance against normalization in implementation, so we sometimes accept a design that is in a lower normal form for performance reasons.

Exercises

6.1   Consider the following universal relation that holds information about the inventory of books in a bookstore:

```
Books (title, isbn, author, publisherName, publisherAdd,
totalCopiesOrdered, copiesInStock, publicationDate, category,
sellingPrice, cost)
```

Assume:

- The `isbn` uniquely identifies a book. (It does not identify each copy of the book, however.)

- A book may have more than one author.

- An author may have more than one book.

- Each publisher name is unique. Each publisher has one unique address—the address of the firm's national headquarters.

- Titles are not unique.

- `totalCopiesOrdered` is the number of copies of a particular book that the bookstore has ever ordered, while `copiesInStock` is the number still unsold in the bookstore.

- Each book has only one publication date. A revision of a book is given a new ISBN.

- The category may be biography, science fiction, poetry, and so on. The title alone is not sufficient to determine the category.

- The `sellingPrice`, which is the amount the bookstore charges for a book, is always 20 percent above the cost, which is the amount the bookstore pays the publisher or distributor for the book.

  a. Using these assumptions and stating any others you need to make, list all the non-trivial functional dependencies for this relation.

  b. What are the candidate keys for this relation? Identify the primary key.

  c. Is the relation in third normal form? If not, find a 3NF lossless join decomposition of `Books` that preserves dependencies.

  d. Is the relation or resulting set of relations in Boyce-Codd Normal Form? If not, find a lossless join decomposition that is in BCNF. Identify any functional dependencies that are not preserved.

6.2 Consider the following relation that stores information about students living in dormitories at a college:

```
College (lastName, stuId, homeAdd, homePhone, dormRoom, roommateName,
dormAdd, status, mealPlan, roomCharge, mealPlanCharge)
```

Assume:

- Each student is assigned to one dormitory room and may have several roommates.

- Names of students are not unique.

- The college has several dorms. `dormRoom` contains a code for the dorm and the number of the particular room assigned to the student. For example, A221 means Adams Hall, room 221. Dorm names are unique.

- The `dormAdd` is the address of the dorm building. Each building has its own unique address. For example, Adams Hall may be 123 Main Street, Anytown, NY 10001.

- `status` tells the student's status: Freshman, Sophomore, Junior, Senior, or Graduate Student.

- `mealPlan` tells how many meals per week the student has chosen as part of his or her meal plan. Each meal plan has a single `mealPlanCharge` associated with it.

- The `roomCharge` is different for different dorms, but all students in the same dorm pay the same amount.

Answer questions (a)–(d) as in Exercise 6.1 for this example.

6.3   Consider the following attributes for tables in a relational model designed to keep track of information for a moving company that moves residential customers, usually from one home or apartment to another:

```
customerID, customerName, customerCurrentAddress, customerCurrentPhone,
customerNewAddress, customerNewPhone, pickupLocation, dropOffLocation,
dateOfMove, startingTime, estimatedWeight, estimatedCost,
truck#Assigned, driverName, driverLicNo, actualCost, amountOfDamages,
truckCapacity, costOfTolls, tax, finalAmount, invoiceNumber, amountPaid,
datePaid, checkNumber, amountDue
```

Assume:

- Although in most cases the `pickupLocation` is the customer's old address and the `dropOffLocation` is the new address, there are exceptions, such as when furniture is moved to or from storage.

- An estimate is provided before the move using a pre-printed invoice containing a unique invoice number. The actual cost is recorded on the same form once the move is complete. The actual cost may differ from the estimated cost. The final amount includes the actual cost of the move, plus tax and tolls.

- In most cases, the customer pays the final amount immediately, but sometimes he or she pays only part of the bill, especially if the amount of damages is high. In those cases, there is an amount due, which is the difference between the final amount and the amount paid.

    (a)–(d) Answer questions (a)–(d) as in Exercise 6.1 for this example.

(e) What tables would you actually implement? Explain any denormalization, omissions, or additions of attributes.

6.4   The owner of a catering company wants a database to keep track of various aspects of the business. Clients may be individuals or businesses who make arrangements for events such as weddings, dances, corporate dinners, fundraisers, etc. The company owns a catering hall in which only one event can take place at a time. In addition, clients can use the services of the company to cater events at their homes, places of business, or places that the client rents, such as historic mansions. Several of these off-site events can take place at the same time. Clients who rent the catering hall must guarantee a minimum of 150 guests, but the hall can accommodate up to 200. Reservations for the hall are accepted up to two years in advance. Clients who provide their own space can have any number of guests. Reservations for off-site events are usually made several months in advance. The firm provides the food, table settings (dishes, silverware, and glassware), linens, waiters, and bartenders for the event, regardless of whether it is in the catering hall or elsewhere. Customers can choose the color of the linen. The firm has set menus that are identified by number. For a given menu number, there is one appetizer, one salad, one main course, and one dessert. (For example, menu number 10 may include shrimp cocktail, Caesar salad, prime rib, and chocolate mousse.) The firm quotes a total price for its services, based on the number of guests, the menu, the location, and intangible factors such as how busy they are on that date. The firm can also contract for floral arrangements, musicians, entertainers, and photographers, if the client requests. The client pays the catering company, which then pays the contractor. The price charged the customer for each of these is always 10% above the cost to the catering company. Assume names are unique. Also assume musicians and entertainers provide only one type of music or entertainment.

Assume the following attributes have been identified:

> clientLName, cFName, cPhone, cStreet, cCity, cState, cZip, eventDate,
> eventStartTime, eventDuration, eventType, numberGuests, locationName,
> locationStreet, locationCity, locationState, locationZip,
> linenColorRequested, numberWaiters, numberBartenders, totalPrice,

```
floristName, floristPhone, floristCost, floristPrice, musicContact,
musicContactPhone, musicType, musicCost, musicPrice, entertainerName,
entertainerPhone, entertainerType, entertainerCost, entertainerPrice,
photographerName, photographerPhone, photographerCost,
photographerPrice, menuNumberChosen, menuAppetizer, menuSalad,
menuMain, menuDessert.
```

(a)–(d) Answer questions (a)–(d) as in Exercise 6.1 for this example.

(e) What tables would you actually implement? Explain any denormalization, omissions, or additions of attributes.

6.5   Consider the following relations, and identify the highest normal form for each, as given, stating any assumptions you need to make.

a. Work1 (empId, empName, dateHired, jobTitle, jobLevel)

b. Work2 (empId, empName, jobTitle, ratingDate, raterName, rating)

c. Work3 (empId, empName, projectNo, projectName, projBudget, empManager, hoursAssigned)

d. Work4 (empId, empName, schoolAttended, degreeAwarded, graduationDate)

e. Work5 (empId, empName, socialSecurityNumber, dependentName, dependentAddress, relationToEmp)

6.6   For each of the relations in Exercise 6.5, identify a primary key and,

a. if the relation is not in third normal form, find a 3NF lossless join decomposition that preserves dependencies.

b. if the relation or resulting set of relations is not in Boyce-Codd Normal Form, find a lossless join decomposition that is in BCNF. Identify any functional dependencies that are not preserved.

6.7   Normalize the relational database schema developed for Exercise 4.6, which was based on Figure 4.4.

6.8   Normalize the relational database schema developed for Exercise 4.7.

6.9   Normalize the relational database schema developed for Exercise 4.8.

6.10   Normalize the relational database schema developed for Exercise 4.9.

6.11   Normalize the relational database schema developed for Exercise 4.10.

6.12   Normalize the relational database schema developed for Exercise 4.11.

6.13 Normalize the relational database schema developed for Exercise 4.12.

On the Companion Website:

- Higher Normal Forms
- Formal Relational Design
- Additional Exercises
- Sample Project
- Student Projects

CHAPTER 7

The Object-Oriented Model

Chapter Objectives

In this chapter you will learn the following:

- The origins of the object-oriented data model

- Fundamental concepts of the object-oriented data model: object, class, inheritance, object identity

- How to construct a UML class diagram

- The basic concepts of the ODMG model

- How to write ODL for an object-oriented schema using a UML class diagram

- How to write simple queries using OQL

- How an object-oriented database is developed and used

7.8 Chapter Summary

Exercises

 On the Companion Website:
- Lab Exercises
- Sample Project
- Student Projects

7.1   Rationale for the Object-Oriented Data Model

The traditional relational model, in which data is represented as tables having rows of single-valued attributes, is limited in its ability to represent the complex data and relationships needed for advanced applications. Just as the E-R model was found to be lacking in its ability to represent a conceptual model for such applications as software engineering, telecommunications, computer-aided design and manufacturing, molecular biology, geographical information systems, engineering design, digital publishing, and many other advanced applications, the traditional relational model lacks the data structures to support the information requirements for these applications. **Object-oriented programming languages**, beginning with Simula and Smalltalk, presented an alternate way of designing programs, in which data structures and their operations had primary importance. Object-oriented programming is widely recognized as a method for producing highly reliable, reusable code. The promise of the early object-oriented languages, the popularity of the object-oriented languages C++, C#, Python, Ruby, and Java, and the addition of object-oriented capabilities to other languages such as Visual Basic.Net, have influenced database modeling as well. The challenge of extending these languages to databases is to move from the temporary objects created and manipulated by programs to **persistent objects** that can be stored in a database. Object-oriented database management systems allow the database designer to create highly complex, interrelated objects and to give them persistence. As discussed in Section 1.6, vendors of relational model database systems have responded to the challenges of object-oriented systems by extending the relational model to incorporate some object-oriented concepts, while retaining the underlying relational structures, creating hybrid object-relational systems (ORDBMS). However, there is considerable overhead involved in mapping the objects used in object-oriented applications to the table structures that the relational model supports. Because relational database vendors have addressed some of the limitations of relational databases, and because users who have a heavy investment in relational systems are disinclined to migrate to an entirely new paradigm, the popularity of object-oriented databases has been limited. However, some strictly object-oriented database management systems (**OODBMS**), such as Objectivity, GemStone, ObjectStore, Caché, and Versant, are in use, particularly in environments having highly complex data requirements.

7.2   Object-Oriented Data Concepts

The Object Management Group (OMG) was founded in 1989 by a group of computer industry leaders for the purpose of developing standards for a common object model that would be portable and interoperable. The nonprofit group has expanded to hundreds of members, including both computer companies and users. One focus of the group has been on developing standards for the object model and services connected with it, and another on modeling standards.

7.2.1   Objects and Literals

The concept of an **object** is fundamental in the object-oriented model. An object corresponds to an entity in our previous terminology, but has both a **state** and a **behavior**. The state includes the internal structure of the object, its descriptive attributes or data elements, as well as the **relationships** it participates in with other objects. The behavior is the set of **methods** (functions or procedures) that can be performed on it. These include methods to create, access, and manipulate the object. Each method has a **signature** giving its name and parameters. Objects are **encapsulated**, which means that their data and methods form a unit, and that access to the data is restricted. Only the object's own methods, created and programmed by the designer of the object, are permitted to access the data, protecting it from changes by outside code. The external appearance of an object, visible to the outside world, is called its **interface** and consists of a description of the object's state and the signatures of its methods. The outside world interacts with the object through its interface, calling the object's own methods to perform any operations on its data elements. Figure 7.1 pictures two objects of a

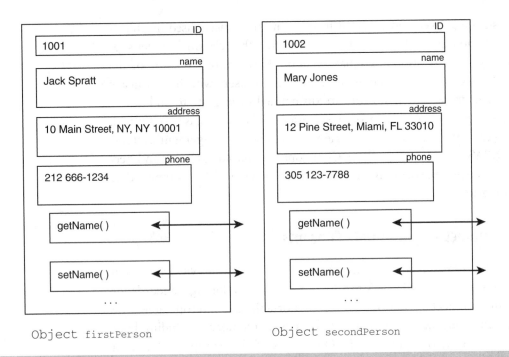

FIGURE 7.1

Two Person Objects

class called `Person`. Each `Person` object instance has its own identifier (`firstPerson` and `secondPerson`, in this example) and attributes `ID`, `name`, `address`, and `telephone`, with its own values for those attributes. Each object is encapsulated, and the values of its attributes are accessible to the outside world only through its methods, such as `getName( )` and `setName( )`. From the names of these methods, we can assume that the programmer who designed these objects has written code for a function that returns the value of the `name` attribute (`getName( )`) and one that allows the user to provide a new value for the `name` attribute (`setName( )`). To make the other attributes accessible, the programmer who designed these objects needs to add `get` and `set` methods for them as well as for any other operations that should be defined for `Person` objects.

A **literal** differs from an object in that it has a state (value) but no object identifier. Atomic literals are the values of the basic built-in types, but we can also have structured literals.

In addition to the fundamental data types, object-oriented systems support user-defined data types; structured types such as records, collections types such as arrays, sets and others; and reference types, which are similar to pointers in programming. New types can be created incorporating previously-defined types.

7.2.2   Classes

A **class** is a description of objects having the same structure, including the same attributes with the same data types, and the same methods and relationships. A class is roughly equivalent to an entity type, except that it includes operations and relationships, not just data elements. Classes are defined by listing their components, which consist of **data members** (attributes, instance variables), the relationships that the objects in the class participate in, and member **methods** (functions or procedures that belong to the class). The general form we will use for a class definition is:

```
class classname {
    list of attributes, relationships, methods
}
```

For example, we can define a `Person` class as:

```
class Person {
    attribute int ID;
    attribute string name;
    attribute string address;
    attribute string phone;
    void setName(in string newName); // method
    string getName( ); //method
    ...
}
```

In this class definition, the four attributes are identified by their data types and names, and two methods are listed. The first, `setName( )`, has a single string parameter, but it has no return value, as indicated by `void`. As the name implies, it is intended to set the value of an object's `name` attribute. The code for this method is written by the designer of the class. It might be defined as follows:

```
void setName(in string newName)
{
    self.name = newName;
}
```

The method is called from a user program to set the name of a `Person` object. For example, if `firstPerson` is created as a `Person` object within the user program, using a declaration such as,

```
Person          firstPerson;
```

or,

```
Person firstPerson = new Person();
```

the user is not able to assign the person's name by referring directly to the `name` attribute of `firstPerson`, because of encapsulation of objects. Instead the user program should contain a command such as:

```
firstPerson.setName('Jack Spratt');
```

Here, `firstPerson` is the "calling object," the object used to call the method, and it becomes the implicit parameter for the method. Within the method, it is referred to as the *self* (or *this*) parameter. We referred to it by name in the assignment line of the method,

```
self.name = newName;
```

For the `getName( )` method, the code written by the designer of the class might be:

```
string getName( )
{
return name;
}
```

Within the user program we would call this method using an object as the implicit parameter. If we write

```
string employeeName = firstPerson.getName( );
```

the `firstPerson` object is the implicit parameter for the method, and the `name` attribute of that object is returned, resulting in the value 'Jack Spratt' being assigned to the user program variable `employeeName`. Methods may be **overloaded**, which means the same method name may be used for different classes, and will have different code for them. Two methods for the same class may also have the same name but if their signatures are different, they are considered different methods.

The set of objects belonging to a class is called the **extent** of the class. An entity set is roughly equivalent to a class extent. The data types in a class can be predefined atomic types including integer, real, character, and boolean, and more complex types as well as user-defined types. The individual objects in the class are called **instances**, **object instances**, or simply **objects**, and they are similar to entity instances.

7.2.3 Class Hierarchies and Inheritance

Classes are organized into **class hierarchies**, consisting of **superclasses** and **subclasses**, in which each subclass has an *isa* relationship with its superclass. We can interpret the relationship to mean an object in the subclass is an object in the superclass—"a student is a person," for example. Subclasses inherit the data members, relationships, and methods of their superclasses, and they may have additional data members, relationships, and methods of their own. Figure 7.2 shows an example of a simplified class hierarchy. Figure 7.3 shows a simplified set of class declarations to correspond to the class hierarchy in Figure 7.2. All objects in the superclass, Person, have data members, ID, name, address, and phone that are common to all people. Those in the Student subclass inherit ID, name, address, and phone and add data members of their own, credits, and GPA. The Faculty subclass also inherits the Person attributes, but has its own data members, dept and rank. In turn, Undergraduate and Graduate

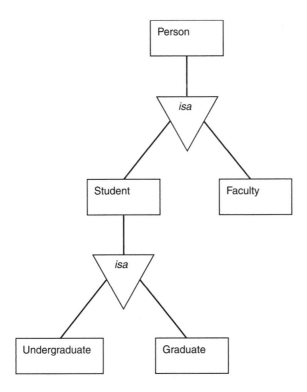

FIGURE 7.2
A Class Hierarchy

FIGURE 7.3

**Simplified Definition
of a Class Hierarchy**

```
class Person {
    attribute int ID;
    attribute string name;
    attribute struct addr(string street, string city, string state, string zip) address;
    attribute string phone;
    string getName( ); //method that returns a string
    void setName(in string newName); // method with no return
    . . .
};
class Student isa Person {
    attribute int credits;
    attribute real(4, 2) GPA;
    int getCredits( );
    void addCredits(in int numCredits);
    . . .
};
class Faculty isa Person {
    attribute string dept;
    attribute enum FacultyRank{instructor, assistant, associate, professor} rank ;
    string getRank( );
    . . .
};
class Undergraduate isa Student{
    attribute string major;
    string getMajor( );
    void setMajor(in string newMajor);
    . . .
};
class Graduate isa Student {
    attribute string program;
    string getProgram( );
    . . .
};
```

subclasses inherit the attributes of both `Person` and `Student`. We have indicated subclasses by using *isa* and we have included some methods for each class. Along with attributes, methods of each superclass are also automatically inherited by the subclass, so that, for example, `Student` and `Faculty` subclasses, as well as `Student`'s `Undergraduate` and `Graduate` subclasses, have the `getName()` and `setName()` methods from `Person`. The subclasses can also have additional methods, as we see for the subclass `Student`, which has methods `getCredits()` and `addCredits()`. The `Undergraduate` and `Graduate` subclasses inherit these methods as well, and each has its own methods: `setMajor()` and `getMajor()` for `Undergraduate`, and `getProgram()` for `Graduate`. We could **override** a method by defining for the subclass a method that has the same **signature** as a method of the superclass, that is, the same name and the same number and types of parameters and return type. In that case the new method will be used on objects of the subclass.

Multiple inheritance means that a subclass belongs to more than one superclass, and that it inherits attributes and methods from the multiple superclasses. An example is shown in Figure 7.4, which shows a class for graduate teaching assistants as a subclass of both `Student` and `Faculty`. Each `TeachingAssistant` object has all the attributes and methods of `Person`, `Faculty`, `Student`, and `Graduate`, as well as attributes and methods of its own. We could add its class definition shown in Figure 7.4 to the one in Figure 7.3. Some OO languages do not support multiple inheritance and others restrict its use to only certain types of classes, because it can cause problems if used carelessly. Our example can illustrate one of the problems. Since `TeachingAssistant` inherits from both `Student` and `Faculty`, each of which inherits the entire structure of `Person`, a `TeachingAssistant` object would have two copies of the `Person` structure, as well as the structures of `Student`, `Faculty`, and `Graduate`. If there are conflicts, there would be a problem deciding which structure should apply to a `TeachingAssistant`. For example, if `Student` has a method `void promote()`, which increases the student's credits by 10, and `Faculty` has a method with the same signature that advances a faculty member's rank to the next level, there is a conflict if we apply the `promote` method to a teaching assistant, since we cannot decide whether to increase the credits or advance the rank. Different object-oriented database management systems treat this in various ways.

FIGURE 7.4
Multiple Inheritance

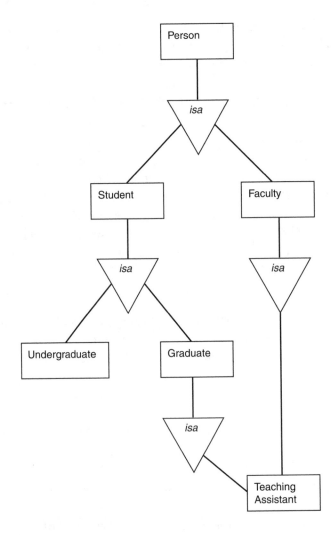

```
...
class TeachingAssistant isa Graduate isa Faculty{
      attribute string fundingSource;
      attribute real(7,2) annualStipend;
      ...
};
```

7.2.4   Object Identity

Object identity is another fundamental concept for object-oriented models. Each object in the database is assigned its own unique object identifier, **OID**, which remains unchanged for the lifetime of the object. Unlike the relational model, where we must identify a primary key for each relation, the object-oriented model provides unique identifiers automatically. The value of the OID does not depend on the value of any attribute of the object, such as `ID` in `Person`, nor is it the same as the name of the object. In the relational model, the primary key value could be updated. However, in the object-oriented model, the OID never changes. Since it is always possible to tell objects apart by their OIDs, it is also possible that two different objects have exactly the same values for all their data items, a situation forbidden in the relational model.

7.3 Object-Oriented Data Modeling Using UML

E-R diagrams are not well suited to representing objects, since they do not allow representation of methods. The Object Management Group defines and maintains standards for Unified Modeling Language (**UML**), which was developed as a standard for software models. **UML** class diagrams allow us to express object-oriented database concepts more naturally than standard E-R diagrams. Figure 7.5 shows a UML class diagram for part of a university database, in which we show many of the features of such diagrams. The choices made in constructing this diagram are intended to demonstrate different features of the diagramming notation, and do not represent the only, or necessarily the best, possible model for the example. In a UML diagram, **rectangles** represent classes. Class rectangles are subdivided into three sections, the top one for the class name, the middle for the attributes, and the bottom for the methods. The string in guillements(<<>>) above the class name is called a stereotype. The <<persistent>> stereotype indicates that the class is persistent, which means it maps to a database and its objects will persist in storage after the program terminates. **Generalization hierarchies** are represented by lines connecting the subclasses to the superclass, with a triangle pointing toward the superclass. In Figure 7.5, `Person` is specialized into `Student` and `Faculty`, and `Student` is specialized into `Undergraduate` and `Graduate`. `Graduate` has a subclass, `TeachingAssistant`. A filled generalization triangle represents **overlapping** subclasses, which means an object can belong to both classes, while a blank (outline only) triangle represents **disjoint** ones. The diagram shows that a `Person` can be both a `Student` and a `Faculty` member, but a `Student` cannot be both `Undergraduate` and `Graduate`. If each member of the superclass must belong to a subclass, we describe the specialization as **mandatory**, as opposed to **optional**. Specialization constraints can be written on the line near the triangle, enclosed in

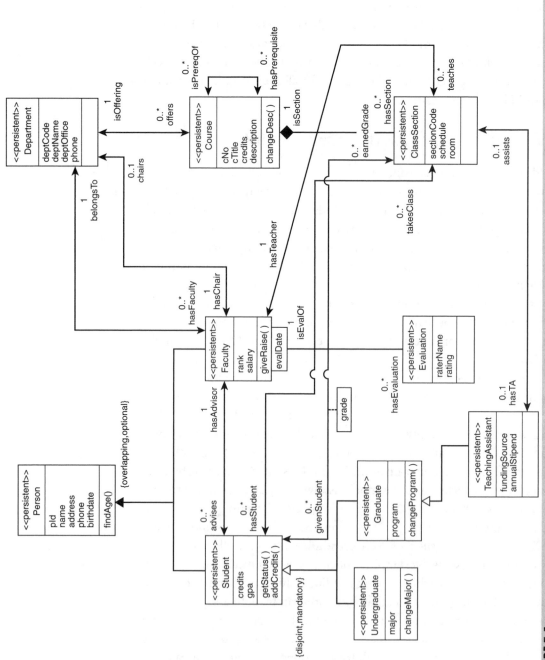

FIGURE 7.5

A UML Class Diagram

curly brackets. For example, we write {overlapping, optional} for the specialization of `Person` into `Student` and `Faculty`, which shows that not every `Person` has to be a `Student` or a `Faculty`, and {disjoint, mandatory} for `Student` into `Undergraduate` and `Graduate` to show that every `Student` must be either `Undergraduate` or `Graduate`. Note that for this example `Graduate Assistant` is not a subclass of `Faculty`.

Relationships between classes are also shown by lines. In UML we distinguish between **associations**, which are either unidirectional or bidirectional relationships between classes, and **aggregation**, which is a type of relationship that connects a whole to its parts. **Associations**, or binary connections between classes, are represented by lines connecting the class rectangles. Several associations, such as the one connecting `Department` and `Course`, are shown in Figure 7.5. The name of the association may optionally appear on the line. Any descriptive attribute of the relationship is shown in a box connected to the association line by a dotted line, as shown in the `grade` attribute of the `Grading` relationship that connects `Student` to `Class Section`. **Rolenames** can also appear on association lines, if they are needed for clarity, but their placement is opposite to that in an E-R diagram, appearing at the head (arrow) of the directed line from a class to the class it relates to. For one of the associations between `Dept` and `Faculty` we have used rolenames `has chair`, from `Department` to `Faculty`, and `chairs`, from `Faculty` to `Department`, to show that it connects the chairperson with the department. **Aggregation** is a special type of relationship that connects a whole to its parts. If the phrase describing the relationship of a class to another is that it "is part of" the other, and the class is clearly subordinate to the other, then aggregation is the better representation of the relationship. We represented the relationship between `Course` and `ClassSection` as an aggregation. The aggregation is represented by a line with a diamond on the side of the class that is the aggregate. If the aggregation is not given a name, the aggregation line is interpreted to mean "has." Participation constraints and cardinality for both association and aggregation relationships are specified using *min..max* notation. In the E-R diagrams described in Chapter 4, we showed relationship cardinality by using "1" for "one" and "M" (or "N") for "many" on the appropriate lines. We used single lines or double lines to show partial or total participation constraints for relationships. An alternative representation that shows both participation and cardinality constraints is the *min..max* notation illustrated in

Figure 7.5. Each relationship line connecting classes has a pair of integers, *min..max*, written at each end, along with the optional rolename. The first integer of the pair, *min*, specifies the least number of relationship instances an object must participate in. If *min* is 0, it means that there may be objects that do not participate in instances of the relationship, so the participation is partial. If *min* is 1 or more, the participation is total. The value of *max* is the greatest number of relationship instances an object can participate in. This value could be 1, *N*, or * (to represent *many*), or some constant integer, such as 10. If both min and max have a value of 1, we simply write the single integer 1 instead of 1..1. In UML diagrams, we call these **multiplicity indicators**, and we place them at the head of the arrow for the relationship. For example, the 0..* with the label `offers` at the head of the arrow going from `Department` to `Course` indicates that a `Department` can offer no courses or many courses, while the 1 with the label `isOffering` at the head of the arrow from `Course` to `Department` means that a `Course` is an offering from exactly one `Department`. Note that similar notation, called (min,max) can be used with E-R diagrams in place of the notation presented in Chapter 4, with some slight differences from its use in UML diagrams. In E-R diagrams, parentheses are used around the values, which are separated by a comma, and the constraints are placed between the entity rectangle and the relationship diamond, essentially placing them opposite their placement in UML.

Recursive relationships between members of the same class, called **reflexive associations** or **reflexive aggregations**, are shown by an association line or aggregation line going from a class back into itself. The relationship that connects courses and their prerequisites is a reflexive association. Rolenames appear on the line, with multiplicity indicators at each end. On the diagram we show that a `course` may have zero to many prerequisites, and that a `course` may be a prerequisite for zero to many other courses.

Weak entities can be represented by a box attached to the associated strong owner entity, with the **discriminator** (partial key) appearing in a box beneath the owner's class rectangle. We show `Evaluation` as a weak entity, dependent on `Faculty`. For this example, we assume the same faculty member is never evaluated twice on the same day, so we use `evalDate` as the discriminator.

7.4   The ODMG Model and ODL

The **Object Database Management Group** (ODMG) was a group of vendors that developed and published standards for object-oriented databases and languages. It was founded in 1991 and published several standards, including the ODMG 3.0 standard published in 1999, before disbanding in 2001. The standards developed by this group have been almost universally adopted by the vendors of object-oriented database management systems. Their work has been taken over by the Object Management Group, which is developing new standards for object databases. The ODMG established standards for the object data model itself, **object definition language** (ODL), **object query language** (OQL), and language bindings for C++, Java, and Smalltalk. ODL is a standard language for describing schemas in object-oriented terms, serving the same function that SQL DDL serves. Figure 7.6 shows the ODL definition for the university schema shown in Figure 7.5.

7.4.1   Class Declarations

Each class declaration begins with the keyword `class`, the name of the class, an optional extent and key declaration in parentheses, and a list of attributes, methods, and relationships enclosed in curly brackets.

7.4.2   Extent

The **extent** of a class can be thought of as the set of object instances for that class that are stored in the database at a given time. Using terms from Chapter 2, the class itself is part of the intension of the database, while the extent is part of the extension of the database. In E-R terms, the class is like the entity type, and the extent is the set of entity instances. It is good practice to choose a name for the extent that is slightly different from the name of the class. For the `Person` class, we called the extent `people`. The parentheses can also contain the name of the key, which we discuss in a later section.

7.4.3   Attributes

The attributes for a class are listed, preceded by their datatypes, within curly brackets. A wide variety of types are permitted in ODL, including simple types and more complex types that can be built from them.

FIGURE 7.6
ODL Definition for the
University Schema

```
class Person(
extent People
key pld)
{
/*define attributes */
    attribute        int pld;
    attribute        string name;
    attribute        Struct Addr(string street, string city, string state, string zip) address;
    attribute        string phone;
    attribute        date birthDate;
/* define methods */
    int              findAge();
};

class Student extends Person
(extent Students)
{
/*define attributes */
    attribute        int credits;
    attribute        real(3,2) gpa;
/*define relationships */
    relationship Set<ClassSection> takesClass Inverse ClassSection::hasStudent;
    relationship Set<Mark> earnedGrade Inverse Mark::givenStudent;
    relationship Faculty hasAdvisor Inverse Faculty::advises;
/*define methods */
    string               getStatus();
    void                 addCredits(in int numCredits);
};

class Faculty extends Person
(extent Fac)
{
/*define attributes */
    attribute        enum FacultyRank{lecturer, instructor, assistant, associate, professor} rank;
    attribute        real(8,2)salary;
/*define relationships */
    relationship Department belongsTo Inverse Department::hasFaculty;
    relationship Set<ClassSection> teaches Inverse ClassSection::hasTeacher;
    relationship Set<Student>advises Inverse Student::hasAdvisor;
```

(Continued)

FIGURE 7.6—Continued

```
    relationship Department chairs Inverse Department::hasChair;
    relationship Set<Evaluation> hasEvaluation Inverse Evaluation::isEvalOf;
/* define methods */
    void            giveRaise(in float amount)raises(Salary out of range);
};

class Undergraduate extends Student
(extent Undergrads)
{
/*define attributes */
    attribute       string major;
/* define methods */
    void            changeMajor(in string newMajor) raises(Invalid major);

};

class Graduate extends Student
(extent Grads)
{
/*define attributes */
    attribute       string program;
/* define methods */
    string          changeProgram(in string newProgram) raises(Invalid program);
};

class TeachingAssistant extends Graduate
(extent TAs)
{
/*define attributes */
    attribute       string fundingSource;
    attribute       real(7,2) Annual Stipend;
/*define relationships */
    relationship ClassSection assists Inverse ClassSection::hasTA;
};

class Department
(extent Departments)
key deptCode, deptName)
```

FIGURE 7.6—Continued

```
{
/*define attributes */
    attribute        string deptCode;
    attribute        string deptName;
    attribute        string deptOffice;
    attribute        string phone;
/*define relationships */
    relationship Set<Faculty> hasFaculty Inverse Faculty::belongsTo;
    relationship Faculty hasChair Inverse Faculty::chairs;
    relationship Set<Course> offers Inverse Course::isOffering;
};

class Course
(extent Courses)
key cNo)
{
/*define attributes */
    attribute        string cNo;
    attribute        string cTitle;
    attribute        int credits;
    attribute        string description;
/*define relationships */
    relationship Set<Course> hasPrerequisite Inverse isPrereqOf;
    relationship Set<Course> isPrereqOf Inverse hasPrerequisite;
    relationship Department isOffering Inverse Department::offers;
};

class ClassSection extends Course
(extent Sections)
{
/*define attributes */
    attribute        string sectionCode;
    attribute        string schedule;
    attribute        string room;
/*define relationships */
    relationship Set<Student> hasStudent Inverse Student::takesClass;
    relationship Faculty hasTeacher Inverse Faculty::teaches;
```

FIGURE 7.6—Continued

```
        relationship TeachingAssistant hasTA Inverse TeachingAssistant::assists;
        relationship Set<Mark> givenIn Inverse Mark::givenTo;
};


class Evaluation
(extent Evaluations)
key (evalDate, isEvalOf)
{
/*define attributes */
        attribute        date evalDate;
        attribute        string raterName;
        attribute        int rating;
/*define relationships */
        relationship Faculty isEvalOf Inverse Faculty::hasEvaluation;
};


class Mark
(extent Grades)
{
/*define attributes */
        attribute string grade;
/*define relationships */
        relationship ClassSection givenTo Inverse ClassSection::givenIn;
        relationship Student givenStudent Inverse Student::earnedGrade;
}
```

Atomic types include integer, float, character, string, boolean, and enumerated types. **Enumerated types** are identified by the keyword `enum`, the user-defined name of the type, a list of literals for the type within curly brackets, and the name of the attribute with that type. For example, we made attribute `rank` in `Faculty` have an enumerated type called `FacultyRank`. We can also have **structured types**, identified by the keyword `Struct`, the name of the type, and curly brackets containing each attribute with its data type. In the `Person` class definition, Addr is a structured type that we have used for the attribute `address`. Since we defined the type, we can use it again for other classes, but we must identify the class it was defined in, using the form `Person::Addr`, called the **scoped name**, consisting of the class name, a double colon, and the structure name. This scoped form is used to refer to any property in a different class. Besides `Struct`, there are type constructors for five collection types, namely `Set`, `List`, `Array`, `Bag`, and `Dictionary`.

7.4.4   Relationships

Relationships represent connections between object instances. For example, faculty members relate to class sections because they teach them, students relate to classes that they take, departments relate to faculty who are employed in them, and so on. The object-oriented model represents these connections using **references**. In ODL, the description of a relationship implies that the system stores and maintains such references. For example, there is a relationship called `takesClass` defined for the `Student` class in this line:

```
relationship Set<ClassSection> takesClass ...
```

which tells us that each `Student` instance can contain a set of references, called `takesClass`, to `ClassSection` instances. Typically, the references are simply the OIDs of the related objects. The keyword `Set` shows that this is a "many" relationship for each student; that is, a `Student` instance can be related to a set of `ClassSection` instances, not just one. The `takesClass` relationship can be seen as a way so that, given a `Student` instance, we can find out what classes the student is taking. We also expect that we would be able to turn the query around and, given a `ClassSection` instance, ask what students are in the class. We see that there is such an inverse relationship, `hasStudent`, defined for `ClassSection`. The phrase,

```
Inverse ClassSection::hasStudent;
```

that appears on the same line means that each `ClassSection` object contains references to the corresponding `Student` instances. We note that in addition to specifying in the `Student` class that the inverse exists, we also specify this relationship in the `ClassSection` class, in this line:

```
relationship Set<Student> hasStudent Inverse Student::takesClass;
```

The connection between `takesClass` and `hasStudent` is that if a class appears in the `takesClass` set of references for a student, that same student should appear in the `hasStudent` set of references for the class. These two relationships are therefore inverses of each other, as indicated. Note that when we identify the inverse relationship we normally use the scoped form for its name,

```
Inverse className::relationshipName,
```

since the inverse relationship is usually in another class definition. ODL allows relationships to have inverses or not. Those without inverses are described as **unidirectional**, while those with inverses are **bidirectional**. Relationships also have **cardinality**, which can be one-to-one, one-to-many, many-to-one, or many-to-many. The bidirectional `Student-classSection` relationship is many-to-many, and both relationship specifications included a **set** of references. If a relationship is one-to-many, like `Department-Faculty`, the relationship on the "one" side, `Department`, is a set. In the `Department` definition we have relationship `Set<Faculty>` since each `Department` instance has references to many `Faculty` instances as shown in the line.

```
relationship Set <Faculty>hasFaculty Inverse Faculty::belongsTo;
```

However, the relationship on the `Faculty` side,

```
relationship Department belongsTo Inverse Department::hasFaculty;
```

specifies just `Department` (not `Set<Department>`), since a faculty record refers to only one department.

7.4.5 Methods

Method declarations in ODL simply specify the **signature**, which is the return type, the name of the method, and the names and types of parameters, which may be identified as IN, OUT, or IN OUT, depending on whether they are input, output, or both. In ODL, classes have automatic get( ) and set( ) methods, so we need not list these, unless we wish to override them. Class member methods are applied to an instance of the class, which is referred to as *self* in the code for the method. The actual code for the method is not part of the ODL, but is written in one of the host languages.

7.4.6 Classes and Inheritance

A subclass is identified by the keyword `extends` and the name of its superclass following the subclass name. The subclass inherits all the attributes, relationships, and methods of the superclass, and it can have some additional properties of its own that appear in the definition. For example, in Figure 7.6, `Faculty` extends `Person`, so it inherits,

```
pId, name, address, phone, birthdate, and findAge( )
```

from `Person`, but adds some additional properties. If the subclass has more than one superclass, we add a colon and the name of the second superclass immediately after the name of the first superclass. As discussed earlier, different systems implement this feature in their own ways, if at all.

7.4.7   *N*-ary Relationships and M:N Relationships with Attributes

Relationships in ODL are binary, but if we must model a ternary or higher-order relationship, we can do so by creating a class for the relationship itself. The class definition would include three or more relationships that connect the new class to the originally related classes. For example, in Section 3.5.1 we described a ternary relationship that connected a class, instructor, and text, shown in Figure 3.12 as `Faculty-Class-Textbook`. In the object-oriented model, we would define the class for the relationship, which we will call `BookOrder`, as shown in the following sketch:

```
Class BookOrder{
relationship Faculty teacher Inverse Faculty::adoptsText;
relationship Book bookFor Inverse Book::usedIn;
relationship ClassSection uses Inverse ClassSection::usesText;
}
```

If the relationship has any descriptive attributes, they would be listed as well. Note that this technique is similar to the way we treated higher-order relationships in the relational model, where we created tables for such relationships.

Binary many-to-many relationships with descriptive attributes cannot be handled by the usual solution of making the relationship a set in both directions, since that leaves no place for descriptive attributes. Referring to the UML diagram in Figure 7.5, we see that `grade` is an example of a descriptive attribute. We use the same solution as for *n*-ary relationships, setting up a class for the relationship. We place the descriptive attributes as attributes of the new class, and we define two one-to-many relationships between the new class and the two original classes. We have done this in Figure 7.6 by defining the class `Mark`. Note that we also kept the many-to-many relationship between `Student` and `ClassSection` that represents enrollment in the section by defining set relationships in both. This relationship did not require a new class definition, since it has no descriptive attributes.

7.4.8   Keys

Keys are optional in ODL, because the unique object identifier (OID) automatically given to each object instance allows the system to tell instances apart. However, the designer may choose to identify any candidate keys as well. This is done at the beginning of the class declaration within the same parentheses as the extent declaration. A key can be a single attribute or a composite, which is identified by placing parentheses around the names of component attributes. For example, we could have written:

```
class Faculty
(extent Fac
key facId, socSecNo, (name, department))
```

This means `facId` is a key, `socSecNo` is a key, and the combination of `name` and `department` is a key. Keys are not restricted to attributes. We can list a relationship or even a method as a key, provided it gives us unique values. Weak entity sets can often be represented as subclasses in which the relationship to the superclass is part of the key, with the discriminator as another part. For example, for the weak entity set `Evaluation`, we wrote:

```
class Evaluation
(extent Evaluations
key (evalDate, IsEvalOf))
{. . .
relationship Faculty isEvalOf Inverse Faculty::hasEvaluation;
. . .
}
```

This means the composite key consists of the date of the evaluation and the identity of the related faculty member.

7.5   Object Query Language

Object Query Language (OQL) uses a syntax that is similar to SQL, but it operates on objects, not tables. One form for queries is:

```
SELECT [DISTINCT] <expression list>
FROM <fromList>
[WHERE <condition>]
[GROUP BY...[HAVING<condition>]]
[ORDER BY <expression>];
```

Although the syntax is similar to SQL, there are some important differences. The expression list may contain the names of attributes of objects, identified by using the dot notation, as in:

```
SELECT s.pId, s.credits
FROM Students s
ORDER BY s.pID;
```

This involves the default `get()` method for the attributes named in the SELECT line. The result will be the values of `pId` and `credits` for each of the `Student` instances in the `Students` extent. In addition to attributes, we can use methods in the expression list. This retrieves the result of applying the method. We could write, for example,

```
SELECT p.name, p.findAge( )
FROM People p
WHERE p.pId = 1001;
```

which will return the `name` and age of the person whose `pId` is 1001, provided the `findAge( )` method has been written correctly. We can also use a relationship in the expression list. This retrieves the object or set of objects related to the "calling" object through the relationship. For example,

```
SELECT s.pId, s.takesClass.cNo, s.takesClass.sectionCode
FROM Students s
WHERE s.pId = '999';
```

retrieves the `cNo` and `sectionCode` of classes that student 999 takes, as well as the `pId`, 999.

The list of variables in the FROM line is similar to defining an alias in SQL. Usually we list the name of an extent, such as `Students` or `People`, and an identifier for the name of the variable, such as `s` or `p`, as we saw above. The variable is actually an **iterator variable**, that ranges over the extent. There are alternate forms for declaring an iterator variable, such as:

```
FROM Students s
FROM s in Students
FROM Students as s
```

In the WHERE clause, we are restricted to a Boolean expression having constants and variables defined in the FROM clause. We can use <, <=, >, >=, !=, AND, OR, and NOT in the expression, as well as IN and quantifiers EXISTS and FORALL. As in SQL, OQL does not eliminate duplicates, so the return is a bag (multiset) rather than a set. If we wish to eliminate duplicates, we can add the keyword DISTINCT as in SQL, producing a set. We can optionally add an ORDER BY clause, as in SQL.

- **Example 1.** Find the ID, name, and major of all undergraduates who have between 60 and 90 credits, in order by name.

```
OQL:
SELECT s.pId, s.name, s.major
FROM Undergrads as s
WHERE s.credits >=60 AND s.credits<=90
ORDER BY s.name;
```

- **Example 2.** We can use a relationship to find records through references. For example, to find the names of all faculty in the biology department, we write the following query:

```
OQL:
SELECT f.name
FROM Departments as d, d.hasFaculty as f
WHERE d.deptName = 'Biology';
```

The first part of the FROM clause says that d is an iterator variable that ranges over the objects in the `Departments` extent, and the second part says that for each of the `Department` objects, the set of faculty identified by the relationship `hasFaculty` for that department is to be identified with the iterator variable f. This type of expression in which one follows a relationship or a method to get to another object is called a **path expression**. We are essentially setting up a nested loop that has d taking on each department in turn, and f taking on each faculty member in that department. The WHERE line restricts the results to the biology department, and the SELECT line displays just the faculty name.

- **Example 3.** We can also do subqueries in OQL. For example, the previous query can be broken up. We can first find the biology department object by writing:

```
OQL:
SELECT d
FROM d in Departments
WHERE d.deptName = 'Biology';
```

We can use this as a subquery to provide the value for an iterator variable, b. Then we declare an iterator variable, f, for the relationship set `hasFaculty` for b. The entire query is expressed as follows.

```
OQL:
SELECT f.name
FROM (SELECT d
    FROM d in Departments
    WHERE d.deptName = 'Biology') as b,
      b.hasFaculty as f;
```

- **Example 4.** It is possible to define structures for returned results right in a query. For example, we can find the name, rank, and salary of all faculty in the English department and put the results in a structure, in descending order by salary.

```
OQL:
SELECT struct(name: f.name, rank: f.rank, salary: f.salary)
FROM Fac as f
WHERE f.belongsTo = 'English'
ORDER BY salary DESC;
```

- **Example 5.** Like SQL, OQL includes the operators COUNT, SUM, AVG, MAX, and MIN, but they are used differently. In OQL, the operator is applied to a collection rather than to a column. COUNT returns an integer, while the return from the other operators has the same type as the collection. The operators can be used on the results of a query. For example, to find the average salary of faculty members in the History department, we write the OQL query as follows:

```
OQL:
AVG(SELECT f.salary
    FROM Fac as f
    WHERE f.belongsTo = 'History');
```

- **Example 6.** To find the number of undergraduates majoring in computer science, we can use the COUNT function.

```
OQL:
COUNT((SELECT u
    FROM Undergrads as u
    WHERE u.majorsIn = 'Computer Science');
```

To find the course number and section of all the class sections that have more than 30 students in them, we can put the COUNT in the WHERE line.

```
OQL:
SELECT   s.cNo, s.section
FROM     Sections as s
WHERE COUNT(s.hasStudents >30);
```

- **Example 7.** Set operations of UNION, INTERSECTION, and EXCEPT (difference) are used as in SQL. For example, to find IDs and names of all students whose undergraduate major or graduate program is computer science, we write a union.

```
OQL:
(SELECT u.pID, u.name
FROM Undergrads as u
WHERE u.major = 'Computer Science')
UNION
(SELECT g.pID, g.name
FROM Grads as g
WHERE g.program = 'Computer Science');
```

- **Example 8.** Defined queries allow us to create views that can be operated on. For example, we can write

```
DEFINE      Juniors AS
    SELECT s
    FROM s in Undergrads
    WHERE s.credits >= 60 AND s.credits<90;
```

This definition can then be used in a query, such as

```
SELECT j.pId, j.name FROM j in Juniors;
```

We have chosen examples that are similar to SQL. OQL has many additional forms and capabilities that are not illustrated here.

7.6   Developing an OO Database

The process of creating an object-oriented database using an OODBMS such as Objectivity or Caché is meant to be a natural extension of application development in an object-oriented programming environment. As discussed previously, there are language bindings specified in the ODMG standard for C++, Java, and Smalltalk. The difference between using objects in programs written in these languages and database objects is the persistence of the database objects. Vendors who support the ODMG standard provide facilities to make program objects persist, and to provide access to database objects for manipulation within programs. A typical development process using, for example, C++ as the host language, is pictured in Figure 7.7. The database designer defines the schema using a data definition language such as ODL or C++ itself. The class definitions in the schema are essentially standard C++ ones that have been extended to provide persistence and to support relationships between objects, as well as inheritance. Persistence is provided by making all objects that are to be persistent inherit from a class provided by the OODBMS just for that

FIGURE 7.7

Typical Object-Oriented Database Development Process

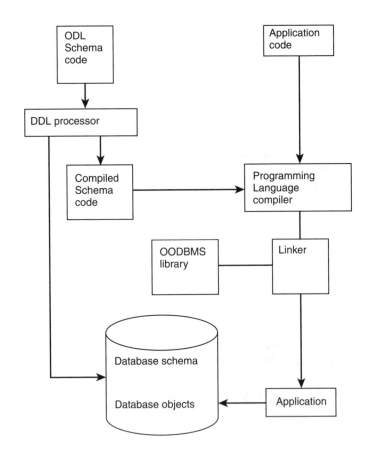

purpose. For example, Objectivity provides the class ooOdb for C++. To make a class permanent, the programmer must specify that it extends ooOdb. For the `Person` class, we would write in C++,

```
class Person: public ooOdb
```

and then continue with the class definition. The persistence will be inherited by `Faculty`, `Student`, and their subclasses as well. If the schema is written in C++, any pointers used must be replaced by references, and the header file must be saved with the extension .ddl.

The DDL processor is then used to process the schema files. This creates the database schema on disk, and generates data model source files. Application code for populating objects in the database can be written in a separate C++ program. In C++, each class has at least one method, called a **constructor**, that generates new object instances. The objects to be stored in the database are created within the C++ application using constructors.

Values of attributes of the object instances can be set either by the constructors using parameters or by methods such as `setName( )`. The program can also manipulate objects retrieved using OQL SELECT statements to update attributes or other properties. C++ classes can also have **destructors** whose function is to destroy objects that are no longer needed. These can be used to delete database objects. When the program is compiled, the C++ compiler uses the schema files created by the DDL processor. The result is then linked with the database run-time library to produce the executable code. The process is similar in Java and Smalltalk.

7.7   Developing an OO Database in Caché

InterSystems Caché is an object-oriented DBMS that provides a variety of ways to define classes, create object instances, make objects persist, access data, and write application code. For example, Caché Studio allows designers to write ODL-type code to create classes whose objects are persistent, simply by adding `Extends (%Persistent)` after the class name. Figure 7.8 shows the class definitions for the University schema, created using Caché Studio. The first class, `Address`, describes a serial object, an object that can be embedded in other classes, such as the `Person` class that follows. `Person` is persistent, which means it can be stored in the database, and it can be automatically populated with random values. It has an index on `perId`, its first attribute. The word "Property" is used for attributes, but it includes relationships as well. Relationships can be one-to-one, one-to-many, parent-to-child, or child-to-parent. When a relationship is defined, its inverse can be defined within the appropriate class automatically. Methods can be coded as part of the initial class definition, or can be added later using Caché Basic or Caché Object Script. Additional classes, such as `Faculty` or `Student`, can be subclasses. Note that `rank` in `Faculty` has a list of possible values, and in `Student` there is an initial value for `credits` and a range for `gpa`. Multiple inheritance is permitted, as shown for `TeachingAssistant`, which extends both `Graduate` and `Faculty` classes. The code shown in Figure 7.8 can be compiled through the Studio IDE and once the classes are created, object instances can be created in several ways, including through the Populate facility that provides random data for instances. The user can input data directly by creating a simple web-based form to accept the values, by using SQL INSERT commands through the Caché System Management Portal, by creating

Figure 7.8

Class Definitions for the University Schema Using Caché Studio

On the Companion Website:

▪ Caché code for this example

```
Class University.Address Extends (%SerialObject, %Populate){
/* define attributes */
Property Street As %String(MAXLEN = 80, POPSPEC = "Street()");
Property City As %String(MAXLEN = 80, POPSPEC = "City()");
Property State As %String(MAXLEN = 2, POPSPEC = "USState()");
Property Zip As %String(MAXLEN = 5, POPSPEC = "USZip()");
}


Class University.Person Extends (%Persistent, %Populate){
Index persidndx On perId [ Unique ];
/* define attributes */
Property perId As %Integer;
Property LName As %String(POPSPEC = "LastName()") [ Required ];
Property FName As %String(POPSPEC = "FirstName()");
Property add As Address;
Property phone As %String(POPSPEC = "USPhone()");
Property birthDate As %Date;
/* define methods */
ClassMethod FindAge() As %Integer{}
}


Class University.Faculty Extends Person{
/* define attributes */
Property rank As %String(VALUELIST = "'Instructor','Assistant','Associate','Professor'");
Property salary As %Numeric;
/* define relationships */
Relationship belongsTo As Department [ Cardinality = one, Inverse = hasFaculty ];
Relationship teaches As ClassSection [ Cardinality = many, Inverse = hasTeacher ];
Relationship advises As Student [ Cardinality = many, Inverse = hasAdvisor ];
Relationship hasEvaluation As Evaluation [ Cardinality = children, Inverse = isEvalOf ];
Relationship chairs As Department [ Cardinality = one, Inverse = hasChair ];
/* define member methods */
ClassMethod giveRaise(amtRaise As %Numeric) { }
}


Class University.Student Extends Person{
/* define properties */
Property credits As %SmallInt(initial = 0);
```

Figure 7.8—Continued

```
Property gpa As %Numeric(MAXVAL = 4.0,MINVAL = 0.0);
/* define relationships */
Relationship hasAdvisor As University.Faculty [ Cardinality = one, Inverse = advises ];
Relationship takesClass As ClassSection [ Cardinality = many, Inverse = hasStudent ];
Relationship earnedGrade As Mark [ Cardinality = many, Inverse = givenStudent ];
/* define member methods */
ClassMethod addCredits(numCredits As %SmallInt){}
ClassMethod getStatus() As %String{}
}

Class University.Undergraduate Extends Student{
/* define attributes*/
Property major As %String;
/* define member methods */
ClassMethod changeMajor(newMajor As %String){}

}
Class University.Graduate Extends University.Student{
/* define attributes*/
Property program As %String;
/* define member methods */
ClassMethod changeProgram(newProgram As %String){}

}

Class University.TeachingAssistant Extends (Graduate, Faculty){
/* define attributes*/
Property fundingSource As %String;
Property tuitionRemission As %Numeric;
/* define relationships */
Relationship assists As ClassSection [ Cardinality = one, Inverse = hasTA ];
}

Class University.Department Extends %Persistent{
/* define attributes */
Property deptCode As %String [ Required ];
Property deptName As %String [ Required ];
Property deptOffice As %String;
Property deptPhone As %String;
/* define relationships */
```

Figure 7.8—Continued

```
Relationship hasFaculty As University.Faculty[ Cardinality = many, Inverse = belongsTo ];
Relationship offers As University.Course [ Cardinality = many, Inverse = isOffering ];
Relationship hasChair As University.Faculty [ Cardinality = many, Inverse = chairs ];
}


Class University.Course Extends %Persistent{
/* define attributes */
Property cNo As %String [ Required ];
Property cTitle As %String [ Required ];
Property credits As %SmallInt;
Property description As %String;
/* define relationships */
Relationship isOffering As University.Department [ Cardinality = one, Inverse = offers ];
Relationship hasPrerequisite As Course [ Cardinality = many, Inverse = isPreqOf ];
Relationship isPreqOf As University.Course [ Cardinality = one, Inverse = hasPrerequisite ];
Relationship hasSection As University.ClassSection [ Cardinality = children, Inverse =
isSectionOf ];
}


Class University.ClassSection Extends %Persistent {
/* define attributes */
Property sectionCode As %String [ Required ];
Property schedule As %String;
Property room As %String;
/* define relationships */
Relationship givenIn As Mark [ Cardinality = many, Inverse = givenTo ];
Relationship hasTeacher As University.Faculty [ Cardinality = one, Inverse = teaches ];
Relationship hasStudent As University.Student[ Cardinality = one, Inverse = takesClass ];
Relationship isSectionOf As University.Course [ Cardinality = parent, Inverse = hasSection ];
Relationship hasTA As University.TeachingAssistant [Cardinality = one, Inverse = assists]
}


Class University.Evaluation Extends %Persistent{
/* define attributes*/
Property evalDate As %Date [ Required ];
Property raterName As %String [ Required ];
Property rating As %String(VALUELIST = "1,2,3,4,5");
/* define relationships */
```

Figure 7.8—Continued

```
Relationship isEvalOf As University.Faculty [ Cardinality = parent, Inverse = hasEvaluation ];
}


Class University.Mark extends %Persistent {
/* define attributes */
Property grade As %String(VALUELIST = "'A','B','C','D','F','I'");
/* define relationships */
Relationship givenStudent As University.Student [ Cardinality = one, Inverse = earnedGrade
];
Relationship givenTo As University.ClassSection [ Cardinality = one, Inverse = givenIn ];
}
```

new objects and assigning values to attributes in command-line mode, by accessing the database from an interface like ODBC through another DBMS such as Access, or by using an application in any of several languages. Queries can also be created and executed in several ways, including through SQL in the System Management Portal.

7.8   Chapter Summary

Object-oriented databases allow database designers and developers to express complex data structures, operations, and relationships more naturally than traditional relational databases. Object-oriented programming languages including C++, Java, and Smalltalk have been extended to allow **persistent** storage of the objects they create and manipulate. The fundamental concepts of the object-oriented paradigm involve an understanding of **objects**, **methods**, **encapsulation**, **classes**, and **inheritance**. In an object-oriented database, the class definitions correspond to class definitions for an object-oriented programming language. The set of object instances in a class is called the **extent** of the class. Each object instance is given a unique object identifier (**OID**) that is independent of any of the values of the object, and that is unchanging. OIDs are used to establish relationships between object instances. **Attributes** in a class can be **atomic types**, **enumerated types**, **structured types**, or **collection types**.

The Object Management Group (**OMG**) has defined standards for the object model and for **UML**, as a modeling standard.

UML diagrams are a useful method of representing classes and relationships, and fit well with the object-oriented data model. From a UML diagram, it is relatively easy to translate the design into class definitions that correspond directly to the items on the diagram, including the relationships between classes. A class is represented by a rectangle having three parts—the class name, the attributes, and the methods. Relationships are shown by lines, with multiplicity indicators of the form *min..max,* but placed on the opposite side to that used in E-R diagrams. Relationships between classes, called **associations**, can be unidirectional or bidirectional, which is represented by defining an inverse for the relationship. They can specify a "one" relationship with a member of a class, or a "many," which is represented by specifying `Set` before the name of the related class. **Aggregation** is a special type of relationship that connects a whole to its parts. **Generalization** is indicated by lines connecting the subclasses to the superclass, with a triangle on the line into the superclass.

Before it disbanded in 2001, the Object Data Management Group (**ODMG**) established industry-accepted standards for object-oriented databases, including standards for Object Definition Language (**ODL**) and Object Query Language (**OQL**). In ODL, we give class declarations, including the name of the class, any inheritance, extent and keys, and descriptions of the attributes, relationships, and methods. OQL uses a syntax that is similar to SQL, but has greater flexibility for dealing with a variety of structures. Because of the ODMG standards for object-oriented language extensions, the process of developing a database using an OODBMS is closely linked to applications in those languages.

Exercises

7.1   Define the following terms:

   a. persistence

   b. encapsulation

   c. method

   d. extent

   e. class hierarchy

   f. OID

g. association

h. aggregation

i. multiplicity indicator

j. reflexive association

k. inverse relationship

l. signature of a method

m. overloading

n. interface

o. overriding a method

7.2 (a) Modify the UML diagram shown in Figure 7.5 by adding additional methods.

   (b) Modify the ODL schema shown in Figure 7.6 to include the new methods you added.

7.3 Develop a UML class diagram for the college student and activities described in Exercise 3.4, but expand it to cover graduate students as well as undergraduates. Graduate students can participate in the clubs as members, or they can serve as moderators of the clubs. A graduate student, like an undergraduate, has one academic advisor, but may also have a thesis advisor, who oversees his or her thesis research.

7.4 Write an ODL schema that corresponds to the UML class diagram you developed in Exercise 7.3.

7.5 Develop a UML diagram for the dental group described in Exercise 3.5, but expand it by assuming that some of the dentists are surgeons, who can perform oral surgery. Also assume some of the professionals are dental hygienists, who can perform routine work such as cleaning and taking X-rays. A patient typically begins an ordinary visit by starting with a dental hygienist who performs routine work, and then a dentist who does a check-up in the same initial visit. The work needed is usually determined at this visit. If follow-up visits are required, each of the next visits will be with one dentist. If a patient requires oral surgery, at least one of his or her visits must be with one of the surgeons, even though the rest of the work needed might be performed by his or her regular dentist. When surgery is performed, there must be a qualified assistant present. Only some of the hygienists are qualified to assist in surgeries. Assume this database does not keep track of appointments, only of actual visits, work, billing, and payments.

7.6   Write an ODL schema that corresponds to the UML class diagram you developed in Exercise 7.5.

7.7   Develop a UML diagram for the interior design firm described in Exercise 3.6, but expand it by assuming the clients can either be individuals or corporations. Also assume the contractors can be licensed professionals with various specialties (such as plumbers, electricians, or carpenters) or hourly laborers.

7.8   Write an ODL schema that corresponds to the UML class diagram you developed in Exercise 7.7.

7.9   Develop a UML diagram for the automobile body repair shop described in Exercise 3.7, but assume the shop is expanding to perform mechanical repairs as well as body work. Body work can be done by a technician, but all mechanical repairs require a licensed mechanic. Jobs now may require one technician to handle the body work (if any) and a licensed mechanic to do the mechanical repairs (if any).

7.10   Write an ODL schema that corresponds to the UML class diagram you developed in Exercise 7.9.

7.11   Develop a UML diagram for the physical therapy center described in Exercise 3.8, but expand it to assume some visits require the use of specialized equipment for electrotherapy, ultrasound, hydrotherapy, and so on, and the patient is charged for each use of such equipment. Patients may also be supplied with special devices to take home, such as exercise bands, neck pillows, and so on, and the patient is charged for these special supplies.

7.12   Write an ODL schema that corresponds to the UML class diagram you developed in Exercise 7.9.

7.13   Convert the E-R diagram shown in Figure 4.4 into a UML diagram, making the additional assumption that some customers may place orders online, and require an email address and optional credit card type and credit card number to be stored. When an online customer shops, a shopping cart is created that shows what items have been selected and the date added.

7.14   Write an ODL schema that corresponds to the UML class diagram you developed in Exercise 7.13.

On the Companion Website:

- Lab Exercises
- Sample Project
- Student Projects

CHAPTER 8

The Enhanced Entity-Relationship Model and the Object-Relational Model

Chapter Objectives

In this chapter you will learn the following:

- Why the E-R model has been extended to the EE-R model

- The meaning of generalization and specialization

- How to represent a generalization hierarchy on an EE-R diagram

- How to represent generalization constraints

- The meaning of union

- How to use (*min,max*) notation for relationship constraints

- How to map an EE-R model to a strictly relational model

- How to use the object-oriented extensions to the relational model with standard SQL

- How Oracle implements the object-relational model

- How to map an EE-R model to an object-relational model

 On the Companion Website:

- Lab Exercises

- Sample Project

- Student Projects

8.1   Rationale for Extending the E-R Model

Although the E-R model is sufficient to represent data needs for traditional applications in business, it is not semantically rich enough to model the more complex environments used for more advanced applications. The databases used for geographic information systems, search engines, data mining, multimedia, digital publishing, financial services, computer-aided design and computer-aided manufacturing (CAD/CAM), software engineering, telecommunications, engineering design, and many other sophisticated applications must be capable of representing more semantic information than the standard E-R model can express. The **Extended Entity-Relationship (EE-R)** model extends the E-R model to allow various types of abstraction to be included, and to express constraints more clearly. Additional symbols have been added to standard E-R diagrams to create EE-R diagrams that express these concepts.

8.2   Generalization and Specialization

The process of generalization and its inverse, specialization, are two abstractions that are used to incorporate more meaning in EE-R diagrams.

8.2.1   Specialization

Often an entity set contains one or more subsets that have special attributes or that participate in relationships that other members of the same entity set do not have. For instance, in the University example whose E-R diagram is shown in Figure 3.12, the `Faculty` entity set can be broken up into subsets, `AdjunctFac` and `FullTimeFac`. Adjunct faculty members teach part-time and are usually appointed on a temporary basis, while full-time faculty are regular employees who work on a continuing basis. Adjunct faculty members are paid per course, while full-time faculty are paid an annual salary. All faculty have attributes `facId`, `lastName`, `firstName`, and `rank`, but `AdjunctFac` members have a local attribute called `coursePayRate` whereas `FullTimeFac` have a local attribute called `annualSalary`.

The method of identifying subsets of existing entity sets, called **specialization**, corresponds to the notion of subclass and class inheritance in object-oriented design, where it is represented by class hierarchies, as discussed in Chapter 7. Figure 8.1(a) shows how this superclass-subclass relationship is represented in EE-R diagrams. In this diagram, the superclass, `Faculty`, has been specialized into two subclasses, `AdjunctFac` and `FullTimeFac`. The circle below `Faculty` is called the **specialization circle**, and it is connected by a line to the superclass. Each subclass is connected to the circle by a line having an **inheritance symbol**, a subset symbol or cup, with the open side facing the superclass. The subclasses inherit the attributes of the superclass, and may optionally have distinct local attributes, such as `coursePayRate` for `AdjunctFac` and `annualSalary` for `FullTimeFac`. Since each member of a subclass **is a** member of the superclass, the specialization circle is sometimes referred to as an *isa* **relationship**.

Sometimes an entity has just one subset with special properties or relationships that we want to keep information about. It contains only one subclass for a specialization. In that case, on the EE-R diagram we omit the circle and simply show the subclass connected by a subset line to the superclass. For example, if some university `Class` entity instances have a lab component for which we want to keep information about the lab used and lab schedule, we could design a subclass just of those entities, as shown in Figure 8.1(b). Note that `LabClass` inherits all the attributes of `Class`, (i.e., `LabClass` *isa* `Class`) in addition to having its local attributes of `labNo` and `labSched`.

Subclasses may also participate in local relationships that do not apply to the superclass or to other subclasses in the same hierarchy. For example, only

FIGURE 8.1(a)

Specialization with Two
Subclasses

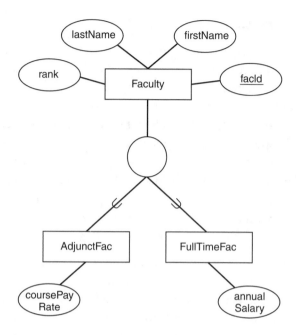

regular faculty members can subscribe to a pension plan. We assume each full-time faculty member can choose one of several companies, and has a unique contract number for his or her pension plan with that company. Each company has several contact persons, of whom one is assigned to correspond with the faculty member. Figure 8.1(c) illustrates this possibility.

8.2.2   Generalization

By the process of specialization, we developed the Faculty class hierarchy by breaking up an existing class into subclasses. Class hierarchies can also be created by recognizing that two or more classes have common properties and identifying a common superclass for them, a process called **generalization**. These two processes are inverses of each other, but they both result in the same type of hierarchy diagram. For example, since students and faculty both have IDs and names as attributes, we could generalize these two entity sets into a new superclass, Person, having the common attributes. The subclasses Student and Faculty would each retain their special attributes, as shown in Figure 8.1(d). Using generalization, we developed this diagram from the bottom up. Note that we would have the

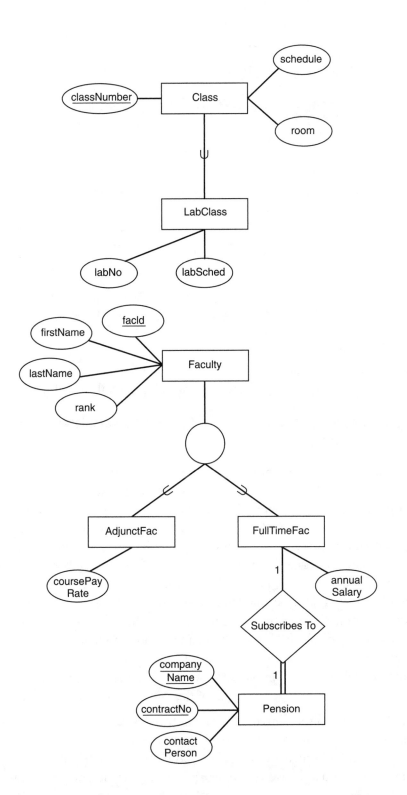

FIGURE 8.1(b)
Specialization with One Subclass

FIGURE 8.1(c)
Subclass with Relationship

FIGURE 8.1(d)

Generalization with Person Superclass

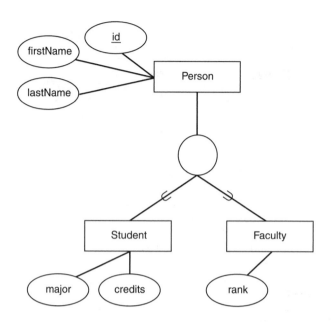

same diagram if we had started with Person and specialized it into Student and Faculty, but we would have been working from the top down.

8.2.3   Generalization Constraints—Disjointness, Completeness, Definition Method

Subclasses can be **overlapping**, which means the same entity instance can belong to more than one of the subclasses, or **disjoint**, which means they have no common members. This is referred to as the **disjointness** constraint, and it is expressed by placing an appropriate letter, d or o, in the specialization circle. A d indicates disjoint subclasses, and an o indicates overlapping subclasses. For example, since a faculty member cannot be both adjunct and full-time, we place a d in the circle for that specialization, as shown on the bottom left in Figure 8.2. We have placed an o in the specialization circle of Person into Faculty and Student to indicate that a person can be both a faculty member and a student. We are assuming, just for this diagram, that a faculty member might be able to take graduate courses, for example, and therefore he or she could be a member of the Student entity set as well as of the Faculty set.

Students are also specialized disjointly in this diagram into undergraduate and graduate. Both types of students have attributes id, lastName, and firstName inherited from Person, both have the attribute credits, but undergraduates have major as an attribute, while graduate students

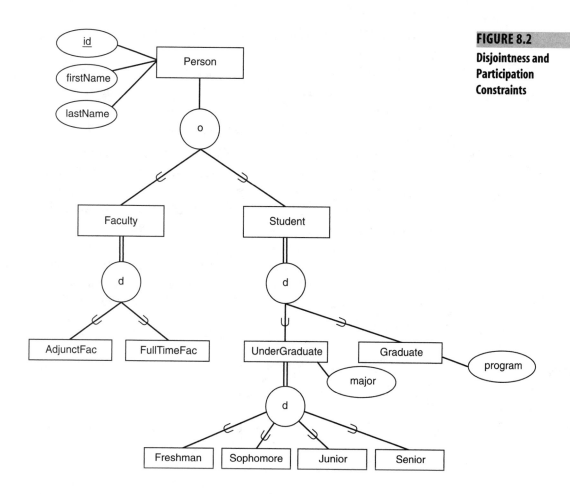

FIGURE 8.2

Disjointness and Participation Constraints

have `program`. Undergraduates are further disjointly specialized into class years, as shown by the `d` in the circle for that specialization. Although we have not listed them, we will assume that each class year has some distinguishing attribute. For example, freshmen could have a peer mentor, seniors could have a thesis supervisor, and so on.

A specialization also has a **completeness** constraint, which shows whether every member of the entity set must participate in it. If every member of the superclass must belong to some subclass, we have a **total** specialization. If some superclass members can be permitted not to belong to any subclass, the specialization is **partial**. For example, since every faculty member must be either `AdjunctFac` or `FullTimeFac`, we have total specialization. In Figure 8.2, this is indicated by the double line connecting the superclass, `Faculty`, to the specialization circle on the bottom left of the diagram. The single line connecting `Person` to its specialization circle indicates that the specialization into `Faculty` and `Student` is partial. There may be some `Person` entities who are neither faculty nor students. The double line below `Student` indicates a total specialization into graduate or undergraduate. The double line below undergraduates shows a total specialization into class years, implying that every undergraduate student must belong to one of the class years.

In some specialization hierarchies, it is possible to identify the subclass that an entity belongs to by examining a specific condition or predicate for each subclass. In the specialization of `UnderGraduate`, if the predicate "credits <30" is true, the student belongs to the freshman subclass, while if the predicate "credits > = 30 AND credits <60" is true, the student is a sophomore, and so on for the other two subclasses. This is an example of a **predicate-defined** specialization, since subclass membership is determined by a predicate. On an EE-R diagram, we can write the defining predicate on the line from the specialization circle to the subclass as shown in Figure 8.3(a).

FIGURE 8.3(a)

Predicate-Defined Specialization

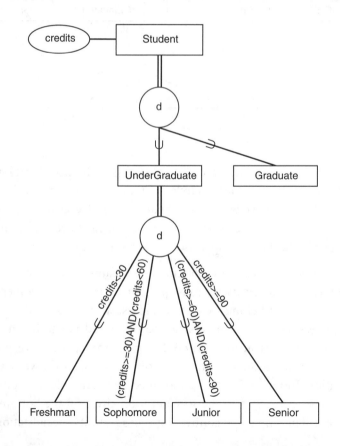

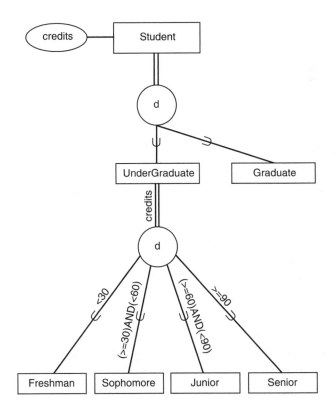

FIGURE 8.3(b)
Attribute-Defined Specialization

Some predicate-defined specializations, including this one, use the value of the same attribute in the defining predicate for all the subclasses. These are called **attribute-defined** specializations. We indicate the defining attribute on the line from the circle to the superclass, and the distinguishing value for each subclass on the line from the subclass to the circle, as shown for the class year specialization in Figure 8.3(b). Specializations that are not predicate-defined are said to be **user-defined**, since the user is responsible for placing the entity instance in the correct subclass. In our example, the specialization of `Person` into `Faculty` and `Student`; of `Faculty` into `Adjunct` and `FullTime`; and `Student` into `Undergraduate` and `Graduate` are all user-defined.

8.2.4 Multiple Hierarchies and Inheritance

In addition to specializing undergraduate students according to the class year, a database designer could decide that it is important to specialize them by their residence status. Figure 8.3(c) shows this further specialization of `UnderGraduate` by residence according to whether a student lives in an on-campus dormitory, an off-campus university property, or

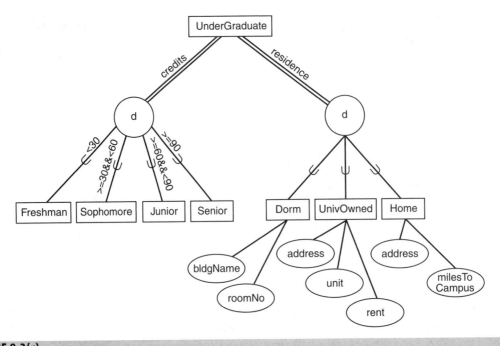

FIGURE 8.3(c)

Multiple Specializations—by Class Year and by Residence

at home. The class year specialization and the residence specialization are independent of each other, and both can appear on the same diagram. In this way, the EE-R model allows us to give the same superclass more than one specialization.

Sometimes the same entity set can be a subclass of two or more superclasses. Such a class is called a **shared subclass**, and it has **multiple inheritance** from its superclasses. For example, adding to our University example, as shown in Figure 8.4, some graduate students might be Teaching Assistants. Teaching Assistants receive some amount of `tuitionremission` for their tuition from a `fundingSource`, and they assist in some introductory classes at the university, for which they receive a `salary` and perhaps a `rank` of Lecturer. Members of the `TeachingAssistant` subclass inherit all the attributes of `Faculty` and of `Graduate`, and of the superclasses of those classes, `Student` and `Person`, in addition to having their own distinguishing attributes of `fundingSource` and `tuitionremission`. As with all subclasses, shared subclasses can participate in relationships. For exam-

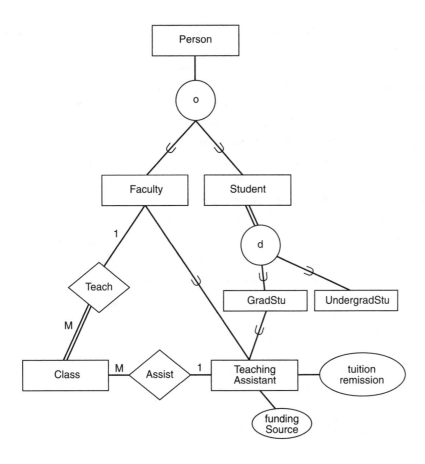

FIGURE 8.4

Multiple Inheritance

ple, we could have `TeachingAssistant` participating in an `Assist` relationship with the `Class` entity set.

8.3 Union

Whereas a shared subclass, as described in the previous section, is a member of all its superclasses and inherits attributes from all of them, a subclass can be related to one of a collection, called a **union** or **category**, of superclasses, rather than belonging to all of them. In that case, an instance of the subclass inherits the attributes of only one of the superclasses, depending on which member of the union that it belongs to. Expanding on our University example, suppose we want to represent sponsors of campus-wide events, which can be sponsored by teams, departments, or clubs. We assume here that a campus-wide event must have exactly one sponsor, but it can be a team, a department, or a club. We could form a union of `Team`, `Department`, and `Club`, which is then the set of all of these entities. `Sponsor` is a subclass of the union representing just one of the many roles that each of these entities might have. The attributes of a particular sponsor will depend on which type it is. Figure 8.5(a) illustrates a union of `Club`, `Team`, and `Department`, represented by the union circle below them, which has a set union symbol inside. The union has subclass `Sponsor`, which is related to `CampusWideEvent`. The three classes are connected to the circle with a set union symbol in it. The circle is connected to the subclass, `Sponsor`, by a line with the subset symbol (cup) on it, facing the circle.

Categories can be partial or total, depending on whether every member of the sets that make up the union must participate in it. The line connecting `Sponsor` to its union circle in Figure 8.5(a) is single, indicating a **partial**

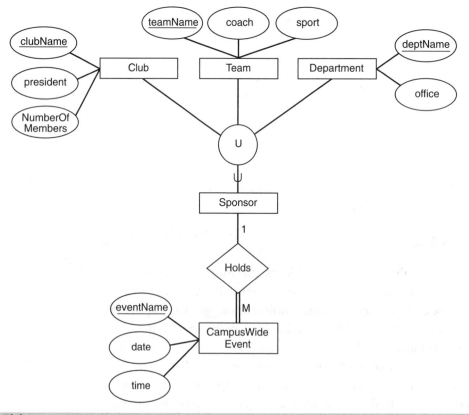

FIGURE 8.5(a)

Example of Union

category. This indicates that not every `Club`, `Team`, or `Department` has to be a `Sponsor`. Elaborating on this example in Figure 8.5(b) we show that `CampusWideEvent` is a union of `Concert` or `Fair`. This indicates that every campus-wide event is either a concert or a fair, and a particular

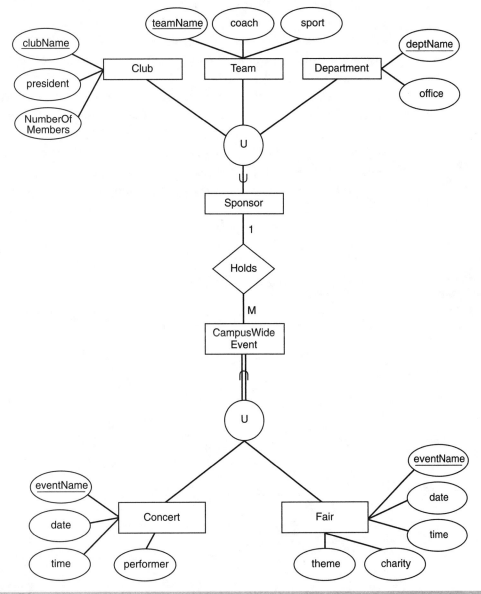

FIGURE 8.5(b)
Partial vs Total Union

campus-wide event will have the attributes of one of these superclasses. The line connecting `CampusWideEvent` to the union circle is double, indicating a **total category**, which means every `Concert` and `Fair` must be a member of `CampusWideEvent`.

Different designers can make different choices about when to use a union or a specialization abstraction. If a union is total, and the superclasses share many attributes, it might be preferable to use specialization. Figure 8.6 shows a specialization of campus-wide events into two subclasses, instead of using the union of concerts and fairs into campus-wide events as we did in Figure 8.5(b). Here we show an attribute-defined specialization, with `type` as the defining attribute. Notice that as a specialization/generalization, it is clear that every concert or fair is a campus event because, in specialization/generalization, every member of a subclass is automatically a member of the superclass. It is a total specialization, as shown by the double line connecting `CampusWideEvent` to the specialization circle, indicating that all campus-wide events are either fairs or concerts.

FIGURE 8.6

Total Union replaced by Specialization/ Generalization

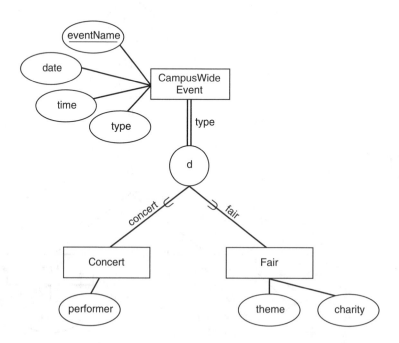

8.4 Using (*min,max*) Notation for Cardinality and Participation

In the E-R and EE-R diagrams thus far, we have used single lines or double lines to show participation constraints for relationships. We have shown relationship cardinality by using "1" for "one" and "M" (or "N") for "many" on the appropriate lines. An alternative representation that shows both participation and cardinality constraints is the (*min,max*) notation illustrated in the E-R diagram in Figure 8.7 for part of the University example. It can

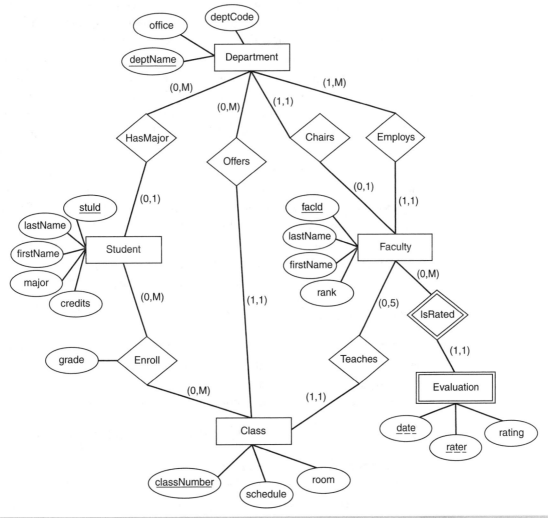

FIGURE 8.7

Part of the University E-R Diagram with (*min, max*) Notation.

be used with either E-R or EE-R diagrams, and it is similar to the multiplicity indicators used in UML diagrams. Each line connecting an entity rectangle to a relationship diamond has a pair of integers, (*min,max*), written in parentheses above it. The first integer of the pair, *min*, specifies the least number of relationship instances an entity instance must participate in. If *min* is 0, it means that there might be entity instances that do not participate in instances of the relationship, so the participation is partial. If *min* is 1 or more, the participation is total. The value of *max* is the greatest number of relationship instances the entity can participate in. This value could be 1, M (to represent *many*), or some constant integer, such as 10. Sometimes * is used to represent *many*. In Figure 8.7, the line connecting `Department` to the `HasMajor` relationship diamond has a min of 0, indicating that a department does not need to have a student majoring in it, and a max of M, indicating that a department can have many student majors. The line from `Student` to the `HasMajor` relationship diamond has (0,1), which means a student does not have to have any major, and has at most one major. The (1,M) on the line connecting `Department` to the `Employs` relationship has a min of 1, meaning a department must have at least one faculty member, and a max of M, since a department can have many faculty. The line from `Faculty` to the relationship has (1,1), indicating that a faculty member belongs to exactly one department. Other participation and cardinality constraints are indicated on the diagram. We note that all of these constraints reflect assumptions about this particular university and that the constraints might be different in another institution. Also note that the placement of the constraints differs from that in the UML diagrams shown in Chapter 7.

8.5   A Sample EE-R Diagram

We now modify our University E-R diagram to show some of the generalizations discussed in previous sections. Figure 8.8 shows an EE-R diagram for the University example, modified to illustrate the use of generalization/specialization, union, and (*min,max*) notation.

8.6   Mapping an EE-R Model to a Relational Model

The techniques discussed in Section 4.8 for mapping an E-R model to a relational model must be extended to take into account the additional features of the EE-R model, namely specialization/generalization, and union.

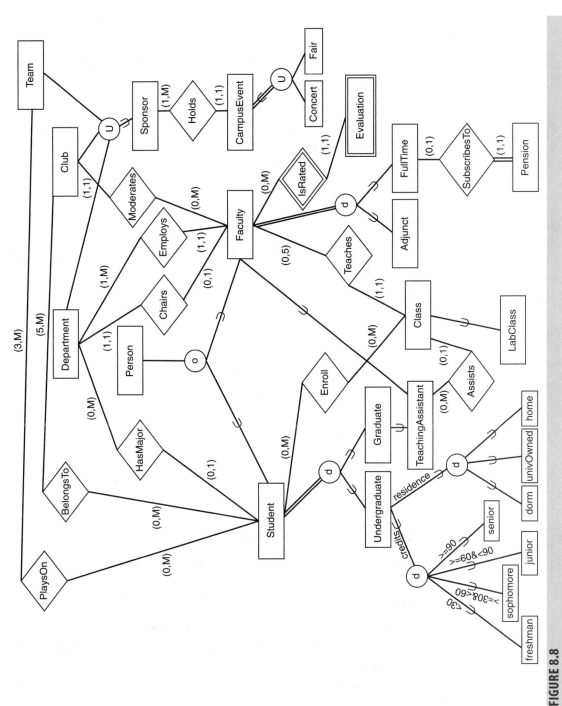

FIGURE 8.8

An EE-R Diagram for the University Example

8.6.1   Summary of E-R to Strictly Relational Mapping Concepts

For entity sets and relationships that are not part of generalizations or unions, the mapping proceeds as for the E-R model.

- We map strong entity sets to tables having a column for each single-valued, non-composite attribute.

  - For composite attributes, we create a column for each component and do not represent the composite. Alternatively, we can create a single column for the composite and ignore the components.

  - For each multi-valued attribute, we create a separate table having the primary key of the entity, along with a column for the multi-valued attribute. Alternatively, if we know the maximum number of values for the attribute, we can create multiple columns for these values. Another method is to use the multi-valued attribute as part of the primary key, thus "flattening" the table.

- For each weak entity set, we create a table that includes the primary key of the owner entity along with the attributes of the weak entity set.

- For one-to-many binary relationships we place the primary key of the one side in the table of the many side, creating a foreign key.

- For one-to-one binary relationships, we place either one of the primary keys in the table for the other entity.

- For many-to-many binary relationships, and for all higher-level relationships, we create a relationship table that consists of the primary keys of the related entities, along with any descriptive attributes of the relationship.

8.6.2   Mapping EE-R Class Hierarchies to Relational Tables

To illustrate the representation of subclasses, we will use Figure 8.1(a), which shows `Faculty` with subclasses `AdjunctFac` and `FullTimeFac`. We can choose one of the following methods.

- **Method 1.** Create a table for the superclass and one for each of the subclasses, placing the primary key of the superclass in each subclass table. For Figure 8.1(a), we create three tables, `Faculty`, `AdjunctFac`, and `FullTimeFac`. Faculty has the attributes shown on the diagram, including a primary key, `facId`. Both `AdjunctFac` and `FullTimeFac` tables have columns for their own attributes, plus columns for the primary key of the superclass, `facId`, which functions both as the primary key and a foreign key in those tables. The tables are:

```
Faculty(facId, lastName, firstName, rank)
AdjunctFac(facId, coursePayRate)
FullTimeFac(facId, annualSalary)
```

- **Method 2.** Create tables for each of the subclasses, and no table for the superclass. Place all of the attributes of the superclass in each of the subclass tables. For this example, we would have tables for `AdjunctFac` and `FullTimeFac`, and none for `Faculty`. The tables are:

```
AdjunctFac(facId, lastName, firstName, rank, coursePayRate)
FullTimeFac(facId, lastName, firstName, rank, annualSalary)
```

- **Method 3.** Create a single table that contains all the attributes of the superclass, along with all the attributes of all subclasses. For our example, we could create the table:

```
AllFac(facId, lastName, firstName, rank, annualSalary,
       coursePayRate)
```

A variation of Method 3 is to add a "type field" to the record, indicating which subclass the entity belongs to. For attribute-defined disjoint specializations, this is simply the defining attribute. For overlapping specializations, we could add a type field for each specialization, indicating whether or not the entity belongs to each of the subclasses.

There are tradeoffs to be considered for each of these methods. The first works for all types of subclasses, regardless of whether the specialization is disjoint or overlapping; partial or total; and attribute-defined or user-defined. For our example, queries about faculty that involve only the common attributes are easily answered using the superclass table. However, queries about members of a subclass will, in general, require a join with the superclass table. The second method handles queries about the subclasses well, since one table has all the information about each subclass. However, it should not be used if the subclasses are overlapping, because data about the instances that belong to more than one subclass will be duplicated. It cannot be used if the specialization is partial, because the entity instances that do not belong to any subclass cannot be represented at all using this method. The third method allows us to answer queries about all the subclasses and the superclass without doing joins, but it will result in storing many null values in the database.

8.6.3   Mapping Unions

To represent unions (categories), we create a table for the union itself, and individual tables for each of the superclasses, using foreign keys to connect them. A problem that often arises with mapping unions is that the superclasses can have different primary keys. Figure 8.5(a) shows `Sponsor` as the union of `Club`, `Team`, and `Department`, which have primary keys `clubName`, `teamName`, and `deptName`, respectively. Although these are all names, they might not be comparable because of differences in length. Other unions might involve grouping together entity sets with radically different keys. The solution is to create a surrogate key that will be the primary key of the union. It will be a foreign key in the tables for each of the superclasses. For the `Sponsor` example, we create a surrogate key for `sponsor`, which we call `sponsorId`, and we insert that attribute as a foreign key in the tables for `Club`, `Team`, and `Department`. We also add `SponsorType` to indicate whether the sponsor is a club, team, or department. The schema will be:

```
Sponsor(sponsorId, sponsorType)
Club(clubName, president, numberOfMembers, sponsorId)
Team(teamName, coach, sport, sponsorId)
Department(deptName, office, sponsorId)
```

If the primary keys of the superclasses are the same, it is not necessary to create a surrogate key. The table for the union will consist of the common primary key field and a type field. The common primary key field will also function as a foreign key for the superclass tables. For the `CampusWideEvent` example shown as a union in Figure 8.5(b), the schema will be:

```
CampusWideEvent(eventName, eventType)
Concert(eventName, date, time, performer)
Fair(eventName, date, time, theme, charity)
```

8.7   Extending the Relational Model

The relational model was designed to represent data that consists of single-valued attributes of a small collection of data types, related in relatively simple ways, typically used in traditional data processing. As discussed in Section 8.1, the model lacks some features needed to represent the more complex types and relationships necessary for advanced applications. The industry responded to this challenge initially by proposing an entirely new data model, the object data model, which is discussed in Chapter 7. Vendors of relational database management systems, including Oracle, IBM, Sybase, Informix, PostgreSQL, and Microsoft have met this competition by capturing some of the features of the object data model, and extending their relational products to incorporate them. The SQL:1999 standard also extended the SQL language to use these new features, which were further extended in 2003, 2006, and 2008. The object-relational model can be viewed as a compromise between the strictly relational model and the object-oriented model described in Chapter 7.

Some of the additional features are:

- Richer fundamental data types, including types for multimedia—text, images, video, audio, and so on

- Collection types that can hold multiple attributes

- User-defined data types, including user-written operations to manipulate them

- Representation of class hierarchies, with inheritance of both data structures and methods

- Reference or pointer types for objects

- Support for XML

- Support for data mining, including expanded statistical functions

8.7.1   New Fundamental Data Types

SQL:1999 added two new fundamental data types, LARGE OBJECT (LOB) and BOOLEAN.

The **LOB** type varities can be used to store text, audio, video, and other multimedia objects. Besides images and audio or video clips, an attribute such as a student's signature might be stored in LOB format. The LOB type has variants **BLOB** (BINARY LARGE OBJECT), and **CLOB** (CHARACTER LARGE

OBJECT). LOB types have very restricted functions, such as substring operations. They allow comparisons only for equality or inequality, and they cannot be used for ordering or in GROUP BY or ORDER BY clauses. Since they are large files, LOBs are normally stored and rarely retrieved again. They can be stored in the table itself if they are not too large, or in a file outside the table, by using a **LOB locator**, a system-generated binary surrogate for the actual address. If we wish to add a student's picture to the `Student` record, we would add the `picture` attribute in the CREATE TABLE command for the `Student` table, using the attribute declaration:

```
picture CLOB REF IS picId SYSTEM GENERATED,
```

The `picId` is a reference pointer to the file containing an image of the picture. We will discuss its use in Section 8.7.4.

Note that Oracle does not support all the features of the standard for LOBs, although it includes BLOB, CLOB, and NCLOB types, as well as Bfile, for extremely large objects.

The SQL standard **BOOLEAN** data type can be used for attributes with possible values of true, false, or unknown. In the table for students, we could add a Boolean attribute, `matriculated`, to indicate whether the student is matriculated or not, using a declaration such as the following within the CREATE TABLE command:

```
matriculated BOOLEAN DEFAULT false,
```

Oracle does not support this data type, but we can simulate it by using string or other type data.

8.7.2   Collection Types

The SQL standard includes structured collection types, including **array** and **row**, as well as sets (unordered collections of distinct elements) and multisets (unordered collections that allow repetition of elements). Oracle has two collection types—**VARRAY** and **nested tables** that perform many of the same functions.

In the SQL standard, **ARRAY[n]** is a structured type that allows an ordered collection of values of the same base data type to be stored as a single attribute. We must specify the base type for the *n* values to be stored in the array, using the form:

attribute-name basetype ARRAY [*n*]

For example, if students are allowed to have double majors, we could use an array for the `majors` attribute in the CREATE TABLE command as in

```
CREATE TABLE Stu (
    stuId        CHAR(6)PRIMARY KEY,
    lastName     VARCHAR(20) NOT NULL,
    firstName    VARCHAR(20) NOT NULL,
    matriculated BOOLEAN DEFAULT false,
    majors       VARCHAR(10) ARRAY[2],
    credits      SMALLINT DEFAULT 0);
```

Values are inserted into an array by invoking a built-in method called a **type constructor**, which creates an instance of the relevant type, using the values the user supplies. For standard arrays, the constructor is called ARRAY. We use it in the standard INSERT statement as follows

```
INSERT  INTO Student VALUES ('S555' , 'Quirk' , 'Sean' , true,
ARRAY['French','Psychology'], 30);
```

The square bracket notation is used in standard SQL to refer to individual elements of an array. For example, we can access a student's majors by writing

```
SELECT s. stuId, s.majors[1], s.majors[2]
FROM    Student s;
```

Oracle uses **VARRAY** in place of the standard syntax. We must specify the base type for the values to be stored in the array, using the form

```
CREATE TYPE arraytypename AS VARRAY(size) OF basetype;
```

For example, if we wish to allow students to have double majors, we can create a user-defined type for an array with two cells to hold major values, and use that type as the data type of the `majors` attribute in the table. Figure 8.9(a) shows the Oracle commands for the type and the table declaration.

To insert a record into a table with an array type, we use the type constructor, listing the values to be inserted into the array, as shown for the three rows inserted in Figure 8.9(b).

Students with only one major get a null value for the second major as shown in the second row inserted. Queries can be written as usual, or we can use the dot notation to get the entire majors array as shown in Figure 8.9(c). However, Oracle does not allow us to access cells of the array individually in queries by using an index directly. Instead we must use

Figure 8.9
VARRAYs in Oracle

Figure 8.9(a)
Oracle VARRAY Type Declaration and Column Definition

```
CREATE TYPE majorstype AS VARRAY(2) OF varchar2(20);

CREATE TABLE Stu (
    stuId           VARCHAR2(6),
    lastName        VARCHAR2(20) NOT NULL,
    firstName       VARCHAR2(20) NOT NULL,
    matriculated    VARCHAR2(5) DEFAULT 'false',
    majors          majorstype,
    credits         NUMBER(3)DEFAULT 0,
    CONSTRAINT Stu_stuId_pk PRIMARY KEY(stuId),
CONSTRAINT Stu_credits_cc CHECK ((credits>=0) AND (credits<150)));
```

Figure 8.9(b)
Using Oracle's VARRAY Constructor to Insert Values

```
INSERT INTO Stu VALUES('S555', 'Quirk','Sean', 'true',
majorstype('French','Psychology'), 30);
INSERT INTO Stu VALUES('S511', 'Marks','Daniel', 'true',
majorstype('History',null), 15);
INSERT INTO Stu VALUES('S599', 'White','Kimberly', 'true',
majorstype('CSC','Math'), 60);
```

Figure 8.9(c)
Retrieving Entire Array

```
select s.*
from Stu s;

select s.stuId, s.majors
from Stu s;
```

PL/SQL, as shown in the `printarray` procedure in Figure 8.9(d). Oracle also permits **nested tables**, which will be discussed in Section 8.7.7.

The ROW type specified in standard SQL is not implemented in Oracle. The SQL standard declaration of the components of **ROW type** consists of a sequence of pairs of field names and data types, like the list of attributes and their data types in a traditional table definition, as shown in Figure 8.10(a) for `team_row_type`. An attribute of a table can itself have a row-type, allowing nested tables. For example, we can have an attribute of a `NewStu` table to represent one team the student belongs to, as shown in Figure 8.10(b) for standard SQL.

The following returns an error, showing we cannot use subscripts to access an array.

```
select s.stuId, s.majors[1] from Stu s;
```

We must use PL/SQL instead, with a loop for the subscript.

```
set serveroutput on;

create or replace procedure printarray as
id          varchar2(6);
fname       varchar2(20);
lname       varchar2(20);
mymajors    majorstype;
cursor majcursor is
   select s.stuid, s.firstname, s.lastname, s.majors
   from Stu s;
begin
   open majcursor;
dbms_output.put_line('Id 'II'      First Name 'II'      Last
Name 'II'    Majoring in');
dbms_output.put_line('-------------------------------------
-------------------------------');
   loop
      fetch majcursor into id, fname, lname, mymajors;
      exit when majcursor%notfound;
      dbms_output.put(idII'      'IIfnameII'      'IIlname);
      for i in 1..2 loop
         if (mymajors(i) is not null) then
            dbms_output.put('        'IImymajors(i));
         end if;
      end loop; -- FOR MAJORS
      dbms_output.put_line(' ');
   end loop; -- FOR STUDENTS
   close majcursor;
end;
```

Figure 8.9(d)
Using PL/SQL to Access Cells of an Array

The ROW constructor can use any data type for its fields, including ROW and ARRAY, and the ARRAY constructor can use a ROW type as a base type. For example, we could put several teams in the student's record by creating the table with an array of the team row type, which we call `teams`, as shown in Figure 8.10(c) in standard SQL. Now each row of the `NewStu2`

Figure 8.10

Using SQL Standard ARRAY and ROW Types

Figure 8.10(a)

Creating an SQL ROW Type

```
CREATE ROW TYPE team_row_type(
    teamName  CHAR(20),
    coach     CHAR(30),
    sport     CHAR(15));
```

Figure 8.10(b)

Declaring an Attribute of an SQL Row Type

```
CREATE TABLE NewStu    (
    stuId   CHAR(6) PRIMARY KEY,
    ...
    team    team_row_type,
    ...);
```

Figure 8.10(c)

Declaring an Array of SQL Row Types

```
CREATE TABLE NewStu2    (
    stuId          CHAR(6)PRIMARY KEY,
    lastName       CHAR(20) NOT NULL,
    firstName      CHAR(20) NOT NULL,
    matriculated   BOOLEAN DEFAULT false,
    teams          team_row_type ARRAY[3],
    majors         CHAR(10) ARRAY[2],
    credits        SMALLINT DEFAULT 0);
```

Figure 8.10(d)

Inserting Values for SQL ROW and ARRAY types

```
INSERT INTO NewStu2 VALUES('S999', 'Smith', 'Michael', true,
ARRAY[ROW('Angels', 'Jones', 'soccer'), ROW('Devils', 'Chin', 'swimming'),
ROW('Tigers', 'Walters', 'basketball')], ARRAY['Math', 'Biology'], 60);
```

table contains an array of up to three teams (each with their names, coaches, and sports) that the student belongs to, so we have nested tables. To insert a NewStu2 record, we use constructors, as shown in Figure 8.10(d).

As mentioned earlier, Oracle has not implemented ROW types, it uses a different syntax for arrays, and it does not support the Boolean type, so the example shown in Figure 8.10 would not work in Oracle.

8.7.3 User-Defined Data Types (UDT)

SQL:1999 also allows a user-defined data type, **DISTINCT**, to be constructed from a base type. For example, if we write,

```
CREATE DISTINCT TYPE studentAgeType AS INTEGER;
```

and also,

```
CREATE DISTINCT TYPE numberOfCreditsType AS INTEGER;
```

These types can then be used as data types for the attributes of a table, as in

```
CREATE TABLE Stu3 (
stuId          CHAR(6) PRIMARY KEY,
...
credits        numberOfCreditsType,
age            studentAgeType,
...);
```

Then, even though both use integers as the base type, we cannot compare a `studentAgeType` attribute with a `numberofCreditsType` attribute. However, Oracle does not support the DISTINCT type.

Both standard SQL and Oracle allow users to create user-defined **structured data types**, called **object types**. They are like classes in the object-oriented model. The attributes can be any SQL type, including other previously-defined structured types, allowing nesting of structured types. An object type can be either the type used for an attribute, or the only type used for a table. For example, we can create an address type as follows:

```
CREATE OR REPLACE TYPE Addresstype AS OBJECT(
street      varchar2(50),
city        varchar2(15),
state       char(2),
zip         varchar2(10));
```

For each such type, SQL provides a default **constructor** to allow new instances of the type to be created. This constructor always has the same name and data type as the user-defined data type, and we can invoke it by simply using the name of the type. Users can also create their own constructors when they define the new type. We can use this new type in defining a column of any table, as in

```
CREATE TABLE Customer (
custID        number(5)PRIMARY KEY,
custName      varchar2(40),
custAdd       Addresstype);
```

When an object type is used in this way, it is called a **column object**. Data is inserted using the default type constructor, which has the same name as the type, as in

```
INSERT INTO Customer values(1001, 'Susan Miller', Addresstype('123 Main
Street', 'Anytown', 'MN', '55144'));
```

Data can be retrieved using the SQL SELECT command, but dot notation is used to refer to the individual attributes of the column object (as in a path expression), and an alias or iterator variable must be used, as in

```
SELECT      c.custId, c.custadd.street, c.custadd.zip
FROM        customer c
WHERE       c.custId=1001;
```

A relational table may contain more than one column object.

An **object table** is one where each row represents an object. Each row, called a **row object**, has a unique OID, and can be referenced by rows in other tables, or other rows in the same table. To create an object table in Oracle we will first define a new `StudentType1` as an object, as shown in Figure 8.11(a).

As this example illustrates, a type definition contains the name of the type, a list of attributes with their data types and member functions and procedures within parentheses, as well as optional specifications `[not]` `instantiable` and `[not] final`. **Not instantiable** means no instances of that type can be created, so such types have no constructors. However, they can be used as base types from which subtypes can inherit and the subtypes can be instantiable. Types that have been created as NOT INSTANTIABLE can be changed later by the statement

```
ALTER TYPE typename INSTANTIABLE;
```

However, altering a type from INSTANTIABLE to NOT INSTANTIABLE is possible only if the type has not been used to create columns, tables, or

```
CREATE OR REPLACE TYPE studentType1 AS object(
    stuId          varchar2(6),
    lastName       varchar2(20),
    firstName      varchar2(20),
    address        Addresstype,
    advisorFacid   varchar2(6),
    credits        NUMBER(3),
    dateofBirth    DATE,
    member function findAge return number,
    member procedure addCredits(numCredits in number)
    )
INSTANTIABLE
NOT FINAL;
/
```

Figure 8.11(a)

Definition of StudentType1 Class.

```
create or replace type body studentType1 is

member function findAge return number is
age    number;
begin
       age := extract(year from (sysdate-dateofBirth) year to month);
       return(age);
end; -- of findAge

member procedure addCredits(numCredits in number) is
begin
       self.credits := self.credits + numCredits;
end; -- of addCredits
end;
/
```

Figure 8.11(b)

Oracle Code for Methods of StudentType1 Class

 On the Companion
Website:
  ■ Oracle code for this
    example

any other items that reference it. NOT FINAL means that we can create subtypes.

Note that we do not indicate primary key or other constraints for the type, because we are defining a type, not a table. The attributes can themselves be previously defined UDTs, as we see in the student `address`, which uses `AddressType`. We can also write declarations of methods as functions or procedures for the type, indicating the parameters and return types. In Oracle, the code body for the methods can be written in PL/SQL, but all the methods must be coded together, as illustrated in Figure 8.11(b) for `StudentType1`. Within the code for a method, the implicit parameter, the calling object, is referred to as *self*. When invoked, a method typically takes an instance of the type as an implicit parameter. Methods are invoked using dot notation because, like attributes, they are members of the type. For example, if `firstStudent` is an instance of the `StudentType1`, we can write in an application program:

```
firstStudent.addCredits(3);
```

Using this new `StudentType1`, we can create a new version of the `Student` table, called `NewStudent1`, which differs slightly from the version used in previous chapters, for purposes of illustration. This is an example of an **object table**, since each row is an instance of `StudentType1`. It also contains an **embedded object**, address.

```
CREATE TABLE NewStudent1 of StudentType1
(CONSTRAINT Student_stuId_pk PRIMARY KEY(stuId),
CONSTRAINT Student_advisorId_fk FOREIGN KEY (advisorId) REFERENCES
Faculty (facId));
```

Any constraints, including foreign keys, are specified for the table, since they apply to the table, not to the type. For the present, we are using the `facId` of the advisor as a foreign key. We can create as many tables as we wish using the same UDT. Although we can insert values in the usual way, it is preferable to use the `StudentType1` type constructor, as in:

```
INSERT INTO NewStudent1
VALUES(StudentType1('S999', 'Fernandes', 'Luis', addressType('101 Pine Lane',
'Madison', 'WI', '53726'), 'F101', 0, '25-Jan-1995'));
```

Besides the constructor `StudentType1`, used in the INSERT here, the new type has the `addCredits()` and `FindAge()` methods that we wrote in Figure 8.11(b), as well as the built-in observer and mutator methods for each of its attributes.

Although the user can override these observer and mutator methods by redefining them, they cannot be overloaded, unlike the corresponding methods in some object-oriented languages. The observer methods (usually called GET in OO terminology) are called using standard SQL DML commands, with path expressions and iterator variables as illustrated in

```
SELECT      s.stuId, s.address.street, s.findAge()
FROM        Newstudent1 s
WHERE       s.stuId='S999';
```

The mutator methods (usually called SET in OO terminology) are invoked using the SQL UPDATE command, again using path expressions and iterator variables, as in

```
UPDATE    Newstudent1 n
SET       n.dateofBirth='20-Jun-1990', n.address.zip='53727'
WHERE     n.stuId ='S999';
```

We saw in Chapter 5 how useful the SQL built-in functions such as MIN and MAX are for a variety of queries. These functions can be used with many different data types. However, when users define their own data types, the built-in functions are not defined for these types, nor are any but a few very basic operations. Therefore, users must also define operations on the new types they create, building on the basic operations defined for the source types. The definition of a new type includes a list of its attributes and its methods, but the methods are defined only for a single user-defined type, and do not apply to other types the user creates. Methods for a type can be classified as **member methods** or **static methods**. **Member methods** have the implicit *self* parameter, as described earlier, and can be either **functions**, which have a single return type, or **procedures**, which have no return but may have input and/or output parameters. We can also create non-member or **static methods**, which are defined for the type, and which do not have an implicit *self* parameter.

User-defined types do not have any automatic ordering of their elements. To provide comparison of objects of the same user-defined type, the user can define equality and ordering relationships for the type as methods. In Oracle, users can impose an order by identifying either a **map method** or an **order method** for the type. A **map method** directs Oracle to apply the comparison method it normally uses for one of its built-in types (normally, one of the attributes) as the comparison method for the entire type. For example, if we had defined a member function

```
MAP MEMBER FUNCTION getstuId RETURN VARCHAR2
```

in the definition of the type, and then coded this function in the type body to return the value of stuId, as follows

```
CREATE OR REPLACE TYPE BODY StudentType IS
MEMBER FUNCTION getstuId RETURN VARCHAR2 IS
BEGIN
      RETURN stuId;
END;
```

then Oracle would use its built-in method of comparing VARCHAR2 values applied to the `stuId` values whenever we compared `StudentType` objects, since we listed this method as MAP. For example for the query

```
SELECT s.stuId, s.lastName, s.firstName
FROM Students s
ORDER BY value(s);
```

the ordering will be by the value of `stuId`.

Users can instead write their own comparison method, called an **order method**, to tell Oracle how to compare two objects of a user-defined type. If we had chosen to write a `compareAge( )` function in the type definition and make it an order method by declaring

```
ORDER MEMBER FUNCTION compareAge(s StudentType) RETURN NUMBER;
```

we could write code for the function in the type body as follows

```
CREATE OR REPLACE TYPE BODY StudentType1 AS
MEMBER FUNCTION compareAge(s StudentType) RETURN NUMBER IS
BEGIN
      IF (self.dateOfBirth < s.dateOfBirth) THEN RETURN 1;
      ELSE IF(self.dateOfBirth> s.dateOfBirth)THEN RETURN -1;
      ELSE RETURN 0;
      END IF;
      END IF;
END;
```

Then Oracle would always compare two `StudentType` objects on the basis of age, not `stuId`. A UDT can have at most one map method or order method for the entire type. A subtype can create its own map method if its root supertype has one, but not its own order method. The previous query would return the rows in order by age.

8.7.4   Reference Types

In strictly relational databases, foreign keys are used to establish relationships between tables. For example, in the relational model, if we assume each student has an advisor who is a faculty member, the corresponding `facId` is identified as a foreign key when we create the `Student` table. Object-relational systems use a similar mechanism, allowing attributes of a type that are actually **references** or pointers to another type. By default, the value for a reference is the OID of the referenced object. When reference types are used, the user must explicitly find and set the reference value when a tuple is inserted. For example, if we define `FacultyType2` as an object and use that type to create the `Faculty2` table, we can create a new `StudentType2` with a reference, `advId`, to `FacultyType2` as shown in Figure 8.12, using Oracle syntax.

Then we can create a new `Student2` table:

```
CREATE TABLE Student2 OF StudentType2;
```

Unlike Oracle, standard SQL requires that the scope for the reference attribute be specified in the table definition, so in the `StudentType2` definition, the standard expression would read

```
advId REF(FacultyType2) SCOPE Faculty2,
```

The reference attribute, `advId`, which is a reference to a `FacultyType2`, refers to tuples in an existing table, `Faculty2`, as indicated by the scope specification for it. Note that the reference itself specifies the type of object referred to, while the scope specifies the table containing row objects of that type. In Oracle, the scope can be specified after both `Faculty2` and `Student2` tables have been created by the following line in Figure 8.12

```
alter table Student2 add (scope for (advId) is faculty2);
```

This limits the allowable values of `advId` to OIDs of rows in the `Faculty2` table. However, we should also ensure that if one of those rows is deleted, the `advId` value in any `Student2` row that points to it is modified, or else we are left with dangling pointers that lead nowhere. This can be done by adding a referential integrity constraint with an ON DELETE option as shown in Figure 8.12

```
alter table Student2 add constraint Stu2_advId_fk foreign key (advId)
references Faculty2 on delete set null;
```

In both standard SQL and Oracle, the system generates an object identifier (OID) when we insert a `Faculty2` tuple, and it can retrieve that value when needed, in response to a query. Note that the value is an internal one that does not appear as part of the row object it refers to. When we wish to insert a `Student2` object, we must get the value of the OID of the

Figure 8.12

StudentType2 with a REF Attribute Replacing a Foreign Key

On the Companion Website:
- Online code for this example

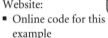

```
CREATE OR REPLACE TYPE FacultyType2 AS object(
facId        varchar2(6),
name         varchar2(20),
dept         varchar2(20),
rank         varchar2(15));

CREATE TABLE Faculty2 of FacultyType2(
constraint Fac2_facId_pk PRIMARY KEY (facId),
constraint Fac2_rank_cc CHECK(rank IN
('Instructor','Assistant','Associate','Professor')));

CREATE OR REPLACE TYPE StudentType2 AS object(
stuId        VARCHAR2(6),
lastName     VARCHAR2(20),
firstName    VARCHAR2(20),
address      AddressType,
advId        REF FacultyType2,
credits      number(3),
dateOfBirth DATE)
instantiable
not final;


CREATE TABLE Student2 OF StudentType2(
constraint Stu2_stuId_pk PRIMARY KEY (stuId));

alter table Student2 add (scope for (advId) is faculty2);
alter table Student2 add constraint Stu2_advId_fk foreign key (advId)
references Faculty2 on delete set null;
```

advisor, using a query. Suppose we have already inserted the faculty record for the advisor, as in

```
insert into faculty2 values(Facultytype2('F101','Smith','History',
'Associate'));
```

We can then insert a `Student2` tuple with a query to obtain the correct reference for the `advId`

```
INSERT INTO Student2 VALUES(studentType2('S555', 'Hughes','John',
AddressType('101 Oak Lane','Austin','TX','73301'),(SELECT REF(f)FROM Faculty2
f WHERE facId = 'F101'), 0, '01-Jan-1988'));
```

Using `REF(f)`, the value placed in the `advId` attribute is the OID of the `Faculty2` record, as you can see if you do a query on the `Student2` record just inserted. Besides ref( ), which takes a row object and returns the REF to that object, the deref( ) and value( ) functions can be used with references. The value( ) function takes a row object and returns the instance, as in

```
SELECT value(f)
FROM Faculty2 as f
WHERE facId='F101';
```

The deref( ) takes a REF to an object (normally found in another object table) and returns the instance for that REF. If we write the following query on the Student2 table, we can follow the reference from the advId and get the Faculty2 row for the advisor

```
SELECT    deref(s.advId)
FROM      Student2 s
WHERE     stuId ='S555';
```

These two queries will return exactly the same result, the values in the Faculty2 object for F101.

In Oracle, we can use the dot notation to create a path expression that allows us to follow the reference. For example, to find a student's first and last name and the name and department of his or her advisor, we can write

```
SELECT stuId, lastname, firstname, s.advId.name, s.advId.dept
FROM Student2 s
WHERE stuId='S555';
```

Notice that this query returns values from both tables, even though only the Student2 table is named in the FROM clause. This is not a join operation. The result is found by following the REF from the Student2 row to the corresponding Faculty2 row.

In addition to system-generated references, the standard allows for user-generated references (for which the user must provide and keep track of the unique identifiers), and derived references, for which the user must specify the attribute from which the reference attribute derives its value. The identifier can either be system generated (the default) or the user can specify that the primary key is to be used as the OID. A system-generated OID is a 16-byte key to which the user has no access, although it can be used for finding and fetching objects, as we saw in earlier examples. Oracle creates an index on the OID column of object tables. In a non-distributed, non-replicated environment, the user can choose the primary key as the OID. The selection is specified in the CREATE TABLE command, as in

```
CREATE TABLE MyStudent of StudentType(
CONSTRAINT MyStudent_stuId_pk PRIMARY KEY(stuId),
CONSTRAINT MyStudent_credits_cc CHECK ((credits>=0) AND (credits <
150)))
OBJECT IDENTIFIER PRIMARY KEY;
```

The last line could have been replaced by OBJECT IDENTIFIER SYSTEM GENERATED, which is the default.

Oracle also uses OIDs to help construct a **reference type** to refer to row objects. We can define a REF attribute, with an optional SCOPE clause that constrains the column to the table specified as the scope, as we saw for standard SQL. The scope clause is required if the object identifier of the referenced object is the primary key. If we do not specify a scope, the reference can be to any row object of the specified type, regardless of where it appears. Since dangling pointers can result from deletion or update of row objects, Oracle provides a referential constraint mechanism, RESTRICT REFERENCES, for reference objects. There is also a test method, IS DANGLING to determine whether the pointer is dangling, and a DEREF dereferencing operator for references.

8.7.5   Type Hierarchies in Standard SQL

Object types can participate in type hierarchies, in which subtypes inherit all attributes and operations of their supertypes, but they may have additional attributes and operations of their own. When defining a new type, the user can declare it as FINAL, which means that no subtypes can be defined for it, or NOT FINAL, which allows subtypes to be created. As discussed in Section 8.7.3, if a class is defined as NOT INSTANTIABLE, we cannot create instances of that type, but if it has subtypes, instances of the subtypes can be created, provided the subtypes themselves are instantiable. Using our previously defined type, StudentType2 from Figure 8.12, which was NOT FINAL, we can define a subtype, UndergraduateType, by writing:

```
CREATE TYPE UndergraduateType UNDER StudentType2 AS (
    major varchar2(15))
INSTANTIABLE,
NOT FINAL;
```

In standard SQL, but not in Oracle, we can create a subtable for Undergraduate under the Student2 table that was previously created for the StudentType2.

```
CREATE TABLE Undergraduate OF UndergraduateType UNDER Student2;
```

`Undergraduate` objects inherit all the attributes of `Student2` tuples and have an additional attribute, `major`. They also inherit any methods defined for `StudentType2` but have their own constructor, observer, and mutator methods for `major`, and they can have their own user-defined methods.

We could continue in this fashion, creating a type called `FreshmanType` under `UndergraduateType`.

```
CREATE TYPE FreshmanType UNDER UndergraduateType AS (
    peerMentor varchar(25))
INSTANTIABLE,
FINAL;
```

In standard SQL, we could then create a `Freshman` subtable using SQL:1999 syntax:

```
CREATE TABLE Freshman OF FreshmanType UNDER Undergraduate;
```

We could continue to create types for Sophomores, Juniors, and Seniors under `UndergraduateType` and their corresponding tables under the `Undergraduate` table.

For graduate students, we would write a definition for `GraduateStudent-Type` under `StudentType2`, similar to the one for `UndergraduateType`, this time specifying the graduate program that the student is enrolled in as an attribute. We could also create a subtype, `TeachingAssistantType`, under `GraduateStudentType`. In our original EE-R diagram, we also had `TeachingAssistant` as a subtype of `Faculty`. However, multiple inheritance is not allowed in the SQL standard or Oracle. We would not be able to make `TeachingAssistant` a subtype of `FacultyType` as well.

SQL queries and DML statements can be written on any of the tables or subtables. When a query is written referring to a table, its scope includes all the subtables for that table in standard SQL. For example

```
SELECT S.*
FROM Student2 S;
```

will include results from all the subtables under `Student2`.

8.7.6   Type Hierarchies in Oracle

Oracle supports the creation of types and subtypes exactly as in the SQL standard, but does not allow subtables to be created under existing tables. Therefore, although we can create subtypes under `StudentType2` as we did in the previous section, as shown in Figure 8.13(a) and (b), we cannot

Figure 8.13(a)

Creating a Subtype in Oracle

```
CREATE OR REPLACE TYPE UndergraduateType UNDER StudentType2 (
    major varchar2(15) )
INSTANTIABLE
NOT FINAL;
```

Figure 8.13(b)

Creating a Subtype of a Subtype in Oracle

```
CREATE OR REPLACE TYPE FreshmanType UNDER UndergraduateType AS (
    peerMentor varchar2(25))
INSTANTIABLE,
FINAL;
```

Figure 8.13(c)

Inserting all Subtypes into Master Table in Oracle

```
INSERT INTO Student2 VALUES
(StudentType2('S444','Klein','Susan', AddressType('123 Hudson Street','New
York','NY','10001'),(SELECT REF(f) FROM Faculty2 f WHERE facId = 'F101'),36,
'14-Mar-1976'));
INSERT INTO Student2 VALUES
(UndergraduateType('S666','Logan','Randolph', null, null, 12,'23-May-
1982','Spanish'));
INSERT INTO Student2 VALUES
(FreshmanType('S777','Miller','Terrence',AddressType('999 Salmon
Street','Sitka','AK','99835'),(SELECT REF(f)FROM Faculty2 f WHERE facId =
'F101'),30,'30-Jun-1985', 'Math','Tom Smith'));
```

On the Companion Website:
- Oracle code for this example

Figure 8.13

Hierarchies in Oracle

create tables for the subtypes under the `Student2` table. Instead, all the subtypes can be placed in the `Student2` table.

In Oracle, subtypes can be substituted for supertypes as object columns or rows, in object tables or views. We can therefore insert Undergraduate records and Freshman records in the `Student2` table by using the appropriate constructor for the subtype, as shown in Figure 8.13(c).

Every row in the table is, of course, a `Student2` tuple, but some belong to other subtypes as well. Every tuple in a hierarchy has a **most specific type**, which is the "closest" subtype it belongs to, the subtype whose constructor was used when it was created.

To retrieve data from a hierarchical table, we can use the **VALUE** function, which ordinarily returns the attribute values of one or more tuples, including all subtypes in the result, as shown in Figure 8.14(a).

This query will show all the data for all the rows, including the reference values. We can improve the format of the results by specifying the attributes to be displayed.

We can limit the query to the supertype and exclude the subtypes by writing the keyword **ONLY**, as in Figure 8.14(b). This query will find only those students who are not undergraduate or freshmen subtypes, or any other subtype of `Student2`, if we had created others. It selects only those whose most specific subtype is `StudentType2`. To limit the query to undergraduate students, we can specify that the row object instances must be of type `UndergraduateType`, using **IS OF (*type*)** as shown in Figure 8.14(c).

```
SELECT VALUE(s)
FROM Student2 s;
```

Figure 8.14(a)

Retrieving all Rows of Student2 Table, Regardless of Type

```
SELECT s.stuId, s.lastName, s.firstName, s.credits
FROM Student2 s
WHERE value(s) IS OF (ONLY StudentType2);
```

Figure 8.14(b)

Retrieving Rows That Are not Subtypes

```
SELECT s.stuId, s.lastName, s.firstName, s.credits
FROM Student2 s
WHERE VALUE(s) IS OF (UndergraduateType);
```

Figure 8.14(c)

Retrieving Rows That Are Undergraduates, Including Freshmen

```
SELECT lastName, firstName, TREAT(VALUE(s) AS FreshmanType).peerMentor
FROM Student2 s
WHERE VALUE(s) IS OF (FreshmanType);
```

Figure 8.14(d)

Retrieving Rows That Are Freshmen, Including the Peer Mentor Attribute

Figure 8.14

Retrieving Hierarchical Data from an Oracle Table

The results include all `UndergraduateType` rows that satisfy the condition, including `FreshmanType` objects. To eliminate the `FreshmanType` objects, we could write `IS OF (ONLY UndergraduateType)`. The ONLY clause limits the return to tuples whose most specific type is `UndergraduateType`.

If we wish to retrieve specific columns we can list them in the SELECT line, as usual. However, for columns that appear only in a subtype, we cannot simply list the column names in the SELECT line, since the column does not appear in the declaration of the type of the table listed in the FROM line. For example, `peerMentor` does not appear as a column in the `Student2` table. There is a **TREAT( )** function that allows us to treat each `Student2` tuple as if it were a `FreshmanType` tuple in order to examine the `peerMentor` attribute as shown in Figure 8.14(d).

If an Oracle type or subtype has a REF attribute, the DEREF operator can be used as described earlier.

8.7.7 Nested Tables in Oracle

A nested table is created using a single built-in type or object type, which is then placed in another table. For example, we could create a nested contact list table type to hold names and telephone numbers of a student's parents, spouse, guardian, or other contacts, as shown in Figure 8.15(a).

Then when we define `StudentType3` we add as an attribute,

```
contactList contactListType
```

as shown in Figure 8.15(b). When we create the `Student3` table, we specify that it has a nested table, as shown in Figure 8.15(c).

Note that we must identify a name for a storage table for the nested table, which we called `contactListStorageTable` in our example. This is a separate table from `Student3`. We specify the primary key of the nested table to include NESTED_TABLE_ID, which is a hidden column created by Oracle that associates the rows of this contact table with the corresponding `Student3` row. All the rows for contacts of a particular student have the same NESTED_TABLE_ID, so we added `lastName` and `firstName` to the primary key to guarantee uniqueness. The compressed indexed organization is specified so that rows belonging to the same student will be clustered together.

```
CREATE OR REPLACE TYPE ContactType AS OBJECT(
    lastName       VARCHAR2(15),
    firstName      VARCHAR2(12),
    relationship   VARCHAR2(15),
    phoneNumber  VARCHAR2(10));
CREATE OR REPLACE TYPE ContactListType AS TABLE OF ContactType;
```

Figure 8.15(a)

Creating a Contact List Table

```
CREATE OR REPLACE TYPE studenttype3 AS OBJECT(
stuId        varchar2(6),
lastName    varchar2(20),
firstName   varchar2(20),
address      Addresstype,
advId        REF FacultyType2,
credits       number(3),
dateOfBirth  date,
contactList contactListType)
INSTANTIABLE
NOT FINAL;
```

Figure 8.15(b)

Creating a UDT with a Nested ContactList Table Type

```
CREATE TABLE Student3 OF StudentType3(
CONSTRAINT Stu3_stuId_pk PRIMARY KEY (stuId))
object id primary key
NESTED TABLE contactList
STORE AS contactListStorageTable(
(primary key (nested_table_id, lastName, firstName))
organization index compress)
return as locator
```

Figure 8.15(c)

Creating the Student3 Table Containing a Nested ContactList Table

```
INSERT INTO Student3(stuId, lastname, firstname,credits, contactList) VALUES
('S999', 'Smith', 'John',0, contactListType());
```

Figure 8.15(d)

Inserting a Row into the Master Table, with an Empty Nested Table

Figure 8.15

Nested Tables in Oracle

Figure 8.15(e)

Inserting Rows into the Nested Table

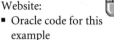

On the Companion Website:
- Oracle code for this example

```
INSERT INTO TABLE(SELECT s.contactList
        FROM    Student3 s
        WHERE   s.stuId = 'S999')
VALUES('Smith','Marjorie','mother','2017771234');
INSERT INTO TABLE(SELECT s.contactList
        FROM    Student3 s
        WHERE   s.stuId = 'S999')
VALUES('Smith','Frank','father','9177778888');
```

Figure 8.15(f)

Retrieving a Table with a Nested Table

```
SELECT  s.lastName, s.firstName, c.*
FROM    Student3 s, TABLE(s.contactList) c
WHERE   s.credits <= 60;
```

Figure 8.15

Nested Tables in Oracle (continued)

To insert data in the subtable, we first create a row for the owner table, Student3, including a parameter-less call to the constructor for the subtable, as shown in Figure 8.15(d).

The constructor creates an empty instance in the subtable, into which we can then insert data using an INSERT INTO TABLE statement as shown in Figure 8.15(e).

We can continue to insert as many contacts as we wish for this student, or go on to create other Student3 rows and their contact lists.

Nested tables can be unnested using the **TABLE** keyword to flatten the table as shown in Figure 8.15(f).

The result will be a multiset with a flattened list where student names will be repeated for each of their contacts (one contact per line). If a type or subtype has a nested table, the TABLE keyword can also be used to unnest the table. ORDER BY and GROUP BY clauses can be used for queries on subtypes just as they were for other types.

8.7.8   Oracle Object Views

Oracle allows users of strictly relational Oracle databases to view them as object-relational ones using a mechanism called an **object view**. An object view is constructed by defining an object type in which each attribute corresponds to a column of an existing relational table. The object view is created using a SELECT statement, in the same manner that we would create a relational view, except that we must specify an object identifier, saying which attribute(s) will be used to identify each row of the view. This identifier, which is usually the primary key, can be used to create reference attributes, if desired. To guarantee safety of updates in the object view, users can write INSTEAD OF triggers. The object view can then be treated as if it were an object table. If we had a purely relational `Faculty` table, defined as shown in Figure 8.16(a), we could define a type, `FacultyType`, as shown in Figure 8.16(b).

```
CREATE TABLE Faculty(
facId       NUMBER(4) PRIMARY KEY,
lastName    VARCHAR2(15),
firstName   VARCHAR2(10),
dept        VARCHAR2(10),
rank        VARCHAR2(10),
salary      NUMBER(8,2));
```

Figure 8.16(a)
Relational Table Faculty

On the Companion Website:
- Oracle code for this example

```
CREATE OR REPLACE TYPE FacultyType as object (
fId             NUMBER(4),
lName           VARCHAR2(15),
fName           VARCHAR2(10),
department      VARCHAR2(10),
rnk             VARCHAR2(10));
```

Figure 8.16(b)
Creating a FacultyType to Correspond to Part of the Relational Faculty Table

```
CREATE VIEW FacultyView OF FacultyType WITH OBJECT
IDENTIFIER (facId) AS SELECT f.facId, f.lastName,
f.firstName, f.dept, f.rank
FROM Faculty f;
```

Figure 8.16(c)
Creating an Object View of FacultyType from the Relational Faculty Table

Figure 8.16
Using Oracle's Object View to Simulate Object Tables

We could create an object view, `FacultyView` as shown in Figure 8.16(c). Note that we include the keywords AS OBJECT as we normally do when we create an object type in Oracle.

Users can then refer to the attributes of the object using dot notation, write methods for the type, and use other object-relational features as if it were a user-defined structured type. Application programmers can treat the relational database as if its structure corresponded directly to the objects they create in their object-oriented programs.

8.8   Converting an EE-R Diagram to an Object-Relational Database Model

The object-relational model provides much more flexibility in mapping an EE-R diagram than does the strictly relational model. As illustrated in our examples, we can make use of new data types, collection types, user-defined structured types, inheritance, and reference types in creating our tables. We modify the mapping algorithm presented in Section 8.6.2 to incorporate the extensions.

For entity sets and relationships that are not part of generalizations or unions, the mapping can proceed in a manner similar to the relational model. Entity sets can be mapped to tables, either using the SQL2 syntax or creating a type and then using that type for the table creation. For composite attributes, we can define a structured type for the composite, with the components as attributes of the type. Multivalued attributes can be expressed as collection types, either as VARRAY, or as nested tables in Oracle or as similar structures in standard SQL. In representing relationships, reference types can be used in place of the foreign key mechanism. For specialization hierarchies, types and subtypes can be defined as needed. Then tables to correspond to the types can be created. However, since no subtypes can have multiple inheritance, the designer must choose among potential supertypes for a shared subtype. The subtype's relationship to the other supertype(s) should be expressed using references. There is no direct representation of unions (categories) in the object-relational model, but we can use the same method as we did for the relational model. We create a table for the union itself, and individual tables for each of the superclasses, using foreign keys or references to connect them.

8.9   Chapter Summary

The EE-R model is an **enhanced E-R** model in which **specialization, gener-alization**, **union**, additional constraints, and other abstractions can be represented. **Specialization** means breaking up an entity set, or class, into the various types of subsets it contains. Its inverse process, **generalization**, means considering objects of different types that have some common features as subclasses of a higher-level class, called the superclass. On an EE-R diagram, generalization/specialization, also called an *isa* relationship, is represented by lines with a **specialization circle** and an **inheritance symbol**. Subclasses inherit the attributes and relationships of their superclasses, but they can have additional attributes or participate in additional relationships. Subclasses may be **disjoint** or **overlapping**, **predicate-defined** (even **attribute-defined**), or **user-defined**. Specialization may be **partial** or **total**. In the EE-R model a subclass can be **shared**, appearing as a subclass of more than one superclass, and having **multiple inheritance** from them.

A subclass may belong to one of a **category** or **union** of superclasses. A union is shown by a circle with the set union symbol. Subclasses of a union inherit the attributes and relationships of only one of the superclasses. A category can be **partial** or **total**. A total category may sometimes be replaced by a specialization. For both E-R and EE-R diagrams, the (*min,max*) notation indicates the minimum and maximum number of relationship instances an entity instance can participate in.

An EE-R diagram can be converted to a strictly relational model in much the same way as an E-R diagram, except for a generalization hierarchy. A hierarchy can be converted to tables by creating a table for the superclass that contains the common attributes, and individual tables for the subclasses. A second method is to create only subclass tables containing columns for all the attributes of the superclass in addition to columns for the subclass attributes. A third method is to create a single large table containing all the attributes of the superclass and all its subclasses. Categories are represented by creating a table for the subclass of the union, and individual tables for each of the superclasses, using their common primary key as a foreign key in the subclass table. It might be necessary to create a surrogate key as the primary key of the union subclass table, and make it a foreign key for each of the superclasses.

The relational model has been extended with additional fundamental data types like BOOLEAN and LOB, collection types, including arrays and nested tables or row types, user-defined data types (**UDTs**), class hierarchies, and reference types. UDTs type definitions include specification of attributes and methods. They can be **final** or not, **instantiable** or not. **Oracle syntax** differs slightly from the SQL standard. In Oracle, UDTs can have a single method, either a **map method** or an **order method**, which defines the order of members. **Object types** can be used to create **column objects** in a table, or **object tables**, in which each row represents an object of the defined type.

Each row in an **object table** has a unique **OID**, either system generated or user-defined. **Reference** types use the OID values as pointers to an object type. They can be used as attributes to represent relationships, similar to foreign keys. A **scope** can be specified that identifies the table referred to. A **DEREF** operator retrieves the tuple referred to, or a **path expression** can be used to retrieve the value of an attribute in the tuple referred to by a reference. **Dangling pointers** can result when referenced objects are deleted, but a **REFERENCES ARE CHECKED** clause provides some integrity protection. If the type is not final, **subtypes** that inherit all attributes and methods can be created, and we can add additional attributes and methods for the subtype. The **type hierarchy** can be extended by creating subtypes of subtypes. However, multiple inheritance is not permitted. In standard SQL, subtables consisting of the subtype can be created under tables that consist of the supertype.

In Oracle, a master table can be created to hold all the objects in a hierarchy. Each tuple has **a most specific type** identified by the constructor used when it is inserted. The **VALUE** function is useful for retrieving data from a hierarchical table. The **ONLY** keyword and the **IS OF** *type* clause can be used to restrict the type of the result, and the **TREAT** keyword provides access to subtype-specific attributes in retrieving subtypes. An **object view** is a mechanism for treating a strictly relational database as if it were an object-relational one. It provides an object-relational view for users.

To convert an EE-R diagram to an object-relational model, we can modify the standard relational conversion mechanism, using new data types and collection types, which are useful for multivalued and composite attributes. Relationships can be represented by reference types instead of by foreign keys. Hierarchies can be represented using supertypes and subtypes.

Exercises

8.1 Define the following terms:

a. specialization

b. generalization

c. union

d. superclass

e. subclass

f. *isa* relationship

g. disjointness constraint

h. completeness constraint

i. attribute-defined specialization

j. multiple inheritance

k. total category

l. LOB, BLOB

m. collection type

n. UDT

o. method

p. reference type

q. nested table

r. most specific type

8.2   a. Assume the entity set Employees is specialized into Clerical, Sales, and Management. Show how the specialization is represented on an EE-R diagram, making up attributes as needed, and stating any assumptions you need to make.

b. For the specialization in Part (a) add relationships that show:

(i)   All employees can have a pension plan

(ii) Sales employees have clients

(iii) Management employees have projects

c. using (*min,max*) notation, add constraints for the relationships, stating any additional assumptions you need to make.

8.3 a. Convert the EE-R diagram you developed for Exercise 8.2 into a strictly relational model, writing out the schema.

b. Convert the EE-R diagram you developed for Exercise 8.2 into an object-relational model, explaining what changes you would make to the relational schema from Part (a).

8.4 Develop an EE-R diagram for the college student and activities described in Exercise 3.4, but expand it to cover graduate students as well as undergraduates. Graduate students can participate in the clubs as members, or they can serve as moderators of the clubs. A graduate student, like an undergraduate, has one academic advisor, but may also have a thesis advisor, who oversees his or her thesis research.

8.5 a. Convert the EE-R diagram you developed for Exercise 8.4 into a strictly relational model, writing out the schema.

b. Convert the EE-R diagram you developed for Exercise 8.4 into an object-relational model, explaining what changes you would make to the relational schema from Part (a).

c. Write the SQL commands to create the object types and tables for your OR model from Part (b).

8.6 Develop an EE-R diagram for the dental group described in Exercise 3.5, but expand it by assuming that some of the dentists are surgeons, who can perform oral surgery. Also assume some of the professionals are dental hygienists, who can perform routine work such as cleaning and taking X-rays. A patient typically begins an ordinary visit by starting with a dental hygienist who performs routine work, and then a dentist who does a checkup in the same initial visit. The work needed is usually determined at this visit. If followup visits are required, each of the next visits will be with one dentist. If a patient requires oral surgery, at least one of his or her visits must be with one of the surgeons, even though the rest of the work needed might be performed by his or her regular dentist. When surgery is performed, there must be a qualified assistant present. Only some of the hygienists are qualified to assist in surgeries. Assume this database does not keep track of appointments, only of actual visits, work, billing, and payments.

8.7   a. Convert the EE-R diagram you developed for Exercise 8.6 into a strictly relational model, writing out the schema.

       b. Convert the EE-R diagram you developed for Exercise 8.6 into an object-relational model, explaining what changes you would make to the relational schema from Part (a).

       c. Write the SQL commands to create the object types and tables for your OR model from Part (b).

8.8   Develop an EE-R diagram for the interior design firm described in Exercise 3.6, but expand it by assuming the clients can either be individuals or corporations. Also assume the contractors can be licensed professionals with various specialties (such as plumbers, electricians, or carpenters) or hourly laborers.

8.9   a. Convert the EE-R diagram you developed for Exercise 8.8 into a strictly relational model, writing out the schema.

       b. Convert the EE-R diagram you developed for Exercise 8.8 into an object-relational model, explaining what changes you would make to the relational schema from Part (a).

       c. Write the SQL commands to create the object types and tables for your OR model from Part (b).

8.10   Develop an EE-R diagram for the automobile body repair shop described in Exercise 3.7, but assume the shop is expanding to perform mechanical repairs as well as body work. Body work can be done by a technician, but all mechanical repairs require a licensed mechanic. Jobs now may require one technician to handle the body work (if any) and a licensed mechanic to do the mechanical repairs (if any).

8.11   a. Convert the EE-R diagram you developed for Exercise 8.10 into a strictly relational model, writing out the schema.

       b. Convert the EE-R diagram you developed for Exercise 8.10 into an object-relational model, explaining what changes you would make to the relational schema from Part (a).

c. Write the SQL commands to create the object types and tables for your OR model from Part (b).

8.12   Develop an EE-R diagram for the physical therapy center described in Exercise 3.8, but expand it to assume some visits require the use of specialized equipment for electrotherapy, ultrasound, hydrotherapy, and so on, and the patient is charged for each use of such equipment. Patients may also be supplied with special devices to take home, such as exercise bands, neck pillows, and so on, and the patient is charged for these special supplies.

8.13   a. Convert the EE-R diagram you developed for Exercise 8.12 into a strictly relational model, writing out the schema.

b. Convert the EE-R diagram you developed for Exercise 8.12 into an object-relational model, explaining what changes you would make to the relational schema from Part (a).

c. Write the SQL commands to create the object types and tables for your OR model from Part (b).

8.14   a. Convert the E-R diagram shown in Figure 4.4 into an EE-R diagram, making the additional assumption that some customers may place orders online, and require an email address and optional credit card type and credit card number to be stored. When an online customer shops, a shopping cart is created that shows what items have been selected and the date added.

b. Convert the EE-R diagram you developed for Part (a) into an object-relational model, listing the object types and tables you would create.

c. Write the SQL commands to create the object types and tables for your OR model from Part (b).

On the Companion Website:

- Lab Exercises
- Sample Project
- Student Projects

CHAPTER 9

Introduction to Database Security

Chapter Objectives

In this chapter you will learn the following:

- The meaning of database security

- How security protects privacy and confidentiality

- Examples of accidental or deliberate threats to security

- Some physical security measures

- The meaning of user authentication

- The meaning of authorization

- How access control can be represented

- How the view functions as a security device

- The purpose of the security log and audit trail

- How and why data encryption is performed

- How security is enforced in some systems

- How Internet security is implemented

9.1   Issues in Database Security

Database security means protecting the database from unauthorized access, modification, or destruction. Since the database represents an essential corporate resource, security is an important goal. In addition to the need to preserve and protect data for the smooth functioning of the organization, database designers have a responsibility to protect the privacy of individuals about whom data is kept. **Privacy** is the right of individuals to have some control over information about themselves. Many countries have laws designed to protect privacy, and every organization that collects and stores information about individuals is legally obliged to adopt policies that conform to local privacy legislation. The database design should reflect the organization's commitment to protection of individual privacy rights by including only those items that the organization has a right to know and keeping them secure. In addition, privacy must be guarded by protecting stored information that is of a sensitive nature. Many organizations also require **confidentiality**, which refers to the need to keep certain information from being known. This might include operational data such as customer lists, receivables, and transaction data, or trade secrets such as formulas or methods the organization uses that provide it with a competitive edge. Database security can also protect confidentiality. Some of the laws and standards requiring controls on access, disclosure, and modification of sensitive data are the European Union Privacy Directive, the U.S. Healthcare Insurance Portability and Accountability Act (HIPAA), the U.S. Sarbanes-Oxley, the U.S. Gramm-Leach-Bliley Act, and the worldwide Payment Card Industry Data Security Standard. Violation of these practices and regulations can lead to fraud, financial losses, and severe penalties. Security threats are events or situations that could harm the system by compromising privacy or confidentiality, or by damaging the database itself. They can occur either **accidentally** or **deliberately**.

9.1.1 Accidental Security Threats

Some examples of accidental security violations are the following:

- The user may unintentionally request an object or an operation for which he should not be authorized, and the request could be granted because of an oversight in authorization procedures or because of an error in the database management system or operating system.

- A person may accidentally be sent a message that should be directed to another user, resulting in unauthorized disclosure of database contents.

- A communications system error might connect a user to a session that belongs to another user with different access privileges.

- The operating system might accidentally overwrite files and destroy part of the database, fetch the wrong files, and then inadvertently send them to the user, or might fail to erase files that should be destroyed.

9.1.2 Deliberate Security Threats

Deliberate security violations occur when a user intentionally gains unauthorized access and/or performs unauthorized operations on the database. A disgruntled employee who is familiar with the organization's computer system poses a tremendous threat to security. Industrial spies seeking information for competitors also threaten security. Privileged users such as DBAs who access end-user data that they should not be permitted to see threaten security. There are many ways deliberate security breaches can be accomplished, including:

- Wiretapping of communication lines to intercept messages to and from the database

- Electronic eavesdropping, to pick up signals from workstations, printers, or other devices within a building

- Reading display screens and reading or copying printouts left unsupervised by authorized users

- Impersonating an authorized user, or a user with greater access, by using his or her log-in and password

- Writing systems programs with illegal code to bypass the database management system and its authorization mechanism, and to access database data directly through the operating system

- Writing applications programs with code that performs unauthorized operations

- Deriving information about hidden data by clever querying of the database

- Removing physical storage devices from the computer facility

- Making physical copies of stored files without going through the database management system, thereby bypassing its security mechanisms

- Bribing, blackmailing, or otherwise influencing authorized users in order to use them as agents in obtaining information or damaging the database

- Using system privileges to grant oneself access to confidential user data

9.2   Physical Security and User Authentication

Database security is best implemented as only one part of a broader security control plan. The plan should begin with physical security measures for the building itself, with special precautions for the computer facilities. Designing a physically secure building is clearly outside the domain of the database designer. However, the DBA or data administrator should be able to suggest measures that would control access to database facilities. Often these begin at the front door, where all employees must be identified visually by guards, or by using badges, handprints, sign-ins, or other mechanisms. Additional identification should be required to enter the computer facilities. Physical security measures should be extended to cover any location where offline data such as backups are stored as well.

Because physical security of individual workstations may be difficult to implement, security control of workstations requires **authentication** of users. Authentication means verifying the identity of the user—checking to ensure that the actual user is who he or she claims to be. It is usually implemented initially at the operating system level. When the user signs on, he or she enters a user ID, which is checked for validity. The system has a user profile for that ID, giving information about the user. The profile normally includes a password, which is supposed to be known only to the user. Passwords should be kept secret and changed frequently. A simple security precaution is for the system to require that passwords be changed monthly. The system should never display passwords at log-in, and the stored profiles should be kept secure, in encrypted form. Although passwords are the most widely used authentication method, they are not very secure, since users sometimes write them down, choose words that are easy to guess, or share them with others. In some organizations, users must insert badges or keys when they log on. In others, voice, fingerprints, retina scans, or other physical characteristics of the user are examined. Some use an authentication procedure rather than a single password. A procedure might consist of answering a series of questions and would take longer and be more difficult to reproduce than a password. Although authentication may be done only at the operating system level, it is desirable to require it again at the database level. At the very least, the user should be required to produce an additional password to access the database.

9.3   Authorization

In addition to authentication, most database management systems designed for multiple users have their own security subsystems. These subsystems provide for **user authorization**, a method by which users are assigned rights to use database objects. Most multiple-user systems have an **authorization language** that is part of the data sublanguage. For example, SQL provides standard authorization commands to grant privileges to users, as discussed in Section 9.8. The DBA uses the authorization language to specify user's rights by means of **authorization rules**, statements that specify which users have access to what information, and what operations they are permitted to use on what data. The authorization mechanism is designed to protect the database by preventing individuals from unauthorized reading, updating, or destruction of database contents. These restrictions are added to the security mechanisms provided by the operating system. However, in a surprisingly large number of cases, database security subsystems are minimal or are not fully utilized. Recognizing that data is a valuable corporate resource, the designer should include available security mechanisms as an important factor in evaluating alternative database management systems, and should develop effective security policies utilizing whatever controls are available with the system chosen.

9.4   Access Control

Access control is the means by which authorizations are implemented. Access control means making sure that data or other resources are accessed only in authorized ways. In planning access, the DBA might use an **access control matrix** for the database, as shown in Figure 9.1. The column headings represent database objects, which may be the names of tables, views, data items, objects, modules, or other categories, depending on the database model and management system used. The row labels represent individuals, roles, groups of users, or applications. The cell entries specify the type of access permitted. Values of entries will also depend on the particular system used, but the choices usually include READ, INSERT, UPDATE, DELETE, EXECUTE, CREATE, and others. Once the access control matrix is complete, the DBA must use the appropriate authorization language to implement it. The DBA, of course, is permitted to create and change the structure of the database, and to use the authorization language to grant data access to others or to revoke access. Some systems allow the DBA to delegate some of this power, granting users the power to

FIGURE 9.1

Access Control Matrix

	OBJECT					
SUBJECT	Student table	StuView1	WrapUp Procedure	Faculty table	Enroll table	CREATE TABLE
User U101	read, update	read	execute	read		yes
User U102		read				no
Role Advisor	read	read			read, insert, update, delete	yes
. . .	. . .	. . .	. . .	. . .	. . .	. . .

authorize other users to perform operations on the database. However, having many such "authorizers" can be extremely dangerous. Since authorizers can create other authorizers, the situation can get out of hand very quickly, making it difficult for the DBA to revoke authorizations.

9.5   Using Views for Access Control

The view is a widely used method for implementing access control. The view mechanism has a twofold purpose. It is a facility for the user, simplifying and customizing the external model through which the user deals with the database, freeing the user from the complexities of the underlying model. It is also a security device, hiding structures and data that the user should not see. In the relational and object-relational models, a user's external model can consist entirely of views, or some combination of base tables and views. By specifying restrictions in the WHERE line of the SELECT statement used to create views, the view can be made **value-dependent**. Figure 9.2(a) gives an example of a view created from the `Student` table by including only data about students whose major is CSC. **Value-independent** views are created by specifying columns of base tables and omitting the WHERE line of the SELECT statement. Figure 9.2(b) gives an example of a view of the `Student` table showing only columns `stuId`, `lastName`, `firstName`, and `major`.

9.6   Security Logs and Audit Trails

Another important security tool is the **security log**, which is a journal that keeps a record of all attempted security violations. The violation can be

```
CREATE VIEW CSCMAJ AS
    SELECT stuId, lastName, firstName, credits
    FROM Student
    WHERE major = 'CSC';
```

FIGURE 9.2(a)
Value-dependent View

On the Companion Website:
- Oracle code for this example

```
CREATE VIEW StuView1 AS
    SELECT stuId, lastName, firstName, major
    FROM Student;
```

FIGURE 9.2(b)
Value-independent View

```
CREATE OR REPLACE TRIGGER EnrollAuditTrail
    BEFORE UPDATE OF grade ON Enroll
    FOR EACH ROW
    BEGIN
        INSERT INTO EnrollAudit
            VALUES(SYSDATE, USER, :OLD.stuId, :OLD.classNumber, :OLD.grade, :NEW.grade);
    END;
```

simply recorded in the log, or it can trigger an immediate message to the system operator or to the DBA. Knowing about the existence of the log can be a deterrent in itself. If the DBA suspects that data is being compromised without triggering security log entries, it is possible to set up an **audit trail**. Such an auditing system records all access to the database, keeping information about the user who requested the access, the operation performed, the workstation used, the exact time of occurrence, the data item, its old value, and its new value, if any. The audit trail can therefore uncover the sources of suspicious operations on the database, even if they are performed by authorized users, such as disgruntled employees. **Triggers** can also be used to set up an audit trail for a table, recording all changes, the time they were made, and the identity of the user who made them. For example, in Oracle, if we wish to monitor changes to grades in the `Enroll` table, we would first set up a table to hold the audit records. The schema for that table might be:

```
EnrollAudit(dateandTimeOfUpdate, userId, oldStuId, oldClassNo, oldGrade,
    newGrade)
```

The trigger should insert a record in the `EnrollAudit` table when a user tries to update a grade in the `Enroll` table. The code to do this is shown in Figure 9.3. It uses SYSDATE and USER, which are referred to as pseudocolumns in Oracle. Both act as functions that return appropriate values. SYSDATE returns the current date and time, while USER returns the ID of the current user.

9.7 Encryption

To counter the possibility of having files accessed directly through the operating system or having files stolen, data can be stored in the database in encrypted form. Only the database management system can unscramble the data, so that anyone who obtains data by any other means will receive jumbled data. When authorized users access the information properly, the DBMS retrieves the data and decodes it automatically. Encryption should also be used whenever data is communicated to other sites, so that wiretappers will also receive scrambled data. Encryption requires a **cipher system**, which consists of the following components:

- An **encrypting algorithm**, which takes the normal text (**plaintext**), as input, performs some operations on it, and produces the encrypted text (**ciphertext**), as output

- An **encryption key**, which is part of the input for the encrypting algorithm, and is chosen from a very large set of possible keys

- A **decrypting algorithm**, which operates on the ciphertext as input and produces the plaintext as output

- A **decryption key**, which is part of the input for the decrypting algorithm, and is chosen from a very large set of possible keys.

One widely used data encryption scheme was the **Data Encryption Standard** (DES), devised by IBM for the U.S. National Bureau of Standards and adopted in 1977. Although it was withdrawn as a standard for government agency use in 2005, a variation of DES, called TripleDES or 3DES, is widely used throughout the world. In the DES scheme, the algorithm itself is public, while the key is private. It uses **symmetric** encryption, in which the decryption key is the same as the encryption key, and the decrypting algorithm is the inverse of the encrypting algorithm. Figure 9.4 gives an overview of the DES process. The DES algorithm uses a 56-bit key on 64-bit blocks of plaintext, producing 64-bit blocks of ciphertext. When data is encoded, it is split up into 64-bit blocks. Within each block, characters are substituted and rearranged according to the value of the key. The decoding algorithm uses the same key to put back the original characters and to restore them to their original positions in each block. Two major challenges with the DES system involve key security and the ease of cracking the code. The key must be kept secure or the encryption is worthless, since anyone with the key has access to the data. Therefore, the security depends on the secrecy of the key, but all authorized users must be told the key. The more people who know the key, the more likely it is that the key will be disclosed to unauthorized users. Also, it is necessary to distribute the key to receivers

FIGURE 9.4
Overview of DES
Encryption

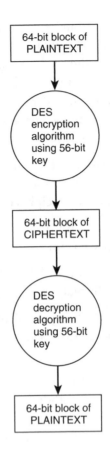

of encrypted messages. If telecommunications lines are used, transmitting the key in plaintext would allow wiretappers easy access to encrypted messages. Often, more secure lines are used for key distribution, or the key is distributed by mail or messenger. DES is not a very secure scheme, since it can be cracked in a reasonable amount of time due to the shortness of the keys. As a result of several famous cases where DES keys were cracked, a more secure version, called **Triple DES** or **3DES**, was recommended in 1999 by the U.S. National Institute of Standards and Technology, the successor to the National Bureau of Standards. Triple DES is now widely used commercially, and is still permitted for some government agency use. The triple DES system uses three keys, and essentially performs the DES encryption three times, once with each key.

In 2001, an improved encryption scheme called the **Advanced Encryption Standard** (AES) was developed. AES was the result of a five-year worldwide competition, with the winning design coming from two Belgian cryptographers, Daemen and Rijmen, who proposed a scheme they called Rijndael. It was adopted as a new standard for U.S. government agency use in 2002, and it is widely used commercially. It uses a symmetric scheme that is more sophisticated than the DES scheme, and it supports three possible key sizes of 128 bits, 192 bits, or 256 bits, depending on the level of security needed. The data itself is broken into 128-bit blocks and it is subjected to four rounds of transformations, each with several steps whose exact nature is determined by the key. Because of the larger key sizes, cracking the scheme is more challenging.

A second approach is **public-key encryption**, an asymmetric algorithm that uses pairs of prime numbers. Figure 9.5 provides an overview of public-key encryption. For each user, a pair of large prime numbers, (p, q) is chosen as the user's **private** key, and the product of the pair, p^*q, becomes the **public** key of that user. Public keys are shared freely, so that anyone wishing to send a message to a user can find his or her public key easily. The public key is then used as input to an encryption algorithm, which

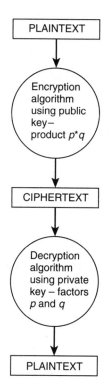

FIGURE 9.5
Overview of Public Key Encryption

produces the ciphertext for that user. When the user receives an encrypted message, he or she must produce the prime factors of the public key to decode it. Since there is no quick method of finding the prime factors of a large number, it is difficult for an intruder to find these factors. However, an intruder who is determined to break the key can do so, provided he or she is willing to commit substantial resources to the task. This method is only as secure as the private key, so users must be given their private keys in some secure fashion, and must protect the private keys against disclosure. One well-known method of public key encryption is **RSA**, named for its developers Rivest, Shamir, and Adleman.

9.8   SQL Authorization Language

SQL has an authorization sublanguage that includes statements to grant privileges to, and to revoke privileges from users. A **privilege** is an action such as creating, executing, reading, updating, or deleting that a user is permitted to perform on database objects. In standard SQL, the creator of a schema is given all privileges on all the objects (tables, views, roles, applications) in it, and can pass those privileges on to others. Ordinarily, only the creator of the schema can modify the schema itself (adding tables, columns, and so on). The statement for granting privileges has the following form:

```
GRANT {ALL PRIVILEGES | privilege-list}
ON {table-name | view-name}
TO {PUBLIC | user-list | role-list} [WITH GRANT OPTION];
```

The possible privileges for base tables are SELECT, DELETE, INSERT, UPDATE, or REFERENCES(col-name). If a table is named in the ON clause, then ALL PRIVILEGES includes all of these operations. If a view is named in the ON clause, and the view was constructed in such a way that it is updatable, the SELECT, DELETE, INSERT, and UPDATE privileges can be granted on that view. For views that are not updatable, only the SELECT can be granted. The UPDATE privilege can be made more restrictive by specifying a column list in parentheses after the word UPDATE, restricting the user to updating only certain columns, as in:

```
GRANT UPDATE ON Student(major) TO U101;
```

The REFERENCES privilege is applied to columns that may be used as foreign keys. This privilege allows the user to refer to those columns in creating foreign key integrity constraints. For example, to allow a user who can update the `Enroll` table to be able to reference `stuId` in the `Student` table in order to match its values for the `Enroll` table, we might write:

```
GRANT REFERENCES (stuId) ON Student TO U101;
```

The user list in the TO clause can include a single user, several users, or all users (the public). The optional WITH GRANT OPTION clause gives the newly authorized user(s) permission to pass the same privileges to others. For example, we could write:

```
GRANT SELECT, INSERT, UPDATE ON Student TO U101, U102, U103 WITH GRANT OPTION;
```

Users U101, U102, and U103 would then be permitted to write SQL SELECT, INSERT, and UPDATE statements for the `Student` table, and to pass that permission on to other users. Because of the ability of users with the grant option to authorize other users, the system must keep track of authorizations using a **grant diagram**, also called an **authorization graph**. Figure 9.6 shows an authorization graph. Here, the DBA, who we assume is the creator of the schema, gave a specific privilege (for example, to read the `Student` table) WITH GRANT OPTION to users U1, U2, and U3. We will use a double arrowhead to mean granting with grant option, and a single arrowhead to mean without it. A solid outline for a node will mean that the node has received the grant option, and a dashed outline will mean it has not. U1 passed along the privilege to U21 and U22, both without the grant option. U2 also passed the privilege to U22, this time with the grant option, and U22 passed the privilege to U31, without the grant option. U3 authorized U23 and U24, both without the grant option. Note that if we give a different privilege to one of these users, we will need a new node to represent the new privilege. Each node on the graph represents a combination of a privilege and a user.

SQL includes the capability to create user roles. A **role** can be thought of as a set of operations that should be performed by an individual or a group of individuals as part of a job. For example, in a university, advisors may need to be able to read student transcripts of selected students, so there may be an Advisor role to permit that. Depending on the policies of the university, the Advisor role might also include the privilege of inserting enrollment records for students at registration time. Students may be permitted to perform SELECT but not UPDATE operations on their personal data, so there may be a Student role that permits such access. Once

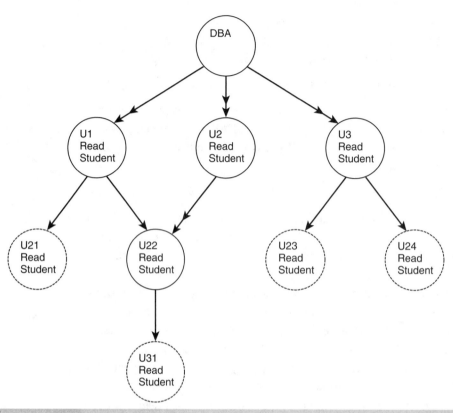

An Authorization Graph

the DBA has identified a role, a set of privileges is granted for the role, and then user accounts can be assigned the role. Some user accounts may have several roles.

To create a role, we write a statement such as:

```
CREATE ROLE AdvisorRole;
CREATE ROLE FacultyRole;
```

We then grant privileges to the role just as we would to individuals, by writing statements such as:

```
GRANT SELECT ON Student TO AdvisorRole;
GRANT SELECT, UPDATE ON Enroll TO AdvisorRole;
GRANT SELECT ON Enroll TO FacultyRole;
```

To assign a role to a user, we write a statement such as:

```
GRANT AdvisorRole TO U999;
```

We can even assign a role to another role by writing, for example:

```
GRANT FacultyRole TO AdvisorRole;
```

This provides a means of inheriting privileges through roles.

The SQL statement to remove privileges has this form:

```
REVOKE {ALL PRIVILEGES | privilege-list}
ON object-list
FROM {PUBLIC | user-list | role-list};
[CASCADE | RESTRICT];
```

For example, for U101 to whom we previously granted SELECT, INSERT, and UPDATE on `Student` with the grant option, we could remove some privileges by writing this:

```
REVOKE INSERT ON Student FROM U101;
```

This revokes U101's ability both to insert `Student` records and to authorize others to insert `Student` records. We can revoke just the grant option, without revoking the insert, by writing this:

```
REVOKE GRANT OPTION FOR INSERT ON Student FROM U101;
```

If an individual has the grant option for a certain privilege and the privilege or the grant option on it is later revoked, all users who have received the privilege from that individual have their privilege revoked as well. In this way, revocations **cascade**, or trigger other revocations. If a user obtained the same privilege from two authorizers, one of whom has authorization revoked, the user still retains the privilege from the other authorizer. Thus, if the DBA revoked the authorization of user U1 in Figure 9.6, U21 would lose all privileges, but U22 would retain whatever privileges were received from U2. Since U22 has the grant option, user U21 could regain privileges from U22. In this way, unscrupulous users could conspire to retain privileges despite attempts by the DBA to revoke them. For this reason, the DBA should be very careful about passing the grant option to others. If the **RESTRICT** option is specified, the system checks to see if there are any cascading revocations, and returns an error if they exist, without executing the revoke statement. CASCADE is the default. When a privilege is revoked, the authorization graph is modified by removing the node(s) that lose their privileges.

9.9   Security in Oracle

Oracle provides robust security that goes far beyond the SQL authorization language commands. There are many different ways to set up and manage the security of an Oracle database besides the methods discussed here. Data stored in the database and data transmitted over networks can be encrypted using advanced AES, 3DES, or similar protocols. Industry standard authentication protocols, including Kerberos, SSL with digital certificates, RADIUS (Remote Authentication Dial-In User Service) and Public Key Infrastructure (PKI) can be used for authentification. Views can be defined to limit user access to base tables. User accounts, roles, and privileges can be defined in several ways.

On installation, Oracle provides four predefined user accounts, SYS, SYSTEM, SYSMAN, and DBSNMP, as well as some sample schemas. SYSMAN is used for administration tasks in Oracle Enterprise Manager, and the management agent can manage and monitor the database using the DBSNMP account. The system prompts for passwords for both the SYS and SYSTEM accounts, although there are default passwords provided. Since these passwords are widely known, it is strongly recommended that new passwords be created to protect the database from attack. The SYS account stores data dictionary information for base tables and views, and should be used only by the DBMS itself, not by users. The SYSTEM account stores other tables and tools used by Oracle and tables for administration. Neither of these accounts should be used to create user tables, and access to them should be strictly controlled. Both SYS and SYSTEM automatically have the DBA role. The DBA role permits a user to create roles and users, to grant privileges, and to create, modify, and delete schemas and objects.

9.9.1   The Oracle Enterprise Manager Database Control Facility

The Oracle Enterprise Manager Database Control is a facility that offers options for granting and revoking privileges. The DBA has to log in using a privileged account such as SYSTEM to the Oracle Database Home Page to access the Database Control. From there, the DBA can choose the Administration icon, then Database Users, then Create User. The DBA fills in the new user name and password. He or she then enters a temporary password, and can choose to have the password expire immediately. This will cause the new user to be prompted for a new password the first time he or she uses the account. The account status should be set to Unlocked. The user role and privileges should be chosen from the list provided, and the CREATE button should be clicked to finish the operation.

9.9.2 Security Control Using SQL*Plus

Users and roles can also be created using SQL*Plus. After signing in to a privileged account such as SYSTEM, the DBA writes a CREATE USER command, which has this form:

```
CREATE USER username IDENTIFIED BY password;
```

For example:

```
CREATE USER U999 IDENTIFIED BY SESAME;
```

However, this command does not give any privileges to the user, so U999 will not be able to establish a session, unless the DBA also writes the following:

```
GRANT CREATE SESSION TO U999;
```

To require the user to change his or her password at the first actual log in, the DBA uses this command:

```
ALTER USER username
PASSWORD EXPIRE;
```

When the user tries to connect, he or she will be given a message saying the password has expired and prompting for a new one before being connected. Once connected, the user can also change his or her own password at any time by writing the following in SQL*Plus:

```
ALTER USER username
IDENTIFIED BY newpassword;
```

Although the user will be connected, he or she will not be able to access any data, since the only privilege given is the one to create a session. To actually use Oracle's facilities, the user needs to be given additional privileges, which can be either system privileges or object privileges.

9.9.3 Object Privileges

In Oracle an **object privilege** is the right to perform an action using DML commands on a table, view, procedure, function, sequence, or package. The creator of a schema automatically has all object privileges on all objects in the schema, and can grant the same object privileges to other users. For tables, the privileges include the SELECT, INSERT, UPDATE, DELETE, and REFERENCES as described in Section 9.8, but also ALTER (the right to use the ALTER TABLE command) and INDEX (the right to use the CREATE INDEX command). For updatable views, privileges are SELECT, INSERT, UPDATE, and DELETE. The syntax for these is the same as the standard SQL authorization language syntax shown in Section 9.8. For example, the DBA might give U999 wide privileges on the `Student` table by writing as follows:

```
GRANT ALL PRIVILEGES ON Student TO U999 WITH GRANT OPTION;
```

If there is a stored procedure called `WrapUp`, the DBA can give U999 permission to run the procedure by writing this command:

```
GRANT EXECUTE ON WrapUp TO U999;
```

9.9.4 System Privileges

In Oracle, **system privileges** include the right to perform actions using DDL commands on database data, schemas, tablespaces, or other Oracle resources, as well as the right to create user accounts. There are about 166 different system privileges possible. A list of them can be seen by writing the following SQL command:

```
SELECT name
FROM SYSTEM_PRIVILEGE_MAP;
```

System privileges can be given through SQL*Plus using a GRANT command of this form:

```
GRANT systemprivilege
TO username
[WITH ADMIN OPTION];
```

For example, we could allow U999 to create tables by writing:

```
GRANT CREATE TABLE TO U999 WITH ADMIN OPTION;
```

Additionally, privileges that are object privileges on single tables can be extended to become system privileges that extend to any table by using the keyword ANY, as in:

```
GRANT SELECT ANY TABLE TO U999;
```

The WITH ADMIN OPTION clause allows the user to pass the privilege on to others.

9.9.5   Roles

As in the SQL standard, Oracle allows privileges to be given to a role as well as to individuals or groups of users. A role consists of a group of privileges. Any number of roles can be granted to a user. Roles can also be granted to other roles, allowing inheritance of privileges. Roles can be created in SQL*Plus using the authorization language commands discussed in Section 9.8.

9.10   Statistical Database Security

Statistical databases are designed to provide data to support statistical analysis on populations. The data itself may contain facts about individuals, but the data is not meant to be retrieved on an individual basis. Users are granted permission to access statistical information such as totals, counts, or averages, but not information about individuals. For example, if a user is permitted statistical access to an employee database, he or she is able to write queries such as:

```
SELECT SUM(Salary)
FROM Employee
WHERE Dept = 10;
```

but not:

```
SELECT Salary
FROM Employee
WHERE empId = 'E101';
```

Special precautions must be taken when users are permitted access to statistical data, to ensure that they are not able to deduce data about individuals. For the preceding example, if there are no restrictions in place except that all queries must involve count, sum, or average, a user who wishes to find the employee of E101 can do so by adding conditions to the WHERE line to narrow the population down to that one individual, as in:

```
SELECT SUM(Salary)
FROM EMPLOYEE
WHERE Dept = 10 AND jobTitle = 'Programmer' AND dateHired > '01-Jan-2004';
```

The system can be modified to refuse to answer any query for which only one record satisfies the predicate. However, this restriction is easily overcome, since the user can ask for total salaries for the department and then ask for the total salary without that of E101. Neither of these queries is limited to one record, but the user can easily deduce the salary of employee E101 from them. To prevent users from deducing information about individuals, the system can restrict queries by requiring that the number of records satisfying the predicate must be above some threshold and that the number of records satisfying a pair of queries simultaneously cannot exceed some limit. It can also disallow sets of queries that repeatedly involve the same records.

9.11   Database Security and the Internet

Unless security software is used, all messages sent over the Internet are transmitted in plaintext, and can be detected by intruders using "packet sniffing" software. Both senders and receivers need to be confident that their communications are kept private. Obviously, customers who wish to purchase products need to have assurance that their credit card information is secure when they send it over the Internet. Companies that allow web connections to their internal networks for access to their database need to be able to protect it from attack. Receivers of messages need to have ways to be sure that those messages are genuine and trustworthy and have not been tampered with. Senders of messages should not be able to repudiate them, denying that they sent them. Web users who download executable content such as Java applets, ActiveX, or VBScript need to have ways to assure that the code will not corrupt their databases or otherwise harm their systems. Several techniques are used to address these issues.

9.11.1   Proxy Servers

A proxy server is a computer or program that acts as an intermediary between a client and another server, handling messages in both directions. When the client requests a service such as a connection or webpage, the proxy evaluates it and determines whether it can fulfill the request itself. If not, it filters the request, perhaps altering it, and requests the service from the server or other resource. It may cache (store a copy of) the server's response so that a subsequent request can be fulfilled from the stored content without using the server again. The proxy server can be used for several purposes, including to maintain security by hiding the actual IP address of the server, to improve performance by caching, to prevent access to sites that an organization wishes to block from its members, to protect the server from malware, and to protect data by scanning outbound messages for data leaks.

9.11.2   Firewalls

A **firewall** is a hardware and/or software barrier that is used to protect an organization's internal network (intranet) from unauthorized access. Various techniques are used to ensure that messages entering or leaving the intranet comply with the organization's standards. For example, a proxy server can be used to hide the actual network address. Another technique is a **packet filter**, which examines each packet of information before it enters or leaves the intranet, making sure it complies with a set of rules. Various gateway techniques can apply security mechanisms to applications or connections.

9.11.3   Digital Signatures

Digital signatures use a double form of public key encryption to create secure two-way communications that cannot be repudiated. They allow users to verify the authenticity of the person they are communicating with, and a means to prove that a message must have come from that person, and that it has not been tampered with in transmission. One method of using digital signatures is for the sender to encode a message first with his or her own private key, and then with the public key of the receiver. The receiver decrypts the message first using his or her private key, and then uses the sender's public key. The double encryption ensures that both parties are authentic, since neither one could have encoded or decoded the message without his or her private key. It also ensures that the message is intact since tampering would invalidate the signature, making it impossible to decode the message.

9.11.4   Certification Authorities

Customers who wish to purchase goods from an e-commerce website need to feel confident that the site they are communicating with is genuine and that their ordering information is transmitted privately. A widely used method of verifying that a site is genuine is by means of **certification authorities** such as Verisign. The process uses public key encryption. The site begins the certification process by generating a public key and a private key, and sending a request to Verisign, along with the site's public key. Verisign issues an encrypted certificate to the site, which stores it for future use. When a customer wishes to place an order using a secure connection to the site, his or her browser asks the site for its Verisign certificate, which it receives in encrypted form. The browser decrypts the certificate using Verisign's public key, and verifies that this is indeed a Verisign certificate, and that the site's URL is the correct one. The certificate also contains the site's public key. The browser creates a session key, which it encrypts using the site's public key from the certificate, and sends the session key to the site. Since the session key is encrypted with the site's public key, only the actual site can decrypt it using its private key. Since both the browser and the site are the sole holders of the session key, they can now exchange messages encrypted with the session key, using a simpler protocol such as 3DES or AES. The process described here is the one used in the **Secure Sockets Layer** (SSL) protocol and is typically used for messages to and from a customer during an order process. An additional measure of security is usually used for transmission of credit card numbers. While the user's browser sends the seller site most of the order information encoded with its public key, when the customer is ready to transmit credit card information at the end of the order process, that information, along with the amount to be charged, is sent directly to the card company site for authorization and approval.

The SET (Secure Electronic Transactions) protocol, which was used for this process, has been superceded by newer protocols such as Visa's Verified by Visa, which provides both authentication and approval of the purchase. It uses an XML-based protocol called 3-D Secure.

Kerberos is an authentication protocol for networks that allows mutual authentication, in which both client and server can verify identity. A trusted Kerberos server is used as a certification authority. It has a key distribution center that stores the secret keys of each client and server on the network, and it uses these as input to generate time-stamped tickets when the client requests service. A ticket is then used to demonstrate to the server that the client is approved for service. Messages can be encrypted using either symmetric key or public key protocols. Both the protocol and free software implementing it were developed at the Massachusetts Institute of Technology. It is used by both Oracle and Caché, as well as many other vendors.

9.12   Chapter Summary

Database **security** means protecting the database from unauthorized access, modification, or destruction. **Privacy** is the right of individuals to have some control over information about themselves, and is protected by law in many countries. **Confidentiality** refers to the need to keep certain information from being known. Both privacy and confidentiality can be protected by database security. Security violations can be accidental or deliberate, and security breaches can be accomplished in a variety of ways. A security control plan should begin with physical security measures for the building and especially for the computer facilities. Security control of workstations involves user **authentication**, verifying the identity of users. The operating system normally has some means of establishing a user's identity, using user profiles, user IDs, passwords, authentication procedures, badges, keys, or physical characteristics of the user. Additional authentication can be required to access the database.

Most database management systems designed for multiple users have a security subsystem. These subsystems provide for **authorization**, by which users are assigned rights to use database objects. Most have an **authorization language** that allows the DBA to write **authorization rules** specifying which users have what type of access to database objects. **Access control** covers the mechanisms for implementing authorizations. An **access control matrix** can be used to identify what types of operations different users are permitted to perform on various database objects. The DBA can sometimes delegate authorization powers to others.

Views can be used as a simple method for implementing access control. A **security log** is a journal for storing records of attempted security violations. An **audit trail** records all access to the database, keeping information about the requester, the operation performed, the workstation used, the time, data items, and values involved. **Triggers** can be used to set up an audit trail. **Encryption** uses a **cipher system** that consists of an **encrypting algorithm** that converts **plaintext** into **ciphertext**, an **encryption key**, a **decrypting algorithm** that reproduces plaintext from ciphertext, and a **decryption key**. Widely used schemes for encryption are the **Triple Data Encryption Standard (3DES)**, the **Advanced Encryption Standard (AES)**, and **public key encryption**. DES/AES uses a standard algorithm, which is often hardware implemented. Public key encryption uses a product of primes as a public key, and the prime factors of the product as a private key.

SQL has an **authorization language** to provide security. The GRANT statement is used for authorization, and the REVOKE statement is used to retract authorization. Privileges can be given to individuals or to a role, and then the role is given to individuals. In Oracle, privileges include **object privileges** and **system privileges**. They can be granted using the authorization sublanguage or through the Oracle Database Manager.

When the database is accessible through the Internet, special security techniques are needed. These include firewalls, certification authorities such as Verisign that issue digital certificates using SSL or S-HTTP, Kerberos or similar protocols for user authentication, stronger protocols for financial information, and digital signatures.

Exercises

9.1   For each of the following, write SQL statements to create views where needed and to grant the indicated privileges for the University database with this schema:

```
Student(stuId, lastName, firstName, major, credits)
Faculty(facId, name, department, rank)
Class(classNumber, facId, schedule, room)
Enroll(stuId, classNumber, grade)
```

a. Give permission to read the tables Student and Class to user 201.

b. Create a view of Enroll that does not include the grade attribute, and give user 201 permission to read and update the view.

c. Create a role that includes reading Student, Class, and the view created in (b). Give that role to all clerks in the dean's office, which includes users 202, 203, 204, and 205.

d. Give permission to user 206, an assistant dean, to read and modify (insert, delete, update) the Faculty and Class tables. This user can authorize others to read and modify Class, but not Faculty.

e. User 206 authorizes user 300 to read Class. Write the command to do this.

f. Create an authorization graph showing all the privileges given so far. You will need a separate node for each combination of privilege and user.

g. Revoke the authorization privilege that the assistant dean was given in (d) but keep his or her own reading and modification privileges. How would you show this change on the authorization graph?

h. Give permission to the Registrar, user 500, to read and modify Student, Class, and Enroll, and to grant those rights to others.

i. For all academic advisors, give permission to read all Class records. For the advisor in the Math department, give permission to read the Student records of students majoring in Math, and to modify Enroll records for these students.

9.2 Assume you have a statistical database with the following schema. The only legal queries are those involving COUNT, SUM, and AVERAGE.

```
newFaculty(facId, lastName, firstName, department, salary, rank,
dateHired)
```

a. Write a legal SQL query to find the salary of the only faculty member who is an Instructor in the Art department.

b. Assume the system will refuse to answer queries for which only one record satisfies the predicate as in (a). Write a legal set of queries that allows the user to deduce the salary of the Art instructor.

c. Assume that there are 10 faculty members in the Art department. The system refuses to answer queries where the number of records satisfying the query is less than six. It will also refuse to answer pairs of queries where the number of records satisfying them simultaneously exceeds three. Would these restrictions make your query for (a) or (b) illegal? If so, is there another legal set of queries that will allow you to deduce the salary of the Art instructor?

9.3 a. Using the University schema shown in Exercise 9.1, write an SQL statement to create a value-dependent view of Student that includes only seniors.

b. Write an SQL statement for a value-independent view of `Faculty`. Do not include the whole table.

c. Write a statement to authorize user 125 to read both views.

9.4 Write a trigger to create an audit trail that will track all updates to the salary field of the `newFaculty` table shown in Exercise 9.2.

9.5 Log on to an e-commerce website, such as a large bookseller. Locate and read the information provided about security of online transactions. Determine whether SSL or some other secure protocol is used. If possible, display and print the information about the Verisign certificate for the site. You may find this in the options in your browser.

9.6 Examine the security features in Access 2010 by reading the online Help on the topic. Then do the following

a. Print the list of trusted publishers, locations, and documents for your computer.

b. Open an Access database you created and encrypt the database with a password.

c. Sign your database and package it for distribution.

 On the Companion Website:

- Lab Exercises
- Sample Project
- Student Projects

CHAPTER 10

Transaction Management

Chapter Objectives

In this chapter you will learn the following:

- Why concurrency control is needed

- The meaning of serializability

- Why and how locking is done

- How the two-phase locking protocol works

- How timestamping is used for serializability

- How optimistic concurrency control techniques operate

- The meaning of database recovery

- The nature and purpose of the transaction log

- Why and how checkpoints are performed

10.1   Properties of Transactions

Regardless of the care with which a database is designed and created, it can be easily damaged or destroyed unless proper concurrency controls and recovery techniques are in place. Database **recovery** means the process of restoring the database to a correct state in the event of a failure. **Concurrency control** is the ability to manage simultaneous processes involving the database without having them interfere with one another. Both are needed to protect the database from data contamination or data loss.

The notion of **transaction** is central to an understanding of both recovery and concurrency control. A transaction can be thought of as a logical unit of work on the database. It might be an entire program, a portion of a program, or a single command. It can involve any number of operations on the database. For the University database, we will use the following relational scheme:

```
Student (stuId, lastName, firstName, major, credits)
Faculty (facId, facname, department, rank)
Class (classNumber, facId, schedule, room)
Enroll (classNumber, stuId, grade)
```

A simple transaction against this database might be to update the number of credits in a Student record, given the stuId. This task involves locating the page containing the appropriate Student record on disk, bringing the page into the database buffer, rewriting the value of the credits field in the record in the buffer, and finally writing the updated page out to disk. Figure 10.1 summarizes the steps in this transaction. A more complicated transaction would be to change the stuId assigned to a particular student. Obviously we need to locate the appropriate Student record, bring its page into the buffer, update the stuId in the buffer, and write the update to disk as before, but we also need to find all the Enroll records having the old stuId and update them. If these updates are not made, we will have an inconsistent state of the database, a state in which the data is contradictory. A transaction should always bring the database from one consistent state to another. While the transaction is in progress, it is permissible to have a temporary inconsistent state. For example, during the stuId update, there will be some moment when one occurrence of the stuId in an Enroll record contains the new value and another still contains the old

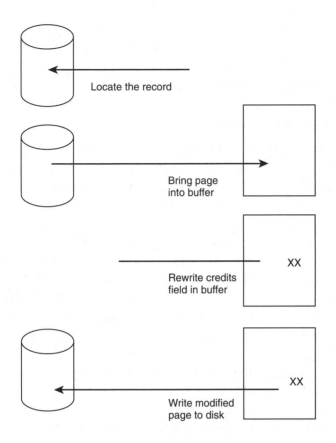

FIGURE 10.1

Steps in a Simple Transaction

one. However, at the end of the transaction, all occurrences will agree. A transaction is the entire series of steps necessary to accomplish a logical unit of work, in order to bring the database to a new consistent state. The transaction is an atomic process, a single "all or none" unit. We cannot allow only part of a transaction to execute—either the entire set of steps must be done or none can be done, because a partial transaction would leave the database in an inconsistent state.

There are two ways a transaction can end or terminate. If it executes to completion successfully, the transaction is said to be **committed**, and the database is brought to a new consistent state. The other possibility is that the transaction cannot execute successfully. In this case, the transaction is **aborted**. If a transaction is aborted, it is essential that the database be restored to the consistent state it was in before the transaction started. Such a transaction is undone or **rolled back**. A committed transaction cannot be aborted. If we decide that the committed transaction was a mistake, we must perform another **compensating transaction** to reverse its effects. However, an aborted transaction that has been rolled back can be restarted at some future time and, depending on the cause of the failure, may successfully execute and commit at that time. Figure 10.2 shows the possible states of a transaction.

It is usually the responsibility of the programmer to identify the beginning and end of each transaction, since the database management system is unable to determine which updates form a single transaction. The words BEGIN TRANSACTION, END TRANSACTION, COMMIT, ABORT, and ROLLBACK are available in some DMLs to delimit transactions. If these delimiters are not used, the entire program is usually regarded as a single transaction, with the system automatically performing a COMMIT when the program terminates correctly and a ROLLBACK when it does not. The active state of the transaction starts with the BEGIN TRANSACTION statement (or its equivalent) and continues until the application program either aborts or terminates successfully. If a fatal error arises while the transaction is active, it is marked as failed and aborted. If any updates were done to the database, they are rolled back. If the program terminates successfully, an END TRANSACTION is reached, and the DBMS prepares to check that it can commit. During this partially committed stage, the DBMS checks that the transaction will not violate the concurrency control protocols discussed beginning in Section 10.4, or any constraints, and that the system is able to make the required changes to the database itself. If no problems arise, the transaction is committed and the process ends.

FIGURE 10.2

Transaction State Diagram

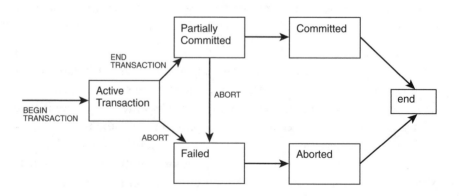

All transactions should demonstrate four important properties, usually called the ACID properties, to ensure that the database maintains a correct state, despite transaction concurrency or system failure. **ACID** is an acronym for the properties, which are:

- **Atomicity.** The transaction is a single, "all or none" unit. Either the entire set of actions is carried out or none are. To ensure this property, the DBMS must be able to roll back transactions that will not be able to complete successfully, undoing their effects on the database. The DBMS' recovery subsystem maintains a **log** of all transaction writes to the database, which is used in the rollback process.

- **Consistency.** The user is responsible for ensuring that his or her transaction, if it were executed by itself, would leave the database in a consistent state. It is the job of the concurrency control subsystem of the DBMS to ensure consistency when multiple transactions execute at the same time.

- **Isolation.** Several transactions may execute at the same time, with interleaving of their operations. The isolation property requires that the final effect is as if the transactions were executed one after another rather than concurrently. Since each transaction leaves the database in a consistent state, the overall result would be a consistent state. The concurrency control system has to guarantee isolation.

- **Durability.** If a transaction has been committed, the DBMS must ensure that its effects are permanently recorded in the database, even if the system crashes before all its writes are made to the database. The recovery subsystem is responsible for guaranteeing durability. It uses the transaction log to ensure this property.

10.2 Need for Concurrency Control

One of the major objectives in developing an enterprise database is to create an information resource that can be shared by many users. If transactions execute one at a time, **serially**, with each transaction doing a commit before the next one begins, there is no problem of interference with one another's transactions. However, users often need to access data simultaneously. If all users are only reading data, there is no way they can interfere with one another and there is no need for concurrency control. If users are accessing different parts of the database, their transactions can run concurrently without a problem. However, when two users try to make updates simultaneously to the same data, or one updates while another reads the same data, there may be conflicts.

Multiprogramming means having two or more programs or transactions processing at the same time. For example, I/O control systems can handle I/O operations independently, while the main processor performs other operations. Such systems can allow two or more transactions to execute simultaneously. The system begins executing the first transaction until it reaches an input or output operation. While the I/O is being performed, the main processor, which would otherwise be idle during I/O, switches over to the second transaction and performs whatever operations it can on the second one. Control then returns to the first transaction and its operations are performed until it again reaches an I/O operation. In this way, operations of the two transactions are **interleaved**, with some operations from one transaction performed, then some from the other, and so forth, until all operations for both transactions are completed. Even though both transactions may be perfectly correct in themselves, the interleaving of operations may produce an incorrect outcome. Some examples of potential problems caused by concurrency are the **lost update problem**, the **uncommitted update problem**, the **problem of inconsistent analysis**, the **nonrepeatable read problem**, and the **phantom data problem**. We illustrate the first three using schedules to show the chronological order in which operations are performed. A **schedule** is a list of the actions that a set of transactions performs, showing the order in which they are performed. In a schedule, we have a column for each transaction, showing the steps of that transaction. The order of operations in each transaction is preserved, but steps from another transaction can be performed during its execution, resulting in an interleaving of operations.

The Lost Update Problem

Suppose Jack and Jill have a joint savings account with a balance of $1000. Jill gets paid and decides to deposit $100 to the account, using a branch office near her job. Meanwhile, Jack finds that he needs some spending money and decides to withdraw $50 from the joint account, using a different branch office. If these transactions were executed serially, one after the other with no interleaving of operations, the final bal-

TIME	Jack's Transaction	Jill's Transaction	BAL
t1	BEGIN TRANSACTION		
t2	read BAL*(reads 1000)*	BEGIN TRANSACTION	1000
t3	. . .	read BAL*(reads 1000)*	1000
t4	BAL = BAL − 50*(950)*	. . .	1000
t5	write BAL*(950)*	BAL = BAL + 100*(1100)*	950
t6	COMMIT	. . .	950
t7		write BAL *(1100)*	1100
t8		COMMMIT	1100

FIGURE 10.3

The Lost Update Problem

ance would be $1050 regardless of which was performed first. However, if they are performed concurrently, the final balance may be incorrect. Figure 10.3 shows a schedule for a concurrent execution that results in a final balance of $1100. The schedule shows sequential units of time as t1, t2, etc., to show the chronological order for operations. The only operations that involve the database are explicitly shown as *read <attribute>* or *write <attribute>*. As shown in Figure 10.1, these operations involve either bringing a value from the database into the buffer (read) or writing a new value to the database page in the buffer (write) and later copying the modified page out to the database. The transaction variables, which we assume for the sake of simplicity have the same name as the database attributes they correspond to, are separate from the database attributes. Updating a transaction variable has no effect on the database, until a *write <attribute>* command is encountered. The value that a transaction reads for a variable is the one it uses for calculations. Each transaction is unaware of any changes made to the database unless it makes them itself. As shown on the schedule, Jack's transaction reads a value of $1000 for BAL at time t2. Jill's transaction does the same slightly later at t3. Jack's transaction subtracts $50 from BAL, and then issues a write to the database at t5, as reflected in the BAL column. At time t5, Jill's transaction still uses the value it read for BAL, not the new value, which it has not read. Her transaction adds $100 and then writes a new value of $1100 to the database, overwriting Jack's update. According to the schedule, Jack's update is lost. If we had delayed Jill's reading until Jack's update had finished, we would have avoided this problem.

The Uncommitted Update Problem

The uncommitted update problem occurs with concurrent transactions when the first transaction is permitted to modify a value, which is then read by the second transaction, and the first transaction subsequently rolls back its update, invalidating the data that the second transaction is using. This is also called the **dirty read** problem, since it is caused by the reading of **dirty data**, values that are intermediate results of an uncommitted transaction. Figure 10.4 shows a schedule containing an example of an uncommitted update that causes an error. For this example, we are assuming a simplified, if unlikely, version of banking activities just to illustrate the concurrency problem. Here, transaction INTEREST calculates the interest for a savings account, using a rate of 5%, while transaction DEPOSIT deposits $1000 in the account, but is rolled back. The starting balance in the account is $1000. If DEPOSIT actually updates the value of the balance to $2000 before INTEREST reads the balance, the amount that INTEREST will store is $2100. However, DEPOSIT is rolled back, which

FIGURE 10.4

The Uncommitted Update Problem

TIME	DEPOSIT Transaction	INTEREST Transaction	BAL
t1	BEGIN TRANSACTION		1000
t2	read BAL *(1000)*	. . .	1000
t3	BAL = BAL + 1000*(2000)*	. . .	1000
t4	write BAL *(2000)*	BEGIN TRANSACTION	2000
t5	. . .	read BAL *(2000)*	2000
t6	. . .	BAL = BAL * 1.05*(2100)*	2000
t7	ROLLBACK	. . .	1000
t8	. . .	write BAL *(2100)*	2100
t9		COMMIT	2100

means the database state should show no effect due to DEPOSIT, so at time t7, the original value, $1000, is restored as part of the rollback. Note that DEPOSIT is unaware that INTEREST has read its write, nor is INTEREST aware that DEPOSIT has rolled back. The reason for the rollback may be that the transaction itself was an error, or it may be the result of a system crash. At t8, the value calculated by INTEREST is written. Since the INTEREST was calculated on the incorrect balance, the final balance will be incorrect. If we had delayed reading the balance for the Interest transaction until after the Deposit transaction had rolled back (or committed), we would have avoided the error.

The Problem of Inconsistent Analysis

The problem of inconsistent analysis occurs when a transaction reads several values but a second transaction updates some of them during the execution of the first. Suppose we want to find the total balance of all savings accounts, but we allow deposits, withdrawals, and transfers to be performed during this transaction. Figure 10.5 contains a schedule that shows how an incorrect result could be produced. SUMBAL finds the sum of the balance on all accounts. We assume there are only three accounts to keep the example small. Notice that this transaction does not update the accounts, but only reads them. Meanwhile transaction TRANSFER transfers $1000 from account A to account C. The TRANSFER transaction executes correctly and commits. However, it interferes with the SUMBAL transaction, which adds the same $1000 twice, once while it is in account A and again when it reaches account C.

There are two other famous problems that can arise from concurrency. They are the

a. **nonrepeatable read problem**, which occurs when a first transaction reads an item, another transaction then writes a new value for the item, and the first transaction then rereads the item and gets a value that is different from its first one.

b. **phantom data problem**, which occurs when a first transaction reads a set of rows (e.g., the tuples in the result of a query), another transaction inserts a row, and then the first transaction reads the rows again and sees the new row.

Time	SUMBAL	TRANSFER	BAL_A	BAL_B	BAL_C	SUM
t1	BEGIN TRANSACTION		5000	5000	5000	–
t2	SUM = 0;	BEGIN TRANSACTION	5000	5000	5000	–
t3	read BAL_A *(5000)*	. . .	5000	5000	5000	–
t4	SUM = SUM + BAL_A *(5000)*	read BAL_A *(5000)*	5000	5000	5000	–
t5	read BAL_B *(5000)*	BAL_A = BAL_A – 1000*(4000)*	5000	5000	5000	–
t6	SUM = SUM + BAL_B *(10000)*	write BAL_A *(4000)*	4000	5000	5000	–
t7	. . .	read BAL_C *(5000)*	4000	5000	5000	–
t8		BAL_C = BAL_C + 1000 *(6000)*	4000	5000	5000	–
t9		write BAL_C *(6000)*	4000	5000	6000	–
t10	Read BAL_C *(6000)*	COMMIT	4000	5000	6000	–
t11	SUM = SUM + BAL_C *(16000)*		4000	5000	6000	–
t12	write SUM *(16000)*		4000	5000	6000	16000
t13	COMMIT		4000	5000	6000	16000

FIGURE 10.5

The Inconsistent Analysis Problem

10.3   Serializability

Serial execution of transactions means that transactions are performed one after another, without any interleaving of operations. If A and B are two transactions, there are only two possible serial executions: all of transaction A is completed first and then all of transaction B is done, or all of B is completed and then all of A is done. In serial execution, there is no interference between transactions, since only one is executing at any given time. The three problems that we illustrated in our figures resulted from concurrency and left the database in an inconsistent state. No serial execution would allow these problems to arise. However, there is no guarantee that the results of all serial executions of a given set of transactions will be identical. In banking, for example, it matters whether INTEREST is calculated for an account *before* a large deposit is made or *after*. In most cases, users do not care in what order their transactions are executed, as long as the results are correct and no user is made to wait too long. For *n* transactions, there are n! possible serial schedules. Regardless of which serial schedule is chosen, a serial execution will never leave the database in an inconsistent state, so every serial execution is considered to be correct, even though different results may be produced by different orders. Our goal is to find ways to allow transactions to execute concurrently while making sure they do not interfere with one another, and to produce a database state that could be produced by a truly serial execution.

If a set of transactions executes concurrently, we say the schedule is **serializable** if it produces the same results as some serial execution. It is essential to guarantee serializability of concurrent transactions in order to ensure database correctness. In serializability, the following factors are important:

- If two transactions are only reading data items, they do not conflict and order is not important

- If two transactions operate on (either reading or writing) completely separate data items, they do not conflict and order is not important

- If one transaction writes to a data item and another either reads or writes to the same data item, then the order of execution is important

Therefore, two operations **conflict** only if all of the following is true:

- They belong to different transactions
- They access the same data item
- At least one of them writes the item

A serializable execution of transactions orders any conflicting operations in the same way as some serial execution, so that the results of the concurrent execution are the same as the results of at least one of the possible serial executions. This type of serializability is called **conflict serializability**, and it is the strictest form of serializability. Figure 10.6 illustrates the two serial schedules and a serializable schedule for two transactions S and T. Figure

Time	S	T	S	T	S	T
t1	BEGIN TRANS				BEGIN TRANS	
t2	read x		BEGIN TRANS		read x	BEGIN TRANS
t3	$x = x*3$		read x		$x=x*3$	
t4	write x		$x=x+2$		write x	
t5	read y		write x			read x
t6	$y=y+2$		read y		read y	$x=x+2$
t7	write y		$y=y+5$		$y=y+2$	write x
t8	COMMIT		write y		write y	
t9		BEGIN TRANS	COMMIT	BEGIN TRANS	COMMIT	read y
t10		read x		read x		$y=y+5$
t11		$x=x+2$		$x=x*3$		write y
t12		write x		write x		COMMIT
t13		read y		read y		
t14		$y=y+5$		$y=y+2$		
t15		write y		write y		
t16		COMMIT		COMMIT		
	(a) Serial S,T		**(b) Serial T,S**		**(c) Serializable**	

FIGURE 10.6

Two Serial schedules and a Serializable Schedule for Transactions S and T

10.6(a) shows the serial schedule S,T while Figure 10.6(b) shows the serial schedule T,S. Figure 10.6(c) shows a serializable schedule that is conflict equivalent to the first serial schedule, S,T. The conflicting reads and writes of the data items are done in the same order in the serializable schedule as they are in the serial schedule S,T. Note that in (a) S reads and writes x before T reads and writes x, and S reads and writes y before T reads and writes y. The same order of reads and writes is preserved in the serializable schedule in (c). Also note that the two serial schedules here are not equivalent, but both are considered correct, and would leave the database in a consistent state. You can verify that the two serial schedules give different results by assigning initial values for x and y, and seeing what final values you get. Using the same initial values, you should see that the schedule in (c) gives the same results as (a). However, it is important to note that showing that a concurrent schedule gives the same results as a serial schedule for some set of values is not sufficient to prove the concurrent schedule is serializable, since another set of values may not give the same results.

It is possible to determine whether a schedule is conflict serializable by examining the order of all its conflicting reads and writes, and comparing them with the order of the same reads and writes in the transactions' serial schedules, to determine if the order matches at least one of them. However, there is a graphical technique, called a **precedence graph**, that allows us to determine whether a schedule is conflict serializable. To construct the graph, we draw nodes and directed edges as follows:

- *Draw a node for each transaction, T1, T2, . . . Tn*
- *If Ti writes X, and then Tj reads X, draw a directed edge from Ti to Tj*
- *If Ti reads X, and then Tj writes X, draw a directed edge from Ti to Tj*
- *If Ti writes X, and then Tj writes X, draw a directed edge from Ti to Tj*

S is serializable if the precedence graph has **no cycles**. A cycle is a path that begins with a particular node and ends up back at the starting node. Figure 10.7 shows a precedence graph for the schedule in Figure 10.5. Since SUMBAL reads BAL_A and then TRANSFER writes BAL_A, we draw an edge from SUMBAL to TRANSFER. Since TRANSFER writes BAL_C and then SUMBAL reads it, we draw an edge from TRANSFER to SUMBAL, resulting in a cycle, and proving that the schedule is not serializable.

If a schedule is serializable, it is possible to use the precedence graph to find an equivalent serial schedule by examining the edges in the graph. Whenever an edge appears from Ti to Tj, put Ti before Tj in the serial schedule. If several nodes appear on the graph, you usually get a partial

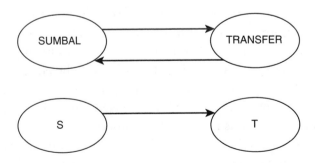

FIGURE 10.7(a)

Precedence Graph for Figure 10.5

FIGURE 10.7(b)

Precedence Graph for Serializable Schedule Shown in Column (c) of Figure 10.6

Figure 10.7

Precedence Graphs for Serializability Testing

ordering of the graph in cases where two or more intermediate nodes must come before a certain node, but the relative order of the intermediate nodes themselves does not matter. There might be several possible serial schedules. If a cycle exists in the graph, no serial schedule is possible, since eventually you will need a node to precede itself. We will apply this test to schedule (c) in Figure 10.6. Let $r_S(x)$ mean transaction S reads x, and $w_S(x)$ mean S writes x. The following string shows the reads and writes in the schedule.

$r_S(x); w_S(x); r_T(x); r_S(y); w_T(x); w_S(y); r_T(y); w_T(y)$

Figure 10.7(b) shows the precedence graph, which is constructed by first drawing nodes for the two transactions, S and T. We read the string in order from left to right, looking for conflicts, which always involve at least one write. The first write occurs with $w_S(x)$, but this does not cause a conflict with the previous read $r_S(x)$, since transaction S did the read, and no transaction ever conflicts with itself. The first conflict is with the third entry in our list, $r_T(x)$. We see that before this, we had $w_S(x)$, which means S wrote x before T read it, so we draw a directed edge from S to T, which essentially means S must precede T with respect to its operations on x. The next conflict comes with $w_T(x)$, which conflicts with both $r_S(x)$ and $w_S(x)$ and would require an edge from S to T, but we have one already so we need not repeat it. The next conflict is for $r_T(y)$, which is in conflict with $w_S(y)$, meaning S wrote y before T read it, so we would draw an edge from S to T, but it already appears. The same is true for $w_T(y)$. We see there is no cycle on the graph, which means the schedule is serializable. From the only edge on the graph, we see that S must precede T, so the schedule is equivalent to the serial schedule S,T.

Serializability can be achieved in several ways, but most systems use the locking, timestamping, or optimistic techniques that will be described here. In general, the DBMS has a concurrency control subsystem that is "part of the package" and not directly controllable by either the users or the DBA. In locking and timestamping, a facility called a **scheduler** is used to allow operations to be executed immediately, delayed, or rejected. If a transaction's operation is rejected, that transaction is aborted, but it may, of course, be restarted after the conflicting transaction completes. Optimistic techniques do not delay or reject transactions, but allow them to proceed as if there were no conflict, and check for conflicts just before a transaction commmits. If a conflict occurs, they abort the transaction.

10.4 Locking

Locking ensures serializability by allowing a transaction to "lock" a database object to prevent another transaction from modifying the object. Objects of various sizes, ranging from the entire database down to a single data item, may be locked. The size of the object determines the fineness, or **granularity**, of the lock. The actual lock might be implemented by inserting a flag in the data item, record, page, or file to indicate that portion of the database is locked, by keeping a list of locked parts of the database, or by other means. Often, there are two categories of locks: **shared** and **exclusive**. A transaction must acquire a lock on any item it needs to read or write. If a transaction has a shared lock on an item, it can read the item but not update it. Thus, many transactions can have shared locks on the same item at the same time. If a transaction has an exclusive lock on an item, it can both read and update the item. To prevent interference with other transactions, only one transaction can hold an exclusive lock on an item at any given time. Figure 10.8 illustrates a **lock compatibility matrix** that shows which type of lock requests can be granted simultaneously. If transaction 1 holds the type of lock indicated on the left, and transaction 2 requests the lock type indicated on the top of the column, the matrix shows whether the lock request can be granted. As shown, if the first transaction holds no lock, the second transaction can be granted either a shared or exclusive lock. If the first transaction holds a shared lock the second transaction can be granted only a shared, not an exclusive lock. All other lock requests will be denied.

If a system uses locks, any transaction that needs to access a data item must first lock the item, requesting a shared lock for read only access or an

	Transaction 2 requests Shared lock	Transaction 2 requests Exclusive lock
Transaction 1 holds No lock	Yes	Yes
Transaction 1 holds Shared lock	Yes	No
Transaction 1 holds Exclusive lock	No	No

FIGURE 10.8

Lock Compatibility Matrix

exclusive lock for write access. If the item is not already locked by another transaction, the lock will be granted. If the item is currently locked, the system determines whether the request is compatible with the existing lock. If a shared lock is requested on an item that has a shared lock on it, the request will be granted; otherwise, the transaction will have to wait until the existing lock is released. A transaction's locks are automatically released when the transaction terminates. In addition, a transaction can sometimes explicitly release locks that it holds prior to termination.

10.4.1 Deadlock

The set of items that a transaction reads is called its **read set**, and the items that a transaction writes is called its **write set**. In database processing, it is often difficult to identify the entire read set and write set of a transaction before executing the transaction. Often, records are accessed because of their relationship to other records. Usually it is impossible to tell in advance exactly which records will be related. For example, in the University database, if we ask for the name and department of all the teachers of a particular student, we are unable to predict exactly which `Enroll` records, `Class` records, and `Faculty` records will be needed.

Since we cannot always specify in advance which items need to be locked by a transaction, we make lock requests during the execution of the transaction. These requests can result in a situation called **deadlock**, which occurs when two transactions are each waiting for locks held by the other to be released. Figure 10.9 shows two transactions, S and T, which are

FIGURE 10.9

Deadlock with Two Transactions

Time	Transaction S	Transaction T
t1	Xlock a	. . .
t2	. . .	Xlock b
t3	request Xlock b	. . .
t4	wait	request Slock a
t5	wait	wait
t6	wait	wait
t7	wait	wait
. . .	. . .	. . .

deadlocked because each is waiting for the other to release a lock on an item it holds. At time t1, transaction S requests and obtains an exclusive lock (Xlock) on item a, and at time t2, transaction T obtains an exclusive lock on item b. Then at t3, S requests a lock on item b. Since T holds an exclusive lock on b, transaction S waits. Then at t4, T requests a shared lock (Slock) on item a, which is held with an exclusive lock by transaction S so transaction T waits. Neither transaction can complete because each is waiting for a lock it cannot obtain until the other completes. Deadlocks involving several transactions can also occur. For example, Figure 10.10 shows four transactions, Q, R, S, and T that are deadlocked because Q is waiting for a data item locked by R, R is waiting for a data item locked by S, S is waiting for a data item locked by T, and T is waiting for a data item locked by Q. Once deadlock occurs, the applications involved cannot resolve the problem. Instead, the system has to recognize that deadlock exists and break the deadlock in some way.

There are two general techniques for handling deadlock: **deadlock prevention**, in which the system looks ahead to see if a transaction would

Time	Trans Q	Trans R	Trans S	Trans T
t1	Xlock Q1	. . .	. . .	. . .
t2	. . .	Xlock R1	. . .	. . .
t3	. . .	. . .	Xlock S1	. . .
t4	. . .	. . .	. . .	Xlock T1
t5	request Slock R1	. . .	. . .	. . .
t6	wait	request Slock S1	. . .	. . .
t7	wait	wait	request Slock T1	. . .
t8	wait	wait	wait	request Slock Q1
t9	wait	wait	wait	wait
. . .	. . .	. . .	. . .	. . .

FIGURE 10.10

Deadlock with Four Transactions

cause a deadlock and never allows deadlock to occur, and **deadlock detection and recovery**, which allows deadlock to occur but, once it has, spots and breaks the deadlock. Since it is easier to test for deadlock and break it when it occurs than to prevent it, many systems use the detection and recovery method. Deadlock detection schemes use a **resource request graph** or **wait-for graph** to show which transactions are waiting for resources locked by other transactions. In such a graph, each node is a transaction. An edge indicates that one transaction is waiting for another to release a lock. For example, Figure 10.11(a) shows two transactions, U and V, with the directed edge from U to V showing that U is waiting for a data item locked by V. The wait-for graph is maintained by the system. As new transactions start, new nodes are added to the graph. When a transaction makes a request for a locked resource that is unavailable, an edge is added to the graph. If the resource is unlocked and obtained by the trans-

FIGURE 10.11
Wait-for Graphs

FIGURE 10.11(a)
U Waits for V

FIGURE 10.11(b)
S and T Deadlocked

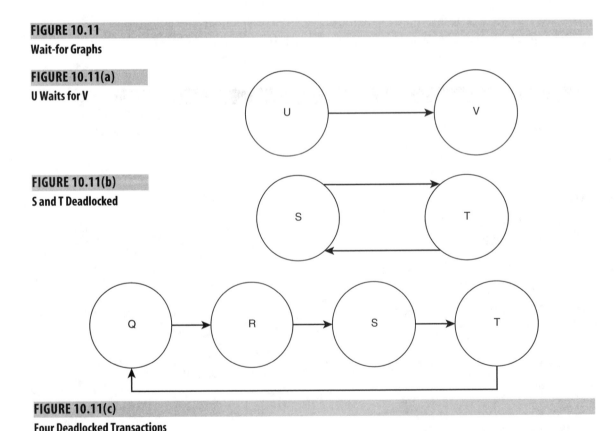

FIGURE 10.11(c)
Four Deadlocked Transactions

action, the edge is erased. In deadlock, the graph will contain a **cycle**. Figure 10.11(b) shows a wait-for graph in which transactions S and T are deadlocked, because there is a cycle starting with S, going to T, and then going back to S. This cycle has length 2, because it contains 2 edges or directed paths, S to T, and T to S. (Of course, there is also a cycle starting at T.) This graph corresponds to the transactions in Figure 10.9. Figure 10.11(c) shows a wait-for graph with a cycle of length 4. This pictures transactions Q, R, S, and T from Figure 10.10.

The system detects deadlock by periodically checking its wait-for graph for cycles. Note that it must check for cycles of any length, since a cycle might involve many transactions. Once a cycle is detected, the system must resolve the deadlock. It does so by choosing one of the transactions in the cycle as the **victim**, a transaction that will be made to fail and will be undone so that the other transactions can proceed. The victim may be the newest transaction, which has not done much work, or the transaction that has made the fewest updates, for example. Care must be taken to avoid always choosing the same transaction as the victim, a situation called **starvation**, because that transaction will never complete. If we chose transaction S shown in Figure 10.11(c) as the victim, then R would obtain its requested data items and could complete and release its locks, so that Q could also complete and, finally, T could obtain its data items. Then transaction S, the victim, could be restarted and could obtain its locks at a later time.

10.4.2 Two-Phase Locking Protocol

One locking scheme that ensures serializability is the **two-phase locking protocol**. According to the rules of this protocol, every transaction can go through two phases: first a **growing phase** in which it acquires all the locks needed for the transaction and then a **shrinking phase** in which it releases its locks. There is no requirement that all locks be obtained simultaneously. Normally the transaction acquires some locks, does some processing, and goes on to acquire additional locks as needed. However, it never releases any lock until it has reached a stage where no new locks will be needed. The rules are:

- A transaction must acquire a lock on an item before operating on the item. For read-only access, a shared lock is sufficient. For write access, an exclusive lock is required.

FIGURE 10.12

Applying Two-Phase Locking Protocol to Figure 10.3

TIME	Jack's Transaction	Jill's Transaction	BAL
t1	BEGIN TRANSACTION		
t2	Xlock BAL		
t3	read BAL *(1000)*	BEGIN TRANSACTION	1000
t4	BAL = BAL − 50 *(950)*	request Xlock Bal	1000
t5	write BAL *(950)*	WAIT	950
t6	COMMIT/UNLOCK BAL	WAIT	950
t7		grant XlockBAL read BAL *(950)*	950
t8		BAL = BAL +100	950
t9		write BAL *(1050)*	1050
t10		COMMMIT/UNLOCK BAL	1050

- Once the transaction releases a single lock, it can never acquire any new locks.

Figure 10.12 shows how the two-phase locking protocol could be applied to Figure 10.3. Note that both transactions needed an exclusive lock on BAL, since both were planning to update it. Jack's transaction requested and obtained the lock first, and held the lock until it finished the update on BAL. Then it released the lock and Jill's transaction, which had been suspended (put in a wait state) while it waited for the lock, could obtain it and complete.

In the **standard** two-phase locking protocol, described by the two rules given above, locks can be released before COMMIT, provided no new locks are requested after any are released. A problem that can arise is that an uncommitted transaction that has released its locks may be rolled back. If a second transaction has been permitted to read a value written by the rolled back transaction, it must also roll back, since it read dirty data. This problem is called a **cascading rollback**. Figure 10.13 shows a case of cascading rollbacks. Transaction R wrote a value of 4 for a, then released its lock, since it was no longer using a. Transaction S read the value of 4 that R had written, and wrote a new value, 8, for a. Transaction T read the value of 8 and calculated yet another value, 18. When R rolled back, the

Time	R	S	T	a
t1	BEGIN TRANS			1
t2	Xlock a	BEGIN TRANS		
t3	read a *(1)*	request Xlock a	BEGIN TRANS	
t4	a=a+3 *(4)*	wait	request Xlock a	
t5	write a *(4)*	wait	wait	4
t6	unlock a	wait	wait	
		grant Xlock a		
t7		read a *(4)*	wait	
t8		a = a*2 *(8)*	wait	
t9		write a *(8)*	wait	8
t10		unlock a	wait	
			grant Xlock a	
t11			read a *(8)*	
t12			a=a+10 *(18)*	
t13			write a *(18)*	18
t14	ROLLBACK			
t15		ROLLBACK		
t16			ROLLBACK	

FIGURE 10.13

Cascading Rollbacks

value of 4 that it wrote became invalid, which caused S to roll back as well. Then its write, 8, became invalid, so T had to roll back as well.

Rollbacks are undesirable because they represent wasted processing time. A variation called **strict** two phase locking requires that transactions hold their exclusive locks until COMMIT, preventing cascading rollbacks. An even stricter protocol is **rigorous** two-phase locking, which requires that transactions hold all locks, both shared and exclusive, until they commit.

The two-phase locking protocol can be refined slightly using **lock upgrading** to maximize concurrency. In this version of two-phase locking, a transaction may at first request shared locks that will allow other concurrent transactions read access to the items. Then when the transaction is ready to do an update, it requests that the shared lock be **upgraded**, or converted into an exclusive lock. Upgrading can take place only during the growing phase, and may require that the transaction wait until another transaction releases a shared lock on the item. Once an item has been updated, its lock can be downgraded—converted from an exclusive to a shared mode. Downgrading can take place only during the shrinking phase.

While all forms of the two-phase protocol guarantee serializability, they can cause deadlock, since transactions can wait for locks on data items. If two transactions each wait for locks on items held by the other, deadlock will occur, and the deadlock detection and recovery scheme described earlier will be needed.

10.4.3 Levels of Locking

Locks can be applied to a single data item, a single record, a file, a group of files, or the entire database. Few systems actually implement data item level locks because of the overhead involved. Some lock pages at a time. We could express the fineness or granularity of locks by a hierarchical structure in which nodes represent data objects of different sizes, as shown in Figure 10.14. Here, the root node represents the entire database, the level 1 nodes tables, the level 2 nodes pages of tables, the level 3 nodes records, and the leaves data items. Whenever a node is locked, all its descendants are also locked. For example, locking page A1 of Figure 10.14 locks records A11 and A12 as well as all their data items. If a second transaction requests an incompatible lock on the same node, the system clearly knows that the lock cannot be granted. For example, a request for an exclusive lock on page A1 will be denied. If the second transaction requests an incompatible lock on any of the descendants of the locked node, the system should check the hierarchical path from the root to the requested node to see if any of its ancestors are locked before deciding whether to grant the lock. Thus if the request is for an exclusive lock on tuple A11, the system should check its parent, page A1, its grandparent, Table A, and the database itself to see if any of them are locked. When it finds that page A1 is already locked, it denies the request. What happens if a transaction requests a lock on a node when a descendant of a node is already locked? For example, if a lock is requested on Table A, the system would have to check every page in the table, every record in those pages, and every data item in those records to see if any of them are locked. To reduce the searching involved in locating locks on descendants, the system can use another type of lock called an **intention** lock. When any node is locked, an intention lock is placed on all the ancestors of the node. Thus if some descendant of Table A (e.g., page A1) is locked, and a request is made for a lock on Table A, the presence of an intention lock on Table A

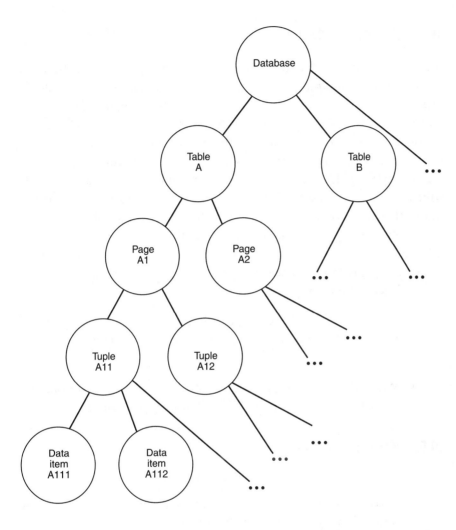

FIGURE 10.14

Levels of Locking

would indicate that some descendant of that node is already locked. Intention locks can use either exclusive or shared mode. To ensure serializability with locking levels, a two-phase protocol is used, meaning no lock can be granted to a transaction once any node has been unlocked by that transaction, no node can be locked by a transaction until its parent is locked by an intention lock, and no node can be unlocked by a transaction until all its descendants are unlocked. The effect of these rules is to apply locking from the root down, using intention locks until the node requiring an actual shared or exclusive lock is reached, and to release locks from leaves up. However, deadlock is still possible, and must be detected and resolved using the methods discussed previously.

10.5 Timestamping

An alternate concurrency control mechanism that eliminates the deadlock problem is **timestamping**. In this scheme, no locks are used, so no deadlocks can occur. A timestamp for a transaction is a unique identifier that indicates the relative starting time of the transaction. It could be the reading on the internal clock at the time the transaction started, or it could be the value of a logical counter that is incremented every time a new transaction starts. In either case, the timestamp value of each transaction T, which we will indicate by TS(T), is unique and indicates how old the transaction is. The effect of timestamping is to assign a serial order to the transactions. The protocol then ensures that the order is met, by not permitting any reads or writes that would violate the order. In addition to transaction timestamps, there are timestamps for data items. Each data item, P, has two timestamps.

- Read-Timestamp(P), giving the timestamp of the last transaction that read the item. It is updated when a read(P) operation is done by a transaction.

- Write-Timestamp(P), giving the timestamp of the last transaction to write (update) the item. It is updated when a write(P) is done.

10.5.1 Basic Timestamping Protocol

Two problems can arise with timestamping:

1. A transaction, T, asks to read an item that has already been updated by a younger (later) transaction

2. T asks to write an item whose current value has already been read or written by a younger transaction

The first problem is a **late read**. The value that T needs to read is no longer available, since it has already been overwritten, so T must roll back and restart with a later timestamp. The second problem is a **late write**, and a younger transaction has already read the old value or written a new one. Again, the solution is to roll back T and restart it using a later timestamp. The following rules summarize this **basic timestamping protocol**. We always test the timestamp of the transaction, TS(T), against WriteTimestamp(P) and/or ReadTimestamp(P) that identify the transaction(s) that last wrote or read the data item, P.

1. If T asks to **read** a data item P, compare its TS(T) with WriteTimestamp(P).

   a. If WriteTimestamp(P) <= TS(T) then proceed using the current data value and replace ReadTimestamp(P) with TS(T). However, if ReadTimestamp(P) is already larger than TS(T), just do the read and do not change ReadTimestamp(P).

   b. If WriteTimestamp(P) > TS(T), then T is late doing its read, and the value of P that it needs is already overwritten, so roll back T.

2. If T asks to **write** a data item P, compare TS(T) with both Write-Timestamp(P) and Read-Timestamp(P).

   a. If Write-Timestamp(P) <= TS(T) and Read-Timestamp(P) <= TS(T) then do the write and replace WriteTimestamp(P) with TS(T).

   b. else roll back T, assign a new timestamp, and restart T.

In the case of a late write, 2(b), the reason why we have to roll back if Read-Timestamp(P) is later than TS(T) is that a younger transaction has already read the current value, and replacing that value now would introduce an error. If Write-Timestamp(P) is later than TS(T), the value T is trying to write is an obsolete value, so it would also introduce an error.

This scheme guarantees that transactions will be serializable and the results will be equivalent to a serial execution schedule in which the transactions are executed in chronological order by the timestamps. Figure 10.15 illustrates what happens when the standard timestamping protocol is applied to the schedule shown in Figure 10.5. At time t1, the values in BAL_A, BAL_B, and BAL_C are all 5000, and their read and write timestamps, which we call R and W respectively, are some earlier time, which we will call t0. Transaction SUMBAL is assigned a timestamp of t1, its starting time. Note that this remains its timestamp throughout its duration, regardless of the clock reading. TRANSFER begins at time t2, and is given transaction timestamp t2. When SUMBAL tries to do a read BAL_A at time t3, its timestamp, t1, is compared with the W value of BAL_A, which is t0. Since this is less than its own timestamp, t1, it reads the value 5000 and, since the R value of BAL_A is less than t1, it replaces the t0 with t1. Similarly when TRANSFER requests a read of BAL_A, it is permitted to do the read and replaces the R value with its timestamp, t2. Processing continues normally until time t10, when SUMBAL tries to do a late read.

Time	SUMBAL	TRANSFER	BAL_A,R,W	BAL_B,R,W	BAL_C,R,W	SUM
t1	BEGIN TRANSACTION- Assign timestamp t1		5000,t0,t0	5000,t0,t0	5000,t0,t0	–
t2	SUM = 0;	BEGIN TRANSACTION- Assign timestamp t2	5000,t0,t0	5000,t0,t0	5000,t0,t0	–
t3	read BAL_A *(5000)*	. . .	5000,t1,t0	5000,t0,t0	5000,t0,t0	–
t4	SUM = SUM + BAL_A *(5000)*	read BAL_A *(5000)*	5000,t2,t0	5000,t0,t0	5000,t0,t0	–
t5	read BAL_B *(5000)*	BAL_A = BAL_A − 1000 *(4000)*	5000,t2,t0	5000,t1,t0	5000,t0,t0	–
t6	SUM = SUM + BAL_B *(10000)*	write BAL_A *(4000)*	4000,t2,t2	5000,t1,t0	5000,t0,t0	–
t7		read BAL_C *(5000)*	4000,t2,t2	5000,t1,t0	5000,t2,t0	–
t8		BAL_C = BAL_C +1000 *(6000)*	4000,t2,t2	5000,t1,t0	5000,t2,t0	–
t9		write BAL_C *(6000)*	4000,t2,t2	5000,t1,t0	6000,t2,t2	–
t10	Read BAL_C *–late read* *ROLLBACK*		4000,t2,t2	5000,t0,t0	6000,t2,t2	–
t11		COMMIT				
t12	restart with timestamp t12					
. . .						

FIGURE 10.15

Timestamping Applied to Figure 10.5

Since the W value of BAL_C is t2, we can see that this value has been written by a later transaction, so SUMBAL cannot read the appropriate value, which has already been overwritten, and it must roll back. It then restarts with a later timestamp, such as t12.

10.5.2 Thomas' Write Rule

A variation of the basic timestamping protocol that allows greater concurrency is one in which some obsolete writes can safely be ignored without rolling back the transaction. It applies in the case where T is trying to do a write to data item P, but a new value has already been written for P by a younger transaction. If a younger transaction has already read P, then it needed the value that T is trying to write, so it is necessary to roll back T and restart it. Otherwise the transaction can proceed, with or without doing a write according to the following write protocol called **Thomas' write rule** that applies to transaction T trying to write P.

1. If Read-timestamp(P) > TS(T), then a younger transaction needed the new value, so T has to be rolled back.

2. If Write-timestamp(P) > TS(T) but Read-timestamp (P) <= TS(T), the write operation can be ignored since it is obsolete, but T can proceed because its write was not needed.

3. else do the write operation and replace Write-timestamp(P) by TS(T).

10.5.3 Multiversion Timestamping

The timestamping protocols discussed so far assume that there is only one version of each data item in the database. Concurrency can be increased if we allow multiple versions to be stored, so that transactions can access the version that is consistent for them. Each data item P has a sequence of versions $<P_1, P_2, . . ., P_n>$, each of which has,

- The content field, a value for P_i

- A Write-Timestamp(P_i), which is the timestamp of the transaction that wrote the value

- A Read-Timestamp(P_i), which is the timestamp of the youngest transaction (i.e., the one with the largest timestamp) that has read version P_i.

Whenever a write(P) is done, a new version of P is created, with appropriate write-timestamp. When a read(P) is done, the system selects the appropriate version of P. The multiversion timestamp protocol is,

1. When Transaction T does a read(P), the value that is returned is the value of the content field associated with the latest Write-Timestamp that is less than or equal to TS(T). The Read-Timestamp is then set to the later of TS(T) or its current value.

2. When T does a write(P), the version we must use is the one whose write timestamp is the largest one that is less than or equal to TS(T). For that version,

a. If Read-Timestamp(P) > TS(T), indicating that P has already been read by a younger transaction, roll back T, because it would be a late write.

b. else create a new version of P, with read and write timestamps equal to TS(T).

For example, in Figure 10.16(a) Transaction 10 requests a data item that has already been updated by Transaction 11. However, an old version of the data item exists with a content value of 100 and a Write-Timestamp of 9. As this is the last Write-Timestamp less than or equal to the transaction's timestamp (10), we use that version for transaction 10. The Read-Timestamp of that

FIGURE 10.16(a)

Transaction Reads an Item Already Updated by a Younger Transaction

Data Item - VAL			
	Content	Read-Timestamp	Write-Timestamp
(old version)	100	9 (←change to 10)	9
(new version)	150	11	11
Transaction with timestamp 10: read VAL (get 100, using old version, and change its Read-Timestamp to 10)			

FIGURE 10.16(b)

Transaction Tries to Write an Item Already Updated by Younger Transaction

Data Item - VAL			
	Value	Read-Timestamp	Write-Timestamp
(old version)	100	10	9
(current version)	150	11	11
Transaction with timestamp 10: read VAL (get 100)			
VAL = VAL −10			
write VAL () (Create a new version of VAL with Value of 90 and Read- and Write-Timestamps of 10)			
(new version of VAL)	90	10	10

FIGURE 10.16

Multiversion Timestamping Examples

version is then changed to 10. The effect of this process is to ensure that the two transactions read data items as if they were actually executed serially. In Figure 10.16(b) transaction 10 is doing a write to an item whose current version was written by a later transaction. However, we examine the version whose Write-Timestamp is less than or equal to 10 (9 in this case). For that version, since the Read-Timestamp is less than or equal to 10, this is not a late write, so we create a new version with both timestamps of 10.

10.6 Optimistic Techniques

In many environments, conflicts between transactions are relatively rare, and the extra processing required to apply locking schemes is unnecessary for most of the transactions. There is a class of techniques that eliminates this overhead. **Validation** techniques, also called **optimistic** techniques, work under the assumption that conflict will normally not occur. They allow transactions to proceed as if there were no concurrency problems, but just before a transaction commits, a check is performed to determine whether a conflict has occurred. If there is a conflict, the transaction must be rolled back. Since the assumption is that conflict rarely occurs, rollback will be rare. The occasional rollback is the price to be paid for eliminating locks. These techniques allow more concurrency than traditional schemes, because no locking is done.

In optimistic schemes, a transaction goes through two or three phases in order, depending on whether it is a read-only or an updating transaction.

1. A **read** phase that extends from the start of the transaction until just before it commits. During this phase, the transaction reads the values of all the data items it needs, and stores them in local variables. If the transaction does any writes, they are done to a local copy of the data, not to the database itself.

2. A **validation** phase that follows the read phase. During this time, the transaction tests to determine whether there is any interference. For a read-only transaction, this consists of checking to see that there was no error caused by another transaction that was active when the data values were read. If no error occurred, the transaction is committed. If interference occurred, the transaction is aborted and restarted. For a transaction that does updates,

validation consists of determining whether the current transaction will leave the database in a consistent state, with serializability maintained. If not, the transaction is aborted. If the update transaction passes the validation test, it goes on to a third phase.

3. A **write** phase that follows the successful validation phase for update transactions. During this phase, the updates made to the local copy are applied to the database itself.

The validation phase is accomplished by examining the reads and writes of transactions that may cause interference. Each transaction, T, is given three timestamps.

- Start(T)—the starting time of the transaction

- Validation(T)—the time when it ends its read phase and enters its validation phase

- Finish(T)—the time it finishes, including its write phase, if any

To pass the validation test, we compare the other transaction's timestamps with Validation(T) and attempt to keep transactions in order. One of the following must be true:

1. All transactions with earlier validation timestamps must have finished (including their writes) before the current transaction started. That means for any transaction S with Validation(S)<Validation(T), we must have

Finish(S)<Start(T),

Else

2. If the current transaction starts before an earlier one finishes, that is, if Start(T)<Finish(S), then both of the following are true:

a. the items written by the earlier transaction, S, are not the ones read by the current transaction, T, and,

b. the earlier transaction, S, completes its write phase before the current transaction, T, enters its validation phase; that is, Finish(S)<Validation(T).

Rule 2(a) guarantees that the writes of the earlier transaction are not read by the current transaction, while rule 2(b) guarantees that the writes are done serially.

Although optimistic techniques are very efficient when there are few conflicts, they can result in rollback of individual transactions. Note that the rollback involves only a local copy of the data, so there are no cascading rollbacks, because the writes have not actually reached the database. However, if the aborted transaction is a long one, valuable processing time will be lost, as the transaction must be restarted. If rollback occurs often, it is an indication that the optimistic method is a poor choice for concurrency control in that particular environment.

10.7 Need for Recovery

Recovery after any failure consists of restoring the database to a correct state. There are many different types of failures that can affect database processing. Some failures affect main memory (including database buffers) only, while others involve disk storage or backup storage devices. Among the causes of failure are:

- Natural physical disasters such as fires, floods, earthquakes, or power outages

- Sabotage or intentional contamination or destruction of data, hardware, or software facilities

- Carelessness or unintentional destruction or contamination of data or facilities by operators or users

- Disk malfunctions such as head crashes, defective disks, or unreadable tracks, which might result in loss of stored data

- System crashes due to hardware malfunction, resulting in loss of main and cache memory

- System software errors that result in abnormal termination or damage to the database management system

- Applications software errors such as logical errors in the program that is accessing the database

Regardless of the cause of the failure, we need to study the possible effects so that we can protect or limit the damage to the database. The principal effects that concern us are the loss of main memory, the loss or corruption of the disk copy of the database, and failure to write data safely to disk storage. Fortunately, there are techniques that can minimize these effects.

10.8   Recovery Techniques

Transactions are used as the basic unit for recovery for a database. The DBMS has a **recovery manager** that is responsible for ensuring **atomicity** and **durability** for transactions in the event of failure. Atomicity requires that all of a transaction be performed or none, so the recovery manager has to ensure that all the effects of committed transactions reach the database, and that the effects of any uncommitted transactions be undone as part of recovery. Durability requires that the effects of a committed transaction be permanent, so they must survive loss of main memory, loss of disk storage, and failures during data transfers to disk.

The possible loss of disk is handled by doing frequent backups, making copies of the database as it appears at a certain point in time. In the event of a disk failure, the database can be recovered to a correct state by starting with the backup copy, and bringing the backup copy up to date using a log of transactions, which will be described shortly. It is desirable to have one or more copies of the database stored in some form of **stable storage**, a non-volatile form of storage that is, in theory, completely safe from destruction. In practice, stable storage can be created by having **mirrored disks**, a version of RAID (Redundant Arrays of Independent Disks) technology in which two independent disks both contain complete copies of the database. Whenever a database page is modified, both copies are updated. A less expensive form of stable storage is to use cheaper versions of RAID technology, spreading the database contents out over multiple independent disks. Another method is to have a live backup copy of the database at a remote site, and to send a copy of each modified database page to the remote disk whenever the local disk is modified. These methods help in recovery both in the event of database failure and in the event of a data transfer failure. To ensure against errors when database writes occur, the modified pages are written first to the local disk and then to the mirror or remote disk. Only after both writes are completed is the output considered to have been done. If a data transfer error is detected, both copies are examined. If they are identical, the data is correct. If one has an error condition, the other copy can be used to replace the faulty data. If neither has an error condition but they have different values, the write is essentially undone by replacing the first copy with the second. If a system failure occurs and the database buffers are lost, the disk copy of the database survives, but it may be incorrect due to partially completed database updates. A transaction can commit once its writes are made to the database buffers, but there might be a delay between the commit and the actual disk writing. Because updates made to buffer pages are not immediately written to disk, even for committed transactions, if there is a system failure during this delay, the system must be able to ensure that these updates reach the disk copy of the database. For some protocols, writes made while a transaction is active, even before it commits, can reach the disk copy of the database. If there is a system failure before the transaction completes, these writes need to be undone. To keep track of database transactions, the system maintains a special file called a **log** that contains information about all updates to the database. The log can contain data transactions records, giving the transaction identifier and some information about it. For example, assuming T is the transaction identifier, there is,

- A record of the form <T starts> showing the start of a transaction

- For each write operation a record of the form <T,X,n> showing the transaction identifier, the attribute name, and the new value, or <T,X,o,n>, showing both the old and new values

- A record of the form <T commits> showing the end of the committed transaction **or** a record of the form <T aborts> showing that a transaction has aborted

- Checkpoint records, which we will describe shortly

10.8.1 Deferred Update Protocol

Using the deferred update recovery protocol, the DBMS records all database writes in the log, and does not write to the database until the transaction is ready to commit.

We can use the log to protect against system failures in the following way:

- When a transaction starts, write a record of the form <T starts> to the log.

- When any write operation is performed, do not actually write the update to the database buffers or the database itself. Instead, write a log record of the form <T,X, n> showing the new value for X.

- When a transaction is about to commit, write a log record of the form <T commits>, write all the log records for the transaction to disk, and then commit the transaction. Use the log records to perform the actual updates to the database.

- If the transaction aborts, simply ignore the log records for the transaction and do not perform the writes.

Note that we write the log records to disk before the transaction is actually committed, so that if a system failure occurs while the actual database updates are in progress, the log records will survive and the updates can be applied later.

Figure 10.17 illustrates a short transaction, the corresponding log transaction entries, and the database data items involved. Note that the database is not updated until after the commit. In the event of a system failure, we examine the log to identify the transactions that may be affected by the failure. Any transaction with log records <T starts> and <T commits> should be **redone** in the order in which they appear in the log. The transaction itself does not have to be executed again. Instead, the **redo procedure** will perform all the writes to the database, using the write log records for the transactions. Recall all of these will have the form <T,X,n>, which

T starts;
read (X);
X = X + 10;
write (X);
read (Y);
Y = 2 * Y;
write (Y);
T commits;

FIGURE 10.17(a)

Transaction T

(Assume at the start that X and Y both have value 100.)

Log	Database Data Items	
	X	Y
<T starts>	100	100
<T,X,110>	100	100
<T,Y,200>	100	100
<T commits>	100	100
	110	200

FIGURE 10.17(b)

Log Entries and Database Data Items

FIGURE 10.17

A Transaction and Its Log

means the procedure will write the value n to the attribute X. If this writing has been done already, prior to the failure, the write will have no effect on the attribute, so there is no damage done if we write unnecessarily. However, this method guarantees that we will update any attribute that was not properly updated prior to the failure. For any transaction with log records <S starts> and <S aborts>, or any transaction with <S starts> but neither a commit nor an abort, we do nothing, as no actual writing was done to the database using the incremental log with deferred updates technique, so these transactions do not have to be undone. This protocol is called a **redo/no undo** method, since we redo committed transactions, and we do not undo any transactions. In the event that a second system crash occurs during recovery, the log records are used again the second time the system is restored. Because of the form of the write log records, it does not matter how many times we redo the writes.

If a system failure occurs while the log records themselves are being written to disk, no database updates have yet been made by the transaction. If the log contains a <T starts> but no <T commits>, or it contains <T starts> followed by <T aborts> we do nothing. If the log contains both <T starts> and <T commits> we perform the redo procedure as described earlier.

10.8.2 Checkpoints

One difficulty with this scheme is that when a failure occurs, we may not know how far back in the log to search. For example, we might wind up redoing a whole day's transactions, even though most of them have been safely written to the database. To put some limit on the log searching we need to do, we can use a technique called a **checkpoint**. Checkpoints are scheduled at predetermined intervals and involve the following operations:

- Writing the modified pages in the database buffers out to disk, a process called **force writing**

- Writing all log records now in main memory out to disk

- Writing a checkpoint record to the log. This record contains the names of all transactions that are active at the time of the checkpoint.

Having checkpoints allows us to limit the log search. If all transactions are performed serially, when a failure occurs, we can check the log to find the last transaction that started before the last checkpoint. In serial execution, any earlier transaction would have committed previously and would have been written to the database at the checkpoint. Therefore, we need only redo the one that was active at the checkpoint, provided it has a commit log record after the checkpoint but before the failure, and any subsequent transactions for which both start and commit records appear in the log. If transactions are performed concurrently, the scheme is only slightly more complicated. Recall that the checkpoint record contains the names of all transactions that were active at checkpoint time. Therefore, we redo all those transactions and all subsequent ones that have committed.

10.8.3 Immediate Update Protocol

A slightly different recovery technique uses a log with immediate updates. In this scheme, updates are applied to the database buffers as they occur and are written to the database itself when convenient. However, a log record is written first, since this is a **write-ahead log protocol**. The scheme for successful transactions is as follows:

- When a transaction starts, write a record of the form <T starts> to the log.

- When a write operation is performed, write a log record containing the name of the transaction, the attribute name, the old value, and the new value of the attribute. This has the form <T,X,o,n>.

- After the log record is written, write the update to the database buffers.

- When convenient, write the log records to disk and then write updates to the database itself.

- When the transaction commits, write a record of the form <T commits> to the log.

If a transaction aborts, the log can be used to undo it, because it contains all the old values for the updated attributes. Because a transaction might have performed several changes to an item, the writes are undone in reverse order. Regardless of whether the transaction's writes have been applied to the database itself, writing the old values guarantees that the database will be restored to its state prior to the start of the transaction.

If the system fails, recovery involves using the log to **undo** or **redo** transactions, making this a **redo/undo** protocol. For any transaction, T, for which both <T starts> and <T commits> records appear in the log, we **redo** by using the log records to write the new values of updated items. Note that if the new values have already been written to the database, these writes, though unnecessary, will have no effect. However, any write that did not actually reach the database will now be performed. For any transaction, S, for which the log contains an <S starts> record, but not an <S commits> record, we will need to **undo** that transaction. This time the log records are used to write the old values of the affected items and thus restore the database to its state prior to the transaction's start.

10.8.4 Shadow Paging

Shadow paging is an alternative to log-based recovery techniques. The DBMS keeps a **page table** that contains pointers to all current database pages on disk. With shadow paging, two page tables are kept, a **current page table** and a **shadow page table**. Initially these tables are identical. All modifications are made to the current page table, and the shadow table is left unchanged. When a transaction needs to make a change to a database page, the system finds an unused page on disk, copies the old database page to the new one, and makes changes to the new page. It also updates the current page table to point to the new page. If the transaction completes successfully, the current page table becomes the shadow page table. If the transaction fails, the new pages are ignored, and the shadow page table becomes the current page table. The commit operation requires that the system do the following:

- Write all modified pages from the database buffer out to disk
- Copy the current page table to disk
- In the disk location where the address of the shadow page table is recorded, write the address of the current page table, making it the new shadow page table

10.8.5 Overview of ARIES Recovery Algorithm

The ARIES recovery algorithm is a very flexible and efficient method for database recovery. It uses a log, in which each log record is given a unique **log sequence number** (LSN), which is assigned in increasing order. Each log record records the LSN of the previous log record for the same transaction, forming a linked list. Each database page also has a **pageLSN**, which is the LSN of the last log record that updated the page. The recovery manager keeps a **transaction table** with an entry for each active transaction, giving the transaction identifier, the status (active, committed, or aborted), and the **lastLSN**, which is the LSN of the latest log record for the transaction. It also keeps a **dirty page table** with an entry for each page in the buffer that has been updated but not yet written to disk, along with the **recLSN**, the LSN of the oldest log record that represented an update to the buffer page. The protocol uses write-ahead logging, which requires that the log record be written to disk before any database disk update. It also does checkpointing to limit log searching in recovery. Unlike other protocols, ARIES tries to repeat history during recovery, by attempting to repeat all database actions done before the crash, even those of incomplete transactions. It then does redo and undo as needed. Recovery after a crash is done in three phases.

1. **Analysis.** The DBMS begins with the most recent checkpoint record and reads forward in the log to identify which transactions were active at the time of failure. It also uses the transaction table and the dirty page table to determine which buffer pages contain updates that were not yet written to disk. It also determines how far back in the log it needs to go to recover, using the linked lists of LSNs.

2. **Redo.** From the starting point in the log identified during analysis, which is the smallest recLSN found in the dirty page table during the analysis phase, the recovery manager goes forward in the log, and applies all the unapplied updates from the log records.

3. **Undo.** Going backward from the end of the log, the recovery manager undoes updates done by uncommitted transactions, ending at the oldest log record of any transaction that was active at the time of the crash.

This algorithm is more efficient than the ones discussed previously, because it avoids unnecessary redo and undo operations, since it knows which updates have already been performed.

10.9   Transaction Management in Oracle

Oracle uses a multiversion concurrency control mechanism, with no read locks. If a transaction is read-only, it works with a consistent view of the database at the point in time when it began, including only those updates that were committed at that time. The DBMS creates **rollback segments** that contain the older versions of data items and that are used for both read consistency and any undo operations that might be needed. It uses a type of timestamp called a **system change number** (SCN) that is associated with each transaction at its start. The system automatically provides locking at the row-level for SQL statements requiring locks. Several types of locks are available, including both DML and DDL locks, the latter being applied at the table level. Deadlock is handled using a deadlock detection scheme, and rolling back of one of the transactions. Oracle supports two **isolation levels**, which are degrees of protection from other transactions. They are:

- **Read committed.** This is statement-level consistency, guaranteeing that each statement in a transaction reads only data committed before the statement started. However, since data can be changed during the transaction containing the statement, there might be nonrepeatable reads and phantom data. This is the default level.

- **Serializable.** This is transaction-level consistency, ensuring that a transaction sees only data committed before the transaction started.

For recovery, Oracle has a **recovery manager** (RMAN), a GUI tool that the DBA can use to control backup and recovery operations. RMAN can be used to make backups of the database or parts thereof, to make backups of recovery logs, to restore data from backups, and to perform recovery operations including redo and undo operations as needed. It maintains control files, rollback segments, redo logs, and archived redo logs. When a redo log is filled, it can be archived automatically. Oracle also provides a backup feature for environments where high availability is important in the form of a managed standby database. This is a copy of the operational database, usually kept at a separate location, that can take over if the regular database fails. It is kept nearly up to date by shipping the archived redo logs and applying the updates to the standby database.

10.10 Chapter Summary

Database **recovery** is the process of restoring the database to a correct state after a failure. **Concurrency control** is the ability to allow simultaneous use of the database without having users interfere with one another. Both protect the database.

A **transaction** is a logical unit of work that takes the database from one consistent state to another. Transactions can terminate successfully and **commit** or unsuccessfully and be **aborted**. Aborted transactions must be undone or **rolled back**. Committed transactions cannot be rolled back.

Without concurrency control, problems such as the **lost update problem**, the **uncommitted update problem**, and the **inconsistent analysis problem** can arise. **Serial execution** means executing one transaction at a time, with no interleaving of operations. There will be more than one possible serial execution for two or more transactions, and they might not all produce the same results, but they are all considered correct. A **schedule** is used to show the timing of the operations of one or more transactions. A schedule is **serializable** if it produces the same results as if the transactions were performed serially in some order. A **precedence graph** shows the order of conflicting read and write operations in a schedule, and proves conflict serializability if it has no cycles. It also shows possible equivalent serial ordering of transactions.

Two methods that guarantee serializability are **locking** and **timestamping**. **Shared locks** are sufficient if a transaction needs only read access, but **exclusive locks** are necessary for write access. A **lock compatibility matrix** shows which type of locks requests can be granted simultaneously. Transactions might be required to wait until locks are released before their lock requests can be granted. Because transactions can wait for locks, **deadlock**, a situation in which two or more transactions wait for locks being held by one another to be released, can occur. Deadlock detection schemes use a **wait-for** graph to identify deadlock. A deadlock is resolved by choosing a **victim**, a transaction that will be made to fail.

Two-phase locking is a widely used locking protocol. Every transaction acquires all its locks before releasing any. Variations to standard two-phase locking include **strict** and **rigorous**. Another variation allows transactions to begin by acquiring shared locks and to **upgrade** them to exclusive locks just before a write. Upgrading can be done only during the growing phase. In the shrinking phase, a transaction can **downgrade** an exclusive lock to a shared lock. The purpose of this refinement is to maximize concurrent access. A tree can be used to represent the **granularity** of locks in a system that allows different sized objects to be locked. When an object is locked, all its descendants in the tree are also locked. When a transaction requests a lock, an intention lock is placed on all the ancestors of any node being locked. Therefore, if a node does not have an intention lock, none of its descendants are locked. Serializability is ensured by using a two-phase locking protocol.

In a **timestamping** protocol, each transaction is given a timestamp, a unique identifier that gives the relative order of the transaction, and each data item has a **Read-Timestamp** and a **Write-Timestamp**. Problems arise when a transaction tries to read an item already updated by a younger transaction, or when a transaction tries to write an item whose value has already been read or updated by a later transaction. The protocol takes care of these problems by rolling back transactions that cannot execute correctly. If multiple versions of data items are kept, late reads can be done.

Optimistic techniques can be used in situations where conflicts are rare. Each transaction starts with a **read phase**, during which it reads all variables it needs, stores them as local variables, and writes to the local copy only. After the read phase, the transaction moves to a **validation phase**, during which the system determines whether there was any interference. If not, it moves on to a **write phase**, during which the updates to the transaction's local copy are applied to the database. If there was interference, the transaction is aborted instead of moving to the write phase.

To facilitate recovery, the system keeps a **log** containing transaction records that identify the start of transactions, giving information about write operations, and identifying the end of transactions. Using an incremental log with **deferred updates**, writes are done initially to the log only, and the log records are used to perform actual updates to the database. If the system fails, it examines the log to determine which transactions it needs to **redo**, namely those that committed but might not have been written to the database. There is no need to undo any writes. At a **checkpoint**, all modified pages in the database buffers are written to disk, all log records are written to disk, and a checkpoint record identifying all transactions active at that time is written to disk. If a failure occurs, the checkpoint records identify which transactions need to be redone. Using an incremental log with **immediate updates**, updates can be made to the database itself at any time after a log record for the update is written. The log can be used to **undo** as well as to **redo** transactions in the event of failure. **Shadow paging** is a recovery technique that uses no logs. Instead, updates are made to a new copy of each page. A **current page table** points to the new page. A **shadow page table** continues to point to the old page until the transaction commits, at which time the current page table becomes the shadow page table. The **ARIES** recovery algorithm is a highly sensitive and flexible algorithm that does recovery by attempting to recreate the exact state the database was in at the time of failure, and then applying undo and redo operations as needed.

Oracle handles concurrency control by using a variety of locking and timestamping techniques. It uses rollback segments for both concurrency and recovery. The Oracle recovery manager maintains control files, rollback segments, redo logs, and archived redo logs for recovery.

Exercises

10.1   Assume a DBMS that uses immediate updates has the following log entries. Figure 10.18 shows a timeline depicting each transaction's starting and ending time, along with the checkpoint. A start and a commit are indicated by a large dot, while an abort is indicated by an X.

<Q starts>

<R starts>

<Q,W,0,20>

<R,X,1,5>

<Q aborts>

<R,Y, − 1,0>

<R commits>

<S starts>

Figure 10.18

Transaction Timeline for Exercise 10.1

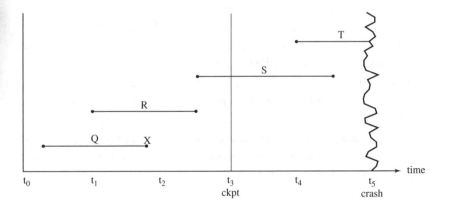

<S,Z,8,12>

<checkpoint record>

<S,X,5,10>

<T starts>

<T,Y,0,15>

<S commits>

————————system crash————————

Assuming a system crash occurs as indicated immediately after the <S commits> log record,

a. Which transactions, if any, need to be redone?

b. Which transactions, if any, need to be undone?

c. Which transactions, if any, are not affected by the crash?

d. Assuming the variables in different transactions refer to database items with the same names, what are the final values of W, X, Y, and Z?

e. If a second system failure occurs while the first recovery is in progress, what needs to be done after the system recovers for the second time?

10.2   Assume the same transactions and operations as shown in Exercise 10.1 are being done by a system that uses the deferred update protocol.

a. Rewrite the log entries for the transactions in Exercise 10.1 for this logging method.

b. Which transactions, if any, need to be redone?

c. Which transactions, if any, need to be undone?

d. Which transactions, if any, are not affected by the crash?

e. What will be the final values of W, X, Y, and Z?

f. If a second system failure occurs while the first recovery is in progress, what needs to be done after the system recovers for the second time?

10.3   Suppose the log in Exercise 10.1 contained the entry
<S aborts> in place of the entry <S commits>.

a. If the system is using immediate updates and the crash
occurred before the rollback took place, what changes, if any,
would you make in the recovery process?

b. If the system were using deferred updates, what changes would
you make in the recovery process of Exercise 10.2?

10.4   Assume the following transactions are to be performed.

Transaction S:

read(a);

$a = a + 10$;

write(a);

read(b);

$b = b*5$;

write(b);

Transaction T:

read(a);

$a = a*2$;

write a;

a. If the initial value of a is 10 and the initial value of b is 20, what
are their final values if we perform the transactions serially,
using order S,T?

b. Using the same initial values, what are the final values of a and
b if the order of execution is T,S?

c. Does this result have any implicatons for serializability?

10.5   Write a concurrent schedule for transactions S and T in Exercise
10.4 that illustrates the lost update problem.

10.6   Apply the standard two-phase locking protocol to the schedule
you devised in Exercise 10.5. Will the protocol allow the execution
of that schedule? Does deadlock occur?

10.7 Apply the standard timestamping protocol to the schedule you devised in Exercise 10.5. In the columns for the attributes, add read and write timestamps, assuming both were last set by a transaction with timestamp t0, as shown in Figure 10.15. Will the protocol allow the execution of that schedule? Are there any rollbacks? If so, are they cascading rollbacks?

10.8 Apply the standard timestamping protocol to the schedule shown in Figure 10.3. Will the protocol allow the execution of that schedule? Are there any rollbacks? If so, are they cascading rollbacks?

10.9 Apply the standard two-phase locking protocol to the schedule shown in Figure 10.4. Does deadlock occur?

10.10 Apply the standard timestamping protocol to the schedule shown in Figure 10.4. Will the protocol allow the execution of that schedule? Are there any rollbacks? If so, are they cascading rollbacks?

10.11 Apply the standard two-phase locking protocol to the schedule shown in Figure 10.5. Does deadlock occur?

10.12 Apply the standard timestamping protocol to the schedule shown in Figure 10.5. Will the protocol allow the execution of that schedule? Are there any rollbacks? If so, are they cascading rollbacks?

10.13 Let T_1, T_2, and T_3 be transactions that operate on the same database items, A, B, and C. Let $r_1(A)$ mean that T_1 reads A, $w_1(A)$ mean that T_1 writes A, and so on for T_2 and T_3. Each of the following shows the order of the reads and writes in a schedule for T_1, T_2, and T_3. In each case, draw a precedence graph with nodes for T_1, T_2, and T_3 and draw edges for conflicts. Determine if each schedule is serializable by examining the precedence graph. If it is serializable, give an equivalent serial schedule.

a. $r_1(A)$; $r_2(A)$; $w_1(A)$; $r_3(A)$; $w_3(A)$; $w_2(A)$

b. $r_1(A)$; $r_1(B)$; $r_2(A)$; $r_3(B)$; $r_3(C)$; $w_2(A)$; $w_2(B)$

c. $r_1(A)$; $r_3(C)$; $r_2(C)$; $w_3(A)$; $r_2(B)$; $r_3(B)$; $w_2(B)$; $w_2(A)$

On the Companion Website:

- Lab Exercises

CHAPTER 11

Relational Query Optimization

Chapter Objectives

In this chapter you will learn the following:

- How a relational query is interpreted

- How a query tree represents relational algebra expressions

- Some rules for equivalence of algebraic operations

- Heuristics for query optimization

- How to estimate the cost of SELECT operations

- How to estimate the cost of JOIN operations

- Methods of processing PROJECT operations

- Methods of processing set operations

- How pipelining can be used for queries

11.1   Query Processing and Query Optimization

In Chapter 5 we saw that some SQL queries could be expressed in different ways. For example, in a SELECT statement involving two or more tables, we could sometimes choose between a join and a subquery. Similarly, in Chapter 4 we considered different sequences of relational algebra commands that produced equivalent results. We noted in passing that certain formulations of these queries were more efficient than others. In this chapter we examine relative efficiency more closely and discuss some techniques for improving the efficiency of queries.

When a relational database management system receives a high-level query in a language such as SQL, it first checks the query syntax to ensure that the language is used correctly. The syntactically correct query is then validated by checking the data dictionary to verify that the attributes, tables, or views referred to are actual database objects and that the operations requested are valid operations on those objects. The query then has to be translated into some form that the system can use. For example, although a query can be expressed in SQL externally, the system must transform it into a lower-level internal representation that it can actually use for processing. Relational algebra can be used for this internal representation, because its operations are easily transformed into system operations. Relational calculus can be used instead, but we will assume relational algebra is used for our examples. The system then examines the internal representation and uses its knowledge of relational algebra operations to determine whether the operations could be rearranged or changed to produce an equivalent, but more efficient, representation. Once the internal representation is as efficient as possible, the system can use its knowledge of table size, indexes, order of tuples, and distribution of values to determine exactly how the query will be processed. In doing so, it estimates the "cost" of alternative execution plans and chooses the plan

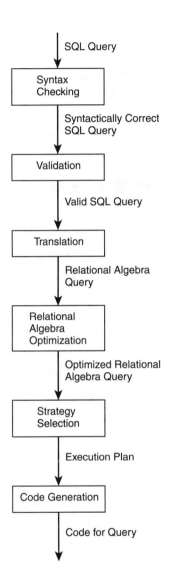

FIGURE 11.1

Interpretation and Optimization Process

with the least estimated cost. To estimate cost, it considers the number and type of disk accesses required, the amount of internal and external memory needed, the processing time required, and communication costs, if any. The execution plan is then coded and executed at the appropriate time. Figure 11.1 summarizes this process for an SQL query. Although optimization of this type is time-consuming, the potential savings in query execution time and reduction in the size of intermediate results can be tremendous, so it is worthwhile to spend the time optimizing before the query is executed. Of course, the optimization itself has a cost associated with it. As we will see in subsequent sections, to make optimization possible the DBMS must maintain metadata about the database, keeping track of the number of records in tables, the number of values for attributes, the size of indexes, and other statistics to use in its estimates. There is the cost of executing the algorithms used for optimization. The trade-off in query efficiency must compensate for these added costs.

11.2   Algebraic Techniques for Query Transformation

The first step in optimization is to choose the relational algebra translation for the high-level query. The relational algebra formulation of a query is of central importance in query processing and optimization, since it specifies the order of operations, and that order can largely determine how efficient the query plan will be. We will use the University database schema to illustrate manipulation of relational algebra queries. We will assume that Student has 10,000 records, Class has 2,500 records, and Enroll has 50,000 records.

```
Student (stuId, lastName, firstName, major, credits)
Class (classNumber, facId, schedule, room)
Faculty (facId, name, department, rank)
Enroll (stuId, classNumber, grade)
```

11.2.1 The Query Tree

A technique that is often used to represent relational algebra expressions is a **query tree** or a **parse tree** as shown in Figure 11.2. Such a tree is a graphical representation of the operations and operands in a relational algebra expression. In constructing a query tree, a leaf node is created for each relation (table) in the expression. For each unary or binary operation on a relation, an upward branch is drawn from the node that represents it. Reading upward from the leaves, as each operation is performed, an internal, nonleaf node is created. In executing a query tree, an internal node can be executed when its operands are available. The node is then replaced by the result of the operation it represents. This process continues until a root node that represents the entire expression is reached. The root node is the last to be executed, and it is replaced by the result of the entire query.

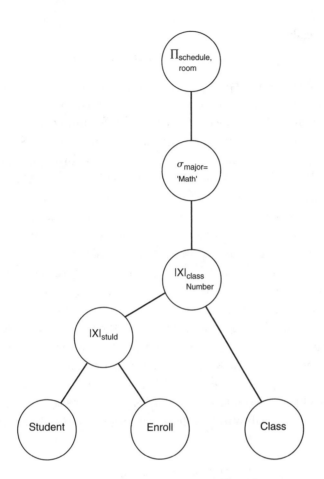

FIGURE 11.2(a)
Initial Query Tree

11.2.2 An SQL Query and Its Relational Algebra Translation

The query "Find the schedules and rooms of all courses taken by any Math major" could be expressed in SQL as:

```
SELECT   schedule, room
FROM     Class, Enroll, Student
WHERE    major = 'Math' AND Class.classNumber = Enroll.classNumber AND
         Enroll.stuId = Student.stuId;
```

One relational algebra translation for this SQL query is,

```
Student JOIN Enroll GIVING Temp1
Temp1 JOIN Class GIVING Temp2
SELECT Temp2 WHERE major = 'Math' GIVING Temp3
PROJECT Temp3 OVER schedule, room
```

or symbolically,

$$\Pi_{schedule,\ room}(\sigma_{major='Math'}\ ((Student\ |\times|\ Enroll)\ |\times|\ Class))$$

The query tree corresponding to this expression is shown in Figure 11.2(a). If we were to execute this relational algebra query as written and as shown in the tree, we would begin by forming the natural join of Student and Enroll over their common column, stuId. Since this is a key for Student as well as an attribute in the key for Enroll, the number of tuples in the join is simply the cardinality of Enroll, since there will be exactly one match in Student for each stuId in Enroll. This operation produces an intermediate table we have called Temp1. Now we join this result with Class, again producing an intermediate table containing one tuple for each tuple in Enroll, since we are joining over classNumber, the key of Class and an attribute in the key for Enroll. The intermediate table consists of 50,000 records and has attributes stuId, lastName, firstName, major, credits, classNumber, grade, facId, schedule, and room. We then perform a selection on the intermediate table, choosing only those rows where the value of major is 'Math'. Finally, we project over two columns, schedule and room, eliminating duplicates, if any. The execution just described would involve producing two intermediate tables with 50,000 fairly long records. Of these, only a small number, those with major = 'Math', are chosen in the SELECT operation.

11.2.3 Performing SELECT Operations Early

We could easily reduce the size of the intermediate tables by doing the SELECT operation earlier and then considering only those students whose major is mathematics. We could rewrite the query as,

```
SELECT Student WHERE major = 'Math' GIVING T1
T1 JOIN Enroll GIVING T2
T2 JOIN Class GIVING T3
PROJECT T3 OVER schedule, room
```

or symbolically,

$$\Pi_{schedule,room}\ (((\sigma_{major\ =\ 'Math'}\ (Student))\ |\times|\ Enroll)\ |\times|\ Class)$$

By reordering the operations in this way, we reduce the size of the intermediate tables. If we assume there are about 400 mathematics majors, each

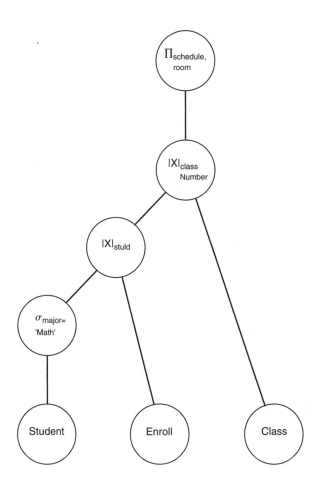

FIGURE 11.2(b)

Revised Query Tree

taking about five courses, we would expect only about 2000 records to result from each join, a significant reduction from the 50,000 expected earlier. This example illustrates the savings possible by performing SELECT operations early. Figure 11.2(b) shows the query tree for the revised expression. Note that we have pushed the SELECT down close to a leaf of the tree.

11.2.4 Evaluating Conjunctive Conditions

If the query involves additional selection criteria, such as finding the schedules and rooms of courses taken by those mathematics majors who have more than 100 credits, we would want to apply the criteria as early as possible, as well. In this case we would have a **conjunctive** condition, so called because it involves a conjunction, an "and" of conditions. The SQL query is:

```
SELECT schedule, room
FROM Student, Class, Enroll
WHERE major='Math' AND credits >100 AND Class.classNumber = Enroll.classNumber
AND Enroll.stuId = Student.stuId;
```

For the relational algebra expression, we could apply both selection criteria directly to the Student relation before doing the first join,

```
SELECT Student WHERE major = 'Math' AND credits > 100 GIVING T1
T1 JOIN Enroll GIVING T2
T2 JOIN Class GIVING T3
PROJECT T3 OVER schedule, room
```

or symbolically,

$$\Pi_{schedule,room}(((\sigma_{major='Math' \& credits>100}(Student)) \bowtie Enroll) \bowtie Class)$$

This reduces the size of the join still further. The query tree is essentially the one shown in Figure 11.2(b), modified by adding the condition on credits to the predicate for the selection.

Even if the second selection criterion in a conjunctive selection refers to another table, it is best to do it early. For example, if we had been asked to find the schedules and rooms for all mathematics majors who have received a grade of F, we would be unable to apply the conjunction condition,

```
major = 'Math' AND grade = 'F'
```

to the Student table, since the grade appears on the Enroll table. We could form the join first and then apply the conjunctive condition and evaluate the rest of the query,

```
Student JOIN Enroll GIVING T1
SELECT T1 WHERE major = 'Math' AND grade ='F' GIVING T2
T2 JOIN Class GIVING T3
PROJECT T3 OVER schedule, room
```

which is:

$$\Pi_{schedule,room} ((\sigma_{major='Math' \& grade='F'}(Student \bowtie Enroll)) \bowtie Class)$$

Figure 11.3(a) shows the query tree for this expression. Unfortunately, this brings us back to an intermediate table size of 50,000 records.

However, if we apply both selections to their corresponding tables before the join, we reduce the size of the intermediate tables,

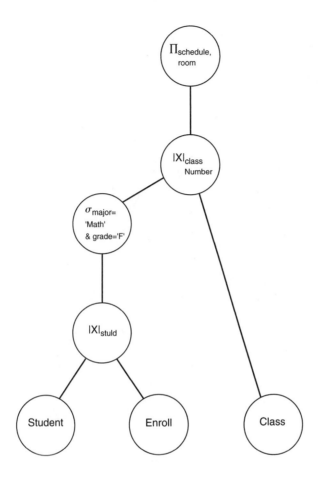

FIGURE 11.3(a)
Initial Query Tree Using Conjunction

```
SELECT Student WHERE major = 'Math' GIVING T1
SELECT Enroll WHERE grade = 'F' GIVING T2
T1 JOIN T2 GIVING T3
T3 JOIN Class GIVING T4
PROJECT T4 OVER schedule, room
```

or symbolically,

$$\Pi_{schedule,room}\ (((\sigma_{major='Math'}(Student))\ |\times|\ (\sigma_{grade='F'}(Enroll)))\ |\times|\ Class)$$

Figure 11.3(b) gives the query tree for this version. It is much more efficient than the earlier version, since it reduces the chosen tuples of both the Student table and the Enroll table before doing the join, keeping joined tuples to a minimum. Note that when the grade condition is applied to the Enroll table, all Enroll records having a grade of F will be returned, not just the ones belonging to mathematics majors. The natural join of these

FIGURE 11.3(b)
Final Query Tree Using Conjunction

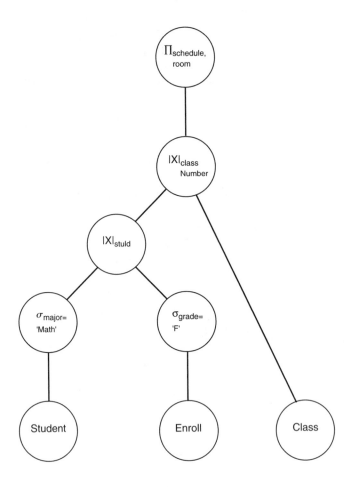

selected Enroll tuples with the selected Student tuples eliminates the Enroll tuples for other majors.

11.2.5 Performing PROJECT Early

We noted earlier that intermediate tables resulting from two joins consisted of very long records. Regardless of when the selections or joins were performed, the intermediate table always had all of the attributes from the original tables. We could use projection to reduce the size of the tuples in the intermediate tables. In doing so, we must be careful not to drop any attributes that will be needed later. Taking as our query, "Find the schedule and room of all courses taken by mathematics majors who have an F in any course," we could add projections to reduce the size of intermediate tables,

```
SELECT Student WHERE major = 'Math' GIVING T1
PROJECT T1 OVER stuId GIVING T2
SELECT Enroll WHERE grade = 'F' GIVING T3
T2 JOIN T3 GIVING T4
PROJECT T4 OVER classNumber GIVING T5
T5 JOIN Class GIVING T6
PROJECT T6 OVER schedule, room
```

or symbolically,

$$\Pi_{\text{schedule,room}}((\Pi_{\text{classNumber}}((\Pi_{\text{stuId}}(\sigma_{\text{major='Math'}} (\text{Student}))) |\times| (\sigma_{\text{grade='F'}} (\text{Enroll})))) |\times| \text{Class})$$

The query tree for this expression is shown in Figure 11.4. Whether it is worthwhile performing all the projections depends on the amount of space saved and the costs involved in processing a projection. In any case, if we decide to do projections, we should do them early, before joins, when possible.

11.2.6 Equivalence of Algebraic Operations

Our examples showed some of the ways that relational algebra expressions can be transformed into equivalent ones that are more efficient. We consider two relations to be equivalent if they have the same attributes, even though the attribute order may be different, and if the values associated with those attributes are identical for corresponding tuples of the two relations. The following list presents some laws governing operations in relational algebra, where R, S, and T represent relations or expressions involving relations. It is possible to prove all of the rules listed here, although we will not present the proofs.

1. *Joins and products are commutative.* The commutative law holds for all types of joins and products. Recall that in Chapter 4 we used theta, θ, to stand for any condition for a theta join. Then we have,

   $R \times S = S \times R$ and
   $R \times_\theta S = S \times_\theta R$ and
   $R |\times| S = S |\times| R$

FIGURE 11.4
**Query Tree Showing
Projection**

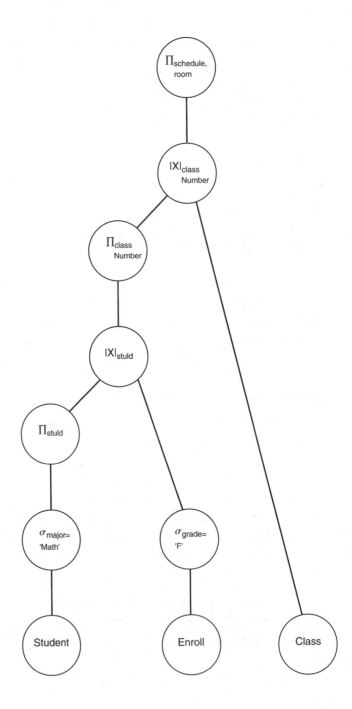

2. *Joins and products are associative.* Natural joins, theta-joins, and products are all associative.

   $(R \times S) \times T = R \times (S \times T)$
   $(R \times_\theta S) \times_\theta T = R \times_\theta (S \times_\theta T)$
   $(R \bowtie S) \bowtie T = R \bowtie (S \bowtie T)$

3. *Select is commutative.* If p and q are selection conditions, then

   $\sigma_p (\sigma_q (R)) = \sigma_q (\sigma_p (R))$

4. *Conjunctive selects can cascade into individual selects.* If we have a series of select conditions connected by "and," we can break up the conjunction into a sequence of individual selects.

   $\sigma_{p \& q \& \ldots \& z} (R) = (\sigma_p (\sigma_q(\ldots(\sigma_z (R))\ldots)))$

   Obviously, we can use the equivalence in the other direction to combine cascading selects into a conjunctive select, when convenient.

5. *Successive projects can be reduced to the final project.* If $list_1$, $list_2$, . . . $list_n$ are lists of attribute names such that each of the $list_i$ contains $list_{i-1}$, then,

   $\Pi_{list1} (\Pi_{list2} (\ldots \Pi_{listn} (R)\ldots) =_{list1}(R)$

   This means that only the last project has to be executed.

6. *Select and project sometimes commute.* If the selection condition involves only the attributes in the projection list, `projlist`, then select and project commute:

   $\Pi_{projlist} (\sigma_p (R)) = \sigma_p (\Pi_{projlist} (R))$

7. *Select and join (or product) sometimes commute.* If the selection condition involves only attributes of one of the tables being joined, then select and join (or select and product) commute. If we assume the predicate p involves only attributes of R, then the following holds:

   $\sigma_p (R \bowtie S) = (\sigma_p (R)) \bowtie S$

   This rule also applies to theta-join and product.

8. *Select sometimes distributes over join (or product).* If the selection condition is a conjunctive condition having the form p AND q,

where p involves only the attributes of relation R and q involves only the attributes of relation S, then the select distributes over the join:

$$\sigma_{p \& q} \ (R \ |\times| \ S) = (\sigma_p \ (R)) \ |\times| \ (\sigma_q \ (S))$$

Again, the rule applies to theta-join and product.

9. *Project sometimes distributes over join (or product).* If the projection list, `projlist`, can be split into separate lists, list1 and list2, so that list1 contains only attributes of R and list2 contains only attributes of S, then:

$$\Pi_{projlist} \ (R \ |\times| \ S) = (\Pi_{ist1} \ (R)) \ |\times| \ (\Pi_{ist2} \ (S))$$

For a theta-join, the distributive law holds if the join condition involves only attributes of `projlist`. If it involves additional attributes, they must first be added to the projection list on the left of the equivalence sign. Then they are placed with either list1 or list2 on the right, depending on which relation or relational expression they are associated with. After the join is performed, a final projection onto the original projection list must be done.

10. *Set operations of union and intersection are commutative.*

$$R \cup S = S \cup R$$
$$R \cap S = S \cap R$$

However, set difference is not commutative.

11. *Set operations of union and intersection are individually associative.*

$$(R \cup S) \cup T = R \cup (S \cup T)$$
$$(R \cap S) \cap T = R \cap (S \cap T)$$

Although union and intersection are associative when used individually, they cannot be mixed in an expression. Set difference is not associative.

12. *Select distributes over set union, set intersection, and set difference.*

$$\sigma_p \ (R \cup S) = \sigma_p \ (R) \cup \sigma_p \ (S)$$
$$\sigma_p \ (R \cap S) = \sigma_p \ (R) \cap \sigma_p \ (S)$$
$$\sigma_p \ (R - S) = \sigma_p \ (R) - \sigma_p \ (S)$$

13. *Project distributes over set union, set intersection, and set difference.*

$$\Pi_{projlist} \ (R \cup S) = (\Pi_{projlist} \ (R)) \cup (\Pi_{projlist} \ (S))$$
$$\Pi_{projlist} \ (R \cap S) = (\Pi_{projlist} \ (R)) \cap (\Pi_{projlist} \ (S))$$
$$\Pi_{projlist} \ (R - S) = (\Pi_{projlist} \ (R)) - (\Pi_{projlist} \ (S))$$

14. *Project is idempotent, meaning repeating it produces the same result.*

$$\Pi_{projlist} (\Pi_{projlist} (R)) = \Pi_{projlist} (R)$$

15. *Select is idempotent.*

$$\sigma_p(\sigma_p (R)) = \sigma_p (R)$$

This list of transformations is not exhaustive, but it is sufficient to illustrate possible substitutions that the query optimizer could consider for given algebraic expressions.

11.2.7 Heuristics for Query Optimization

Heuristics are "rules of thumb" that can be used to help solve problems. They are not always guaranteed to work in a particular situation, but they are techniques that we can try out to see if they produce a good result. We now examine some heuristics that have been developed for optimizing relational algebra expressions. A cardinal rule is to try to reduce the size of intermediate results by doing selects and projects as early as possible, and to execute first those selects and projects that reduce the table sizes as much as possible. The heuristics are:

1. Do selection as early as possible. If appropriate, use cascading of selects, commutativity of selects with projects, joins, and products, and distributivity of select over set union, set intersection, and set difference to move the selection as far down the query tree as possible.

2. Use associativity of join, product, union, and intersection to rearrange relations in the query tree so that the selection operation that will produce the smallest table will be executed first.

3. If a product appears as an argument for a selection, where the selection involves attributes of the tables in the product, transform the product into a join. If the selection involves attributes of only one of the tables in the product, apply the selection to that table first.

4. Do projection early. If appropriate, use cascading of projects, distributivity of projection over product and set union, intersection, and difference, and commutativity of selection and projection to

move the projection as far down the query tree as possible. Examine all projections to see if some are unnecessary.

5.   If there is a sequence of selections and/or projections with the same argument, use commutativity or cascading to combine them into one selection, one projection, or a selection followed by a projection.

6.   If a subexpression appears more than once in the query tree, and the result it produces is not too large, compute it once and save it. This technique is especially useful when querying on views, since the same subexpression must be used to construct the view each time.

These heuristics can be incorporated into an algorithm that a query optimizer could use to produce the optimized relational algebra query, as shown for the University example queries in Figures 11.2(b), 11.3(b), and 11.4. In fact, we used these rules to optimize the queries for those examples.

11.3   Processing Techniques and Cost Estimation

The next step in optimization is for the strategy selector to choose an execution plan.

To develop an execution plan, the strategy selector must consider the various ways each of the operations in the query tree could be executed. It "prices" each method by considering the costs of the processes involved.

11.3.1 Cost Factors

The cost of executing a query is determined by the cost of reading files, the processing costs once data is in main memory, the cost of writing and storing any intermediate results, the communication costs, and the cost of writing the final results to storage. Of these, the most significant factor is the number of disk accesses, the read and write costs. In calculating these costs, the system must use statistics stored in the system catalog and knowledge about the size, distribution of values, structure, and access methods of each file.

A table can be stored in **packed form**, in which blocks or pages contain only tuples from that table, or in **unpacked form**, in which tuples from the table are interspersed with tuples from other tables. If the storage form is unpacked, it is difficult to calculate the number of blocks needed. In the worst case, we would have to assume every tuple of the relation is in a different block. If the storage form is packed, we could estimate the number of blocks needed to hold the table if we knew the tuple size, number of tuples, and capacity of the blocks. We will ordinarily assume all tables are in packed form.

The access cost for a table is the number of blocks that must be brought into main memory for reading or that must be written out to secondary storage for writing. The values associated with access cost are:

- $t(R)$, the number of tuples in the relation R

- $b(R)$, the number of blocks needed to store the relation R

- $bf(R)$, the number of tuples of R per block, also called the **blocking factor** of R

If R is packed, then:

- $b(R) = t(R)/bf(R)$

For the University example, if the `Student` relation is stored in packed form in blocks of 4K bytes, and each record is 200 bytes long, then 20 records fit per block (4096/200), ignoring any overhead for block headers and so on, giving a blocking factor of 20. Note that records are not split across blocks, so we ignore any fractional space that is not large enough for an entire record. Since there are 10,000 Student records, we need 10000/20 or 500 blocks to hold this file in packed form.

The tuples in the blocks containing table R can be arranged in some order, often by increasing value of a primary key, but sometimes by the value of a secondary key. Alternatively, they can be in random order (as in a heap), or hashed on the value of a primary key. The access method used determines the storage structure. The file can be accessed by an index on the primary key, secondary indexes on non-primary key attributes, or a hashing function. For each table, we can have one **clustered index**, which means that tuples are in physical order by the value of the indexed field, with tuples having the same value of the index appearing in the same block. Other indexes will then be **nonclustered**. An index can be **dense**, having an entry for each tuple of the relation, or **nondense**. The index normally is a multilevel structure such as a **B+ tree** or a similar organization. The purpose of the index is to speed access to the data file, but we must first access the index itself, so the additional overhead of accessing the index must be considered in the access cost. However, it is usually slight compared to the cost of accessing the data records by other methods. When using indexes, we will use the following notation:

- $l(index$-$name)$, the number of levels in a multi-level index or the average number of index accesses needed to find an entry.

An index tells us which records of the file have a particular value for an attribute. For cost estimation, we often need an estimate of the number of such records. The data dictionary can store this statistic:

- $n(A,R)$, the number of distinct values of attribute A in relation R.

From this statistic, we can approximate the number of tuples that have a particular value for A. If we assume that the values of A are **uniformly distributed** in R, then the number of tuples expected to have a particular value, c, for A, which we will call the **selection size** or $s(A = c,R)$, is:

- $s(A=c,R) = t(R)/n(A,R)$

If the attribute, A, is a candidate key, then each tuple will have a unique value for that attribute, so $n(A,R) = t(R)$ and the selection size is 1.

To illustrate the use of the formula, suppose we try to estimate the number of students in the university with a major of Mathematics. We know there are 10,000 students, so $t(\texttt{Student}) = 10000$. Let us assume there are 25 possible major subjects, so $n(\texttt{major, Student}) = 25$. Then we can estimate the number of mathematics majors as:

```
s(major='Math',Student) = t(Student)/n(major,Student) = 10000/25 = 400
```

Notice that we assumed that majors are uniformly distributed, that the number of students choosing each major is about equal. Some systems, including Oracle, store more information about the distribution of values, maintaining **histograms**, which are graphs that display the frequencies of different values of attributes. The histogram would be used to give a more accurate estimate of the selection size for a particular value. Many systems also store the minimum and maximum values for each attribute. In our examples, we will continue to assume uniform distribution.

11.3.2 Cost of Processing Selects

We use these cost factors to estimate the reading cost of various techniques for performing a selection of the form $\sigma_{A=c}(R)$. Our choice of method depends to a great extent on what access paths exist—whether the file is hashed on the selection attribute(s), whether the file has an index on the attribute(s), and if so, whether the index is clustered, or whether the file is in order by the selection attribute(s).

1. *Using a full table scan.* We begin with the "worst case" method, also called a **full table scan**. This is the method used when there is no access path for the attribute, such as an index, hash key, or ordering on the attribute, and the attribute is not a candidate key. Since this is the default method, we will always compare the cost of other methods with this one, and choose the one with lower cost. The cost is the number of blocks in the table, since we have to examine every tuple in the table to see if it qualifies for the selection, that is:

    - $b(R)$

    For example, if we want to find all students who have a first name of "Tom," we need to access each block of Student. We previously calculated the number of blocks of Student to be 10000/20 or 500, so:

    Reading Cost $(\sigma_{firstName='Tom'}(\text{Student})) = b(\text{Student}) = 500$

2. *Using a hash key to retrieve a single record.* If A is a hash key having unique values, then we apply the hashing algorithm to calculate the target address for the record. If there is no overflow, the expected number of accesses is 1. If there is overflow, we need an estimate of the average number of accesses required to reach a record, depending on the amount of overflow and the overflow handling method used. This statistic, which we call h, can be available to the optimizer. The cost is:

    - h

    For example, if we are told that the Faculty file is hashed on facId and $h = 2$, then:

    Reading Cost $(\sigma_{facId='F101'}(\text{Faculty})) = 2$

3. *Selection for equality on a key using an index.* When we have an index on a key field, we retrieve whatever index blocks are needed and then go directly to the record from the index. The system may store the number of levels in indexes. Therefore, using l to represent the number of index levels, the cost is:

   - l(index-name) + 1

   since we must read all the levels of the index and then perform another access to read the record itself.

   Consider the simple selection $\sigma_{\text{stuId} = \text{'S1001'}}$ (Student). Since stuId is the primary key, if we have an index on stuId, called Student_stuId_ix, having 3 levels, we have:

   Reading Cost ($\sigma_{\text{stuId='S1001'}}$(Student)) = 1(Student_stuId_ix) + 1 = 3+1 = 4

4. *Selection for equality on a non-clustered index on an attribute.* For the predicate A = c with non-clustered index on attribute A, the number of tuples that satisfy the condition is the selection size of the indexed attribute, $s(A=c,R)$, and we must assume the tuples are on different blocks, which we have to access individually. We will assume that all the tuples having value A=c are pointed to by the index, perhaps using a linked list or an array of pointers. The cost is the number of index accesses plus the number of blocks for the tuples that satisfy the condition, or:

   - l(index-name) + s(A=c,R)

   For example, suppose we have a non-clustered index on major in Student and we wish to do the selection $\sigma_{\text{major='CSC'}}$ (Student). We would find records having a major value of 'CSC' by reading the index node for 'CSC' and going from there to each tuple it points to. If the index has 2 levels, the cost will be:

   Reading Cost($\sigma_{\text{major='CSC'}}$ (Student)) = 1(Student_major_ix) + s(major='CSC', Student)= 2 + (10000/25) = 2+400 = 402

   We note that this is only slightly less than the worst case cost, which is 500.

5. *Selection for equality using a clustered index on an attribute.* If our selection involves an attribute, A, and we have a clustered index on A, we use the selection size for the indexed attribute divided by the blocking factor to estimate the number of blocks we have to

retrieve. Note that we assume the tuples of R having value A = c reside on contiguous blocks, so this calculation estimates the number of blocks needed to store these tuples. We add that to the number of index blocks needed. Then the cost is:

- l(index-name) + $(s(A=c,R))/bf(R)$

For example, if the index on major in the `Student` file were a clustered index, then to select students with a major of CSC, we would assume that the 400 records expected to have this value for major would be stored on contiguous blocks and the index would point to the first block. Then we could simply retrieve the following blocks to find all 400 records. The cost is:

Reading Cost($\sigma_{major='CSC'}$ (Student)) = 1(Student_major_ix) + s(major='CSC', Student)/bf(Student) =2+(400/20) = 22

6. *Selection on an ordered file.* If the predicate has the form A = c, where A is a key with unique values and records are arranged in order by A, a binary search can be used to access the record with A value of c. Using the cost of the binary search, the cost of this method under these conditions is approximately:

- $\log_2 b(R)$

For example, suppose we want to find a class record for a given `classNumber`, and we are told the `Class` file is in order by `classNumber`. We first calculate the number of blocks in the table. If there are 2500 `Class` records, each 100 bytes long, stored in blocks of size 4K, the blocking factor is 4096/100, or 40, so the number of blocks is 2500/40 or 63. (Note that we round up if part of a block is needed.) Then using the formula, we get the cost estimate:

$\sigma_{classNumber='Eng201A'}$ (Class) $= \log_2(63) \approx 6$

If A is not a key attribute, there can be several records with A value of c, and the estimate must be adjusted to consider the selection size, $s(A=c,R)$ divided by the number of records per block. In that case, we get an estimate of:

- $\log_2 b(R) + s(A=c,R)/bf(R)$

7. *Conjunctive selection with a composite index.* If the predicate is a conjunction and a composite index exists for the attributes in the

predicate, this case reduces to one of the previous cases, depending on whether the attributes represent a composite key, and whether the index is clustered or a B+ tree.

8. *Conjunctive selection without a composite index.* If one of the conditions involves an attribute that is used for ordering records in the file, or has an index or a hash key, then we use the appropriate method from those previously described to retrieve records that satisfy that part of the predicate, using the cost estimates given previously. Once we retrieve the records, we check to see if they satisfy the rest of the conditions. If no attribute can be used for efficient retrieval, we use the full table scan and check all the conditions simultaneously for each tuple.

11.3.3 Processing Joins

The join is generally the most expensive operation to perform in a relational system, and since it is often used in queries, it is important to be able to estimate its cost. The access cost depends on the method of processing as well as the size of the results. Unlike selection, where the result is likely to be a small number of records, a join can produce a large number of records, so we need to add the cost of writing the results to the access cost when doing a join.

Estimating the Size of the Result

An important cost factor to consider in processing joins is the size of the result. If R and S are relations of size $t(R)$ and $t(S)$ respectively, then to calculate the size of their join, we need to estimate the number of tuples of R that will match tuples of S on the corresponding attributes. Two special cases exist.

- If the tables have no common attributes, then the join becomes a product, and the number of tuples in the result is $t(R) * t(S)$. For example, if we join Class and Student, which have no common attributes, there are 10,000*2500 tuples in the result.

- If the set of common attributes is a key for one of the relations and a foreign key in the second, the number of tuples in the join can be no larger than the number of tuples in the second relation, since each of these can match no more than one of the key values in the first relation. For R |×| S, if the common attributes are a key for R, then the size of the join is **less than or equal to t(S)**. For example, if we form the natural join of `Student` and `Enroll`, since `stuId` is the primary key of `Student`, the number of tuples in the result will be the same as the number of tuples in `Enroll`, or 50,000, since each `Enroll` tuple has exactly one matching `Student` tuple. Joining on a foreign key is the most common type of natural join.

The difficult case is the general one in which the common attributes do not form a key of either relation. We must estimate the number of matches. Let us assume that there is one common attribute, A, and that its values are uniformly distributed in both relations. For a particular value, c, of A in R, we would expect the number of tuples in S having a matching value of c for A to be the selection size of A in S, or $s(A=c,S)$. We saw earlier that an estimate of the selection size is the number of tuples in S divided by the number of different values for A in S, or $t(S)/n(A,S)$. This gives us the number of matches in S for a particular tuple in R. However, since there are $t(R)$ tuples in R, each of which may have this number of matches, the total expected number of matches in the join is given by:

- $t(R \mathbin{|\times|} S) = t(R)^* t(S) / n(A,S)$

If we had started by considering tuples in S and looked for matches in R, we would have derived a slightly different formula.

- $t(R \mathbin{|\times|} S) = t(S)^* t(R) / n(A,R)$

Normally, we use the formula that gives the smaller result.

The number of blocks needed to write the result of a join depends on the blocking factor. If we know the number of bytes in each of R and S, we can estimate the number of bytes in the joined tuples to be roughly their sum, and divide the block size by that number to get the blocking factor of the result. Then we can find the number of blocks by dividing the expected number of tuples by the blocking factor.

Methods of Performing Joins

Now we consider the read costs of different methods of performing a join. The choice of method depends on the size of the files, whether the files are sorted on the join attribute(s), whether indexes or hash keys exist for the join attribute(s).

1. *Nested Loops.* This is the default method, which must be used when no special access paths exist. If we assume both R and S are packed relations, having $b(R)$ and $b(S)$ blocks respectively, and we have two buffers for reading, plus one for writing the result, we can bring the first block of R into the first buffer, and then bring each block of S, in turn, into the second buffer. We compare each tuple of the R block with each tuple of the S block before switching in the next S block. When we have finished all the S blocks, we bring in the next R block into the first buffer, and go through all the S blocks again. We repeat this process until all of R has been compared with all of S. Figure 11.5 illustrates the process. The algorithm is:

```
for each block of R
    for each block of S
        for each tuple in the R block
            for each tuple in the S block
                if the tuples satisfy the condition then add to join
            end
        end
    end
end
```

The number of accesses to read the data for this method is given by,

- Read cost $(R \mid \times \mid S) = b(R) + (b(R)*b(S))$

since each block of R has to be read, and each block of S has to be read once for each block of R. For the example shown in Figure 11.5, there are 4 blocks of R and 3 blocks of S, giving us $4+4*3 = 16$ blocks read. They are read in the order shown below the figure.

We could use the nested loop method to compute the reading cost for performing the join Student $\mid \times \mid$ Enroll, assuming both are packed. Let us assume that Student has 10,000 tuples, occupying 500 blocks, as calculated previously, and Enroll has 50,000 tuples, each 100 bytes. Assuming blocks are 4K as before, the

FIGURE 11.5

**Nested Loop Join with
Two Buffers for Reading**

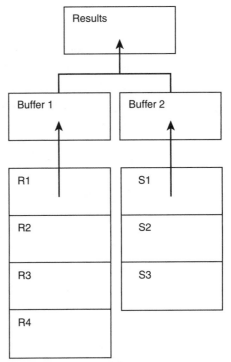

Blocks read in order R1,S1,S2,S3
R2,S1,S2,S3
R3,S1,S2,S3
R4,S1,S2,S3

blocking factor for `Enroll` is 4096/100, or 40, so the file occupies 50000/40 or 1250 blocks. Using `Student` for the outside loop, our reading cost for this example is:

$b(\texttt{Student}) + (b(\texttt{Student}) * b(\texttt{Enroll})) = 500 + (500*1250) = 625,500$

It is important to note that the size of the file chosen for the outer loop has a significant effect on the reading cost, since the number of blocks in the outer loop file must be added to the product of the sizes of the two files. Therefore, we should pick the smaller file for the outside loop. If we had chosen to use `Enroll` for the outer loop, our result would have been 626,250.

If the buffer can hold more than three blocks, the best strategy is to read into the buffer as many blocks as possible from the file in the outer loop, and save buffer space for only one block from the file in the inner loop, plus the space for writing the result. For example, if $b(B)$ is the number of blocks the buffer can hold, then, using R as the file for the outer loop and S as the file for the inner loop, we should read $b(B)$–2 blocks of R into the buffer at a time, and only 1 block of S, saving one buffer block for the result. The total number of blocks of R accessed is still $b(R)$, but the total number of S blocks that need to be accessed is reduced to approximately $b(S)*(b(R)/(b((B) - 2))$. The cost of accessing the files then becomes:

- $b(R) + ((b(S)*(b(R))/(b((B) - 2))$

However, if there is enough space in the buffer to allow one of the relations to fit with room for one more block from the other file, plus the block for storing the results, then we should choose that one for the inner loop. For example, suppose S fits in main memory. Then S has to be read only once, and we should store it in the buffer while switching in blocks of R one at a time. The cost of reading the two packed files then reduces to the most efficient possible cost, which is:

- $b(R) + b(S)$

2. *Sort-Merge Join.* A very efficient join strategy is achieved when both files are sorted on the attribute(s) to be joined. In this case, the join algorithm is a variation on the algorithm for merging two sorted files. When the files are sorted, we would expect that all tuples having a specific value, say c, for the join attribute, A, would be on a single block in each relation. We begin the join by bringing the first block of each relation into the buffer and finding all the records in R with the first value for A, and then all the records in S with that same value. These are then joined and written to the result file. Then we move on to the next value in each of the files, and so forth. Each block of each file will be read only once, unless there are some records with the same A value in different blocks, which is relatively rare. Therefore the cost for accessing the two files is just:

- $b(R) + b(S)$

Because this join is so efficient, it might be worthwhile to sort the files before a join. In that case, the cost of sorting, which depends on the sorting method used, would have to be added to the cost of accessing the files.

3. *Using an Index or Hash Key.* If one of the files, S, has an index on the common attribute A, or if A is a hash key for S, then each tuple of R would be retrieved in the usual way by reading in the R blocks, and the index or hashing algorithm would be used to find all the matching records of S. The cost of this method depends on the type of index. For example, if A is the primary key of S, we have a primary index on S and the access cost is the cost of accessing all the blocks of R plus the cost of reading the index and accessing one record of S for each of the tuples in R:

- $b(R) + (t(R) * (l(\text{indexname}) + 1))$

We could use this to find Student $|\times|$ Enroll if we assume that Student has an index on its primary key stuId. We access each Enroll block in sequence and then, for each Enroll tuple in each block, we use the index on stuId to find each matching Student record. If the index has 2 levels, the read cost is,

$b(\text{Enroll}) + (t(\text{Enroll}) * (2+1)) = 1250 + (50000*3) = 151{,}250$

which is about four times as efficient as the nested loop method we priced earlier.

If the index is on an attribute that is not a primary key, we have to consider the number of matches in S per tuple of R, which increases the read cost to:

- $b(R) + (t(R) * (l(\text{indexname}) + s(A=c,S)))$

However, if the index is a clustered index, we can reduce the estimate by dividing by the blocking factor, since several S records on each block will have the same value for A.

- $b(R) + (t(R) * (l(\text{indexname}) + s(A=c,S)/bf(S))$

If we have a hash function in S instead of an index, then the cost is,

- $b(R) + (t(R) * h)$

where h is the average number of accesses to get to a block from its key in S.

11.3.4 Processing Other Operations

Projection

A projection operation involves finding the values of the attributes on the projection list for each tuple of the relation, and eliminating duplicates, if any exist. If a projection has a projection list containing a key of the relation, then the projection can be performed by reading each tuple of the relation and copying to the results file only the values of the attributes in the projection list. There will be no duplicates, because of the presence of the key. The read cost is the number of blocks in the relation, which is,

- $b(R)$

and the number of tuples in the result will be the number of tuples in the relation, $t(R)$. However, depending on the size of the projection list, the resulting tuples might be considerably smaller than the tuples of R, so the number of blocks needed to write the result might be much smaller than the blocks needed for R.

If the projection list consists of non-key attributes only, then we must eliminate duplicates. One method is sorting the results so that duplicates will appear next to one another, and then eliminating any tuple that is a duplicate of the previous one until no duplicates remain. To calculate the cost, we find the sum of the cost of accessing all the blocks of the relation to create a temporary file with only attributes on the projection list, plus the cost of writing the temporary file, the cost of sorting the temporary file, the cost of accessing the sorted temporary file from secondary storage to eliminate duplicates, and the cost of writing the final results file. The sorting operation is the most expensive of these steps. In general, external sorting is required in a database environment, since files are too large to fit in main memory. A simple two-way merge sort can be used if there are three buffers available. This sort is illustrated in Figure 11.6. The process involves creating sorted subfiles called **runs** at each step. The runs are then merged at the next step. In the first step shown on the left in Figure 11.6(b), each page of the input file is read in and sorted internally using a standard in-memory sort algorithm such as Quicksort. The second step is performed

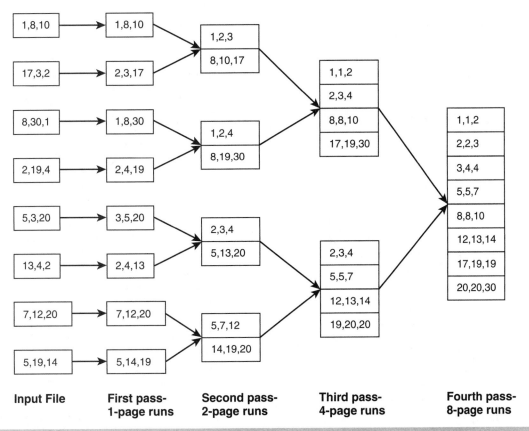

FIGURE 11.6(a)

External Two-Way Merge Sort

by reading in pairs of runs from the previous results, merging them to produce runs of length two pages each. Two pages are read at a time, each in its own buffer. The first value in the first buffer is compared with the first value in the second buffer, and the smaller of the two is written to the output buffer and eliminated from the values to be compared. The larger of the two is then compared with the next value in the buffer from which the first was eliminated. The process continues until all values from both pages have been written to two output pages. Then the next two pages are compared, and so on until all pages have been read. In the third step, the previous runs of length two pages are compared, creating runs of four pages. In the fourth step, a single sorted run is created. The number of

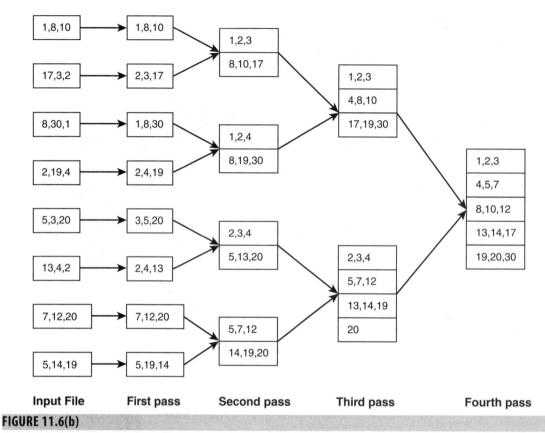

| Input File | First pass | Second pass | Third pass | Fourth pass |

FIGURE 11.6(b)
Revised External Two-Way Merge Sort

disk accesses for this example is 64, because in each step, each of the eight pages must be read and written, resulting in 16 input/output operations for each step. For the four steps, 64 operations are needed. In general, if there are n pages in the file, the number of passes needed will be $(\log_2 n)+1$, and the number of disk accesses required just for the sorting phase will be:

- $2n((\log_2 n)+1)$

In our example, we had eight pages, and we needed $(\log_2 8)+1$, which is 3+1, or 4 passes. We needed $2*8((\log_2 8)+1))$, which is 16(4) or 64 disk accesses. The cost can be reduced if more than three buffers are used. The initial cost of reading the entire input file to choose only attributes on the projection list can be eliminated if the first sorting pass is

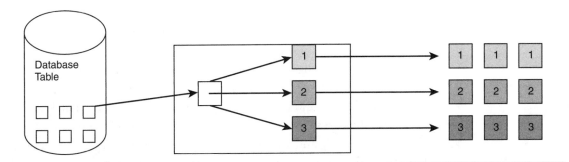

FIGURE 11.7

Projection Using Hashing

used to drop unwanted attributes, as well as to sort. We can also eliminate duplicates at each merge step, resulting in the improvement
shown in Figure 11.6(b) for our example, which requires only 58 disk
accesses.

Another method can be used if there are several buffers available. It uses
hashing, which requires two phases, a partitioning phase and a duplicate
elimination phase. In the partitioning phase, one buffer page is used for
reading the table, one page at a time. The remaining buffers form the output pages for the hash partitions. Figure 11.7 shows the partitioning
phase. Each tuple in the input page is reduced to its projection list attributes, and then a hashing function is used on the combination of these
attributes. The value of the output determines which buffer page the
reduced tuple will be placed in, and which partition it will end up in. Since
two tuples with the same value on the projection list attributes would hash
to the same partition, any duplicates will be placed in the same partition.
Therefore, duplicate elimination is performed for each partition. This
phase can be accomplished by using a new hashing function on the pages
of the partition. Each page of the partition is read in, one at a time, and an
in-memory hash table is created. If two tuples hash to the same value, they
are compared, and any duplicate is eliminated. When the entire partition
has been read, the hash table is written to disk, the buffers are cleared, and
the next partition is processed.

Set Operations

The set operations of union, intersection, and difference can be done only
on files that are union-compatible, having identical structures. If we sort

both files on the same attributes, we can then modify the sort-merge algorithm to do union, placing in the results file any tuple that appears in either of the original files, but dropping duplicates. To do intersection, we use the same basic algorithm, but place in the results file only the tuples that appear in both of the original files. For set difference, R − S, we examine each tuple of R and place it in the results file if it has no match in S. In each case, the cost is the sum of the cost of accessing all the blocks of both files, sorting both and writing the temporary sorted files, accessing the temporary files to do the merge, and writing the final file.

11.4   Pipelining

In our discussion so far we have assumed that a query involving several relational algebra operations is executed by performing each operation on the relation or relations involved, constructing a temporary results table, and using that table as input for the next operation. This process, known as **materialization**, can be quite expensive, since we have to consider not just the sum of all the costs of the operations, but the cost of writing the intermediate tables. An alternative to materialization is **pipelining**, in which tuples "pass through" from one operation to the next in the pipeline, without creation of a temporary file. For example, if we were to perform the relational algebra operations of join followed by project, as in,

$$\Pi_{firstName, lastName} (Student \; |\times| \; Enroll)$$

using pipelining, we would perform the join as one process, and place the joined tuples in a buffer, from which they would be taken as input to the project process, without writing the join out to disk. Although pipelining can be more efficient than materialization, it cannot be used in algorithms that require that the entire relation be available as input, such as the sort-merge join.

11.5   Query Optimization in Oracle

Earlier versions of Oracle provide two types of optimization for relational databases—**cost-based**, which is the default, and **rule-based**. Its rule-based optimizer provides efficiency rankings for different types of access paths. The predicate in each SQL statement is examined to determine which of the access paths apply to the query, and the system chooses the path with the best score from among those available. For example, the highest ranking (1) is given to using the primary key to retrieve a single tuple of a table, a middle rank (7) to an indexed cluster key, and the lowest ranking (15) a full table scan. If the query is,

```
SELECT stuId, firstName, lastName
FROM Student
WHERE major = 'CSC';
```

the optimizer cannot use the primary key rule, since the primary key is not given in the predicate. If the table has a clustered index on major, the optimizer will choose that indexed cluster key, which has rank 7, rather than the full table scan, with rank 15.

Oracle's cost-based optimizer, which was an option for previous releases, is the only type used in the current version. It uses statistics to generate estimates of the cost of various methods of executing queries. The user is responsible for requesting that the system gather statistics for objects such as specific columns, tables, or the schema, by executing the package DBMS_STATS. There is also a COMPUTE STATISTICS command that generates some statistics. Frequencies of column values are recorded using histograms. The system prices out various execution plans for a query and chooses the one that uses minimum resources. However, the user can influence the choice by providing **hints** in the form of formatted comments in the query. For example, the user can force the system to use a particular index by modifying the SQL statement to include a commented +INDEX hint, as in:

```
SELECT /*+ INDEX(Student_major_ndx)*/ stuId, firstName, lastName
FROM Student
WHERE major = 'CSC';
```

Users can examine execution plans for an SQL statement by using the EXPLAIN PLAN command. Oracle also allows users to extend optimization to user-defined types by using its extensible optimization option, which gives the user control over many aspects of query plans.

11.6 Chapter Summary

Relational database management systems check each query for syntax errors, translate the query into an internal representation, rearrange or change the operations to produce an efficient order of operations, estimate the cost of executing the query using various plans, and choose the most efficient plan. A **query tree** can be used to represent relational algebra operations. Using properties such as commutativity, associativity, and distributivity, operations can be rearranged to produce an equivalent but more efficient query tree. Heuristics guide in the selection of properties to apply. Simple rules such as, "Do selection early" can result in tremendous cost savings. To choose the actual execution plan, the system considers factors such as file access cost, processing costs, costs of writing and storing intermediate results, communication costs, and the cost of writing final results. The size, distribution of values, structure, and access paths for files must be considered. The system stores statistics such as the number of tuples in each relation, the number of blocks, the blocking factor, the number of levels in each index, and the number of distinct values for each attribute. When choosing a plan involving an index, the type of index is very significant.

There are several methods of processing selects and joins, and the system uses its statistics to estimate the cost of methods before choosing one. Other operations such as projection and set operations have simpler access plans. When a query involves several operations, the cost of materializing the intermediate tables and accessing them must be considered in addition to the cost of the operations. An alternative to materialization is pipelining, in which tuples produced by one operation are passed to the next in a pipeline. Oracle used both rule-based and cost-based optimizers, but now cost-based is the default method. Users are responsible for telling the system to collect appropriate statistics either by running the DBMS_STATS package or using the COMPUTE STATISTICS option. They can also influence the execution plan by providing hints as part of the SQL queries.

Exercises

Schema for Exercises 11.1–11.5

```
Student (stuId, lastName, firstName, major, credits)
Faculty (facId, facName, department, rank)
Class (classNumber, facId, schedule, room)
Enroll (classNumber, stuId, grade)
```

11.1   Write the query tree for the following relational algebra expression:

```
SELECT Class WHERE room = 'A205' GIVING T1
T1 JOIN Faculty GIVING T2
PROJECT T2 OVER facName,dept
```

or symbolically,

$\Pi_{facName,dept} ((\sigma_{room='A205'} (Class)) |\times| Faculty)$

11.2   Consider the following SQL query for the University example:

```
SELECT   facName, schedule
FROM     Faculty, Class, Enroll, Student
WHERE    lastName = 'Burns' AND firstName='Edward'
         AND Class.classNumber =
         Enroll.classNumber AND Faculty.facId = Class.facId AND
         Student.stuId = Enroll.stuId;
```

   a. Write an initial relational algebra expression for this query.

   b. Using equivalences of relational algebra expressions, rewrite
   your relational algebra expression in a more efficient form, if
   possible. Explain why the new expression is efficient.

11.3   Write an efficient relational algebra expression for the following
   SQL query:

```
SELECT   lastName, firstName, grade
FROM     Student, Enroll, Class, Faculty
WHERE    facName = 'Tanaka' AND schedule= 'MTHF12' AND
         Class.classNumber = Enroll.classNumber AND Faculty.facId =
         Class.facId AND Student.stuId = Enroll.stuId;
```

   Explain why your relational algebra expression is efficient.

11.4   Write an initial query tree for the following relational algebra
   expression:

```
Class JOIN Enroll GIVING T1
T1 JOIN Student GIVING T2
SELECT T2 WHERE facId = 'F101' GIVING T3
SELECT T3 WHERE major = 'Art' GIVING T4
PROJECT T4 OVER lastName, firstName
```

   or symbolically,

$\Pi_{lastName, firstName}(\sigma_{major='Art'} (\sigma_{facId='F101'} ((Class |\times| Enroll) |\times| Student)))$

Using the heuristics given in Section 11.2.3, optimize the query tree.

11.5   Consider the query tree shown in Figure 11.8. Using the heuristics
   given in Section 11.2.3, write two different optimized query trees
   for this expression.

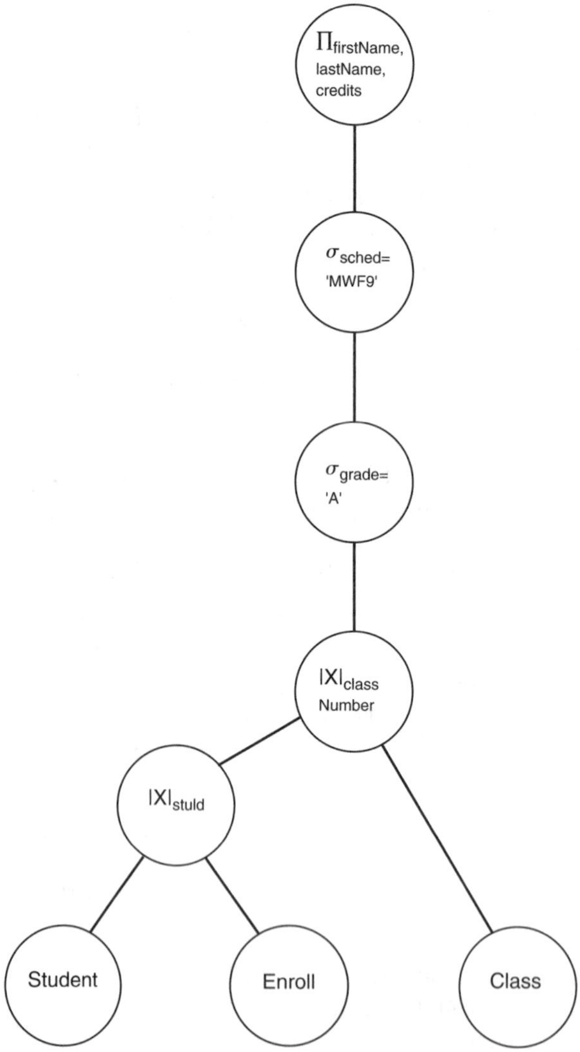

FIGURE 11.8

Query Tree for Exercise 11.5

Information for Exercises 11.6–11.12: Assume we have the following information about the University database:

All tables are stored in packed form in blocks of length 4096 bytes.

Student has 10,000 tuples, each 200 bytes long. It is hashed on stuId, the primary key, and has a secondary non-clustered index on lastName, with 3 levels. There are 8,000 values for lastName, 2,000 values for firstName, 25 values for major, and 150 values for credits.

Faculty has 800 tuples of length 100 bytes. It has an index on facId, the primary key, with 2 levels. There is a secondary non-clustered index on department, with one level. facName has 650 values, department has 25 values, and rank has 4 values.

Class has 2,500 tuples with length of 100 bytes. It is hashed on classNumber, the primary key, and has no secondary indexes. facId has 700 values here, schedule has 35 values, and room has 350 values.

Enroll has 50,000 tuples with length of 100 bytes. It has a composite index on the primary key, {classNumber, stuId}, with 4 levels, and no other index. The attribute grade has 10 values.

11.6   a. Find the blocking factor and total number of blocks needed for each of the four relations. Use this information for the questions that follow.

   b. Calculate the following selection sizes, assuming uniform distribution of attribute values:

```
s(major='Art',Student)
s(rank='Professor',Faculty)
s(grade='A',Enroll)
s(room='A205',Class)
```

11.7   a. Estimate the number of tuples in the result of Class $|\times|$ Enroll. Approximately how many blocks are needed to store the result?

   b. Estimate the number of tuples and the number of blocks in the result of Student $|\times|$ Faculty, where major in Student is compared with department in Faculty.

   c. Estimate the number of tuples and blocks for Faculty $|\times|$ Class.

   d. Estimate the number of tuples and blocks for Faculty $|\times|$ Enroll.

11.8   Find the read cost only (no writing costs) of Class $|\times|$ Enroll using nested loops with:

a. Class as the outside loop and buffer size of only two blocks

b. Enroll as the outside loop and buffer size of two blocks

c. Class as the outside loop and buffer size of 10 blocks

d. Enroll as the outside loop and buffer size of 10 blocks

11.9 Find the total access cost for Faculty |×| Student using major and department as the joined fields and assuming that the buffer holds only two blocks, using:

a. Nested loops, where you choose the best placement of relations in inside and outside loops. Include the cost of writing the results.

b. The secondary index (a B+ tree having one level) on department in Faculty. Include the cost of writing the results, as found for Part (a).

11.10 Find the access cost for performing Enroll |×| Student, using the hash key on stuId. Assume the average number of accesses to retrieve a Student record given stuId is 2.

11.11 Give an efficient strategy for each of the following SELECT operations and give the cost of each:

a. SELECT Student WHERE stuId = 'S1001'

b. SELECT Student WHERE lastName = 'Smith'

c. SELECT Student WHERE major = 'Art'

d. SELECT Student WHERE credits >= 100

e. SELECT Faculty WHERE department = 'History' and rank = 'Professor'

f. SELECT Class WHERE facId = 'F101'

g. SELECT Enroll WHERE grade = 'A'

11.12 Assume we wish to form the three-way join:

Class |×| Enroll |×| Student

a. Estimate the cost of (Class |×| Enroll) |×| Student, using the most efficient strategies for each of the two joins.

b. Estimate the cost of Class |×| (Enroll |×| Student), using the most efficient strategies for the two joins.

c. Consider the following method:

```
for each block of Enroll
    for each tuple in the Enroll block
        use the value of stuId from the Enroll tuple as the hash
            key for Student and get the matching Student tuple
        use the value of classNumber from the Enroll tuple as the
            hash key for Class and get the matching Class tuple
        write out the join of the three tuples
    end
end
```

Find the estimated cost of this method. Assume the average number of access for a hash key value is 2.

On the Companion Website:

- Additional Exercises

CHAPTER 12

Distributed Databases

Chapter Objectives

In this chapter you will learn the following:

- The definition of a distributed database system

- The advantages of distribution

- The factors to be considered in designing a distributed database system

- Alternative architectures for a distributed system

- The identity and functions of the components of a distributed database system

- Data placement alternatives

- How distributed database system components are placed

- Update synchronization techniques

- How the DDBMS processes requests for data

12.8 Chapter Summary

Exercises

 On the Companion Website:

- Sample Project

- Student Projects

12.1   Rationale for Distribution

A **distributed database system** is one in which multiple database sites are linked by a communications system in such a way that the data at any site is available to users at other sites. Normally, each site or node has a complete information processing system, with its own data administration function, personnel, users, hardware, and software—including a local database, database management system, and communications software. At the very least, a site must have memory and a communications processor. The sites are usually geographically remote and are linked by a telecommunications system, although it is possible to have a distributed system linked by a local area network within a single building or small area. Ideally, users need not be aware of the true location of the data they access, and the system appears to be a local database to them. Depending on the needs of the organization, distributed databases can have the following advantages over a single, centralized system that provides remote access to users.

1. *Local Autonomy.* An important objective of any distributed system is to allow the user to have more direct control over the system he or she uses. If each site has its own system, more of the basic information processing functions such as systems analysis, applications programming, operations, and data entry can be done locally, resulting in greater local control and user satisfaction than if these functions were performed at a central site, remote from user concerns and issues. At the same time, there should be centralized planning and coordination, so that standards can be developed and enforced, and the individual systems will be compatible.

2. *Improved reliability.* A distributed system is more reliable than a centralized one, because processing is done at several sites, so fail-

ure of a single node does not halt the entire system. Distributed systems can be designed to continue to function despite failure of a node or of a communications link.

3. *Better data availability.* Distributed database systems often provide for replication of data. If a node fails, or the only link to a node is down, its data is still available, provided a copy is kept somewhere else in the system.

4. *Increased performance.* As the organizational information processing requirements increase, the existing system may be unable to handle the processing load. In a centralized system, a system upgrade might be necessary to provide the performance increase required. A distributed system is basically modular, allowing new processors to be added as needed. Depending on the network topology, or physical layout, new sites may be easy to integrate.

5. *Reduced response time.* A distributed system should be designed so that data is stored at the location where it is used most often. This allows faster access to local data than a centralized system serving remote sites. However, in a poorly designed distributed system, the communications system might be heavily used, resulting in greater response time.

6. *Lower communications costs.* If data used locally is stored locally, communications costs will be lower, since the network will not be used for most requests. In a centralized system, the communications network is needed for all remote requests. However, we must consider the additional cost for the database software, additional storage costs for multiple copies of data items and software, higher hardware costs, and higher operating costs that distribution can entail.

12.2 Architectures for a Distributed System

Factors the designer of a distributed database system must consider in choosing an architecture include data placement, type of communications system, data models supported, and types of applications. Data placement alternatives are discussed in detail in Section 12.5. They differ in the amount of data replication they permit. Each alternative dictates a different type of system, using different update and request decomposition procedures. If the communications system is slow and expensive to use, this favors local storage and processing. A fast, inexpensive communications system favors centralized storage and processing. Various data models and accompanying manipulation languages are supported in distributed systems. In general, a designer should avoid models that use record-at-a-time retrieval, and choose instead those that allow set level operations, because of the number of messages that are required for programmer-navigated retrieval. This is one reason why the relational model is the one most often used for distributed databases. In considering the types of applications to be performed against the chosen database, the designer needs to estimate the size of the database, the number of transactions, the amount of data the transactions require, the complexity of transactions, the number of retrievals relative to the number of updates, and the number of transactions that refer to local data as opposed to remote data.

12.2.1 Distributed Processing Using a Centralized Database

In this architecture, shown in Figure 12.1, the database itself is not distributed, but users access it over a computer network. Processing can be performed at multiple sites, using data from the central database site. The central site also does processing, often both for its local applications and for some centralized applications. Local sites communicate only with the central site, not with one another, when they access data from the database for processing.

12.2.2 Client-Server Systems

In client-server systems, as shown in Figure 12.2, the database resides on a back-end machine, a **server**, and users typically access the data through their workstations, which function as **clients**. The database functions are divided between client and server. The client provides the user interface and runs the application logic, while the server manages the data and processes data requests. In a typical interactive transaction, the user interacts with the client workstation, using a graphical user interface provided either by the database system or by a third-party vendor. Besides handling the application logic, the client performs initial editing of data requests (usually SQL), checks the syntax of the request, and generates a database

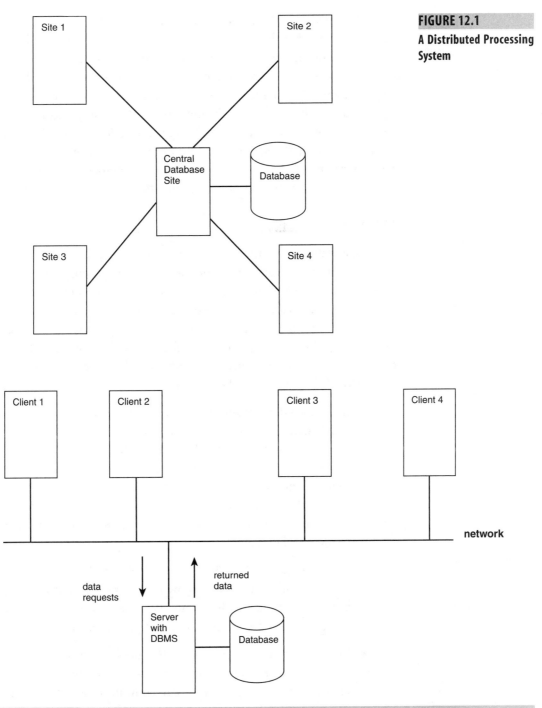

FIGURE 12.1
A Distributed Processing System

FIGURE 12.2
A Client-Server System

request, which is sent via the network to the server. The server validates the request by checking the data dictionary, authorization, and integrity constraints; optimizes the query; applies concurrency controls and recovery techniques; retrieves the data; and sends it back to the client. The client presents the data to the user. Application programs also run on the client, passing data requests through an **application program interface** (API) to the server in a similar fashion. If the client adheres to a standard such as ODBC or JDBC, it can communicate with any server that provides a standard interface. Unlike the centralized database environment, the server does not do application processing itself.

12.2.3 Parallel Databases

In parallel database architecture, there are multiple processors that control multiple disk units containing the database. The database may be partitioned on the disks, or possibly replicated. If fault-tolerance is a high priority, the system can be set up so that each component can serve as a backup for the other components of the same type, taking over the functions of any similar component that fails. Parallel database system architectures can be **shared-memory**, **shared-disk**, **shared-nothing**, or **hierarchical**, which is also called **cluster**.

- In a **shared-memory** system, all processors have access to the same memory and to shared disks, as shown in Figure 12.3(a). The database resides on the disks, either replicated on them or partitioned across them. When a processor makes a data request, the data can be fetched from any of the disks to memory buffers that are shared by all processors. The DBMS informs the processor what page in memory contains the requested data page.

- In the **shared-disk** design, shown in Figure 12.3(b), each processor has exclusive access to its own memory, but all processors have access to the shared disk units. When a processor requests data, database pages are brought into that processor's memory.

- In **shared-nothing** systems, each processor has exclusive control of its own disk unit or units and its own memory, as shown in Figure 12.3(c), but processors can communicate with one another.

FIGURE 12.3

Architectures for Parallel Databases

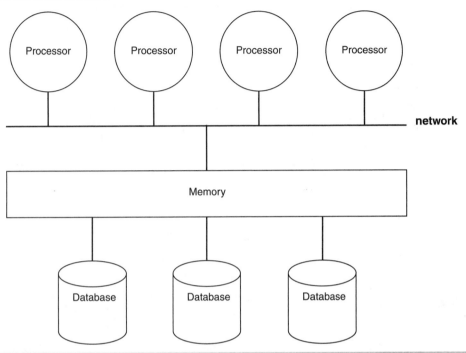

FIGURE 12.3(a)

Shared Memory

- In **hierarchical** or **cluster** architecture, systems made up of nodes that are shared-memory, are connected by an interconnection network, as seen in Figure 12.3(d). The systems share only communications with one another, making the overall inter-system architecture shared nothing.

The purpose of parallel databases is to improve performance by executing operations in a parallel fashion on the various devices. Careful partitioning of data is essential so that parallel evaluation of queries is possible. Data partitioning can be done by **range partitioning**, which means placing records on designated disks according to a range of values for a certain attribute. Other methods are by **hashing** on some attribute, or by placing new records on successive disks in **round-robin** fashion. When a query is

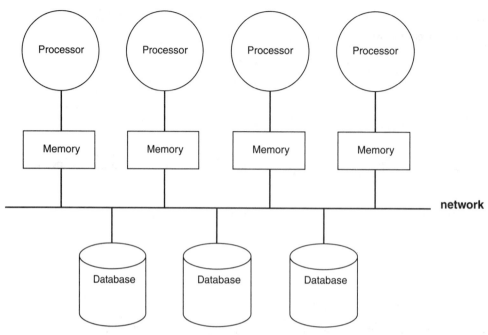

FIGURE 12.3(b)
Shared Disk

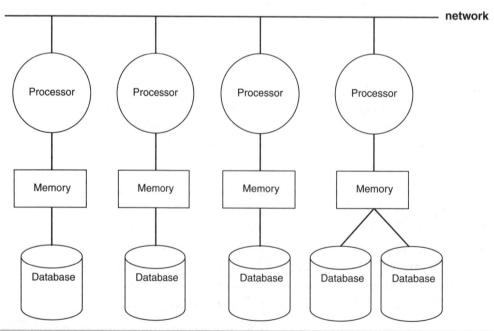

FIGURE 12.3(c)
Shared Nothing

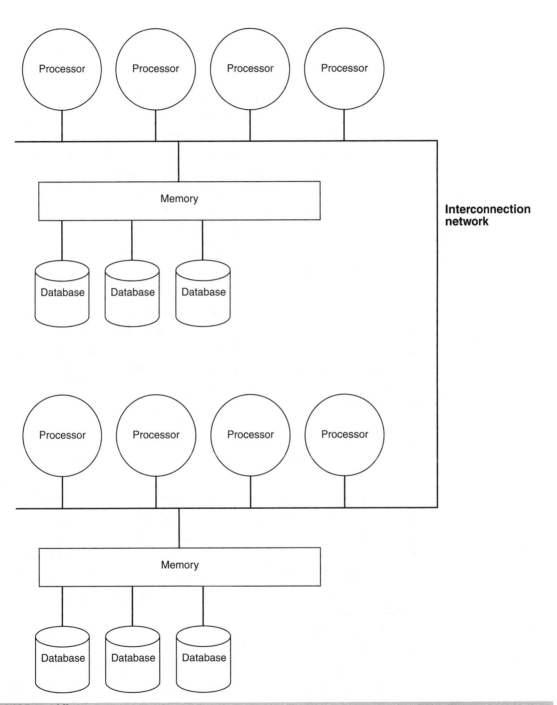

FIGURE 12.3(d)
Hierarchical

processed, since the required data may reside on different disks, the query is decomposed into subqueries that are then processed in parallel using the appropriate partition of the database.

Parallel databases using shared-nothing architecture provide linear **speed-up**, which means that as the number of processors and disks increase, the speed of operations increases in a linear fashion. They also provide linear **scale-up**, which means that they are scalable, so that if more processors and disks are added, the performance level is sustained. This allows us to increase the amount of data stored and processed without sacrificing performance. These characteristics of shared nothing have made this the architecture of choice for web applications.

12.2.4   Distributed Databases

In this architecture, the database is distributed, possibly with replication, among several relatively autonomous sites. The distribution is transparent to the user, who does not need to specify where the data is located (**location transparency**). A distributed system can be **homogeneous** or **heterogeneous**. In a homogeneous system, all nodes use the same hardware and software for the database system. In a heterogeneous system, nodes can have different hardware and/or software. Since a homogeneous system is much easier to design and manage, a designer would normally choose such a system. Heterogeneous systems usually result when individual sites make their own hardware and software decisions, and communications are added later, which is the norm. The designer then has the task of tying together the disparate systems. In a heterogeneous system, translations are needed to allow the databases to communicate. Since transparency is a major objective, the user at a particular site makes requests in the language of the database management system at that site. The system then has the responsibility of locating the data, which might be at another site that has different hardware and software. The request might even require coordination of data stored at several sites, all using different facilities. If two sites have different hardware but the same database management systems, the translation is not too difficult, consisting mainly of changing codes and word lengths. If they have the same hardware, but different software, the translation is difficult, requiring that the data model and data structures of one system be expressed in terms of the models and structures of another. For example, if one database is relational and the other uses the object-oriented model, objects must be presented in table form to users of the relational database. In addition, the query languages must be translated. The most challenging environment involves different hardware and software. This requires translation of data models, data structures, query language, word lengths, and codes.

12.3 Components of a Distributed Database System

A distributed database system normally has the following software components, as illustrated in Figure 12.4. Note that some sites contain all these components, while others might not.

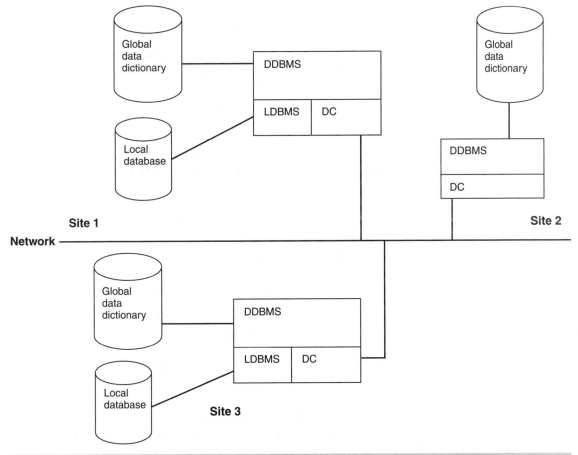

FIGURE 12.4

Components of a Distributed Database System

- **Data communications component (DC).** The data communications component is the software at each node that links it to the network. This DC component includes a complete description of the network's nodes and lines. For each node, it identifies processing performed, storage capacity, processing power, and current state. For each link, it identifies the nodes it connects, type of link, bandwidth, protocols required, and the current state of the link.

- **Local database management component (LDBMS).** The local database management component functions as a standard database management system, responsible for controlling the local data at each site that has a database. It has its own data dictionary for local data, as well as the usual subsystems for concurrency control, recovery, query optimization, and so on.

- **Global data dictionary (GDD).** The global data dictionary is a repository of information about the distributed database. It includes a list of all data items with their location and other information about data stored anywhere in the distributed system.

- **Distributed database management component (DDBMS).** The distributed database component is the management system for the global database. It has many functions, including the following:

  1. *Provides the user interface.* **Location transparency** is one of the major objectives of distributed databases. Ideally, the user need not specify the node at which data is located, but acts as if all data is stored locally and accessed by the local DBMS. The local DBMS, however, is unaware of the distribution, so only requests that can be satisfied locally should be sent to the local DBMS. The DDBMS, therefore, intercepts all requests for data and directs them to the proper site(s).

  2. *Locates the data.* After receiving a request for data, the DDBMS consults the global data dictionary to find the node or nodes where the data is stored. If the request can be filled entirely at the local node, it passes the query on to the local DBMS, which processes it. Otherwise, it must devise and carry out a plan for getting the data.

  3. *Processes queries.* Queries can be categorized as **local, remote,** or **compound.** A local request is one that can be filled by the

local DBMS. Local requests are simply handed down to the local DBMS, which finds the data and passes it back to the DDBMS, which in turn passes it to the user. (Recall the local DBMS has no user interface.) A remote request is one that can be filled completely at another node. In this case, the DDBMS passes the request to the DBMS at that node and waits for the response, which it then presents to the user. A compound request, also called a **global** request, is one that requires information from several nodes. To process a compound request, the DDBMS has to decompose the query into several remote and local requests that together will provide the information needed. It then directs each query to the appropriate DBMS, which processes it and returns the data to the DDBMS. The DDBMS then coordinates the data received to formulate a response for the user.

4. *Provides network-wide concurrency control and recovery procedures.* Although each local DBMS is responsible for handling update and recovery for its own data, only the DDBMS is aware of system-wide problems. Network-wide concurrency control is needed to prevent simultaneous users from interfering with one another. Network-wide recovery procedures are needed because, if a local node fails, although the local DBMS can recover its data to its condition at the time of failure, only the DDBMS can keep track of and apply changes made while the node was inactive.

5. *Provides translation of queries and data in heterogeneous systems.* In heterogeneous systems with different hardware but the same local DBMS, minor translations of codes and word lengths, and slight changes due to differences in implementation are needed. If the local DBMSs are different, major translation is needed. This includes changing from the query language of one DBMS into that of another and changing data models and data structures. If both hardware and DBMSs are different, both types of translation are needed.

12.4 Data Placement

One of the most important decisions a distributed database designer has to make is data placement. Proper data placement is a crucial factor in determining the success of a distributed database system. There are four basic alternatives, namely **centralized**, **replicated**, **partitioned**, or **hybrid**. Some of these require additional analysis to fine-tune the placement of data. In deciding among data placement alternatives, the following factors need to be considered.

1. *Locality of data reference.* The data should be placed at the site where it is used most often. The designer studies the applications to identify the sites where they are performed, and attempts to place the data in such a way that most accesses are local.

2. *Reliability of the data.* By storing multiple copies of the data in geographically remote sites, the designer maximizes the probability that the data will be recoverable in case of physical damage to any site.

3. *Data availability.* As with reliability, storing multiple copies assures users that data items will be available to them, even if the site from which the items are normally accessed is unavailable due to failure of the node or its only link.

4. *Storage capacities and costs.* Although the cost of data storage is lower than the cost of data transmission, nodes can have different storage capacities and storage costs. These must be considered in deciding where data should be kept. Storage costs are minimized when a single copy of each data item is kept, but the plunging costs of data storage make this consideration less important.

5. *Distribution of processing load.* One of the reasons for choosing a distributed system is to distribute the workload so that processing power will be used most effectively. This objective must be balanced against locality of data reference.

6. *Communications costs.* The designer must consider the cost of using the communications network to retrieve data. Retrieval costs and retrieval time are minimized when each site has its own copy of all the data. However, when the data is updated, the changes must then be sent to all sites. If the data is very volatile, this results in high communications costs for update synchronization.

The four placement alternatives, as shown in Figure 12.5, are the following.

1. *Centralized.* This alternative consists of a single database and DBMS stored in one location, with users distributed, as illustrated in Figure 12.1. There is no need for a DDBMS or global data dictionary,

	Alternative			
Criterion	Centralized	Replicated	Partitioned	Hybrid
LOCALITY OF REFERENCE	lowest	highest	* should be high	*should be high
RELIABILITY	lowest	highest	high for system, low for item	*
AVAILABILITY	lowest	highest	high for system, low for item	*
STORAGE COSTS	lowest	highest	lowest	* should be average
LOAD DISTRIBUTION	poor	best	good	* should be good
COMMUNICATION COSTS	highest	low, except for updates	* should be low	* should be low

* Depends on exact data placement decisions made

FIGURE 12.5

Evaluation of Data Placement Alternatives

because there is no real distribution of data, only of processing. Retrieval costs are high, because all users, except those at the central site, use the network for all accesses. Storage costs are low, since only one copy of each item is kept. There is no need for update synchronization, and the standard concurrency control mechanism is sufficient. Reliability is low and availability is poor, because a failure at the central node results in the loss of the entire system. The workload can be distributed, but remote nodes need to access the database to perform applications, so locality of data reference is low. This alternative is not a true distributed database system.

2. *Replicated.* With this alternative, a complete copy of the database is kept at each node. Advantages are maximum locality of reference, reliability, data availability, and processing load distribution. Storage costs are highest in this alternative. Communications costs for retrievals are low, but cost of updates is high, since every site must receive every update. If updates are very infrequent, this alternative is a good one.

3. *Partitioned.* Here, there is only one copy of each data item, but the data is distributed across nodes. To allow this, the database is split into disjoint **fragments** or parts. If the database is a relational one, fragments can be vertical table subsets (formed by projection) or horizontal subsets (formed by selection) of global relations. Figure

FIGURE 12.6

Fragmentation

FIGURE 12.6(a)

Horizontal Fragment:
$\sigma_{major='Math'}$ (Student)

Student				
stuId	**lastName**	**firstName**	**major**	**credits**
S1001	Smith	Tom	History	90
S1002	Chin	Ann	Math	36
S1005	Lee	Perry	History	3
S1010	Burns	Edward	Art	63
S1013	McCarthy	Owen	Math	0
S1015	Jones	Mary	Math	42
S1020	Rivera	Jane	CSC	15

FIGURE 12.6(b)

Vertical Fragment:
$\Pi_{stuId, major}$ (Student)

Student				
stuId	**lastName**	**firstName**	**major**	**credits**
S1001	Smith	Tom	History	90
S1002	Chin	Ann	Math	36
S1005	Lee	Perry	History	3
S1010	Burns	Edward	Art	63
S1013	McCarthy	Owen	Math	0
S1015	Jones	Mary	Math	42
S1020	Rivera	Jane	CSC	15

FIGURE 12.6(c)

Mixed Fragment:
$\Pi_{stuId, major}$ ($\sigma_{major='Math'}$
(Student))

Student				
stuId	**lastName**	**firstName**	**major**	**credits**
S1001	Smith	Tom	History	90
S1002	Chin	Ann	Math	36
S1005	Lee	Perry	History	3
S1010	Burns	Edward	Art	63
S1013	McCarthy	Owen	Math	0
S1015	Jones	Mary	Math	42
S1020	Rivera	Jane	CSC	15

12.6 provides examples of fragmentation. In any **horizontal frag-mentation scheme**, each tuple of every relation must be assigned to one or more fragments such that taking the union of the fragments results in the original relation; for the horizontally partitioned case, a tuple is assigned to exactly one fragment. In a **vertical fragmentation scheme**, the projections must be lossless, so that the original relations can be reconstructed by taking the join of the fragments. The easiest method of ensuring that projections are lossless is, of course, to include the key in each fragment; however, this violates the disjointness condition, because key attributes would then be replicated. The designer can choose to accept key replication, or the system can add a **tuple ID**—a unique identifier for each tuple—invisible to the user. The system would then include the tuple ID in each vertical fragment of the tuple, and would use that identifier to perform joins. Besides vertical and horizontal fragments, there can be **mixed fragments**, obtained by successive applications of select and project operations. This alternative requires careful analysis to ensure that data items are assigned to the appropriate site. If data items have been assigned to the site where they are used most often, locality of data reference will be high with this alternative. Because only one copy of each item is stored, data reliability and availability for a specific item are low. However, failure of a node results in the loss of only that node's data, so the systemwide reliability and availability are higher than in the centralized case. Storage costs are low, and communications costs of a well-designed system should be low. The processing load should also be well distributed if the data is properly distributed.

4. *Hybrid.* In this alternative, different portions of the database are distributed differently. For example, those records or tables with high locality of reference are partitioned, while those commonly used by all nodes are replicated, if updates are infrequent. Those that are needed by all nodes, but updated so frequently that synchronization would be a problem, might be centralized. This alternative is designed to optimize data placement, so that all the advantages and none of the disadvantages of the other methods are possible. However, very careful analysis of data and processing is required with this plan.

As an example, let us consider how the University database schema might be distributed. We assume that the university has a main campus and four branch campuses (North, South, East, and West), and that students have a home campus where they normally register and take classes. However, students can register for any class at any campus. Faculty members teach at a single campus. Each class is offered at a single campus. We will modify the schema slightly to include campus information in our new global schema:

```
Student(stuId, lastName, firstName, major, credits, homecampus)
Faculty(facId, name, department, rank, teachcampus)
Class(classNumber, campusoffered, facId, schedule, room)
Enroll(stuId, classNumber, grade)
```

It is reasonable to assume that `Student` records are used most often at the student's home campus, so we would partition the `Student` relation, placing each student's record at his or her home campus. The same is true for `Faculty` records. The `Class` relation could also be partitioned according to the campus where the class if offered However, this would mean that queries about offerings at other campuses would always require use of the network. If such queries are frequent, an alternative would be to replicate the entire `Class` relation at all sites. Because updates to this table are relatively infrequent, and most accesses are read-only, replication would reduce communication costs, so we will choose this alternative. The `Enroll` table would not be a good candidate for replication, because during registration, updates must be done quickly and updating multiple copies is time consuming. It is desirable to have the `Enroll` records at the same site as the `Student` record and as the `Class` record, but these may not be the same site. Therefore we might choose to centralize the `Enroll` records at the main site, possibly with copies at the `Student` site and the `Class` site. We can designate the main site as the primary copy for `Enroll`. The fragmentation scheme would be expressed by specifying the conditions for selecting records, as in:

$$\text{Student}_{Main} = \sigma_{homecampus='Main'}(\text{Student})$$
$$\text{Student}_{North} = \sigma_{homecampus='North'}(\text{Student})$$
. . . .
$$\text{Faculty}_{Main} = \sigma_{teachcampus='Main'}(\text{Faculty})$$
$$\text{Faculty}_{North} = \sigma_{teachcampus='North'}(\text{Faculty})$$
. . . .
$$\text{Enroll}_{North} = \Pi_{stuId,classNumber,grade}(\sigma_{Student.homecampus='North'}(\text{Enroll} |\times| \text{Student})) \cup$$
$$\Pi_{stuId,classNumber,grade}(\sigma_{Class.campusoffered='North'}(\text{Enroll} |\times| \text{Class}))$$

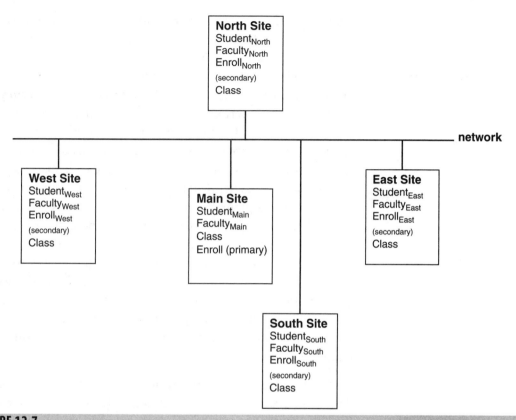

FIGURE 12.7

Data Placement for the Distributed University Schema

We are not fragmenting the `Class` relation. Because we have made different decisions for different parts of the database, this is a hybrid fragmentation scheme. Figure 12.7 illustrates the data placement decisions for this example.

12.5 Transparency

Ideally, the distribution in a distributed database system should be transparent to the user, whose interaction with the database should be similar to that provided by a single, centralized database. Forms of transparency that are desirable are as follows:

- **Data distribution transparency.** This type of transparency can take several forms. The user should not have to know how the data is fragmented, a property called **fragmentation transparency**. Users should be unaware of the actual location of the data items they access, a property called **location transparency**. If data is replicated, users should be unaware of the fact that multiple copies exist, a property called **replication transparency**. To support these properties, it is essential that data item names be unique. In a centralized system, it is easy to verify uniqueness. However, in a distributed system, it can be difficult to ensure that no two sites use the same name for different data items. It is possible to guarantee systemwide uniqueness of names if each data item name has a prefix that is the identifier of the site where the item originated, called the **birth site**. Often the URL of the site is used. However, this technique compromises location transparency. The problem can be solved by using aliases for data items, which the system can then map to the composite name. Another approach is to have a **name server** where all names are checked for uniqueness and registered. However, the server might become a bottleneck, compromising performance, and if the server fails, the entire system is affected.

- **DBMS heterogeneity transparency.** Users who need to access data from a remote site with a different DBMS from their local one should not be aware of the fact that they are using a different DBMS. Their queries should be submitted in the language that they normally use. For example, if they are Access users, and the remote site uses Oracle, they should be able to use the Access query form to submit queries. The system should take care of any translations needed. The problem of providing such transparency becomes more difficult if the two systems use different data models.

- **Transaction transparency.** The ACID properties of transactions, discussed in Chapter 10 for centralized databases, must also be guaranteed for distributed transactions. The system must therefore guarantee **concurrency transparency**, which ensures that concurrent transactions do not interfere with one another. It must also provide **recovery transparency**, handling systemwide database recovery. These issues will be examined further in Section 12.6.

- **Performance transparency.** A distributed database system should deliver performance that is comparable to one using a centralized architecture. For example, a query optimizer should be used to minimize response time for queries, so that users do not wait too long for results. This issue will be discussed in Section 12.7.

12.6 Transaction Control for Distributed Databases

Each local database management system in a distributed database system has a **transaction manager** including a concurrency controller and a recovery manager that function in the usual manner. Each site that initiates transactions also has a **transaction coordinator** whose function is to manage all transactions—whether local, remote, or global—that originate at that site. For local or remote transactions, the transaction manager at the data site itself takes over. For global transactions, a typical sequence of events when such a transaction is entered at a site requires the transaction coordinator at that particular site to:

- Start executing the transaction

- Consult the global data dictionary to divide the transaction into subtransactions and identify where they will be carried out

- Send the subtransactions to the target sites, using the communications system

- Receive the results of the subtransactions back from the target sites

- Manage the completion of the transaction, which is either a commit at all sites or an abort at all sites

The transaction coordinator is responsible for ensuring distributed concurrency control and distributed recovery. It follows a global concurrency control protocol to ensure serializability of global transactions, and maintains a log for recovery.

12.6.1 Concurrency Control

We have already considered problems of concurrency control in a centralized system in Chapter 10. The **lost update problem**, the **uncommitted update problem**, the **problem of inconsistent analysis**, the **nonrepeatable read problem**, and the **phantom data problem**, which we discussed in that chapter, can all occur in a distributed database as well. We discussed serializability of transactions, and we can now extend that notion for the distributed environment. Locking was the first solution we considered, and we examined the problem of deadlock, the situation in which two transactions each wait for data items being held by the other. We looked at deadlock detection methods, using a wait-for graph. We also examined timestamping as a method for concurrency control. In a distributed database system, if the database is either centralized or partitioned so that there is only one copy of each item, and all requests are either local (can be filled at local site) or remote (can be filled completely at one other site), then the usual locking and timestamping mechanisms are sufficient. More difficult concurrency problems arise when there are multiple copies of data items spread across the system. To solve this **multiple-copy consistency problem**, we must be sure that each location receives and performs the updates to the common data items. We also have to manage compound transactions that require updates to different data items located at different sites. These issues are dealt with using protocols that employ locking or timestamping on a more global level.

Locking Protocols

In Chapter 10, we discussed the **two-phase locking protocol**, which guaranteed serializability for transactions in a centralized database. Using this protocol, each transaction acquires all the required locks during its growing phase and releases its locks during its shrinking phase. The transaction cannot acquire any new lock once it releases any lock. We can extend the solution to a distributed environment by managing locks in one of several ways.

- **Single-site lock manager.** In this design, there is a central lock manager site, to which all requests for locks are sent. Regardless of which site originates a transaction, the locking site determines whether the necessary locks can be granted, using the rules of the two-phase locking protocol, as described in Chapter 10. The requesting site can read data from any site that has a replica of an item. However, updates must be performed at all the sites where the item is replicated. This is referred to as **Read-One-Write-All** replica handling. The single-site lock manager scheme is relatively simple and easy to implement. Deadlock detection and recovery are also simple, involving only the techniques discussed in Chapter 10, since only one site manages locking information. However, the site might become a bottleneck, because all lock requests must go through it. Another disadvantage is that the failure of the lock manager site stops all processing. This can be avoided by having a backup site take over lock management in the event of failure.

- **Distributed lock manager.** In this scheme, several sites (possibly all sites) have a local lock manager that handles locks for data items at that site. If a transaction requests a lock on a data item that resides only at a given site, that site's lock manager is sent a request for an appropriate lock, and the lock site proceeds as in standard two-phase locking. The situation is more complicated if the item is replicated, since several sites might have copies. Using the Read-One-Write-All rule, the requesting site requires only a shared lock at one site for reading, but it needs exclusive locks at all sites where a replica is stored for updates. There are several techniques for determining whether the locks have been granted, the simplest being that the requesting site waits for each of the other sites to inform it that the locks have been granted. Another scheme requires that the requesting site wait until a majority of the other sites grant the locks. The distributed manager scheme eliminates the bottleneck problem, but deadlock is more difficult to determine, because it involves multiple sites. If the data item to be updated is heavily replicated, communications costs are higher than for the previous method.

- **Primary copy.** This method can be used with replicated or hybrid data distribution where locality of reference is high, updates are infrequent, and nodes do not always need the very latest version of data. For each replicated data item, one copy is chosen as the **primary copy**, and the node where it is stored is the **dominant node**. Normally, different nodes are dominant for different parts of the data. The global data dictionary must show which copy is the primary copy of each data item. When an update is entered at any node, the DDBMS determines where the primary copy is, and sends the update there first, even before doing any local update. To begin the update, the dominant node locks its local copy of the data item(s), but no other node does so. If the dominant node is unable to obtain a lock, then another transaction has already locked the item, so the update must wait for that transaction to complete. This ensures serializability for each item. Once the lock has been obtained, the dominant node performs its update and then controls updates of all other copies, usually starting at the node where the request was entered. The user at that node can be notified when the local copy is updated, even though there might be some remote nodes where the new values have not yet been entered. Alternatively, the notification might not be done until all copies have been updated. To improve reliability in the event of dominant node failure, a backup node can be chosen for the dominant node. In that case, before the dominant node does an update, it should send a copy of the request to its backup. If the dominant node does not send notification of update completion shortly after this message, the backup node uses a time-out to determine whether the dominant node has failed. If a failure occurs, the backup node then acts as the dominant node. It notifies all other nodes that it is now dominant, sends a copy of the request to its own backup node, locks data and performs its own update, and supervises the updates at the other nodes. It is also responsible for supplying data needed when the original dominant node recovers. If nondominant nodes fail, the system continues to function, and the dominant node is responsible for keeping a log of changes made while the node was down, to be used in recovery. The primary copy approach has lower communications costs and better performance than distributed locking.

- **Majority locking protocol.** In this scheme, lock managers exist at all sites where data items are stored. If a data item is replicated at several sites, a transaction requiring a lock on the item sends its request to at least half of the sites having a replica. Each of these sites grants the local lock if possible, or delays the grant if necessary. When the transaction has received grants from at least half of the replica sites, it can proceed. Note that while several transactions can hold a majority of the shared locks on an item, only one transaction can have the majority of the exclusive locks on a particular item. This protocol is more complex than the previous ones, and requires more messages. Deadlock between sites is also difficult to determine.

Regardless of how the locks are managed, the two-phase locking protocol is applied. The transaction must obtain all of its locks before releasing any lock. Once it releases any lock, no further locks can be obtained.

Global Deadlock Detection

Locking mechanisms can result in deadlock, a situation in which transactions wait for each other, as discussed in Chapter 10. Deadlock detection in a centralized database involves constructing a **wait-for** graph, with transactions represented by nodes, and an edge from node T1 to node T2 indicating that transaction T1 is waiting for a resource held by transaction T2. A **cycle** in the graph indicates that deadlock has occurred. In a distributed environment, each site can construct its **local wait-for graph**. Nodes on the graph can represent both local transactions using local data and non-local transactions that are using the data at that site. Any transaction that is using a site's data is therefore represented by a node on the graph, even if the transaction itself is executing at another site. If a cycle occurs on a local wait-for graph, deadlock has occurred at that site, and it is detected and broken in the usual way: by choosing a victim and rolling it back. However, **distributed deadlock** can occur without showing up as a cycle in any local wait-for graph. Figure 12.8(a) shows a global schedule with four sites executing transactions concurrently. At site 1, transaction T2 is waiting for a shared lock on data item a, currently locked exclusively by T1. In Figure 12.8(b), the local wait-for graph for site 1 shows an edge from T2 to T1, but no cycle. Similarly, sites 2 through 4 have wait-for graphs, each of which has no cycle, indicating no deadlock at that site. However, when we take the union of the graphs, Figure 12.8(c), we see that the global wait-for graph has a cycle. At site 4, T1 is waiting for T4, which is waiting at site 3 for T3, which is waiting at site 2 for T2, which is waiting at site 1 for T1. Therefore we have a cycle indicating distributed deadlock. No single site could detect that deadlock by using its local graph alone. Therefore the system needs to maintain a **global wait-for graph** as well as the local ones. There can be a single site identified as the **deadlock detection coordinator** that maintains the graph, or the responsibility could be shared by several sites, to avoid bottlenecks and improve reliability.

The deadlock detection coordinator is responsible for constructing a global graph using information from the lock managers at all sites. These managers transmit messages informing the coordinator whenever an edge is added to or deleted from their local graphs. The coordinator continuously checks for cycles in the global graph and, if one is detected, the coordinator is responsible for selecting a victim and informing all participating sites that they must roll back that transaction.

FIGURE 12.8
Wait-for Graphs for Deadlock Detection

Time	Site1	Site2	Site3	Site4
t1	T1: Xlock a	T2: Slock g	T3: Slock m	T4: Xlock q
t2	T1: Xlock b	T2: Xlock h	T3: Xlock n	T4: Slock r
t3	T2: request Slock a	T3: request Xlock g	T4: request Slock n	T1: request Slock q
t4	. . . T2wait . . .	. . . T3wait . . .	. . . T4wait . . .	. . . T1wait . . .

FIGURE 12.8(a)
Global Schedule of Transactions T1, T2, T3, T4

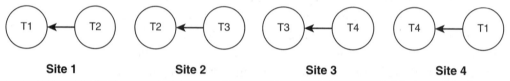

Site 1   Site 2   Site 3   Site 4

FIGURE 12.8(b)
Local Wait-for Graphs with No Cycle

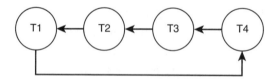

FIGURE 12.8(c)
Global Wait-for Graph with Cycle

Timestamping Protocols

In Chapter 10, we discussed timestamping in a centralized system, and examined protocols that guaranteed that transactions were executed as if in timestamp order. We can apply essentially the same protocols to distributed systems, if we can guarantee unique timestamps. This can be done either by issuing timestamps from only one site, or by specifying that timestamps will have two parts. The first is the usual timestamp generated by the local clock or logical counter, and the second part is the node identifier. Since the clock or counter is advanced at each node for each transaction, this guarantees that every transaction will have a unique timestamp, although two transaction timestamps can have the same first part. It would be desirable to have some type of global clock, so we could determine which of two transactions entered at different sites was actually first, but it is virtually impossible to fully synchronize all the local clocks involved. Instead, there is usually a scheme to prevent local timestamps from diverging too much. For example, there can be a rule that if a node receives a timestamp with first part, t, greater than its current clock reading, it automatically advances its clock to $t+1$. This prevents nodes that have frequent transactions from getting too far ahead of less active nodes. As in the centralized case, the protocol includes resolution procedures to follow in the case of conflicting transactions. The basic timestamping protocol, Thomas' Write Rule, and multiversion timestamping can all be applied directly to the distributed environment using the unique timestamps.

12.6.2 Recovery

As with a centralized database, a distributed database management system must ensure that its transactions are atomic and durable, despite system failures. If the transaction aborts, its effects must be completely undone throughout all the sites it affected. If it commits, its effects must persist at all the sites where they should.

Failures and Recovery

In addition to the types of failures that can occur in a centralized database, such as disk crashes or system failures, distributed databases can suffer from failures due to loss of messages, failure of a site, or failure of a communications line. They must also be able to deal with a situation called **network partitioning**. This occurs when failure of a line or node that had provided a link between parts of the network fails, resulting in splitting the network into groups of nodes so that nodes within a group can communicate, but there is no communication between the groups.

It is difficult to tell whether one of the nodes or links has failed. If a site is unable to communicate with a node, it may be due to the fact that the node is busy, that the node itself has failed, that the communications link has failed, or that the network is partitioned due to the failure of a different node or another link. In the case of a link failure, rerouting may be used, and the system could continue as before. If no other link exists, the node is isolated, and the link failure is treated as a node failure. The system can recognize a node failure either by self-reporting of the failed node or, if that is not possible, by a time-out method. In that case, if a node fails to respond to a message within a prespecified time, it is assumed to have failed, and recovery procedures are started. It is essential that the timeout be sufficiently long that recovery procedures are not triggered unnecessarily. The following steps are used to allow the system to continue following the failure of a node.

1. The system should flag the node or link as failed, to prevent any other node from trying to use it and thus generating a second recovery procedure.

2. The system should abort and roll back any transactions affected by the failure.

3. The system should check periodically to see if the node has recovered or, alternatively, the node should report when it has recovered.

4. Once restarted, the failed node must do local recovery, rolling back any partial transactions that were active at the time of failure.

5. After local recovery, the failed node must update its copy of the data so that it matches the current state of the database. The system keeps a log of changes made during the node's failure for this purpose.

Commit Protocols

The transaction coordinator is responsible for determining whether a transaction commits or aborts. If the transaction involves several sites as participants, it must commit at all of them or abort at all of them. The coordinator must use a protocol to determine the outcome of a transaction and to handle any failure. The simplest protocol is the two-phase commit protocol. The three-phase commit protocol in an enhanced version that addresses some additional problems.

1. **Two-Phase Commit Protocol.** This relatively simple protocol consists of a **voting phase** and a **resolution phase**. At the end of a transaction's execution, the transaction coordinator asks the participant sites whether they can commit the transaction T. If all agree to commit, the coordinator commits; otherwise it aborts the transaction. The phases consist of the following activities.

   • **Phase 1—Voting Phase.** The coordinator writes a <begin commit T> record to its log, and force-writes the log to write to disk. The coordinator sends a <prepare T> message to all participant sites. Each site determines whether it can commit its portion of T. If it can, it adds a <ready T> message to its own log, force-writes the log to disk, and returns a <ready T> message to the coordinator. If a site cannot commit, it adds an <abort T> to its log, force-writes the log, and returns an <abort T> vote to the coordinator.

- **Phase 2—Resolution Phase.** The coordinator resolves the fate of the transaction according to the responses it receives.

  a. If the coordinator receives an <abort T> message from any site, it writes an <abort T> message to its log and force-writes the log. It sends an <abort T> message to all participant sites. Each site records the message in its own log and aborts the transaction.

  b. If a site fails to vote within a specified time (the timeout period), the coordinator assumes a vote of <abort T> from that site and proceeds to abort as specified above.

  c. If the coordinator receives <ready T> messages from all participating sites, it writes a <commit T> record to its log, force-writes the log, and sends a <commit T> message to all participants. Each site records the message in its own log and responds to the coordinator. When all acknowledgments are received, the coordinator writes an <end T> message to its log. If any acknowledgment is not received during the timeout, the coordinator assumes that the site has failed. In the event of failure of either the coordinator or a participating site, the protocol determines the actions to be taken.

     (1) *Failure of a participating site.* As described above, if the coordinator does not receive a vote from a site within the timeout, it assumes an <abort T> vote and aborts the transaction. If the site votes to accept the commit and fails afterward, the coordinator continues executing the protocol for the other sites. When the failed site recovers, the site consults its log to determine what it should do for each transaction that was active at the time of failure.

        i. If the log has a <commit T> record, it does a redo(T).

        ii. If the log has an <abort T> record, it does an undo(T).

        iii. If the log does not have ready, abort, or commit records for T, then it must have failed before responding with a vote, so it knows the coordinator had to abort the transaction. Therefore it does an undo(T).

iv. If the log has a <ready T> record, the site tries to determine the fate of the transaction. It consults the coordinator, and if the coordinator responds that the transaction committed, the site does a redo(T). If the coordinator responds that the transaction was aborted, the site does an undo(T). If the coordinator does not respond, the site assumes the coordinator has failed, and the site may attempt to determine the transaction's fate by consulting other participant sites. If it cannot determine the fate, the site is **blocked** and must wait until the coordinator has recovered.

(2) *Failure of the coordinator.* If the coordinator fails during the commit protocol, the participating sites try to determine the fate of the transaction. Several possibilities exist:

  i. If one of the sites has an <abort T> in its log, T is aborted.

  ii. If one of the sites has a <commit T> in its log, T is committed.

  iii. If a site exists without a <ready T> in its log, that site cannot have voted to commit T, so the coordinator cannot have decided to do a commit. Therefore, T can now be aborted.

  iv. In all other cases (all active sites have a <ready T> but no site has either <abort T> or <commit T>), it is impossible to tell whether the coordinator has made a decision about the fate of T. T is **blocked** until the coordinator recovers.

2. **Three-Phase Commit Protocol.** As discussed, the two-phase commit protocol can result in blocking under certain conditions. The three-phase commit protocol is a non-blocking protocol, unless all of the sites fail. Conditions for the protocol to work are:

  ▪ At least one site has not failed

  ▪ There is no network partitioning

- For some predetermined number *k,* no more than *k* sites can fail simultaneously

The protocol adds a third phase after the voting phase but before the resolution phase. The coordinator first notifies at least *k* other sites that it intends to commit, even before it force-writes its own commit log record. If the coordinator fails before issuing the global commit, the remaining sites elect a new coordinator, which checks with the other sites to determine the status of T. Since no more than *k* sites can fail, and *k* sites have the "intend to commit" message, those sites can ensure that T commits. Therefore blocking does not occur unless *k* sites fail. However, network partitioning can make it appear that more than *k* sites have failed, and unless the protocol is carefully managed, it is possible that the transaction will appear to be committed in one partition and aborted in another.

12.7 Distributed Query Processing

In Chapter 11 we discussed techniques for transforming SQL queries into a low-level representation such as relational algebra, and methods of transforming relational algebra expressions into equivalent but more efficient ones. We also presented various methods for estimating the cost of processing queries for various relational algebra operations. The dominant factor in the cost estimates was the number of disk accesses required. A distributed environment requires that we also consider the cost of transmitting data over the network. If the network is relatively slow, this factor can become the dominant cost factor. If the data is replicated, we have to consider the issue of choosing the best of several possible sites for performing all or part of a query. Partitioning of data complicates queries that require the use of more than one of the partitions. Therefore, in a distributed database system, we must consider additional query optimization procedures.

As described earlier, database queries can be categorized as **local**, **remote**, or **compound** (also called **global**). A local request is one that can be satisfied at the node where it is entered. A remote request can be satisfied at a single, remote node. A compound request is one that requires access to more than one node. In satisfying a compound request, the DDBMS is responsible for breaking down the query into several subqueries, each of which is directed to a specific node for processing. The DDBMS must then collect and coordinate the responses to obtain an overall result. Ideally, the user should not be aware of the distribution of data, and should not need to specify where the data items are located.

12.7.1 Steps in Distributed Query Processing

Some or all of the following steps must be performed by the DDBMS in answering a query.

1. *Accept the user's request.* The user interface is the responsibility of the DDBMS, rather than the local DBMS at each node. Because the local DBMS is not aware of the distribution, it is unable to handle queries about data items not stored locally.

2. *Check the validity of the request.* This requires checking that the correct query language syntax is used, and that the data items referred to actually exist. This is external level validity checking, which requires that the DDBMS have access to the user's subschema.

3. *Check authorization.* Access control information must be available to the DDBMS, so that it can check whether the user is authorized to perform the operations requested on the data items specified. This checking should be done both at the user's node and at every node where the request is processed. This is logical-level checking, and requires that the schema be available to the DDBMS.

4. *Map external to logical level.* The DDBMS maps the user's data names and views to the corresponding logical-level objects.

5. *Determine a request processing strategy.* The DDBMS must consult the global data dictionary to determine the location of the data items requested. If the request is local, it forwards it to the local DBMS for processing. If the request is remote, it goes on to the next step. If the request is compound, it must break it into sub-queries and direct each to a node. There may be several ways of breaking up the query, so the DDBMS normally uses some form of optimization to determine which decomposition to use. Optimization in a centralized system involves several techniques. For example, if there are multiple conditions, testing can be done first on the condition that eliminates the largest number of records, or the one that requires the fewest I/O operations. In accessing records, the shortest access paths are chosen. In a distributed sys-

tem, the optimization also includes the use of the communications system. An objective of optimization might be to minimize response time, which would dictate decomposing the request in such a manner that parallel processing could be performed at several nodes, especially if the communications system is fast and the processing load is light. Sometimes several nodes perform the same process, and results are obtained from the one that finishes first. If the system is heavily used, other objectives might be more appropriate. These include minimizing total processing time, which consists of the sum of the (possibly simultaneous) processing times of the nodes and the time used for executing communications software and consolidating the results. In selecting an algorithm, true optimization requires that the DDBMS find all the ways of processing the query and then "cost out" each one by using mathematical formulas that include processing costs, communications costs, and storage costs. Because of the difficulty of finding all possible processing methods, a "hill climbing" method is often used. This consists of finding an initial solution and costing it out, then evaluating a slightly different alternative, choosing the better of the two. The better one then becomes the basis for a comparison with another alternative, and the process continues until no other method can be found or a certain number of iterations fail to produce substantial improvement.

6. *If the system is heterogeneous, translate each query into the DML of the data node.* In remote or compound requests, the node where the data is located may use a different DBMS from the user's node. Therefore, the DDBMS must provide translation due to hardware and software differences. In the worst case, different data models and data structures as well as different codes and word lengths might be involved.

7. *Encrypt the request.* Security is improved if every request and every response is encrypted before being passed to the communications system. The receiving node must then decrypt the message before processing.

8. *Depending on the system, the local data communications component may determine the routing.* The requesting node must provide logical identifiers for each node that is to receive a subrequest. The

function of translating a logical identifier to a physical identifier and choosing a path requires a network description, which is available to the DC component. Routing may be direct or indirect, requiring that the message pass through intermediate nodes. If indirect, the routing may be determined by the originating node in advance, or may be dynamically determined by the intermediate nodes.

9. *The DC component transmits the message through the communications system.* Since communications between databases are process-to-process communications, the message must pass down through all the data communication layers at the source node, be transmitted to the destination, and pass back up through all the communication layers at the destination node.

10. *Decrypt the request.* If the message was encrypted at the source, it must now be decrypted at the destination node before processing can begin.

11. *Perform update synchronization, if needed.* If the request is an update, the DDBMS at the receiving node must go through synchronization procedures, as described in Section 12.6.

12. *Local DBMS does its processing.* The local DBMS at the data node performs logical and physical binding, determines local processing strategy, and retrieves the data requested of it.

13. *If the system is heterogeneous, translate the data.* The requesting node, data node, or some intermediate node can perform any necessary translation.

14. *Send the results to the destination node.* Normally, query results are returned to the requesting node, but other nodes might also be specified as destinations. The results might be encrypted before they are returned.

15. *Consolidate the results, edit, and format the response for the user.* The requesting node usually coordinates the entire query decomposition process, and it is normally the site where final consolidation of partial results is performed. In addition, the DDBMS at that node consults the user's external model to present data in the

form the user expects. However, other nodes may perform some of these functions.

16. *Return the results to the user.* Since the user interface is provided by the DDBMS, it is responsible for displaying the results.

12.7.2 Estimating Data Communications Costs

We will assume we have the schema discussed in Section 12.4, with the number of bytes for each attribute indicated as follows.

```
Student(stuId(5), lastName(15), firstName(15), major(12), credits(4),
homecampus(10))
Faculty(facId(5), name(15), department(15), rank(20), teachcampus(10))
Class(classNumber(10), campusoffered(10), facId(5), schedule(10), room(5))
Enroll(stuId(5), classNumber(10), grade(3))
```

Example 1

We wish to find class schedule information for all CSC majors using the data distribution shown in Figure 12.7. The query is: Find the `stuId`, `lastName`, `firstName`, `classNumber`, `campusoffered`, `schedule`, and `room` of all CSC majors, regardless of campus. In SQL, we write:

```
SELECT stuId, lastName, firstName, classNumber, campusoffered, schedule, room
FROM Student, Enroll, Class
WHERE major='CSC' AND Student.stuId = Enroll.stuId AND
Enroll.classNumber=Class.classNumber;
```

Strategy 1.

1. At each site, select the CSC majors, $(\sigma_{major='CSC'}(\text{Student}))$.

2. At each site, join those tables with `Enroll` over the `stuId`.

   $(\sigma_{major='CSC'}(\text{Student})) |\times| \text{Enroll}$

3. **Project results onto** `classNumber, stuId, firstName, lastName` at each site.

   $\Pi_{classNumber, stuId, firstName, lastName}((\sigma_{major='CSC'}(\text{Student})) |\times| \text{Enroll})$

4. Ship the results from the four remote sites to Main.

5. At Main, join with `Class`.

   $(\Pi_{classNumber, stuId, firstName, lastName}((\sigma_{major='CSC'}(\text{Student})) |\times| \text{Enroll})) |\times| \text{Class}$

6. At Main, project onto `stuId`, `lastName`, `firstName`, `classNumber`, `campusoffered`, `schedule`, `room`.

In Step 4, we need to determine the cost of shipping the results from each of the remote sites. Assume there are 25 major fields available at all five campuses, and each campus has 2000 students. There should be 2000/25 or 80 CSC majors at each campus. When we join these with `Enroll`, assuming students take an average of five classes each, we get 5*80 or 400 records. We project onto the desired attributes, which total 45 bytes, for a total of 45*400 or 18,000 bytes from each of the 4 sites, or **72,000** bytes. The rest of the query is executed at the Main site, as indicted in Steps 5 and 6. The cost is determined by the methods discussed in Chapter 11. If the query is entered at the Main site, there are no additional shipping costs. However, if it is entered at another site, we would have to add the costs of shipping the results back to that site.

Strategy 2.

1. At each site, select the CSC majors and project the results onto `stuId`, `lastName`, `firstName`. The relational algebra operations are:

$\Pi_{stuId, lastName, firstName}\ (\sigma_{major='CSC'}(\text{Student}))$

2. Ship the four intermediate tables from North, South, East, and West to the Main site.

3. Join all five intermediate tables with `Enroll` at Main.

$(\Pi_{stuId, lastName, firstName}\ (\sigma_{major='CSC'}(\text{Student}))) |\times| \text{Enroll}$

4. Join the resulting table with `Class` at Main.

$((\Pi_{classNumber, stuId, firstName,\ lastName}(\sigma_{major='CSC'}(\text{Student}))) |\times| \text{Enroll}) |\times| \text{Class}$

5. Still at Main, project the results onto `stuId`, `lastName`, `firstName`, `classNumber`, `campusoffered`, `schedule`, `room`.

The only shipping costs are the costs of sending each of the four intermediate tables (from North, South, East, and West) to Main. The result of the SELECT has 80 records, each 61 bytes. When the project is performed, the size is 35 bytes, so we need to ship 80*35 or 2800 bytes from each of the four sites, for a total of **11,200** bytes shipped. The rest of the query is executed at the Main site, as indicted in Steps 3, 4, and 5.

Comparing the two strategies, the shipping costs for the first are about six times those of the second.

Example 2

For each faculty member from all campuses, find the faculty `name` and the `classNumber`, `campus`, and `schedule` of all courses that the faculty member teaches. We assume there are 2500 `Class` tuples and 800 `Faculty` tuples. The query is entered at the West campus. In SQL, it is:

```
SELECT name, classNumber, campusoffered, schedule
FROM Faculty, Class
WHERE Faculty.facId = Class.facId;
```

Strategy 1. Send `Faculty` subtables from the other campuses to the West campus. Complete the entire query at the West campus. The communications costs are:

Four `Faculty` subtables: 640 tuples total, each with 65 bytes, for a total of 41,600 bytes shipped.

Grand total of **41,600** bytes shipped.

Strategy 2. Send each `Faculty` subtable to the Main site, and join with `Class` there. Project onto `name`, `classNumber`, `campusoffered`, `schedule` and send the results to the West campus.

`Faculty` subtables: 640 tuples total, each with 65 bytes, for a total of 41,600 bytes shipped.

`Results` subtable: 2500 tuples, each 45 bytes, for a total of 112,500 bytes shipped.

Grand total of **154,100** bytes shipped.

For this example, the first strategy is more efficient because there is no need to ship the results file. Note that if the query were entered at the Main campus, the second strategy would have the same cost as the first.

12.7.3 The Semijoin Operation

For many distributed databases, an operation called a **semijoin** can be very cost effective. If A and B are tables, then the left-semijoin A |× B, is found by taking the natural join of A and B and then projecting the result onto the attributes of A. The result will be just those tuples of A that participate in the join. We defined the right-semijoin in a similar fashion. As an example of the use of the semijoin in a distributed environment, we will use the following simple schema.

```
Department(deptCode(5), deptName(20), chairpersonId(5),
telephone(10), office(5)
```

stored at site A. Assume there are 100 records, 45 bytes each.

```
Faculty(facId(5), deptCode(5), firstName(15),
lastName(15), birthDate(12), rank(10),
socialSecurityNumber(9))
```

stored at site B. Assume there are 1000 records, 71 bytes each.

Consider the query "Find the name of each department, and the name of the chairperson of that department," entered at site A. In SQL, we write:

```
SELECT firstName, lastName, deptName
FROM Faculty, Department
WHERE Department.chairpersonId = Faculty.facId;
```

Strategy 1

Ship the entire `Faculty` file to site A and do the join there. Shipping cost is 1000*71 or **71,000** bytes. Then project the results onto `firstName`, `lastName`, `deptName` and present the results to the user at site A, with no further shipping.

Strategy 2

Ship the entire `Department` file to site B and do the join there. Shipping cost is 100*45 or 4500 bytes. Then ship the results to site A. Shipping cost is 50*1000 or 50,000 bytes, for a total of **54,500** bytes.

Strategy 3

Project `Department` onto `chairpersonId` and ship only `chairpersonId` to site B. Since `chairpersonId` is 5 bytes and we assumed 100 records, we ship 5*100 or 500 bytes so far.

At site B, join with `Faculty` over `facId`. Project the result and transfer only `firstName`, `lastName`, and `deptCode` back to site A. Cost is 35*100 or 3500 bytes.

At site A, join the result with `Department` on `DeptCode`, and project the result onto `firstName`, `lastName`, and `departmentName`. No further shipping costs are involved.

Total shipping cost is **4,000** bytes.

Note that the initial projection identified only the Ids of chairpersons, substantially reducing the amount of data to be shipped. The semijoin was done at site B, where we did a join and then projected the results onto the attributes of `Faculty` (`firstName`, `lastName`, and `deptCode`) that were in the join.

The semijoin is often used this way in distributed systems, especially in queries where few tuples will participate in the join. The optimizer considers a semijoin in place of a join when the tables to be joined reside at different sites.

12.8 Chapter Summary

A **distributed database system** has multiple sites connected by a communications system, so that data at any site is available to users at other sites. The system can consist of sites that are geographically far apart but linked by telecommunications, or the sites can be close together, and linked by a **local area network**. Advantages of distribution may include **local autonomy, improved reliability, better data availability, increased performance, reduced response time**, and **lower communications costs**.

The designer of a distributed database system must consider the **type of communications system, data models supported, types of applications**, and **data placement alternatives**. Final design choices include **distributed processing using a centralized database, client-server systems, parallel databases**, or **true distributed databases**. A distributed database can be **homogeneous**, where all nodes use the same hardware and software, or **heterogeneous**, where nodes have different hardware or software. Heterogeneous systems require translations of codes and word lengths due to hardware differences, or of data models and data structures due to software differences.

A distributed database system has the following software components: **data communications component (DC)**, **local database management system (DBMS)**, **global data dictionary (GDD)**, and **distributed database management system component (DDBMS)**. The responsibilities of the distributed database management system include providing the user interface, locating the data, processing queries, providing network-wide concurrency control and recovery procedures, and providing translation in heterogeneous systems. **Data placement alternatives** are **centralized**, **replicated**, **partitioned**, and **hybrid**. Factors to be considered in making the data placement decision are locality of reference, reliability of data, availability of data, storage capacities and costs, distribution of processing load, and communications costs. The other components of a distributed database system may be placed using any of the four alternatives.

Forms of transparency that are desirable in a distributed database include **data distribution transparency**, (which includes **fragmentation transparency**, **location transparency**, and **replication transparency**), DBMS **heterogeneity transparency**, **transaction transparency**, (which includes **concurrency transparency** and **recovery transparency**), and **performance transparency**.

One of the most difficult tasks of a distributed database management system is **transaction management**. Each site that initiates transactions also has a **transaction coordinator** whose function it is to manage all transactions, whether local, remote, or global, that originate at that site. **Concurrency control** problems that can arise include the **lost update problem**, the **uncommitted update problem**, the **problem of inconsistent analysis**, the **nonrepeatable read problem**, and the **phantom data problem**, as well as the **multiple-copy inconsistency** problem, which is unique to distributed databases. As for the centralized case, solutions for the distributed case include techniques such as **locking** and **timestamping**. The two-phase locking protocol has variations in the distributed environment that include **single-site lock manager**, **distributed lock managers**, **primary copy**, or **majority locking**. The **Read-One-Write-All** rule is often used for replicated data. Distributed deadlock is detected using a **global wait-for graph**. Timestamping can also be used to guarantee serializability. Timestamps may include two parts—a normal timestamp and a node identifier. To prevent timestamps from different sites from diverging too much, each site can automatically advance its timestamps whenever it receives a later timestamp than its current time. Recovery protocols include the **two-phase commit** and the **three-phase commit** protocols.

Another important task of the distributed database management system is **distributed query processing**, which includes several steps, the most difficult of which is to **determine a request processing strategy** and supervise its execution. Standard query optimization techniques must be extended to consider the cost of transferring data between sites. The semijoin operation is sometimes used when a join of data stored at different sites is required. It can result in substantial savings when a join is required.

Exercises

12.1   Using the data distribution scheme shown in Figure 12.7 for the distributed University example, describe at least two strategies for each of the following queries. Estimate the data transfer cost for each strategy.

   a. Find the `className` and the `names` of all students enrolled in all classes with schedule 'MWF9'.

   b. Find the `classNumber`, `facId` of the teacher, and the campus of all classes being taken by Rosemary Hughes, who is a student at the North campus.

12.2   Consider the query "Find the `classNumber`, `schedule`, and `lastName` of all enrolled students for all classes being taught by Professor Smith of the North campus." The query is entered at the North campus.

   a. Describe a strategy that does not use the semijoin and estimate the data transfer cost of that strategy.

   b. Describe a semijoin strategy for the same query and estimate the data transfer cost.

12.3   For the distributed `Department`, `Faculty` schema described in Section 12.7.3:

   a. Consider the query "For each faculty member, print the `first name`, `last name`, and `department name`."

      i. Give two different strategies for processing this query without using a semijoin and the communications cost of each.

      ii. Give a strategy using a semijoin and the cost of this strategy.

   b. Consider the query "For each faculty member, print the `first name`, `last name`, `department name`, and `chairperson name`."

      i. Explain why this query is more complex than the previous one.

      ii. Devise an efficient strategy for executing this query and give the communications cost for it.

12.4 A database is to store listing information for a residential real estate agency that uses a multiple listing service. A multiple listing service is a cooperative service in which different real estate agencies agree to list and show one another's properties for sale, dividing the sales commission. People who wish to sell homes contact one of the agencies and register with only that agency. Properties to be offered for sale are visited by an agent (the listing agent) who collects information. Once listed, the property can be sold by any agent in any agency (the selling agent). However, when a binder (a declaration of a buyer's intention to purchase) and a deposit are placed on the property, no agent can show the property to another prospective buyer. If no contract follows within a month, or if the buyer retracts the bid, the property becomes available again. If the sale goes through and a contract is signed by all parties, the binder status and the listing status are marked as sold, and the contract date is recorded in the binder table. At the end of each month, the listing and binder information for all houses sold that month (i.e., for which contracts have been signed) are removed from their corresponding tables, and the information is put in the Sold table. Prospective buyers can register with only one agent. When the property is sold, the commission is divided between the listing agent and the selling agent, who can be the same person. The commission is always 10% of the selling price. Assume the following schema is used:

```
AgencySalesOffice(name, address, numberOfAgents, generalTelephone)
Agent(agentName, salesOfficeName, agentTelephone)
ActiveListing(address, type, style, size, askingPrice, dateListed,
  ownerName, ownerTelephone, lotSize, houseSize, numBedrooms, numBaths,
  numFloors, features, status, listingAgent)
Sold(address, type, style, size, askingPrice, dateListed, ownerName,
  ownerTelephone, lotSize, houseSize, numBedrooms, numBaths, numFloors,
  features, status, listingAgent, sellingAgent, buyerName, sellingPrice,
  dateOfContract)
ProspectiveBuyer(name, address, telephone, typeWanted, styleWanted,
  sizeWanted, bedroomsWanted, highestPrice, dateRegistered,
  specialRequests, agentName)
Binder(buyerName, listingAddress, sellingPrice, dateBid, dateAccepted,
  amountDeposit, status, dateCancelled, dateOfContract)
```

For simplicity, assume all names are unique. The attribute `features` in `ActiveListing` is a description of the property containing at most 100 characters. The `specialRequests` attribute in `ProspectiveBuyer` lists any special needs of the client.

a. Chose a data distribution plan for this data and justify your choice, using the criteria listed in Section 12.5.

b. Write a fragmentation schema as follows: Decide how the data should be fragmented to fit the distribution plan. Use relational algebra or SQL commands to create the fragments. For each fragment, identify the location(s) where it will be stored.

c. Explain how the following query would be answered: Find the names and addresses of all prospective buyers and their agents for a new listing. It is a residence (i.e., `type` = 'residence') colonial style, with four bedrooms and asking price of $800,000.

d. Explain how the following query would be answered: Find all the houses that are suitable to show a prospective buyer who is interested in a two-story residence with three bedrooms and two baths that cost under $500,000. For each house, show all the listing information, plus the name and telephone number of the listing agent.

e. Explain how the following query would be answered: For all houses sold last month for which Jane Hayward was the listing agent, find the name of the selling agent.

12.5 Assume a chain of computer stores that sells computers, components, and parts uses the following global schema for a relational database that keeps information about items at each store:

```
Item(itemNo, itemName, supplier, unitCost)
Store(storeName, address, manager, telephone)
Stock(itemNo, store, qtyOnHand, qtyOnOrder, reorderPoint)
```

The company has 20 stores that stock about 15,000 different items. Each item comes from only one supplier, but there are different suppliers for different items. The database keeps track of what items are in what store, what items have been reordered at each store, and the reorder point, which is the number of items that is the minimum each store wishes to keep in stock. When the quantity on hand falls to the reorder point, a new order is placed, unless the item has already been reordered. Each store serves customers in its own geographical area, but if an item is out of stock, the manager can obtain the item from another store. All information is currently stored in a central database. We wish to design a distributed system to make operations more efficient.

a. Choose a data distribution plan and justify your choice.

b. Write a fragmentation scheme, using relational algebra or SQL to create the fragments. For each fragment, identify the location(s) where it will be stored.

c. Explain how the following query would be answered: Find the total quantity of item number 1001 on hand in all stores.

d. If the number of bytes in each data item is 10, find the communications cost involved in the strategy you used for the query in (c).

e. Assume a customer at store A has requested a large quantity of an item that is out of stock in store A. Explain how the database will enable the manager of that store to locate stores that would provide enough items to fill the order, assuming no single store would have sufficient quantities to fill the entire order. Write the SQL or relational algebra query for the request.

f. Assuming each data item occupies 10 bytes, estimate the communications cost involved in the strategy you used for the query in (e), making assumptions as needed.

 On the Companion Website:

- Sample Project
- Student Projects

CHAPTER 13

Databases and the Internet

Chapter Objectives

In this chapter you will learn the following:

- Fundamental concepts and terminology for the World Wide Web

- The origins of the Internet and the World Wide Web

- Characteristics of HTTP

- Fundamentals of HTML and XML

- Characteristics of XML documents

- The structure of a DTD

- The structure of an XML Schema

- The characteristics of tiered architecture

- The functions of the data layer

- Fundamentals of web programming using PL/SQL

- Fundamentals of web programming using JDBC

- The characteristics and graphical representation of the semi-structured data model

- Some fundamental XML query operations

- Some methods used to convert between XML and relational database formats

13.1 Introduction

E-commerce is revolutionizing the way businesses interact with their customers, suppliers, and contractors. Organizations are developing web-based applications to create worldwide markets for their products, to deliver information, to provide cheaper and better customer service, to communicate with their suppliers, to provide training for employees, to expand the workplace, and to implement many other innovative activities. Increasingly, organizations are choosing to provide dynamic access to their databases directly from the Web. The Web itself can be viewed as a huge, loosely organized information resource whose potential is enormous. To cultivate and manage this resource requires a combination of communications technology, information retrieval technology, and database technology. There has been a rush to develop standards for providing and accessing data on the Internet, and many competing models have been proposed. XML has emerged as a robust standard for document storage, exchange, and retrieval that may lead to the integration of competing technologies. The XML standard for describing the content of documents facilitates the development of online applications, including e-commerce applications.

13.2   Fundamental Concepts of the Internet and the World Wide Web

In order to understand the technologies and standards used on the World Wide Web, some background information about the Internet is needed.

13.2.1 Origins of the World Wide Web

The terms **Internet** and **World Wide Web** are sometimes used interchangeably, but they actually have different meanings. The Internet predates the Web by a few decades. The Internet is a large network composed of smaller networks (internetwork). It developed from **Arpanet**, a communications network that was created in the 1960s using funds from the U.S. Department of Defense Advanced Research Project Agency (DARPA) for the purpose of linking government and academic research institutions. The network used a common protocol, **TCP/IP** (Transmission Control Protocol/Internet Protocol), to facilitate communications between sites. Later, the National Science Foundation took over the responsibility for managing the network, which was now referred to as the Internet. Although the Internet allowed access to resources at distant sites, it required considerable sophistication on the part of the user, who had to find the resources of interest, log on to the remote system containing them, navigate the directories of that system to find the desired files, copy the files to a local directory, and then display them correctly.

In 1989 Tim Berners-Lee proposed a method of simplifying access to resources that led to the development of the World Wide Web. His proposal included:

- A method to identify the location of resources, called a **Uniform Resource Locator (URL)**

- A standard protocol, Hypertext Transfer Protocol (**HTTP**), for transferring documents over the Internet

- A language, Hypertext Markup Language (**HTML**) that integrated instructions for displaying documents into the documents themselves

- **Hypertext**, a technique for using embedded links in documents to reference other resources

- A **graphical browser** that displayed content in a window, which could contain embedded links

Berners-Lee's proposal made it possible to automate the complicated process of finding, downloading, and displaying files on the Internet.

13.2.2 Browsers, Links, and URIs

When users access the Web using a browser such as Microsoft Internet Explorer, Mozilla Firefox, Google Chrome, or Apple Safari, they may type in the URL that identifies the site's web server. A URL is a specific type of **Uniform Resource Identifier (URI)**, which is a string that identifies the location of any type of resource on the Internet, including web pages, mailboxes, downloadable files, and so on. An example of a URI is `http://www.iona.edu/about.htm`. The first part identifies the protocol, `http`, that is to be used for accessing the resource. The next part, `www.iona.edu`, identifies the server where the resource is located. The last part, the path name, identifies the document, `about.htm`, to be accessed. The site may have a number of web pages, each of which has a corresponding root document that tells how the page is to be displayed. The pages may have links that contain the URLs of other resources. Clicking on links allows the user to visit the sites that contain those resources and display the information from them without typing in their URL.

13.2.3 HTTP

The Hypertext Transfer Protocol (HTTP) is the most widely used protocol on the Internet. A **communications protocol** is a set of standards for the structure of messages between parties. Using this protocol, a web browser, functioning as an HTTP client, first sends a request to an HTTP server. An HTTP request usually has a few lines of text, with an empty line at the end. An example is:

```
GET about.htm HTTP/1.1
Host: www.myComputer.1:80

User-agent: Mozilla/5.0
Accept: text/html, image/gif, image/jpeg
```

The first line, the request line, has three fields.

- The HTTP method field, which can be GET or POST; here it is GET
- The URI field, which gives the local path to and the name of the object to get or post; here it is `about.htm`. The local path is the part of the URL that follows the host name.

- The HTTP version field, which tells what version of the protocol the client is using; here it is 1.1

The second line, the host header, gives the host name and the HTTP port being used. It is followed by a blank line. The next line, the user agent line, shows the type of the client. The fourth line tells the types of files the client will accept. Both of these are optional.

After receiving such a request message, the server sends back an HTTP response message. The server retrieves the object requested (about.htm in this example), uses the page or resource to assemble the HTTP response message, and sends the message back to the client. It has several lines, including a status line, some header lines, and the body of the message, which usually contains the requested object. The status line is the first line. It gives the HTTP version, a status code, and a server message. For example, a status line such as,

```
HTTP/1.1 200 OK
```

means that the request was successful, (indicated by the status code of 200 and the message OK), and the requested object is in the body of the message that follows. Other status code values and corresponding messages indicate that the resource was not found, or that an error occurred. Common codes are 404, Not Found and 500, Server Error. Header lines can include information about the date and time of the response, the date the object was modified, the number of bytes in the content of the object, and the type of the content. The body of the message, which contains the actual object, follows the header lines. It usually contains HTML formatting information as well as the content.

If the user wanted to send a request message asking that the server run an application requiring input data, or to submit input data from an HTML form, the client request message would be a POST rather than a GET. For example,

```
POST /cgi-bin/CSServer/processStu HTTP/1.0
 . . .
stuId=S1099&credits=30
```

would request that the server run an application named processStu stored at the location indicated by the local path /cgi-bin/CSServer/, using the input values S1099 and 30. The response might be a message or an HTML page.

When the client browser gets the response message containing the requested object, it uses the HTML in the file to display the object properly. If the object contains links, it uses the HTTP protocol and the URIs to establish a connection with each resource to retrieve the associated objects.

HTTP is a **stateless** protocol. Each request message and its response are self-contained, with no facility for remembering previous interactions. This creates a problem in the context of e-commerce, which requires a continuous session with the user. The application must encode any state information either in the client or the server, not in the protocol.

13.2.4 HTML

HTML, Hypertext Markup Language, is a data format used for presenting content on the Internet. It is a **markup** language, so called because HTML documents contain marks or tags that provide formatting information for the text. Markup languages have been used for many years to specify the format of documents; for example, they specify what part of a document should be underlined, where to insert spaces, where a new paragraph should start, and so on. HTML tags are enclosed in angled brackets, < >. Most of the tags occur in pairs, having the form <*tag*> and </*tag*>. The first of the pair specifies where the special formatting is to start, and the second where it is to end. For example, <**B**> means bold, so that in,

```
The last word in this sentence is in <B> boldface</B>.
```

we can interpret the <B> to mean "turn on bolding" and </B> to mean "turn off bolding." An HTML document starts with the tag <**HTML**> and ends with </**HTML**>. The heading of a document can be enclosed in tags <**HEAD**> and </**HEAD**>, and the body can be enclosed in tags <**BODY**> and </**BODY**>. There are many other tags, but some of the most useful ones are:

- <UL> for unordered list, used to identify a list of items to follow

- <LI> for list item, used for each item on the list

- <H1> for Heading 1, which specifies that the usual format for a level-1 heading should be used

- <H2> through <H6>, for level 2 through level 6 headings

- <I> for italics

- <U> for underline

These tags all require an ending tag, but some tags, such as the one for a new paragraph, <P>, do not always require an ending tag.

Besides text, an HTML document can contain a wide variety of objects such as Java applets, audio files, images, video files, and others. When the document is retrieved by the user's browser, the text is displayed in accordance with the formatting commands, the applets are executed, the audio files play, the video is displayed, and so on, at the user's workstation. Figure 13.1(a) shows a sample HTML document, and Figure 13.1(b) shows the result when the document is opened in a browser.

13.2.5 XML

Although HTML works well for displaying text, it uses a limited set of tags with fixed meanings, making it relatively inflexible. In the example shown in Figure 13.1, we can infer the meanings of the items, but the document does not describe them. HTML is an application of a more powerful and general language, Standard Generalized Markup Language (**SGML**). SGML is actually a meta-language that allows users to define their own markup languages. However, SGML is quite complex. A simpler language based on SGML and HTML, called **XML** (Extensible Markup Language), was created in 1996 by the World Wide Web Consortium XML Special Interest Group. The objective was to retain the flexibility of SGML and the simplicity of HTML. XML also allows users to define their own markup language. For example, users can create tags that describe the data items in a document. The database community has a great interest in XML as a means of describing documents of all types, including databases. Using XML, it is possible to define the structure of heterogeneous databases, facilitating translation of data between different databases.

Standalone XML Documents

Figure 13.2 shows an example of an XML document. An XML document usually begins with an optional **declaration** that identifies the XML version used for the document, and, optionally, the coding system used, and/or whether the document has an external document type definition

FIGURE 13.1(a)

HTML Document Showing a Customer List

```
<HTML>
<HEAD>
<TITLE>Customer List</TITLE>
</HEAD>
<BODY>
<H2>Corporate Customer List</H2>
<UL>
        <LI> WorldWide Travel Agency</LI>
        <LI> 10 Main Street, New York, NY 10001</LI>
        <LI> 212 123 4567</LI>
</UL>
<H2>Individual Customer List</H2>
<UL>
        <LI> Mary Jones</LI>
        <LI> 25 Spruce Street, San Diego, CA 92101</LI>
        <LI> 619 555 6789</LI>
</UL>
<UL>
        <LI> Alice Adams</LI>
        <LI> 25 Orange Blossom Street, Miami, FL 60601</LI>
        <LI> 305 987 6543</LI>
</UL>
</BODY>
</HTML>
```

Figure 13.1(b)

Customer List Document Shown in a Browser

Corporate Customer List
- WorldWide Travel Agency
- 10 Main Street, New York, NY 10001
- 212 123 4567

Individual Customer List
- Mary Jones
- 25 Spruce Street, San Diego, CA 92101
- 619 555 6789

- Alice Adams
- 25 Orange Blossom Street, Miami, FL 60601
- 305 987 6543

FIGURE 13.2

XML Instance Document Showing Customer List

```xml
<?xml version="1.0" encoding="UTF–8" standalone="yes"?>
<CUSTOMERLIST>
<CUSTOMER TYPE="Corporate" STATUS="Active">
        <NAME>WorldWide Travel Agency</NAME>
        <ADDRESS>
        <STREET>10 Main Street</STREET>
        <CITY>New York</CITY>
        <STATE>NY</STATE>
        <ZIP>10001</ZIP>
        </ADDRESS>
        <TELEPHONE>
        <AREACODE>212</AREACODE>
        <PHONE>123 4567</PHONE>
        </TELEPHONE>
</CUSTOMER>
<CUSTOMER TYPE="Individual"> <!--start of individual customers-->
        <NAME>Mary Jones</NAME>
        <ADDRESS>
        <STREET>25 Spruce Street</STREET>
        <CITY>San Diego</CITY>
        <STATE>CA</STATE>
        <ZIP>92101</ZIP>
        </ADDRESS>
        <TELEPHONE>
        <AREACODE>619</AREACODE>
        <PHONE>555 6789</PHONE>
        </TELEPHONE>
</CUSTOMER>
<CUSTOMER TYPE="Individual" STATUS="Inactive">
        <NAME>Alice Adams</NAME>
        <ADDRESS>
        <STREET>25 Orange Blossom Street</STREET>
        <CITY>Miami</CITY>
        <STATE>FL</STATE>
        <ZIP>60601</ZIP>
        </ADDRESS>
        <TELEPHONE>
        <AREACODE>305</AREACODE>
        <PHONE>987 6543</PHONE>
        </TELEPHONE>
</CUSTOMER>
</CUSTOMERLIST>
```

(DTD) or not. A DTD is a specification for the structure of an XML document and will be described in the next section. The most common coding system for XML documents is Unicode, identified by UTF-8. A document without an external DTD is described as "standalone." An example of a declaration for a standalone document is:

```
<?xml version="1.0" encoding="UTF-8" standalone="yes"?>
```

If there is an external DTD, the name of the file containing the DTD appears on the second line, as in:

```
<?xml version="1.0" encoding="UTF-8"?>
<!DOCTYPE CUSTOMERLIST SYSTEM "C:\BOOK\EXAMPLES\CUSTOMERLIST.DTD">
```

The declaration is followed by one or more XML **elements**, each of which has a **start tag** showing the name of the element, some **character data**, and an **end tag**. XML is case-sensitive. An element is the basic component of an XML document. Elements can be subelements of other elements. Elements must be properly nested, so that if an element's start tag appears inside the body of another element, its end tag must also appear before the end tag of the enclosing element. The first element in the DTD must be a single root element, in which every other element is nested. Figure 13.2 shows the root element CUSTOMERLIST, which contains all the information about customers. Within this element, the element CUSTOMER gives all the information about one customer. An element can also be empty, which can be indicated using the self-terminating tag:

```
<EMPTYELEMENT/>.
```

Elements can have **attributes** whose names and values are shown inside the element's start tag. Note that CUSTOMER has an attribute named `type` whose values appear as either "Corporate" or "Individual," and an attribute named `status` whose values appear as "Active" or "Inactive." The attribute values are shown in quotes. The designer has a choice of whether to represent data using an element or an attribute. Attributes occur only once within each element, while subelements can occur any number of times.

We can insert **comments** wherever we wish in the document. A comment starts with <!-- and ends with -->, and can contain any explanatory text, except the string --, as shown in Figure 13.2 for the second customer.

We can refer to external files, common text, Unicode characters, or some reserved symbols by using an **entity reference**. The reference begins with the ampersand character, &, and ends with a semicolon, ;. When the document is displayed in a browser, the reference will be replaced by its content. To include reserved symbols that have special meaning in XML, it is necessary to use the **&. . .;** as an **escape sequence**. These predefined entities are &, <, >, ' and ", which we refer to by their mnemonic names `amp`, `lt`, `gt`, `apos`, and `quot`. For example, to indicate the string,

```
X<1
```

we would write

```
x&lt;1
```

and to write

```
value>'a'&value<'z'
```

we would write:

```
value&gt;&apos;a&apos;&amp;value&lt;&apos;z&apos;
```

References are also used to insert Unicode characters in the text. For example, to insert the symbol © we write `&00A9;` since the Unicode character for © is 00A9.

An XML document, such as the one shown in Figure 13.2, is said to be **well formed** if it obeys the rules of XML. It must conform to the following guidelines:

- It starts with an XML declaration like the one shown in the first line of Figure 13.2.

- It has a root element that contains all the other elements, such as the element CUSTOMERLIST in Figure 13.2.

- All elements are properly nested. If the start tag of an element occurs within another element, the end tag occurs within the element as well. For example, each NAME element is nested within the CUSTOMER element.

DTDs

Users can define their own markup language by writing a **Document Type Declaration (DTD)** or by writing an **XML Schema**. Domain-specific DTDs have been developed for a number of fields. They allow seamless data exchange between documents with the same DTD. For example

MathML, Mathematics Markup Language, is a widely-used DTD for documents in mathematics, specifying both the display of equations and the meaning of mathematical expressions. Although DTDs are still used for specialized fields, XML schemas have largely replaced them for many applications. A DTD is a specification for a set of rules for the elements, attributes, and entities of a document. A document, which we will now refer to as an instance document as opposed to a DTD, that obeys the rules of its associated DTD is said to be **type-valid**. Processors can validate XML instance documents by checking their DTDs. Several instance documents can share the same DTD. Figure 13.3 shows a sample DTD that describes the structure of the instance document CUSTOMERLIST. A DTD must obey these rules:

- The DTD is enclosed in <!DOCTYPE *name[DTDdeclaration]>*

- *name* is the name of the outermost enclosing tag, which is CUSTOMERLIST in our example.

- The *DTDdeclaration,* which is enclosed in square brackets, gives the rules for documents that use this DTD.

- Each **element** is declared using a type declaration with the structure <!ELEMENT *(content type)>* where the content type can be

FIGURE 13.3

Possible DTD for CUSTOMERLIST Document

```
<!DOCTYPE CUSTOMERLIST [
    <!ELEMENT CUSTOMERLIST (CUSTOMER*)>
        <!ELEMENT CUSTOMER (NAME,ADDRESS+,TELEPHONE?)>
            <!ELEMENT NAME (#PCDATA)>
            <!ELEMENT ADDRESS (STREET,CITY,STATE,ZIP)>
                <!ELEMENT STREET (#PCDATA)>
                <!ELEMENT CITY (#PCDATA)>
                <!ELEMENT STATE (#PCDATA)>
                <!ELEMENT ZIP (#PCDATA)>
            <!ELEMENT TELEPHONE (AREACODE,PHONE)>
                <!ELEMENT AREACODE (#PCDATA)>
                <!ELEMENT PHONE (#PCDATA)>
    <!ATTLIST CUSTOMER TYPE (Corporate|Individual) #REQUIRED>
    <!ATTLIST CUSTOMER STATUS (Active|Inactive) "Active">
]>
```

- Other elements that are subelements of the declared element. In Figure 13.3 the element CUSTOMERLIST has subelement CUSTOMER, the element CUSTOMER has subelements NAME, ADDRESS, and TELEPHONE, and both ADDRESS and TELEPHONE in turn have subelements.

- #PCDATA, which means the element value consists of parsed character data. In Figure 13.3, the element NAME has this content type, as do STREET, CITY, STATE, ZIP, AREACODE, and PHONE.

- The empty element, indicated by <EMPTYELEMENT/>.

- The symbol ANY, which means any content is permitted.

- A regular expression that is constructed from these four choices.

- In an element declaration, the name of any subelement can optionally be followed by one of the symbols *, +, or ?, to indicate the number of times the subelement occurs within its enclosing element. The meanings are:

  * The element occurs zero or more times. In Figure 13.3, CUSTOMER elements can occur zero or more times, indicating that a CUSTOMERLIST could have no customers, or many.

  + The element occurs one or more times. In Figure 13.3, ADDRESS can occur one or more times for each customer.

  ? The element occurs zero or one times. In Figure 13.3, TELEPHONE occurs zero or one time for each customer.

- **Attribute** list declarations for elements are declared outside the element. They specify which elements have attributes, the name of each attribute, the data type, possible values (optional), whether the attribute is required, and default value, if any. They have the form <!ATTLIST elementName attName (attType)default>. Several attribute types exist, including string types and enumerated types. String type is declared as **CDATA**. An enumerated type is shown by listing all its possible values. An attribute declaration can also have a default specification. A required attribute is identified by writing #REQUIRED. If the attribute is not required, a default value may appear. The default value will be provided when no other value is specified for the attribute. In Figure 13.3, the

CUSTOMER element has two attributes, TYPE and STATUS. The TYPE attribute is an enumerated type having possible values Corporate and Individual. It is a required attribute. The STATUS attribute has possible values Active and Inactive, with Active being the default. It is not required.

A DTD can be **external**, which means it is stored separately from the instance documents that use it, or **internal**, embedded in the instance document. For the example shown in Figure 13.2 and Figure 13.3, the internal format would be

```
<?xml version="1.0" encoding="UTF-8"?>
<!DOCTYPE CUSTOMERLIST[
. . .
]>
<CUSTOMERLIST>
<CUSTOMER type="Corporate" status="Active">
. . .
</CUSTOMERLIST>
```

An external DTD can be used to specify the structure of many instance documents. Each document instance that uses an external DTD must contain a declaration identifying it, by giving its name and storage location. For the instance document in Figure 13.2, the format could be

```
<?xml version="1.0" encoding="UTF-8"?>
<!DOCTYPE CUSTOMERLIST SYSTEM "customerlist.dtd">
<CUSTOMERLIST>
<CUSTOMER type="Corporate" status="Active">
. . .
</CUSTOMERLIST>
```

When the instance document is opened in a browser, the user is given the option to see the source code for the DTD.

XML Schemas

XML Schema is a more powerful way to describe the structure of documents than DTDs. It permits more complex structure, additional fundamental data types, user-defined data types, user-created domain vocabulary (namespaces), and also supports uniqueness and foreign key constraints. An XML schema defines the organization and data types of an XML structure.

If an instance document conforms to an XML schema, it is called **schema-valid**. XML schemas are themselves XML documents, and can be schema-validated against the standards provided by the World Wide Web Consortium, W3C, as specified at www.w3.org. This site contains an XML standard schema document for all user-defined XML schema documents. There are several sites that can validate schemas, allowing users to upload documents to ensure that they are valid. XML schema is a very large topic, and a comprehensive treatment of it is beyond the scope of this book, but a brief introduction to provide the basic flavor of it follows.

A simple XML schema is shown in Figure 13.4. Like a DTD, an XML schema lists elements and attributes. Elements may be complex, which means they have subelements, or simple. In Figure 13.4 the element CustomerList is of complex type, consisting of any number of Customer elements. Customer is also a complex type element, consisting of Name, Address, and Telephone. Name is a simple element of string type. Address is a complex type consisting of the simple string-type elements Street, City, State, and Zip. Telephone is a complex type consisting of the simple string type elements AreaCode and Phone. Customer has two attributes, Type and Status. Type is a required attribute that is an enumerated type. Its base type is string and its possible values are "Corporate" or "Individual." Status is a string type with default value of "Active."

Attributes or elements can be used to store data values. Attributes can be used for simple values that are not repeated, such as Type and Status. Elements can be complex or simple, and can occur multiple times. Type and Status could be represented as elements instead of attributes, as shown in Figure 13.5.

13.3 Tiered Architectures

For data-intensive applications, we can identify three major functions that are required in an Internet environment: presentation, application logic, and data management. The placement of these functions depends on the architecture of the system.

13.3.1 Single-Tier Architecture

Initially, databases were created in a centralized mainframe environment, accessed by batch processes from dumb terminals. The database itself

FIGURE 13.4

Possible XML Schema
for CustomerList

```
<xsd:schema xmlns:xsd="http://www.w3.org/2001/XMLSchema">
<xsd:element name ="CustomerList">
 <xsd:sequence>
   <xsd:element name="Customer" minoccurs="0" maxoccurs="unbounded">
      <xsd:complexType>
         <xsd:sequence>
            <xsd:element name="Name" type="xsd:string"/>
            <xsd:element name="Address" minoccurs="1" maxoccurs="unbounded">
               <xsd:complexType>
                  <xsd:sequence>
                     <xsd:element name="Street" type="xsd:string"/>
                     <xsd:element name="City" type="xsd:string"/>
                     <xsd:element name="State" type="xsd:string"/>
                     <xsd:element name="Zip" type="xsd:string"/>
                  </xsd:sequence>
               </xsd:complexType>
            </xsd:element>
            <xsd:element name="Telephone" minoccurs="0" maxoccurs="unbounded">
               <xsd:complexType>
                  <xsd:sequence>
                     <xsd:element name="AreaCode" type="xsd:string"/>
                     <xsd:element name="Phone" type="xsd:string"/>
                  </xsd:sequence>
               </xsd:complexType>
            </xsd:element>
         </xsd:sequence>
         <xsd:attribute name="Type" use="required">
            <xsd:simpleType>
               <xsd:restriction base="xsd:string">
                  <xsd:enumeration value="Corporate"/>
                  <xsd:enumeration value="Individual"/>
               </xsd:restriction>
            </xsd:simpleType>
         </xsd:attribute>
         <xsd:attribute name="Status" type="xsd:string" default="Active"/>
      </xsd:complexType>
   </xsd:element>
 </xsd:sequence>
</xsd:element>
</xsd:schema>
```

FIGURE 13.5

Another XML Schema
for CustomerList

```
<xsd:schema xmlns:xsd="http://www.w3.org/2001/XMLSchema">
 <xsd:element name ="CustomerList">
  <xsd:sequence>
   <xsd:element name="Customer" minoccurs="0" maxoccurs="unbounded">
    <xsd:complexType>
     <xsd:sequence>
      <xsd:element name="Name" type="xsd:string"/>
      <xsd:element name="Address" minoccurs="1" maxoccurs="unbounded">
       <xsd:complexType>
        <xsd:sequence>
         <xsd:element name="Street" type="xsd:string"/>
         <xsd:element name="City" type="xsd:string"/>
         <xsd:element name="State" type="xsd:string"/>
         <xsd:element name="Zip" type="xsd:string"/>
        </xsd:sequence>
       </xsd:complexType>
      </xsd:element>
      <xsd:element name="Telephone" minoccurs="0" maxoccurs="unbounded">
       <xsd:complexType>
        <xsd:sequence>
         <xsd:element name="AreaCode" type="xsd:string"/>
         <xsd:element name="Phone" type="xsd:string"/>
        </xsd:sequence>
       </xsd:complexType>
      </xsd:element>
      <xsd:element name="Type" type="xsd:string"/>
      <xsd:element name="Status" type="xsd:string"/>
     </xsd:sequence>
    </xsd:complexType>
   </xsd:element>
  </xsd:sequence>
 </xsd:element>
</xsd:schema>
```

FIGURE 13.6(a)

Single-tier Architecture

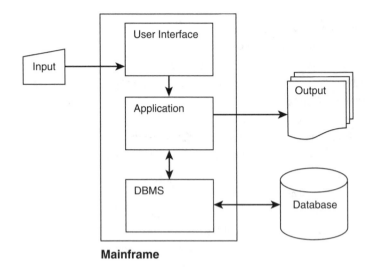

Mainframe

FIGURE 13.6(b)

Two-tier Architecture for
Thin Clients

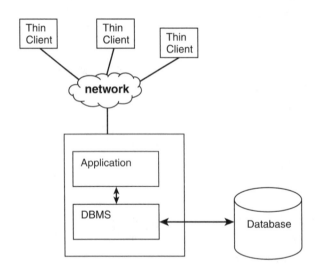

resided on secondary storage, and the database management system, the application, and the user interface all resided on a single computer, as illustrated in Figure 13.6(a)

13.3.2 Two-Tier Architecture

As PCs became cheaper and more widely used, two-tier architecture developed. In this architecture, the user's workstation or other device functions as a client, and the database management system resides on a server. The two systems interact using a networking protocol. If the client provides only the user interface, and the server runs the application as well as han-

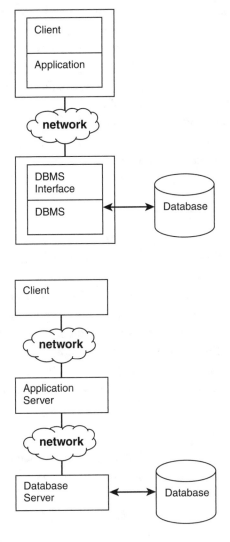

FIGURE 13.6(c)
Two-tier Architecture for Thick Clients

FIGURE 13.6(d)
Three-tier Architecture

dling data access, the client functions as a **thin client**. This architecture, which is illustrated in Figure 13.6(b), is typical when simple devices such as PDAs or cell phones are used as clients.

If the client takes on some of the application processing as well as handling the user interface, it functions as a **thick** or **fat client**, as shown in Figure 13.6(c). PCs and workstations can function as thick clients in two-tier architecture, because they provide the needed processing power and storage. The server handles tasks such as validation as well as data access.

Several problems arise in this environment. The first is a problem of scalability, because the server is unable to handle a large number of clients simultaneously. The number of independent connections to the database is limited. Second, since the application logic is handled primarily by the client, the server has to trust that the application code will not damage the database. The applications themselves have to include transaction management routines, including exception handling and rollback if needed. The trust problem can be addressed by requiring registration of programs with the server. The server will then reject any unregistered applications. The third problem is that there may be a large number of clients running applications, and there is no central place to maintain business logic.

13.3.3 Three-Tier Architecture

Three-tier architectures completely separate application logic from data management. The client handles the user interface, which is called the **presentation layer** or the first tier. The interface can be web-based. A separate **application server** executes the application logic and forms the **middle tier**. The database server, which runs the DBMS and handles the data access, forms the third tier. The communications network connects each tier to the next one. This layered architecture is similar to the layering found in communications protocols and other fields, and its purpose is to support standardization among vendors and provide flexibility. The three-tier architecture allows:

- Support for thin clients, because clients need only handle the presentation layer

- Independence of tiers. Each tier can use whatever platform or software is best suited to its environment. Well-defined APIs can be used to standardize and control the interactions between layers. Code at any tier can be modified independently without affecting the other tiers.

- Easier application maintenance, because the application server is a central location where most business logic is stored

- Integrated data access, because data from several heterogeneous databases can be handled by the middle layer in a fashion that is transparent to the client

- Scalability, because the middle tier can share database connections with many clients simultaneously

The Presentation Layer

At the first tier, a user-friendly interface that is suitable for the device must be presented. At this layer, the user typically sees forms through which he or she issues requests and sees responses to those requests. HTML forms are often used for this purpose. Script code in JavaScript, JScript, VBScript, and similar **scripting languages** can be embedded in the HTML to provide some simple client-side processing. **Style sheets** that specify how data is presented on specific devices may also be used.

HTML forms can be used to pass input values from the client to the middle tier. The user's browser displays a web page containing a form with input fields, text areas, drop-down lists, and other objects in which the user can enter input data. An HTML document can contain multiple forms. Each form can have any HTML tags except another FORM tag. The HTML code for a simple sign-on form is shown in Figure 13.7. The HTML for a form begins with a FORM tag, and has the general format

```
<FORM ACTION=''applicationURL'' METHOD=''GET'' NAME=''formName''>
<INPUT TYPE=''inputType'' SIZE=size NAME=''name'' VALUE=''value''>
. . .
</FORM>
```

A FORM tag has the following fields:

- ACTION—gives the URI of the application that will process the input provided on the form. It is a relative reference that specifies

```
<FORM ACTION="/cgi-bin/signon.cgi" METHOD="GET" NAME="UserLogin"
    <P>
    User ID:<INPUT TYPE="text" SIZE=20 NAME="userID">
    <P>
    Password:<INPUT TYPE="password" SIZE=20 NAME="password">
    <P>
    <INPUT TYPE="submit" VALUE="Log on">
    <INPUT TYPE="reset" VALUE="Clear">
<FORM>
```

FIGURE 13.7
A Simple HTML Form

the directory and the program to be executed. If no directory is specified, it uses the URI of the current page.

- METHOD—specifies the method used to submit input from the filled-in form to the server. Possible values are GET or POST. A GET method sends the program name and the input information from the form in a single step. With a POST method the program name is part of the URL, and the input information is transmitted in a separate message.

- NAME—optionally allows the form to be given a name, so that programs can refer to the form and its fields by name.

Forms can include INPUT, SELECT, and TEXTAREA tags that specify user input objects. The INPUT tag has no terminating tag. Input tag attributes include TYPE, SIZE, NAME, and VALUE. TYPE specifies the type of the input field. If the type is text, the input box appears as a blank rectangle of the size specified in SIZE where the user can type in text. If the type is password, the characters entered will be obscured to protect the password. If the type is reset, a labeled button will appear. If the user presses that button, all input fields in the form will be reset to their defaults. If the type is submit, a labeled button appears that sends values of all input fields to the server when the user presses it. The NAME provides a name for the field to identify the field contents to the server. The name must be provided for all input types except submit and reset. VALUE is an optional field that can be used to specify the default value of an input field. It is also used to provide a label for the button for submit or reset.

User input can also come from TEXTAREA and SELECT tags in a manner similar to INPUT tags.

The URI that appears in the ACTION attribute of the FORM tag must be that of an application, page, or script. If the method is GET, the action and each input area name and value are concatenated into a request URI having the form:

action?inputName1=inputValue1&inputName2=inputValue2&inputName3=inputValue3

For example, for the form shown in Figure 13.7, if the user entered the name Adam Adams and the password sesame, the request URI would be:

```
http://localhost/cgi-bin/signon.cgi?userID=Adam+Adams&password=sesame
```

Note that blanks are replaced by + and names are connected to their values by =. Any special characters are encoded using the form %xxx, where xxx is the ASCII value for the character.

Scripting Languages Scripting languages including JavaScript, JScript, and VBScript can be used to add simple programs that run at the client tier. Scripts are identified by a SCRIPT tag embedded in an HTML document. Its form is:

```
<SCRIPT LANGUAGE="scriptLanguageName" SRC="externalFileName"></SCRIPT>
```

The LANGUAGE attribute gives the name of the scripting language, such as "JavaScript." The SCR attribute gives the name of the external file with the script code, such as "checkForm.js." The code is automatically embedded in the HTML document. Scripts are used at the client for processes such as checking the validity of data that the user has entered in the form, identifying the type of browser the client is running, and controlling some browser functions.

Style Sheets: CSS and XSL Style sheets contain instructions that tell a web browser or other display controller how to present data in a manner that is suitable for the client's display. For example, the same web page can be rendered slightly differently by Netscape and Explorer, and considerably different by a cellphone or PDA display. The style sheet dictates how fonts, colors, margins, and placement of windows are tailored for the specific device.

Cascading Style Sheets (CSS) can be used with HTML documents. The same style sheet can be used for many documents, allowing web designers to apply a design template to all the pages at a given site, if the organization wishes to have a uniform look to the pages. A link to the style sheet can be included in the HTML document by writing a link tag having the form:

```
<LINK REL="StyleSheet" HREF="nameOfStyleSheet">
```

The style sheet itself consists of a set of specifications for properties of the document, such as colors, fonts, spacing, and so on. Each specification is given by a line of the style sheet having the form:

```
Attribute {property: value}
```

For example, to set a font size and color for the level-one headings, we would write in CSS:

```
H1 {FONT-SIZE: 24pt; COLOR: blue}
```

Then an HTML document that uses the style sheet would replace any H1 tags with the specifications given in the style sheet.

The Extensible Stylesheet Language (XSL) is a language for writing style sheets for XML files. XSL files contain specifications of attributes that control the display of XML documents in a manner similar to the way CSS controls HTML displays. It is a much more powerful language than CSS, allowing the structure of documents to be changed using XSL Transformation Language (XSLT), allowing parts of the documents to be referenced using XML Path Language (XPath), and formatting objects for display.

The Middle Tier

The application server at the middle tier is responsible for executing applications. This tier determines the flow of control, acquires input data from the presentation layer, makes data requests to the database server, accepts query results from the database layer, and uses them to assemble dynamically generated HTML pages.

CGI (Common Gateway Interface) can be used to connect HTML forms with application programs. This protocol defines how inputs from forms are passed to programs executing at the middle tier. Programs that use this protocol are called **CGI scripts**, and are often written in Perl. A typical Perl script extracts the input arguments from the HTML form, and constructs as output from the program a dynamically constructed web page that it sends to the browser.

It is possible for each page request to start up a new process on the server, but this limits the number of simultaneous requests that can be handled. Instead, an application server maintains a pool of threads and uses these to execute requests, avoiding the overhead of creating a new process for each request. They allow concurrent access to several data sources. The application server also manages sessions, detecting when a session starts, identifying which sessions belong to which users, and detecting when a session ends. To identify a session, the server can use cookies, hidden fields in HTML forms, and URI extensions. A **cookie** is a small text string that the server sends to the user's browser when the browser connects to it. It is essentially a session identifier that is stored in the memory of the browser and remains stored after the connection ends. Whenever the user reconnects to the server, the browser returns a copy of the cookie to the server, thereby establishing that the user is the same as for the previous session. Cookies are therefore used to store user information between sessions.

A major job of the application server is to **maintain state**, since HTTP is a stateless protocol. Any multi-step transaction that requires several interactions with a user requires that the state of the transaction be maintained. In a typical e-commerce transaction, the user will sign in, view products recommended for purchase based on his or her interests, browse through the site's offerings, place items in a shopping basket, modify the shopping basket several times, and then move on to the purchase. At that time, the shopper has to enter the shipping name and address, enter or confirm his or her own name and address, provide a credit card number and expiration date, and request any special services such as gift wrapping, express shipping, and so on. The final total, including any tax and extra charges, must be calculated and displayed, and the shopper must agree to the amount before the purchase is complete. A confirmation message is then sent back to the shopper. These steps require that the state of the transaction be maintained. Since HTTP is a stateless protocol, either the client or the server must be able to maintain state. On the client side, cookies are used for this purpose. Cookies are easily generated at the middle tier using Java's Cookie class and sent to the client, where they can be stored in the browser cache. The client's browser sends the cookie to the server with each request. A problem with this solution is that users might refuse to accept cookies, or might clean up the browser cache before the cookie expires, erasing the cookie. State could also be maintained in the database itself, but all queries or updates to the state, such as signing in or modifying the shopping basket, would require a database access. This solution is best used for relatively permanent information such as past orders, customer name and address, customer preferences, and so on. It is also possible to maintain state at the middle tier, using local files at that level.

Server-side processing can use many different technologies such as ASP, PHP, Java servlets, JavaServer pages, Server-Side Java Script, Python, or others. Java servlets are Java programs that implement the Servlet interface. They can use the HttpServlet class, which provides methods for receiving input from HTML forms and for constructing dynamic web pages from the program results. Both the request and the response are passed as servlet parameters. Servlets have all the functionality of standard Java programs, allowing them to implement complicated transactions involving the database. Because they are Java programs, they are platform independent, and they run in containers. They can access all APIs including JDBC. They run on the middle tier, either in a web server or an application server.

JavaServer pages are written in HTML but contain special tags that allow some servlet-type code, using JavaScript. JavaScript is a full-featured programming language that can be embedded in HTML. JavaServer pages do not usually support complex applications, but are used for building user interfaces. However, they are executed like servlets.

13.4   Web Programming with Oracle

There are several ways users can be provided with dynamic access to an Oracle database. Two methods using PL/SQL are the PL/SQL Web Toolkit, which allows programmers to implement all three layers of a web application using PL/SQL, and PL/SQL Server Pages (PSP), which allows programmers to embed PL/SQL code in HTML pages. A third method, using JDBC, will be discussed in Section 13.5.

13.4.1   PL/SQL Web Toolkit

Figure 13.8 provides an overview of the process of accessing an Oracle database from a web page using the Web Toolkit. The steps are

1. Using a browser on a client computer, the user follows a link on a web page or fills in an HTML form, which sends a request to a web server, possibly passing input values.

2. The server sends a message to the database server, invoking a PL/SQL stored procedure in the Oracle database, passing parameters as needed.

3. The stored procedure invokes subprograms in the PL/SQL Web Toolkit, which generate a web page dynamically.

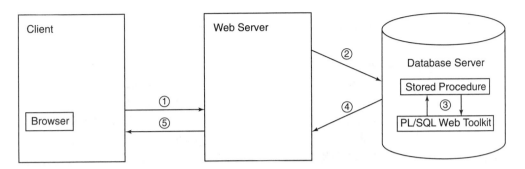

Figure 13.8
Using PL/SQL Web Toolkit

4. The generated page is passed to the web server.

5. The Web server displays the page on the client's browser.

For submitting requests, it may be necessary to first find the local host name and IP address of the database server. These can be obtained using the PL/SQL anonymous procedure shown in Figure 13.9, which the user can enter and execute at the database site using the standard method for a PL/SQL procedure. If the client and the server are on the same machine, "localhost" may be used in place of the actual address in requests.

The Web Toolkit has packages to perform various tasks for producing a dynamic web page. One of the most commonly used is the .htp package, which has functions that generate HTML tags, as illustrated in Figure 13.10(a). This procedure can be written and compiled in SQL*Plus and stored in the database space like any other stored PL/SQL procedure. As described earlier, it is invoked within a browser, which passes the URL for the procedure to the Web server. When the procedure is called, it generates the HTML indicated in the comments, as shown in Figure 13.10(b), which in turn displays a page as shown in Figure 13.10(c) in the user's browser.

```
SET serveroutput on
BEGIN
  DBMS_OUTPUT.PUT_LINE(UTL_INADDR.GET_HOST_NAME); -- gets local host name
  DBMS_OUTPUT.PUT_LINE(UTL_INADDR.GET_HOST_ADDRESS); -- gets local IP addr
END;
/
```

Figure 13.9
PL/SQL Procedure to Get Name and Address of Local Host

On the Companion Website:
- Code for Examples

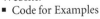

Figure 13.10(a)
PL/SQL Procedure to Produce HTML Tags

```
CREATE OR REPLACE PROCEDURE example_page
IS
BEGIN
  HTP.HTMLOPEN;                        -- produces <HTML>
  HTP.HEADOPEN;                        -- produces <HEAD>
  HTP.TITLE('Customer Report');        -- produces <TITLE>Customer Report</TITLE>
  HTP.HEADCLOSE;                       -- produces </HEAD>
  HTP.BODYOPEN;                        -- produces <BODY>
  HTP.HEADER(1,'Customer Name');       -- produces <H1>Customer Name</H1>
  HTP.PARA;                            -- produces <P>
  HTP.PRINT('Line of text ');          -- will print Line of text
  HTP.BODYCLOSE;                       -- produces </BODY>
  HTP.HTMLCLOSE;                       -- produces </HTML>
END;
```

Figure 13.10(b)
HTML Produced by HTP Package

```
<HTML>
<HEAD>
<TITLE>Customer Report</TITLE>
</HEAD>
<BODY>
<H1>Customer Name</H1>
<P>
Line of text
</BODY>
</HTML>
```

Figure 13.10(c)
Contents of Web page Produced by HTML

Customer Name
Line of text

Instead of the simple header and line of text shown in Figure 13.10(c), most database applications display forms in which the user can choose menu options, provide input values for the application, or display results. Values for these options must be passed as parameters to the PL/SQL application, using either HTML form tags or coded into the URL. First the form must be created, using the formOpen procedure, which has the syntax shown in Figure 13.11(a). The corresponding HTML tag is shown in Figure 13.11(b). Within an application, after the `htp.bodyopen` line you might open a form with the command

```
htp.FormOpen(owa_util.get_owa_service_path||'process_user_option')
```

The `owa_util.get_owa_service_path` function dynamically determines the virtual path to the PL/SQL gateway for the request, which makes the code more portable. When the user chooses one of the options on the form and submits the form, the procedure named, `process_user_option` in this case, is invoked. An HTML form contains elements such as list boxes, drop-down lists, radio buttons, text fields, and submit buttons to provide the user choices. PL/SQL uses several htp procedures to create forms that contain these elements, including htp.formText, htp.formCheckbox, htp.formRadio, htp.formTextarea, and others. Figure 13.11(c) provides an example for a drop-down list element that could appear in a form. The application should validate the values entered, checking that they have the correct format, that they are in range, and so forth, displaying appropriate messages to the user. To transmit the data from a form, the htp.formSubmit procedure with syntax shown in Figure 13.11(d) must be added. This procedure creates a button with no name and a default label of 'Submit', unless the user chooses to provide a name and a different label for the button, as in

```
formSubmit(option2, 'Add Student');
```

The form must be closed using the procedure htp.formClose, also shown in Figure 13.11(d), which produces the HTML </FORM> tag. This line should appear before the `htp.bodyclose` line. Details of the required syntax for all these procedures can be found in the online Oracle documentation for the Web Toolkit.

13.4.2 PL/SQL Server Pages (PSP)

While the Web Toolkit provides a way to generate dynamic web pages, it can be time-consuming to use htp procedures and functions to create pages most of whose content could be more easily created using HTML

Figure 13.11(a)
htp formOpen Procedure Syntax

```
htp.formOpen (
    curl          in     varchar2,
    cmethod       in     varchar2  DEFAULT 'POST',
    ctarget       in     varchar2  DEFAULT NULL,
    cenctype      in     varchar2  DEFAULT NULL,
    cattributes   in     varchar2  DEFAULT NULL);
```

Figure 13.11(b)
HTML Tag for formOpen Procedure

```
<FORM ACTION="curl" METHOD="cmethod" TARGET="ctarget"
ENCTYPE="cenctype" cattributes>
```

Figure 13.11(c)
Example of Using htp to Create a Drop-down List in a Form

```
htp.formSelectOpen('Choose color','Choose your favorite color:')

htp.formSelectOption('red');
htp.formSelectOption('blue');
htp.formSelectOption('green');

htp.formSelectClose;
```

Figure 13.11(d)
htp formSubmit and formClose Procedures

```
htp.formSubmit (
    cname         in     varchar2  DEFAULT NULL,
    cvalue        in     varchar2  DEFAULT 'Submit',
    cattributes   in     varchar2  DEFAULT NULL);

htp.formClose;
```

directly. PSP allows programmers to embed PL/SQL statements in HTML pages, so that the HTML script can be written directly as if for a static page and then PL/SQL commands can be added later to provide the dynamic database content, using the delimiters <% and %> to identify them. The resulting pages, called PSP pages, are handled by the Oracle PL/SQL Web gateway (mod_plsql) and reside on the server side. Programmers can also add Web Toolkit calls in the same application. Figure 13.12 shows a PSP script to print the names of students in the Student table. The PSP page is loaded into the Oracle database space using a utility program called loadpsp, which is found in the $ORACLE_HOME/bin directory. To load the StudentList procedure a command line like the following can be used, assuming the userId is *Jones* and the password is *sesame*, and there is already a procedure called StudentList in the database space:

```
loadpsp -replace -user Jones/sesame StudentList.psp
```

A URL is then used to access the procedure once it is stored, as in

```
http://hostname:port/pathname/StudentList
```

More complete details about PSP scripts can be found in the online Oracle documentation.

13.5   JDBC

JDBC is an Application Programming Interface (**API**) that provides a standard for relational database access from Java. The interface includes a set of Java classes and interfaces. While the java.sql standard covers the common features, various vendors, including Oracle, have added extended functionality to their JDBC drivers. Using standard JDBC, Java applications are platform independent, allowing them to run on a variety of servers and DBMSs.

To develop JDBC applications, the following steps are necessary

- At the start of the application, write import java.sql.*, to import all the standard JDBC classes and interfaces, as well as import java.io.* for Java input and output. For an Oracle database, to add the extensions, you might add

```
import oracle.jdbc.*
```

- Load the JDBC drivers using a command like the following, which loads the Oracle JDBC drivers:

```
Class.forName("oracle.jdbc.driver.OracleDriver")
```

Figure 13.12

A PSP Script to Display Student Names

```
<%@ page language="PL/SQL"%>
<%@ page contentType="text/html"%>
<%@ plsql procedure="StudentList"%>
<% /** This example displays the last name and first name of every
              student in the Student table. **/ %>

<%
  CURSOR stu_cursor IS
  SELECT lastName, firstName
  FROM Student
  ORDER BY lastName;
%>

<html>
<head>
<meta http-equiv="Content-Type" content="text/html">
<title>Student List</title>
</head>
<body TEXT="#000000" BGCOLOR="#FFFF00">
<h1>Student List</h1>
<table width="50%" border="1">
<tr>
<th align="left">Last Name</th>
<th align="left">First Name</th>
</tr>
<% FOR stu IN stu_cursor LOOP %>
  <tr>
   <td> <%= stu.lastName %> </td>
   <td> <%= stu.firstName %> </td>
   </tr>
<% END LOOP; %>
</table>
</body>
</html>
```

- Connect to the database using the DriverManager class. The get-Connection method can be used to create a Connection object as follows, using the url for the database and the user's own ID and password as indicated by italics. Alternatively, the user can be prompted for the ID and password.

```
conn = DriverManager.getConnection("jdbc:oracle:oci8:url","yourId",
"yourpassword")
```

The Connection object, conn, will then be used for all communication with the database.

- Use SQL to interact with the database and Java for the logic in the application program.

- Close the connection object to disconnect from the database using a statement like

```
conn.close()
```

The bulk of the code for a JDBC program involves the SQL and Java statements for interacting with the database. The Connection object is used for communicating with the database using statements. Three JDBC classes may be used for this purpose

- **Statement** is used for SQL statements with no parameters.

- **PreparedStatement** is used when the SQL statement has parameters or is to be executed many times. It is precompiled.

- **CallableStatement** is used for executing stored procedures.

To create object instances for these classes, the Connection class has three methods

- **createStatement**, which returns a new Statement object.

- **prepareStatement**, which takes an SQL statement with input parameters (if any), precompiles it, and stores it in a Prepared-Statement object.

- **prepareCall**, which is used for a call to a stored procedure. It has methods for handling input and output parameters and executing the procedure. It returns a CallableStatement.

Once a statement has been created by using one of these methods on a Connection object, the Statement object is used for executing SQL statements. Depending on the type of SQL statement, the appropriate method, such as executeUpdate or executeQuery is called. The executeQuery method executes an SQL statement and returns a **ResultSet** object, which contains the results returned by the query. The ResultSet class provides many useful methods, and includes a cursor that is initially positioned before the first row of returned data, and can be advanced to each subsequent row using the class next method. Within each row, the columns can be retrieved using a get method, with the columns referenced either by their names or by their positions, using an index that counts the first column as position 1. Other useful ResultSet methods include isFirst, wasNull, close, and several others. Figure 13.13 shows the basic elements of a Java program using JDBC.

13.6   The Semi-Structured Data Model

The Web can be viewed as a massive collection of documents that includes links and multimedia content such as sound, images, or video as well as text. Techniques for searching text documents were originally developed in the field of information retrieval, which was the domain of librarians rather than the public or database managers. However, with the development of the Web, the creation of collections of documents and the searching of those documents became an activity that was done primarily by ordinary computer users rather than by librarians. Because of the availability of the rich information resources the Web provides, the fields of information retrieval and database management have converged. In the database field, the documents on the Web are viewed as data sources similar to other databases, and the process of searching them can be seen as akin to querying a database. XML provides a bridge between the disciplines of information retrieval, which has traditionally included markup languages, and database management, which has relied on structured data models. XML allows documents to be marked up with meta-data, and can include tags that give some structure to documents. The semi-structured data model is a method of describing such partial structure. A semi-structured model contains a collection of nodes, each containing data, possibly with different schemas. The node itself contains information about the structure of its contents.

13.6.1 Graphical Representation

The semi-structured data model can be represented using a graph consisting of nodes and edges. Each document can be represented as a **tree,**

```
import java.sql.*;
import java.io.*;

class Test{

 public static void main(String args[]) {

        try {
   Class.forName("oracle.jdbc.driver.OracleDriver");
        }
        catch (ClassNotFoundException e) {
        System.out.println("Cannot load OracleDriver");
        }

        Connection conn = null;
        Statement stmt = null;
        ResultSet rset = null;

  try {
   conn = DriverManager.getConnection("jdbc:oracle:oci8", "Jones", "sesame");
   stmt = conn.createStatement();
   rset = stmt.executeQuery("select stuId, lastName, firstName from Student");
   while (rset.next())
    System.out.println(rset.getString(1)+" " + rset.getString(2)+" " +rset.getString(3));

   rset.close();
   stmt.close();
   conn.close();
        }
  catch (SQLException e) {
   System.out.println("SQL error:" + e.getMessage());
        }
 }
}
```

Figure 13.13

Basic Elements of a Java Program Using JDBC

having a single **root** node and a sequence of **child** nodes. Each child node can itself have child nodes, which in turn can have child nodes, and so on. A strict rule for trees is that every node, except the root, has exactly one parent node, which is at the level above it in the tree. The nodes can represent either complex objects or atomic values. An edge can represent either the relationship between an object and its sub-object, or the relationship between an object and its value. Leaf nodes, which have no sub-objects, represent values. There is no separate schema, since the graph is self-describing. For example, Figure 13.14 shows a hierarchical representation for the `CustomerList` data that corresponds to the XML schema of Figure 13.5. The entire document, `CustomerList`, becomes the root of the tree. Each `Customer` element is represented as a child of the root. The sub-elements of `Customer`, namely `Name`, `Address`, `Telephone`, `Type`, and `Status`, are represented as children of `Customer`. The sub-elements of `Address` and `Telephone` are represented as their children. An instance document for this schema is shown in Figure 13.15. The instance document mirrors

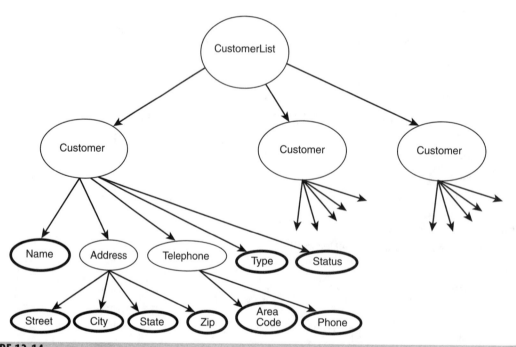

FIGURE 13.14

Hierarchical Representation of CustomerList

```
<CustomerList xmlns:xsi="http://www.w3.org/2001/XMLSchema-instance"
        xsi:noNamespaceSchemaLocation="C:\XML\XMLExample1">
  <Customer>
    <Name>WorldWide Travel Agency</Name>
    <Address>
       <Street> 10 Main Street </Street>
       <City> New York </City>
       <State> NY </State>
       <Zip> 10001 </Zip>
    </Address>
    <Telephone>
       <AreaCode> 212 </AreaCode>
       <Phone> 123 4567 </Phone>
    </Telephone>
    <Type>Corporate</Type>
    <Status>Active</Status>
  </Customer>
  <Customer>
    <Name>Mary Jones</Name>
    <Address>
       <Street> 25 Spruce Street </Street>
       <City> San Diego </City>
       <State> CA </State>
       <Zip> 92101 </Zip>
    </Address>
    <Telephone>
       <AreaCode> 619 </AreaCode>
       <Phone> 555 6789 </Phone>
    </Telephone>
    <Type>Individual</Type>
    <Status>Active</Status>
  </Customer>
```

FIGURE 13.15

Instance Document for CustomerList Schema of Figure 13.5

FIGURE 13.15

Continued

```
<Customer>
    <Name>Alice Adams</Name>
    <Address>
        <Street> 25 Orange Blossom Street </Street>
        <City> Miami </City>
        <State> FL </State>
        <Zip> 60601 </Zip>
    </Address>
    <Telephone>
        <AreaCode> 305 </AreaCode>
        <Phone> 987 6543 </Phone>
    </Telephone>
    <Type>Individual</Type>
    <Status>Inactive</Status>
  </Customer>
</CustomerList>
```

the structure of the XML schema (or of a DTD, if applicable), and shows the values provided for leaf nodes of the tree. All data resides in leaf nodes. If any attributes are present, they also become leaf nodes.

13.6.2   XML Parsers

For XML to be used in an application, it is necessary to parse XML documents. An XML parser reads in the XML document as a string and uses a parsing technique based on either an event-driven model in which only a single pass is made through the document, or a tree-based model in which an entire parsing tree is built in memory. Parsers that implement slight variations of these two basic models also exist. **DOM** (Document Object Model) is a W3C standard for the tree-based model, which implements the semi-structured data model as shown in Figure 13.14, with nodes representing the elements of the XML document and the data. The parser has methods to restructure the tree, to create nodes, modify nodes, and delete nodes. It stores the entire tree in memory, which consumes both time and memory, but which allows the programmer to navigate the tree structure as needed and supports dynamic data updating. **SAX** (Simple API for XML) parsing uses the event-driven model. As the parser reads the XML document and recognizes each fragment of XML syntax, it streams a series of events, which are sent to event handlers for processing the elements or data in the document. The basic types of event handlers are document handlers, for processing DTDs, schemas, and data, and error handlers for accessing errors generated in parsing. This approach is faster and less memory intensive, but since each fragment is seen only once, in document order, it does not permit revisiting or modification of segments.

13.6.3 XML Data Manipulation

XQuery is the current W3C standard query language for XML data. It uses the abstract logical structure of a document as it is encoded in XML, possibly in a DTD or an XML Schema definition.

XPath Expressions

Queries make use of the notion of a **path expression**, which comes from an earlier language, **XPath**. A path expression usually consists of the name of the document and a specification of the elements to be retrieved, using a path relationship. An example is:

```
Document("CustomerList.xml")//Customer/Name
```

The expression specifies the name of the document that is to be searched and one or more steps specified by / or //. The separator // means the next element can be nested anywhere within the preceding one (i.e., any descendant of the preceding node), while the separator / means the next element named must be nested immediately under the preceding one (i.e., in the graph it must be a child node of the preceding one). The steps in the path expression cause reading to advance through the document. The nodes of the graph for a structured XML document are ordered using pre-order traversal, which is a depth-first, left-to-right order. For an XML document, the entire document is the root node, which is followed by element nodes, other node types that we have not discussed here, and attribute nodes. Each element precedes its children, and all children of an element node precede the node's siblings. The nodes of the entire document are seen to be totally ordered by the language processor. In Figure 13.16, the numbers in the nodes show the order in which each node is encountered using normal (forward) traversal. Each node is given an object identifier based on this order. In the instance document in Figure 13.15 the nodes are listed in the same order. The path expression is normally evaluated by

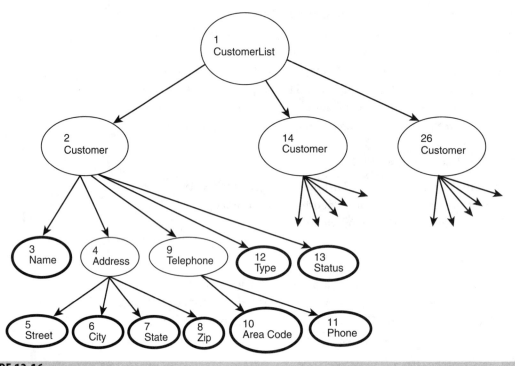

FIGURE 13.16

Pre-order Traversal of Graph

reading forward in the document until a node of the specified type is encountered. For the path expression in this example, the first customer node is found and the name of that customer, WorldWide Travel Agency, is targeted. We can add conditions to any nodes in a path expression. For example, if we write,

```
doc("CustomerList.xml")//Customer/Address[State="CA"]
```

the first node that satisfies this condition is the Address node of the second customer. The condition forces the reading to advance through the nodes of the document until it finds one that satisfies the condition. XQuery allows both forward and backward directions for reading. The user can specify an axis or direction for searching. A forward axis allows a search for a child, descendant, self, attribute, following sibling, and so on. A reverse axis allows a search for a parent, ancestor, self, preceding sibling, and so on.

XQuery Expressions

A simple query using a path expression usually returns a set of nodes that qualify for the expression. For example, for the query,

```
FOR
    $N IN doc("CustomerList.xml")//Customer/Name
RETURN <Result> $N </Result>
```

the variable $N is bound to each Name node in turn. Query evaluation begins by reading the root node, then advancing to the first Customer node, then to the Name node that is a child of the customer. This node becomes the **context node**, also called the current node, which is bound to the variable. From this position, reading advances to the next node that satisfies, i.e., the next Name node, which becomes the new context node, and so on. The query constructs a list of names and the RETURN clause generates an XML document containing the list of values to which $N is bound in turn. The Result tag is applied to each of the Name nodes found by the query. The result of this query is this XML document:

```
<Result><Name> WorldWide Travel Agency </Name></Result>
<Result><Name> Mary Jones </Name></Result>
<Result><Name> Alice Adams </Name></Result>
```

FLWOR Expressions

XQuery uses a general form called a FLWOR expression. FLWOR, pronounced "flower" stands for FOR, LET, WHERE, ORDER BY, and RETURN, which are the clauses found in such expressions. Not all of these clauses are required. The expressions allow for binding of variables to results, and also for iterating through the nodes of a document. They also allow joins to be performed, and data to be restructured. An example is,

```
FOR $C IN
    doc("CustomerList.xml")//Customer)
WHERE $C/Type="Individual"
ORDER BY Name
RETURN <Result> $C/Name, $C/Status </Result>
```

which produces the following XML document:

```
<Result><Name>Alice Adams</Name><Status>Inactive</Status></Result>
<Result><Name>Mary Jones</Name><Status>Active</Status></Result>
```

The results are ordered by `Name`, as specified in the query. If no order is specified, results appear in the order in which they are encountered in the document.

XQuery also allows nodes to be constructed, and joins to be performed. For example, let the schema shown in Figure 13.17 describe a second XML document that represents orders placed by customers. An instance document is shown in Figure 13.18. We can use XQuery to form a join of the `CustomerList` document with the `OrdersList` document. For example,

FIGURE 13.17

XML Schema for OrdersList

```
<xsd:schema xmlns:xsd="http://www.w3.org/2001/XMLSchema">
  <xsd:element name ="OrdersList">
   <xsd:sequence>
    <xsd:element name="Order" minoccurs="0" maxoccurs="unbounded">
     <xsd:complexType>
      <xsd:sequence>
       <xsd:element name="OrderNumber" type="xsd:integer"/>
       <xsd:element name="Customer" type="xsd:string" minoccurs="1"/>
       <xsd:element name="OrderDate" type="xsd:date" minoccurs="1"/>
       <xsd:element name="Item" minoccurs="1" maxoccurs="unbounded">
       <xsd:complexType>
         <xsd:sequence>
          <xsd:element name="ItemName" type="xsd:string"/>
          <xsd:element name="Price" type="xsd:decimal"/>
          <xsd:element name="Quantity" type="xsd:integer"/>
         </xsd:sequence>
        </xsd:complexType>
       </xsd:element>
      </xsd:sequence>
     </xsd:complexType>
    </xsd:element>
   </xsd:sequence>
  </xsd:element>
</xsd:schema>
```

```
<OrdersList xmlns:xsi="http://www.w3.org/2001/XMLSchema-instance"
        xsi:noNamespaceSchemaLocation="C:\XML\XMLExample2">
  <Order>
    <OrderNumber>1001</OrderNumber>
    <Customer>Mary Jones</Customer>
    <OrderDate>08-Feb-2011</OrderDate>
    <Item>
      <ItemName>pen</ItemName>
      <Price>15.99</Price>
      <Quantity>1</Quantity>
    </Item>
    <Item>
      <ItemName>desk lamp</ItemName>
      <Price>34.98</Price>
      <Quantity>1</Quantity>
    </Item>
  </Order>
<Order>
    <OrderNumber>1002</OrderNumber>
    <Customer>WorldWide Travel Agency</Customer>
    <OrderDate>8-Feb-2011</OrderDate>
    <Item>
      <ItemName>folder</ItemName>
      <Price>1.59</Price>
      <Quantity>12</Quantity>
    </Item>
    <Item>
      <ItemName>printer</ItemName>
      <Price>336.49</Price>
      <Quantity>1</Quantity>
    </Item>
    <Item>
      <ItemName>telephone</ItemName>
      <Price>95.00</Price>
      <Quantity>1</Quantity>
    </Item>
  </Order>
```

FIGURE 13.18

Instance Document OrdersList

FIGURE 13.18

Continued

```
<Order>
   <OrderNumber>1003</OrderNumber>
   <Customer>Mary Jones</Customer>
   <OrderDate>10-Feb-2011</OrderDate>
   <Item>
      <ItemName>filing cabinet</ItemName>
      <Price>45.00</Price>
      <Quantity>1</Quantity>
   </Item>
  </Order>
</OrdersList>
```

the query "Find the name and address of the customer for each order" requires a join of these documents. The query can be expressed as,

```
<Result>
{ FOR $O IN doc("OrdersList.xml")/Order,
    $C IN doc("CustomerList.xml")/Customer[Name=$O/Customer]
ORDER BY Customer
RETURN
    <OrderCust>
       {$O/OrderNumber, $O/Customer, $C/Address}
    </OrderCust>
</Result>
```

This expression constructs an XML document consisting of OrderCust elements, each of which has an order number, customer name, and customer address, arranged in order by the customer name. The condition [Name=$O/Customer] specifies that the Name node of the Customer element in the CustomerList document matches the Customer element in the Orders document, which is a join condition.

XQuery provides many predefined functions, including count, avg, max, min, and sum, which can be used in FLWOR expressions. For example, the following example lists customers who have two or more orders:

```
<RepeatList>
FOR $C IN DISTINCT(doc("CustomerList.xml"))
LET $O := doc("OrderList.xml")/Customer[Customer=$C.Name]
WHERE count($O)>1
RETURN
```

```
<RepeatCustomer>
{$C/Name,$C/Address}
</RepeatCustomer>
</RepeatList>
```

For the data shown in the instance documents in Figures 13.15 and 13.18, the `RepeatList` XML document will be:

```
<RepeatCustomer>
<Name>Mary Jones</Name>
<Address>
<Street>25 Spruce Street</Street>
<City>San Diego</City>
<State>CA</State>
<Zip>92101</Zip>
</Address>
</RepeatCustomer>
```

XQuery is a very powerful language with many additional features that are beyond the scope of this book. Complete details of the current specifications for the language can be found at the W3C website.

13.7 XML and Relational Databases

It is sometimes desirable to store XML data in a relational or object-relational database in a manner that allows retrieval and update of the data. The basic issue is how to map the hierarchical structure of XML documents into a relational or object-relational model. A simple but not very flexible solution is to let the entire document be represented as a single attribute. A more satisfactory solution is to "shred" the document into parts that are represented as attributes. However, this requires an intelligent mapping algorithm. The XML Schema can be used to facilitate this mapping. We might also wish to be able to transform relational data into XML form and to publish it in that form. Ultimately, what is needed is the ability to do "round-tripping" between XML and databases, which means being able to accept data in XML form, transform it into a relational database, query and update the database in the usual way, access it using SQL, and transform the output back into XML format, without loss of content.

Many vendors of relational database management systems have extended their native data types to allow storage of XML content. One method of handling XML documents is to create a table in which each document is a single tuple of CLOB type.

This solution is limited because of the limitations on CLOB operators. If we wish to access individual elements of the documents, we have to resort to XPath or XQuery operators and we are limited to character data as a return.

An alternative is to use an XML Schema or DTD and to create a table in which the XML elements are mapped to objects in an object-relational database. For example, if we have a schema such as the one shown in Figure 13.5, we can create a table in which each `Customer` element is a tuple, by writing code like the following:

```
CREATE SCHEMA xml_Orders OF XMLTYPE
XMLSCHEMA "schema location"
ELEMENT "Order";
```

The columns of the table then correspond to the elements of `Order` in the XML document.

A parser can then be used to convert the elements of the XML document to a relational or object-relational structure and to store the data in that form. Once the data is stored, it can be treated as a relational database using SQL. With this solution, it is also possible to use SQL with XPath expressions to retrieve values with a variety of datatypes from the database. To achieve true round-tripping, the query language has to have facilities that can tag and structure relational data into XML format. This technique can also be used to facilitate data exchange between existing heterogeneous databases, which can be queried using standard languages such as SQL, with the query results being placed into XML instance documents to be used as input to another database.

13.8   XML in Oracle

Oracle supports XML both as a native datatype for use in Oracle databases and as an input and output type for object-relational databases whose structure mirrors that of XML documents.

13.8.1   XML DB

Oracle XML DB is a standard feature of the Oracle database management system that allows the creation of databases in which the **XMLType** is used as a native datatype. XMLType is actually an object type, and can be used as a type for a column or a type for the entire table, as well as for parameters and PL/SQL variables. Oracle XML DB incorporates the W3C recommendations for XML, and provides methods for accessing and querying XML content, using XML and SQL syntax. Figure 13.19(a) shows an SQL command to create a simple table containing a numeric `custid` column and an XMLType column called `contactinfo`. Inserting records individually is easily done by using `XMLType` (or `XMLType.createXML`) in the same way that we used constructors in object oriented and object-relational databases, as shown in Figure 13.19(b). The XML input data is formatted exactly as shown earlier in Figure 13.2, with each element tagged. For this example, the other two records shown in Figure 13.2 were inserted in the same manner. The XML data is stored as a CLOB, and we can query the XML column as a single CLOB value using the `getClobval()` method on

Figure 13.19

Using XMLType for a Column

```
create table customers (
custid            number(4) primary key,
contactinfo       XMLtype);
```

Figure 13.19(a)

Creating a Table with an XMLType Column

```
insert into customers values(1, XMLtype(
'<CUSTOMER TYPE="Corporate" STATUS="Active">
        <NAME>WorldWide Travel Agency</NAME>
        <ADDRESS>
        <STREET>10 Main Street</STREET>
        <CITY>New York</CITY>
        <STATE>NY</STATE>
        <ZIP>10001</ZIP>
        </ADDRESS>
        <TELEPHONE>
        <AREACODE>212</AREACODE>
        <PHONE>123 4567</PHONE>
        </TELEPHONE>
</CUSTOMER>'));
```

Figure 13.19(b)

Inserting Records with XMLType Column

On the Companion Website:
■ Code for Examples

Figure 13.19(c)

SQL Query Using getClobval with Results

```
set long 1000

select C.contactinfo.getClobval()as Customer
from   Customers C
where custid=1;

CUSTOMER
------------------------------------------------------
<CUSTOMER TYPE="Corporate" STATUS="Active">
    <NAME>WorldWide Travel Agency</NAME>
    <ADDRESS>
    <STREET>10 Main Street</STREET>
    <CITY>New York</CITY>
    <STATE>NY</STATE>
    <ZIP>10001</ZIP>
    </ADDRESS>
    <TELEPHONE>
    <AREACODE>212</AREACODE>
    <PHONE>123 4567</PHONE>
    </TELEPHONE>
</CUSTOMER>
```

the `contactinfo` column, as shown in Figure 13.19(c), which returns the entire XML record, complete with XML tags. Note that we set the width of the SQL output to accommodate the long return values. We can also retrieve individual tagged elements, using the XML `extract` method and Xpath notation to indicate the node to be retrieved, as shown in Figure 13.19(d) and (e). To eliminate the tags in the result, we can add `text()`, as shown in Figure 13.19(e). We can add a condition for the XMLType column in the WHERE line as shown in Figure 13.19(f), or we could have used the `existsNode` method to test for a node with a specific value. In this query, the `@TYPE` returns the value of the attribute TYPE as an XMLType, and the `getStringVal` method converts the result to a string so that we can compare it with the string value 'Individual'.

Oracle also supports object tables that consist entirely of native XML type entries, which can be created as illustrated in Figure 13.20(a). Although

```
Select C.contactinfo.extract('/CUSTOMER/NAME') as CustomerName
from Customers C;

CUSTOMERNAME
-----------------------
<NAME>Mary Jones</NAME>
<NAME>Alice Adams</NAME>
<NAME>WorldWide Travel Agency</NAME>



select C.contactinfo.extract('/CUSTOMER//STATE') as CustomerStates
from    Customers C;

CUSTOMERSTATES
------------------
<STATE>CA</STATE>
<STATE>FL</STATE>
<STATE>NY</STATE>
```

Figure 13.19(d)
Queries Using Extract and Xpath Notation with Results

```
select C.contactinfo.extract('/CUSTOMER//STATE/text()') as CustomerStates
from    Customers C;

CUSTOMERSTATES
----------------------------
CA
FL
NY
```

Figure 13.19(e)
Query Using text() to Eliminate Tags

the usual method of populating such tables is by reading directly from an XML document in a file, it is possible to insert XML records individually, as shown in Figure 13.20(b). To retrieve all the data, we can use SELECT object_value, as shown in Figure 13.20(c), or we can simply use SELECT value() as we did in Chapter 8 for Oracle object-relational tables. The command shown in Figure 13.20(d) gives exactly the same results as the previous command. We can use Xpath expressions to specify

Figure 13.19(f)
Query Using a Condition

```
select C.contactinfo.extract('/CUSTOMER/NAME/text()') as IndividualCustomers
from Customers C
where C.contactinfo.extract('/CUSTOMER/@TYPE').getstringval()='Individual';


INDIVIDUALCUSTOMERS

---------------------------------------

Mary Jones
Alice Adams
```

Figure 13.20
Using a Table of XMLType

Figure 13.20(a)
**Creating an Object Table
of XMLType**

```
create table Customers2 of XMLtype;
```

Figure 13.20(b)
**Inserting into an XML-
Type Table**

```
insert into customers2 values(XMLType(
'<CUSTOMER TYPE="Corporate" STATUS="Active">
        <NAME>WorldWide Travel Agency</NAME>
        <ADDRESS>
        <STREET>10 Main Street</STREET>
        <CITY>New York</CITY>
        <STATE>NY</STATE>
        <ZIP>10001</ZIP>
        </ADDRESS>
        <TELEPHONE>
        <AREACODE>212</AREACODE>
        <PHONE>123 4567</PHONE>
        </TELEPHONE>
</CUSTOMER>'));
```

elements to be extracted, as shown for the Name element in Figure 13.20(e). Using extractValue gives us the results without tags, as shown in Figure 13.20(f). This example also illustrates retrieval of multiple nodes. We can also add conditions to the query, as shown in Figure 13.20(g). Notice that the value was extracted as a string, and other datatypes such as DATE can be retrieved using extractValue.

```
select object_value from customers2;

OBJECT_VALUE
---------------------------------------------

<CUSTOMER TYPE="Corporate" STATUS="Active">
        <NAME>WorldWide Travel Agency</NAME>
        <ADDRESS>
        <STREET>10 Main Street</STREET>
        <CITY>New York</CITY>
        <STATE>NY</STATE>
        <ZIP>10001</ZIP>
        </ADDRESS>
        <TELEPHONE>
        <AREACODE>212</AREACODE>
        <PHONE>123 4567</PHONE>
        </TELEPHONE>
</CUSTOMER>

. . .
 (similar returns for 2 other records)
```

Figure 13.20(c)
Query Using object_value

```
select value(c) from customers2 c;
```

Figure 13.20(d)
Query Using value( ) for the Object Table

```
select extract(object_value,'/CUSTOMER/NAME') from customers2;

EXTRACT(OBJECT_VALUE,'/CUSTOMER/NAME')
--------------------------------------

<NAME>WorldWide Travel Agency</NAME>
<NAME>Mary Jones</NAME>
<NAME>Alice Adams</NAME>
```

Figure 13.20(e)
Using XPath Notation to Retrieve a Node

Figure 13.20(f)

Using extractValue and Retrieving Multiple Nodes

```
select extractValue(object_value,'/CUSTOMER/NAME'), extractValue(object_value,'/CUS-
TOMER/ADDRESS/CITY')
from customers2;


EXTRACTVALUE(OBJECT_VALUE,'/CUSTOMER/NAME')
-------------------------------------------

EXTRACTVALUE(OBJECT_VALUE,'/CUSTOMER/ADDRESS/CITY')
---------------------------------------------------

WorldWide Travel Agency
New York

Mary Jones
San Diego

Alice Adams
Miami
```

Figure 13.20(g)

Using a Condition

```
select extractValue(object_value,'/CUSTOMER/NAME')
from customers2
where extractValue(object_value,'/CUSTOMER/ADDRESS/CITY')='Miami';

EXTRACTVALUE(OBJECT_VALUE,'/CUSTOMER/NAME')
-------------------------------------------
Alice Adams
```

To input data to an XML object table from an XML instance document requires registering the XML schema for the document. Registration also permits XML DB to create an object-relational database structure that best fits the XML schema, matching up datatypes for elements and attributes, creating structures for objects, and using VARRAYs or nested tables for repeating elements. XML instance documents used as input can then be shredded automatically, and their components stored in the object-relational database. The registration process and the XML schema creation can be done in a single step through PL/SQL using the `registerschema` method, which has the general form

```
BEGIN
  DBMS_XMLSCHEMA.registerschema(
   'customer.xsd',
   '<xs:schema xmlns:xdb="http://xmlns.oracle.com/xdb"
   xmlns:xs="http://www.w3.org/2001/XMLSchema"
      body of XML schema
END
```

As the first argument for the method, we specify the name under which we are registering the schema, and as the second argument we write the schema itself, so we are able to create and register the schema in a single step. An alternative method to use when the schema is already written is to store the schema in a directory in the XML DB `repository` and then use the `registerschema` method, giving the location of the schema as an argument.

Once a schema is registered, Oracle can do a mapping to an object-relational table, unless the programmer has chosen other options. The document root corresponds to the name of the table, and elements and attributes are mapped to table columns. VARRAYs and nested tables can store complex data. Shredding the documents provides better performance than storing them as CLOBs, but queries can be written as shown previously. However, Oracle does a hidden rewrite to change the query to its corresponding SQL form, and it can then use the optimizer before executing it.

13.8.2   Oracle XML Developer's Kits

Oracle provides XML Developer's Kits (**XDK**s) for PL/SQL, Java, C, and C++, which include libraries and utilities for applications using XML with those host languages. Using an XDK allows more control over XML content, because the documents can be parsed. The PL/SQL XDK supports DOM parsing only, but the Java, C, and C++ parsers provide both DOM and SAX interfaces. Using the XDK allows programmers to use the appropriate parser to obtain and parse an XML document, and to process the elements in the host language, exploiting the best features of both XML and the host language.

The Oracle XML SQL Utility (**XSU**) is an XDK component that allows two-way mapping between XML and SQL. Using XSU, programmers can

- Extract data from XML documents and insert it into database tables or views, using a standard canonical mapping. The elements and attributes of the XML document become attributes of the table.

- Update or delete data in the database tables or views from data in an XML document using SQL.

- Extract data from object-relational tables or views and transform the Results Set into XML. In the resulting document, the table name becomes the root element, and each row of the table is tagged as a ROW element, within which each attribute is tagged with the name of the database column.

13.9   Chapter Summary

The emergence of e-commerce has pushed organizations to develop web-based database applications to create worldwide markets and many other innovative activities.

In 1989 Tim Berners-Lee proposed a method of simplifying access to Internet resources that led to the development of the **World Wide Web**. His proposal included the notions of **URL**, **HTTP**, **HTML**, **hypertext**, and **graphical browsers** with embedded **links**.

HTTP is a **stateless** protocol with no facility for remembering previous interactions, which creates a problem for e-commerce. HTML is a data format used for presenting content on the Internet. It is called a **markup** language because HTML documents contain marks or tags that provide formatting information for the text. An HTML document can contain Java applets, audio files, images, video files, and content. **XML** or Extensible Markup Language allows users to define their own markup language. Using XML, it is possible to define the structure of heterogeneous databases and support translation of data between different databases.

An XML document contains one or more elements, each of which has a **start tag** showing its name, some **character data**, and an **end tag**. Elements can be **sub-elements** of other elements. Sub-elements must be properly nested. Elements can have **attributes** whose names and values are shown inside the element's start tag. Attributes occur only once within each element, while sub-elements can occur any number of times. A document can contain **entity references** to refer to external files, common text, Unicode characters, or some reserved symbols. An XML document is said to be **well formed** if it obeys the rules of XML. Users can define their own markup language by writing a **Document Type Declaration** (DTD) or by writing an **XML Schema**. An instance document that obeys the rules of its associated DTD is said to be **type-valid**. **XML Schema** is a more powerful way to describe the structure of documents than DTDs. If an instance document conforms to an XML schema, it is called **schema-valid**. An XML schema lists elements and attributes. Elements may be complex, which means they have sub-elements, or simple. Attributes or elements can be used to store data values. Attributes can be used for simple values that are not repeated while elements can be complex or simple, and can occur multiple times.

Three major functions required in an Internet environment are presentation, application logic, and data management. The placement of these functions depends on the architecture of the system. **Three-tier architectures** completely separate application logic from data management. The client handles the user interface, which is called the **presentation layer** or the first tier. A separate **application server** executes the application logic and forms the **middle tier**. The **database server** forms the third tier. The communications network connects each tier to the next one. The three-tier architecture allows support for **thin clients** that need only handle the presentation layer, independence of tiers that can use different platforms, easier application maintenance on the application server, integrated transparent data access to heterogeneous data sources, and scalability.

HTML forms are often used at the presentation layer. Code in JavaScript, JScript, VBScript, and similar scripting languages can be embedded in the HTML to provide some client-side processing. **Style sheets** specify how data is presented on specific devices. The application server at the middle tier is responsible for executing applications. It determines the flow of control, acquires input data from the presentation layer, makes data requests to the database server, accepts query results from the database layer, and uses them to assemble dynamically generated HTML pages. Server-side processing can involve many different technologies such as Java Servlets, Java Server pages, and others. **CGI**, Common Gateway Interface, can be used to connect HTML forms with application programs. To maintain state during a session, servers may use **cookies**, hidden fields in HTML forms, and URI extensions. Cookies are easily generated at the middle tier using Java's Cookie class and sent to the client, where they can be stored in the browser cache.

Oracle supports web programming for databases using SQL with the **PL/SQL Web Toolkit**, which allows the programmer to generate HTML tags from within PL/SQL, and with **PL/SQL Server Pages** (PSP), which supports SQL statements in standard HTML scripts. Both reside on the server side. **JDBC** provides a standard way of accessing relational databases, allowing SQL statements to appear in Java applications or applets. To use JDBC to execute an SQL query, the programmer has to import the JDBC classes and interfaces, load the JDBC Drivers, create a connection object or objects, create a statement object, and use the statement object to create a ResultSet from an SQL query. The Java code is used to process the results.

XML allows documents to be marked up with meta-data, and can include tags that give some structure to documents. A **semi-structured data model** contains a collection of nodes, each containing data, possibly with different schemas. Each document can be represented as a **tree**, having a single **root** node and a sequence of **child** nodes. Each child node can itself have child nodes, which in turn can have child nodes, and so on. The nodes can represent either **complex objects** or **atomic values**. An **edge** can represent either the relationship between an object and its sub-object, or the relationship between an object and its value. **Leaf** nodes represent values. The nodes of the graph for a structured XML document are ordered using **pre-order traversal**, which is a depth-first, left-to-right order. There is no separate schema, since the graph is self-describing.

XQuery is the current W3C standard query language for XML data. It uses the abstract logical structure of a document as it is encoded in XML, possibly in a DTD or an XML Schema definition. Queries make use of the notion of a **path expression**, which comes from an earlier language, **XPath**. A path expression usually consists of the name of the document and a specification of the elements to be retrieved, using a path relationship. We can add conditions to any nodes in a path expression. The path expression is normally evaluated by reading forward in the document until a node of the specified type and condition is encountered. The user can specify an axis or direction for searching. XQuery uses a general form called a **FLWOR** expression, for FOR, LET, WHERE, ORDER BY, and RETURN clauses. The expressions allow for binding of variables to results, and also for iterating through the nodes of a document. They also allow joins to be performed, and data to be restructured. XQuery provides many predefined functions, including count, avg, max, min, and sum, which can be used in FLWOR expressions.

Many vendors of relational database management systems have extended their native data types to allow storage of XML documents. It is also possible to use SQL with XPath expressions to retrieve values from the database. Existing heterogeneous databases can be queried using standard languages such as SQL, and the query results can be placed into an XML instance document. The query language has to have facilities that can tag and structure relational data into XML format. Oracle includes an **XML-Type** datatype, which can be used as an attribute type or an object table type and stores data in CLOB form, allowing only limited operations. However, using an Oracle **XDK** provides much more flexibility, allowing parsing of the XML document, and mapping to an object-relational database. Oracle's **XSU** is an XDK utility that allows two-way mapping between SQL and XML.

Exercises

13.1 Define the following terms.

   a. e-commerce

   b. HTML

   c. HTTP

   d. URI

   e. browser

   f. stateless protocol

   g. SGML

   h. XML

   i. markup language

   j. entity reference

   k. well-formed document

   l. type-valid document

   m. schema-valid document

n. W3C

o. thin client

p. presentation layer

q. style sheet

r. cookie

s. semi-structured model

t. XQuery

u. XPath

v. document shredding

w. DOM parsing

x. SAX parsing

y. FLWOR expression

z. XDK

aa. XSU

13.2 Explain what is meant by the convergence of database processing and document processing.

13.3 If a website uses static linked HTML files for displaying data, what problems can arise?

13.4 What are HTML forms used for in e-commerce?

13.5 How is state maintained during a long e-commerce transaction?

13.6 How are HTML, SGML, and XML related?

13.7 What is the purpose of style sheets?

13.8 What makes an XML document well-formed?

13.9 When is an XML document type-valid?

13.10 What makes an XML document schema-valid?

13.11 How can you determine whether an XML schema document is schema-valid?

13.12 Explain the difference between an element and an attribute in an XML document.

13.13 Create an HTML document similar to the one shown in Figure 13.1 for a list of products, and test it using a browser.

13.14 For the list of products in Exercise 13.13, create a well-formed XML document, similar to the one shown in Figure 13.2.

13.15 Write a DTD for the list of products in Exercise 13.13, making sure the instance document is type-valid for the DTD.

13.16 Write an XML schema for the same list of products.

13.17 Write a new instance document listing products, making sure the new list is schema-valid.

13.18 Draw a hierarchical diagram for the data in Figure 13.18.

13.19 Using XQuery, write two queries for the data in Figure 13.18.

On the Companion Website:

- Laboratory Exercises
- Sample Project
- Student Projects

CHAPTER 14

Social and Ethical Issues

Chapter Objectives

In this chapter you will learn the following:

- Some ethical issues and standards for computer professionals

- The meaning of intellectual property

- What forms of protection exist for intellectual property

- How software can be protected

- How privacy and security are related

- The history and state of privacy legislation in the United States

- The history and state of privacy legislation in the European Union

- How differences in U.S. and European Union privacy laws affect trade
- How human factors are considered in software development
- Factors in the human-database interface
- The importance of usability

 On the Companion Website:

- Additional Exercises

- Sample Project

- Student Projects

14.1   Computerization and Society

The effect of computerization on society is often described as a revolution that surpasses the industrial revolution. Like other emerging technologies, computers have created new situations and possibilities that challenge society's moral codes. It takes time and reflection for society to develop and apply values, moral principles, and codes to deal with the issues created by any new technology. Since computer technology advances so quickly, products come on the market before society has had a chance to consider the moral issues they raise and to formulate the application of values and moral principles to guide their use. Given the vacuum created by this lag, individuals or groups formulate their own rules for behavior, often without adequate consideration of the implications of their actions.

Legislation may later be enacted to regulate behavior, and frequently challenges to those laws result in changes, refinements, or new interpretations of the laws. All information technology workers, especially those who design or administer databases, need to be aware of the ethical and social issues created by computer technology, to ensure that their conduct meets ethical and professional standards. In addition, where laws or regulations exist, they need to be aware of the restrictions that affect them, and to be responsible for ensuring that their organizations comply with the laws that govern them.

14.1.1 Ethical Issues

The rule of law that is recognized in well-ordered societies is challenged by the Internet. Since it is a global entity, no single country can apply its laws to the entire Internet. In cyberspace, individuality is highly prized, and the Internet community is very resistant to attempts by governments to control it. The Internet provides a forum for people to express themselves freely to a vast audience, exercising their fundamental human right to freedom of speech. Without some controls on content, however, abuses such as pornography, hate rhetoric, and spam can become rampant. Another major area of disagreement is how intellectual property laws should be applied on the Internet, or whether they should apply at all to digital media. In addition to whether one should be able to copy documents or other material available on the Web, the issue of linking to content on other websites can also be controversial. For example, if a link brings a browser to a web page with copyrighted material, does it violate the copyright? If a link bypasses the home page of another site to bring the user to an internal page, thereby avoiding the advertisements that may appear on the home page, does that violate the rights of the site owner, since it diminishes the value of the advertising space?

The issues of software ownership and software licensing are also hotly debated. Privacy is another issue that is controversial. Individual privacy is challenged by the widespread use of computer technology to collect and share personal information that is stored in databases.

Users of social networking websites are concerned with balancing their desire for interpersonal communication with respect for their privacy. The use of cookies and spyware to collect "clickstream data," which is a record of every keystroke on a user's computer, and the increasing use of data mining can further erode privacy. Most countries have laws that protect the privacy of individuals from intrusion by the government and private businesses, on the grounds that privacy is a fundamental human right.

Opponents of privacy legislation claim that the collection and sharing of customer data among businesses is a form of free speech that should be protected. Cybercrime, including identity theft, poses new hazards for individuals and organizations. The responsibilities that computer professionals have to make their products easier and safer for users, and the best ways to do that are also debated. Local, national, and international organizations such as the American Civil Liberties Union and the Electronic Frontier Foundation work to defend individual rights against what they consider to be undue government and commercial interference.

14.1.2   Ethical Standards for Computing Professionals

In their work, professionals encounter situations that require moral judgments. Many professions have codes of ethics that guide their members' actions in such situations. The Association for Computing Machinery publishes a Code of Ethics and Professional Conduct that outlines general moral imperatives as well as professional and leadership responsibilities for computing professionals. In addition, ACM and IEEE (The Institute for Electrical and Electronics Engineers), which are the two leading professional organizations in computing, have jointly created a Software Engineering Code of Ethics and Professional Practice to guide software engineers. These guidelines apply to professionals who design any software, including database management systems, software that enhances the capabilities of database management systems, or database applications developed for a client. Both codes are posted on the organizations' websites.

On the Companion Website:

- Codes of Ethics

14.2   Intellectual Property

A large area of disagreement centers on how intellectual property laws and protections such as copyrights, patents, trade secrets, and trademarks can be adapted to the changing environment of the digital age, or whether they should apply at all to digital media.

The question of who owns intellectual property and what rights the owners have to that property, including software and databases, is complex and controversial. On one side are those who believe that virtually all non-personal information that could be useful to people should be freely available. Dorothy Denning quotes Richard Stallman, who opposes the term "intellectual property":

> I believe that all generally useful information should be free. By 'free' I am not referring to price, but rather to the freedom to copy the information and to adapt it to one's own uses. ...When information

is generally useful, redistributing it makes humanity wealthier no matter who is distributing and no matter who is receiving. (Denning, Dorothy E. *Concerning Hackers Who Break into Computer Systems*, Proceedings of the 13th National Computer Security Conference, Washington, D.C., Oct., 1990, pp. 653–664.)

Many people argue that intellectual property laws should not apply to software. There is a strong "free software" movement that supports the notion that all software should be free and freely copied. The Free Software Foundation challenges the protection of software on philosophical and practical grounds. Richard Stallman, who founded The Free Software Foundation, has written and spoken extensively about the reasons why software should not be compared to property, and why ownership of programs is unethical. The Open Source movement is also opposed to proprietary software. In his seminal book *The Cathedral and the Bazaar,* Eric Raymond provides an analogy used by open source advocates. He explains that when the source code for software is made freely available, the independent programmers and hackers who work on it can develop better software than a select group of highly-paid programmers at a software company. The "cathedral" represents a software company such as Microsoft that employs a professional team, while the "bazaar" represents a loosely affiliated group of independent programmers. The argument is that the bazaar approach is better because the collective intelligence of the independents can be used to fix bugs and improve the software more rapidly.

On the other side there are those who believe that every use of copyrighted works of all types, including transmission of them to personal computers for personal use and storage of them in temporary Internet files, is subject to copyright restrictions. Commercial software is usually protected by copyright or other means. The justification for such protection is based on notions of justice and the desire to foster enterprise. Legislation exists in most countries to protect intellectual property rights, and international agreements have been signed to attempt to guarantee these rights throughout the world.

14.2.1 Definition of Intellectual Property

Property ownership is a fundamental concept in most well-ordered societies. Legal systems devote considerable attention to rights and obligations of property owners. Sir William Blackstone described the origins and nature of the rights of property owners in the eighteenth century. He wrote:

> There is nothing which so generally strikes the imagination, and engages the affections of mankind, as the right of property; or that sole and despotic dominion which one man claims and exercises over the external things of the world, in total exclusion of the right of any other individual in the universe (Blackstone, Sir William *Commentaries on the Laws of England*, 1765–1769).

Property originally referred to land, but the meaning has been extended to cover other assets. Blackstone listed among the rights of an owner of a piece of land the right to use it as he sees fit, to receive income from it, to transfer ownership, and to exclude others from it. The collection of property rights forms what came to be known as the **Blackstonian bundle**. A person who owns a plot of land, a bank account, a piece of jewelry, or a car can use it, can control who else can use it, and can transfer ownership of it, as long as it does not interfere with the safety or property of other people.

Compared with tangible property, intellectual property is harder to define and the rights associated with it are more difficult to identify. Unlike land, intellectual property is usually intangible. Intellectual property refers to products of the mind—such as literature, music, art, architecture, inventions, formulas for products, software, and databases. A broad definition is, "the legal rights which result from intellectual activity in the industrial, scientific, literary, and artistic fields" (World Intellectual Property Organization, *WIPO Intellectual Property Handbook: Policy, Law and Use*, p. 3). WIPO is an agency of the United Nations that administers international treaties in the area of intellectual property.

In the case of tangible property such as a piece of land or a car, use of it is exclusive, since only one person can use it at a time. Intellectual property differs because it is non-exclusive in that many people can use it at the same time, and their simultaneous use of it does not diminish its value. The cost of providing additional access to it is usually low, even though the cost of producing it originally might have been high. The notion of justice is at the foundation of intellectual property rights. Since the creator or inventor of an original work has invested his or her time and resources in its creation, he or she is entitled to reap the rewards. By guaranteeing a return for intellectual work, society encourages authors and other creative people to continue to develop new works. In the case of a software writer, a database designer, or a database developer, the individual has spent time, effort, and money in both acquiring the knowledge to be able to do those tasks and in creating the product. The individual is entitled to some return. If the person is an employee who created the work for hire, the employer is entitled to a return.

14.2.2 Legal Protections for Intellectual Property

The rights of owners of intellectual property are protected by a variety of mechanisms, including by copyright, patent, trade secret, trademarks, and service marks.

WIPO divides intellectual property into two branches—**industrial property**, which covers inventions, and **copyright**, which covers literary and artistic works.

Industrial property takes a range of forms. These include patents to protect inventions, and industrial designs, which are aesthetic creations determining the appearance of industrial products. Industrial property also covers trademarks, service marks, layout designs of integrated circuits, commercial names and designations, as well as geographical indications, and protection against unfair competition.

Copyright relates to artistic creations, such as books, music, paintings and sculptures, films and technology-based works such as computer programs and electronic databases. (WIPO, *Understanding Copyright and Related Rights,* p. 6)

Meaning of Copyright

Copyright is a right given to the creator of a literary or artistic work. The copyright is given by the government of the country of origin for a limited period of time. During that time, the author of the work has sole, exclusive rights to copy, distribute, rent, and communicate the work to the public. Article 2 of the Berne Convention, which is the international treaty covering copyright, specifies the type of works covered by the original agreement:

The expression "literary and artistic works" shall include every production in the literary, scientific and artistic domain, whatever may be the mode or form of its expression, such as books, pamphlets and other writings; lectures, addresses, sermons and other works of the same nature; dramatic or dramatico-musical works; choreographic works and entertainments in dumb show; musical compositions with or without words; cinematographic works to which are assimilated works expressed by a process analogous to cinematography; works of drawing, painting, architecture, sculpture, engraving and lithography; photographic works to which are assimilated works expressed by a process analogous to photography; works of applied art; illustrations, maps, plans, sketches and three-dimensional works relative to geography, topography, architecture or science (WIPO, *Berne Convention for the Protection of Literary and Artistic Works*, 1979, p. 4)

The WIPO Copyright Treaty of 1996 specifically mentions computer programs and databases as matters to be protected by copyright. Article 4 of the treaty states

Computer programs are protected as literary works within the meaning of <u>Article 2 of the Berne Convention</u>. Such protection applies to computer programs, whatever may be the mode or form of their expression.

Article 5 states

Compilations of data or other material, in any form, which by reason of the selection or arrangement of their contents constitute intellectual creations, are protected as such. This protection does not extend to the data or the material itself and is without prejudice to any copyright subsisting in the data or material contained in the compilation. (WIPO, *WIPO Copyright Treaty*, 1996, pp. 2–3).

To be eligible for copyright protection, the work must be original, it must have a tangible form, and it must be fixed in a medium, conditions generally referred to as **originality**, **expression**, and **fixation**. Anyone who creates a work that could be copyrighted automatically owns the copyright. It is not necessary to publish the work, to use the copyright symbol, ©, on it, or to make a formal application for a copyright. It is automatic. Therefore every web page, software program, multimedia presentation, essay, database, term paper, and so on that is original and fixed in a medium (e.g., a paper, a recording, a disk, a server) is automatically copyrighted. Copyright protects the owner's right to make copies of the work, to use it as the basis of a new work (called a **derivative** work), to distribute or publish it, to rent it, to publicly display the work, and to publicly perform the work. Publishing the work includes posting it on the Internet. Distributing the work includes electronic distribution. Publicly displaying the work can include displaying it on a computer screen. Publicly performing the work includes publicly playing a recording of it. The owner has exclusive rights in these areas, with limited exceptions that are in a category called **fair use**, such as in reviews of the work. Anyone who wants to use the copyrighted work must obtain permission from the owner of the copyright, and possibly pay a fee, unless the use is fair use.

Works protected by copyright can always be used freely for personal use, such as reading. Fair use of a copyrighted work also allows limited non-personal use of copyrighted materials without the author's permission. This area includes using a small amount of the material for educational purposes, quotation in reviews, parody, or other limited uses. It is often difficult to determine whether the use of a work falls under the category of fair use. There are four factors to be considered when making such a decision. The judgment requires that all four factors lean in the direction of fair use. They are:

1. **The character of the use.** If the use is for review, parody, commentary, reporting, or similar purposes, and it is personal, educational, or nonprofit, it is more likely to be considered fair use. If the use is commercial, it is likely not fair use.

2. **The nature of the work to be used.** If the work is factual and published, the use is more likely to be fair use, while if it is imaginative and unpublished, it is less likely to be fair use.

3. **The amount of the work to be used.** A small amount is likely to be fair use, while a significant portion of the work is not fair use.

4. **The effect it would have on the market for the original work or for permissions, if the kind of use were widespread.** This factor should be considered only after evaluating the first three factors. If the use takes away from sales of the original work, or avoids paying royalties on the original work, it is not fair use. However, if the original is not available for purchase, or if the owner of the copyright cannot be identified, it is more likely to be fair use.

Some intellectual works are not protected by copyright. This category includes works that are considered utilitarian or trivial, as indicated by the following list from the U.S. Copyright Office.

- Titles, names, short phrases, and slogans; familiar symbols or designs; mere variations of typographic ornamentation, lettering, or coloring; mere listings of ingredients or contents

- Ideas, procedures, methods, systems, processes, concepts, principles, discoveries, or devices—as distinguished from a description, explanation, or illustration

- Works consisting entirely of information that is common property and containing no original authorship (for example: standard calendars, height and weight charts, tape measures and rulers, and lists or tables taken from public documents or other common sources). (U.S. Copyright Office, *Copyright Basics, Circular 1*, p. 3.)

Facts are always in the public domain, but a specific arrangement and expression of them, such as that found in a database, can be copyrighted. Ideas are also in the public domain, but a particular explanation of them, such as an essay, can be copyrighted. Mathematical and chemical formulas are in the public domain, but product formulas can be copyrighted. Some of the other exceptions, such as symbols, are eligible for protection under trademark laws, and others, such as processes, are eligible for patents or trade secret protection.

Other works in the public domain include works on which the copyright has expired and has not been renewed, those on which the copyright has been lost, and those that the author has intentionally put in the public domain. Works in the public domain can be used freely by anyone, without permission.

International Copyright Laws and U.S. Copyright Laws

Copyrights are recognized internationally, but each country makes its own laws concerning them. The United States, the United Kingdom, and France originally had copyright laws dating back to the eighteenth century. Most copyright laws are based on the **Berne Convention** for the protection of Literary and Artistic Works, which first convened in 1886 at the instigation of Victor Hugo. Revisions to the Berne Convention were made in 1896, 1908, 1914, 1928, 1967, 1971, and 1979. The purpose of the convention was to ensure that each country recognized copyrights of works published in other member countries. The convention did not require that the work be registered or that it display the copyright symbol. It set the duration of copyright as the lifetime of the author plus 50 years. Although the Berne Convention set guidelines, each member country made its own laws to adhere to the guidelines. The Berne Convention is now administered by the World Intellectual Property Organization (**WIPO**), which was founded in 1967.

Copyright protection in the United States has its origins in the Constitution. Article 1, Section 8 of the Constitution of the United States gives Congress the power,

> To promote the Progress of Science and useful Arts, by securing for limited Times to Authors and Inventors the exclusive Right to their respective Writings and Discoveries, . . . (*The Constitution of the United States,* Article 1, Section 8, Clause 7.)

The first U.S. copyright law, designed by Congress to protect those rights, was passed in 1790. The law was amended in 1831 and 1870. The Copyright Act was adopted in 1909 and remained in effect, with slight modifications, until 1978. In 1976 a new Copyright Act was passed by Congress, and it went into effect in 1978. Several modifications have been made to the law, including extensions of the length of time protection exists, and addition of criminal penalties for various computer-related activities.

The U.S. Copyright Office lists the type of works that can be protected by copyright under the current Act:

> Copyright protects "original works of authorship" that are fixed in a tangible form of expression. The fixation need not be directly perceptible so long as it may be communicated with the aid of a machine or device. Copyrightable works include the following categories:

1. literary works
2. musical works, including any accompanying words
3. dramatic works, including any accompanying music
4. pantomimes and choreographic works
5. pictorial, graphic, and sculptural works
6. motion pictures and other audiovisual works

7. sound recordings

8. architectural works

These categories should be viewed broadly. For example, computer programs and most "compilations" may be registered as "literary works"; maps and architectural plans may be registered as "pictorial, graphic, and sculptural works" (U.S. Copyright Office. *Copyright Basics*, p. 3).

This law requires originality, fixation, and expression, but it does not require publication, use of the copyright symbol, or registration of the work with the Copyright Office. However, for the purpose of protecting the copyright and determining the dates of protection, the Copyright Office advises authors to register the work, and to affix the claim of copyright, which should include the copyright symbol or word, the author's name, and the date of publication. To complete the registration process, the author must fill out a registration form, pay a fee, and send two copies of the published work to the Copyright Office for deposit in the Library of Congress. Registration allows the author to claim copyright protection in a court of law in the case of infringement. The U.S. Copyright Office offers guidelines for copyright registration.

In general, copyright registration is a legal formality intended to make a public record of the basic facts of a particular copyright. However, registration is not a condition of copyright protection. Even though registration is not a requirement for protection, the copyright law provides several inducements or advantages to encourage copyright owners to make registration. Among these advantages are the following:

- Registration establishes a public record of the copyright claim.

- Before an infringement suit may be filed in court, registration is necessary for works of U.S. origin.

- If made before or within five years of publication, registration will establish *prima facie* evidence in court of the validity of the copyright and of the facts stated in the certificate.

- If registration is made within three months after publication of the work or prior to an infringement of the work, statutory damages and attorney's fees will be available to the copyright owner in court actions. Otherwise, only an award of actual damages and profits is available to the copyright owner.

- Registration allows the owner of the copyright to record the registration with the U.S. Customs Service for protection against the importation of infringing copies (U.S. Copyright Office, *Copyright Basics*, p. 7).

The published work must be deposited with the Library of Congress. In fact, the law requires that any work published in the U.S. be deposited with the Library of Congress within three months of publication, regardless of whether it is registered. The 1976 Copyright Act specified the duration of copyright but the terms were extended by the Sonny Bono Copyright Term Extension Act, so that for works created before 1978 copyrights are for 95 years, but copyrights for post-1978 works are for the lifetime of the author plus 70 years, and works for hire 95 years from publication or 120 years from creation. A 1980 amendment was made to cover software, both source code and object code.

In 1998, The **Digital Millennium Copyright Act** (DMCA) was enacted by Congress. It has some controversial provisions relating to tools designed to circumvent protection or encryption systems, making it a crime to use such a tool.

No person shall circumvent a technological measure that effectively controls access to a work protected under this title (Digital Millennium Copyright Act, Sect 1201,1(a)).

It is also a crime to manufacture or offer a tool that is designed primarily for the purpose of circumventing protection technologies.

No person shall manufacture, import, offer to the public, provide, or otherwise traffic in any technology, product, service, device, component, or part thereof, that:

A. Is primarily designed or produced for the purpose of circumventing a technological measure that effectively controls access to a work protected under this title;

B. Has only limited commercially significant purpose or use other than to circumvent a technological measure that effectively controls access to a work protected under this title; or

    C. Is marketed by that person or another acting in concert with that person with that person's knowledge for use in circumventing a technological measure that effectively controls access to a work protected under this title (Digital Millennium Copyright Act, Sect 1201, 2(a)).

Specific exceptions are made for libraries, archives, and educational institutions, but only for the purpose of evaluating the work to determine whether to acquire a copy of it. Exceptions are also made for law enforcement agencies, and under limited circumstances, for reverse engineering to allow interoperability of products, for encryption research, for computer repairs, and similar uses. The law also limits the liability of Internet service providers for online copyright infringement by subscribers to the Internet service.

Copyright **infringement** means that a person uses or sells an item protected by copyright, or intentionally supports others in doing so, violating the owner's property rights. The owner of the copyright has to prove that the person did not make fair use of the item. Courts usually want the copyright owner to prove that he or she owns the work, that the violator had knowledge of the work, and that the new work produced is not substantially different from the copyrighted one. The penalties can include injunction, monetary damages, and imprisonment for certain offenses.

Patents

Another form of protection for intellectual property is a patent, which is designed to protect an invention or discovery. According to WIPO,

> Inventions may be defined in a non-legal sense as new solutions to technical problems. These new solutions are ideas, and are protected as such; protection of inventions under patent law does not require that the invention be represented in a physical embodiment. The protection accorded to inventors is, therefore, protection against any use of the invention without the authorization of the owner. Even a person who later makes the same invention independently, without copying or even being aware of the first inventor's work, must obtain authorization before he can exploit it. (WIPO, *Understanding Copyright and Related Rights*, p. 7.)

A patent is the grant of a property right to the inventor. Patents are issued by the governments of individual countries, although there are some international treaties concerning them. In the United States, patents are issued by the Patent and Trademark Office, which is an agency of the Department of Commerce. A patent gives the inventor the right to prevent others from making, using, offering to sell, or selling the invention in the United States or its territories or possessions, or from importing the invention into the United States. It is up to the inventor to enforce his or her right to exclude these activities. The term of the patent is generally 20 years from the time of the filing of the application. During this time, the inventor has the opportunity to recover the costs of creating the invention.

United States patent laws, like copyright laws, have their origins in Article 2, Section 8 of the Constitution. Congress enacted the first U.S. patent law in 1790, and revised it in 1952. In 1999, Congress enacted the American Inventors Protection Act (AIPA), which was amended by the Intellectual Property and High Technology Amendments Act of 2002. According to the patent law,

> . . . any person who invents or discovers any new and useful process, machine, manufacture, or composition of matter, or any new and useful improvement thereof, may obtain a patent, subject to the conditions and requirements of the law. The word "process" is defined by law as a process, act or method, and primarily includes industrial or technical processes (United States Patent and Trademark Office, *General Information Concerning Patents*, Jan. 2005).

The invention must be **useful**, which means that it has a useful purpose and can actually work. An idea or suggestion for a useful device is not sufficient. It must be demonstrated that the creation works. The invention must be **new**, which means it must not have been known, published, or used previously. It must be **non-obvious** to a person who has ordinary skill in the area. The inventor must file an application that includes a specification, describing the invention in detail:

> The specification must include a written description of the invention and of the manner and process of making and using it, and is required to be in such full, clear, concise, and exact terms as to enable any person skilled in the technological area to which the invention pertains, or with which it is most nearly connected, to make and use

the same (United States Patent and Trademark Office, *General Information Concerning Patents,* Jan. 2005).

Drawings may also be required to further describe the invention. The Patent Office reviews the application and sends it to one of its technology centers to determine whether the invention is new, useful, and nonobvious. If the patent is granted, it remains in effect for 20 years. During that time, others can use the ideas but not the process of the patent. After the patent expires, anyone can examine the disclosures and use the invention.

Patents given in one country have no automatic legal basis in another. However, under the **Paris Convention** for the Protection of Industrial Property, of which the United States is a member, a treaty was signed that provides that each of the 173 member countries guarantees to give citizens of the other countries the right to patent (and trademark) that it offers its own citizens. In addition, if an inventor files a regular first patent application in one of the member countries, he or she can, within a specified period, file for patent protection in all the member countries. Even if this filing was made later, it will be considered to have been filed on the same date as the first regular application, for purposes of determining right of priority if another person should file for the same invention. The Patent Cooperation Treaty of 1970 creates a standard application format and a centralized filing procedure for the filing of patents in all the member countries. The Patent Law Treaty of 2000 further streamlined and harmonized the application process.

Owners of patented inventions normally display the patent number on the product. People who have applied for a patent for an invention are permitted to display the words "Patent Pending" or "Patent Applied For" on the product while the patent application is being reviewed. Both of these practices are methods of warning the public that a patent exists or may exist, and of helping the inventor to identify violations by having the public report any suspected infringement. It is up to the patent owner to identify and investigate any infringement, but it can be costly and time-consuming to do so. If the patent owner can prove infringement, the penalties are heavy.

Trade Secrets

Trade secrets provide another way to protect intellectual property. A trade secret is any information that is used in the operation of a business that is kept secret and that gives it a competitive edge. It can be a formula, process, pattern, compilation, program, method, technique, device, or any other information. The formula for a soft drink, the secret ingredients of a cosmetic, and the process for manufacturing a distinctive product are all examples of trade secrets. Unlike copyrights and patents, there is no way to register a trade secret under any national or international law. In the United States, trade secrets are protected by states, most of which have adopted laws based on the work of the National Conference of Commissioners of Uniform State Laws, which drafted the Uniform Trade Secrets Act in 1970 as a model law and amended it in 1985. The Economic Espionage Act of 1996 makes the theft or misappropriation of a trade secret for a product produced for or placed in interstate commerce, or one whose theft would benefit a foreign power, a federal crime. These laws protect the company from misappropriation of the secret, making it a crime to improperly acquire a trade secret. The protection remains as long as the information is kept secret. The biggest threat to a trade secret usually comes from within the company itself. Current employees may reveal the secret accidentally in casual discussions at business meetings, at professional conferences, or in personal conversations, or they may be bribed by business competitors to reveal it. Former employees bring with them knowledge of the business processes of a company and other proprietary information, and they may reveal this information to their new employers. Companies usually protect trade secrets by limiting the number of employees who have access to them, by guarding the documents containing them carefully, and by requiring employees who have access to them to sign nondisclosure agreements.

Litigation often results when a trade secret is revealed. The courts must determine whether the information constitutes a trade secret. They consider factors such as how widely the information is known both inside and outside the company, what measures have been taken to guard the secret, how valuable the information is to the company and its competitors, the amount of time, effort, and financial investment involved in developing the secret, and how difficult it is to duplicate the information.

If the owner can establish that it was a trade secret using the factors previously described, and that the secret was obtained by improper means such as bribery, the owner can receive compensation. There are heavy fines and possible prison sentences for violating trade secret laws.

Since protection under patent laws requires full disclosure but protection under trade secret laws requires that the secret never be disclosed, a company cannot claim a trade secret and also apply for a patent for the same information.

Trademarks and Service Marks

Trademarks and service marks are also eligible for protection under intellectual property laws. Marks can include one or more letters, numbers, or words. They can also be drawings, symbols, colors, sounds, fragrances, or the shape or packaging of goods that are distinctive. According to the United States Patent and Trademark Office,

- A **trademark** is a word, phrase, symbol, or design, or a combination of words, phrases, symbols, or designs, that identifies and distinguishes the source of the goods of one party from those of others.

- A **service mark** is the same as a trademark, except that it identifies and distinguishes the source of a service rather than a product (U.S. Patent and Trademark Office, *Basic Facts About Trademarks*).

In the United States trademarks are protected by both federal law under the **Lanham Act** (Trademark Law of 1946) and by state laws. Registration of them is not required. A company can establish its right to a mark simply by using it, and can designate it as a trademark by using the TM symbol, or as a service mark by using the SM symbol. However, marks used in interstate or foreign commerce can be protected by registering them with the Patent and Trademark Office. Registration requires a clear reproduction of the mark, including any three-dimensional aspects, a sample of it in use, a list of goods and services for which the mark will be used, as well as other requirements. A search is then conducted to ensure that the mark is appropriate and distinctive and does not infringe upon any other registered mark. Once registered, owners can use the federal registration symbol ® to designate the mark. Registering the mark allows the owner to notify the public of ownership of the mark, establishes the legal right to ownership and exclusive right to use it, allows the owner to bring a court action concerning infringement of the mark, allows him or her to use it as a basis of registration of the mark in foreign countries, and allows the owner to file the registration with the U.S. Custom Service to prevent infringing foreign goods from being imported.

To prove infringement, an owner must show that consumers are likely to be misled by the use of the infringing mark. Registration is valid for 10 years, but it can be renewed. Many countries have adopted either the **Madrid Protocol** of 1989 or the Madrid Agreement Concerning the International Registration of Marks of 1891. WIPO administers a system of international registration of marks based on these two treaties. More than 76 countries form the Madrid Union, and have signed one or both of these agreements. To register the mark, the owner must first file an application with the trademark office of one of the member countries. Once the mark has been registered in a member country, the owner can use that as the basis for getting an international registration that is valid in the member countries of the Madrid Union.

14.2.3 Intellectual Property Protection for Software

Software and its packaging can be protected by copyright, by patent or trade secret laws, by trademark, or by some combination of these devices. Although the algorithms that are used to create software cannot be copyrighted because they are ideas, software programs themselves can be copyrighted because they are classified as expressions. Both U.S. copyright laws and the Berne Convention specifically mention software as subject to copyright. Software does not have to be published in order to be copyrighted. As soon as it is created, the program is copyrighted and all rights belong to the owner, who can be the programmer or an employer, in the case of a work for hire. Therefore it is illegal for anyone to make a copy of any program, unless the owner gives permission to do so, except for the limited fair use described earlier. The documentation that accompanies software, including all the manuals, is also protected by copyright, regardless of whether it displays a copyright symbol. Except for fair use, it is also illegal to copy manuals unless permission to do so has been given. Often, there is also a trademark associated with software. It is illegal to market competing software using a mark that is so similar to the trademark that customers might be misled into thinking it is the original product. Sometimes the software contains a technical protection device to prevent copying. Tampering with that device or creating technology to facilitate tampering in order to circumvent the protection violates the DMCA in the United States, and violates the Berne Convention standards.

A customer who buys proprietary software is normally buying a **license to use** the software, not the software itself, which remains the property of the owner. The terms of the license are often displayed on an opening screen when the software is installed, and the customer signifies agreement to the terms before installing the product. The usual terms are that the customer has a right to use the software, and to make a backup copy, but only one copy of the program can be used at a time. In that case, it is illegal for the customer to run the backup on a second computer at the same time the original is being used. It is certainly illegal, and constitutes software piracy, for the customer to give a copy of the software to another person to use. Often, product registration using a unique license number is required by the vendor, but the protection applies even if registration is not required. A business or other organization may purchase a license to use a certain number of copies of software at a time. The organization should use some mechanism to count the number of copies being used simultaneously to prevent abuse of the license. Some organizations purchase site licenses that allow an unlimited number of copies of software to be used only at a certain site. It would then be software piracy to allow the software to be used at a second location, such as a branch office.

Some software is free and available for copying. This type of software, which includes the MySQL database management system, may have enhancements, manuals, or trademarks that are protected by intellectual property rules. Although copying the open source software is legal, copying any related product that is protected is clearly not.

Another category of software is **shareware**, which allows people to download and use the software in order to evaluate it. If they wish to continue to use the software after the trial period, they are asked to pay for its use. In some cases, the vendor states that although the trial software can be downloaded free, the customer is required to register. Then it is illegal for the customer to give a copy to another person, since that person should also register. Some products have protective devices that disable the software after the trial period or after a certain number of uses. However, even if the software continues to function after the trial period, any further use violates the agreement the user makes in downloading the product, and is illegal.

Commercial database management system software, such as that from major vendors, is usually protected using the same intellectual property protection methods as other software. The custom applications that may have been written by a company for a database, such as a customized user interface or customized reports, also qualify for the software protections mentioned. The same rules that apply to other software apply to this software. Some major DBMS vendors allow customers to download a free personal edition of their database software, for their own use. Others offer the personal edition only for a limited trial period. Editions for an enterprise are usually not available free.

Databases themselves are also qualified for different kinds of intellectual property protection. For example, the database can be copyrighted, because it is an expression, even though the facts contained in the database cannot be copyrighted. This protection applies even if the owner has published the data on the Web. Since all expressions are automatically copyrighted, even if they are published without a copyright symbol, users should assume that all data on the Web is copyrighted, unless otherwise stated. Therefore, except for fair use, making copies of data on the Web is illegal, unless the data is clearly identified as copyright-free. The information in a database can also be treated as a trade secret, since it can be used to provide a competitive advantage. In that case, of course, the data is not published. However, if a person gains access to this proprietary information, he or she is not free to use it because of trade secret laws. Sensitive data or data that should be kept secure under privacy laws should be protected using the security subsystem of the database management system and possibly other security safeguards, and should be stored in encrypted form, as well as being encrypted whenever it is transmitted. Bypassing the security devices to gain unauthorized access to the data is illegal.

14.3   Databases and Privacy Issues

Much of the data that people provide about themselves in the regular course of their lives ends up in databases. School records, which contain personal information such as name, address, date of birth, and details about performance in school, are often kept in a database. When people apply for employment, information about their goals, their job history, their educational background, and their references may be stored in a database long after they have completed the application process. When people file their income tax returns, they provide detailed information about the sources and amounts of their income, as well as name, address, and social security number. Sometimes people unwittingly provide information about their buying habits. Whenever a consumer makes a purchase and pays by personal check, credit card, debit card, or uses a "preferred customer" card with an identifying number, that purchase can be linked with the buyer. If the purchase is made via a website, by telephone, or by mail order, or if the customer registers for a warrantee or service agreement, the same link can be made. In the registration process, customers might unknowingly provide personal information such as education level, family income, hobbies, and other data unrelated to the purchase. People provide similar background information in the process of filling out survey forms, or when they enter sweepstakes or other contests. When they apply for a loan or a credit card, they authorize companies to check their credit records. Cookies or spyware installed on user's computers, often without their express consent, can provide an endless stream of data, called "clickstream data," by capturing their every keystroke.

Database technology makes it possible to store massive amounts of data about individuals. Data matching software could be used to match records obtained from databases developed by different companies or government agencies. Communication technology makes it possible to transfer all kinds of data to third parties, who could compile their databases containing profiles of individuals. Data mining could be used to discover patterns of an individual's behavior. All of these technologies could potentially be used to compile information about individuals without their knowledge or consent. The issues of whether it is ethical to collect certain data about an individual, to use it without the consent of the individual, and to share it with third parties are the subject of much debate. There is a conflict between the individual's right to privacy and the desire of governments and businesses to have information that would be useful to them.

14.3.1 Privacy and Security

In Chapter 9, we loosely defined **privacy** as the right of individuals to have some control over information about themselves. Personal data that is collected and stored in databases forms the bulk of the information that individuals might be concerned about. In general, people provide this information willingly, often without realizing that it can be stored and possibly misused. By providing or allowing access to personal information, consumers surrender what they consider to be a small amount of privacy for real or perceived benefits. However, if the organizations or people who initially collect the data pass on or sell the information to a third party without the consumer's consent, the consumer's privacy might be violated. There is disagreement about how much privacy people are entitled to, and what constitutes a violation of privacy.

Database security means protecting the database from unauthorized access, modification, or destruction. Chapter 9 dealt with database security from a technical standpoint. In addition to the need to preserve and protect data for the smooth functioning of the organization, database designers have a responsibility to protect the privacy of individuals about whom data is kept. Database designers and database administrators should be aware of applicable privacy legislation and should be able to set and to implement corporate policies that respect the privacy rights of people. The security mechanisms discussed in Chapter 9 should be used in implementing these policies.

14.3.2 Privacy as a Human Right

In an 1890 article, Justice Louis Brandeis and Samuel Warren defined privacy as the "right to be left alone" ("The Right to Privacy," *Harvard Law Review* 4, 1890 pp. 193–220). Justice Brandeis wrote that modern devices (faster photographic equipment, in that case) allow violations of privacy to be committed against a person without his or her knowledge, and argued that the law needed to be extended to cover such circumstances. The collection and dissemination of massive amounts of personal information made possible by databases and communications technology certainly fall into the category of potential violations of privacy under this definition.

Recent scholars have defined privacy in more complete terms and provided a philosophical basis for privacy. Alan Westin, author of the seminal 1967 work *Privacy and Freedom,* defined privacy as "the desire of people to choose freely under what circumstances and to what extent they will expose themselves, their attitude and their behavior to others" (*Privacy and Freedom,* New York: Atheneum, 1967, p. 7). In 1990, the Calcutt Committee provided its own definition in its first report on privacy: "The right of the individual to be protected against intrusion into his personal life or affairs, or those of his family, by direct physical means or by publication of information" (*Report of the Committee on Privacy and*

Related Matters, Chairman David Calcutt QC, 1990, Cmnd. 1102, London: HMSO, 1990, p. 7). Deborah Johnson, in her book on computer ethics (*Computer Ethics 4th ed.,* Prentice Hall, 2008) argued that privacy has intrinsic value because it is "an essential aspect of autonomy," and autonomy is an intrinsic good. James Moor, in his 1997 article, "Towards a Theory of Privacy for the Information Age" (*Computers and Society* (27)3, pp. 27–32), states that, "As societies become larger and highly interactive, but less intimate, privacy becomes a natural expression of the need for security." Richard Spinello says "A primary moral foundation for the value of privacy is its role as a condition of freedom (or autonomy)." He identifies "information privacy" in his book *CyberEthics* as having two components, restricted access and limited control. By restricted access he means "a capacity to shield personal data from some parties while sharing it with others." Limited control means "In situations where a user provides his or her personal information to a vendor or a professional party, the user will be informed when that information will be shared with a third party. In addition, under normal conditions the user will have the capacity to limit the sharing of that information." (*CyberEthics,* Jones and Bartlett, 4th ed., 2011, p. 151–152.)

Privacy is recognized as a fundamental human right enshrined in the constitutions of many countries, in a declaration of human rights by the United Nations, in conventions adopted by the European Union, and in laws enacted both in the United States and throughout the world. In the Universal Declaration of Human Rights adopted in 1948, the General Assembly of the United Nations proclaimed in Article 12,

> No one shall be subjected to arbitrary interference with his privacy, family, home, or correspondence, nor to attacks upon his honour and reputation. Everyone has the right to the protection of the law against such interference or attacks.

Despite the adoption of this declaration by the United Nations, privacy is not universally protected, even among the member nations. Among countries where privacy legislation exists, there is considerable variation in the definition of privacy and the degree to which privacy is protected.

Privacy Legislation in the United States

The Constitution of the United States does not address individual privacy directly, but the Fourth Amendment to the Constitution, ratified in 1791, protects people against unreasonable searches, by guaranteeing that,

> The right of the people to be secure in their persons, houses, papers, and effects, against unreasonable searches and seizures, shall not be violated, and no warrants shall issue, but upon probable cause, supported by oath or affirmation, and particularly describing the place to be searched, and the persons or things to be seized. (The Constitution of the United States, 4th Amendment.)

The history of privacy law and attempts at legislation in the United States demonstrates a growing awareness on the part of the public and legislators of the value of privacy. An early set of principles governing private information was the Code of Fair Information Practices, which were part of a 1972 report prepared for the U.S. Department of Health, Education, and Welfare (HEW). The Fair Information practices included these principles:

1. There must be no personal data record keeping systems whose very existence is secret.

2. There must be a way for a person to find out what information about the person is in a record and how it is used.

3. There must be a way for a person to prevent information about the person that was obtained for one purpose from being used or made available for other purposes without the person's consent.

4. There must be a way for a person to correct or amend a record of identifiable information about the person.

5. Any organization creating, maintaining, using, or disseminating records of identifiable personal data must assure the reliability of the data for their intended use and must take precautions to prevent misuses of the data.

(U.S. Department of Health, Education, and Welfare, Secretary's Advisory Committee on Automated Personal Data Systems, Records, Computers, and the Rights of Citizens viii (1973).)

These principles can be considered the basis for many of the privacy laws that have been enacted in the United States. United States privacy laws are divided into two categories—those that provide protection from government interference and those that provide protection from interference by others, including businesses.

U.S. Privacy Laws Concerning Government Agencies The Freedom of Information Act of 1966 requires that agencies of the executive branch of the federal government, including cabinet and military departments, government corporations, regulatory agencies and others, provide access to their records. With certain exceptions defined in the law, these agencies must provide copies of agency rules, opinions, orders, records, and proceedings to individuals who request them. The subject of the records need not be the person making the request. Several amendments have been made to this law in recent years.

The Privacy Act of 1974 was an important step in protecting the privacy rights of individuals from government interference. It allows individuals access to government records about themselves. Its stated purpose was,

> . . . to balance the government's need to maintain information about individuals with the rights of individuals to be protected against unwarranted invasions of their privacy stemming from federal agencies' collection, maintenance, use, and disclosure of personal information about them. (U.S. Department of Justice, *Overview of the Privacy Act of 1974,* 2010 ed., p. 4.)

A component of this legislation was an attempt to prevent the government from using social security numbers as "universal identifiers" that could possibly be used to link information from different sources. The overview states that,

> [Congress was] . . . concerned with potential abuses presented by the government's increasing use of computers to store and retrieve personal data by means of a universal identifier—such as an individual's social security number. (U.S. Department of Justice, *Overview of the Privacy Act of 1974,* 2010 ed., p. 4.)

There were four basic policy objectives on which the Act focused:

1. To restrict *disclosure* of personally identifiable records maintained by agencies.

2. To grant individuals increased rights of *access* to agency records maintained on themselves.

3. To grant individuals the right to seek *amendment* of agency records maintained on themselves upon a showing that the records are not accurate, relevant, timely, or complete.

4. To establish a code of *"fair information practices,"* which requires agencies to comply with statutory norms for collection, maintenance, and dissemination of records.

In 1988, Congress enacted the Computer Matching and Privacy Protection Act to protect individuals from certain computer matching activities by government agencies. It states,

> These provisions add procedural requirements for agencies to follow when engaging in computer-matching activities; provide matching subjects with opportunities to receive notice and to refute adverse information before having a benefit denied or terminated; and require that agencies engaged in matching activities establish Data Protection Boards to oversee those activities.

The Computer Matching and Privacy Protection Amendments of 1990 added to the due process provisions of the Act. In 2007, an exemption from the Privacy Act was granted for the Advance Passenger Information System to provide data about airline passengers to and from the U.S. to the Office of Homeland Security.

The Patriot Act enacted in 2001 and extended in 2006, weakened the provisions of some of the privacy laws, in the interests of national security. The purpose of the law is to combat terrorism by allowing law enforcement agencies more access to information about potential terrorist plans. The law relaxes restrictions on information sharing among federal agencies, allows law enforcement officials to obtain "roving wiretaps" to monitor cellular telephone conversations of suspected terrorists, provides greater subpoena power to obtain email records of terror suspects, and gives law enforcement agencies easier access to banking records to prevent money laundering. This law is highly controversial and a number of challenges to it have been filed.

United States Privacy Legislation Concerning Private Businesses The laws discussed above restricted the government's use of personal data, but did not apply to private businesses, in general, except for government contractors. Instead, individual laws were passed to deal with practices in various business sectors. These include:

- Fair Credit Reporting Act of 1970
- Family Educational Rights and Privacy Act of 1974

- Right to Financial Privacy Act of 1978

- Federal Managers Financial Integrity Act of 1982

- Cable Privacy Protection Act of 1984

- Cable Communications Policy Act of 1984

- Electronic Communication Privacy Act of 1986

- Computer Security Act of 1987

- Video Privacy Protection Act of 1988

- Telephone Consumer Protection Act of 1991

- Driver's Privacy Protection Act of 1994

- Health Insurance Portability and Accountability Act of 1996

- Children's Online Privacy Protection Act of 1998

- Gramm-Leach-Bliley Financial Services Modernization Act of 1999

- Sarbanes-Oxley Act of 2002

- The Fair and Accurate Credit Transactions Act of 2003

- Check Clearing for the 21st Century Act of 2004

- Identity Theft Penalty Enhancement Act of 2004

- Genetic Information Nondiscrimination Act of 2008

In general, privacy laws in the United States attempted to apply the principles of the HEW Code of Fair Information Practices Act to the industry to which they apply. Except for instances explicitly covered by privacy legislation, they do not prevent businesses from collecting information about their customers and sharing that information with third parties. Even in instances where the sharing of customer information is restricted, such as in the Gramm-Leach-Bliley Financial Services Modernization Act of 1999, Congress has chosen to apply the restrictions using an "opt-out" rather than an "opt-in" mechanism. With "opt-in," an organization cannot share customer information unless the customer specifically agrees to the sharing, while with "opt-out" the data can be shared unless the customer requests that it not be shared. Organizations are required to notify customers of their right to opt-out of data sharing, but if a customer fails to respond, the organization can assume that permission has been granted. It is generally agreed that it is more restrictive to require opt-in than opt-out, and many privacy advocates in the United States were disappointed by the approval of the opt-out provisions.

Privacy Legislation in the European Union

In the European Union, a different standard exists, and that difference has some important implications for U.S. firms doing business in the European market, since it limits the flow of data across borders. While U.S. laws have historically restricted government activities and handled business activities only on a sector-by-sector basis, European laws are more restrictive of business activities. They also require opt-in rather than opt-out as the mechanism for obtaining customer approval of data sharing. The European Union based its directives on principles developed by the Organization of Economic Cooperation and Development (OECD), an international organization with 32 member countries and cooperative relationships with many others. In 1980, the organization developed standards called the Fair Information Practices, including these eight principles taken from the OECD Guidelines on the Protection of Privacy and Transborder Flows of Personal Data (OECD, Paris, 1981):

- **Collection Limitation Principle.**
  - There should be limits to the collection of personal data
  - The data should be obtained by lawful and fair means
  - Data should be collected with the knowledge or consent of the subject, where possible and appropriate.

- **Data Quality Principle.** Personal data should be:
  - Relevant to the purposes for which they are to be used
  - Collected only to the extent necessary for those purposes
  - Accurate, complete and up-to-date.

- **Purpose Specification Principle.**
  - The purposes for which personal data are collected should be specified in advance of data collection
  - Data should not used again except for fulfilling those purposes

- **Use Limitation Principle.** Personal data should not be shared or used for purposes other than those stated in the Purpose Specification Principle except with the consent of the subject or by the authority of law.

- **Security Safeguards Principle.** Reasonable security measures should be used to protect personal data against unauthorized access, use, disclosure, modification, destruction, and loss.

- **Openness Principle.** There should be a general policy of openness about practices concerning personal data. It should be easily possible to know about its existence, nature, purpose of use, and the name and contact information of the person who controls it (called the **data controller**).

- **Individual Participation Principle.** An individual should be able to:

  - Find out whether the data controller has data relating to him or her

  - Find out what that data is within a reasonable time, at a reasonable charge (if any), and in a form that is understandable

  - Challenge the denial of any such request and to challenge data related to him or her. If the challenge is successful, the individual has the right to have the data corrected or erased.

- **Accountability Principle.** A data controller should be accountable for complying with the principles.

In the Convention for the Protection of Individuals with Regard to Automatic Processing of Personal Data, which was proposed in 1981 and adopted in 1985, the Council of Europe set policy for its member countries regarding processing of personal information. The summary of the convention states:

> This Convention is the first binding international instrument which protects the individual against abuses which may accompany the collection and processing of personal data and which seeks to regulate at the same time the transfrontier flow of personal data.

> In addition to providing guarantees in relation to the collection and processing of personal data, it outlaws the processing of "sensitive" data such as a person's race, politics, health, religion, sexual life, or criminal record, in the absence of proper legal safeguards.

The Convention also enshrines the individual's right to know that information is stored on him or her and, if necessary, to have it corrected.

Restriction on the rights laid down in the Convention are only possible when overriding interests (e.g., State security, defence, etc.) are at stake.

The Convention also imposes some restrictions on transborder flows of personal data to States where legal regulation does not provide equivalent protection. (Council of Europe. Strasbourg, 1981.)

Both the OECD principles and the Council of Europe's Convention, which is similar, have been used as the basis of privacy laws in dozens of countries. The exact provisions and phrasing varies by country, but in general they require that personal information must be obtained fairly, be used only for the purpose originally specified, be relevant and adequate for the purpose, not be excessive for the purpose, be accurate, and that it be destroyed after its purpose is completed.

In 1995, the European Union adopted the European Data Protection Directive, "Protection of Individuals with regard to the processing of personal data and on the free movement of such data," which required all of its member countries to adopt legislation by 1998 that enforced the same privacy protection standards, which are essentially those of the OECD and COE. The directive included a provision that data about citizens of European Union countries must be afforded the same level of protection when it leaves the country. Other countries have ensured that they can safely receive such data by adopting laws using the same standards, but the United States has not. Therefore, U.S. companies doing business in or having business partners in the European Union and countries having EU-type privacy laws had problems obtaining the data needed for their business, since they could not legally obtain customer information from those countries. A partial solution was worked out in 2000 between the European Union and the U.S. Federal Trade Commission using the **Safe Harbor** mechanism. United States companies can certify that they follow the rules of the safe harbor agreement, which means that they comply with the EU rules in the way they treat data. The companies must annually certify to the U.S. Department of Commerce that they meet the standards, and state in their public privacy policy statements that they do so. They may also display the Safe Harbor program certification mark on their website and in publicity releases. The list of companies that belong to the safe harbor program is published by the Department of Commerce. Enforcement is the responsibility of the Federal Trade Commission or other federal or state agencies. Punishment is by severe fines and by expulsion of the offending company from the safe harbor program.

14.4 Human Factors

14.4.1 Human Factors in Software Development

Human factors in software development refers to factors that promote or facilitate optimal performance on the part of the user. These factors include both physical characteristics of the user and psychological factors, and should be considered as part of any database system development project. Human factors are vitally important in critical software such as that used in life-support systems, nuclear power plants, medical treatment devices, airplanes, and many other areas where error or failure can have life-threatening consequences. In business, design for human factors can reduce errors and increase productivity, especially in repetitive tasks such as order entry. Good design resulting from consideration of human factors promotes user acceptance and satisfaction. By careful design for human factors, physical problems such as fatigue and psychological problems such as stress can be reduced. The result of user-centered design is an increase in user comfort and user safety, greater productivity, increased user satisfaction, and a reduction in errors. It also reduces training costs, as well as the costs of dealing with and recovering from errors.

A human factors system engineering approach includes consideration of the user at every stage of the system project. A typical system project can include these stages:

- **Conceptualization.** Designers identify the objectives of the system and define specifications for it.

- **Definition.** Designers define the system, including any subsystems. They describe the environment in which it will be used and the way it will be used.

- **Overall design.** Designers identify all system components and their functions. Components include hardware, software, and human components. They analyze tasks and requirements.

- **Interface design.** Designers use appropriate design standards to create user interfaces. They apply design principles, statistical data, mathematical modeling, results of empirical studies, and experience.

- **Development.** Developers implement the system, test it, and modify it if indicated by the testing.

- **Deployment.** When the system is deployed, developers evaluate its use and make modifications as needed.

- **Maintenance.** Once the system is operational, procedures for continued evaluation, system evolution, and improvement are put in place.

At every stage, the designers and developers benefit by considering human factors. Including users in discussions during the conceptualization, definition, and design stages to capture their input about the proposed system at these early points helps to ensure that the system design is user-centered. Human factors specialists who are employed by the enterprise or who work as consultants can be valuable members of the design team. At the interface design stage, designers should incorporate interface design principles that have been developed by experts in the field. The field of Human–Computer Interaction (HCI) is a speciality that involves aspects of computer science, cognitive psychology, graphic design, communications, and other fields of study. The Association for Computing Machinery Special Interest Group in Computer–Human Interaction defines the field as follows: "Human–computer interaction is a discipline concerned with the design, evaluation and implementation of interactive computing systems for human use and with the study of major phenomena surrounding them."(Hewett, Baecker, Card, et al. *ACM SIGCHI Curricula for Human–Computer Interaction*, 1996.) The ACM curriculum provides an overview of the field. Other sources for design principles include a number of excellent books, conferences, and research institutes, such as the University of Maryland Human–Computer Interaction Lab, the Human–Computer Interaction Institute at Carnegie-Mellon University, the Media Lab at the Massachusetts Institute of Technology, and the Stanford University Program in Human–Computer Interaction.

14.4.2 The Human-Database Interface

The ultimate measure of the success of a database project is the extent to which the users actually use it to obtain the information they need. A database designer normally spends a considerable amount of time making sure that the database is useful, that it actually satisfies the information needs of the enterprise. As explained in Chapter 2 and illustrated throughout later chapters, the designer interviews users to determine their data needs, designs the conceptual model, applies techniques such as normalization to ensure the quality of the model, chooses the most appropriate database management system, does the logical mapping, designs the internal model, creates the system, and develops the database. The designer may be satisfied if the database itself is well designed and highly efficient. However, if it is not usable because of a poor user interface, end users will not be satisfied and will be disinclined to use the database. Usability is an aspect of quality that merits the same kind of careful attention that the rest of database design does.

When designing for interactive users, database designers should consider the elements of interactive design, which include use of metaphors (e.g., desktop look and feel), quality and consistency of navigational cues, quality of error messages, effective feedback, and visual components such as layout, fonts, and color. The layout should be consistent from screen to screen, the screen should not be too crowded, the colors and fonts should enhance readability, and the language should be unambiguous, simple, clear, and appropriate for the users. Care should be taken to use language and symbols that do not offend any group or subgroup. Illustrations and examples that demonstrate and enhance diversity should be chosen.

Jakob Nielsen, an expert in usability, distinguishes between **utility**, which means the functionality of the design, and **usability**. Both are attributes of quality, and both are essential to the success of a database project. Without utility, the database does not provide what users need, and without usability, users cannot get what they need because the user interface is too difficult. Both utility and usability can be measured by user research methods.

Nielsen describes usability as "a quality attribute that assesses how easy user interfaces are to use" (Jakob Nielsen. *Usability 101: Introduction to Usability,* http://www.useit.com/alertbox/20030825.html). He lists five components of usability.

1. **Learnability** refers to the ease with which users can accomplish tasks the first time they see the design.

2. **Efficiency** refers to how quickly users can accomplish tasks once they have mastered the design.

3. **Memorability** refers to how easily users can reestablish proficiency in using the design after a period of not using it.

4. **Errors** refers to the number and severity of errors that users make, and how easily they can recover from them.

5. **Satisfaction** refers to how pleasant it is to use the design.

For end users, usability is closely tied to productivity. Nielsen suggests that about 10 percent of a project's budget should be spent on usability. He claims that such an investment will substantially improve software, will double a website's quality metrics, and will improve an intranet's quality metrics almost as much. In gross measures, such improvements mean cutting training costs in half and doubling the number of transactions that can be performed by employees or customers.

14.4.3 Usability Testing for Database Applications

Some basic techniques can be used for studying usability. Nielsen suggests repeated user-testing. The process consists of finding some representative users, having them perform representative tasks, and observing their actions, noting where they succeed and where they have problems with the interface. As few as five users can provide valuable information. Nielsen suggests conducting many small tests as the design progresses, revising the design in an iterative fashion between tests. Using the elements of interactive design mentioned above, it is straightforward to create test designs using various components and layouts and to conduct small studies to see the effect of changes. Usability testing should continue during development, deployment, and maintenance phases, because even slight changes that seem insignificant to the developers can have a large impact on usability. Small studies can be done as case studies. It is possible to perform formal hypothesis testing using a limited number of subjects, provided appropriate statistical distributions such as the Student's t distribution are used. However, before deployment of the final system, formal hypothesis testing should be done using statistically robust methods on a larger sample.

14.5 Chapter Summary

Computerization has created new situations that challenge society's moral codes. ACM and IEEE publish ethical standards to help guide computer and software professionals, but ethical questions about computer use remain. The Internet is largely unregulated because it is not subject to the rules of any single country, and because of its culture. It provides a forum for free speech, but abuses such as pornography, spam, and hate rhetoric can become rampant. Another issue is intellectual property protection both for Internet and database content and for software. Individual privacy is compromised by the widespread use of computer technology to share personal information stored in databases, and the increased use of data mining. Responsibilities of computer professionals to make their products easier and safer for users, and the best ways to do that are also debated.

The foundation of **intellectual property** rights is that the creator is entitled to a just return, which in turn encourages creative people to develop new works. Intellectual property is protected by a variety of mechanisms, including copyright, patent, trade secret, trademarks, and service marks.

Software and its packaging can be protected by copyright, by patent or trade secret laws, by trademark, or by some combination of these devices. A customer who buys proprietary software is actually buying a **license to use** the software, not the software itself, which remains the property of the owner. **Open source** software is free and available for copying. **Shareware** allows people to download and use the software for an evaluation period, after which they should pay for its continued use. Commercial database management system software and custom applications written for it are usually protected using the same intellectual property protection methods as other software. Databases themselves are also qualified for different kinds of intellectual property protection. For example, the database can be copyrighted, because it is an expression, even though the facts contained in the database cannot be copyrighted. The information in a database can also be treated as a trade secret, since it can be used to provide a competitive advantage.

Database technology makes it possible to store massive amounts of data about individuals. Data matching, spyware, data mining, and communication technologies could be used to compile and share information about individuals without their knowledge or consent. The issues of whether it is ethical to collect certain data about an individual, to use it without the consent of the individual, and to share it with third parties are the subject of much debate, and practices in the United States and the European Union differ significantly. In the U.S., several federal laws protect privacy of individuals from interference by government agencies. The Patriot Act has weakened the provisions of some of the privacy laws, in the interests of national security. Individual laws deal with practices in various business sectors. Generally, they require that consumers have to **opt-out** to prevent their information from being shared. European laws are more restrictive of business activities. They also require **opt-in** rather than opt-out as the mechanism for obtaining customer approval of data sharing. They are based on principles of collection limitation, data quality, purpose specification, use limitation, security safeguards, openness, individual participation, and accountability. Data about EU citizens must be afforded the same level of protection when it leaves the country. However, U.S. companies can certify that they follow the rules of the **Safe Harbor** agreement, which means that they comply with the EU rules in the way they treat data, and can receive such data.

Human factors in software development refers to physical and psychological factors that promote or facilitate optimal performance on the part of the user. User-centered design increases user comfort, safety, productivity, and satisfaction, and reduces training costs and errors. A human factors systems engineering approach includes consideration of the user at every stage of the system project. Usability is an important determinant of the success of a database project. Components of **usability** include learnability, efficiency, memorability, error reduction, and satisfaction. The field of Human–Computer Interaction (HCI) covers design, evaluation, and implementation of computer systems for human interaction.

Exercises

14.1   Define the following terms.

   a. intellectual property

   b. copyright

   c. patent

    d. trade secret

    e. trademark

    f. service mark

    g. infringement

    h. open source

    i. freeware

    j. Blackstonian bundle

    k. fair use

    l. public domain

    m. Berne Convention

    n. WIPO

    o. copyright infringement

    p. Digital Millennium Copyright Act

    q. Freedom of Information Act

    r. Privacy Act of 1974

    s. universal identifier

    t. Patriot Act of 2002

    u. Gramm-Leach-Bliley Financial Services Modernization Act of 1999

    v. Lanhan Act

    w. opt-out

    x. OECD

    y. data controller

    z. Safe Harbor

14.2   Choose one of the U.S. laws mentioned in this chapter and research its origins, its provisions, and its legislative history. Summarize the arguments in favor of the law and against the law. Prepare a presentation describing your findings.

14.3   Choose one of the international conventions or agreements mentioned in this chapter and research its history, its provisions, the countries that participate in it, and its relationship to U.S. law in the same area. Summarize the arguments in favor of the agreement and against it. If you were the president of the United States, would you subscribe to the agreement? Prepare a presentation describing your findings.

14.4   Research the open source software movement and read about its philosophical basis. Write an essay defending your position on this issue.

14.5   Assume you and a group of friends have developed an innovative piece of software for which you wish to protect your intellectual property rights. Identify the mechanism you would choose, and describe what you would need to do (if anything) to establish your ownership and to enforce your ownership of the software. Would your rights be recognized in other countries? If not, is there any mechanism you can use to enforce them overseas?

14.6   Assume you have a position as database administrator in a large corporation. The company has been collecting data about employees, including monitoring their working habits by recording their keystrokes, timing their telephone interactions with clients, and scanning their email for personal correspondence. As DBA, you are asked to help set up a recordkeeping system to store such data. Does the company have a legal right to perform this kind of monitoring? What is your professional responsibility in this situation? Do the ACM and IEEE Codes of Ethics have any provisions to guide you?

On the Companion Website:

- Additional Exercises
- Sample Project
- Student Projects

CHAPTER 15

Data Warehouses and Data Mining

Chapter Objectives

In this chapter you will learn the following:

- How data warehouses differ from operational databases

- The basic architecture of a data warehouse

- The meaning of the terms rollup, drill-down, cross-tabulation, and slice and dice

- How data warehouse queries are expressed in SQL

- How bitmap indexes and join indexes can be used

- How view materialization and view maintenance are handled

- The purpose of data mining

- The types of knowledge data mining can produce
- How decision trees, regression, neural networks, genetic algorithms, and clustering are used
- Some application areas for data mining

15.1   Origins of Data Warehouses

Beginning in the 1960s, many organizations started to use standard database technology to collect, store, and process massive amounts of their operational data. The primary purpose of these databases is to support current transactions, using real-time processing. Often, there are several operational databases in an organization to serve different business areas, rather than a single enterprise-wide database. Businesses with an enterprise-wide database system have a competitive advantage because decision makers can be provided with a view of the entire organization's current operations. As data become outdated, old records are usually archived, and the operational database is refreshed and populated with more current data. In the 1980s, business leaders began to realize that the historical data has value as well. In combination with current data, it can be used to help them make better business decisions. Decisions such as where to open a new store, what audience to target for an advertising campaign, which customers to approve loans for, and when to order additional stock can be made with more confidence when they are based on a careful examination of patterns found in existing data. Computer-based **Decision Support Systems** (DSS) and **Executive Information Systems**

(EIS) were developed to support these uses. An important component of such systems is the data warehouse, a repository of enterprise-wide historical data. The data in a data warehouse is often collected from various departments or sites belonging to a large enterprise. The term was coined by W. H. Inmon, who described a data warehouse as, "a subject-oriented, integrated, nonvolatile, time-varying collection of data that is used primarily in organizational decision making" (Inmon, *Building the Data Warehouse*, John Wiley and Sons, 1991). A data warehouse is intended for decision-support applications rather than for processing of ordinary transactions. It is optimized for data retrieval, as opposed to processing transactions.

Vendors of DBMSs including Oracle, IBM, and Microsoft were quick to add features to their product line to allow warehousing of the data from their operational database systems. New and powerful analytical processing (OLAP) tools were developed to draw more information from data stored in such warehouses and to provide enhanced methods of presenting information. SQL was extended to support the functions required by data warehouses.

Hardware advances including parallel machines, cheaper and faster data storage devices, and better data communications technology have also contributed to the popularity of data warehouses. The development of data mining, the process of developing new information by searching large amounts of data to identify patterns, trends, and anomalies, allows more sophisticated analysis and modeling. The volume of data available through cloud computing, the explosion in digitized content, and the availability of an almost unlimited supply of clickstream data, have made the prospect of harnessing and exploiting these resources more attractive. The term **Business Intelligence** (BI) was coined by Howard Dresner in 1989 as an umbrella term to mean "concepts and methods to improve business decision making by using fact-based support systems." A data warehouse with historical and current data, enriched with other information streams, is a prime source for BI.

15.2 Operational Databases and Data Warehouses

Traditional operational databases support **online transaction processing** (**OLTP**), which characteristically involves a limited number of repetitive transactions, each of which affects a few records at a time. Most operational databases today use the relational, object-oriented, or object-relational model to store data. Data is normalized to reduce redundancy, which promotes data integrity. Such a database is developed to serve the information needs of end users, and is designed to support their day-to-day business operations. High availability and efficient performance are critical factors in the success of an operational database. It must provide support for a large volume of transactions, and it must produce reports and deliver responses to user queries or other online operations in a short time frame. An operational database is updated in real-time, as transactions occur. Updates, insertions, and deletions must be done quickly to keep the database in a state that reflects the current environment of the enterprise. To preserve performance, older data is periodically purged.

By contrast, data warehouses support **OLAP** as well as decision making. The data in a data warehouse can be taken directly from multiple operational databases, at different periods of time (historical data), and may also include data from other sources, lightly and highly summarized data, and metadata. The sources may have different models or standards, or the source data may be unstructured, but the data warehouse integrates the data so that users see a consistent model. Often, the data model is dimensional, rather than relational, and the data may be repeated rather than normalized. The data warehouse typically contains a very large amount of data, and it is optimized for efficient query processing and presentation of results for decision support. Today's data warehouses are in the terabyte (trillion byte) to petabyte (quadrillion byte) range, but forecasters see exabyte (quintillion byte) range data as clickstream data, social network data, and other Internet traffic data is stored. In data warehouses, updates are not as frequent as they are in the operational database, but are done periodically. Since the data is relatively stable, more sophisticated indexing methods may be used to optimize data retrieval. OLAP applications typically must go through large amounts of data in order to produce results. Analysts examine the data stored in the warehouse using complex queries, generally involving grouping and aggregation operators. They may do time-series analysis using the historical data, data mining, or other complex operations. The queries and reports are usually less predictable than in standard databases.

15.3   Architecture of a Data Warehouse

Unlike an operational database, for which requirements can be specified in advance, a data warehouse must be designed to support *ad hoc* queries and new and unanticipated types of analysis and reporting. A typical

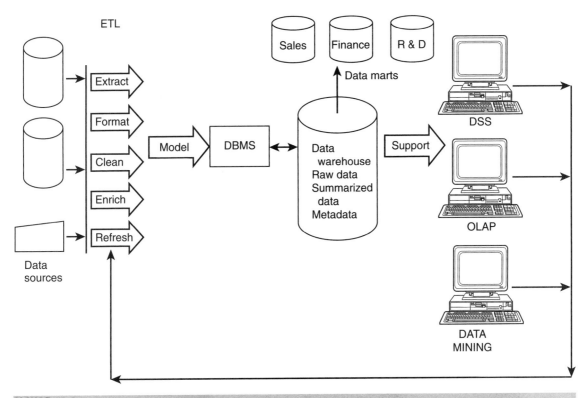

FIGURE 15.1
Data Warehouse Architecture

architecture is shown in Figure 15.1. Data is taken from data sources, which may include multiple operational databases, other inputs such as independent files, and environmental data such as geographic information or global or local financial data. The **ETL** (**Extraction, Transformation, and Loading**) system accesses data stores, transforms and integrates the data, loads the database files, creates indexes, and performs associated tasks. The data must be extracted from the sources using back-end system tools that can accommodate the differences among the heterogeneous sources. Additional processing such as summarizing may be done to enrich the data. The data is reformatted into a consistent form. The data can also be checked for integrity and validity, a process called **data cleaning**, to ensure its quality prior to loading it into the warehouse. Data is then put into the data model for the warehouse and loaded. The loading process is a long transaction, since a large volume of data is typically involved, so the system must use transaction management tools to ensure proper recovery in the event of failure during the loading transaction. The database management system that supports the data warehouse has a system catalog that stores metadata, as well as other database system components. The data warehouse is then used to support queries for OLAP, to provide information for decision support systems that are used by management for making strategic decisions, and to provide the data for data mining tools that discover new information about patterns in the data. Certain segments of the data are organized into subsets called **data marts**, which focus on specific subjects. For example, a data mart could contain specialized information about a single department within the organization. All of these uses can result in new knowledge, which can then be used as a data source from which data can be formatted and put into the warehouse. Data from all data sources must be periodically refreshed. If there is sufficient storage space, the new data is simply added to the existing warehouse, and the old data is kept as long as it is useful. Otherwise, data that is no longer used is purged periodically, and new data is added. The frequency and scope of the updates depend on the environment. Factors that must be considered in formulating the update policy include how much storage is available, whether the warehouse needs recent data, whether it can be off-line during refresh, and how long the process for transmitting the data, cleaning, formatting, loading, and building indexes will take. The usual policy is to do a partial refresh periodically.

15.4 Developing a Data Warehouse

There are two competing methodologies for designing data warehouses, called top-down and bottom-up, respectively.

15.4.1 Top-Down Method

In the first influential book in the field, *Designing the Data Warehouse,* first published by Wiley in 1991, W. H. Inmon defined a data warehouse as a resource for organizational decision making having these four characteristics:

- subject-oriented—the data items that describe a subject area (e.g., an entity) are linked together. Examples of subjects might be Customer, Product, Student, and so on.

- non-volatile—data warehouse data is static—not updated or deleted once it is stored

- integrated—data that may be from disparate sources is made coherent and consistent

- time-variant—all data stored in the warehouse is identified as belonging to a specific time period

His method calls for building a data warehouse as the centerpiece for a **Corporate Information Factory**, which is a delivery framework for Business Intelligence. Since the data warehouse has to support unanticipated queries and reports, it is impossible to determine all the system requirements in advance. Therefore, Inmon recommends going rapidly through the design and development stages and making the initial data warehouse operational quickly, then iterating the process. He recommends working within a "time box," setting a deadline of one week to six months, so that the project moves forward quickly. As users have an opportunity to provide feedback from their experiences with the first iteration, additional requirements become known. The second iteration incorporates these requirements, and the data warehouse design is refined. This process can continue as long as needed. The major steps in the process, as outlined in Inmon's 2000 white paper *Building the Data Warehouse: Getting Started* are the following:

1. Constructing a data model for the data warehouse

Unless there is an existing enterprise model, the process begins with constructing the enterprise data model, using traditional database design techniques. The designer or design team interviews potential users and managers to develop a set of requirements for the enterprise model. Existing (non-enterprise) operational databases and other data sources such as spreadsheets, flat files, and environmental data stores are examined to identify possible sources of data for the data warehouse, and those responsible for these sources are interviewed to determine whether the sources can be relied upon. The designer constructs an Entity-Relationship model for the enterprise, and maps it to normalized tables. Using this data model, or the model for the existing enterprise database if there is one, the designer takes additional steps described in Inmon's 2000 white paper *Creating the Data Warehouse Data Model from the Corporate Data Model* to transform the enterprise data model into the data warehouse model:

- Remove all purely operational data. This includes any data item that is kept in the operational database that will never be used in the applications for the data warehouse. For example, in Student records an item that keeps track of student library fines may not be necessary in the data warehouse, especially if they have to be cleared up at the end of each semester. Similarly, for Customer records we might have a temporary alternate telephone number that need not be stored in the data warehouse.

- Add a time element to the key, if one is not already there. For example, Student enrollment records should have a semester and year added.

- Add derived data. This is data that is calculated once and will be needed many times. For example, we might choose to keep the total amount of each Customer's yearly spending.

- Create relationship artifacts. Some data in an operational database shows relationships that exist at a given moment, such as what faculty member is teaching a course during the current semester, which may be indicated by having the faculty ID appear as a foreign key in the course record. If the faculty member record is deleted, that foreign key value is changed. However, it may be useful to know who has taught a given course over a period of time. Therefore the data warehouse might have a table showing a history of course offerings that includes a record for each time a course is offered, with the ID of the faculty member. There may also be a faculty teaching history table, showing each course a faculty member has taught over a number of semesters.

- Decide on levels of summarization for data. In addition to operational data, which may or may not be stored directly in the data warehouse, summaries of some data may be kept. It may be desirable to store summaries of each month's sales totals for each salesperson, or weekly sales for each branch of a business. These summaries may correspond to regular reports produced from the operational database.

- Merge tables if appropriate. The normalization process often produces tables with the same primary key. For the data warehouse, it may be desirable to combine such tables, provided the data they contain is often used together, and the insertion patterns are similar.

- Create arrays of data if appropriate. Because normalized records cannot have repeating fields, an operational database may require multiple occurrences of records with the same basic data. For example, there might be twelve records each year showing each salesperson's total sales for the month. For the data warehouse, we could create a single record for each salesperson for the entire year with an array of data items for each month, showing that month's total sales.

- Organize data according to its stability. For each entity, data items might be categorized according to whether they never change, sometimes change, or often change. For a stock record, data items that never change might be `itemNumber` and `itemName`; items that sometimes change might be `supplierName`, `reorderPoint`, and `unitPrice`; and items that often change might be `quantityOnHand` and `quantityOnOrder`. For the data warehouse, the stock record could then be split into three parts, each containing `itemNumber` and those data items with the same speed of change.

The result of these modifications to the enterprise model will be a data model for the data warehouse.

2. Selecting data warehouse hardware and software

The designer has to choose the technology to be used before the first iteration can be created. Considerations in the selection include the volume of data, user reporting and querying requirements, the budget, the types of applications, and many others. The software includes a database management system that can handle data warehousing and software for data capture and transformation. The hardware could be general-purpose or a specialized machine called a database appliance.

3. Sizing the data warehouse

The designer has to estimate the volume of data that will eventually be stored and processed, and ensure that the technology chosen is neither too large nor too small for the data.

4. Collecting obvious informational requirements

By examining existing reports, spreadsheets, and information systems output, and by interviewing end users, the designer can determine the obvious information requirements for a first iteration.

5. Choosing subsets of data for initial loading into the data warehouse

The designer should determine who the first users of the first iteration will be, and identify the data that they will need. The users should be from functional areas where data warehousing will be most effective, such as marketing, finance, sales, or process control, depending on the industry or environment.

6. Selecting a subject area for design

Within the functional area selected for the initial loading, there may be several subject areas that could be chosen. Examination of the data model should reveal what subjects or subsets of subjects can be implemented without conflict, and about five to fifteen tables should be chosen.

7. Identifying physical characteristics of the subject area

The physical attributes of the stored records, including all keys and data items, along with the volume of data, is determined next.

8. Identifying the unit of time for the data

Each key attribute should have a unit of time—hour, day, week, month, quarter, year, or other unit. Determining the unit is important because it has a great effect on the number of records that will be needed. The smaller the time unit, the larger the number of records.

9. Identifying the system of record

The system of record is the source data that will be used to populate the warehouse record. It should be the source that is most accurate, complete, timely, similar in structure to the target record, and near the point of entry. Identifying the system of record may be complicated because for a particular warehouse record there may be multiple data sources, no source, a different data format, or data may need to be combined, summarized, or otherwise altered from the source.

10. Determining whether delta data should be used

Besides data stored in the operational database, there are often records of potential changes to data warehouse records, called "delta data," which may be stored in files or other small data stores. These changes will be applied at the next warehouse refresh. Delta data may be used if the data warehouse records are relatively stable, and only a small number of records need to be refreshed. The alternative is a complete refresh.

11. Loading transformation data to metadata

After source data and data transformations have been specified, this information is stored in the metadata for the data warehouse. The result is a complete description of what is in the data warehouse, where it came from, and how it was transformed.

12. Specifying the frequency of transformation

For each record type in the warehouse, a frequency of transformation is chosen, depending on many factors such as the amount to be transformed, whether the user needs the most current data, whether a delta file is used, how complex the transformation is, how much summarization is needed, and so on.

13. Executing DDL

This step creates the structure of the data warehouse.

14. Creating code that embodies the transformations

The code for the ETL system for accessing data from the data sources and performing the data transformations can be done manually or the designer may use an automatic code generator. This is one of the most difficult and time-consuming parts of the project.

15. Allocating space

Data must be mapped to the physical devices that will house the data warehouse. In a parallel environment, data must be carefully mapped across the available devices.

16. Population of data into the warehouse

Executing the code described in Step 14 results in the population of the data warehouse.

17. Providing the end user with access to the data

The end user is provided with direct access or access through various reporting tools. At this final step in the process the first iteration is complete. The end user is encouraged to explore the data and provide feedback that will be used in the next iteration, to design and create a better data warehouse.

The cycle repeats as necessary so that the data warehouse serves the information needs of the entire organization. Once the warehouse is in place, individual business units can identify the subject areas that are of interest to them. These subsets are called **data marts**.

15.4.2   Bottom-Up Method

A competing methodology for building a data warehouse was first decribed by Ralph Kimball in his influential book, *The Data Warehouse Toolkit*, first published by Wiley in 1996. His method begins with building a data mart rather than a complete data warehouse. The aim is to eventually develop data marts for the entire enterprise, and combine them into a single data warehouse. His method is summarized in the **Business Dimensional Lifecycle**, which is illustrated in Figure 15.2.

1. Program Planning

Since the final goal is a complete set of data marts to form a data warehouse, there should be a **program plan**, which is the overall plan to develop a Business Intelligence resource, and may involve several lifecycle iterations. A document called the **enterprise data warehouse bus matrix** that gives an overall view of the organization's data needs may be constructed to ensure that data from various projects can be integrated. The bus matrix ensures that the various data marts that are constructed can be integrated through a method called conformed dimensions. A system for monitoring and managing the program and all its projects is also set up.

2. Project Planning

A project is a single iteration of the lifecycle, which is generally the development and deployment of one data mart. The project planning phase will produce an integrated **project plan**, specifying the staffing requirements, timeline, tasks, sequencing, and so forth for the project. Project management software may be used to monitor the project.

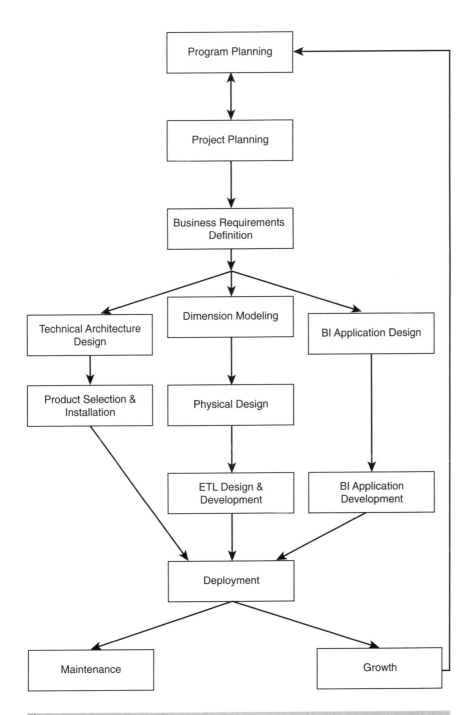

Figure 15.2

Kimball's Business Dimensional Lifecycle

3. Business Requirements Definition

A business requirements analyst, a person who understands business and Business Intelligence and who has good communication skills, interviews representatives from the segments that the project will serve, and constructs a matrix of business processes mapped to strategic business initiatives or other requirements document. This document provides the plan for the three tracks that follow—technology, data, and BI.

4. Development of Technology, Data, and BI Tracks

The three development tracks can be done concurrently, although there are some dependencies involved among the tracks.

- For the **technology track**, the technical architecture design is created to specify the capabilities that will be needed. Designers must consider the business requirements specified, the current technology, and the long-term strategic technology plan in their design. Hardware and software are then selected, acquired, and installed according to the project plan's specifications.

- For the **data track**, the designers do a detailed data analysis for the business segment that will be served by the data mart and produce a dimensional model, a logical model of the type that will be described in Section 15.5. The physical model is then developed and the physical database structure is created. The labor-intensive ETL system design and development is done.

- For the Business Intelligence track, designers work with end users to identify the applications needed and to create the appropriate interfaces, applications, and tools for the users.

5. Deployment

When the tasks in all three tracks have been completed, integrated, tested and validated, users are trained, and support infrastructure is put into place, the system is put into operation.

6. Maintenance

Once in operation, the system performance should be monitored and tuning or other types of maintenance may be needed to ensure optimal performance. Additional user training, application development, or other support may be necessary.

7. Growth

Typically, a successful project will lead to calls for additional projects, as users explore the capabilities of their data marts. The program plan is examined again and the cycle repeats.

15.4.3   Comparison of Methods

With top-down design, the data warehouse provides an integrated, consistent overview of the data for the entire enterprise, and constructing the data marts from the warehouse is a relatively simple matter, involving choosing the data of interest from the data warehouse. The designs of the data marts are consistent, since they come from the same source. Changes to the business do not require major changes to the data model, since it is based on subjects, not business processes. However, the data warehouse project is an enormous one, and the resources required for such a daunting task may not be available. With bottom-up design projects are more easily completed within a limited budget and shorter timeframe, so the return on investment is seen more quickly. However, integrating the data marts produced by different projects may be difficult, and it may happen that a true enterprise data warehouse is never produced. Many organizations use a hybrid methodology, combining features of both methods.

15.5   Data Models for Data Warehouses

15.5.1   ROLAP and MOLAP

Although the models in the data sources may vary, the data warehouse itself must use a single consistent model that accommodates the needs of users. Inmon uses a highly-normalized relational model based on the Entity-Relationship corporate data model. If a relational model is used, we describe the system as a **relational OLAP (ROLAP)** system. A ROLAP warehouse consists of multiple relational tables. Kimball uses a multidimensional model. A data warehouse that stores data using multidimensional arrays is called a **multidimensional OLAP (MOLAP)** system.

15.5.2   Data Cubes and Hypercubes

In a MOLAP system, data can be thought of as residing in a multidimensional matrix called a **data cube**. Figure 15.3(a) shows a three-dimensional data cube called Sales. On the front, visible face of the cube, we see sales figures for the month of June for four departments (dairy, grocery, produce, pharmacy) in three supermarkets (store 1, store 2, store 3). Note that all stores have these same four departments, which correspond to categories of products sold in supermarkets. The figures might represent sales in thousands of dollars. The sales data for each month appears in spreadsheet form, which is a presentation style that would be familiar to many users. The third dimension in this example is time, as indicated by the labels for the months of June, July, August, September, and October. Each month's sales figures for each department in each supermarket appear in a cell in the three-dimensional matrix. Users can view the data by whatever dimension is of interest to them. For example, if a user wishes to see data about sales for each department, the cube can be **pivoted**, or rotated to display a different dimension of interest, as shown in Figure 15.3(b). Here,

FIGURE 15.3(a)

Sales Data Cube

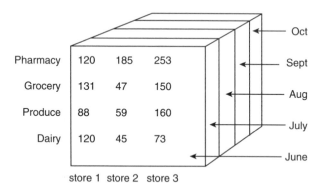

FIGURE 15.3(b)

Pivoted Sales Data Cube

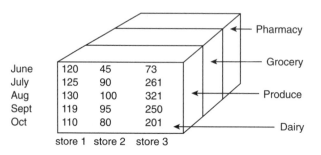

the visible face of the cube shows the dairy department sales for the months of June through October for each of the three supermarkets. If we rotated on another axis, we could examine data for each store. The front face of the cube would show, for a single store, the sales for each department during each month.

In a multidimensional model, a coarser level of data granularity can be created by combining or aggregating data, a process called **rollup**. For example, using the data cube shown in Figure 15.3(a) we could roll up on department, combining data from all departments of each store, to give the total sales for each store for each month, as shown in Figure 15.4(a). We could have rolled up on stores, giving the data for each department, regardless of store, for each month. Similarly, we could have rolled up on the month. A different granularity of rollup would be generated by combining the months into seasons, showing summer season sales by department and store on one spreadsheet display, and similarly for fall, winter, and spring.

The inverse process is **drill-down**. In this process, we provide more detail on some dimension, using finer granularity for the data. For example, we might drill down on department, showing the sub-departments or categories in each of the departments. Figure 15.4(b) provides an example in which departments are broken down into categories for the month of June. The remainder of the cube would show the same breakdown for the other months. This data could not be obtained from the data cube shown in Figure 15.3(a), but requires that the more detailed data be stored, or that it be possible to obtain it from data stored in the data warehouse.

When pivoting and/or rollup of a data cube results in a two-dimensional spreadsheet-style display, it is natural to add totals for the rows and columns, forming a **cross-tabulation**, as illustrated in Figure 15.4(c). This example shows a cross-tabulation of the sales figures by store and month, showing totals for each store, totals for each month, and the total for both. Using pivoting, we could get cross-tabulations by department and store, or by department and month.

If we examine a portion of the data cube by using a selection where we specify equality conditions for one or more dimensions, this type of operation is also called **slicing** the data cube, because it appears as if the user has cut through the cube in the selected direction(s). For example, for the

FIGURE 15.4(a)
Rollup of Sales on Department

	June	July	Aug	Sept	Oct
Store1	459	351	340	345	360
Store2	336	340	334	330	370
Store3	636	650	645	599	700

FIGURE 15.4(b)
Drill-Down of Sales on Department Showing Month of June

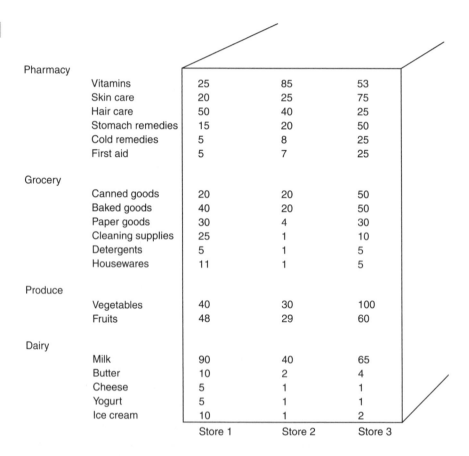

FIGURE 15.4(c)
Cross-Tabulation of Sales by Store and Month

	June	July	Aug	Sept	Oct	Total
Store1	459	351	340	345	360	**1855**
Store2	336	340	334	330	370	**1710**
Store3	636	650	645	599	570	**3100**
Total	**1431**	**1341**	**1319**	**1274**	**1300**	**6665**

data cube shown in Figure 15.3(a), if we specify the condition WHERE month = 'July', we would get the spreadsheet for that month, taking a slice of the cube. For the rotated cube in Figure 15.3(b), if we write WHERE department = 'grocery' we get a similar slice of the cube. An additional operation, called **dicing**, is performed if we specify a range of values in a selection. For example, if we sliced the data cube in Figure 15.3(a) by specifying the month of July, we can dice further by specifying WHERE store = 'store2' OR store ='store 3'.

There is no reason to limit the data in a data cube to two or three dimensions. Designers can store data using as many dimensions as they wish, if those dimensions are of interest to them. However, beyond the third dimension, we cannot draw a physical representation of the data cubes. The cubes of these higher dimensions are referred to as **hypercubes**. It is still possible to apply the processes of pivoting, rollup, and drilling down to hypercubes.

15.5.3 Star Schema

A widely used schema for data warehouses is a **star schema**. There is a central table of raw data, called the **fact table**, that stores unaggregated, observed data. The fact table has some attributes that represent dimensions and other, dependent attributes that are of interest. Each dimension is represented by its own table, and the **dimension tables** can be thought of as the points of a star whose center is the fact table. For example, in Figure 15.5(a) the fact table, ORDER, is shown in the center. Each tuple of the fact table provides information about one order, which involves the sale of one product to one customer on a particular day. For each order, the fact table records the orderNumber, productNumber, customerId, salespersonId, date, unitPrice, and numberOrdered. There are dimension tables for the product, customer, salesperson, and date. Each of these could be used as a dimension in a hypercube, allowing us to ask queries about the sales of a particular product, the sales to a particular customer, the sales made by a specific salesperson, or the sales made on a specific date. The dimension tables—Product, Customer, Salesperson, and Date—are shown relating to their corresponding dimension attributes of the fact table. Normally those attributes are foreign keys in the fact table. The dimension tables provide additional information about each dimension. For example, the Salesperson dimension table provides more details about the salesperson who took the order. The remaining

FIGURE 15.5(a)

A Star Schema

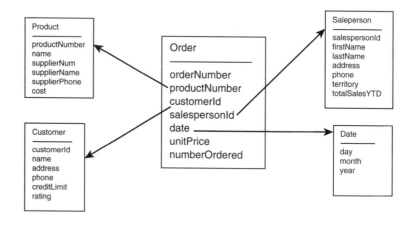

FIGURE 15.5(b)

A Snowflake Schema

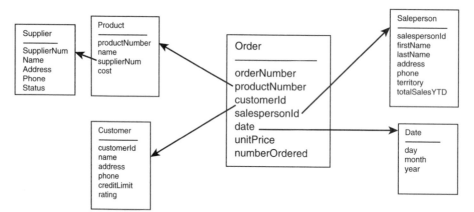

Figure 15.5(c)

Columnar Data Storage

File 1—stuId	S1001,S1002,S1005,S1010,S1013,S1015,S1020
File 2—lastName	Smith,Chin,Lee,Burns,McCarthy,Jones,Rivera
File 3—firstName	Tom,Ann,Perry,Edward,Owen,Mary,Jane
File 4—major	History,Math,History,Art,Math,Math,CSC
File 5—credits	90,36,3,63,0,42,15

attributes of the fact table, `orderNumber`, `unitPrice`, and `numberOrdered`, are dependent attributes.

15.5.4   Snowflake Schema

A variation of the star schema is the **snowflake schema**, in which the dimension tables themselves have dimensions, because they are normalized. For example, in Figure 15.5(b) we show the `Product` dimension having a `Supplier` dimension table. We removed from the `Product` table all the supplier attributes except `supplierNum`, as those attributes are functionally dependent on `supplierNum`, and placed them in a separate `Supplier` table. If any of the other dimension tables were not normalized, we would have done the same for them, creating a snowflake with the fact table as the center.

15.5.5   Columnar Data

A newer approach to storing data, especially within data warehouses, is to use columnar storage. With this approach, each attribute of the database is stored separately, and the values of the column are stored one after another, contiguously, densely packed, in compressed form. Figure 15.5(c) illustrates this type of storage for the `Student` table. Columnar storage uses the relative positioning of data values to determine which ones belong to the same record. For example, all the values belonging to S1005 will be the third ones in their respective column files. An advantage of columnar storage is that since the data in a column is all the same type, it can be compressed very efficiently. Another advantage is that for some queries that are often used in OLAP, such as finding the sum, average, standard deviation or similar functions for a single column or the correlation between two columns, only the files containing those columns need to be retrieved. The disadvantage is that retrieving an entire tuple is slower.

15.6   Data Warehouse Queries and SQL

SQL:1999 added some OLAP functions as an amendment to the standard, and many vendors have included such functions in their offerings. In the current SQL standard, the OLAP functions have been merged into the SQL Foundation portion.

15.6.1   Aggregate Functions

The traditional aggregate functions of SUM, COUNT, MAX, MIN, and AVG can be used in some limited slicing and dicing queries for a data warehouse. The general form of such a query is:

```
SELECT <grouping attributes> <aggregation function>
FROM <fact table> NATURAL JOIN <dimension table(s)>
WHERE <attribute = constant> . . . <attribute = constant>
GROUP BY <grouping attributes>;
```

For example, for the fact table Order shown in Figure 15.5(a) with schema,

```
Order (orderNumber, productNumber, customerId, salespersonId, date, unitPrice,
numberOrdered)
```

and the dimension table Product with schema,

```
Product (productNumber, name, supplierNum, supplierName, supplierPhone, cost)
```

we could write,

```
SELECT O.productNumber, SUM(numberOrdered)
FROM Order O NATURAL JOIN Product P
WHERE P.supplierNum = 'S101'
GROUP BY P.productNumber;
```

which gives us a list of the products supplied by S101 and the total number of each. Note that we sliced on Product and diced on supplierNum for this query.

Typical queries for data warehouses require additional aggregate functions. SQL includes the functions **stddev** (standard deviation), and **variance** for single attributes. These are standard statistical measures that indicate how "spread out" a set of data values are from the mean. For example, a high standard deviation for total monthly sales in the dairy department would mean that the amount of sales fluctuates widely from month to month, while a low standard deviation would indicate that sales remain fairly constant throughout the period. Additional statistical functions are **correlation** and **regression**, which apply to pairs of attributes.

15.6.2   RANK Functions

SQL also has functions to calculate **rank** for data values. For example, if the `Salesperson` table has schema,

```
Salesperson(salespersonId, firstName, lastName, address, phone, territory,
totalSalesYTD)
```

we might want to be able to find the rank of salespeople according to their `totalSalesYTD`. The command,

```
SELECT salespersonId, rank( ) over(order by (totalSalesYTD) desc)
FROM Salesperson;
```

will display the `salespersonId` and the `rank` of all salespeople. If two people have the same sales amount, they are given the same rank, but the next rank value is skipped. For example, if two salespeople are tied for the highest sales, they are both ranked number 1, but the next person is ranked number 3. If we do not wish to skip numbers, we can use the dense_rank( ) option in place of the rank( ) option. Note that in standard SQL the "order by" phrase in the SELECT line simply tells what attribute to use for the ranking. It does not specify that the tuples are to be displayed in the order of the ranking. If we wish to have the results for all salespeople displayed with the highest ranking first rather than the order of existing tuples, we must add an ORDER BY line, as in:

```
SELECT salespersonId, dense_rank( ) over(order by (totalSalesYTD) desc) as
   salesRank
FROM Salesperson
ORDER BY salesRank;
```

However, Oracle SQL displays the results in the order of the ranking attribute.

15.6.3   CUBE and ROLLUP Functions

The GROUP BY clause has also been extended in SQL:1999 with special **CUBE** and **ROLLUP** options for data cubes. For example, if we have a fact table `Sales` with schema,

```
Sales(store, dept, month, amount)
```

and dimension tables for store, department, and month for the supermarket data represented by the data cube in Figure 15.3(a), the query,

```
SELECT dept, store, month, sum(amount)
FROM Sales
GROUP BY CUBE(dept, store, month);
```

produces all 80 possible GROUP BY combinations for the three attributes department, store, and month for the original 36 tuples in the three-month data as shown in Figure 15.6(a). The grouping is done by department alone, by store alone, by month alone, by the combination of store and month, the combination of store and department, the combination of month and department, the combination of all three, and of none. In contrast to the cube, which gives grouping on all possible combinations of attributes named, the ROLLUP option allows users to specify what attributes are to be used for aggregation. If we write,

```
SELECT dept, store, month, sum(amount)
FROM Sales
GROUP BY ROLLUP(dept, store, month);
```

we aggregate on all combinations of `department`, `storeNumber`, and `month` values, and also on `department` alone, and `department` and `store` alone, but not on `month` alone, producing 53 rows for the original 36 tuples, as shown in Figure 15.6(b).

15.6.4   Analytic Functions

These functions use a group of tuples, called the **window**, and compute aggregate values for the group. The window can be moved to compute a moving, centered, or cumulative aggregate. Examples are CORR (correlation), REGR (regression), CUME_DIST (cumulative distribution), percentile, RATIO_TO_REPORT, and many others.

15.7   Optimization and Index Techniques

The amount of data in a warehouse can be so large that efficient indexes are important so that queries can be executed in a reasonable amount of time. Since the data in a data warehouse is not updated by ordinary transactions, it is relatively static. Therefore once indexes are created for the data, the cost of maintaining them is not a factor. Special indexing techniques, including bitmap indexing and join indexing, that are efficient for a large amount of static data are applied to the data warehouse environment.

```
SQL> select dept, store, month, sum(amount)
  2  from sales
  3  group by cube(dept, store, month);
```

DEPT	STORE	MONTH	SUM(AMOUNT)
			4322
dairy			708
grocery			992
produce			943
pharmacy			1679
	1		1387
dairy	1		353
grocery	1		403
produce	1		266
pharmacy	1		365
	2		1018
dairy	2		137
grocery	2		139
produce	2		184
pharmacy	2		558
	3		1917
dairy	3		218
grocery	3		450
produce	3		493
pharmacy	3		756
		July	1417
dairy		July	242
grocery		July	321
produce		July	313
pharmacy		July	541
	1	July	461
dairy	1	July	123
grocery	1	July	138
produce	1	July	90
pharmacy	1	July	110
	2	July	319
dairy	2	July	49
grocery	2	July	40
produce	2	July	55
pharmacy	2	July	175
	3	July	637
dairy	3	July	70
grocery	3	July	143
produce	3	July	168
pharmacy	3	July	256
		June	1431
dairy		June	238
grocery		June	328
produce		June	307
pharmacy		June	558
	1	June	459
dairy	1	June	120
grocery	1	June	131
produce	1	June	88
pharmacy	1	June	120
	2	June	336
dairy	2	June	45
grocery	2	June	47
produce	2	June	59
pharmacy	2	June	185
	3	June	636
dairy	3	June	73
grocery	3	June	150
produce	3	June	160
pharmacy	3	June	253
		August	1474
dairy		August	228
grocery		August	343
produce		August	323
pharmacy		August	580
	1	August	467
dairy	1	August	110
grocery	1	August	134
produce	1	August	88
pharmacy	1	August	135
	2	August	363
dairy	2	August	43
grocery	2	August	52
produce	2	August	70
pharmacy	2	August	198
	3	August	644
dairy	3	August	75
grocery	3	August	157
produce	3	August	165
pharmacy	3	August	247

80 rows selected.

Figure 15.6(a)

Using the SQL CUBE Option

```
SQL> select dept,store, month, sum(amount)
  2  from sales
  3  group by rollup(dept, store, month);
```

DEPT	STORE	MONTH	SUM(AMOUNT)
dairy	1	July	123
dairy	1	June	120
dairy	1	August	110
dairy	1		353
dairy	2	July	49
dairy	2	June	45
dairy	2	August	43
dairy	2		137
dairy	3	July	70
dairy	3	June	73
dairy	3	August	75
dairy	3		218
dairy			708
grocery	1	July	138
grocery	1	June	131
grocery	1	August	134
grocery	1		403
grocery	2	July	40
grocery	2	June	47
grocery	2	August	52
grocery	2		139
grocery	3	July	143
grocery	3	June	150
grocery	3	August	157
grocery	3		450
grocery			992
produce	1	July	90
produce	1	June	88
produce	1	August	88
produce	1		266
produce	2	July	55
produce	2	June	59
produce	2	August	70
produce	2		184
produce	3	July	168
produce	3	June	160
produce	3	August	165
produce	3		493
produce			943
pharmacy	1	July	110
pharmacy	1	June	120
pharmacy	1	August	135
pharmacy	1		365
pharmacy	2	July	175
pharmacy	2	June	185
pharmacy	2	August	198
pharmacy	2		558
pharmacy	3	July	256
pharmacy	3	June	253
pharmacy	3	August	247
pharmacy	3		756
pharmacy			1679
			4322

53 rows selected.

Figure 15.6(b)

Using the SQL ROLLUP Option

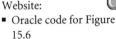

On the Companion
Website:
- Oracle code for Figure
  15.6

Bitmap indexes can be constructed for any attributes that have a limited number of distinct possible values. They are especially appropriate if the domain is small. For each value in the domain, a bit vector is constructed to represent that value, by placing a 1 in the position for that value. For example, Figure 15.7 shows the Faculty table with a bitmap index for rank and another one for department. Because the first Faculty record has a rank

FIGURE 15.7(a)

The Faculty Table

Faculty

facId	name	department	rank
F101	Adams	Art	Professor
F105	Tanaka	CSC	Instructor
F110	Byrne	Math	Assistant
F115	Smith	History	Associate
F221	Smith	CSC	Professor

FIGURE 15.7(b)

A Bitmap Index for Rank

Instructor	Assistant	Associate	Professor
0	0	0	1
1	0	0	0
0	1	0	0
0	0	1	0
0	0	0	1

FIGURE 15.7(c)

A Bitmap Index for Department

Art	CSC	History	Math
1	0	0	0
0	1	0	0
0	0	0	1
0	0	1	0
0	1	0	0

of Professor, the first row of the rank index has a 1 in the `Professor` column. Because the department of the first Faculty record is Art, there is a 1 in the `Art` column of the first row department index. Bitmap indexes take much less space than standard indexes, and they allow efficient processing of some queries directly from the index. For example, for the SQL query,

```
SELECT COUNT(*)
FROM Faculty
WHERE rank = 'Professor' AND department = 'Art';
```

the two indexes can be compared by constructing a new bit vector by using a bitwise AND, comparing the fourth bit of the rank vector with the first bit of the department vector. The number of 1s in the new bit vector is the number of Professors in the Art department. Similar procedures can be used to speed up other operations, including the join.

Because the join is difficult when tables are large, data warehouses can use join indexes to speed up join queries. Most join operations are done on foreign keys. In a data warehouse using a star schema, the join operation often involves comparing the fact table with dimension tables. A **join index** relates the values of a dimension table to the rows of the fact table. For each value of the indexed attribute in the dimension table, the index stores the tuple IDs of all the tuples in the fact table having that value.

Another technique for speeding up a join operation is hashing. For large tables, each of the two tables is hashed on the common attributes and written out to disk, where they are stored in blocks in partitions according to the order determined by the hashing algorithm and the values of the hashed attributes. The blocks are then accessed in pairs, and matching tuples are joined.

Other optimization techniques already discussed in Chapter 11 can be applied in data warehouses. For example, Oracle Exadata uses the Oracle cost-based optimizer.

15.8 Views and View Materialization

Views play an important role in data warehouses, as they do in operational databases, in customizing the user's environment. SQL operators, including the OLAP extension operators of CUBE and ROLLUP, can be performed on views as well as on base tables. The SQL CREATE VIEW command simply defines the view, and does not create any new tables. When a query is written on a view, one way it can be executed is through **query modification**, which replaces the reference in the WHERE line by the view definition. For example, we can have a view, `BestSalespeople` defined by,

```
CREATE VIEW BestSalespeople
AS SELECT S.salespersonId, S.lastName, S.firstName, S.phone, S.salesYTD
FROM Salesperson S
WHERE S.salesYTD > (SELECT AVG(salesYTD)
                    FROM Salesperson);
```

If we write a query using the view such as,

```
SELECT SUM (B.salesYTD)
FROM BestSalespeople B;
```

then if query modification is used, the reference in the FROM line is replaced by the view definition, resulting in:

```
SELECT SUM (B.salesYTD)
FROM (SELECT S.salespersonId, S.lastName, S.firstName, S.phone, S.salesYTD
   FROM Salesperson S
   WHERE S.salesYTD > (SELECT AVG(salesYTD)
                       FROM Salesperson) )AS B;
```

In a data warehouse environment, where queries and views are very complex and where analysts use the system in an interactive environment, query modification might result in unacceptable delays in response time. Therefore, an alternative method of handling views is to **materialize** them, pre-computing them from the definition and storing them for later use. To further speed up processing, indexes can be created for the materialized views.

The data warehouse designer must consider which views should be materialized, weighing the storage constraints against the possible benefits of speeding up the most important queries. The designer must also decide on a maintenance policy for materialized views. When the underlying base tables change, the view should also be updated. This can be done as part of the update transaction for the base tables, a policy called **immediate view maintenance**, which slows down the refresh transaction for the data warehouse. An alternative is to use **deferred view maintenance**. Several policies are possible, including:

- **Lazy refresh**, which updates the view when a query using the view is executed and the current materialized version is obsolete

- **Periodic refresh**, which updates the view at regular intervals of time
- **Forced refresh**, which updates the view after a specified number of updates have been made to the underlying base tables

The refresh process can be done by re-computing the entire materialized view. However, for complex views, especially those with joins or aggregations, this can be too expensive. Instead, the refreshing can be done incrementally, incorporating only the changes made to the underlying tables.

Oracle uses a special SQL statement to create materialized views

```
CREATE MATERIALIZED VIEW        <materialized_view-name>
[BUILD {IMMEDIATE|DEFERRED}]
[REFRESH{FAST|COMPLETE|FORCE} {ON COMMIT|ON DEMAND…}]
…
AS SELECT <view-query>;
```

The BUILD clause allows the view either to be populated immediately, or to defer population until data is inserted later. The FAST refresh clause causes an incremental refresh, so that if the underlying tables are updated, only the changed items are updated in the view, as opposed to the COMPLETE, which updates all rows of the view. FORCE, which is the default, will attempt a fast update, but will do a complete one if a fast one is not possible.

For example, we could create a view for the star schema in Figure 15.5(a) to retrieve the customer name, salesperson name, and product name and quantity of products for each order.

On the Companion Website:

- Oracle Code for This Example

```
CREATE MATERIALIZED VIEW order_mv
BUILD IMMEDIATE
REFRESH FAST ON COMMIT

AS SELECT O.orderNumber, S.lastName AS Salesper, C.name AS Cust, P.name
AS Prod, O.numberOrdered AS Quan
FROM Order O, Product P,  Customer C, Salesperson S
WHERE O.productNumber = P.productNumber AND O.customerId=C.CustomerId
AND O.salespersonId=S.SalespersonId
GROUP BY O.orderNumber, O.productNumber;
```

This view, which is updated whenever any of the four underlying tables is updated, can be treated as if it were an actual table for queries. Prior to executing this command, the user has to be authorized to create materialized views and has to set up certain logs.

15.9   Data Warehouse Vendors

Data warehouses require a combination of specialized software and hardware platforms. Among the most popular are offerings from Teradata, Oracle, IBM, Netezza, Microsoft, Sybase, and SAP. Some of these are integrated systems called **data warehouse appliances**, which include a complete package of servers, operating sytems, and DBMSs already installed and optimized for data warehouse creation and processing. They are descendants of database machines, which had integrated DBMS software and customized operating systems running on specialized hardware optimized for data storage and retrieval. They were first developed in the 1980s by vendors such as Teradata, Britton-Lee (later acquired by Teradata), and Tandem (later acquired by Compaq, which was then acquired by Hewlett-Packard). These appliances generally use massively parallel processing on shared-nothing architecture. Teradata, formerly owned by NCR Corporation, is a leader in the field of data warehouse appliances and has several products including its Active Enterprise Data Warehouse, Data Warehouse Appliance, and Data Mart Appliance lines. Oracle offers another leading database appliance, the Sun Oracle Database Machine, which combines Oracle Exadata storage servers with the Oracle DBMS and its Oracle Warehouse Builder. The DBMS and Warehouse Builder can also run on many other hardware and software platforms, making Oracle's data warehouse offerings very flexible. IBM has its InfoSphere Warehouse, which uses a massively parallel shared-nothing distributed architecture for its DB2 DBMS. Like Oracle, DB2 can be used to create data warehouses on many different platforms. Microsoft SQL Server 2000 is a data warehouse platform that is relatively low-cost, integrates seamlessly with Microsoft Office, and can be easily combined with various hardware platforms using data warehouse reference architectures for Dell, Hewlett-Packard, IBM, and other hardware vendors. Sybase (now owned by SAP Corporation) offers its Analytic Appliance combining IBM servers with its own DBMS at a low cost. Its Sybase IQ software for data warehousing and BI uses a relational model, but uses columnar data storage. Netezza is a smaller vendor that offers a true database warehouse appliance with integrated database, server, and hardware.

15.10 Data Mining

In the area of Business Intelligence, one of the most important processes is using data to discover new knowledge that can provide a competitive advantage.

Data mining means discovering new information from very large data sets. In addition to database technology, data mining uses techniques from the fields of statistics and artificial intelligence, especially machine learning. Because it involves large amounts of data, it is necessary to have a large database or a data warehouse. An enterprise data warehouse can be an ideal data source because the data stored there is already extracted from original sources, cleansed, integrated, and formatted. If no data warehouse exists these processes have to be performed before data mining can begin.

We previously described data mining as one of the primary applications for a data warehouse, along with OLAP and decision support systems. Data mining differs from ordinary database querying or reporting, and from OLAP. Standard database queries or reports can only tell users what is in the database, merely reporting facts already stored. In OLAP, an analyst can use the database to test hypotheses about relationships or patterns in the data. The analyst has to formulate the hypothesis first, and then study the data to verify it. Data mining, on the other hand, is used to study the data without formulating a hypothesis first. It uncovers relationships or patterns by induction, exploring existing data and possibly finding important factors that an analyst would never have included in a hypothesis.

A data warehouse that is used as a source for data mining should include summarized data as well as raw data taken from original data sources such as operational databases. Since the types of operations used in data mining differ from the analytic ones for OLAP and decision support systems, the data mining application should be considered in the original design of the warehouse. A separate data mart may be constructed from the data warehouse data specifically for the purpose of data mining. Data mining generally requires knowledge of the domain (e.g., the environment of the business being studied) as well as knowledge of the data mining process. The data format required most often is a "flat file" or a vector in which all the data for each case of observed values appears as a single record, rather than as normalized relational tables or objects. Data values may be either **numerical** or **categorical**, which means the values are discrete and non-numeric. Some categorical values may be **ordinal**, having a natural order (e.g., poor, fair, good, excellent) while others may be **nominal**, unordered (e.g., male, female). If data is not represented as individual cases, or if joins are needed in order to place all data for a case together, considerable effort must be expended in preparing the data and reformatting it. Therefore, the warehouse design should be created with data mining in mind.

15.11 Purpose of Data Mining

For most businesses, the ultimate purpose of data mining is to provide knowledge that will give the company a competitive advantage, enabling it to earn a greater profit. Other enterprises such as public agencies, scientific research organizations, or non-profit groups can use data mining to provide better service, advance scientific knowledge, or to make better use of their resources. Organizations use data mining in the hope that they will be able to accomplish the following:

- **Predict** the future behavior. For example, by studying the data from the three supermarkets as shown in Figure 15.6, we are probably able to predict sales figures for the same period next year. If we have a public health database that contains data about the spread of influenza for the past five winters, we are probably able to predict the number, timing, and location of such infections for the coming winter.

- **Classify** items by placing them in the correct categories. For example, given data about the credit worthiness of customers in the past, we can classify a new customer as credit worthy or not credit worthy. Classification is also used in medicine, to determine which of several possible diagnoses is the appropriate one for a patient, based on past data about other patients and symptoms.

- **Identify** the existence of an activity or an event. For example, if we know the typical patterns of stock sales that were present in previous cases of insider trading, and we see the same pattern occurring again, we might be able to identify a current case of insider trading. Insurance companies study patterns and characteristics of prior claims known to be fraudulent to determine which new claims might be fraudulent. Credit card companies use similar methods to identify possible misuse of subscriber's cards.

- **Optimize** the use of the organization's resources. Data mining can model scenarios to help determine the best placement of equipment, the type and placing of advertisements that will bring the best results, the most lucrative way to invest money, or the most efficient way to use available time or equipment in order to maximize productivity or reach some other goal.

15.12 Types of Knowledge Discovered

Knowledge can be represented in a variety of ways, including as rules, decision trees, neural networks, frames, or other methods.

Outputs can include:

- **Association rules**, which have the form $\{x\} \Rightarrow \{y\}$, where x and y are events that occur at the same time. A typical example involves pairs of products that customers often purchase together, using **market basket** data, which shows what items were purchased for a transaction. For example, if a customer buys bread, he or she is likely to buy butter at the same time. The rule can be expressed as an implication:

```
{bread} ⇒ {butter}
```

Note that both the left-hand side (bread in this example) and the right-hand side (here, butter) can be sets of items rather than individual items. Two important measures connected with association rules are **support** and **confidence**. For a set of items, the support is the percentage of transactions in the data set that contain all these items included in both left- and right-hand sides. Note that the transaction can include additional items that are not part of the association. For example, if we have one million sales records, and 100,000 of them include both bread and butter, the support for the rule bread $\Rightarrow$ butter is 10%. Confidence is a measure of how often the rule proves to be true; that is, for the cases where the left-hand side of the implication is present, confidence is the percentage of those in which the right-hand side is present as well. For one million sales records, perhaps 500,000 include bread, but only 100,000 of the ones that include bread also include butter, so the confidence in this rule is 20%.

- **Classification rules.** Classification is the problem of placing instances into the correct one of several possible categories. The system is developed by providing a set of past instances for which the correct classification is known, called a **training set**. Using these examples, the system develops a method for correctly classifying a new item whose class is currently unknown. A classical example of a classification rule is the problem of deciding which customers should be granted credit, based on factors such as income, home ownership, and such.

- **Sequential patterns.** A typical application of sequential patterns is the prediction that a customer who buys a particular product in one transaction will follow up with the purchase of a related product in another transaction. For example, a person who buys a printer in a computer supply store will probably buy paper on a subsequent visit. Such patterns are represented as sequences. The sequence {printer}{paper} represents two visits by the same customer in which the sequential pattern is observed, that is, the customer purchased a printer on the first visit and paper on a subsequent visit. The percentage of times such a sequence occurs in the entire set of sales transactions is the support for the pattern. We refer to the first subsequence, {printer}, as a **predictor** of the second subsequence {paper}. The confidence for this prediction is the probability that when {printer} occurs on a visit, {paper} will occur on a subsequent visit. This probability can be calculated by examining the raw data from observed sales transactions. Sequential patterns might involve more than one item in each subsequence, and more than one subsequence. In general terms, if the sequence $S_1, S_2, \ldots S_n$, where each S_i is a set of items, has been found to be valid, then S_1 is a predictor of S_2 through S_n.

- **Time series patterns.** A **time series** is a sequence of events that are all the same type. For example, if the sales total for a supermarket is calculated and recorded at the end of each month over a long period of time, these measures constitute a time series. Time series data can be studied to discover patterns and sequences. For example, we can look at the data and find the longest period when the sales figures continue to rise each month, or find the steepest decline from one month to the next. Stock prices, interest rates, inflation rates, and many other quantities can be analyzed using time series.

15.13 Models and Methods Used

A variety of models such as functions, trees, and graphs are used for the data mining process, and the choice of representation model depends on the kind of output desired. The model itself can be constructed by several different algorithms as well.

15.13.1 Data Mining Process Model

Data mining is a process that involves several steps, as summarized in Figure 15.8, which is adapted from a model called **CRISP-DM** (Cross Industry Standard Model for Data Mining) developed by a consortium of vendors to be a standard model for the data mining process.

1. **Business Understanding.** The process begins with understanding the requirements and the objectives of the project, within the context of the business or other enterprise. It requires a clear statement of the problem to be solved, which is usually either predicting behavior or classifying phenomena.

2. **Data Understanding.** In the data understanding phase, data from a data warehouse or data mining mart would be examined to gain insight into the data, and to detect any obvious subsets. **Visualization methods** such as charts and graphs may be used. This step may lead back to a better business understanding.

3. **Data Preparation.** This step includes the activities involved in constructing the data that will be used as input for the modeling tools. Data is selected and any problems in quality or format are

Figure 15.8

Steps in CRISP-DM Process Model

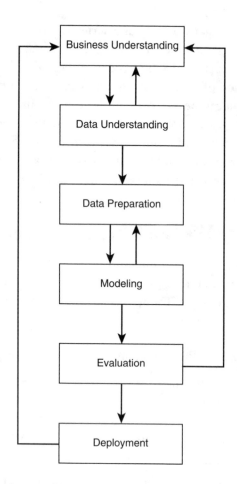

identified. Cleaning and reformatting are done if necessary. Depending on the nature of the problem, **outliers**, which are cases where the values lie outside the normal range, might be detected and either eliminated or highlighted.

4. **Modeling.** This step involves selecting the type of model that best corresponds to the desired outcome, such as a decision tree for a classification, a neural network for prediction, or a statistical model. The models are constructed using algorithms on the available data. For predictive models we identify the dependent or **target variable**, which is the attribute whose value we wish to be able to predict. The model is used to find the attributes, called inde-

pendent or **predictor variables,** whose values influence the value of the target variable. For example, if we wish to predict how much a particular customer will spend on our products, the amount spent at the end of the year might be a target variable. For these models, a training set, a set of cases for which the value of the target variable is already known, is used to construct the model. The data mining system should uncover the predictor variables, which might turn out to be yearly income, age, or other factors, by examining the data. For classification models the objective is to identify those characteristics that enable us to determine which group each individual case belongs to. The algorithms for building these models examine already classified cases to find which factors contribute most to determining the correct grouping. Often the same types of models can be used for either prediction or classification. It may be necessary to return to the data preparation phase if the necessary data for the selected model is not available in the correct form.

5. **Evaluation.** The model constructed must be thoroughly tested and evaluated to be sure it works correctly, is validated, and achieves the objectives specified in the first phase. It may be necessary to return to that phase at this point.

6. **Deployment.** The model developed is put into use. This may involve simply sharing the knowledge gained from the model by means of a report. Often, however, the model is developed so that end users can employ it, replicating it for their own needs. In that case, there must be user education to ensure that users understand how to employ the model.

15.13.2 Regression

Regression is a statistical method for predicting the value of an attribute, Y, (the **dependent variable**), given the values of attributes $X_1, X_2, . . ., X_n$ (the **independent variables**). An example is using a student's SAT scores and high school average as independent variables to predict his or her cumulative grade-point average at the end of four years of college, which is the dependent variable. Many statistical software packages allow users to identify the potential factors that are useful for predicting the value of the dependent variable. Using **linear regression**, the package then finds the contribution or weight of each independent variable for the prediction, in the form of the coefficients, $a_0, a_1, \ldots, a_n$ for a linear function having the form:

$$Y = a_0 + a_1 X_1 + a_2 X_2 + \ldots + a_n X_n$$

The formula derived represents a curve that fits the observed values as closely as possible. For example, the formula may show that the SAT score should be given a weight of .4, and the high school average a weight of .3 in predicting the final grade point average.

In data mining, the system itself is asked to identify the independent variables, as well as to find the regression function. Data mining systems can also use non-linear regression, using a curve-fitting approach, finding the equation of the curve that fits the observed values as closely as possible. They can also deal with non-numerical data. For example, the formula may show that the SAT score should be given a weight of .4, and the high school average a weight of .3 in predicting the final grade point average.

15.13.3   Decision Trees

One method of developing classification rules is to develop a **decision tree**, an example of which is shown in Figure 15.9. This tree is used to make decisions about whether to accept a student at a university, based on a prediction of whether the student will be a poor, average, good, or excellent student. It considers the student's high school average and total SAT score. If the average is below 70% and the SAT is below 1500, the prediction is that the applicant will be a poor student in college. At the other

FIGURE 15.9

A Decision Tree

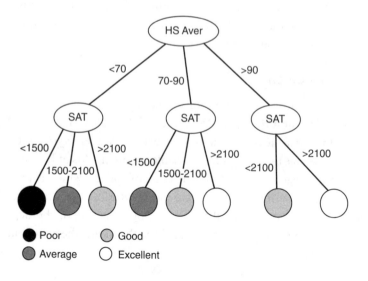

extreme, if the average is above 90 and the SAT is above 2100, the system predicts that the student will be excellent. The tree would be constructed initially by examining the records of past students, considering their entering characteristics of `HSAver` and `SAT`. These attributes are called **partitioning attributes**, because they allow the set of training instances to be broken up or partitioned into disjoint classes. The **partitioning conditions** are shown on the branches. Note that the conditions do not have to be identical for all branches. For example, if the high school average is above 90, we consider only SAT scores of above or below 2100, and do not use the value 1500, as we did for the other branches.

Two popular types of decision trees are Classification and Regression Trees (**CART**) and Chi Square Automatic Interaction Detection (**CHAID**)trees. A CART tree is constructed as a binary tree, with each node having only two options. For a CART tree for this example, each node must have a yes/no question like "Is the HS average >90?" which would cause branching to a second level, where a node with a subsequent question such as "Is the HS average >80" in the false case and "Is the SAT >2100?" in the true case. The tree is built by splitting the data into two groups at each level, with the algorithm using some method of measuring **distance**, which is a number that indicates the amount of difference between the groups. The algorithm seeks to maximize the distance between groups, that is, to find some way to make the groups as different from each other as possible. Various statistical methods can be used to measure such distance. The division process continues, building the tree as it progresses. A CHAID tree algorithm allows multi-way splits and uses the chi-square distribution in measuring distances.

15.13.4 Artificial Neural Networks

Artificial neural networks are non-linear models that resemble biological neural networks in structure. This technique includes a variety of methods using a set of samples for all variables to find the strongest relationships between variables and observations. The methods originated in the field of artificial intelligence. They use a generalized form of regression, using a curve-fitting technique to find a function from the set of samples. Neural networks use a learning method, adapting as they learn new information by examining additional samples. Figure 15.10 shows a very simple model of a neural network that represents purchases from websites. The aim of the system is to predict which potential customers will order from specific websites. Several input variables involving age, education, and income are

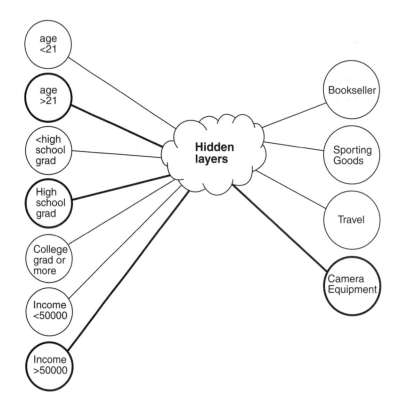

used in the prediction. The sample shows that high school graduates over age 21 with income greater than $50,000 are most likely to order from a camera equipment website. In the learning stage, the network is provided with a training set of cases that provide facts about these input values for a sample of customers, and also the websites that the customers ordered from. The hidden layers are developed by the system as it examines these cases, using generalized regression techniques. As additional cases are provided, the system refines its hidden layers until it has learned to predict correctly a certain percentage of the time. Then test cases are provided to evaluate the system. If it performs well on the test cases, the system can be used on new data where the outcome is unknown.

Building a neural network may require several hidden layers, each with several nodes. Paths from the input nodes to the nodes in the hidden layer are assigned weights, which are determined by the system from the training set data. Figure 15.11 shows a simple neural network with one hidden layer. The input layer consists of nodes 1, 2, and 3, which are the predictor

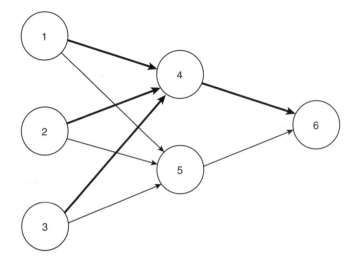

Figure 15.11

Neural Network with One Hidden Layer

variables. The hidden layer has nodes 4 and 5, and the output layer is node 6, which represents the target variable. The inner nodes are determined by the system, and each input node is connected to every inner node. The path from each input node, i, to each inner node, j, is given a weight, W_{ij}, which is also calculated by the system. Each node in the inner layer takes an input value from each node in the input layer, multiplies that by the appropriate connection weight, adds the results, applies a function called the **activation function** to the sum, and passes the output to the node(s) in the next layer. The activation function for each node is also computed by the system. For example, the value that node 4 passes to node 6 is the value of the activation function for node 4 applied to the sum of the values from nodes 1, 2, and 3 times their corresponding weights, or

$$f_4(W_{14}*v(\text{node } 1))+W_{24}*v(\text{node } 2)+W_{34}*v(\text{node } 3))$$

where f_4 is the activation function of node 4 and $v(\text{node } i)$ is the value of node i. If there were a second hidden layer, values would have been passed to them from the first hidden layer, they in turn would apply their activation functions to the sum of these values times the corresponding weights, and pass their results either to the nodes of a third layer or to the output layer.

Neural networks have several drawbacks that make them difficult to work with. A major problem is **overfitting** the curve. The training set data, like any real raw data, always has a certain amount of **noise**, inconsistencies or variations that are not actually significant and that should be ignored. Instead, the network can accommodate its prediction function to account for these values, producing a curve that fits the training set data perfectly. The prediction function will then perform poorly on new data. A second problem is that the knowledge of how the system makes its predictions is in the hidden layers, so users do not have a good view of the reasoning used. Unlike the regression model, where the coefficients show the contribution of each attribute, the weights assigned to the factors in the model cannot be interpreted in a natural way by users. Although the model might work well, the output can be difficult to understand and interpret.

15.13.5 Clustering

Clustering or segmentation refers to methods used to place tuples into clusters or groups that can be disjoint or overlapping. Using a training set of data, the system identifies a finite set of clusters into which the tuples of the database can be grouped. The tuples in each cluster are similar, sharing some properties, and they are dissimilar to the tuples in other clusters. Similarity is measured by using some type of distance function that is defined for the data. For example, if age is an attribute, the difference in people's ages could be used as the distance function. In some problems, the categories can be organized hierarchically. Figure 15.12 shows an example in which people are clustered by education and income levels. It shows the highest grade completed by each person on the x-axis and the annual income of each on the y-axis. From the data, it appears that there are three clusters. There are people with a lower education level who have low income, people with a low education level with moderately high income, and people with a high education level with high income.

FIGURE 15.12

Clustering

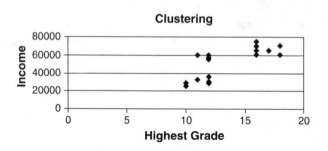

15.13.6   Genetic Algorithms

Genetic algorithms can be used as a method in constructing models. These techniques simulate evolution by using processes similar to genetic combination, mutation, and natural selection. An algorithm begins with a population of candidate solutions (called **individuals**), which may be randomly generated and which are usually represented as arrays of bits. Each solution in that population is evaluated and given a score by means of a **fitness function**, which measures desirable properties of individuals. For the next generation, the fittest individuals are selected and then modified by recombination or mutation to form a new generation whose individuals, called **chromosomes**, have many of the characteristics of their parents, and generally have a higher fitness score. The process is then repeated, stopping either when the evaluation scores of the evolved population are sufficiently high or when a predefined number of generations has been propagated. These algorithms can be used to construct models such as decision trees or the layers of neural networks.

15.14 Applications of Data Mining

Data mining has been used in a wide variety of applications. Among the most successful are the following:

15.14.1   Retailing

- **Customer relations management (CRM)** is an emerging application of data mining. CRM allows a retailer to provide a personalized shopping experience to customers in order to build customer loyalty. Data mining is used to identify and anticipate customer needs, so that the retailer will have the items they request and will be able to suggest related items that the customer will buy. For example, consumer websites often analyze the customer's previous purchase history to suggest new purchases, or to suggest purchases related to the current one.

- **Advertising campaign management** uses data mining to identify the customers who will be most likely to make purchases in response to advertising. For mail-order firms, it is used to identify the households that will respond positively to catalogs. Data can come from responses to previous direct mail items or to test items. Data mining identifies the factors that are associated with a positive response to build a model. That model, which includes demographic and geographic data, is used to identify the people most likely to respond positively to new campaigns, based on their demographic and other attributes.

15.14.2   Banking and Finance

- **Credit scoring.** Retailers, banks, and others who extend credit to customers can use a variety of data mining techniques to build a model to determine whether to extend credit to new applicants.

- **Fraud detection and prevention.** Data mining has been used successfully to detect fraudulent credit card transactions, either after the fact or in real-time, to deny the potential transaction. Insurance companies have also used data mining to determine whether claims are fraudulent. Stock trades are routinely investigated to identify possible cases of insider trading or other illegal activity. The telecommunications industry also uses data mining to detect fraudulent use of telephone systems.

15.14.3   Manufacturing

- **Optimizing use of resources.** Data mining models can be used to determine the best deployment of equipment, human resources, and materials.

- **Manufacturing process optimization.** The manufacturing process itself can be analyzed to determine the most cost-effective and/or efficient way to produce products.

- **Product design.** By examining data about product defects and repairs, manufacturers can eliminate parts that are likely to be defective, improving the design. Results of market research can also be used to design products that consumers would prefer.

15.14.4   Science and Medicine

- **Determining effectiveness of treatments.** Patients, healthcare providers, and health insurers all benefit from being able to determine which courses of treatment are most effective. Data mining not only provides the basis for sound statistical results of studies of various treatments, but it can reveal hidden factors that influence the treatment outcome.

- **Analyzing effects of drugs.** Both before and after new drugs come to market, a vast amount of data must be collected and provided about the drugs' effects. Large scale drug studies, involving huge amounts of data, play a vital role in the health-care industry.

- **Finding relationships.** Patterns among patient care and the outcome of treatments can be determined. In addition to the obvious relationships between course of treatment or drugs and patient outcomes, hidden relationships among other factors, such as the setting where care is provided, and outcomes can be discovered using data mining.

- **Astronomy** requires storage and exploration of data taken from telescopes throughout the world. The amount of data stored in this field is massive and continually growing, and is beyond the ability of humans to examine it all. Data extracted from these observations is used to create digital catalogs of the sky, listing the positions and features of objects. Astronomers use data mining to discover new phenomena, new relationships, and other knowledge about the universe.

- **In weather prediction** the amount of data produced by observations from weather satellites and other observers far exceeds the ability of humans to process. Data mining techniques allow scientists to study ecosystem disturbances such as storms, global warming, and other phenomena.

- **Bioinformatics** is the science of managing, mining, and interpreting information from biological data, including genomic data. The development of a variety of genome projects and new developments such as microarray technology have contributed to an exponential growth in DNA and protein sequence databases, which require data mining techniques to identify and extract useful information about the structure and functions of genes.

15.14.5   Homeland Security

- **Identify and track terrorist activities**. Unusual patterns of money transfers and communications can reveal the existence of potential terrorist plots.

- **Identify individual terrorists**. Travel and immigration records can be used to identify and locate terrorists. For airline travel, Secure Flight is a program created by the U.S. Transportation Safety Administration to check airline passenger information prior to flights. It uses data mining to identify those individuals who are on the No Fly list or those who should be subject to additional screening. For automobile, train, ship, or rail travel that crosses a U.S. border, a similar system, Automated Targeting System, is used to determine whether travelers should be placed in a high-risk group. Cargo is also subject to this system.

15.14.6   Search Engines

Search engines represent one of the most obvious uses of data mining, requiring examination of the massive amount of data on the Internet to identify and classify resources for user queries.

15.15   Data Mining Software Providers

There are many vendors offering data mining software, either as a stand-alone product or as part of a database or data warehouse management system. SAS offers Enterprise Miner, which includes tools for the entire data mining process, from data preparation to scoring. It uses in-database analytics and offers several advanced algorithms for building both predicting and classifying models. It has partnered with Teradata to offer its Analytic Advantage Program. Oracle offers ODM (Oracle Data Mining) as an option to its Oracle Database Enterprise Edition as well as on its Exadata database appliance. Since the mining can be done inside the operational database, there is no need for a separate data extraction and movement operation. The models are then stored inside the Oracle database. It offers multiple in-database advanced mining algorithms for anomaly detection, regression, classification, association rules, clustering, and other models for both data and text. It has a graphical user interface, Oracle Data

Miner, that guides the user through the model-building process using the CRISP-DM steps, and allows analysts to explore patterns in their Oracle databases. It also offers an opportunity to try out data mining using a pre-installed Oracle database and data sets on the Amazon Cloud using its Oracle Data Mining Amazon Machine Image (AMI). IBM's SPSS Modeler software integrates with IBM's Cognos Business Intelligence software and its Info Sphere Warehouse, as well as with other databases, spreadsheets, and flat files on a variety of platforms. It offers automated data preparation, advanced analytic functions, advanced algorithms, and interactive data visualization. KXEN offers an impressive line of data mining tools for a variety of applications, including social network analysis. It can access data from any ODBC-compliant database, including Oracle, Teradata, DB2, MySQL, Access, and SQLServer, as well as files including SAS, SPSS, Excel, and both fixed length and delimited text files. Portrait Software specializes in customer analytics. FICO has specialized in the financial services industry but has expanded its offerings to other sectors. TIBCO Spotfire Software and Angoss Software are other leading providers of data mining software. There are also open-source data mining tools such as Weka, which is managed by the open-source software company Pentaho.

15.16 Chapter Summary

Data warehouses store massive amounts of data taken from the operational databases used by an enterprise, as well as from other data sources. They are used for **decision support systems (DSS)**, **online analytical processing (OLAP)**, and **data mining**. Data is taken from data sources using back-end system tools. The extracted data is reformatted, cleaned, enriched, put into the proper model, and loaded into the warehouse. **Data marts** containing specialized data can also be created. The warehouse can be developed using either a **top-down** or **bottom-up** methodology, or a hybrid. Warehouses often use a **multidimensional model**. Data can be represented using multidimensional **data cubes**, which can be **pivoted** or rotated to display a different dimension. If the dimension is more than three, we use the term **hypercube**. **Rollup** is a process of aggregating data along dimensions, while its inverse, **drill-down**, is a process of providing more detail for some dimension. A **cross-tabulation** is a spreadsheet-like display with totals added to the data. **Slicing** a data cube is equivalent to performing a selection with equality condition for one or more dimensions, while **dicing** is equivalent to a range selection.

Multidimensional OLAP systems store data as multidimensional arrays, and are called **MOLAP** systems. Relational OLAP, called **ROLAP** systems, use multiple relational tables. A **star schema** uses a central table of data values called the **fact table**, with attributes that represent dimensions. Each dimension has its own **dimension table** that is connected to the fact table. In a variation called a **snowflake schema**, the dimension tables themselves have dimension tables because they are normalized. **Columnar data** storage can also be used.

Queries for a data warehouse can use the standard aggregate functions from SQL, usually with GROUP BY options. SQL provides additional functions for the statistical measures of **standard deviation**, **variance**, **correlation**, **regression**, **percentile**, and others. There is also a **rank** function that returns the rank of a tuple with respect to some attribute. The GROUP BY clause can include the option **GROUP BY CUBE** and **GROUP BY ROLLUP** for data cubes.

Special index techniques can be used in a data warehouse environment to speed up queries. **Bitmap indexes** are useful if the domain of values for an attribute is small. It is possible to answer some queries directly from the index, without accessing the data records. A **join index** is constructed by storing, for each value of the indexed attribute in a dimension table, the tuple Ids of all tuples in the fact table having that value for the attribute. **Hashing** on the join attributes may also be used to speed up queries.

For the sake of efficiency, views are often created by **view materialization**, pre-computing them and storing them for future use. Indexes can also be created for materialized views. A view maintenance policy is needed for materialized views. It can be immediate or deferred. If deferred, the refresh policy can be lazy, periodic, or forced.

Data mining means discovering new information from very large data sets. The purpose is to gain a competitive advantage by being able to predict behavior, classify items, identify an activity or event, or optimize the use of resources. Knowledge discovered can be **association rules**, which have measures of support and confidence. Knowledge can also be expressed as **classification rules**, sequential patterns, or **time series pat-**

terns. The data set that is used to teach the system is called the **training set**. The **CRISP-DM** model may be used for the data mining process. Data mining methods include **decision trees**, **regression**, **artificial neural networks**, **clustering**, **genetic algorithms**, and others. Application areas include retailing, banking and finance, manufacturing, science and medicine, weather forecasting, search engines, and many others.

Exercises

15.1   Define the following terms:

   a. data warehouse

   b. decision support system

   c. OLAP

   d. OLTP

   e. data mining

   f. data mart

   g. data cleaning

   h. data cube

   i. rollup

   j. drill-down

   k. pivoting

   l. slice and dice

   m. bitmap index

   n. join index

   o. view materialization

   p. star schema

   q. regression

   r. artificial neural network

   s. clustering

   t. decision tree

   u. association rule support and confidence

v. training set

w. time series

x. overfitting

y. genetic algorithms

z. customer relations management

15.2 Let the following relations represent a fact table, `Orders`, and associated dimension tables `Customers`, `Salespeople`, and `Products`.

Orders			
custId	prodId	salesPersonId	Quantity
101	1	10	20
101	2	11	8
101	3	10	15
102	1	11	10
102	2	10	12
102	3	10	15
103	1	11	9
103	2	10	40
103	3	10	12

Customers		
custId	name	creditRating
101	Adams	10
102	Burke	12
103	Collins	15

Products		
prodId	name	Price
1	Widget	3
2	Bolt	1
3	Drill	10

Salespeople		
salesPersonId	lastName	firstName
10	Yates	Tom
11	Zorn	Steve

a. Draw a star schema for this data.

b. Draw a data cube similar to the one shown in Figure 15.3, showing the quantity of orders placed by customers for products through salesperson 10 as the visible face. Let customer be the x-axis and product be the y-axis on this face. Salespeople should be the z-axis for the third dimension. If no order has been placed by a customer for a product through salesperson 10, place a 0 in the cell.

c. Pivot the cube to show orders placed by customers and salesperson, with product as the third dimension. The visible face should be for product 1.

d. Pivot the cube to show orders placed by salesperson and product. The visible face should be for customer 101. Add totals to make this a cross tabulation.

15.3   a. For the data cube for Exercise 15.2(b) show the rollup on salesperson.

b. Assume there are two types of widgets, bolts, and drills—small and large. Show a drill-down on product for the data cube in Exercise 15.2(b).

c. For the data cube for Exercise 15.2(b) show the slice that corresponds to the selection WHERE salesPersonId = 2.

d. For the slice in Exercise 15.3(c) dice for the range prodId < 2.

15.4   a. For the data in the `Orders` table in Exercise 15.2, write out bitmap indexes on `custId`, `prodId`, and `salesPersonId`.

b. Devise a query that can be answered by using the indexes alone.

c. Write out join indexes for customers, products, and salespeople.

15.5   The following transactions were observed at a supermarket.

TransNo	CustId	Date	Time	Market Basket
1	10	Jun 06	10:00	{bread, milk, juice}
2	11	Jun 06	10:10	{coffee, milk}
3	12	Jun 06	10:20	{bread, butter, milk}
4	13	Jun 06	10:25	{bread, eggs}

TransNo	CustId	Date	Time	Market Basket
5	14	Jun 06	10:30	{milk, juice}
6	10	Jun 07	10:00	{butter, meat}
7	11	Jun 07	10:05	{paper towels, juice}
8	13	Jun 07	10:30	{butter, paper towels}
9	14	Jun 07	10:45	{milk, bread}

a. What is the support for the association rule bread ⇒ milk? What is the confidence for this rule?

b. What is the support for the sequential pattern {bread}{butter}? What is the confidence for this pattern?

c. Can you find any other associations or sequential patterns of interest in this data? If so, give the support and confidence for them.

d. Add some items or transactions that will yield a new association rule with both support and confidence of at least 50%.

e. Add some transactions that will yield a new sequential pattern with both support and confidence of at least 50%.

 On the Companion Website:

- Laboratory Exercises

- Oracle Code for Examples

Index

(*Note:* Page numbers in *italics* indicate tables and figures.)